1080 RECIPES

Simone and Inés Ortega

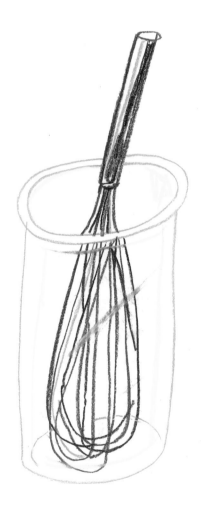

illustrations
Javier Mariscal

CONTENTS

PREFACES

From the Publisher

The popularity of Spanish food has grown exponentially throughout the world during the past decade. Tapas bars and Spanish restaurants are opening in every major city and, thanks to the growing reputations of the country's many fine chefs, including Ferran Adrià of El Bulli and others, gastronomic attention has been well and truly turned on the food of contemporary Spain. As *The New York Times* recently reported, Spanish cuisine currently enjoys a reputation for innovation and creativity previously only awarded to the food of France.

However, the imaginative recipes being developed by Spain's leading chefs are, despite their innovation, based on the solid traditions of Spanish food, which is unpretentious, healthy, simple and delicious.

As different cultures settled in various parts of Spain over the ages, each brought their own contribution to the development of its cuisine. The Greeks introduced the quintessentential Spanish ingredient, olive oil, while seasonings, spices and the many combinations of meat and fruit that we associate today with Spanish food are a legacy of the Moors. The diverse cultures of the country's history can be clearly traced through the variety and combination of ingredients in its dishes, the most famous of which is the surprising marriage of fish and meat in the country's national dish, paella.

1080 Recipes was written by Simone Ortega, who has been writing about food for over fifty years, and is the foremost authority on traditional Spanish cooking. It has been Spain's favorite cookery book since its first publication over thirty years ago, with millions of copies now sold. Over the years, Simone has been joined by her daughter Inés, also a respected food writer, and together, they have revised and updated the recipes to reflect modern methods without losing the traditional character of Spanish food.

This first edition in English has been further adapted for the English-speaking market, adding explanation and introduction to specialist ingredients and particular techniques of cooking. The great Spanish illustrator Javier Mariscal has filled the pages of *1080 Recipes* with hundreds of specially created colorful and evocative drawings depicting the food and atmosphere of Spain, and the recipes are also accompanied by more than 100 color photographs showing the completed dishes.

With *1080 Recipes* on your table, you will quickly learn to love a cuisine that is filled with variety, subtlety and flavor.

Buen provecho!

From the authors

I am confident that this book has helped to improve the way people in Spain eat: it has made learning to cook easier for those who don't have much time to spend in the kitchen; the recipes are tasty and simple; and my readers have told me over the years that I have included clear and precise explanations that ensure my recipes always work, even in the hands of the most inexperienced of cooks.

Each recipe is numbered and the book is fully indexed, using the recipe numbers to direct you quickly and easily to the dish you are looking for. You will also see that the recipes do not have grandiose titles but, instead, I have given them names that describe the main ingredients in the dish—although there are just one or two exceptions to this rule, when I have used a name by which a dish is widely recognized, such as gazpacho.

Finally, I hope that this English edition will encourage a host of new readers to grab their pans with increasing enthusiasm.

Simone Ortega

My family has always regarded three things as important in our lives: reading, writing and cooking. I spent years watching my mother cook and later, as I grew up, I started to help her in the kitchen. As a result of constant nagging from her friends, my mother was eventually persuaded to collect her recipes together into a book. My father, being a publisher, then decided to publish this as *1080 Recipes*, a title that was taken from the number of recipes that the book contained. We never for a moment imagined that over the course of a little more than 3 decades this book would become a cookery classic and that we would soon be celebrating millions of copies sold!

Later, as I began writing and publishing my own cookery books, my mother began to ask me to update or modify recipes with her so that they were more in tune with contemporary styles of cooking and eating. Since then she and I have worked together to ensure that *1080 Recipes* is as relevant to contemporary lifestyles as it was when it was first published.

Over time, cooking habits may have changed, but *1080 Recipes* remains fresh. It is always up-to-date, always accessible, and its pages contain dishes that can be made successfully in any home and by any cook, thus ensuring the book's continuing success. Its aim has never changed: to offer the best of Spanish cuisine in a simple and accessible way, while maintaining an international and contemporary outlook. This was Simone Ortega's great secret when she created her classic first edition, and I am proud to follow in her footsteps.

Inés Ortega

From Ferran Adrià

I have great pleasure in writing a preface to this classic cookery book, which was written by one of the first people to raise food and cooks to their rightful places in society. *1080 Recipes* has now been translated into English, with Simone's daughter Inés helping to update and revise its recipes. This English edition proves that, for Simone Ortega, cooking has no borders.

The first time Simone came to El Bulli, I was very interested to know what she thought of my food, and I was pleased when I realized that she instinctively understood and enjoyed what we do in our restaurant. Simone is a sensitive and intuitive woman, traditional but at the same time evolutionary in her outlook. She has an instinctive feel for creating new flavors, demonstrating that she has the intuition necessary to be a great cook.

In this book, Simone and Inés offer us a wealth of gastronomic experience and wisdom and *1080 Recipes* will quickly transport you to the heart of Spain. This is a timeless book. When you read it, you suddenly realize the glories of the food in front of you, those that, until now, you have not fully appreciated. Ours is a splendid cuisine, born out of the pleasure of eating, and it is also one that is perfect for those who have little time to cook, but who don't want to give up the enjoyment of eating well and, thus, of feeding their souls as well as their stomachs.

In this book, we travel on a delicious journey through 1080 recipes with Simone and Inés, each recipe demonstrating its two authors' dedication to a job well done and their passion for creativity and good food.

One thousand and eighty thank yous!

APPETIZERS

Olives

How to cure

Fresh olives are inedible and must be cured to remove their bitterness. (Commercially available olives will already have been cured.) Put fresh olives into a container of caustic soda so that they are just covered. The proportions are 2 ¼ pounds olives to 1 ounce caustic soda. Leave the olives for 24 hours. It does not matter if they become a little soft because the salt used for preserving the olives will make them firmer.

Note: Caustic Soda, whose chemical name is sodium hydroxide, is a form of lye. It can be found in some craft stores and hardware stores on the internet. Be sure the label says sodium hydroxide. It is a strong chemical so handle it carefully.

How to preserve

Wash the olives thoroughly, put them into containers, and add enough water to cover them. Add salt to taste, a few sprigs of savory, some lemon rind, and a few cloves of unpeeled garlic. Leave the olives in this mixture for a few days before eating them.

A dressing for black olives

Black olives preserved in brine can be eaten as they are or dressed with a little paprika, onion, and olive oil.

1

Pastry for tartlets

- **2 ¼ cups all-purpose flour, plus extra for dusting**
- **½ teaspoon salt**
- **generous ½ cup butter, margarine, or lard, or a mixture of equal quantities of any two of these, plus extra for greasing (optional)**
- **2 teaspoons peanut oil, plus extra for greasing (optional)**
- **1 egg, lightly beaten**

Makes 20

Sift the flour into a large bowl, add the salt, and mix, lifting up the flour with a spoon and letting it fall back into the bowl to aerate it. Add the fat, oil, and egg and quickly mix together with your fingertips until the mixture resembles bread crumbs. Gradually add about ¾ cup water, a little at a time, and lightly mix with your hands to form a smooth dough that comes away from the sides of the bowl. (The exact quantity of water required depends on the type of flour.) Leave the ball of dough in the bowl, cover with a clean dish towel, and let rest in a cool place for 30 minutes. Preheat the oven to 400°F and grease 20 tartlet pans, 1 ½ inches in diameter, with butter or oil. (You could also use boat-shaped barquette pans.) Roll out the dough on a lightly floured surface until it is quite thin (about ⅛ inch). Cut out 20 rounds with a 1 ½-inch fluted cutter, re-rolling the dough as necessary, and use to line the prepared pans. Prick the base of each with a fork, line with waxed paper, and fill with pie weights or dried beans. Bake for 15 minutes. Remove the paper and weights, return the tartlets to the oven, and bake for 5 minutes more, until golden brown. This process of pre-cooking pastry before adding the filling is called 'baking blind', and is done to prevent a wet filling causing the pastry to go soggy. Transfer the tartlets to wire racks and let cool completely. If you are not using them immediately, store in an airtight container.

2

French pastry for tartlets

MASA FRANCESA PARA TARTALETAS

- ¾ ounce (a little less than ½ large cake) fresh yeast
- 3 tablespoons lukewarm milk
- 2 egg yolks
- scant ½ cup (a little less than 1 stick) butter, plus extra for greasing
- 2¼ cups all-purpose flour, plus extra for dusting
- pinch of salt

Makes 25

Mash the yeast with the milk in a cup or small bowl until smooth, then let stand for about 10 minutes, until the mixture is foamy. Transfer the yeast mixture to a mixing bowl and add the egg yolks and butter. Sift in the flour and salt and mix with your hands. Roll out the dough on a lightly floured surface until very thin (about 3mm/⅛ inch). Cut out 25 rounds with a 1⅛-inch fluted cutter, re-rolling the dough as necessary. Grease 25 tartlet pans, 1½ inches, with butter and line with the dough rounds. Cover with a clean dishtowel, and let rise for 30 minutes. Preheat the oven to 400°F. Prick the base of the tartlets with a fork, then line each of the tartlets with waxed paper, and fill with pie weights or dried beans. Transfer to the oven and bake blind for 15 minutes. Remove the paper and weights, return the tartlets to the oven, and bake for 5 minutes more, until golden brown. Transfer the tartlets to wire racks and let them cool completely. Once cold, they are ready to use. If not using immediately, you can store the tartlets in an airtight container.

3

Muffins with chopped ham

MUFFINS CON JAMÓN PICADO

- 10 muffins
- 2 ounces butter, softened
- 5 ounces cured ham, chopped

Makes 30

Cut the muffins into thirds. Spread them with a little softened butter and top with chopped cured ham. Use the back of a spoon to press the ham down to prevent it falling off the muffin when it is picked up.

4

Muffins with foie gras and gelatin

MUFFINS CON FOIE-GRAS Y GELATINA

- 10 muffins
- 3½ ounces fresh or canned foie gras paté
- set gelatin (see recipe 42), finely chopped

Makes 30

Cut the muffins into thirds and spread generously with fresh or canned foie gras paté. Cover with the chopped gelatin and press down with the back of a spoon to prevent the gelatin falling off the muffin when it is picked up.

5

Little ham turnovers
EMPANADILLAS DE JAMÓN

- 1 quantity Pastry for Turnovers (see recipe 43)
- 7 ounces cured ham, chopped
- sunflower oil, for deep-frying

Makes 30

Fill the turnovers with the chopped cured ham. Heat the oil in a deep fryer or deep pan to 350–375°F or until a cube of day-old bread browns in 30 seconds. Add the turnovers, in batches, and cook for 6–8 minutes, turning during the cooking to brown both sides. Serve the turnovers immediately.

6

Ham and pineapple canapés
CANAPÉS DE JAMÓN Y PIÑA

- 5 slices of bread, each cut into 4 x 1½ inch rounds and toasted
- 2 ounces butter
- 5 slices cured ham, each cut into 4 pieces
- 20 pieces canned pineapple
- 2½ ounces grated cheese

Makes 20

Preheat the oven to 350°F. Spread the rounds of toasted bread with a little butter. Place a slice of cured ham on each, top with a piece of drained cann ed pineapple, and sprinkle with grated cheese. Place on a baking sheet and bake for 5 minutes. Serve hot.

7

Foie gras canapés
CANAPÉS DE FOIE-GRAS

- 3½ ounces fresh or canned foie gras paté
- 1 tablespoon evaporated milk or lightly beaten heavy cream
- 1 tablespoon brandy
- ¼ teaspoon paprika
- 5 slices of bread, each cut into 4 x 1½ inch rounds and toasted
- 20 capers

Makes 20

Combine the foie gras paté, evaporated milk or heavy cream, brandy, and paprika in a bowl until thoroughly mixed. Spoon the mixture into a pastry bag and pipe onto the rounds of toasted bread. Garnish each canapé with a caper, rinsed if salted.

8 Ham and cream cheese rolls

ROLLITOS DE JAMÓN Y QUESO BLANCO

- 2–3 medium-thick slices
  of cured ham
- salted spreadable cream cheese

Makes approx. 12

Spread each slice of ham with cream cheese, then roll up, wrap in aluminum foil, and place in the freezer for 30 minutes. Unwrap the foil and cut the rolled ham into ½ inch slices before serving.

9 Shrimp barquettes

BARQUITAS DE GAMBAS

- 20 pastry barquettes
  (see recipe 1)
- 3½ ounces Classic Mayonnaise
  (see recipe 105)
- 40 medium sized cooked,
  peeled shrimp
- set gelatin (see recipe 42),
  finely chopped (optional)

Makes 20

Spread the base of each pastry barquette with mayonnaise. For each one, put two shrimp on top of the mayonnaise, then cover with the gelatin. Chill for at least 30 minutes before serving.

10 Tuna canapés

CANAPÉS DE ATÚN

- 1 x 7 ounce can tuna
- 2 tablespoons Thick Mayonnaise
  (see recipe 106)
- 5 slices of bread, each cut into
  4 x 1½ inch rounds and toasted

Makes 20

Drain the tuna, place in a bowl, and mash well with a fork. Stir in the mayonnaise until thoroughly combined, then spread the mixture on the rounds of toasted bread.

11

Caviar canapés
CANAPÉS DE CAVIAR

- 5 slices of bread, each cut into 4 x 1½ inch rounds and toasted
- 2 ounces butter
- 3½ ounces caviar
- 1 lemon
- 2 hard-cooked eggs, chopped

Makes 20

Spread the rounds of toasted bread with butter and spoon a little caviar on top. Squeeze 2 drops of lemon juice onto each canapé and top with the chopped eggs. Halved quail eggs may also be used for this recipe.

12

Smoked salmon canapés
CANAPÉS DE SALMÓN AHUMADO

- 5 slices of bread, each cut into 4 x 1½ inch rounds and toasted
- 2 ounces butter
- 7 ounces smoked salmon, thickly sliced
- 1 lemon (optional)

Makes 20

Spread the rounds of toasted bread with butter and place the sliced smoked salmon on top. If you like, sprinkle each canapé with a few drops of lemon juice.

Variation: You can also sprinkle the canapés with a little finely chopped scallion on the butter before adding the smoked salmon.

13

Smoked trout or smoked eel canapés
CANAPÉS DE TRUCHA O ANGUILA AHUMADA

- 5 slices of bread, each cut into 4 x 1½ inch rounds and toasted
- 2 ounces butter
- 7 ounces smoked trout or smoked eel fillet, finely chopped
- 1 lemon

Makes 20

Spread the rounds of toasted bread with butter and top with the smoked trout or smoked eel fillet. Sprinkle 2 drops of lemon juice on each canapé.

Snails

Snails gathered in the wild should be fed only flour for 5–6 days to eliminate any toxins. Live cultivated snails should be cooked on the day of purchase. You can also use freshly cooked, frozen, or canned snails. If using live snails, wash them well in plenty of salted water mixed with a little vinegar before cooking.

14

Snails (first version)
CARACOLES

- 24 snails
- 2 tablespoons olive oil
- 1 onion, chopped
- 1 red or green bell pepper,
  seeded and finely chopped
- 3 tomatoes,
  finely chopped and seeded
- 2 tablespoons all-purpose flour
- pinch of paprika
- 1 bay leaf
- 5 ounces Serrano ham or other
  dry-cured ham, diced
- 2 cloves garlic, finely chopped
- 5 sprigs fresh parsley, chopped
- 1 hard-cooked egg, chopped
- salt and pepper

Serves 6

If you are using fresh snails, put them in a large pan and pour in just enough lukewarm water to cover. Heat gently until the snails emerge from their shells, then increase the heat to high, and cook for 30 minutes. Drain well, discard the shells and return the snails to the pan. Set aside. If you are using canned snails, drain and set aside. Heat the oil in another pan. Add the onion and pepper. Cook over low heat, stirring occasionally, for about 10 minutes, until the onion begins to brown. Add the tomato and cook, stirring occasionally, for 10 minutes more. Sprinkle the flour over the mixture, stir in, then remove the pan from the heat, and season with paprika to taste. Stir in sufficient water to make a fairly thick sauce and add a bay leaf. Season with salt and pepper to taste. (The mixture should be quite spicy.) Stir in the Serrano ham, then add the garlic and parsley. Pour the sauce into the pan with the snails and heat through. If you are using canned snails, just add them to the sauce and heat through. If you like, you can add chopped hard-cooked egg.

15

Snails (second version)
CARACOLES

- 24 snails
- 1 onion, cut into wedges
- 1 bay leaf
- 2 tablespoons olive oil
- 1 onion, chopped
- 1 chile, chopped
- 2 ounces bacon, diced
- 2 ounces chorizo, thinly sliced
- 2 tablespoons all-purpose flour
- 1 meat bouillon cube

Serves 6

If you are using fresh snails, put them, some onion wedges, and a bay leaf in a pan, pour in just enough water to cover, and bring to a boil. Cook for 15 minutes. If you are using canned snails, skip this step. Meanwhile, heat the oil in another pan. Add the chopped onion and chile to taste (seeded if you prefer a milder flavor), bacon and chorizo. Sprinkle with the flour, crumble in the meat bouillon cube, and cook over low heat, stirring frequently, for about 10 minutes, until lightly browned. Add the onion and chile mixture to the snails, which should now be in just a little water, and simmer for about 20 minutes.

Fish croquettes
CROQUETAS DE PESCADO

- **½ quantity Croquettes (see recipe 62)**
- **sunflower oil, for deep frying**

Makes 20

Make a half quantity of croquettes according to recipe 62. Shape the mixture into small sized croquettes. Heat the oil in a deep-fryer or deep skillet to 350–375°F or until a cube of day-old bread browns in 30 seconds. Place several croquettes into the oil, being careful not to overcrowd the pan, and cook for 2 minutes, or until golden brown. Remove with a slotted spoon and keep warm while you quickly cook the remaining croquettes. Serve immediately.

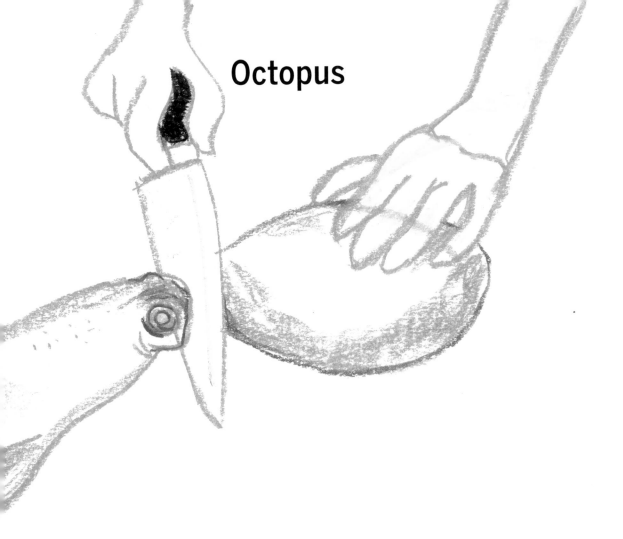

Octopus

How to cook

Octopus must be tenderized or it can be tough. It is sold fresh or frozen; the frozen is usually pre-cleaned. If you buy it fresh, to make sure that octopus will be tender enough, freeze it for up to 2 weeks. With either one, when you are ready to cook it, put the frozen octopus straight into boiling water and cook for about 35 minutes, until tender. The time will depend on the size and tenderness of the octopus. Alternatively, pour plenty of water into a pressure cooker, add a bay leaf and a piece of onion, and bring to a boil. Add the octopus, cover, bring to high pressure, and cook for 15 minutes. Let the pressure cooker cool completely before opening it. The following is a more classic way of cooking octopus: clean and rinse the octopus and prick it all over with a fork. Bring a large pan of water to a boil with a bay leaf and a piece of onion. Add the octopus and cook for 1 minute, then remove it from the pan. When the water comes back to a boil, add the octopus again for 1 minute. Do this three times in a row, leaving the octopus to cook for 45 minutes the last time. Drain the octopus and rinse under cold running water.

17   📷   Octopus with paprika
PULPO CON PIMENTÓN

- **2¼ pounds octopus**
- **¾ cup olive oil**
- **pinch of hot paprika**
- **salt (optional)**

Serves 6

Prepare and cook the octopus (see page 21). Drain well and rinse under cold running water. Remove and discard any remaining dark stain and cut the meat into small pieces with kitchen scissors. Place the pieces in a bowl, pour the oil over them, season with salt if necessary, and sprinkle with hot paprika to taste. Mix well to ensure the octopus is thoroughly coated and serve immediately. If this is not possible transfer the octopus to a heatproof bowl, cover with aluminum foil, and keep warm in the oven.

- **6 fl oz olive oil**
- **¼ small onion (about 1 ounce), chopped**
- **1 clove garlic, finely chopped**
- **pinch of sweet paprika**
- **2¼ pounds octopus**

Serves 6

Variation
Heat the oil in a pan. Add the onion and garlic and cook over low heat, stirring occasionally, for 10 minutes, until lightly browned. Remove the onion and garlic with a slotted spoon and discard. Remove the pan from the heat and stir in sweet paprika to taste. Add the flavored oil to the octopus pieces, mix well, and serve immediately.

18   Octopus in vinaigrette
PULPO EN VINAGRETA

- **2¼ pounds octopus**
- **⅔ cup olive oil**
- **1½ tablespoons white-wine vinegar**
- **1 onion, finely chopped**
- **1 green bell pepper, halved, seeded and diced**
- **2¼ cups cooked or drained canned peas**
- **salt and pepper**

Serves 6

Prepare and cook the octopus (see page 21). Meanwhile, prepare the vinaigrette. Whisk together the oil and vinegar in a bowl and season to taste with salt and pepper. Stir in the onion and green bell pepper and set aside. Drain the octopus well and rinse under cold running water. Remove and discard any remaining dark skin and cut the meat into medium-size pieces with kitchen scissors. Put the octopus pieces in a bowl, pour the vinaigrette over them, and add the peas. Taste and adjust the marinade if necessary. Cover the bowl and let marinate in the refrigerator, stirring occasionally, for 2 hours before serving.

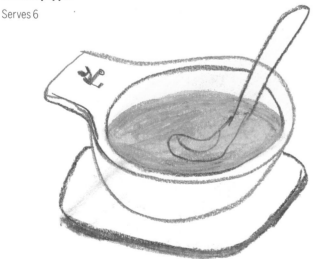

19

Little Pavian Soldiers

SOLDADITOS DE PAVÍA

- 1 pound 2 ounces skinless salt cod fillet, cut into strips
- 2 teaspoons paprika
- pinch of freshly ground black pepper
- juice of 1 lemon
- about 2¼ cups olive oil
- all-purpose flour, for dusting
- 1 egg

Serves 4

Put the cod strips in a bowl and add water to cover. Let soak, changing the water once, for 24–48 hours. Drain well and pat dry thoroughly with paper towel. Combine the paprika, black pepper, and lemon juice in a large bowl and stir in ¾ cup of the oil. Add the cod strips and mix well. Cover and let marinate, stirring occasionally, for at least 2 hours. Drain the cod and pat dry with paper towel. Heat the remaining oil in a deep-fryer or deep skillet to 350–375°F or until a cube of day-old bread browns in 30 seconds. Pour the flour into a shallow dish and lightly beat the egg in another shallow dish. Roll each strip of fish in the flour, shaking off any excess, then roll in the beaten egg. When the oil is hot enough, add the cod, in batches, and cook for 5 minutes until golden brown. Remove with a slotted spoon, drain on paper towel, then transfer to a warm oven while you cook the remaining strips.

20

Stuffed mushrooms

CHAMPIÑONES RELLENOS

- 6 tablespoons (¾ stick) butter, plus extra for greasing
- ½ cup bread crumbs
- 3–4 tablespoons warm milk
- 12 large, fresh mushrooms
- juice of ½ lemon
- ⅓ cup chopped Serrano ham or prosciutto
- 1 tablespoon chopped fresh parsley
- salt and pepper

Makes 12

Preheat the oven to 350°F. Generously grease an ovenproof baking dish with butter. Put the bread crumbs in a bowl, add the milk, and let soak. Remove the stalks from the mushrooms and chop them. Reserve the caps. Put the stalks in a pan with 2 tablespoons of the butter and the lemon juice and season with salt. Place the pan over low heat and cook gently for 6 minutes. Put the mushroom caps, gill sides up, in a single layer in the prepared ovenproof baking dish and dot with the remaining butter. Bake for 10 minutes. Meanwhile, drain the bread crumbs if they have not absorbed all the milk. Combine the mushroom stalks, bread crumbs, ham, and parsley in a bowl. Season with salt and pepper. Divide the mixture among the mushroom caps and return them to the oven for about 30 minutes. If the tops have not lightly browned, place the mushrooms under a preheated broiler for the last 10 minutes. Serve immediately, straight from the dish.

Russian salad

ENSALADILLA RUSA

- **9 ounces potatoes,
  diced and boiled**
- **1 pound 2 ounces carrots,
  diced and boiled**
- **2¼ pounds fresh peas, boiled**
- **7 ounces Classic Mayonnaise
  (see recipe 105)**

Serves 6

Drain the vegetables, transfer to a bowl and allow to cool. Add the mayonnaise and toss to combine thoroughly. Refrigerate until ready to use.

Note: The base for this salad is a thick mayonnaise, which is mixed with a combination of vegetables and the above is the classic version. Delicious variations include adding pieces of tart apple (such as Granny Smith or Fuji), walnut or celery to the vegetables. Cooked, peeled shrimp may also be added, and give an exquisite flavor to a simple Russian salad.

22

Watercress salad
ENSALADILLA DE BERROS

- 1 pound 2 ounces potatoes, diced
- 1 pound 2 ounces tart apples, such as Granny Smith or Fuji
- 9 ounces celery, sliced
- 2 bunches watercress, leaves picked and coarsely chopped
- 7 ounces Thick Mayonnaise (see recipe 106)
- 1 quantity tartlet cases (see recipe 1), optional

Serves 6

Cook the potato in salted water for 15–20 minutes, until tender but still firm to the bite. Drain and let cool completely. When the potato is cold, peel core and dice the apples, then mix with the potato. Add the celery and watercress. Stir in the mayonnaise, cover, and chill in the refrigerator for at least 1 hour. Serve the salad in a large bowl, or in individual tartlet cases for a special occasion.

23

Fried canapés
CANAPÉS FRITOS

- scant ½ cup milk
- 6 tablespoons (¼ stick) butter, plus extra for spreading
- ¼ cup all-purpose flour
- ½ cup grated gruyere cheese
- 1 egg
- 5 slices of bread
- olive oil, for frying
- salt and pepper

Makes 10

Put the milk and butter in a small pan, season, and bring to a boil. Add the flour and cook, stirring constantly to prevent lumps. When the mixture is thick and smooth, remove the pan from the heat and let cool slightly, then stir in the gruyere. Let cool until only just warm, then stir in the egg until incorporated. Season to taste. Spread the slices of bread with a little butter and a thick layer of the cheese mixture. Cut off the crusts and cut each slice diagonally to form two triangles. Heat the oil in a heavy skillet. Add several bread triangles, topping sides down, and fry until golden brown. Remove with a spatula and transfer to a warm oven while you cook the remaining triangles. Serve hot.

24

Hot cheese and mayonnaise canapés
CANAPÉS DE MAYONESA Y QUESO, CALIENTES

- 5 slices of bread, each cut into 4 x 1½ inch rounds and toasted
- 1 quantity Thick Mayonnaise (see recipe 106)
- 4 ounces grated cheese
- 2 onions

Makes 20

Preheat the oven to 350°F. Mix the mayonnaise with the grated cheese in a bowl. Spread the mixture generously on the toasted bread rounds, reserving a little. Slice the centers of the onions very thinly and sprinkle them over the toasts. Top each toast with a small pat of the reserved cheese mixture. Place the toasts on a baking sheet and bake for a few minutes, until they are golden brown. (Watch carefully as they burn very easily.) Serve hot

25

Cheese, tomato, and bacon canapés
CANAPÉS DE QUESO, TOMATE Y BACON

- 5 slices of bread, each cut into
  4 x 1½ inch rounds and toasted
- 4 tablespoons (½ stick) butter
- 3½ ounces cheese triangles,
  sliced, or other spreadable
  mild cheese
- 3 ripe tomatoes, thinly sliced
- 10 slices bacon,
  halved widthways
  Makes 20

Preheat the oven to 400°F. Spread the bread rounds lightly and evenly with a little softened butter. Place a slice of cheese on each, then add a slice of tomato. Place a slice of bacon (or half a slice if the slices are very long) doubled over on top of each. Put the canapés on a baking sheet and bake for about 15 minutes, until the cheese has melted and the bacon is crisp. Serve hot.

26

Soft cheese and paprika canapés
CANAPÉS DE QUESO BLANDO Y PIMENTÓN

- 5 slices of bread, each cut into
  4 x 1½ inch rounds and toasted
- 3½ ounces ricotta, or other soft
  white cheese
- pinch of paprika
  Makes 20

Preheat the oven to 350°F. Spread the toasted bread rounds with a generous layer of ricotta. Sprinkle each one with a little paprika, then place on a baking sheet, and bake for about 5 minutes, until the cheese has melted.

27

Soft cheese sandwiches
EMPAREDADOS DE QUESO BLANDO

- 3½ ounces ricotta
- 3½ ounces mascarpone
- 2 tablespoons heavy cream,
  or unsweetened evaporated milk
- 1 teaspoon finely chopped chives
  or shallot or scallion
- 10 slices white bread,
  crusts removed
- 10 slices rye bread,
  crusts removed
  Makes 20

Beat together the cheeses until combined, then beat in the cream or unsweetened evaporated milk. Stir in the chives, shallot, or scallion. Spread the mixture on the slices of white bread and top each with a slice of rye bread. Cut each sandwich diagonally in half to form two triangles. They may be kept in the refrigerator for a short time.

28

Baked cheese sticks

PALITOS DE QUESO AL HORNO

- Scant ½ cup (a little
  less than 1 stick) butter
- ⅔ cup all-purpose flour
- generous 1 cup grated
  Parmesan cheese
- 1 cup bread crumbs
- salt (optional)

Makes about 20

Preheat the oven to 400°F. Put the butter in a pan and melt it over low heat but do not let it brown, then remove the pan from the heat. Stir in the flour, then stir in the Parmesan. Season with salt if necessary. Pour the bread crumbs into a shallow dish spreading them out with a spoon. Shape scoops of the cheese mixture into long, fat sticks, about the size of your little finger. Roll the cheese sticks in the bread crumbs and place on a baking sheet. Bake for 8–10 minutes, until golden brown. Carefully transfer the cheese sticks to a wire rack (they will break easily) and let cool completely before serving.

29

Fried gruyere cheese

FRITOS DE QUESO GRUYÈRE

- 5 ounces gruyere cheese
- 1½ cups milk
- all-purpose flour, for dusting
- 1 egg, lightly beaten
- 1 cup bread crumbs
- peanut or sunflower oil,
  for deep frying

Makes 20

Cut the gruyere into ½ x ¾ x 1¼-inch pieces. Place in a bowl, add the milk and let soak for 2 hours. Drain the cheese and pat dry with paper towel. Roll each piece of cheese lightly in the flour, then the beaten egg, and finally in the bread crumbs. Heat the oil in a deep-fryer or deep skillet to 350–375°F or until a cube of day-old bread browns in 30 seconds. Add the cheese pieces, in batches, and cook for about 2 minutes, until golden. Drain well and serve immediately.

30

Fried gruyere cheese and bacon

FRITOS DE QUESO GRUYÈRE Y BACON

- 7 ounces gruyere cheese
- 5 slices thin rindless bacon
- 2–3 tablespoons oil

Makes about 15

Cut the cheese into strips about ½ inch thick and a little longer than the shorter side of the thin slices of bacon. If necessary, cut off the bacon rind with kitchen scissors and discard, then cut the slices in half. Place a piece of cheese on each half, roll up the bacon, and secure it with a wooden toothpick. Heat 2–3 tablespoons oil in a skillet. Add the bacon rolls and cook, turning frequently, for 10–15 minutes, until the bacon is browned and cooked through. Drain well and serve immediately, leaving the toothpicks in place.

31

Choux puffs with Roquefort or foie gras

PETITS-CHOUX AL ROQUEFORT O AL FOIE-GRAS

Choux pastry:
- 1¼ cups milk
- 4 tablespoons (½ stick) butter, plus extra for greasing
- ⅓ cup lard or white vegetable shortening
- 1¼ cups all-purpose flour
- 3 eggs
- 2 egg whites
- salt

Filling:
- 3½ ounces foie gras paté mixed with 4 tablespoons lightly whipped cream or 3½ ounces Roquefort cheese mixed with 3½ ounces softened butter

Makes approx. 65

Pour the milk into a pan and add the butter, lard or vegetable shortening, and a pinch of salt. Melt over low heat, stir the mixture with a wooden spoon, and bring to a boil. Immediately pour in all the flour and cook, stirring constantly, for 3 minutes. Remove the pan from the heat and let cool. Meanwhile, preheat the oven to 350°C. Lightly grease one or two baking sheets with butter. When the dough is nearly cooled, beat in the eggs, one at a time, making sure that each one has been fully incorporated before adding the next. Whisk the egg whites in a clean, dry bowl until they form soft peaks, then fold them into the mixture. Using a teaspoon, make small mounds of the mixture on the prepared baking sheet, spacing them well apart as they spread during cooking. Bake for 8–10 minutes, until puffed up and golden brown. Transfer to wire racks and let cool. Slit the puffs on one side with kitchen scissors and open them with your fingers. Choose your preferred filling, mix the ingredients, then use a small spoon to fill the puffs with the filling.

32

Celery with Roquefort

APIO CON ROQUEFORT

- 1 head celery, trimmed and washed
- 2 ounces Roquefort cheese
- 2 ounces butter, softened

Makes approx. 25

Cut the celery stalks into 1¼-inch lengths. Beat the Roquefort and butter in a bowl. Fill each piece of celery with the mixture, spreading it out evenly. Put the filled celery on a plate, cover, and chill in the refrigerator for at least 1 hour before serving.

33 Fried date and bacon rolls

PINCHOS DE DÁTILES Y BACON FRITOS

- **20 dried dates**
- **20 slices thin rindless bacon**
- **2–3 tablespoons peanut oil**

Makes 20

Slit the dates along the longest sides and carefully remove and discard the pits. Wrap each date in a slice of bacon. Heat the oil in a skillet, add the bacon rolls, and cook, turning occasionally, for about 10 minutes, until the bacon is cooked through and lightly browned. Drain well and serve immediately.

34 Prunes stuffed with Roquefort, raisins, and pine nuts

CIRUELAS RELLENAS DE ROQUEFORT, PASAS Y PIÑONES

- **3½ ounces Roquefort cheese**
- **12 pine nuts**
- **scant ¼ cup raisins**
- **1 tablespoon wine from Malaga or sweet sherry**
- **4 tablespoons light cream**
- **12 ready-to-eat pitted prunes**

Makes 12

Crumble the Roquefort into a bowl and mash lightly with a fork. Add the pine nuts, raisins, wine or sherry, and cream and mix to a paste. Open the cavities of the prunes with your fingers and use a small spoon to fill the prunes with the Roquefort paste. Close the prunes and secure with wooden toothpicks. Put the prunes on a plate, cover, and chill in the refrigerator for at least 2 hours before serving.

Note: To use standard prunes, soak them in warm water to rehydrate, following the instructions on the packet, then remove the pits.

35

Mushroom tartlets

TARTALETAS DE CHAMPIÑON

- 1 quantity tartlet cases
  (see recipe 1)
- 4 ounces white mushrooms,
  sliced
- 4 tablespoons (½ stick) butter
- juice of ½ lemon
- 1 tablespoon sunflower oil
- 1 tablespoon all-purpose flour
- 1 cup milk
- pinch of curry powder
- salt

Makes 20

Put the mushrooms in a pan with half the butter and the lemon juice. Cover and cook over low heat for 10–15 minutes, until tender. Heat the remaining butter with the oil in a pan. Stir in the flour, then gradually stir in the milk. Cook, stirring constantly, for about 8 minutes, until thickened and smooth. Season with salt and stir in a very small pinch of curry powder. Mix the sauce with the mushrooms and their cooking juices, then spoon the mixture into the tartlet shells, and serve hot.

36

Asparagus éclairs

ÉCLAIRS DE ESPÁRRAGOS

- 1 quantity Choux Pastry
  (see recipe 31)
- butter, for greasing
- 1 quantity Thick Mayonnaise
  (see recipe 106)
- 1 jar asparagus tips, drained

Makes 20

Preheat the oven to 350°F and lightly grease 2 baking sheets with butter. Make the choux pastry as described in recipe 31 but instead of making small balls, pipe finger shapes onto the baking sheet. Cook for 8–10 minutes until puffed up. Remove from the oven and let cool on the trays. When the baked éclairs are cold, slit each one along one side with kitchen scissors. Fill with thick mayonnaise and asparagus tips, before gently closing. Serve reasonably soon after making or the pastry will go soggy.

COLD PLATE SUGGESTIONS

37

Salad with yogurt dressing
ENSALADA CON SALSA DE YOGUR

- ⅔ cup plain yogurt
- juice of ½ lemon
- 1 head lettuce,
  cored and trimmed
- 1 tart apple,
  such as Granny Smith or Fuji
- ½ cup hazelnuts
- 1 tablespoon chopped
  fresh parsley
- salt and pepper

Serves 4

Combine the yogurt and lemon juice in a small bowl and season to taste with salt and pepper. Line a salad bowl with the lettuce. Core the apple, cut it into very thin slices, and add to the bowl. Coarsley chop the hazlenuts and sprinkle over the top. Pour the dressing over the salad and toss lightly. Sprinkle with the parsley before serving.

Note: When in season, green asparagus may also be added to this recipe. It should be cooked (see page 309), cooled, and cut into 2-inch lengths.

38

Salad with asparagus, York ham, and mayonnaise
ENSALADA DE ESPÁRRAGOS, JAMÓN DE YORK Y MAYONESA

- 1 bunch white asparagus or
  14 ounces canned white
  asparagus
- 3 firm tomatoes
- 1 cucumber
- 3 hard-cooked eggs
- 7 ounces Smithfield,
  or Black Forest Ham, prosciutto,
  or other dry-cured ham, diced
- 1 tablespoon chopped onion
- 1 tablespoon chopped
  fresh parsley
- salt

Mayonnaise
- 1 egg
- 1¼ cups olive oil
- 1 tablespoon white-wine vinegar
  or lemon juice

Serves 6

Make the mayonnaise as described in recipe 105. If using fresh asparagus, trim, peel, and cook (see page 309). Drain the cooked (or canned) asparagus well and leave on a clean dishtowel to dry. Dice the tomatoes, put them in a colander, sprinkle with a little salt, and let drain. Peel and dice the cucumber, put it in another colander, sprinkle with a little salt, and let drain. Rinse both ingredients and pat dry. Cut the asparagus spears into 1-inch lengths. Chop 1½ of the hard-cooked eggs and slice the remaining eggs. Combine the asparagus, tomato, cucumber, chopped eggs, ham, onion, and half the parsley in a bowl. Stir in the mayonnaise, cover, and chill in the refrigerator for 1 hour. To serve, garnish the salad with the sliced eggs and sprinkle with the remaining parsley.

Roasted mixed vegetables
ESCALIBADA

- 2 large green bell peppers
- 1 large red bell pepper
- 3 eggplants,
  about 1¾ pounds total weight
- 1 large onion
- 4 potatoes,
  about 1¾ pounds total weight
- 1½ cups olive oil
- 2 tomatoes
- 6 tablespoons white-wine
  vinegar
- 1 clove garlic, finely chopped
- salt and pepper

Serves 4

Preheat the oven to 400°F. Put the bell peppers, eggplants, onion, and potatoes (unpeeled) into a roasting pan. Pour in half the oil and toss to coat. Roast for 25 minutes. Stir gently, add the tomatoes, and roast for 20 minutes more. Remove the roasting pan from the oven and let the vegetables stand until they are cool enough to handle. Peel, halve and seed the bell peppers, then cut them into strips. Peel the eggplants and cut into strips. Cut the onion into wedges. Peel the tomatoes and cut into pieces. Place them in a bowl. Whisk together the remaining oil and the vinegar to make a vinaigrette. Season each vegetable separately with salt and pepper and sprinkle with the vinaigrette. Cut the potatoes in half and scoop out the flesh with a teaspoon, taking care not to pierce the skins. Chop the flesh, season to taste with salt and pepper, and return it to the potato skins. The escalibada may be served in one large dish or four individual dishes. Put the potatoes in the center and arrange the other vegetables around them. Stir the garlic into the vinaigrette remaining after the vegetables have been dressed and pour it over the salad.

Note: It may be better to use fresh vinaigrette for pouring over the salad at the end, as the vinaigrette used with the vegetables can take on a strong flavor, particularly from the bell peppers.

40

Rolls of ham with Russian salad and gelatin

CANUTILLOS DE JAMÓN DE YORK CON ENSALADA RUSA Y GELATINA

- **2 carrots**
- **1 envelope (¼ ounce)
  unflavored powdered gelatin**
- **3 ½ ounces canned peas,
  drained**
- **6 slices of Smithfield,
  or Black Forest Ham, prosciutto,
  or other dry-cured ham**
- **1 pound 2 ounces Russian Salad
  (see recipe 21)**
- **lettuce leaves, sliced tomato,
  and sliced hard-cooked egg
  (optional)**
- **salt**

Serves 6

Cook the carrots in a pan of salted boiling water for about 15 minutes, until tender. Drain and slice thinly, then let cool. Pour 2 ½ cups water into a heatproof bowl. Sprinkle the gelatin over the surface and let stand for 5 minutes, until spongy. Set the bowl over a pan of barely simmering water and heat until the gelatin has dissolved and the mixture is clear. Do not stir. Remove the bowl from the heat. Pour a thin layer of gelatin into the base of a round cake pan, 9 inches in diameter and 1½ inches deep. Put the pan in the refrigerator and leave until the gelatin has set, then arrange the carrot slices and peas decoratively over the base. Place a slice of ham on a plate and put 1 ½ tablespoons of the Russian salad on top, then roll up the ham and se-cure it with a toothpick. Repeat with the remaining slices of ham and Russian salad. Place the ham rolls in the pan, arranging them like the spokes of a wheel with the toothpicks sticking up. Pour in the remain-ing gelatin and put the pan in the refrigerator for 3–4 hours, until set. To serve, carefully remove and discard the toothpicks. Warm a palette knife in hot water and run it around the edge of the pan and turn the salad out onto a round plate. A typical Spanish garnish for this dish would include lettuce leaves, tomato slices and slices of hard-cooked egg.

41

Rolls of ham with asparagus and mayonnaise

ROLLOS DE JAMÓN DE YORK CON ESPÁRRAGOS Y MAYONESA

- 1 tablespoon capers,
  rinsed, drained and chopped
- 1 quantity Classic Mayonnaise
  (see recipe 105)
- 6 slices of Smithfield,
  or Black Forest Ham, prosciutto,
  or other dry-cured ham
- 6 fat, canned asparagus spears
  or 18 thin, canned asparagus
  spears, drained
- 1 hard-cooked egg, chopped
- 2 sprigs fresh parsley, chopped
- 6 dried pitted dates
- 3 tablespoons sunflower oil
- 1 tablespoon white-wine vinegar
  or lemon juice
- 3 carrots, cut into julienne strips
- salt

Serves 6

Stir the capers into the mayonnaise. Spread out a slice of ham and place 1 tablespoon mayonnaise mixture in the middle. Place 1 fat asparagus spear or 3 thin asparagus spears on top of the mayonnaise. Roll up the ham carefully with the asparagus in the middle, its tip poking out of the end. Repeat with the remaining ham and asparagus. Place the rolls on a serving dish. Set a little egg white to one side, then combine the remaining chopped egg with the parsley. Sprinkle the mixture over the ham rolls. Place a date on the middle of each roll. Whisk together the oil and vinegar or lemon juice in a bowl and season to taste with salt. Add the carrot strips and toss, then decorate the serving dish with four mounds of carrot strips. If you are not serving the dish immediately, cover with aluminum foil and store in the refrigerator.

42

Foie-gras aspic mousse

ASPIC-MOUSSE DE FOIE-GRAS

- ½ envelope (⅓ ounce)
  unflavored powdered gelatin
- 1 black truffle, sliced (optional)
- 2 ounces goose or duck
  foie gras, fresh or canned
- ¾ cup heavy cream, whipped,
  until slightly thickened
- iceberg lettuce leaves
  or arugula (optional)

Serves 4

Pour 1¼ cups water into a heatproof bowl. Sprinkle the gelatin over the surface and let stand for 5 minutes. Set the bowl over a pan of barely simmering water and heat until the gelatin has dissolved and the mixture is clear. Do not stir. Remove the bowl from the heat and let stand until the gelatin is almost cold but still liquid. Pour a thin layer over the base of a quiche pan. Arrange slices of truffle, if using, on top and put in the refrigerator until the gelatin has set. Put the foie gras in a bowl and mash with a fork, then stir in one-third of the heavy cream. When fully incorporated, stir in half the remaining cream, and when that has been fully incorporated, stir in the rest. Gradually, add the remaining gelatin, whisking constantly. Pour the mixture into the pan with the gelatin and chill in the refrigerator for at least 3 hours, longer if time allows. To serve, warm a metal spatula in hot water and run it around the edge of the pan and turn out the mousse onto a round plate. Garnish with iceberg lettuce leaves or arugula.

For more dishes that could be served as cold plates, see the following recipes:

Soups
Gazpacho (recipe 168)
Chunky gazpacho (recipe 169)
Chilled gazpachuelo (recipe 170)
Tomato juice soup (recipe 138)
Vichyssoise (recipe 172)

Fish and shellfish
Tuna, mayonnaise, and potato roll (recipe 239)
Cold bonito pie (recipe 562)
Fisherman's cold spider crab (recipe 651)
Bonito in aspic with mayonnaise (recipe 565)
Shellfish cocktail (recipe 658)
Glasses of fish and shellfish with vegetable sauce (recipe 679)

Chicken

Chicken supremes (recipe 822)

Eggs

Eggs mimosa (recipe 483)
Hard-cooked eggs with salad (recipe 486)
Poached eggs in jelly (recipe 494)

Vegetables

Red bell peppers with hard-cooked eggs (recipe 431)
Tomatoes filled with sardines, green bell peppers, and olives
  (recipe 455)

Vegetables and potatoes

Cold rice with vegetables and vinaigrette (recipe 186)
Cold rice with tuna and mayonnaise (recipe 183)
Lentil salad (recipe 229)
Potatoes with mayonnaise, tomato, and anchovies (recipe 268)
Potato salad with tuna and hard-cooked egg (recipe 266)

Aspic mousses

Bonito in aspic with mayonnaise (recipe 565)

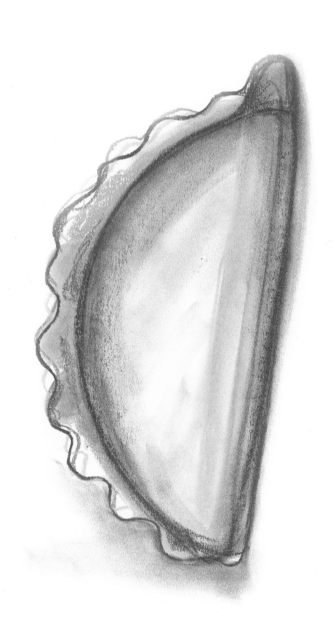

FRIED DISHES, SAVORY TARTLETS, LITTLE TURNOVERS AND MOUSSES

Pastry for little turnovers (first version)
MASA DE EMPANADILLAS

- ½ cup dry white wine
- 2 tablespoons butter
- 2 tablespoons lard or
  vegetable shortening
- 2¾ cups all-purpose flour,
  plus extra for dusting
- vegetable oil, for deep frying
- salt

Makes 30–36

Pour the wine into a pan and add ½ cup water, the butter, and lard or shortening. Heat gently, stirring, until the fat has melted. Once the mixture is warm but not boiling, remove the pan from the heat, sift in the flour and a pinch of salt, and stir well with a wooden spoon. Turn out the dough onto a floured surface and knead well until smooth. Form the dough into a ball, put it on a plate, cover with a clean dish towel, and let rest for about 2 hours. To make the turnovers, roll out the dough on a floured surface until it is ⅛ inch thick. Place mounds of your chosen filling (see recipe 45) on half the dough and fold the other half over to cover them. Cut into half-moon shapes, leaving a small margin around the filling. To do this, you can use a crescent-shaped cutter, a pastry wheel, or a fine-edged glass. Press the pastry edges securely together with your fingers to prevent the filling leaking out when the turnovers are deep-fried. Heat the oil in a deep-fryer or deep skillet to 350–375° F or until a cube of day-old bread browns in 30 seconds. Carefully add the empanadas to the hot oil, in batches, and cook for 6–8 minutes, until golden brown. Remove from the oil with a slotted spatula, drain on paper towels, season lightly with salt and serve hot.

44

Pastry for little turnovers (second version)
MASA DE EMPANADILLAS

- 2 tablespoons butter
- 3 tablespoons sunflower oil
- 2¾ cups all-purpose flour,
  plus extra for dusting
- 1 egg
- vegetable oil, for deep-frying
- salt

Makes about 30–36

Pour 1 cup water into a pan, add a pinch of salt, the butter, and oil, and heat gently to melt the butter. When the mixture is warm but not boiling, remove the pan from the heat, add the flour, and stir well. Stir in the egg. Mix in the pan until it forms a dough then turn it out onto a floured surface and knead well (more flour can be added to the mixture if necessary). Cover the dough with a clean dish towel and let rest for at least 30 minutes. Make the turnovers as described in the previous recipe.

45 Fillings for little turnovers

RELLENOS PARA LAS EMPANADILLAS

Filling suggestions:
- 1 onion, chopped and sautéed in olive oil for 5 minutes until softened and translucent
- 3 tablespoons tomato paste
- about 2 cups leftover cooked ground meat, or dry-cured ham, or cooked chicken, or cooked fish, or canned, drained tuna
- 1 slice bread, crusts removed, soaked in warm milk, and drained slightly, or a chopped hard-cooked egg
- 1 anchovy (optional)
- pepper, chopped fresh parsley, or grated nutmeg

The principle for preparing the filling for the turnovers is almost always the same. Choose your prefered filling and combine the ingredients well. Use about 2 generous teaspoons of filling per turnover, and fill the turnovers (see recipe 43).

Note: Some people prefer to mix the meat or fish with a thick béchamel sauce (see recipe 77) instead of onion and tomato. The taste is also good, but milder in flavor.

46 Puff pastry for pies

EMPANADAS DE HOJALDRE

- 1¾ cups all-purpose flour, plus extra for dusting
- ⅔ cup lard, softened
- ½ cup margarine, softened
- juice of 1 lemon
- 1 egg, lightly beaten
- salt

Makes 1 pie

Make the puff pastry dough as described in recipe 9. Divide the pastry into 2 equal pieces. Roll each piece into a circle 10 inches wide, ¼ inch thick. Preheat the oven to 350°F. Arrange the filling (see recipes 47–49) on one circle of dough, carefully leaving a ¾ inch margin around the edge so that the dough can be sealed around the filling. When you are happy with the filling, gently lay the second circle of dough over the top, pressing down around the edge to seal the pastry. Transfer to the oven and cook until lightly browned on top.

Note: You can vary the filling as much as you like, although the classic recipe is a thick tomato sauce with strips of fresh, roasted or preserved red bell pepper.

47

Puff-pastry tuna pie
EMPANADA DE HOJALDRE CON BONITO EN ESCABECHE

• 1 quantity Puff Pastry dough
  (see recipe 968)
• 1 quantity Classic Tomato Sauce
  (see recipe 73)
• 1 x 7-ounce canned tuna,
  drained
• 2 bottled or canned bell peppers,
  cut into strips
Makes 1 pie

Prepare the dough as described in recipe 46. Spread the tomato sauce over the dough. Coarsely flake the tuna. Scatter evenly over the dough, and add the peppers. Proceed as in recipe 46.

48

Puff-pastry lean pork and black pudding pie
EMPANADA DE HOJALDRE CON MAGRO DE CERDO Y MORCILLA

• 1 quantity Puff Pastry dough
  (see recipe 968)
• 1 quantity Classic Tomato Sauce
  (see recipe 73)
• 14 ounces lean pork,
  cut into cubes
• 1 blood sausage (morcilla) cut
  into ¾-inch thick slices
Makes 1 pie

Prepare the dough as described in recipe 46. Spread the tomato sauce over the dough. Heat a little oil in a skillet and add the pork. Cook for 5 minutes or until cooked through and lightly browned. Scatter the pork and slices of blood or other sausage evenly over the dough. Proceed as in recipe 46.

49

Puff-pastry chicken and pepper pie
EMPANADA DE HOJALDRE CON POLLO

• 1 quantity Puff Pastry dough
  (see recipe 968)
• 1 quantity Classic Tomato Sauce
  (see recipe 73)
• 2 roasted, boneless chicken
  breast halves, or other leftover
  cooked chicken, cut into bite-
  sized pieces
• 2 bottled or canned bell peppers,
  cut into strips
Makes 1 pie

Prepare the dough as described in recipe 46. Spread the tomato sauce over the dough. Arrange the chicken and peppers evenly on top. Proceed as in recipe 46.

Galician pie

EMPANADA GALLEGA

- ¼ ounce (1 package) active-dry
  yeast
- ¾ cup lukewarm water
- 3 eggs
- 3½ cups all-purpose flour,
  plus extra for dusting
- 1 tablespoon margarine,
  at room temperature
- 2 tablespoons sunflower oil,
  plus extra for brushing
- 14 ounces pork tenderloin
  or skinless, boneless chicken
  breast halves, cut into strips
- 2 canned or bottled bell peppers,
  or roasted bell peppers, drained
  and cut into strips
- salt

"Rustido:"
- 2 tablespoons olive oil
- 3 onions, coarsely chopped
- 1 clove garlic, crushed
- 1 tablespoon chopped
  fresh parsley
- 1 chorizo sausage, sliced

Serves 4–5

Mash the yeast with a pinch of salt and the lukewarm water in a cup or small bowl until smooth, then let stand for about 10 minutes, until the mixture is frothy. Beat two of the eggs in a bowl. Sift the flour with a pinch of salt onto a work surface. Make a well in the center and pour in the beaten egg and yeast mixture. Gradually incorporate the flour into the liquid, then knead well for 10 minutes. Dust the surface lightly with flour to prevent the dough sticking. Add the margarine and knead for 10 minutes more, banging the dough onto the surface. Add a little water to the dough if necessary. Once the dough is smooth and elastic, form it into a ball, place it in a bowl, and cover with a clean dish towel. Let rise in a warm place for 1–2 hours, until doubled in volume. Meanwhile, make the "rustido." Heat the olive oil in a skillet. Add the onions and cook over low heat, stirring occasionally, for 10 minutes, until softened and translucent. Add the garlic and parsley and cook for 5 minutes more. Stir in the chorizo and cook for 2 minutes more. Remove the skillet from the heat and set aside. Heat the sunflower oil in a skillet. Add the strips of meat and cook over medium-low heat, stirring frequently, for about 8 minutes, until golden brown. Remove from the skillet with a slotted spoon and set aside. Preheat the oven to 350°F. Brush a 12-inch baking pan or ovenproof baking dish with oil. Divide the dough into two pieces, one slightly bigger than the other. Roll out the larger piece on a lightly floured surface and use to line the pan or dish. Spread half the rustido over the dough. Lay the strips of meat on the rustido and add the strips of bell pepper. Spoon the remaining rustido over the top. Roll out the remaining dough and use it to cover the mixture. Seal the edges of the dough carefully, pressing them together and rolling them slightly. Pinch the dough in the center of the pie with two fingers to create a chimney to allow the steam to escape. Beat the remaining egg and brush it over the dough to glaze. Bake for 15 minutes, then increase the oven temperature to 375°F, and bake for 15 minutes longer. Increase the oven temperature to 400°F and bake for 15 minutes more, until golden brown. Remove the pie from the oven. Serve hot or warm, straight from the dish, if you prefer.

Note: You can vary the filling as much as you like. Try fresh sardines (scaled, cleaned, and the heads, tails, and backbones removed) or salt cod (soaked and blanched). Raisins can be added to a cod pie. Squid can also be used for the filling; fry it with the "rustido."

51

Puff-pastry pie with farmer's cheese and mushrooms

EMPANADA DE HOJALDRE CONGELADO, QUESO DE BURGOS Y CHAMPIÑONES

- 5 ounces mushrooms,
  thickly sliced
- 1½ tablespoons margarine
- 2 tablespoons lemon juice
- 14 ounces frozen puff pastry
  dough, thawed
- all-purpose flour, for dusting
- scant 1 cup farmer's cheese
- 1 tablespoon chopped
  fresh parsley
- 1 extra large egg or 2 medium
  eggs, lightly beaten
- salt (optional)

Serves 4

Preheat the oven to 400°F. Put the mushrooms, margarine, and lemon juice into a pan and cook over low heat, stirring occasionally, for about 6 minutes. Remove the pan from the heat and set aside. Gently roll the thawed dough with a rolling pin, first in one direction and then the other (across and down) to make it thinner. Roll out on a lightly floured surface to ⅛ inch thick. Cut a 9-inch round from the dough and use it to line the base and sides of an 8-inch baking pan with removable base. Reserve the remaining dough. Lightly prick the base with a fork and bake for about 10 minutes. Meanwhile, mash the cheese in a bowl with a fork. Drain the mushrooms and add them to the cheese with the parsley and most of the beaten egg, leaving just enough egg to glaze the pastry. Season lightly with salt if necessary. Remove the piecrust from the oven and spread the filling over the base. Roll out the remaining dough and place it on top of the filling, carefully sealing the sides. Make a hole in the center of the lid with a knife to let the steam escape during cooking. Brush the remaining beaten egg over the pastry and bake for 15–20 minutes, until golden brown. (It may be necessary to put the pie under the broiler for a short time to brown the top.) Let the pie stand on a work surface for 10 minutes until cooled slightly before transferring it to a serving dish. Serve warm.

52

Shrimp and béchamel toasts

PAN DE MOLDE CON GAMBAS Y BECHAMEL

- 1 pounds 2 ounces raw shrimp,
  shelled and deveined
- 2 tablespoons butter
- 3 tablespoons olive oil
- 1 heaping tablespoon
  all-purpose flour
- 2¼ cups milk
- pinch of curry powder (optional)
- 12 slices of bread
- ½ cup grated gruyere cheese
- salt

Serves 6

If the shrimp are quite large, cut them in half. Set aside. Preheat the oven to 350°F. Melt the butter with the oil in a pan over low heat. Add the shrimp and cook, stirring occasionally, for 3–4 minutes, until pink and cooked through. Using a slotted spoon, transfer the shrimp to a plate. Stir the flour into the pan, then gradually add the milk, a little at a time, stirring constantly with a whisk or wooden spoon. Simmer gently for 10 minutes, then stir in the curry powder, if using, and season to taste with salt. Add the shrimp and mix well before spreading the mixture on the slices of bread. Sprinkle the gruyere on top, place on a baking sheet, and bake for about 5 minutes, until golden brown. Transfer to a large dish and serve immediately.

53

Mushroom, béchamel, and cheese toasts
PAN DE MOLDE CON CHAMPIÑONES, BECHAMEL Y QUESO RALLADO

- **14 ounces mushrooms**
- **¼ cup (½ stick) butter**
- **juice of 1 lemon**
- **2 tablespoons sunflower oil**
- **1 heaping tablespoon flour**
- **2 ¼ cups milk**
- **12 slices of bread**
- **½ cup grated gruyere or**
  ⅔ cup grated Parmesan cheese
- **salt and pepper**

Serves 6

Prepare the mushrooms (see page 379), cutting them into thick slices and using 1 ½ tablespoons of the butter and the lemon juice. Preheat the oven to 350°F. Melt the remaining butter with the oil in a pan over low heat. Stir in the flour, then gradually add the milk, a little at a time, stirring constantly with a whisk. Season with salt and a little pepper. Simmer gently for about 10 minutes, then add the mushrooms and their cooking juices. Stir well, remove the pan from the heat, and let cool slightly. Spread the mixture on the slices of bread and sprinkle with the gruyere or Parmesan. Place on a baking sheet and bake for about 5 minutes, until golden brown. Transfer to a large dish and serve immediately.

54

Cheese toasts
PAN DE MOLDE CON QUESO RALLADO

- **generous 1 cup milk**
- **6 tablepoons butter**
- **3 tablespoons all-purpose flour**
- **3 eggs**
- **1 ¼ cups grated gruyere cheese**
- **12 slices of bread**
- **vegetable oil, for deep-frying**
- **salt and pepper**

Serves 6

Pour the milk into a pan, add the butter, season with salt and pepper, and bring to a rolling boil. Add the flour and cook, stirring constantly with a wooden spoon, until the mixture thickens and comes away from the sides of the pan. Remove the pan from the heat and let cool slightly. Stir in the eggs (unbeaten), one at a time, making sure each one is fully incorporated before adding the next. Stir in the gruyere. Spread the mixture on the slices of bread, covering them generously, and let stand in a cool place for 30 minutes. Heat the oil in a deep-fryer or skillet to 350–375°F or until a cube of day-old bread browns in 30 seconds. Working in batches, carefully add the slices of bread, coated sides down, and cook for a few minutes, until golden brown. Remove with a slotted spatula, drain well, and keep warm in the oven until all the toasts are cooked. Serve warm.

Note: These toasts can also be cooked in the oven. They taste equally good but do not look as attractive as the fried version. If cooking in the oven, sprinkle some extra gruyere on each slice, as this cheese melts well in the oven.

55

Pizza

Dough:
- 1 ounce (½ large cake) fresh yeast
- 1¼ cups lukewarm water
- 2¼ cups all-purpose flour, plus extra for dusting
- 1 teaspoon salt
- 2 tablespoons olive oil, plus extra for greasing

Serves 4

Mash the yeast with the lukewarm water in a cup or small bowl until smooth, then let stand for about 10 minutes, until the mixture is frothy. Sift the flour and salt onto a surface and make a well in the center. Pour in the oil and gradually add the yeast mixture. Using your fingers, gradually incorporate the flour into the liquid, then knead the dough until it is smooth and elastic. Dust the work surface lightly with flour to prevent the dough sticking. Form the dough into a ball, place it in a ceramic or glass bowl, cover with a clean dish towel, and let rise in a warm place for 1–2 hours, until doubled in volume. Lightly grease a baking pan with a removeable base. Roll out the dough into a round and transfer it to the baking pan. Add the topping (see Note), cover the pizza with aluminum foil and let stand for about 30 minutes before baking in a preheated oven at 400°F. It will take 20–30 minutes to cook.

Note: It is usual to cover the dough base with a thick tomato sauce (see recipe 73). On top of this place slices of mozzarella or other cheeses that will melt easily. Add some anchovies if you like and pitted olives (usually black) and slices of tomato. Use ripe tomatoes and slice them in advance to give them time to drain. Additional ingredients, such as bacon, mussels, etc, are a matter of personal taste. Sprinkle oregano over the pizza and season with salt and pepper.

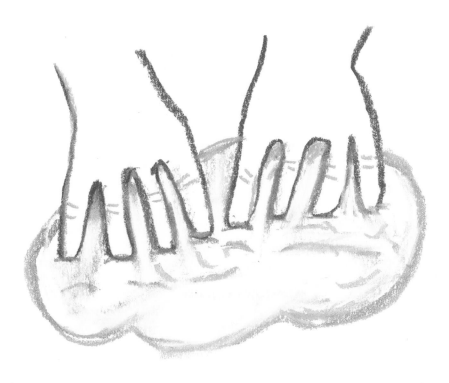

Bacon and cheese tart: quiche

TARTA DE BACON Y QUESO: QUICHE

Pastry:
- 1¾ cups all-purpose flour,
  plus extra for dusting
- 6½ tablespoons butter,
  cut into small pieces,
  plus extra for greasing
- 1 egg yolk
- 1 tablespoon sunflower oil
- salt

Filling:
- 3¼ ounces gruyere cheese
- 2 bacon or ham slices, diced
- 4 eggs, beaten
- generous 1 cup heavy cream
- ¾ cup milk
- salt

Serves 6–8

Make the pastry dough at least 2 hours before preparing the quiche. Sift the flour and a pinch of salt into a bowl, add the butter, and rub it into the flour with your fingertips. Try to handle the ingredients as little as possible. Add the egg yolk and oil and work the mixture until it has the texture of bread crumbs. Gradually stir in 1¼ cups water, a little at a time. Turn out onto a lightly floured surface and knead gently to form a dough. Roll it into a ball, put on a plate, cover, and let rest in a cool place. Preheat the oven to 350°F. Lightly grease with butter a loose-based quiche pan, 10 inches in diameter and about 1½ inches deep. Roll out the dough to a round on a lightly floured surface. Lift the dough on the rolling pin into the prepared pan and press down with your fingers to make sure it is even over the base. Trim the excess dough with a sharp knife and lightly prick the base all over with a fork. For the filling, thinly slice 1½ ounces of the gruyere and grate the remainder. Place the bacon or ham and the cheese slices in the piecrust and bake for about 20 minutes, until the pastry is cooked but not browned. Meanwhile, beat the eggs with the cream and milk in a bowl and season with salt. Remove the piecrust from the oven and increase the oven temperature to 425°F. Pour the egg mixture into the piecrust, sprinkle the remaining grated cheese on top, and return the quiche to the oven. Bake for 15 minutes, then lower the oven temperature to 350°F, and bake for 25 minutes more, until golden brown. Remove the quiche from the oven and allow to cool slightly. Transfer to a serving dish and serve warm.

Onion tart

TARTA DE CEBOLLA

Pastry:
- 1¾ cups all-purpose flour, plus extra for dusting
- 6 tablespoons butter, cut into small cubes, plus extra for greasing
- 1 egg, separated
- 1 tablespoon olive oil
- salt

Filling:
- 6 tablespoons olive oil
- 2 tablespoons margarine
- 2¼ pounds onions, thinly sliced
- 1 heaping tablespoon all-purpose flour
- scant 1 cup light cream
- ½ cup grated gruyere cheese
- salt and pepper

Serves 6–8

Make the pastry dough as described in recipe 56, using the egg yolk but reserving the white. Let rest in a cool place for at least 2 hours. Preheat the oven to 450°F. Lightly grease with butter an 11-inch quiche pan with a removeable base. Roll out the dough to a round on a lightly floured surface. Lift the dough on the rolling pin into the prepared pan and press down with your fingers to make sure it is even over the base. Trim the excess dough with a sharp knife and lightly prick the base all over with a fork. Bake for 15 minutes. Meanwhile, lightly whisk the egg white in a small, clean, dry bowl until it is frothy but not stiff. Brush the egg white over the base of the piecrust, then return the pan to the oven for 5 minutes more. To make the filling, heat the oil in a large pan and, when it is hot, add the margarine. Add the onion and cook over low heat, stirring occasionally, for about 5 minutes, until softened and translucent. Drain off the fat, return the pan to the heat, sprinkle in the flour, and season with salt and pepper. Stir well, then stir in the cream. Spoon the mixture into the piecrust and spread it evenly over the base. Sprinkle the gruyere on top and bake for about 25 minutes, until golden brown. Remove the tart from the oven and let cool slightly. Serve warm.

58

Fritter batter (first version)
MASA PARA BUÑUELOS

- 2 ¾ cups all-purpose flour
- 3 tablespoons white wine
- 3 tablespoons sunflower oil
- 1 ¼ cups milk
- ½ teaspoon baking powder
- vegetable oil, for deep-frying
- salt

Serves 4–6

Sift the flour and a pinch of salt into a bowl. Make a well in the center, and pour in the wine and sunflower oil. Stir with a wooden spoon, then stir in the milk. Let the mixture rest for at least 30 minutes. Mix the baking powder into the batter. Heat the vegetable oil in a deep-fryer or deep saucepan to 350–375°f or until a cube of day-old bread browns in 30 seconds. Working quickly, but carefully, add some filling of your choice to one heaped teaspoon of fritter batter at a time and cook, in batches, for 3–5 minutes or until golden brown. Drain on paper towel and season lightly with salt.

59

Fritter batter (second version)
MASA PARA BUÑUELOS

- 1 ¼ cups all-purpose flour
- 1 egg, separated
- 1 tablespoon sunflower oil
- 1 cup beer
- salt

Serves 4

This batter is good for frying fish, courgette, apple, etc. Sift the flour and a pinch of salt into a bowl. Make a well in the center, and pour in the egg yolk and oil. Stir well, then gradually stir in the beer, a little at a time, until a thick batter forms. Just before cooking, whisk the egg white with a pinch of salt in a clean, dry bowl until soft peaks form. Fold the egg white into the batter. Form the batter into fritters, add your chosen filling, and cook as described in recipe 58.

60

Fritter batter (third version)
MASA PARA BUÑUELOS

- 1 ¼ cups all-purpose flour
- 1 cup soda water
- very small amount of baking powder (just enough to cover the tip of a knife)
- pinch of salt
- pinch of powdered saffron

Serves 4

This batter can be used for brains, squid, onions, etc. Mix all the ingredients to form a thick batter. Shape into fritters, add your chosen filling and cook as described in recipe 58.

Cheese fritters with tomato sauce
BUÑUELOS DE QUESO CON SALSA DE TOMATE

- **2 tablespoons butter**
- **1 cup all-purpose flour**
- **4 eggs**
- **1¼ cups grated gruyere cheese**
- **vegetable oil, for deep-frying**
- **1 quantity Classic Tomato Sauce
  (see recipe 73)**
- **salt**

Serves 6

Pour 1⅔ cups water into a pan, add the butter and a pinch of salt, and heat gently until the fat has melted. Bring to a boil, pour in the flour, and stir vigorously with a wooden spoon until the mixture comes together and leaves the sides of the pan. Remove the pan from the heat and stir for about 5 minutes, until the mixture is cool. Stir in the eggs (unbeaten), one at a time, making sure each one is fully incorporated before adding the next. Stir in the gruyere and let the mixture stand for 2 hours. Heat the oil in a large deep pan. While it is still heating, scoop up a little of the cheese mixture on a teaspoon and use your finger to push it off the spoon into the oil. It should sink to the base of the pan. Repeat the process, but don't add too many fritters to the pan at the same time, as they expand considerably during cooking and it is better to fry them with plenty of space. As the oil heats up, the fritters will begin to rise to the surface. When they are golden brown remove them from the oil with a slotted spoon and place them in a large colander set over a baking dish in a warm oven until all the fritters are fried. Remove the pan from the heat between each batch of fritters to let the oil cool until it is just warm. Then repeat the cooking process again. Serve the fritters in a napkin-lined dish and offer the warmed tomato sauce separately.

Croquettes

CROQUETAS

- 2 tablespoons sunflower oil
- 3 tablespoons butter
- 4 tablespoons all-purpose flour
- 3 cups milk
- 2 eggs
- 3 cups bread crumbs
- vegetable oil, for deep-frying
- salt
- fresh or deep-fried parsley
  sprigs (see recipe 918), optional

Filling:
- 1 pound 2 ounces cooked,
  peeled and deveined shrimp or
  12 ounces cooked white fish,
  such as hake or 2 chopped hard-
  cooked eggs or generous 1 cup
  diced Serrano ham or prosciutto
  or 1 diced cooked boneless
  chicken breast half or 1 ⅓ cups
  diced leftover roast chicken

Serves 6

Make a béchamel sauce by heating the sunflower oil in a pan. Add the butter, and when it has melted, stir in the flour with a wooden spoon. Gradually stir in the milk, a little at a time, and cook, stirring constantly, until the béchamel sauce thickens. Season with salt and stir in your chosen filling, then spread the mixture out in a large dish to cool for at least 2 hours. Using two tablespoons, shape scoops of the mixture into croquettes. Finish forming the croquettes with your hands. Beat the eggs in a shallow dish. Pour the bread crumbs into another shallow dish. Roll each croquette lightly in the bread crumbs, then in the beaten egg, and finally in the bread crumbs again, making sure that each one is evenly covered. If the croquettes are being prepared in advance, cover them with a damp dish towel to prevent them drying out. Heat the vegetable oil in a deep-fryer or deep pan to 350–375°F or until a cube of day-old bread browns in 30 seconds. Add the croquettes, in batches of about six at a time, and cook until crisp and golden brown. Using a slotted spoon, transfer them to a large colander set over a baking dish and place in a warm oven until all the croquettes have been cooked. Serve immediately on a dish garnished with sprigs of fresh or deep-fried parsley.

63

Cheese and egg croquettes
CROQUETAS DE QUESO RALLADO Y HUEVO

- 2 tablespoons sunflower oil
- ¼ cup (½ stick) butter
- 4 tablespoons all-purpose flour
- 3¼ cups milk
- 2 eggs
- 1½ cups grated gruyere
  cheese

Serves 6

Make a thick béchamel sauce as described in recipe 77. Remove the pan from the heat and let cool slightly. Stir in the eggs (unbeaten), one at a time, making sure each one is fully incorporated before adding the next. Stir in the gruyere. Spread the mixture out in a large dish to cool for at least 2 hours, then proceed as directed in recipe 62.

64

Salt cod and potato croquettes
CROQUETAS DE PATATA Y BACALAO

- 9 ounces salt cod fillet
- 3¼ pounds potatoes
- 1–2 tablespoons olive oil
- 1 clove garlic
- 2 eggs, separated
- all-purpose flour, for dusting
- vegetable oil, for deep-frying
- 1 quantity Classic Tomato Sauce
  (see recipe 73)
- salt

Serves 6

If the salt cod is dried, place it in a bowl, add water to cover, and let soak for about 2 hours without changing the water, then drain. If it is vacuum packed, this is not necessary. Put the potatoes (unpeeled) and cod in a pan and add enough water to cover generously. Bring to a boil, then lower the heat, and simmer for about 30 minutes, until the potatoes are tender. Drain well. Peel the potatoes, place in a bowl, and mash well. Lift out the cod with a fish slice and remove any remaining skin and bones, then finely flake the flesh with your fingers and add to the mashed potato. Heat the olive oil in a small pan. Add the garlic and cook, stirring frequently, until lightly browned. Transfer the garlic and a pinch of salt to a mini-food processor and process briefly, or place in a mortar and pound. Stir the garlic mixture into the mashed potato. Beat in the egg yolks, one at a time, making sure that each is fully incorporated before adding the next. Whisk the egg whites with a pinch of salt in a clean, dry bowl until soft peaks form. Fold the egg whites into the mashed potato. Shape the mixture into croquettes with your hands and roll lightly in flour. Heat the vegetable oil in a deep-fryer or deep pan to 350–375°F or until a cube of day-old bread browns in 30 seconds. Add the croquettes, in batches if necessary, and cook until crisp and golden brown. Using a slotted spoon, transfer them to a large colander set over a baking dish and place in a warm oven until all the croquettes have been cooked. Drain well and serve immediately, offering the tomato sauce separately.

Portuguese salt cod fritters

BUÑUELOS DE BACALAO PORTUGUESES

- 1½ pounds salt cod
- 3¼ pounds potatoes
- 1 clove garlic, finely chopped
- 1 teaspoon finely chopped fresh parsley
- 3 egg yolks
- vegetable oil for deep-frying
- 1 quantity Classic Tomato Sauce (see recipe 73), optional

Serves 6

Put the salt cod in a bowl, add water to cover, and let soak for a few hours, changing the water only once, then drain. Put the potatoes (unpeeled) and cod in a pan and add enough water to cover generously. Bring to a boil, then lower the heat, and simmer for 30 minutes, until the potatoes are tender. Drain well. Peel the potatoes, place in a bowl, and mash well. Lift out the cod with a slotted spatula and remove any remaining skin and bones, then finely flake the flesh with your fingers. Add to the mashed potato, then stir in the garlic and parsley. Beat in the egg yolks, one at a time, making sure that each is incorporated before adding the next. Heat the vegetable oil in a deep-fryer or deep pan to 350–375°F or until a cube of day-old bread browns in 30 seconds. Drop tablespoons of the fish mixture into the hot oil and cook until crisp and golden brown. You will need to do this in batches. Remove with a slotted spoon, transfer to a large colander set over a baking pan and place in a warm oven until all the fritters have been cooked. Serve the fritters hot, offering the tomato sauce separately, if using.

Mushroom tart

TARTA DE CHAMPIÑONES

Pastry:
- 1¾ cups all-purpose flour, plus extra for dusting
- 6½ tablespoons butter, cut into small pieces, plus extra for greasing
- 1 egg, separated
- 1 tablespoon sunflower oil
- salt

Filling:
- 1 pounds 2 ounces cremini mushrooms, thickly sliced
- 3 tablespoons butter
- few drops of lemon juice
- 1 tablespoon sunflower oil
- 1 heaping tablespoon all-purpose flour
- 1¼ cups milk
- 1 egg yolk
- salt

Serves 6–8

First make the pastry dough as described in recipe 56, using the egg yolk but reserving the white. Let rest in a cool place for at least 2 hours. Preheat the oven to 350°F. Grease with butter a quiche pan with a removeable base, 10 inches in diameter and about 1½ inches deep. Roll out the dough to a round on a lightly floured surface. Lift the dough on the rolling pin into the prepared pan and press down with your fingers to make sure it is even over the base. Trim the excess dough with a sharp knife and lightly prick the base all over with a fork. Lightly whisk the egg white in a clean, dry bowl until frothy but not stiff. Brush over the inside of the piecrust. Bake for about 25 minutes, until firm and golden brown. Meanwhile, put the mushrooms in a pan, add 1 tablespoon of the butter and the lemon juice, and season lightly with salt. Cover and cook over low heat for about 6 minutes. Make a béchamel sauce by melting the remaining butter with the oil in another pan. Stir in the flour, then gradually whisk in the milk, a little at a time. Season with salt and cook, stirring constantly, for about 6 minutes. Lightly beat the egg yolk in a heatproof bowl, then very carefully stir in the béchamel sauce, a little at a time to prevent it separating. Pour the mixture back into the pan and stir well before adding the cooked mushrooms. When the pastry case is golden brown, remove from the oven and turn out onto a serving dish. Fill with the mushroom and béchamel mixture and serve immediately.

Green asparagus and béchamel tart

TARTA DE BECHAMEL Y ESPÁRRAGOS VERDES

Pastry:
- 1¾ cups all-purpose flour, plus extra for dusting
- 6½ tablespoons butter, cut into small pieces, plus extra for greasing
- 1 tablespoon peanut oil
- 1 egg yolk
- salt

Filling:
- 2¼ cups milk
- 1 heaping tablespoon cornstarch
- scant 1 cup grated gruyere cheese
- 3 eggs, lightly beaten
- ½ bunch of green asparagus, cooked and cut into 1½-inch pieces
- salt

Serves 6–8

First make the pastry dough according to the directions in recipe 56. Let rest in a cool place for at least 2 hours. Preheat the oven to 350°F. Grease with butter a quiche pan with a removeable base, 11 inches in diameter and about 1½ inches deep. Roll out the dough to a round on a lightly floured surface. Lift the dough on the rolling pin into the prepared pan and press down with your fingers to make sure it is even over the base. Trim the excess dough with a sharp knife and lightly prick the base all over with a fork. Bake for about 15 minutes, until set but not browned. Meanwhile, make the filling. Pour the milk into a pan and bring to just below the boiling point. Add the corn-starch and cook, stirring constantly, for 3 minutes. Remove the pan from the heat and stir in nearly all the gruyere, leaving just enough to sprinkle over the top of the tart. Remove the piecrust from the oven and brush a little of the beaten egg around the edges. Do not switch off the oven. Gradually stir the remaining eggs into the filling mixture, season to taste with salt, and pour the mixture into the piecrust. Gently press the pieces of asparagus deeper into the filling mixture to prevent them from drying out during cooking. Sprinkle the remaining cheese over the top and bake for 15 minutes, until golden brown. Remove the tart from the oven, transfer to a serving dish and serve immediately.

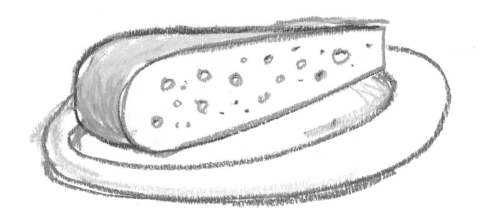

Hot asparagus mousse

MOUSSE CALIENTE DE ESPÁRRAGOS

- **butter, for greasing**
- **9 ounces canned green or white asparagus, drained**
- **2 ¾ cups bread crumbs**
- **¾ cup warm milk**
- **2 egg yolks**
- **1 extra large egg, lightly beaten**
- **½ quantity Classic Béchamel Sauce (see recipe 77)**
- **3 ½ ounces cooked spinach or green asparagus**
- **salt and pepper**

Serves 4

Preheat the oven to 300°F. Line the base and ends of a loaf pan 9 ½ x 4 inches with aluminum foil and grease generously with butter. Pat the asparagus dry with paper towel. Pour the bread crumbs in a bowl, add the warm milk, and let soak for 10 minutes. Put the asparagus in a food processor or blender and process briefly to chop, then add the bread crumbs. Scrape the mixture into a bowl and beat in the egg yolks, one at a time, making sure that the first is fully incorporated before adding the second. Beat in the whole egg and season to taste with salt and pepper, bearing in mind that the asparagus is already salted. Pour the mousse mixture into the prepared pan and smooth the top. Place the pan in a roasting pan and pour in boiling water to come about halfway up the sides. Place in the oven and bake for about 1 ¼ hours until set. Meanwhile, pour the béchamel sauce into a food processor or blender. Add the cooked spinach or asparagus and process until combined. Remove the mousse from the pan, using the aluminum foil to help you, and serve immediately with the green béchamel sauce.

69

Cold asparagus mousse

MOUSSE DE ESPÁRRAGOS FRÍA

- 12 ounces canned white
  asparagus, drained
- 6 tablespoons unflavored,
  powdered gelatin
- 1½ cups boiling water
- 4 heaping tablespoons
  Thick Mayonnaise
  (see recipe 106)
- escarole or lettuce, hard-cooked
  egg, and tomato (optional)
- salt and pepper

Serves 6

Pat the asparagus dry with paper towel. Put the gelatin in a food processor or blender, add the boiling water, and process for 10 seconds. Immediately add the asparagus and process until finely chopped. Add the mayonnaise and process briefly again, until it has been incorporated. Taste and season with salt and pepper if necessary. Line the base and ends of a loaf pan 9 ½ x 4 inches with aluminum foil and pour in the mixture. Cover and chill in the refrigerator for 5–6 hours, until set. To serve, turn out, using the aluminum foil to help you. A typical Spanish garnish would include escarole or chopped lettuce, slices of hard-cooked egg, and pieces of tomato.

70

Leek mousse

MOUSSE DE PUERROS

- 6 leeks, about 9 ounces total
  weight, trimmed and rinsed well
- 1 cup bread crumbs
- generous 1 cup warm milk
- butter, for greasing
- 3 extra large eggs
- ¾ cup whipping cream,
  whipped until slightly thickened
- ½ quantity Classic Béchamel
  Sauce, (see recipe 77)
- 3½ ounces cooked,
  drained spinach
- salt

Serves 4

Cook the leeks in a pan of salted boiling water for 20–30 minutes, until tender. Drain well and pat dry with paper towel. Meanwhile, put the bread crumbs in a bowl, add the warm milk, and let soak. Preheat the oven to 325°F. Line the base and ends of an 8-inch long pan with aluminum foil and grease generously with butter. Cut off and reserve the bulbs and tops of the leeks and cut the remainder into ¾-inch lengths. Put the reserved bulbs and tops in a food processor or blender and add the bread crumb and milk mixture. Process briefly, then with the motor running, add the eggs one at a time. When the mixture is smooth and thoroughly combined, pour it into a ceramic or glass bowl, and stir in the cream. Stir in the remaining leek. Pour the mixture into the prepared pan. Place the pan in a roasting pan and pour in boiling water to come about halfway up the sides. Place in the oven and bake for about 1 hour, until set. Meanwhile, pour the béchamel sauce into a food processor or blender. Add the spinach and process until combined. Serve the mousse hot and offer the sauce separately.

71

Individual fish mousses
PEQUEÑAS MOUSSES DE PESCADO

- 1 pound 2 ounces white fish fillets, skinned
- 5 tablespoons lemon juice
- 3 tablespoons olive oil, plus extra for brushing
- 7 ounces smoked salmon or smoked trout, thinly sliced
- 14 ounces farmer cheese
- 1 tablespoon chopped fresh parsley
- lettuce or escarole leaves (optional)
- salt

Serves 6

Cut the white fish fillets into cubes, put in a shallow bowl, and pour the lemon juice over them. Let marinate in the refrigerator, stirring occasionally, for about 3 hours. Brush 6 ramekins or individual ceramic or glass dishes with a little oil. Line the base and the sides of the dishes with the slices of smoked fish, letting them overhang the rims. Drain the white fish, reserving the lemon juice. Put half the white fish in a food processor or blender with half the cheese, 1 tablespoon of the reserved lemon juice, and half the oil. Process briefly and scrape into a bowl. Put the remaining white fish, the remaining cheese, 1 tablespoon of the reserved lemon juice, and the remaining oil in the food processor or blender and process until smooth. Stir into the first batch of white fish, add the parsley, and season to taste with salt. Spoon the mixture into the prepared dishes and fold over the overhanging smoked fish. Put the dishes on a tray, cover completely with foil, and chill in the refrigerator for 5–6 hours, until set. (The mousses can be prepared up to a day in advance.) To serve, turn the mousses onto plates and garnish with lettuce or escarole leaves.

72

Tomato gelatin
GELATINA DE TOMATE

- 2¼ pounds ripe, fleshy tomatoes
- 1 large canned or bottled red bell pepper, chopped
- 1 tablespoon coarsely chopped fresh mint
- 3 ounces unflavored powdered gelatin
- 1½ cups heavy cream
- lettuce or escarole leaves (optional)
- salt

Serves 8

Cut a cross in the stalk end of each tomato with a sharp knife, put the tomatoes in a heatproof bowl, and pour in boiling water to cover. Let stand for 1–2 minutes, then drain, and peel off the skins. Cut the tomatoes in half, scoop out the seeds with a teaspoon, and coarsely chop the flesh. Put in a food processor or blender, together with any juice remaining on the cutting board, and add the bell pepper and mint. Process briefly to combine then transfer to a large heatproof bowl. Pour 1½ cups water into a pan, bring to a boil, and stir in the gelatin with a wooden spoon. Remove the pan from the heat and pour the gelatin into the tomato mixture. Lightly whisk the cream and fold it into the tomato mixture. Season to taste with salt. Pour the mixture into a mold 9½ x 4 inches and chill in the refrigerator for at least 4 hours. Turn out the gelatin and garnish with lettuce or escarole leaves. (It's easier to turn out the gelatin from a plastic rather than a metal mold.)

SAUCES

Hot sauces

73 📷 ## Classic tomato sauce
SALSA DE TOMATE CLÁSICA

- 3 tablespoons sunflower oil
- 1 onion, chopped (optional)
- 2¼ pounds ripe tomatoes, seeded and chopped
- 1 teaspoon sugar
- salt

Serves 6

Heat the oil in a skillet. Add the onion, if using, and cook over low heat, stirring occasionally, for about 5 minutes, until softened but not browned. (If you're not using the onion, add the tomato immediately). Add the tomato and cook over low heat, breaking up the flesh with the edge of a slotted spoon, for about 15 minutes. Allow the mixture to cool slightly then transfer to a food processor or blender and process. Add the sugar, season to taste with salt, and process briefly again. Serve the sauce either in a sauceboat or poured directly over a dish.

74 ## Canned tomato sauce
SALSA DE TOMATE EN CONSERVA

- 3 tablespoons sunflower oil
- 1 onion, chopped
- 1 pound 2 ounces canned tomatoes
- 1 teaspoon sugar
- salt

Serves 6

The sauce may also be made using canned tomatoes. To do this, follow the method described in recipe 73 but use the quantities of ingredients listed here.

Note: Making tomato sauce with either fresh of canned tomatoes in a cast-iron skillet will cause the pan to lose its "seasoning" and turn a metallic, almost silver color. If you have done so and you want to use the skillet for other dishes (omelets, fried food, etc.), set it over the heat with nothing in it until the base turns black again. This re-seasons it and you can use it without ingredients sticking.

75 Tomato sauce with onion and wine

SALSA DE TOMATE CON CEBOLLA Y VINO

- 3 tablespoons sunflower oil
- 1 onion, chopped
- 2 ¼ pounds ripe tomatoes, chopped
- bouquet garni (1 fresh sprig parsley, 1 clove garlic, and 1 bay leaf tied in cheesecloth)
- 3 tablespoons dry white wine
- 1 teaspoon sugar
- salt

Serves 6

Heat the oil in a skillet. Add the onion and cook over low heat, stirring occasionally, for 7–8 minutes, until lightly browned. Increase the heat to medium, add the tomato, bouquet garni, and wine, and cook, breaking up the tomatoes with the side of a slotted spoon, for about 15 minutes. Remove and discard the bouquet garni. Transfer the contents of the pan to a food processor or blender and process. Add the sugar, season to taste with salt, and process briefly to mix. The sauce is now ready to be served. If you prefer a thicker texture, return the sauce to the pan and cook over high heat until some of the liquid has evaporated.

76 Chinese sweet-and-sour sauce

SALSA AGRIDULCE CHINA

- 1 ½ tablespoons sugar
- 2 tablespoons vinegar
- 1 tablespoon tomato paste
- 1 tablespoon soy sauce
- 3 tablespoons orange juice
- 1 teaspoon cornstarch

Serves 4

Put the sugar, vinegar, tomato paste, soy sauce, and orange juice in a pan. Mix the cornstarch with 4 tablespoons water to a paste in a cup, then pour it into the pan. Bring the sauce to a boil over low heat, stirring constantly, and serve hot. This sauce makes a good accompaniment for roast pork, chops, etc.

Béchamel

Tricks

- To prevent lumps forming when making béchamel, remove the pan from the heat when stirring in the flour. Stir briefly with a wooden spoon, return the pan to the heat, and proceed as normal
- To avoid a skin forming on top of a béchamel sauce prepared in advance, cover the surface with a disk of waxed paper lightly greased with butter. Béchamel sauce can be stored in the refrigerator for a few days or frozen
- To reheat, put it into a heatproof bowl set over a pan of barely simmering water.

77 Classic béchamel sauce
SALSA BECHAMEL CORRIENTE

- ¼ cup (½ stick) butter
- 2 tablespoons sunflower oil
- 2 tablespoons all-purpose flour
- 3 cups milk
- salt

Serves 6

Melt the butter with the oil in a pan and stir in the flour. Gradually stir in the milk, a little at a time, and bring to a boil, stirring constantly. Add salt to taste and simmer over medium heat, stirring constantly, for 8–10 minutes. If a thinner sauce is required, add more milk. If the béchamel needs to be thicker, simmer the sauce longer, until it reaches the required consistency.

78 Béchamel sauce with tomato
SALSA BECHAMEL CON TOMATE

- 1 quantity Classsic béchamel sauce (see recipe 77)
- 1 tablespoon tomato purée

Serves 6

Spoon a little of the béchamel sauce into a bowl and stir in the tomato paste. Pour the mixture back into the pan and mix well.

79

Béchamel sauce with egg yolks

SALSA BECHAMEL CON YEMAS

- 2 egg yolks
- 1 quantity Classic Béchamel
  Sauce (see recipe 77)

Serves 6

Put 2 egg yolks in a bowl and gradually add a little of the béchamel sauce, stirring constantly to prevent the eggs curdling. Then return the mixture to the sauce in the pan and reheat gently but do not allow it to boil.

80

Béchamel sauce with capers

SALSA BECHAMEL CON ALCAPARRAS

- ¼ cup (½ stick) butter
- 2 tablespoons sunflower oil
- 2 tablespoons all-purpose flour
- 1½ cups milk
- 1½ cups fish stock
  (use the cooking liquid
  left over after poaching fish)
- 1–2 tablespoons capers,
  rinsed and drained

Serves 6

This sauce is usually made to accompany poached fish. Make the béchamel sauce as described in recipe 77, adding the stock at the same time you add the milk. When the sauce is ready, stir in the capers.

Note: For added flavor, add 1–2 egg yolks as described in recipe 79.

81

Béchamel sauce with stock

SALSA BECHAMEL CON CALDO

- 2 tablespoons (¼ stick) butter
- 2 tablespoons sunflower oil
- 2 tablespoons all-purpose flour
- scant 2 cups milk
- scant 2 cups chicken stock
  (homemade, canned or
  made with a bouillon cube)
- salt

Serves 6

Make the béchamel sauce as described in recipe 77 but using the ingredients listed here. Both homemade stock and stock made from a cube contain salt, so bear this in mind when seasoning the sauce. This sauce is clearer and lighter than the previous recipes and is good for cannelloni, vegetables, or baked fish dishes.

Spanish sauce

SALSA ESPAÑOLA

- 1 pound 2 ounces boneless veal or beef, trimmed of visible fat
- 3 tablespoons sunflower oil
- 1 onion, chopped
- 3 carrots, diced
- 1 tablespoon all-purpose flour
- bouquet garni
  (1 fresh sprig parsley, 1 clove garlic, and 1 bay leaf tied together in cheesecloth)
- 1 whole clove
- 1 small veal shank bone
- salt

Serves 6

Dice the veal or beef very finely. Heat the oil in a pan. Add the onion and cook over low heat, stirring occasionally, for about 10 minutes, until golden brown. Add the meat and cook, stirring frequently, for 8–10 minutes, until evenly browned. Stir in the carrot, then stir in the flour. Cook, stirring constantly, for about 5 minutes, then gradually stir in 4 cups water. Add the bouquet garni, clove, and veal shank and simmer gently for 30 minutes. Remove and discard the veal shank, clove, and bouquet garni and pour the sauce through a fine strainer into a bowl, pressing it with a wooden spoon to get all the liquid. Return the sauce to the pan and stir well. Season to taste with salt and simmer until the sauce reaches the required consistency.

83 Bolognese sauce

SALSA BOLOÑESA

- **5 ounces lean steak**
- **2 tablespoons olive oil**
- **⅓ cup finely chopped bacon**
- **1 small onion, finely chopped**
- **1 carrot, finely chopped**
- **1–2 stalks celery, finely chopped**
- **1 whole clove**
- **6 tablespoons canned tomato purée**
- **2 tablespoons white wine**
- **salt**

Serves 6

Finely chop the steak. Heat the oil in a deep pan. Add the bacon and cook over low heat, stirring occasionally, for 5 minutes. Add the steak, onion, carrot, celery, and clove, season with salt, and cook, stirring frequently, for about 10 minutes, until the meat is browned and the vegetables have softened. Stir in the tomatoes and wine, cover, and simmer gently for 10 minutes.

Note: This sauce is enough for 11 ounces Spaghetti. Toss the freshly cooked pasta in 1 generous cup light cream and the bolognese sauce, and serve with freshly grated Parmesan cheese.

84 Béarnaise sauce

SALSA BEARNESA

- **1 tablespoon finely chopped scallion or shallot**
- **2 tablespoons white-wine vinegar**
- **⅔ cup butter**
- **juice of ½ lemon**
- **4 egg yolks**
- **pinch of potato starch**
- **1 tablespoon chopped fresh parsley**
- **salt and pepper**

Serves 6

Put the scallion or shallot in a small pan, pour in the vinegar, and cook for a few minutes until the liquid has reduced by half. Remove the pan from the heat and let cool. Melt the butter in another pan, but do not let brown. Stir 2 tablespoons water and the lemon juice into the cooled vinegar mixture. Make a water bath with a pan or skillet large enough to hold the smaller pan. Half-fill the pan with water and bring to just below boiling point. Lower the heat so that the water is barely simmering. Add the egg yolks to the vinegar mixture and, using the tip of a knife, add a pinch of potato starch. Whisk well, then place the pan in the simmering water, and cook, whisking constantly, until the sauce thickens. Remove from the heat and take the pan out of the water bath. Gradually whisk in the butter, a little at a time. When all the butter has been fully incorporated, add the parsley and season to taste with salt and pepper. Serve in a warmed sauceboat.

Note: This sauce is somewhere between a mayonnaise and a hollandaise, and is always served hot. It is delicious but a little fiddly to make as it curdles easily. If the butter seems to be separating in the sauce, whisk it well just before serving. This sauce goes well with tenderloin, sirloin, or round steak or with broiled fish. To make a hollandaise sauce, follow the method above but leave out the vinegar reduction, potato starch and parsley, and use 3 egg yolks, 200 g/7 oz butter and the juice of ½ lemon.

85

Cumberland sauce
SALSA CUMBERLAND

- **thinly pared rind of ½ orange**
- **juice and thinly pared rind of 1 lemon**
- **3 tablespoons red currant jelly**
- **½ teaspoon Dijon mustard**
- **1½ teaspoons Worcestershire sauce**

Serves 4

Cut the orange and lemon rind into very fine julienne strips. Bring a small pan of water to the boil. Add the orange and lemon rind and blanch for 2 minutes. Drain and reserve. Melt the jelly in the pan and add the lemon juice. Stir in the mustard and the Worcestershire sauce. Stir in the reserved citrus rind just before serving. The sauce may be served hot or cold and is good with fish or roasted meat.

86

Savory lemon sauce
SALSA CON ZUMO DE LIMÓN

- **4½ tablespoons butter**
- **1 heaping tablespoon all-purpose flour**
- **1 chicken bouillon cube**
- **2 egg yolks**
- **juice of 1 lemon**
- **pinch of freshly grated nutmeg**
- **1 tablespoon chopped fresh parsley**
- **salt**

Serves 4

Melt the butter in a pan, then stir in the flour. Gradually stir in scant 2 cups water, a little at a time, then cook, stirring constantly, for 5 minutes. Crumble in the bouillon cube and remove the pan from the heat. Put the egg yolks and lemon juice in a bowl, spoon in a little of the hot sauce, and stir immediately to prevent the yolks curdling. Stir in a little more sauce and then pour the mixture back into the pan. The sauce does not require further cooking but should be kept warm. Season to taste with salt and stir in the nutmeg and parsley. Serve in a warmed sauceboat. This sauce goes well with fried or roast meat and baked fish. It is similar to Béarnaise sauce but easier to make.

Note : You can also make this sauce using half stock and half milk.

87

Mousseline sauce for fish
SALSA MOUSSELINA PARA PESCADO

- ¼ cup (½ stick) butter
- 2 tablespoons all-purpose flour
- 3 cups fish stock
- 1 egg white
- 2 egg yolks
- salt

Serves 6

Melt the butter in a pan, then stir in the flour. Gradually whisk in the fish stock, a little at a time, then remove the pan from the heat, and continue to whisk until the sauce is smooth. Return the pan to the heat and cook, stirring constantly, for 4 minutes. Season to taste with salt. Transfer the sauce to a heatproof bowl and place over a pan of barely simmering water to keep warm. Just before serving, whisk the egg white in a clean, dry bowl until soft peaks form. Gently fold the egg yolks into the whites, then gradually fold in the hot sauce, a little at a time. Serve immediately in a warmed sauceboat.

88

Red wine sauce
SALSA DE VINO TINTO

- 1½ tablespoons olive oil
- 2 large shallots, chopped
- 2¼ cups red wine
- 3 tablespoons butter
- 1 tablespoon all-purpose flour
- 1 tablespoon chopped
  fresh parsley
- salt and pepper

Serves 6

Heat the oil in a skillet. Add the shallots and cook over low heat, stirring occasionally, for about 7 minutes, until beginning to brown. Add the wine and ¾ cup water and simmer gently for 10 minutes. Blend the butter and flour in a bowl with a fork to form a paste. Gradually stir the paste into the skillet a small amount at a time. When the meat is ready, pour any cooking juices into the sauce. Stir in the parsley and season to taste with salt and pepper. Pour the sauce over the meat. This sauce goes well with sirloin or round steak.

89

Madeira sauce
SALSA DE VINO DE MADEIRA

- 3 tablespoons olive oil
- 1 small onion, thinly sliced
- 1 tablespoon all-purpose flour
- 1 cup water mixed with
  ½ teaspoon meat extract,
  or Maggi Seasoning
- ⅔ cup Madeira wine
- 1½ tablespoons butter
- salt

Serves 4

Heat the oil in a pan. Add the onion and cook over low heat, stirring occasionally, for about 7 minutes, until lightly browned. Stir in the flour, then gradually stir in the water with the meat extract or Maggi Seasoning, a little at a time. When incorporated, gradually stir in the Madeira. Simmer gently for 10 minutes. Strain through a coarse strainer into a clean pan and reheat. Season with salt if necessary (bearing in mind that the meat extract and Maggi Seasoning are salty). Just before serving, remove the pan from the heat and whisk in the butter. Serve with cured ham and spinach.

Sherry and mushroom sauce
SALSA DE JEREZ Y CHAMPIÑONES

- 4 ounces mushrooms, sliced
- 4½ tablespoons butter
- juice of ½ lemon
- 1 tablespoon sunflower oil
- 1 tablespoon all-purpose flour
- 5 tablespoons sherry
- ½ teaspoon meat extract
  or Maggi Seasoning
- 1 tablespoon chopped
  fresh parsley (optional)
- salt

Serves 4–6

Put the mushrooms into a small pan. Add 2 tablespoons of the butter, the lemon juice, and a pinch of salt. Cover and cook over low heat for 10 minutes. Remove the pan from the heat and set aside. Melt the remaining butter with the oil in another pan. Stir in the flour and cook, stirring constantly, for a few minutes, until lightly browned. Gradually stir in the sherry and 1¼ cups water. Cook over medium heat for 8 minutes, then strain the mixture into a clean pan to remove any lumps. Add the mushrooms with their cooking juices and the meat extract or Maggi Seasoning and parsley, if using, and reheat gently. Season with salt, if necessary, and serve in a warmed sauceboat. This sauce is a good one to serve with meat, sweetbreads and poached or lightly boiled eggs.

Sherry and olive sauce
SALSA DE JEREZ Y ACEITUNAS

- 2 tablespoons sunflower oil
- 1 onion, chopped
- 1 tablespoon all-purpose flour
- 1 tablespoon tomato paste
- 5 tablespoons sherry
- ½ cup olives, pitted and sliced
- ½ teaspoon meat extract
  or Maggi Seasoning
- salt

Serves 6

Heat the oil in a small pan. Add the onion and cook over low heat, stirring occasionally, for about 7 minutes, until beginning to brown. Stir in the flour and cook, stirring constantly, for 2 minutes. Stir in the tomato paste, then gradually stir in scant 2 cups water, a little at a time. Stir in the sherry and olives. Simmer gently for about 5 minutes, then stir in the meat extract of Maggi Seasoning, and season with salt if necessary (bearing in mind that the meat extract, Maggi Seasoning and olives are salty). Serve in a warmed sauceboat. This sauce goes well with meat, sweetbreads, and poached eggs.

92
White wine sauce
SALSA DE VINO BLANCO

- 3 tablespoons olive oil
- 1 onion, chopped
- 1 tablespoon all-purpose flour
- 2 tomatoes,
  peeled, seeded, and chopped
- ¾ cup white wine
- generous ½ cup chopped
  Serrano ham or prosciutto
- ½ teaspoon meat extract or
  Maggi Seasoning
- salt and pepper

Serves 6

Heat the oil in a pan. Add the onion and cook over low heat, stirring occasionally, for about 7 minutes, until beginning to brown. Stir in the flour and cook, stirring constantly, for 2 minutes. Add the tomato and cook for 5 minutes, then add the wine and 1¼ cups water. Simmer gently for about 10 minutes, then remove from the heat and allow to cool a little. Transfer the mixture to a food processor or blender, and process until smooth. Return the sauce to the pan, add the ham, and cook over low heat for 3 minutes. Add a little cold or hot water if the sauce is too thick, then keep warm until ready to serve. Just before serving, stir in the meat extract or Maggi Seasoning and season with salt, if necessary, and pepper (bearing in mind that the meat extract, Maggi Seasoning and ham are salty). This sauce goes well with lightly boiled or poached eggs and omelets and should be served immediately after pouring.

93
Shallot sauce for fried meat
SALSA DE CHALOTAS PARA LA CARNE

- 2 shallots, finely chopped
- 1 teaspoon chopped
  fresh parsley
- ¾ cup dry white wine
- salt

Serves 4

Fry steaks or other cuts of meat in a skillet, then transfer them to a plate and set aside in a warm place. Add the shallots, parsley and wine to the cooking juices in the skillet. Add ⅔ cup water and cook over high heat for 5 minutes, then lower the heat to medium, and cook for 5 minutes more. To serve, pour the sauce over the meat.

94
Cream and meat extract sauce
SALSA DE NATA LÍQUIDA Y EXTRACTO DE CARNE

- 1 cup light cream
- ½ teaspoon meat extract or
  Maggi Seasoning

Serves 4–6

Combine the cream and the meat extract or Maggi Seasoning in a heatproof bowl. Set the bowl over a pan of barely simmering water to heat the sauce, but do not let it boil. Serve in a warmed sauceboat. This sauce is a good one to serve with leftover meat.

Note: Meat extract is a seasoning that can add a meaty, salty flavor to sauces, soups and stews. One popular brand is Bovril. If you can't find it, use Maggi Seasoning or some beef bouillon.

Butter and anchovy sauce

SALSA DE MANTEQUILLA Y ANCHOAS

- **6 canned anchovy fillets, drained**
- **scant ½ cup butter (a little less than 1 stick), softened**
- **juice of 1 lemon**
- **1 tablespoon chopped fresh parsley**

Serves 4

Mash the anchovies with half the butter in a mortar or process in a mini-food processor. When the mixture is smooth, beat in the remaining butter. Put the mixture in a pan and heat gently, but do not let color. Stir in the lemon juice and parsley. Pour the sauce over the dish you're serving or serve in a previously warmed sauceboat. This sauce goes well with beef tenderloin, roasted fish such as grouper, fried fish such as sole, or oven-cooked fish suchas halibut.

96

Black butter and caper sauce

SALSA DE MANTEQUILLA NEGRA Y ALCAPARRAS

- ⅔ cup butter
- ½ teaspoon white-wine vinegar
- 2 tablespoons capers,
  rinsed and drained
- salt

Serves 4

Melt the butter in a pan over low heat until it begins to color but not burn, then remove from the heat, and add the vinegar, capers, and a pinch of salt. Return to the heat and cook, stirring constantly, for 1–2 min-utes. Serve in a warmed sauceboat. This sauce is usually served with skate and halibut.

97

Red currant sauce for venison

SALSA DE GROSELLA PARA VENADO, CORZO O CIERVO

- 4 tablespoons olive oil
- 2 shallots, chopped
- 1 small stalk celery, chopped
- 7 ounces boneless venison,
  chopped
- 3 cups red wine (such as
  Burdeos or Bordeaux, or other
  dry wine made from Cabernet
  Sauvignon or Merlot grapes)
- bouquet garni (1 bay leaf,
  1 sprig fresh thyme, 1 sprig
  fresh parsley, and 1 clove garlic
  tied together in cheesecloth)
- 5 tablespoons brandy
- scant 1 cup red currant jelly
- 1 tablespoon potato starch
- 3–4 drops of red food coloring
  (optional)
- salt and pepper

Serves 8

Heat the oil in a pan. Add the shallots, celery, and venison and cook over low heat, stirring occasionally, for 5 minutes, until the shallots are softened but not browned. Pour in the wine, add the bouquet garni, and cook until the liquid has reduced by half. Pass the sauce through a strainer into a bowl, pressing down well, then return the sauce to the pan and place over the heat. Stir in the brandy and red currant jelly, and season to taste with salt and pepper. Mix the potato starch to a paste with a little water in a bowl, then stir into the pan, and cook, stirring constantly, for 2 minutes. Add the food coloring, if using, and serve in a warmed sauceboat. If you need to keep the sauce warm while you prepare the rest of the meal, pour it into a heatproof bowl, put a pat of butter on top to prevent a skin forming, and set the bowl over a pan of barely simmering water.

Note: The thickness of the sauce will depend on the type of red cur-rant jelly. If the sauce is too thick, add a little water. If it is too thin, add a little more potato starch mixed to a paste with water.

Cold sauces

Vinaigrette

The ideal proportions for a vinaigrette are 3 tablespoons oil to 1 tablespoon vinegar, but if the flavor of the vinaigrette is too strong, add more lemon juice to the mixture.

Tricks
- If too much vinegar has been used, put a large piece of bread into the dish to absorb the dressing. Discard the bread and make a fresh vinaigrette. The salad will still be useable
- Personalize the vinaigrette by adding chopped onion, chopped hard-cooked egg, a pinch of curry powder or saffron, capers, etc
- See the glossary (page 964) for information on different types of vinegar.

98

Vinaigrette
SALSA VINAGRETA

- **pinch of salt**
- **1 tablespoon white- or red-wine vinegar**
- **3 tablespoons olive oil**

Serves 2–4

Dissolve the salt in the vinegar in a bowl, then add the oil, whisking well with a fork until the ingredients are amalgamated.

Note: The vinaigrette can be varied in many ways: adding mustard, a little finely chopped onion and parsley; chopped capers, or chopped hard-cooked egg, for example.

99

Special vinaigrette (first version)

SALSA VINAGRETA HISTORIADA

- 2 hard-cooked eggs
- 1 teaspoon Dijon mustard
- 1 tablespoon white-wine vinegar
- 1¼ cups sunflower oil
- 1 tablespoon chopped
  fresh parsley
- salt

Serves 4

Cut the hard-cooked eggs in half and scoop out the yolks with a teaspoon into a bowl. Finely chop and reserve the whites. Add the mustard to the bowl and mash into the egg yolks using the back of a spoon. Add the vinegar, then gradually whisk in the oil, a little at a time, as if making mayonnaise. When the oil has been fully incorporated, season to taste with salt. Just before serving, stir in the parsley and egg whites. Serve the vinaigrette in a sauceboat. This dressing is an excellent accompaniment to hot or cold fish, garbanzo beans, and hot or cold asparagus.

100

Special vinaigrette (second version)

SALSA VINAGRETA HISTORIADA

- 3 tablespoons white-wine
  vinegar
- generous ½ cup sunflower oil
- ¾ cup vegetable stock
- 1 hard-cooked egg
- 1 tablespoon chopped
  fresh parsley
- 1 tablespoon finely chopped
  scallion (optional)
- salt

Serves 4

Put the vinegar in a bowl and stir in a pinch of salt. Gradually whisk in the oil, a little at a time, followed by the stock. Chop the hard-cooked egg and add it to the vinaigrette with the parsley and scallion, if using, just before serving. Serve the vinaigrette in a sauceboat. This dressing is an excellent accompaniment to hot or cold fish, garbanzo beans, and hot or cold asparagus.

101

Vinaigrette with garlic

SALSA VINAGRETA CON AJO

- 1 clove garlic
- 2 tablespoons white-wine
  vinegar
- 6 tablespoons sunflower oil
- 1 tablespoon finely chopped
  fresh parsley
- salt

Serves 4

Pound the garlic with a pinch of salt to a paste in a mortar or process in a mini-food processor. Transfer to a bowl and gradually whisk in the vinegar with a fork, then gradually whisk in the oil. Finally, add the parsley. Let stand in a cool place for 30 minutes before serving in a sauceboat. This sauce goes well with cold fish.

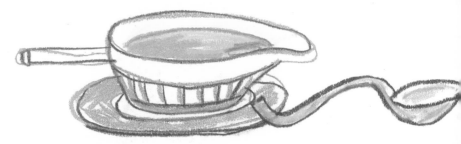

102

Roquefort sauce with cream
SALSA ROQUEFORT CON CREMA

- 3 ounces Roquefort cheese
- 1 tablespoon olive oil
- 1 teaspoon vinegar
- salt
- 3½ ounces light cream
  (optional)

Serves 2–4

Mash the Roquefort with the oil in a bowl, then add the vinegar, and season with salt. Transfer to a food processor or blender and process briefly. Return to the bowl and chill in the refrigerator for 30 minutes. Just before serving, if the sauce is too thick, add a little light cream. Serve the sauce with poultry, cooked ham, and other cold meats.

103

Roquefort sauce with yogurt
SALSA ROQUEFORT CON YOGUR

- 3 ounces Roquefort Cheese
- 1 tablespoon olive oil
- 1 teaspoon lemon juice
- 2 teaspoons plain yogurt
- salt and pepper

Serves 2–4

Mash the Roquefort with the oil in a bowl, then add the juice. Season with salt and pepper to taste, then gradually stir in the yogurt. This sauce goes well with poultry, cooked ham, and endive salad, amongst other things.

104

Little butter mountains
MONTONCITOS DE MANTEQUILLA

- 1 tablespoon very finely chopped
  fresh parsley
- ¼ cup (½ stick) butter, softened
- 1 teaspoon lemon juice
- 6 very thin slices lemon

- ¼ cup (½ stick) butter, softened
- 3 teaspoons white-wine vinegar
- ½ teaspoon dried tarragon
- 6 very thin slices lemon
- salt
- 6 small sprigs fresh parsley

Makes 6

First version
Combine the parsley, butter, and lemon juice in a bowl. Divide the mixture into six small mounds and place each one on a slice of lemon. Store in the refrigerator or a cool place until required. Place a lemon slice topped with butter on each steak just before serving.

Second version
Put the butter into a bowl and gradually add the white wine vinegar, a little at a time, whisking as if making mayonnaise. Season with salt and stir in the tarragon. Divide the mixture into six small mounds and place each one on a slice of lemon, then top each with a sprig of fresh parsley. Store the slices in the refrigerator until required. Place a lemon slice topped with butter on each steak before serving.

Note: To serve these butters with roasts and fried foods, make three times the quantity shown and serve the butter in a small serving bowl at the table.

Mayonnaise

Tricks

- For successful mayonnaise, make sure all the ingredients are at room temperature. If any are usually stored in the refrigerator, remove them at least 1 hour before they are needed
- If there is no wine vinegar available, use lemon juice instead
- When the mayonnaise is finished, add 1 teaspoon hot water. This makes it lighter and prevents it curdling. If the mayonnaise needs to be lighter still, you can use unsweetened condensed milk in place of the oil
- To change the color, add tomato sauce or chopped parsley
- For mayonnaise intended to accompany seafood, add 1 tablespoon tomato sauce and 1 tablespoon brandy
- If, even after you have carefully followed the instructions, the mayonnaise does not "come together," mix it with a little egg white in a separate bowl
- If the mayonnaise separates, transfer to a chilled bowl and gradually beat in an egg yolk or 1 teaspoon vinegar.
- If the mayonnaise is too thick, add a little cold water or 1 tablespoon chilled light cream
- Give the mayonnaise a special touch by adding a little chopped fresh parsley or tarragon.

105

Classic mayonnaise
SALSA MAYONESA CLÁSICA

- 2 egg yolks,
  at room temperature
- 2 tablespoons white-wine
  vinegar or lemon juice
- 2¼ cups sunflower oil
- salt

Serves 4

Put the egg yolks in a bowl with 1½ teaspoons of the vinegar or lemon juice and a small pinch of salt. Stir lightly with a whisk or fork and then gradually whisk in the oil, 1–2 teaspoons at a time, until about a fourth has been added. Whisk in the remaining oil in a slow, steady stream. Add the remaining vinegar or lemon juice, then taste, and adjust the seasoning. It is a good idea to make the mayonnaise in a cool place and store it in the refrigerator.

106

Thick mayonnaise

SALSA MAYONESA

- 1 egg, at room temperature
- juice of ½ lemon
- ¼ teaspoon Dijon mustard (optional)
- 2 ¼ cups sunflower oil
- salt

Serves 4

Put the egg, lemon juice, mustard, if using, a pinch of salt, and a dash of oil in a food processor or blender. (These ingredients should not quite cover its blades.) Gently combine the ingredients with a spatula or the handle of a spoon, then process for 20 seconds. Add the remaining oil, combine again with a spatula or the handle of a spoon, then process for about 35 seconds, until the mayonnaise is thick and creamy. Taste and add more salt, mustard, or lemon juice to taste. Store it in the refrigerator.

Note: Instead of adding all the remaining oil at once, pour it gradually through the feeder hole with the motor running.

107

Green mayonnaise

SALSA MAYONESA VERDE

- 1 egg, at room temperature
- juice of ½ lemon
- 1 cup sunflower oil
- ½ bunch fresh parsley, leaves only
- 2 tablespoons coarsely chopped, and rinsed and drained capers
- 2 pickled gherkins, coarsely chopped
- a few drops of green food coloring (optional)
- salt

Serves 4

Make the mayonnaise as described in recipe 106, omitting the mustard, and transfer to a bowl. Pound the parsley leaves in a mortar or process briefly in a mini-food processor, then add 1 tablespoon of the mayonnaise. Mix well, then stir the mixture into the rest of the mayonnaise until thoroughly and evenly combined. Stir in the capers and pickled gherkins and add the green food coloring, if using. Store the green mayonnaise in the refrigerator until required.

108 Mayonnaise with tomato and brandy

SALSA MAYONESA CON TOMATE Y COÑAC

- 1 egg, at room temperature
- juice of ½ lemon
- 1 cup sunflower oil
- 1 tablespoon brandy
- 1 teaspoon Dijon mustard
- 1 teaspoon tomato paste
- a few drops of Worcestershire
  sauce
- salt

Serves 4

Make the mayonnaise as described in recipe 106, omitting the mustard, and transfer to a bowl. Gradually stir in the brandy, a little at a time, then the mustard, tomato paste, and Worcestershire sauce. Mix well, then store in the refrigerator until required.

109 Egg-free mayonnaise with tomato

SALSA TIPO MAYONESA CON TOMATE, SIN HUEVO

- 2 stalks celery, with leaves
- 1 tablespoon tomato paste
- ¾ cup milk
- ¾ cup sunflower oil
- juice of ½ lemon
- 10 blanched almonds
- 4 black peppercorns, crushed
- salt

Serves 4

Cut the celery stalks into ¾-inch lengths and coarsely chop the leaves. Place all the ingredients in a food processor or blender and process until thoroughly combined. Pour into a sauceboat and chill in the refrigerator for at least 1 hour.

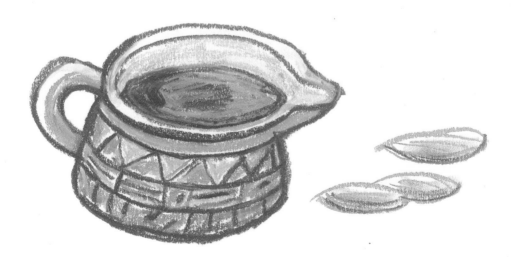

Garlic mayonnaise
ALIOLI

- **3 cloves garlic**
- **1–2 egg yolks**
- **2¼ cups sunflower oil**
- **2 tablespoons white-wine vinegar or lemon juice**

Serves 4

Crush the garlic with a little salt to a paste in a mortar or process in a mini-food processor. Transfer to a bowl, add the egg yolks, then gradually add the oil as described in recipe 105. Finally, add the vinegar or lemon juice and 1–2 tablespoons warm water, then serve. This garlic mayonnaise can be served with all kinds of cold meat. It also makes a good accompaniment to poached salt cod or potatoes and vegetables such as artichokes, leeks, turnips or carrots.

111

Quick garlic mayonnaise
ALIOLI RÁPIDO

- **3 cloves garlic**
- **1 quantity Classic Mayonnaise (see recipe 105)**
- **salt**

Serves 4

Crush the garlic with a little salt to a paste in a mortar or process in a mini-food processor: the salt absorbs the aroma of the garlic. Gradually stir the garlic paste into the mayonnaise, then serve.

112

Romesco sauce
SALSA ROMESCU

- 2 romesco or other hot dried
  red chile peppers
- 1¾ cups almonds
- scant 1 cup hazelnuts
- 3 tomatoes
- 1 cup light olive oil,
  plus extra for drizzling
- 2 Marie cookies or tea biscuits
- 1 tablespoon white-wine vinegar
- 1 tablespoon chopped
  fresh parsley
- 1 tablespoon chopped fresh mint
- salt and pepper

Serves 6

Preheat the oven to 400°F. Put the chile peppers in a bowl, pour in warm water to cover, and let soak for 30 minutes, then drain, and peel. Place the almonds, hazelnuts, and tomatoes on a baking sheet, drizzle with oil, and roast in the oven for 10 minutes. Transfer the nuts to a bowl and return the tomatoes to the oven for 30 minutes more. Process the almonds, hazelnuts, and cookies or biscuits together in a food processor or pound in a mortar. Remove the tomatoes from the oven and, when cool enough to handle, peel and add to the nut mixture. Add the chile peppers, and pound or process. Gradually add the oil, a little at a time, as if making mayonnaise (see recipe 105). Finally, add the vinegar, parsley, and mint. Season to taste with salt and pepper and stir in a little water if the sauce is too thick. This sauce goes very well with shellfish, especially if broiled or grilled. It has a strong flavor so it should be used in moderation.

113

Vegetable sauce
SALSA DE HORTALIZAS – PIPIRRANA·

- 2 large, ripe tomatoes,
  seeded and finely chopped
- 1 cucumber, finely chopped
- 1 green bell pepper,
  seeded and finely chopped
- 1 small onion, finely chopped
- 3 tablespoons white-wine
  vinegar
- 6 tablespoons sunflower oil
- salt and pepper

Serves 6

This sauce should be made 30 minutes prior to being served. This gives it enough time to marinate but not enough time for the tomato to break down and become very watery. Combine the tomato, cucumber, bell pepper, and onion in a bowl. Whisk the vinegar with a pinch of salt and pepper in a separate bowl and whisk in the oil. Pour the dressing over the vegetables and mix well. Let stand in a cool place for about 30 minutes before serving. To serve, pour the sauce over fish or shellfish. If the sauce is to be served with meat, offer it separately in a ceramic or glass bowl. More than just a sauce, this recipe is like a very finely chopped salad and goes very well with fish, shellfish, and cold meat.

Guacamole

GUACAMOLE

- 1 large, very ripe avocado
- 1 tablespoon finely
  chopped onion
- 1 piece green bell pepper,
  finely chopped
- 2 slices green chile or
  3 small green chiles
- ½ tomato, finely chopped
- 4 coriander seeds, crushed
- a few drops of lemon juice
- salt

Serves 3

Halve the avocado and remove and reserve the pit. Scoop out the flesh into a bowl with a spoon. Mash with a fork until smooth. Add the onion, bell pepper, chiles, tomato, and coriander seeds, season with salt, and stir in the lemon juice to prevent discoloration. Mix together well, spoon into a serving bowl, and place the reserved avocado pit in the middle. Cover tightly with plastic wrap and place in the refrigerator until ready to serve. Remove the chile just before serving. Serve this spicy avocado sauce as an accompaniment to cold meat or as an appetizer on crackers.

115

Sauce for seafood salad

SALSA PARA SALPICÓN DE MARISCOS

- 1 onion, very finely chopped
- oil
- 1 ¼ cups white-wine vinegar
- 1 hard-cooked egg,
  roughly chopped
- ½ red bell pepper,
  very finely chopped
- 1 tablespoon brandy
- salt

Serves 4

Place the onion and oil in a bowl and set aside for 5 minutes to steep. Make a vinaigrette with the vinegar, salt, and the oil and onion mixture. Add the egg, pepper and brandy.

116

Marinade for game

- 1 bottle red wine, to cover meat
- 1 thinly sliced onion
- 2 sliced carrots
- 3 sprigs fresh parsley
- 2 bay leaves or sprigs thyme
- 12 black peppercorns
- 2 ground cloves
- dash of olive oil
- salt

Makes enough for 1 joint

Combine all the ingredients in a ceramic or glass dish; a metal dish will affect the flavor. Add the meat, turning well to coat. Cover the dish to prevent the aroma of the ingredients escaping and place in the refrigerator. The meat should be left to marinate for at least 5 hours and up to 24 hours. Turn the meat in the marinade from time to time, then re-cover. When the meat is ready to be cooked, remove it from the marinade and discard the marinade. Cook the meat as desired. This type of marinade is used to make meat more tender and improve flavor. Use it for strong meats such as venison for example.

Sweet sauces

117

Caramel sauce

CARAMELO LÍQUIDO

- **1 tablespoon superfine sugar**
- **a few drops of lemon juice**
- **¾ cup hot water**

Serves 4

Put the sugar, lemon juice, and 2 tablespoons cold water into a pan. Cook over high heat, whisking constantly, until golden brown. Remove from the heat and add the hot water very carefully as there will be a lot of steam. Return the pan to the heat and cook for about 5 minutes, until the sauce thickens a little. Remove from the heat and let cool before serving in a small pitcher.

118

Chocolate sauce
SALSA DE CHOCOLATE

- 7 ounces semisweet chocolate, broken into squares
- 1 teaspoon potato starch
- 2½ cups milk
- 4 tablespoons superfine sugar

Serves 4

Put the chocolate in a pan, add 4 tablespoons water, and heat gently, stirring occasionally, until the chocolate has melted and the mixture is smooth. Mix the potato starch to a paste with 1 tablespoon of the milk in a cup. Gradually stir the remaining milk into the chocolate and add the sugar and the potato starch mixture. Cook, stirring constantly, for 2 minutes, then remove the pan from the heat. Let the sauce cool, then strain it through a coarse strainer into a sauceboat. This sauce goes well with baked desserts, vanilla ice cream, and poached pears.

119

Jam sauce
SALSA DE MERMELADA

- 2 tablespoons superfine sugar
- 3 tablespoons jam (such as red currant, raspberry, or apricot)
- 2 teaspoons potato starch
- a few drops of lemon juice

Serves 4

Put the sugar and jam into a pan, pour in scant 2 cups water, and cook over medium heat, stirring constantly, for 10 minutes. Stir the potato starch to a paste with 2 tablespoons water in a cup, then stir into the jam mixture. Cook, stirring constantly, for 5 minutes more. Add the lemon juice, strain, and serve. This sauce goes well with steamed desserts and ice cream.

120

Orange sauce
SALSA DE ZUMO DE NARANJA

- juice of 4 large oranges
- 1 thinly sliced strip lemon rind
- 1 cup superfine sugar
- 1 teaspoon potato starch or rice flour
- 2 tablespoons Curaçao or Cointreau (optional)

Serves 6

Extract the orange juice using a juicer or food processor, as both methods produce a thicker juice. Otherwise, squeeze the fruit in the usual way and use a little extra potato starch to thicken the sauce. Pour the orange juice into a pan, add the lemon rind and sugar, and heat gently, stirring until the sugar has dissolved. Stir the potato starch to a thin paste with 3 tablespoons water in a cup. (If using rice flour, stir it with 1 tablespoon water.) Stir into the juice mixture and cook, stirring constantly, for 2 minutes. Remove from the heat, add the liqueur, if using, strain into a pitcher, and let cool. Store in the refrigerator until required. This sauce can be served with baked desserts and ice cream.

STEWS & SOUPS

121 · Swiss chard, potato, navy beans, and rice stew

POTAJE CON ACELGAS, PATATAS, JUDÍAS BLANCAS Y ARROZ

- 1¾ cups dried haricot beans,
  soaked overnight in cold water
  and drained
- 4 Swiss chard leaves,
  finely chopped
- 9 ounces lean pork, diced
- scant 1½ cups diced turnips
- 3 tablespoons olive oil
- 1 small onion, finely chopped
- 1 tomato, peeled and seeded
- pinch of saffron threads
- 3 potatoes, diced
- ½ cup rice
- salt

Serves 6

Put the beans in a pan and add cold water to cover. Bring to a boil and drain. Add fresh cold water to cover and bring back to a boil, then lower the heat, and simmer for 25–30 minutes. Drain well. Put the Swiss chard leaves, pork, and turnips into another pan and add water to cover and a pinch of salt. Bring to a boil, then lower the heat, and simmer for about 1 hour, until quite tender. Add the beans, stir well, and continue to simmer for 30 minutes more, until very tender. Heat the oil in a skillet. Add the onion and cook over low heat, stirring occasionally, for about 7 minutes, until lightly browned. Add the tomato and cook for 5 minutes more. Transfer the contents of the pan to the stew. Put the saffron in a mortar, or small bowl. add a spoonful of stock from the stew, and crush. Add to the stew. About 30 minutes before serving, add the potatoes to the stew, and 15 minutes after adding the potatoes, add the rice. If necessary, cook a little longer, until the potato and rice are tender. Serve in a soup tureen.

122 Simple stew

POTAJE SENCILLO

- scant 1½ cups dried navy beans,
  soaked overnight in cold water
  and drained
- 1 bay leaf
- ½ onion, halved
- 2 cloves garlic
- 2 tablespoons lard or
  vegetable shortening
- 4 ounces lean cured ham
  in a single piece
- 4 ounces slab bacon,
  rind removed if necessary
- 4 cups warm water
- 2¼ pounds cabbage,
  preferably Savoy, shredded
- 1 pound 2 ounces potatoes,
  diced
- salt

Serves 6

Put the beans, bay leaf, onion, garlic, lard or shortening, ham, and bacon into a large pan and pour in 4 cups cold water. Bring to a boil, then lower the heat, and simmer for 15 minutes. Add 1 cup fresh cold water, bring back to a boil, and simmer for 15 minutes more. Do this twice more at 15-minute intervals, then simmer for 15 minutes more (making a total cooking time of about 1¼ hours.) Using a slotted spoon, remove the beans from the pan. Put about half the beans in a bowl, add some of the stock from the stew, and set aside. Put the remaining beans in a blender or food processor and process to a purée. Scrape the bean purée into the stew. Add the warm water and when the stew comes back to simmering point, stir in the cabbage. Continue to simmer for 1 hour, then add the potatoes, and season with salt. Cook for 45 minutes more, until the potato and cabbage are tender. Add the reserved beans. Remove the pieces of ham and bacon, cut them into small cubes, and return them to the stew. Taste and adjust the seasoning, if necessary. Serve in a soup tureen.

123 Galician stew

POTE GALLEGO

- scant 1½ cups dried haricot beans, soaked overnight in cold water and drained
- 5 ounces ham
- 2 beef shanks
- 1 pound 2 ounces lean beef
- 4 potatoes
- 1 pound turnip green or cabbage
- 1 tablespoon lard or vegetable shortening
- salt

Serves 6

Put the beans in a pan and add cold water to cover. Bring to a boil and drain. Add fresh cold water to cover and bring back to a boil, then lower the heat and simmer for 25–30 minutes. Drain well. Put the ham, shin bones, beef, potatoes, turnip tops or Savoy cabbage and lard into a large stockpot. Add enough water to cover. Bring to a simmer and simmer for 1 hour. Add the beans, simmer for 30 minutes more and serve hot.

124 Thick garbanzo soup

PURÉ DE GARBANZOS

- 2 tablespoons olive oil
- 2 leeks, chopped and rinsed well
- 6¼ cups beef or veal stock (home-made, canned, or from a bouillon cube)
- 1⅔ cups canned or cooked garbanzo beans
- 1 tablespoon cornstarch
- croûtons
- salt

Serves 6

Heat the oil in a large pan. Add the leek and cook over low heat, stirring occasionally, for about 15 minutes, until beginning to brown. Add 1¼ cups of the stock and simmer for 5 minutes, then remove the pan from the heat. Add the leek mixture to the rest of the stock. Process the garbanzos, in batches, in a blender or food processor with all but 2 tablespoons of the leek and stock. Pour the processed garbanzo beans into a pan and heat gently. Mix the cornstarch to a paste with the reserved stock and leek mixture in a cup and stir into the soup. Simmer gently for about 5 minutes. Season to taste with salt and serve in a soup tureen with the croûtons.

125

Thick bean soup

PURÉ DE JUDÍAS BLANCAS

- 1 ⅔ cups dried navy beans,
  soaked for 3–5 hours in
  cold water and drained
- 2 cloves garlic
- 1 bay leaf
- 1 tablespoon olive oil
- 2 tablespoons all-purpose flour
- 2 tablespoons (¼ stick) butter
- croûtons
- salt

Serves 6

Put the beans in a large pan, pour in water to cover, and bring to a boil. Drain well and add 8 ¾ cups fresh cold water, the garlic, bay leaf, and oil. Bring to a boil, then lower the heat, and simmer for 1–1 ½ hours, until tender. (The cooking time depends on the type and age of the beans and the type of water, so the best way to check is by testing a few beans.) Remove the pan from the heat and let cool slightly. Remove and discard the garlic and bay leaf. Process the beans, in batches, in a blender or food processor, then push through a fine strainer into a clean pan. Mix the flour to a paste with a little of the cold puréed beans in a bowl. Add this to the rest of the bean purée in the pan and simmer, stirring constantly, for about 8 minutes. Season to taste with salt and, just before serving, add the butter to the hot soup so that it melts without cooking. Serve in a soup tureen with croûtons if you like.

Note: This soup can also be made with leftover cooked beans or leftover stew. The method is the same as for the thick garbanzo soup (see recipe 124).

126

Thick lentil soup

PURÉ DE LENTEJAS

- generous ½ cup rice
- scant 3 cups cooked lentils,
  drained and the cooking stock
  reserved
- salt

Serves 6

Bring a large pan of water to a boil, but do not add salt. Add the rice, bring back to a boil, and cook for about 15–18 minutes, or until tender. Drain well, refresh under cold running water, and drain again. Set half the rice aside. Process the rest of the rice with the lentils, and some of the cooking stock, in batches, in a blender or food processor to form a thick soup. Pour into a clean pan. Add more stock if necessary. Heat the soup well and season to taste with salt. Season the reserved rice and place small mounds on top of the soup. Do this just before serving so that the rice does not have time to sink.

Note: A chicken bouillon cube dissolved in a little hot water will provide added flavor. Add it at the end, just before serving.

Thick pea soup

PURÉ DE GUISANTES SECOS

• **5 ounces slab bacon,
   rind removed if necessary**
• **2¾ cups dried peas,
   soaked for 6–8 hours in
   cold water and drained**
• **4 ounces carrots**
• **1 onion, coarsely chopped**
• **salt**

Serves 6

Separate the fatty part of the bacon from the leaner part. Pour 10⅔ cups water into a large pan and add the peas. Bring to a boil and skim off the froth that rises to the surface with a skimmer or slotted spoon. Add the carrots, onion, and the fattier part of the bacon. Lower the heat and simmer gently for 1½–2 hours, until the peas are very tender. Remove the pan from the heat and let cool slightly. Remove the bacon. Process the mixture, in batches, in a blender or food processor and return to a clean pan. Dice the remaining bacon and put it into another pan. Add hot water to cover, bring to a boil, and simmer for 5 minutes. Meanwhile, gently reheat the soup and season to taste with salt. Drain the bacon, add to the soup, and simmer for 10 minutes. Serve in a soup tureen.

128

Thick pea soup with milk

PURÉ DE GUISANTES SECOS CON LECHE

• **scant 2 cups dried peas,
   soaked for 12 hours in
   cold water and drained**
• **1 small onion, halved**
• **1 veal shank bone**
• **1 bouquet garni
   (1 bay leaf, 1 clove garlic,
   and 1 sprig fresh parsley
   tied together in cheesecloth)**
• **1¼ cups hot milk**
• **3 tablespoons butter**
• **croûtons**
• **salt**

Serves 6

Pour 8¾ cups water into a large pan and add the peas, onion, veal shank bone, and bouquet garni. Bring to a boil over medium heat, then lower the heat, and simmer for 2½–3 hours. Remove the onion, veal shank, and bouquet garni and reserve most of the cooking stock. Process the peas with some of the stock in a blender or food processor and return to a clean pan. Season to taste with salt, stir in the hot milk, and, if necessary, a little more of the stock. Reheat the soup and stir in the butter. Serve in a soup tureen and offer the croûtons separately.

129

Thin onion soup

SOPA DE CEBOLLA CLARA

- **3 tablespoons olive oil**
- **2 onions, thinly sliced**
- **2 tablespoons all-purpose flour**
- **8¾ cups chicken stock (homemade, canned or made with a bouillon cube)**
- **1 tablespoon finely chopped fresh parsley**
- **generous 1 cup grated Parmesan cheese (optional)**
- **salt**

Serves 6

Heat the oil in a large pan. Add the onion and cook over low heat, stirring occasionally, for about 10 minutes, until browned. Using a slotted spoon, transfer the onion to a plate and set aside. Add the flour to the pan and cook, stirring constantly, for about 2 minutes, until lightly colored. Gradually stir in the stock. Return the onion to the pan and simmer for 20 minutes. Remove the pan from the heat, season to taste with salt and add the parsley. Serve in a soup tureen and hand the Parmesan separately, if using.

130

Garlic soup with eggs

SOPA DE AJO CON HUEVOS

- **1 cup olive oil**
- **5 ounces day-old bread, thinly sliced**
- **5 cloves garlic**
- **1 tablespoon chopped onion**
- **1 teaspoon paprika**
- **6¼ cups boiling water**
- **1 sprig fresh parsley**
- **6 eggs**
- **salt**

Serves 6

Heat the oil in a skillet over a medium heat. Add the bread slices, in batches, and fry for 2 minutes until golden brown on both sides. Remove with a slotted spatula and drain on paper towels. Drain off all but 4 tablespoons of the oil in the skillet and return the pan to the heat. Add the garlic and onion and cook over low heat, stirring occasionally, for 5 minutes until softened. Remove the skillet from the heat and stir in the paprika. Preheat the oven to 350°F. Put the fried bread in an ovenproof casserole that can be used on the stovetop. Remove and discard the garlic and pour the onion and paprika mixture onto the fried bread. Add the boiling water and season with salt. Stir well, add the parsley, and bring to a boil, then lower the heat, and simmer for 5 minutes. Transfer the casserole to the oven and bake for 7 minutes until it forms a crust. Crack the eggs onto the crust, season each with a little salt, and return the casserole to the oven. Bake until the whites are set. Serve immediately.

131 Creamy carrot soup

CREMA DE ZANAHORIAS

- 1 pound 2 ounces potatoes,
  cut into large pieces
- 1 pound 2 ounces carrots, sliced
- ½ onion, coarsely chopped
- 2 tomatoes, peeled and seeded
  or ½ teaspoon tomato paste
- 1 sprig fresh parsley
- 3 tablespoons sunflower oil
- croûtons
- salt

Serves 6

Pour 8 ¾ cups water into a large pan. Add the potato, carrot, onion, tomato, parsley, and oil and season with salt. Bring to a boil, then lower the heat, and simmer for about 1 hour, until the carrots and potatoes are tender. Check the liquid in the pan during cooking and add cold water if necessary. Remove the pan from the heat and discard the parsley. Let the mixture cool slightly, then process, in batches, in a blender or food processor. Return to a clean pan and reheat. Serve hot and offer the croûtons separately.

Note: This soup can be made in advance but it is important to process the mixture in a blender or food processor before it gets cold. Once it has been processed, it can be allowed to cool and then reheated before serving.

132 Pumpkin soup

SOPA DE CALABAZA

- 3 tablespoons olive oil
- 2 leeks, chopped and rinsed well
- scant 1 cup diced potatoes
- about 1½ pounds West Indian
  pumpkin or butternut squash
- 2¼ cups hot milk
- ½ teaspoon meat extract, Maggi
  Seasoning or beef soup base
- salt

Makes 3 ½ quarts

Heat the oil in a large pan. Add the leek and cook over low heat, stirring occasionally, for about 5 minutes, until softened. Add the potato and pumpkin, pour in 6 ¼ cups water, and season lightly with salt (remember that the meat extract or Maggi Seasoning will be salty). Bring to a boil, lower the heat, and simmer for about 45 minutes. Remove the pan from the heat and let cool slightly. Process the mixture, in batches, in a blender or food processor. Return to a clean pan and add the milk. Reheat gently and stir in the meat extract or Maggi Seasoning. Serve in a soup tureen.

Note: If you prefer, you can omit the potatoes from the soup and use 3 ¼ pounds pumpkin instead.

Porrusalda

PORRUSALDA

- **9 ounces salt cod fillet**
- **4 tablespoons olive oil**
- **6 leeks, chopped and rinsed well**
- **2 ⅔ cups diced potatoes**
- **salt**

Serves 6

Put the cod in a bowl and add water to cover. Let soak for up to 24 hours, changing the water several times. Drain well. Put the fish in a pan, pour in 2 ¼ cups water, and bring to a boil. Remove the pan from the heat and lift out the cod with a slotted spatula. Remove any remaining bones and skin, flake the flesh with a fork, and return it to the water in which it has been cooked. Heat the oil in another large pan. Add the leek and cook over low heat, stirring occasionally, for about 5 minutes, until beginning to brown. Add the potato and cook for 5 minutes more. Pour in 8 ¾ cups water, bring to a boil, and simmer for about 35 minutes, until the potatoes are tender but not disintegrating. Add the cod and its cooking water and simmer for 10 minutes more. Season, if necessary, and serve in a soup tureen.

Note: Porrusalada is a traditional soup from the Basque region.

134 Leek and potato soup
SOPA DE PUERROS Y PATATAS

- 3 large leeks, rinsed well
- 3 tablespoons olive oil
- 6 potatoes, diced
- 1 chicken bouillon cube
- salt

Serves 6

Trim the leeks, halve them lengthwise, and cut into ¾ inch lengths. Rinse well and drain. Heat the oil in a large pan. Add the leek and cook over low heat, stirring occasionally, for about 10 minutes, until beginning to brown. Pour in 8 ¾ cups water and season lightly with salt (bearing in mind that the bouillon cube will be salty). Bring to a boil and simmer for 5 minutes, then add the potato, and simmer for 30 minutes more, until the potato is tender. Crumble the bouillon cube into a pitcher or cup and stir in a ladleful of soup, then pour back into the soup. Serve immediately.

135 Minestrone soup
MINESTRONE

- ½ cup navy beans,
  soaked overnight in
  cold water and drained
- 1 ⅔ cups green beans,
  cut into short lengths
- 1¼ cups peas
- 1 zucchini, diced
- 1 cup diced carrots
- 9 ounces butternut squash
  or pumpkin, peeled, seeded
  and diced
- 1 leek, cut into ¼ inch slices
  and rinsed well
- 2 tomatoes, diced
- 2 stalks celery, sliced
- scant 1 cup small pasta shapes
  (such as shells, spirals or tubes),
  cooked
- 3 tablespoons olive oil
- 1 onion, chopped
- 1 clove garlic
- 1 sprig fresh mint
- 2 tablespoons chopped
  fresh mint
- freshly grated Parmesan cheese

Serves 6

Put the navy beans in a pan, pour in water to cover, and bring to a boil. Lower the heat and simmer for 1–1½ hours, until tender. (Top up the pan with cold water a couple of times during cooking, as this will make the beans softer.) Drain and set aside. Pour 8 ¾ cups water into a large pan and bring to a boil. Add the green beans, peas, zucchini, carrot, pumpkin, leek, tomato, and celery and bring back to a boil. Lower the heat and simmer gently for about 30 minutes, until all the vegetables are tender but not disintegrating. Stir in the cooked navy beans and the pasta shapes. Heat 2 tablespoons of the oil in a skillet. Add the onion and cook over medium heat, stirring occasionally, for 5–6 minutes, until just beginning to brown. Add the contents of the skillet to the soup. Crush the garlic and mint sprig in a mortar, or process in a mini-food processor, stir in the remaining oil to make a paste, and add to the soup.Serve in a soup tureen, sprinkled with the chopped mint. Offer the Parmesan separately.

136

Leek soup with milk

SOPA DE PUERROS CON LECHE

- 2 tablespoons olive oil
- 4 leeks, sliced and rinsed well
- 5 potatoes, cut into pieces
- 2¼ cups hot milk
- ½ teaspoon meat extract
- salt

Serves 6

Heat the oil in a large pan. Add the leek and cook over low heat, stirring occasionally, for about 5 minutes, until softened but not colored. Pour in 6¼ cups water and add the potato and a pinch of salt. Bring to a boil, then lower the heat, and simmer for 1 hour. Remove the pan from the heat and let cool slightly, then process in a blender or food processor. Stir in the hot milk and meat extract or Maggi Seasoning and serve in a soup tureen.

137

Green bean and tomato soup

SOPA DE TOMATE Y JUDÍAS VERDES

- 9 ounces potatoes,
  cut into large pieces
- 3¼ pounds very ripe tomatoes,
  peeled, seeded and chopped
- 2 tablespoons olive oil
- 1 sprig fresh parsley
- 1 bay leaf
- pinch of baking soda
- 1⅔ cups green beans, trimmed
  and cut into ¾-inch lengths
- salt

Serves 6

Put the potato, tomato, oil, parsley, bay leaf, and a pinch of salt into a large pan, pour in 8¾ cups water, and bring to a boil, then lower the heat, and simmer for 45 minutes. Remove the pan from the heat and let cool slightly. Remove and discard the parsley and bay leaf, then process in a blender or food processor, in batches if necessary. Bring a small pan of lightly salted water to a boil and add the baking soda. Add the beans and cook for about 15 minutes, until tender. Drain well. Reheat the soup, if necessary, then pour into a soup tureen, and sprinkle the green beans on top. Serve immediately.

138

Tomato juice soup
SOPA DE JUGO DE TOMATE

- 2¼ cups chicken stock
  (homemade, canned or
  made with a bouillon cube)
- 1 heaping tablespoon cornstarch
  or 1 tablespoon potato starch
- 2¼ cups tomato juice
- 2 tablespoons dry sherry
- 4 tablespoons light cream
- 1 tablespoon chopped
  fresh parsley
- salt
  Serves 4

Pour the stock into a large pan and heat gently. Mix the cornstarch or potato starch to a paste with 2 tablespoons water in a cup or small bowl and stir into the stock. Cook, stirring constantly, for 2 minutes. Shake the tomato juice well and add to the pan, then stir in the sherry, and season to taste with salt. Heat through gently but do not let the soup boil. If serving the soup hot, ladle it into warm bowls. Swirl 1 tablespoon of cream into each bowl and sprinkle with the parsley. If serving the soup cold, use a little less cornstarch in the stock. Let the soup cool, then chill in the refrigerator. Garnish with the cream and parsley before serving.

139

Zucchini soup with cheese triangles
SOPA DE CALABACINES CON QUESITOS

- 4 zucchini
- 4 cheese triangles (Laughing
  Cow or similar) or other cheese,
  cut into 4 bite-size pieces
- salt
  Serves 4

Peel half of each zucchini and slice each whole zucchini thinly. Put the slices in a pan and pour in just enough water to cover. Add a pinch of salt and bring to a boil, then lower the heat, and simmer for about 20 minutes, until tender. Remove from the heat and let cool, then process, in batches, in a blender or food processor. Taste and adjust the seasoning and serve immediately.

Note: Do not leave more than half the peel on the zucchini as this can make the soup bitter. This soup is also very good if a crumbled chicken bouillon cube is added to the cooking water.

140

Cream of asparagus soup

SOPA-CREMA DE ESPÁRRAGOS

- 30 asparagus spears
- 3 cups milk (see method)
- ¼ cup (½ stick) butter
- 3 tablespoons all-purpose flour
- 3 egg yolks
- 1 teaspoon finely chopped
  fresh parsley
- salt

Serves 6

Trim and, if necessary, peel the asparagus spears. Wash well, then cook in a pan of salted boiling water for about 20 minutes, until tender. (Test by piercing one of the spears with the point of a knife.) Remove the asparagus from the pan, reserving the cooking liquid. Cut off and reserve the tips. Cut the remaining stalks into two or three pieces and process to a purée in a blender or food processor with a little of the reserved cooking liquid. Push the purée through a coarse strainer into a bowl. Measure the remaining cooking liquid and add enough milk to make 4 cups. Melt the butter in a pan over a low heat, stir in the flour, and cook, stirring constantly, for 2 minutes. Gradually stir in the milk mixture, a little at a time. Add the asparagus purée, season to taste with salt, and cook, stirring, until thickened to the required consistency. (Bear in mind that the egg yolks will thin the soup slightly). Just before serving, put the egg yolks into a soup tureen and, very gradually to prevent them curdling, add the hot soup. Finally, add the reserved asparagus tips to the soup and sprinkle with the parsley.

141

Watercress soup

CREMA DE BERROS

- 3 tablespoons olive oil
- 1 thick leek, halved lengthwise,
  sliced and rinsed well
- 1 onion, coarsely chopped
- 2¼ pounds potatoes,
  cut into pieces
- 2 bunches watercress,
  coarse stalks removed
- 6¼ cups hot water
- 1 cup milk
- ½ teaspoon meat extract
  or Maggi Seasoning
- salt and pepper

Serves 6

Heat the oil in a large pan. Add the leek and onion and cook over low heat, stirring occasionally, for 4–6 minutes, until softened. Add the potato and 1½ bunches of the watercress. Pour in the hot water, stir in 1 teaspoon salt, and bring to a boil, then lower the heat, cover, and simmer for 1 hour. Meanwhile, finely chop the remaining watercress. Remove the pan from the heat and let cool slightly, then process in a blender or food processor. Return the soup to a clean pan and reheat gently. Just before serving, stir together the milk and meat extract or Maggi Seasoning and add to the soup. Simmer for 6 minutes more. Season with salt and pepper to taste and pour into a soup tureen. Add the chopped watercress and serve immediately.

142   Rice and mint soup

SOPA DE ARROZ CON MENTA

- **4 cups chicken stock (homemade, canned or made with a bouillon cube)**
- **2 tablespoons rice**
- **⅔ cup plain yogurt**
- **1 egg yolk, lightly beaten**
- **1 tablespoon all-purpose flour**
- **3 tablespoons butter**
- **1 tablespoon chopped fresh mint**
- **salt and pepper**

Serves 4

Pour the stock into a pan and bring to a boil. Add the rice, bring back to a boil, and cook over medium–high heat for 15 minutes. Season with salt (bearing in mind that the stock is salty). Combine the yogurt, egg yolk, and flour in a separate, large pan, then gradually stir in 1 cup water, a little at a time. Simmer gently for 5 minutes, then stir in the rice and stock mixture, and cook for 5 minutes more. Melt the butter in a small pan, remove from the heat, and stir in the mint. Add this mixture to the soup just before serving.

143   Celery and potato soup

SOPA DE APIO COY PATATAS

- **4 tablespoons olive oil**
- **2 bunches of celery, cut into 2 inch lengths**
- **3 onions, coarsely chopped**
- **1½ pounds potatoes, cut into pieces**
- **2 veal shank bones**
- **1 tablespoon finely chopped celery leaves or fresh parsley**
- **salt**

Makes 4 quarts.

Heat the oil in a large stockpot. Add the celery and onion and cook over low heat, stirring occasionally, for about 10 minutes, until beginning to soften. Add the potato, veal shanks, and 11 cups water. Bring to a boil, then lower the heat, and simmer for 1 hour. Remove the pan from the heat and let cool slightly. Remove the veal shanks and process the soup, in batches, in a blender or food processor. Return the soup to a clean pan, season to taste with salt and reheat gently. Serve hot in a soup tureen, garnished with the celery leaves or parsley.

144

Mushroom soup

CREMA DE CHAMPIÑONES

- 3 ⅔ cups finely chopped cremini
  mushrooms
- 2 tablespoons (¼ stick) butter
- a few drops of lemon juice
- 4 tablespoons all-purpose flour
- 6 ¼ cups chicken stock
  (homemade, canned or
  made with a bouillon cube)
- 1 egg yolk
- salt

Serves 6

Put the mushrooms, butter, lemon juice, and a pinch of salt in a pan, cover, and cook over low heat for about 6 minutes. Put the flour in a separate, large pan over low heat and cook, stirring constantly, for about 5–7 minutes, until lightly colored. Gradually stir in the stock, a little at a time. Simmer, stirring constantly with a whisk, for 10 minutes. Add the mushrooms and their cooking juices and simmer for 5 minutes more. Put the egg yolk into a soup tureen and gradually pour in the hot soup. Stir with a spoon and serve immediately.

145

Soup with rice, hard-cooked egg, and chopped parsley

CALDO DE COCIDO CON ARROZ, HUEVO DURO Y PEREJIL PICADO

- 8 ¾ cups vegetable stock
- 4 tablespoons rice
- 2 hard-cooked eggs
- 1 tablespoon chopped
  fresh parsley
- salt

Serves 6

Pour the stock into a pan and bring to a boil. Add the rice, bring back to a boil, and cook over a medium–high heat for about 15–18 minutes, or until tender. Meanwhile, chop the yolks and 1 ½ of the whites (all the egg whites would be too much). Pour the stock and rice into a soup tureen, season to taste with salt, add the parsley and eggs, and serve immediately.

Consommé

CONSOMÉ

- **1 beef shank**
- **1 pound 2 ounces lean beef,**
  cut into small pieces
- **7 ounces carrots, thickly sliced**
- **7 ounces turnips, thickly sliced**
- **1 small onion, halved**
- **1 leek, halved lengthwise**
  and rinsed well
- **1 stalk celery**
- **1 whole clove**
- **2 egg whites**
- **salt**

Makes 6 ¼ cups

Put the beef shank and pieces of beef into a large pan, pour in 8 ¾ cups water, and bring to a boil. Lower the heat and simmer for 30 minutes, then skim off the froth that has risen to the surface with a skimmer or slotted spoon. Add the carrot, turnip, onion, leek, celery, and clove and season to taste with salt. Bring back to a boil, then simmer over low heat, stirring occasionally, for 1 ½ hours. Twice during this cooking time, add 5 tablespoons cold water to help any froth rise to the surface. In a clean, dry bowl, whisk the egg whites until they form soft peaks then transfer them to a pan. Carefully and slowly pour the stock (including the vegetables) onto the egg whites, stirring constantly with a wooden spoon. Simmer for about 20 minutes. Strain the stock into a bowl, then strain again through a fine cheesecloth-lined strainer into another bowl. Season to taste with salt. Serve in indiviual soup bowls with your choice of garnish (see recipes 147–150).

Note: If the consommé is very pale, you can use a little meat extract, Maggi Seasoning or beef bouillon to darken the color or a little caramel made with a teaspoon of sugar and a few drops of water heated in a pan until the sugar browns. (Be careful not to burn it as this will give the stock a bitter flavor.) Add a few spoonfuls of the consommé to the caramel and then return the mixture to the consommé, and it will take on a good golden color.

147

Egg squares
FLAN

- 2 egg yolks
- 1 cup stock or milk
- salt

Serves 2–4

Preheat the oven to 325°F. Lightly beat the egg yolks with the stock or milk, season with salt, and pour into a lightly greased cast-iron egg dish or small gratin dish. Put the dish in a roasting pan and pour in hot water to come about halfway up the sides. Bake for 10–15 minutes, until the mixture has set. Remove the dish from the roasting pan and let cool, then turn out the set egg mixture, and cut into small squares. Add the squares to the soup bowls just before serving.

148

Egg cubes
FLAN

- butter, for greasing
- 1 egg
- 3 egg yolks
- scant 1 cup hot stock
- salt

Serves 2–4

Preheat the oven to 325°F. Grease a gratin dish with butter. Beat the egg and the egg yolks in a bowl and gradually beat in the hot stock a little at a time (taking care that it does not curdle them). Season with salt and pour into the prepared dish. Put the dish in a roasting pan and pour in hot water to come about halfway up the sides. Bake for 1 hour but do not let the water boil as this will cause small holes to form in the mixture. Remove the dish from the pan and let cool completely before cutting the set mixture into small cube to serve.

149

Chopped ham and hard-cooked egg
PICADO DE JAMON DE YORK Y HUEVO DURO

- 3½ ounces very lean prosciutto or other dry-cured ham
- 2 hard-cooked eggs

Serves 2–4

Cut the ham into very thin strips about ¾ inch long and chop the hard-cooked eggs. Put a little of each ingredient into each soup bowl before pouring in the consommé.

150

Dumplings
BOLITAS

- 1 thick slice bread
- 1 egg, beaten
- 1 clove garlic, finely chopped
- 2 sprigs fresh parsley, finely chopped

Serves 2–4

Cut the crusts off the bread, leaving a piece about the size of a large egg. Crumble it into a bowl and add the egg, garlic, and parsley. Mix well to make a dough. Form the dough into small balls or one large sausage shape. Add the dumplings to the soup 5 minutes before the end of the cooking time. Or roll in bread crumbs and fry in olive oil until golden brown all over, then add to the soup just before serving.

151

Simple noodle soup

SOPA DE FIDEOS SIMPLE

- 8¾ cups chicken stock
  (homemade, canned or
  made with a bouillon cube)
- 4 ounces fine noodles
- salt

Serves 6

Pour the stock into a pan and bring to a boil. Gradually add the noodles in batches and cook for about 15 minutes. (The cooking time will depend on the type of noodles. To test whether they are ready, bite a piece between your teeth.) Make sure the noodles don't begin to disintegrate, as this will turn the liquid cloudy and they will not taste as good. Skim off the froth that rises to the surface of the water with a slotted spoon, season to taste with salt, and serve immediately. This soup should not be made in advance.

152

Toasted flour soup

SOPA DE HARINA TOSTADA

- 6 tablespoons all-purpose flour
- 7½ cups cold chicken stock
  (homemade, canned or made
  with a bouillon cube)
- 2 egg yolks
- 2 tablespoons (¼ stick) butter
- croûtons
- salt

Serves 6

Put the flour into a pan and cook over low heat, stirring constantly with a wooden spoon, for 5–7 minutes, until lightly toasted. Gradually stir in the cold stock, a little at a time. Bring to a boil, stirring constantly, then lower the heat and simmer for about 8 minutes. Season to taste with salt. Put the egg yolks into a soup tureen and, very slowly to prevent the eggs curdling, pour in the soup. Add the butter and when it has melted, stir the hot soup, and serve, adding croûtons at the last minute.

153

Chilled cucumber soup

SOPA DE PEPINOS FRÍA

- 4 cucumbers,
  each about 7 ounces
- 1¼ cups plain yogurt
- 1 small clove garlic
- 3 tablespoons white-wine
  vinegar
- 3 sprigs fresh mint
- 1 cup light cream
- 2 tablespoons chopped
  fresh mint
- salt and pepper

Serves 6

Peel two of the cucumbers and coarsely dice all of them. Put the cucumber, yogurt, garlic, vinegar, and mint sprigs into a food processor or blender and process until smooth. Pour the soup into a ceramic or glass bowl and gradually add the cream. Season to taste with salt and pepper. Cover and chill in the refrigerator until required. Serve chilled, sprinkled with the chopped mint.

Chicken soup

CREMA DE GALLINA

- **14 ounces skinless chicken breasts**
- **9 ounce beef shank bone**
- **2 carrots, thickly sliced**
- **1 onion, halved**
- **1 stalk celery, including leaves**
- **bouquet garni (1 sprig fresh parsley, 1 clove garlic, and ½ bay leaf tied together in cheesecloth)**
- **1½ tablespoons butter**
- **1 tablespoon sunflower oil**
- **2 tablespoons all-purpose flour**
- **1¼ cups milk**
- **1 egg yolk**
- **salt and pepper**

Serves 6

Put the chicken, beef shank, carrot, onion, celery, bouquet garni, and a pinch of salt in a pan and pour in 8 ¾ cups water. Bring to a boil over medium–low heat, then lower the heat, and simmer for 1–1 ½ hours, until the chicken is tender and cooked through. Lift the chicken out of the pan, cut the meat into bite-size pieces and set aside. Remove and discard the beef bone and bouquet garni. Reserve the stock and vegetables. Melt the butter with the oil in another pan. Stir in the flour, then gradually add the milk, a little at a time, stirring constantly with a wooden spoon. Simmer for about 4 minutes and then stir in 5 cups of the reserved stock. Remove the pan from the heat and let cool slightly, then process in a food processor or blender with the carrot, celery and onion from the stock. Lightly beat the egg yolk with a little of the remaining stock in a cup and add to the soup. Reheat the soup but do not allow to boil. Put the chicken pieces into a soup tureen and pour in the soup through a coarse strainer. Serve immediately.

155

Belgian chicken soup

SOPA DE POLLO A LA BELGA

- 3 carrots
- 1 beef shank bone
- 3¼ pound chicken
- 2 leeks, trimmed and rinsed well
- bunch of celery, including leaves
- 5 tablespoons olive oil
- a pinch of dried aromatic herbs
  or 1 bouquet garni
  (1 sprig fresh thyme, 1 bay leaf,
  and 1 sprig fresh parsley tied
  together in cheesecloth)
- 2 tablespoons (¼ stick) butter
- 1 heaping tablespoon
  all-purpose flour
- 2 egg yolks
- juice of ½ lemon
- fried bread (see recipe 130)
  or toasted bread
- salt and pepper

Serves 8

Slice 1 carrot. Put the beef bone, chicken, 1 leek, half the celery including the leaves, the sliced carrot, and a pinch of salt into a pan and pour in 10⅔ cups water. Bring to a boil, then lower the heat, and simmer for 1 hour. Remove the pan from the heat and strain the stock into a bowl. Reserve the chicken and, when it is cool enough to handle, remove and discard the skin, and cut the meat off the bones. Chop the remaining, uncooked carrots, leek, and celery. Heat 3 tablespoons of the oil in another pan. Add the chopped carrots, leek, and celery and cook over low heat, stirring occasionally, for about 5 minutes, until the vegetables are softened but not colored. Add the chicken meat and aromatic herbs or bouquet garni and season with a pinch of pepper. Pour in the stock and simmer gently for about 20 minutes. Melt the butter with the remaining oil in another pan. Stir in the flour, then gradually add 2¼ cups of the chicken stock, a little at a time, stirring constantly. Cook for about 8 minutes, then stir back into the soup. Simmer for 10 minutes more. Lightly beat the egg yolks with the lemon juice in a bowl and then, very slowly to prevent the eggs curdling, stir in a little chicken stock. Pour into the soup and transfer to a soup tureen. Serve immediately, offering the fried or toasted bread separately.

156

Chicken liver soup

SOPA DE HIGADITOS

- 3 tablespoons sunflower oil
- 1 clove garlic
- generous ½ cup blanched
  almonds
- 6 chicken livers
- a few saffron threads
- 6¼ cups chicken stock
- 1 tablespoon potato starch
- 1 egg yolk
- fried bread (see recipe 130)
  or toasted bread
- salt

Serves 6

Heat the oil in a skillet. Add the garlic and cook for a few minutes, until just colored. Remove with a slotted spoon and discard. Add the almonds to the skillet and cook, stirring frequently, for 2–3 minutes, until golden brown. Remove with a slotted spoon and set aside. Add the chicken livers, season with salt, cover, and cook over low heat, stirring occasionally, for about 5 minutes, until evenly browned. Crush the saffron in a mortar, or small bowl, and stir in a little of the stock.Remove the chicken livers from the pan with a slotted spatula. Put the livers, almonds, and saffron mixture in a blender or food processor, add a little stock, and process until smooth. Transfer to a pan and stir in the remaining stock. Simmer over low heat for 10 minutes. Mix the potato starch with 3 tablespoons water in a small bowl and add to the soup. Bring the soup to a boil. Beat the egg yolk in a bowl and gradually whisk in a few spoonfuls of hot soup, then stir into the soup. Serve in a soup tureen, offering the bread separately.

157

- 1 pound 2 ounces mixed pre-cut fresh vegetables such as carrots, parsnip, celery, green beans, etc (often sold in bags)
- 1 veal shank bone
- 1 tablespoon olive oil
- 1 tablespoon cornstarch
- ½ teaspoon meat extract
- salt

Serves 6

Vegetable soup
SOPA DE VERDURAS

Put 8 ¾ cups water into a pan and add the vegetables, veal shank, oil, and a pinch of salt. Bring to a boil, then lower the heat, and simmer for about 30 minutes, until the vegetables are tender. Mix the cornstarch to a paste with 2 tablespoons water in a small bowl, then stir in a little soup. Pour back into the soup and stir well with a wooden spoon. Simmer for 5 minutes more. Remove the veal shank, stir in the meat extract or Maggi Seasoning, and serve in a soup tureen.

158

- 3 tablespoons olive oil
- ⅔ cup diced bacon
- 1 large onion, finely chopped
- 1 pound 2 ounces Savoy cabbage, shredded
- 8 ¾ cups boiling water
- 4 tablespoons rice
- ½ teaspoon meat extract or Maggi Seasoning
- salt

Serves 6

Cabbage soup
SOPA DE REPOLLO

Heat the oil in a large pan. Add the bacon and onion and cook over low heat, stirring occasionally, for 8–10 minutes, until the onion is beginning to brown. Add the cabbage, cover, and cook, stirring occasionally, for about 15 minutes. Pour in the boiling water and simmer for 10 minutes, then add the rice, and cook for 30 minutes more. Stir in the meat extract or Maggi Seasoning and serve in a soup tureen.

159

Russian beet soup
SOPA RUSA DE REMOLACHA

- 2 tablespoons margarine
- 1 pound 2 ounces cooked beet, peeled and sliced, or canned beef, sliced
- 4 cups hot chicken stock (homemade, canned or made with a bouillon cube)
- 1 tablespoon red-wine vinegar
- 6 tablespoons light cream
- salt and pepper

Garnish (optional):
- 2 tablespoons finely chopped red cabbage
- 1 tablespoon red-wine vinegar

Serves 6

If making the garnish, put the red cabbage in a ceramic or glass bowl, add the vinegar, and toss lightly. Set aside until ready to serve. Melt the margarine in a large pan. Add the beet and cook over a low heat, stirring occasionally, for 10 minutes. Pour in the hot stock, add the vinegar, and season with salt and pepper and simmer over low heat for 15 minutes. Remove the pan from the heat and let the mixture cool slightly, then process in a food processor or blender. If serving chilled, pour the soup into a bowl, cover, and chill in the refrigerator for at least 3 hours. Serve in individual bowls, adding a swirl of cream to each. If serving hot, pour the processed soup into a soup tureen, add the cream, and mix lightly to create a marbled effect. Strain the red cabbage garnish, if using, and add to the soup.

Note: Versions of this hearty soup are popular throughout Eastern and Central Europe.

160

Grouper soup
SOPA DE MERO

- 3 tablespoons olive oil
- 2 leeks, thickly sliced and rinsed
- 2 onions, thickly sliced
- 1 cup white wine
- 1 white fish head, such as hake or whiting, gills removed
- 1 x 14 oz grouper fillet
- bouquet garni (1 sprig fresh parsley, 1 clove garlic, and 1 bay leaf tied together in cheesecloth)
- 2¼ pounds potatoes
- ¾ cup hot milk
- 2 egg yolks
- 1 teaspoon chopped fresh parsley
- croûtons
- salt

Serves 8

Heat the oil in a large pan. Add the leek and onion and cook over low heat, stirring occasionally, for about 10 minutes, until beginning to brown. Pour in 4 cups water and the wine and bring to a boil. Add the fish head, grouper, and bouquet garni. Bring back to a boil. Cut the potatoes into large pieces, and add to the pan along with a pinch of salt. Cook for 30 minutes more. Re-move and discard the fish head and leave the mixture to cool slightly. Lift out the grouper with a slotted spatula and remove the skin and bones if any. Flake the flesh with a fork, put in a food processor or blender with the potatoes and stock, and process until smooth and combined. Add the hot milk and process briefly again to combine. Lightly beat the egg yolks in a bowl and stir in a few spoonfuls of the soup, then add to the hot soup. Serve in a soup tureen, sprinkled with the parsley, and offer the croûtons separately.

Sailor's Soup

SOPA MARINERA

- 2 tablespoons olive oil
- 2 leeks, sliced and rinsed well
- ½ onion, chopped
- 2 tomatoes, seeded and chopped
- ½ bay leaf
- 2 cloves garlic, lightly crushed
- 1 pound 2 ounces raw shrimp, shells on and heads attached, if available
- 9 ounces monkfish tail
- a few saffron threads
- 4 ounces fine noodles
- salt and pepper

Serves 6

Heat the oil in a large pan. Add the leek and onion and cook over low heat, stirring occasionally, for 5 minutes, until softened. Stir in the tomato, add the bay leaf and garlic, and pour in 8 ¾ cups water. Season with salt, add the shrimp and monkfish, and bring to a boil. Cook over medium-high heat for 15 minutes, then remove the pan from the heat, and strain the stock into a clean pan. Cut out the monkfish bone and discard. Shell the shrimp and remove and reserve the heads, if attached. Put the heads, if using, in a mortar and pound with a pestle, or pulse in a food processor or blender, straining the liquid produced into the stock. Put the monkfish and shrimp in a food processor or blender, add some of the stock, and process until thoroughly combined. Push the mixture through a fine strainer into the stock, pressing down hard with a spoon to make sure all the liquid is extracted. Crush the saffron with 2 tablespoons of the stock in a mortar and add to the soup. Reheat the soup over low heat. Add the noodles and simmer for 15–20 minutes. Season with salt and pepper to taste and serve in a soup tureen.

Cream of shellfish soup

CREMA DE CARABINEROS, GAMBAS O CANGREJOS

- 1 pound 2 ounces raw royal red
  shrimp, shells on, or crayfish
- 1 pound 2 ounces raw jumbo
  shrimp, shells on and heads
  attached if available
  (see glossary)
- 7 tablespoons butter
- scant 1 cup rice flour
- 2 tablespoons brandy
- scant ½ cup light cream
- salt and pepper

Concentrated stock:
- scant 1 cup white wine
- 2 carrots, sliced
- 1 onion, cut into 4 wedges
- 1 sprig fresh parsley
- 1 bay leaf
- pinch of salt

Serves 6–8

First make the concentrated stock. Put all the stock ingredients into a pan, add 8 ¾ cups water, and bring to a boil. Lower the heat and simmer for 30 minutes, then remove from the heat, and let cool completely. (This step can be done several hours in advance). Put the royal red shrimp or crayfish and the jumbo shrimp in the cooled concentrated stock. Bring to a boil, then lower the heat, and cook for about 5 minutes, depending on the size of the shellfish. Remove the shellfish with a slotted spoon and reserve the stock. Preheat the oven to 300°F. Peel some of the jumbo shrimp for the garnish and remove their heads, if necessary. Reserve the heads and shells. Cut the peeled jumbo shrimp in half, put in a bowl, and cover with a plate to prevent them drying out. Remove and discard the royal red shrimp heads, if attached, as they have a very strong flavor. Use all the remaining shellfish and all the reserved shells and heads to prepare a flavored butter. To do this, mash them with the butter, in batches, in a mortar with a pestle, or pulse in a food processor, to a purée. Transfer the purée to an ovenproof baking dish and bake for 25 minutes. Strain the concentrated stock into a measuring cup and, if necessary, add enough water to make 6 ¼ cups. Line a colander with cheesecloth, set it over a bowl, and pour in the shellfish butter purée and some of the concentrated stock. Squeeze the cheesecloth tightly to extract as much liquid as possible, then add the liquid to the concentrated stock. Mix the rice flour with a little of the concentrated stock or water in a bowl. Pour the stock into a pan, add the brandy, and heat gently. When the stock is hot, stir in the rice flour mixture, and simmer, stirring constantly, for 5–10 minutes. Season to taste with salt and pepper. Put the cream into a soup tureen and stir in a little hot soup to prevent it curdling. Gradually add the remaining soup and the shelled jumbo shrimp tails. Serve immediately.

Note: This recipe can also be made using only crayfish or only shrimp and the results are equally delicious.

163

Shrimp soup
CREMA DE GAMBAS

- 1 pound 2 ounces raw prawns, shells on and heads attached if available (see glossary)
- 4 tablespoons butter or sunflower oil
- 3 tablespoons all-purpose flour
- 2 tablespoons tomato paste
- 8 ¾ cups warm fish stock (homemade, canned or made with a bouillon cube)
- 2 tablespoons brandy
- scant ½ cup light cream
- salt and pepper

Serves 6

Remove the heads from all the shrimp, if necesary, and peel 1 ½ cups of them. Reserve the heads. Set the peeled tails aside for the garnish. Mash the remaining shrimp in their shells with the shrimp heads in a mortar with a pestle. Alternatively, process them in a food processor or blender in two or three batches, adding 2 tablespoons water to each batch. Heat the butter or oil in a pan. Stir in the flour and cook for a few minutes, stirring constantly, until lightly colored. Add the shrimp purée and tomato paste, then stir in the warm stock. Simmer over low heat for 30 minutes, occasionally skimming off the froth that rises to the surface. Strain the soup into a clean pan and season to taste with salt and pepper. Reheat gently, then add the brandy and reserved peeled shrimp and reheat gently, ensuring that the prawn tails turn pink and are cooked through. Put the cream in a soup tureen and gradually add the hot soup, very slowly. Serve immediately.

164

Fish soup with cream and curry
CREMA DE PESCADO CON NATA Y CURRY

- 2 tablespoons rice
- 2 ¼ pounds white fish fillets
- 4 tablespoons olive oil
- 1 onion, chopped
- 1 carrot, chopped
- 1 turnip, chopped
- 1 ½ tablespoons flour
- ½ teaspoon curry powder
- juice of ½ lemon
- ½ cup light cream
- 2 sprigs chopped fresh parsley
- salt

Concentrated stock:
- 1 carrot, thickly sliced
- 1 turnip, thickly sliced
- 1 onion, halved
- ⅔ cup dry white wine
- 1 bay leaf
- pinch of salt

Serves 6

Cook the rice (see recipe 173) but do not fry it. Refresh under cold water and set aside. Cut the fish into pieces, put in a pan, pour in water to cover, and add all the ingredients for the concentrated stock. Bring to a boil over high heat, then lower the heat, and simmer for 10 minutes. Remove the pan from the heat and let cool. Reserve some of the fish in a bowl with a little of the stock to prevent it drying out and set aside. Remove and discard the bay leaf. Heat the oil in a pan. Add the chopped onion, carrot, and turnip and cook over low heat, stirring occasionally, for about 8 minutes, until softened. Stir in the flour and curry powder, then gradually add the concentrated stock (including the fish), a little at a time, stirring constantly. Cook over low heat for 30 minutes, then remove the pan from the heat, and let cool slightly before processing in a blender or food processor. Return the soup to a clean pan and reheat gently. Stir in the lemon juice and season to taste with salt, then add the rice. Just before serving, stir in the cream and the reserved fish. Pour the soup into a soup tureen, sprinkle with the parsley and serve immediately.

Fish soup

SOPA DE PESCADO DESMENUZADO

- 3½ ounces salt cod fillet
- 5 tablespoons olive oil
- 1 small onion, chopped
- 1 pound 2 ounces tomatoes, seeded and chopped
- 1 pound 2 ounces mixed fish fillets
- 1 pound 2 ounces raw large shrimp, shells on and heads attached if available or crayfish
- 1 bay leaf
- 3½ ounces bread
- 1 teaspoon paprika
- salt and pepper

Serves 6

Put the salt cod in a bowl, add water to cover, and let soak for several hours without changing the water. Heat the oil in a pan. Add the onion and cook over low heat, stirring occasionally, for 6–8 minutes, until beginning to brown. Add the tomato and cook for 15 minutes more, occasionally mashing them with the side of a slotted spoon. Let the mixture cool a little, then transfer to a food processor or blender and process. Scrape into a bowl, and set aside. Put the mixed fish and the shrimp or crayfish into a pan, pour in water to cover, and add the bay leaf and a pinch of salt. Bring to a boil over high heat and boil for 2 minutes, then remove the pan from the heat. Lift out the fish with a slotted spatula and transfer to a plate. Remove and discard the bay leaf, and reserve the stock. Tear the bread into pieces, place in a bowl, add a ladleful of the stock, and let soak. Drain the salt cod. Remove the skin and any remaining bones from the mixed fish and the salt cod. Pass all the fish, together with the soaked bread, through a food mill fitted with a coarse disk into a bowl, or process in a blender or food processor. Lift out the shrimp or crayfish from the stock with a slotted spoon. Remove and discard the shells and heads if attached. Pass the shellfish through the food mill, then pour through a little stock to make sure that all the flavor has been extracted, or process in the food processor or blender. Put the reserved tomato mixture into a pan. Add the paprika and cook over low heat, stirring constantly, for 2 minutes. Add the cod, mixed fish, bread, and shellfish and pour in 6 ¼–8 ¾ cups of the stock. Season to taste with salt and pepper and simmer for 5–10 minutes. Serve in a soup tureen.

Mussel soup

SOPA DE MEJILLONES

- 3¼ pounds mussels
- scant ½ cup dry white wine
- 1 sprig fresh thyme
- ½ bay leaf
- 3 tablespoons olive oil
- 5 ounces onions, chopped
- 1 clove garlic, lightly crushed
- 3 tablespoons potato starch
- 2¼ cups hot milk
- 2 egg yolks
- 1 teaspoon chopped
  fresh parsley
- salt and pepper

Serves 6

If your mussels have not been pre-scrubbed, scrape the shells with the blade of a knife and remove the "beards," then scrub under cold running water. Discard any mussels with broken shells or any that do not shut immediately when sharply tapped. Put the mussels in a pan, pour in the wine, and add the thyme, bay leaf, and a pinch of salt. Cover tightly and cook over high heat, shaking the pan occasionally, for about 6 minutes, until all the shells have opened. Remove the mussels with a slotted spoon and discard any that remain closed. Strain the cooking liquid through a cheesecloth-lined strainer and reserve. Remove the mussels from their shells, put them on a plate, and cover with a damp dishtowel to prevent them drying out. Heat the oil in another pan. Add the onion and garlic and cook over low heat, stirring occasionally, for 5 minutes, until softened. Pour in 6¼ cups water and the mussel cooking liquid and simmer for about 10 minutes. Mix the potato starch with 6 tablespoons water in a small bowl, then stir into the soup. Simmer for 5 minutes more, then add the hot milk. Season to taste with salt and pepper. Put the egg yolks into a soup tureen and add the soup very slowly to prevent the yolks curdling. Add the mussels (cut in half with kitchen scissors if they are very large), sprinkle with the parsley, and serve.

167

Fish soup with noodles

SOPA DE PESCADO BARATA CON FIDEOS GORDOS

- 1 large onion
- 5 tablespoons white wine
- 1 bay leaf
- backbone of a white fish
- 1 hake or other white fish head,
  gills removed
- 3 tablespoons olive oil
- 2 tablespoons all-purpose flour
- 1 tablespoon tomato paste
- a few saffron threads
- ½ clove garlic
- 4 ounces noodles
- salt

Serves 6

Cut a thick slice from the onion and finely chop the remainder. Pour 8 ¾ cups water into a pan, and add the wine, onion slice, bay leaf, and a pinch of salt. Add and submerge the fish backbone and head and bring to a boil, then lower the heat, and simmer for 10 minutes. Remove the pan from the heat and strain the stock through a fine strainer into a bowl. Heat the oil in another pan. Add the chopped onion and cook over low heat, stirring occasionally, for 8 minutes. Stir in the flour and cook, stirring constantly, for 2–4 minutes, until lightly colored. Stir in the tomato paste and pour in the strained fish stock. Pound the saffron with the garlic and a pinch of salt in a mortar with a pestle, or process in a mini-food processor. Stir in a little of the fish stock, then pour into the pan. Bring to a boil, then lower the heat, and simmer for 15 minutes. Strain the soup through a coarse strainer into another pan. Add the noodles, and cook for about 15 minutes, until tender. Serve in a soup tureen.

Note: Some of the water in this recipe can be replaced with shellfish stock (or cooking liquid). This will give soup added flavor.

Gazpacho with goat cheese balls coated in chopped olives

GAZPACHO CON BOLAS DE QUESO DE CABRA ENVUELTAS
EN ACEITUNAS PICADAS

- 2 ¼ pounds ripe tomatoes, peeled, seeded, and coarsely chopped
- ¼ onion, coarsely chopped
- 1 small cucumber, peeled and coarsely chopped
- ½ small green (bell) pepper, seeded and coarsely chopped
- 4 ½ cups bread crumbs
- ¾ cup olive oil
- 2 tablespoons white-wine vinegar
- 3/12 ounces fresh goat cheese
- 6 black olives, pitted and chopped
- chopped fresh basil
- salt

Serves 4–6

Working in batches, put the tomato, onion, cucumber, bell pepper, bread crumbs, oil, and vinegar into a food processor or blender and process until smooth. Transfer to a bowl and if the mixture is too thick, add a little cold water. (This is not usually necessary as the tomatoes usually provide enough liquid.) Cover the bowl with plastic wrap and chill in the refrigerator for at least 2 hours before serving. Just before serving, shape the goat cheese into little balls using a melon baller or with your hands. Roll the balls in the chopped olives. Season the soup with salt to taste, stir well and garnish with the basil. Serve with the cheese balls.

Notes: To give the gazpacho a special touch, use sherry vinegar instead of white-wine vinegar. If the soup is not cold enough when it is time to serve, add a few ice cubes. You can add a little freshly ground black pepper at the last minute, if you like.

169   Chunky gazpacho

GAZPACHO EN TROZOS

- 1½ tablespoons white-wine vinegar
- 3 tablespoons sunflower oil
- 2 tablespoons bread crumbs
- ½ clove garlic
- 1 sprig fresh parsley
- 3 plump ripe tomatoes, peeled, seeded, and chopped
- 2 tablespoons finely chopped onion
- 1 small cucumber, peeled and finely chopped
- 1 small green bell pepper, seeded and finely chopped
- salt

Serves 4–5

Stir the vinegar and a pinch of salt in a pitcher until the salt has dissolved, then whisk in the oil with a fork. Pour into a soup tureen and gradually whisk in 5 cups water, a little at a time. Add the bread-crumbs. Pound the garlic with the parsley and 1 tablespoon of the mixture from the soup tureen in a mortar with a pestle, or process in a mini-food processor, then add to the tureen. Cover and chill in the refrigerator for at least 1 hour. Add the tomato, onion, cucumber, and bell pepper to the tureen. If the soup is not sufficiently chilled when you're ready to serve, add a few ice cubes.

170   Chilled gazpachuelo

GAZPACHUELO FRÍO

- 3 egg yolks or 2 eggs, at room temperature
- 1½ tablespoons white-wine vinegar
- 2¼ cups sunflower oil
- 4 cups ice water
- scant 1 cup olives, pitted and chopped
- 2 tomatoes, peeled, seeded, and chopped
- salt and pepper

Serves 4–5

Make a classic mayonnaise with the egg yolks, vinegar, and oil as described in recipe 105 and season with salt and pepper. Alternatively, make the mayonnaise with the whole eggs in a blender as described in recipe 106. In either case, the mayonnaise should be very thick. Put the mayonnaise into a soup tureen and gradually stir in the ice water, a little at a time. Add the olives and the tomato and serve immediately.

Note: Gazpachuelo is another traditional Spanish soup. It is usually served chilled. It is similar to gazpacho with a mayonnaise base.

Hot fish gazpachuelo
GAZPACHUELO CALIENTE DE PESCADO

- ½ small onion, halved
- 1 bay leaf
- 2 tablespoons white wine
- 1 pound 2 ounces white fish, such as monkfish or grouper
- 9 ounces live littleneck or steamer clams (optional)
- 2 egg yolks, at room temperature
- 1½ tablespoons white-wine vinegar
- 1 cup sunflower oil
- about 1½ pounds waxy potatoes, cut into ¼ inch slices
- thinly sliced and toasted or fried (see recipe 130) day-old bread
- salt and pepper

Serves 6

Pour 6¼ cups water into a pan and add the onion, bay leaf, wine, fish, and a pinch of salt. Bring to a boil and cook for 2 minutes, then remove the pan from the heat, cover, and set aside. Wash the clams under cold running water, if using. Discard any with broken shells or any that do not shut immediately when sharply tapped. Put them in a pan, add ½ cup water, cover, and cook over high heat, shaking the pan occasionally, for about 5 minutes, until they have opened. Remove the clams with a slotted spoon and discard any that have not opened. Strain the cooking liquid through a cheesecloth-lined strainer and add to the pan with the fish. Remove the clams from their shells, cover with a damp dishtowel, and set aside. Make a mayonnaise with the egg yolks, vinegar, and oil (see recipe 105) and season with salt and pepper. Pour most of the fish stock into another pan, leaving just enough in the original pan to cover the fish and prevent it drying out. Add the potato and bring to a boil, then lower the heat, and cook for about 30 minutes, until tender. Add more water if necessary to make sure there is enough soup. Remove any skin and bones from the fish and cut the flesh into pieces. Put the mayonnaise into a soup tureen and gradually pour in the hot soup, a little at a time, stirring constantly to prevent the mayonnaise separating. Add the potato and fish, and the clams, if using. Serve the bread separately or add it to the soup just before serving.

Vichyssoise

VICHYSSOISE FRÍA

- 3 tablespoons butter
- 1 large onion, finely chopped
- 4 large leeks,
  finely chopped and rinsed well
- 2¼ pounds potatoes,
  thinly sliced
- 3 cups chicken stock
  (homemade, canned or
  made with a bouillon cube)
- 2¼ cups milk
- 1 cup light cream
- 2 teaspoons chopped
  fresh parsley
- salt

Serves 8

Melt the butter in a pan. Add the onion and cook over low heat, stirring occasionally, for 5 minutes, until softened. Add the leek and cook, stirring occasionally, for 5 minutes more, until beginning to brown. Add the potato, pour in the stock, and bring to a boil. (If using a bouillon cube, add 3 cups water to the pan and when it comes to a boil, stir in the bouillon cube). Simmer for about 40 minutes. Remove the pan from the heat and let cool slightly before processing in a food processor or blender. Add the milk and process briefly again to mix. Pour the soup into a ceramic or glass bowl, season to taste with salt, and stir in the cream. Cover and chill in the refrigerator for at least 12 hours, 24 if possible. Serve in individual soup bowls, sprinkled with the parsley.

RICE, PULSES, POTATOES AND PASTA

Rice

Rice is a rich source of vitamins B and E and also contains useful amounts of phosphorous, potassium, sodium, iron, copper, zinc, magnesium, and silicon. Refined white rice, that is, after the rice has been husked, does not contain any vitamin B. Rice contains more carbohydrates than wheat but has fewer proteins and minerals. Rice is easily digested and is absorbed by the body almost in its entirety. It is widely used as an infant food and is useful for those suffering from diarrhea and gastrointestinal problems. Rice goes well with most other foods and, given its high calorie and carbohydrate contents, it is most ideally partnered by foods that provide proteins, minerals, and vitamins.

Tricks and tips

Each type of rice has its own cooking time. Follow the instructions on the package carefully to obtain perfect rice.

- When cooking white rice, add a few drops of lemon juice to the cooking water to ensure that the grains are separated and sparkling white
- Never stir rice with a fork while it is cooking as this will make it stick
- Always wait until the water is boiling before adding the rice, otherwise it will stick
- For perfect rice pilaf, cook the grains in a little hot oil, stirring constantly, until they turn transparent, then add all the water or stock at once. The proportions are twice as much liquid as rice. Cover the saucepan and cook for 15 minutes without stirring. When the liquid has evaporated, remove the lid and leave the rice to finish cooking over very low heat
- For perfect paella, leave the cooked dish to stand for 5 minutes on a folded damp dishtowel before serving
- When serving rice as an accompaniment, make it more interesting by putting a little food coloring or a pinch of saffron in the cooking water. This will turn it yellow.

173
White rice
ARROZ BLANCO

- **2½ cups long-grain rice**
- **¼ cup (½ stick) butter**
- **salt**

Serves 6

Bring a large pan of unsalted water to a boil. Add the rice, stir with a wooden spoon to prevent the grains clumping together, and cook over high heat for 12–18 minutes, until tender. (The cooking time depends on the type of rice.) Drain the rice in a fine-mesh sieve and rinse well under cold running water, stirring to make sure that it is well washed. Leave the rice draining in the sieve until required. Melt the butter in another pan. Add the rice, season with salt, and heat through, stirring with a wooden spoon. Serve immediately.

Note: When reheating the rice you could add scant ½ cup drained canned peas.

174
White rice with garlic
ARROZ BLANCO CON AJO

- **2½ cups long-grain rice**
- **5 tablespoons olive oil**
- **1 clove garlic,**
  peeled and lightly crushed
- **salt**

Serves 4–6

Cook the rice in boiling water and rinse under cold running water as described in recipe 173. Heat the oil in a large skillet, add the garlic, and cook over low heat for about 5 minutes. Remove and discard the garlic, then add the rice, and heat through.

Rice with shrimp, monkfish, and mussels

ARROZ BLANCO CON GAMBAS, RAPE Y MEJILLONES

- 2½ cups long-grain rice
- 2¼ pounds mussels
- 5 tablespoons white wine
- 1 bay leaf or sprig fresh parsley
- 9 ounces raw shrimp, shells on and heads attached, if available
- 5 tablespoons butter
- 2 tablespoons sunflower oil
- 1 tablespoon chopped onion
- 2 tablespoons all-purpose flour
- scant 2 cups milk
- 1 tablespoon tomato paste
- 9 ounces boneless monkfish fillet, cut into pieces
- 1 tablespoon chopped fresh parsley
- salt

Serves 6

Cook the rice in boiling water and rinse under cold running water as described in recipe 173. Drain well and set aside. If your mussels have not been pre-scrubbed, scrape their shells with the blade of a knife and remove the "beards," then scrub under cold running water. Discard any mussels with broken shells or any that do not shut immediately when sharply tapped. Put them in a heavy pan with the wine and bay leaf or parsley. Cover and cook over low heat for about 10 minutes, until the shells have opened. Remove the mussels with a slotted spoon, reserving the cooking liquid, and discard any that remain closed. Remove the mussels from their shells and if they are very large, cut them in half with kitchen scissors. Put them on a plate, cover with another plate to prevent them drying out, and set aside. Strain the reserved cooking liquid through a cheesecloth-lined strainer into a bowl and set aside. Shell the shrimp, remove the heads, if attached and reserve the heads and shells. Set the shrimp aside. Put the heads and shells in a pan, add water to cover and a pinch of salt, and bring to a boil. Lower the heat and simmer for 10 minutes, then strain the shrimp stock into the bowl of strained mussel stock. Make a béchamel sauce: Melt 2 tablespoons of the butter with the oil in a skillet. Add the onion and cook over low heat, stirring occasionally, for a few minutes, until softened. Stir in the flour and cook, stirring constantly, for 1 minute, then gradually stir in the milk, alternating with scant 2 cups of the shellfish stock. Simmer for 10 minutes, season to taste with salt, and stir in the tomato paste. The sauce should be quite thick. Add the monkfish and reserved shrimp tails to the sauce and cook for 6 minutes, then add the mussels and reheat briefly. Melt the remaining butter in another pan. Add the rice, season with salt, and heat through, stirring with a wooden spoon. To serve, spoon the rice into a ring mold, then turn it out onto a warm serving dish. Fill the center with the fish and sauce and sprinkle with the chopped parsley. Alternatively, serve the rice on the side.

Rice with fish and shellfish

ARROZ A BANDA

- ¾ cup olive oil
- 5 ounces onions, chopped
- 11 ounces tomatoes,
  peeled and chopped
- 1 bay leaf
- 1 sprig fresh parsley
- 1 sprig fresh thyme
- 1 clove garlic
- pinch of saffron threads
- 5 ounces monkfish fillet,
  cut into chunks
- 5 ounces conger eel steak, cut
  into chunks and bones removed
- 5 ounces gurnard (sea robin)
  fillet, cut into chunks
- 7 ounces ocean perch, rockfish
  or racasse (scorpion fish) fillet,
  cut into chunks
- 5 ounces raw jumbo shrimp,
  peeled
- scant 3½ cups long-grain rice
- salt and pepper

Serves 4

Heat the oil in a pan. Add the onion and cook over low heat, stirring occasionally, for about 8 minutes, until beginning to brown. Add the tomato, bay leaf, parsley, and thyme and pour in 6¼ cups water. Pound the garlic with the saffron in a mortar or process in a mini-food processor and add to the pan. Bring to a boil and add the fish and shrimp. Season with salt and pepper and cook over high to medium–high heat for 15 minutes. Using a slotted spoon, transfer the fish and shrimp to a serving dish and keep warm. Strain the fish stock into a stove-top safe casserole and bring to a boil. Add the rice, cover, and cook for 20 minutes. Remove the casserole from the heat and let stand, still covered, for 5 minutes. Lightly stir with a fork to separate the grains. Serve the rice in the casserole and the fish and shrimp on the serving dish.

177

Murcian rice and fish stew
ARROZ CALDERO

- 3¼-pound striped mullet,
  cleaned and filleted,
  head reserved
- 1 pound 2 ounces gurnard
  (sea robin), cleaned and filleted,
  head reserved, or monkfish
  fillets
- 1 pound-2 ounce grouper
  or porgy, cleaned and filleted,
  head reserved
- scant 1 cup olive oil
- 2 ñoras or other small dried
  red chiles
- 2 ripe tomatoes,
  peeled and chopped
- 2 cloves garlic
- 2 cups long-grain rice
- 7 ounces raw jumbo shrimp,
  peeled
- salt

Serves 4

Ask your fish supplier to reserve the heads of the fish. Cut out and discard the gills from the reserved heads, then set aside. Cut the fish into thick slices. Heat the oil in a Dutch oven or large stovetop-safe casserole. Add the chilies and cook over low heat, stirring frequently, for 2–4 minutes. Remove with a slotted spoon and set aside. Add the fish heads to the pan and cook, turning occasionally, for 10 minutes. Remove and discard, then add the tomato, and cook, stirring occasionally, for 5 minutes. Pour in 8¾ cups water and bring to a boil. Meanwhile, pound the chilies with 1 garlic clove in a mortar, or process in a mini-food processor, then add to the pan, and simmer for 5 minutes. Season the slices of fish with salt, add to the pan, and simmer gently for 5–10 minutes, until the flesh is opaque and flakes easily. Carefully remove the fish from the pan using a fish slice, put on a serving dish, and keep warm. Strain the stock and return to a clean pan. Pound the remaining garlic in a mortar, or process in a mini-food processor, and stir in 1 cup of the fish stock. Set aside. Taste the remaining stock, season with salt, if necessary, and bring to a boil. Add the rice and bring back to a boil, then lower the heat, cover, and cook for 15 minutes. Put the shrimp on top of the rice, re-cover the pan, and cook for 5 minutes more, until the rice is tender and the shrimp are cooked through. The rice is served first and the fish is eaten afterward with the garlic and stock mixture poured over it just before serving.

Note: the rice may be served with alioli, garlic mayonnaise (see recipe 110) or ajoaceite garlic oil. To make this, mix 2 crushed garlic cloves with olive oil and salt, stirring until smooth.

One of the most famous restaurants in Madrid for Murcian cooking is El Caldero, run by Antonio Valero and his son Alfredo. Their style of cooking is very precise and individual, with very little influence from the cuisines of other regions of Spain. In general, Murcian dishes are strongly flavored. Sauces, such as tártara sauce and alioli are a specialty. The region of Murcia in the southeast of the country is richly supplied with fish. Among the most important are mullet, gilthead bream, 'lobarro' and Mediterranean shrimp. The latter are available only at certain times of the year, making them one of Murcia's most expensive products. It is a longstanding local tradition to serve certain fish with rice, especially with caldero rice, literally "cauldron rice." The dish has traditional roots in the fishing villages of the region. The fishermen made a tripod with three canes stuck in the sand, hung an iron cooking pot from the top, and lit a fire using dry seaweed. Seawater was used as stock to cook the fish and once they were cooked, they were removed and eaten while the rice cooked in the pot. The most important characteristics of caldero rice are its aroma, color, and flavor, all produced by 'ñora' chiles, an essential ingredient. The rice is always cooked in the same stock as the fish, creating a very intense partnership. The caldero is an iron pot still made today by specialist ironmongers. It is seasoned with heat to give caldero rice its special flavor. A Dutch oven is a fairly good substitute.

Sailors' rice

ARROZ CALDOSO A LA MARINERA

- **9 ounces clams**
- **5 tablespoons olive oil**
- **1 large onion, chopped**
- **1 clove garlic, chopped**
- **9 ounces tomatoes,**
  peeled and chopped
- **1 teaspoon paprika**
- **9 ounces raw shrimp, peeled**
- **2 cups long-grain rice**
- **1 bay leaf**
- **1¼ cups shelled peas**
- **6 young globe artichokes,**
  halved lengthwise
- **salt**

Serves 4

Scrub the clams under cold running water and discard any with broken shells or any that do not shut immediately when sharply tapped. Pour about 5 tablespoons water into a skillet, add a pinch of salt and the clams, cover, and cook over high heat, shaking the pan occasionally, for 5–7 minutes, until the clams have opened. Remove with a slotted spoon and discard the empty half shells and any clams that remain closed. Put the clams on the half shell into a dish and keep warm. Strain the cooking liquid into a bowl through a cheesecloth-lined strainer and add enough water to make 4 cups. Heat the oil in a stovetop-safe casserole. Add the onion and cook over low heat, stirring occasionally, for about 10 minutes, until lightly browned. Add the garlic and tomatoes and cook, stirring occasionally, for 10 minutes. Stir in the paprika and add the shrimp, rice, and bay leaf. Stir well, pour in the diluted cooking liquid, and bring to a boil. Simmer for 5 minutes, then add the peas and artichokes, and cook for 20 minutes more. Remove the casserole from the heat, remove the bay leaf, place the clams on top, and serve immediately.

179

Castilian rice

ARROZ CASTIZO

- 4 tablespoons olive oil
- 2 onions, very finely chopped
- 1 green bell pepper,
  seeded and diced
- 2 cloves garlic, finely chopped
- 1 tablespoon finely chopped
  fresh parsley
- 2 tomatoes,
  peeled, seeded, and chopped
- 4 dozen littleneck
  or cherrystone clams
- 2½ cups long-grain rice
- 1 teaspoon paprika
- pinch of saffron threads,
  toasted and crushed
- salt

Serves 6

Heat the oil in a stovetop-safe casserole. Add the onion and bell pepper and cook over low heat, stirring occasionally, for 5 minutes, until softened. Add the garlic and parsley and cook, stirring occasionally, for 3 minutes more. Add the tomato and stir well. Meanwhile, scrub the clams under cold running water and discard any with broken shells or any that do not shut immediately when sharply tapped. Pour ⅔ cup water into a skillet, add the clams, cover, and cook over high heat, shaking the pan occasionally, for 3–5 minutes, until the clams have opened. Remove the clams with a slotted spoon and discard the empty half shells and any clams that remain closed. Put the clams on the half shell into a dish and keep warm. Strain the cooking liquid into a bowl through a cheesecloth-lined strainer and add enough water to make 4 cups. Add the rice to the casserole, stir in the paprika, and season with salt. Cook, stirring constantly, for 2 minutes, then pour in the diluted cooking liquid. Bring to a boil and cook for about 12 to 18 minutes, until the rice is tender. Stir in the saffron and add the clams. Remove the casserole from the heat and let stand for 5 minutes before serving.

Rice with cauliflower and cuttlefish

ARROZ CON COLIFLOR Y SEPIA

- 4 tablespoons olive oil
- 5 ounces onion, finely chopped
- 2 cloves garlic, finely chopped
- 1 pound 2 ounces cuttlefish or squid, cleaned (see page 468) and cut into strips
- 1 teaspoon paprika
- pinch of ground cinnamon
- 3¼ pounds cauliflower, separated into flowerets
- 2½ cups long-grain rice
- pinch of saffron threads
- pepper

Serves 6

Heat the oil in a stovetop-safe casserole. Add the onion and garlic and cook over low heat, stirring occasionally, for about 10 minutes, until lightly browned. Increase the heat to medium, add the cuttlefish or squid, and cook, stirring constantly, for 2–3 minutes, until lightly browned. Stir in the paprika, cinnamon, and a pinch of pepper. Pour in water to cover and cook, stirring constantly, for 5 minutes, until the seafood is tender. Add the cauliflower and rice. Crush the saffron in a mortar and stir in a little water, then add to the pan. Add a little more water to cover the rice, if necessary, and bring to a boil. Lower the heat and cook, uncovered, for 20–25 minutes, until the rice is tender and the liquid has been absorbed. Serve immediately.

Black rice

ARROZ NEGRO

- 14 ounces small squid, cleaned
  with their ink sacs reserved
  (see page 468)
- generous 1 cup olive oil
- 2 cloves garlic, finely chopped
- 3 tomatoes,
  peeled, seeded, and chopped
- 6¼ cups fish stock (homemade
  or made with a bouillon cube)
- 2½ cups long-grain rice
- 1 canned or bottled red bell
  pepper, drained and cut
  into strips
- salt

Serves 6

Put the ink sacs into a bowl of water. Using a sharp knife, cut the sac into thin rings. Heat the oil in a stovetop-safe earthenware pot, a paella pan or a large heavy skillet. Add the squid rings, and the tenta-cles if you like, and cook over medium–high heat, stirring frequently, for 5 minutes. Stir in the garlic, add the tomato, and pour in ⅔ cup of the stock. Lower the heat, cover, and cook for 20 minutes. Mean-while, carefully remove the ink pouches from the bowl of water and break them into a measuring cup. Add enough fish stock to make 5 cups. Stir the rice into the pan, then add the squid ink and stock mixture. Season with salt, mix well, cover, and cook over high heat for 10 minutes, then lower the heat to medium, stir in the bell pepper strips, re-cover and cook for 10 minutes more. Remove the pan from the heat and let stand, still covered, for 5 minutes before serving.

Rice with chicken, mushrooms, and truffles

ARROZ BLANCO CON PECHUGA DE GALLINA, CHAPIÑONES Y TRUFAS

- 1 skinless boneless chicken
  breast portion
- 1 small leek,
  halved and rinsed well
- 1 carrot, sliced
- ½ bay leaf
- 2½ cups long-grain rice
- 1 pound 2 ounces mushrooms,
  trimmed
- ½ cup (1 stick) butter
- a few drops of lemon juice
- 2 tablespoons olive oil
- 2 tablespoons all-purpose flour
- 2 truffles, sliced
- scant 2 cups milk
- 2 egg yolks
- salt

Serves 6

Put the chicken breast portion (a fourth of a good chicken), leek, carrot, and bay leaf into a pan and pour in water to cover. Add a pinch of salt and bring to a boil, then lower the heat to medium, and cook for 20–30 minutes, until the chicken is cooked through. (Check by cutting into the thickest part with the tip of a knife. If the juices run clear and the meat is no longer pink, the chicken is ready.) Remove the chicken from the pan and reserve 1 cup of the stock. When the chicken is cool enough to handle, cut into bite-size pieces. Cook the rice in boiling water and rinse under cold running water as described in recipe 173. Drain well and set aside. Remove the mushroom stalks from the caps and cut both into fairly thick slices. Put into a pan with 2 tablespoons of the butter, the lemon juice, and a pinch of salt. Cover and cook over low heat for 5 minutes. Meanwhile, make a béchamel sauce by melting 2 tablespoons of the remaining butter with the oil in a pan. Stir in the flour and cook, stirring constantly, for 2 minutes. Gradually stir in the milk, alternating with the reserved chicken stock. Season with salt and cook, stirring constantly, for 10 minutes. Add the mushrooms and their cooking juices, then add the truffles and chicken. Melt the remaining butter in another pan. Add the rice, season with salt, and heat through, stirring with a wooden spoon. Spoon it into a ring mold, then turn it out onto a warm serving dish. Whisk the egg yolks with a little of the béchamel sauce in a bowl, then stir into the pan with the chicken mixture. Remove the pan from the heat and spoon the mixture into the center of the rice. Serve immediately.

Note: In Spain, this dish is made with hen instead of chicken. If you are cooking it with hen, you will need to increase the cooking time for the meat to 45–60 minutes.

Cold rice with tuna and mayonnaise

ARROZ BLANCO FRÍO CON MAYONESA Y ATÚN

- 2 ½ cups long-grain rice
- 9 ounces canned tuna, drained and flaked
- sunflower oil, for brushing
- salt

Garnish:
- baby lettuce leaves
- 3 tomatoes, sliced
- 1 hard-cooked egg, sliced

Mayonnaise (or use good-quality, thick bottled):
- 2 eggs
- 2 tablespoons white-wine vinegar or lemon juice
- 3 cups sunflower oil
- salt

Serves 6

Make the mayonnaise in a blender as described in recipe 105, as it will be thicker. Cook the rice in boiling water and rinse under cold running water as described in recipe 173. Drain well, pour into a large bowl, add a little salt, and mix. Reserve a little of the tuna for the garnish. Stir the remainder into the rice with a little more than half the mayonnaise. Brush the inside of a cake mold with sunflower oil. Spoon the rice mixture into it, pressing down well to make sure there are no holes. Cover with plastic wrap and chill in the refrigerator for at least 1 hour. To serve, run a round-bladed knife around the edge of the mold and invert the rice mixture onto a round serving dish. Top with the remaining mayonnaise and garnish with lettuce, tomatoes, hard-cooked egg, and the reserved tuna. Serve immediately.

Notes: If you like, season the tomato slices with salt and put a little tuna and mayonnaise on the lettuce leaves. As an alternative, the hard-cooked egg may be chopped and put on top of the rice.

184

Rice with tomato sauce, green beans, and omelet

ARROZ BLANCO CON SALSA DE TOMATE, JUDÍAS VERDES Y TORTILLA

- 2 tablespoons sunflower oil
- 2¼ pounds tomatoes, seeded and chopped
- 1 teaspoon sugar
- 2½ cups long-grain rice
- 1 pound 10 ounces green beans, trimmed
- pinch of baking soda
- 6 tablespoons (¾ stick) butter
- 3 tablespoons olive oil
- 3 eggs, beaten
- salt

Serves 6

Make a thick tomato sauce with the sunflower oil, tomato, and sugar as described in recipe 73. Cook the rice in boiling water and rinse under cold running water as described in recipe 173. Drain well and set aside. If the beans are very fat, cut them into small cubes; otherwise cut into short lengths. Bring a pan of water to a boil and add a pinch of salt and the baking soda. Add the beans and cook for about 20 minutes, until tender. (The cooking time will depend on the freshness of the beans.) Drain the beans well. Melt half the butter in a skillet. Add the beans and cook for a few minutes. Heat the olive oil in another skillet over medium heat. Season the eggs with salt, pour them into the pan, and tilt the pan to cover the base evenly. Cook until the underside has set, flip over the omelet, using a spatula, and leave it in the skillet over low heat. Melt the remaining butter in a pan. Add the rice, season with a little salt, and heat through, stirring with a wooden spoon. Spoon the rice along the center of a warm oval serving dish and spoon the tomato sauce around the rice. Put the green beans on top of the rice and at place some at either end. Cut the omelet into ¾-inch wide strips and sprinkle over the beans, to garnish. Serve immediately.

185

Rice with Swiss chard

ARROZ CON ACELGAS

- 4 tablespoons olive oil
- 1 pound 10 ounces Swiss chard, chopped
- 3½ ounces bacon, cut into strips
- 1 cup long-grain rice
- 2 cups beef stock (homemade, canned or made with a bouillon cube)
- grated Parmesan cheese

Serves 4

Heat the oil in a pan. Add the Swiss chard and bacon and cook over medium–low heat, stirring occasionally, for 5 minutes. Add the rice, pour in the stock, and bring to a boil. Lower the heat, cover, and cook for about 20 minutes, until the rice is tender and the stock has been absorbed. Serve immediately, offering the Parmesan separately.

Cold rice with vegetables and vinaigrette

ARROZ BLANCO FRÍO CON VERDURAS Y VINAGRETA

- 2 cups long-grain rice
- 1 pound 10 ounces green beans,
  cut into short lengths or
  3 ¼ pounds peas, shelled
- pinch of baking soda (optional)
- salt

Vinaigrette:
- 2 tablespoons white-wine
  vinegar
- 6 tablespoons olive oil
- 1 teaspoon chopped
  fresh parsley
- 1 hard-cooked egg,
  finely chopped
- salt

Garnish:
- iceberg lettuce leaves
- 1 pound 2 ounces ripe tomatoes,
  sliced
- 3 hard-cooked eggs,
  cut into segments

Serves 6

Cook the rice in boiling water and rinse under cold running water as described in recipe 173. Drain well and season with salt while it is still in the sieve. Spoon the rice into a ring mold and set aside. Make the vinaigrette as described in recipe 98 and pour into a sauceboat. Set aside. If using the green beans, cook them in a large pan of salted boiling water for 20–30 minutes, until tender. (The cooking time will depend on the freshness of the beans.) If you like, add a pinch of baking soda to the water to make the beans greener. Drain the beans and let cool. If using the peas, cook them in a large pan of salted boiling water for 15–30 minutes until tender. (The cooking time will depend on the size and freshness of the peas.) Drain well and let cool. Turn the rice out onto a serving dish. Spoon the green beans or peas into the center of the ring. Arrange alternating lettuce leaves and tomato slices around the outside of the ring. Garnish with the hard-cooked egg segments and serve, offering the vinaigrette separately.

Note: The dish may be kept in the refrigerator without its deteriorating for up to 1 hour before serving.

Cold rice salad

ENSALADA FRÍA DE ARROZ

- 2½ cups long-grain rice
- 1 pound 10 ounces tomatoes, peeled, seeded, and chopped
- 9 ounces mushrooms, thinly sliced
- juice of ½ lemon
- 1 canned or bottled red bell pepper, drained and diced
- 2 tablespoons chopped fresh parsley
- 2 tablespoons white-wine vinegar
- 6 tablespoons olive oil
- 1 hard-cooked egg, chopped
- salt

Serves 6

Cook the rice in boiling water and rinse under cold running water as described in recipe 173. Drain well and set aside. Put the tomato in a colander, sprinkle with salt, and let drain. Put the mushrooms in a bowl, add the lemon juice, and mix well. Put the rice in a large salad bowl and add the tomato, mushrooms, bell pepper, and parsley. Whisk together the vinegar and oil in a pitcher and season with salt. Pour the dressing over the salad and mix well. Sprinkle the chopped hard-cooked egg over the salad just before serving. The salad can be served in the salad bowl or in a serving dish garnished with lettuce leaves around the edge.

Rice with chicken

ARROZ BLANCO CON GALLINA

- 1 chicken, about 3¼ pounds
- 1 onion
- 2 whole cloves
- 2 carrots, thickly sliced
- 1 bay leaf
- ¾ cup white wine
- 2½ cups long-grain rice
- 6 tablespoons (¾ stick) butter
- 2 tablespoons sunflower oil
- 2 tablespoons all-purpose flour
- 2 egg yolks, lightly beaten
- ¼ teaspoon meat extract
  or Maggi Seasoning
- 1 teaspoon chopped parsley
- salt

Serves 6

Put the chicken into a pan, pour in enough water to cover, and add a pinch of salt. Stud the onion with the cloves and add to the pan with the carrots, bay leaf, and white wine. Cover and bring to a boil, then lower the heat, and simmer gently for 1½–2 hours, until tender. While the chicken is cooking, occasionally skim off the froth that rises to the surface with a slotted spoon. (Check whether the chicken is done by cutting into the thickest part of the thigh with the tip of a knife. If the juices run clear and the meat is no longer pink, the chicken is ready.) Meanwhile, cook the rice in boiling water and rinse under cold running water as described in recipe 173. Drain well and set aside. Lift the chicken out of the pan and carve the meat. Put the meat in a dish and ladle some of the stock over it to keep it warm. Strain and reserve the remaining stock. To make the sauce, melt half the butter with the oil in a pan. Stir in the flour and cook, stirring constantly, for 2 minutes. Gradually stir in 3 cups of the reserved chicken stock and cook, stirring constantly to prevent lumps forming. Gradually stir a little of the stock into the egg yolks in a bowl, taking care that the yolks do not curdle. Add to the sauce, together with the meat extract or Maggi Seasoning and parsley. Season with salt if necessary. Add the chicken meat and keep the sauce warm but do not let it cook any more. Melt the remaining butter in a pan. Add the rice, season with salt, and heat through, stirring with a wooden spoon. Spoon the rice into a ring mold, then turn out onto a warm serving dish. Spoon the chicken mixture into the center of the ring. Serve immediately.

Note: In Spain, this dish is made with hen instead of chicken. If you are cooking it with hen, you will need to increase the cooking time for the meat to 1½–3 hours.

Rice with ground meat
ARROZ CON CARNE PICADA

- 4 tablespoons olive oil
- 1 onion, thinly sliced
- 1 green bell pepper,
  seeded and cut into strips
- 2 tomatoes,
  peeled, seeded, and chopped
- 14 ounces ground beef
- pinch of paprika
- 1¼ cups long-grain rice
- 2¼ cups boiling beef stock
  (homemade, canned or
  made with a bouillon cube)
- salt and pepper

Serves 4–6

Heat the oil in a pan. Add the onion and bell pepper and cook over low heat, stirring occasionally, for 5 minutes, until softened. Add the tomato and beef and cook, breaking up the meat with a wooden spoon, for 5 minutes, until lightly browned. Add the paprika, season with salt and pepper, and mix well, then stir in the rice, and cook, stirring constantly, for 2 minutes. Pour in the stock, cover, and cook for about 15 to 18 minutes, until the rice is tender and all the liquid has been absorbed. Serve immediately.

190

Rice with kidneys

ARROZ BLANCO CON RIÑONES

- 1 kidney, about 1 pound 2 ounces
- 2½ cups long-grain rice
- 5 tablespoons olive oil
- 2 tablespoons all-purpose flour
- ¾ cup sherry
- 3 tablepoons butter
- salt

Serves 6

Prepare the kidney as described on page 768. Cook the rice in boiling water and rinse under cold running water as described in recipe 173. Drain well and set aside. To make the sauce, heat the oil in a pan. Stir in the flour and cook, stirring constantly, for 4–5 minutes, until beginning to brown. Gradually stir in the sherry and 2½ cups water and season with salt. Simmer for 5 minutes, then add the pieces of kidney, and cook for 4 minutes more. Melt the butter in another pan. Add the rice, season with salt, and heat through, stirring with a wooden spoon. Spoon into a ring mold, then turn out onto a warm serving dish. Spoon the kidney mixture into the center of the rice and serve immediately.

191

Yellow rice with peas

ARROZ DE ADORNO, AMARILLO Y CON GUISANTES

- pinch of saffron threads
- 2½ cups long-grain rice
- scant 1 cup fresh or frozen peas
- 3 tablespoons butter
- salt

Serves 6

Crush the saffron threads in a mortar, then stir in 2 tablespoons water. Cook the rice in boiling water, adding the saffron mixture to the water, and rinse under cold running water as described in recipe 173. If using fresh peas, cook in a pan of salted boiling water for 15–30 minutes, until tender. (Cook frozen peas according to the instructions on the package.) Melt the butter in another pan. Add the rice, season with salt, and heat through, stirring with a wooden spoon. Drain the peas and stir into the rice. Serve immediately.

192

Yellow rice with scrambled eggs
ARROZ AMARILLO CON HUEVOS REVUELTOS

- 2½ cups long-grain rice
- scant 1 cup baby peas, cooked
- pinch of saffron threads
- 3 tablespoons butter
- salt

Eggs:
- 8 eggs, beaten
- 1½ tablespoons butter
- 3 tablespoons milk
- 9 ounces raw shrimp, peeled and
  halved, or 2 truffles, thinly sliced
- salt

Serves 6

Prepare the rice and peas as described in recipe 191 and keep warm. It needs to be ready as the eggs must be served as soon as they are cooked. Half fill a large, deep pan or roasting pan with water and bring to a boil, then lower the heat so that the water is just simmering. Put the eggs, butter, milk, and shrimp, if using, into a pan and season with salt. Put the pan in the simmering water and cook, stirring constantly with a fork especially around the edge of the pan as this is where the eggs will set first. When the egg mixture begins to turn creamy, remove the pan from the simmering water, stir in the truffles, if using, and continue to stir well until the eggs have set. The total cooking time required depends on how firm you like your scrambled eggs; it is usually about 10 minutes. Spoon the rice into a ring mold and turn out onto a warm serving dish. Spoon the scrambled eggs into the center and serve immediately. Alternatively, serve the rice in a mound on the side.

193

Milanese rice
ARROZ MILANESA

- 2½ cups long-grain rice
- 3 tablespoons olive oil
- 1 onion, finely chopped
- generous ½ cup diced
  Serrano ham, prosciutto
  or other dry-cured ham
- scant 1 cup diced chorizo
  sausage
- 9 ounces canned peas, drained
- generous 1 cup grated
  Parmesan cheese
- salt

Serves 6

Cook the rice in boiling water and rinse under cold running water as described in recipe 173. Drain well and set aside. Heat the oil in a large pan. Add the onion and cook over low heat, stirring occasionally, for 5–8 minutes, until lightly browned. Stir in the ham and chorizo, then add the rice, and cook for 5 minutes, stirring constantly with a wooden spoon. Season to taste with salt and stir in the peas. Cook, stirring, for a few minutes more. Serve immediately, offering the Parmesan separately.

194

Indian rice with raisins and pine nuts
ARROZ HINDÚ CON PASAS Y PIÑONES

- **2 tablespoons raisins**
- **1½ cups long-grain rice**
- **2 tablespoons (¼ stick) butter**
- **2 tablespoons pine nuts**
- **curry powder or soy sauce,**
  to taste
- **salt**

Serves 4

Put the raisins in a bowl, add warm water to cover, and let soak for 15–30 minutes. Meanwhile, cook the rice in boiling water and rinse under cold running water as described in recipe 173. Drain well and set aside. Drain the raisins and pat dry with a dishtowel. Melt the butter in a pan. Add the pine nuts and cook, stirring frequently, for 2–3 minutes, until light golden brown. Add the raisins and the rice and cook over low heat, stirring constantly, for 10 minutes. If using the curry powder, stir it in and season with salt. If using the soy sauce, stir it in but do not add salt. Serve immediately.

Note: This dish is usually served as an accompaniment and the quantities shown reflect this. You can multiply them to serve more.

195

Rice with sausages and bacon
ARROZ CON SALCHICHAS Y BACON

- **generous 1 cup long-grain rice**
- **5 tablespoons olive oil**
- **5 ounces bacon, cut into strips**
- **4 frankfurters,**
  each cut into 4 pieces
- **1 green bell pepper,**
  seeded and diced
- **2 stalks celery, thinly sliced**
- **1 large onion, diced**
- **½ cup olives, pitted and halved**
- **soy sauce, to taste**
- **salt**

Serves 4

Cook the rice in boiling water and rinse under cold running water as described in recipe 173. Drain well and set aside. Heat the oil in a large skillet. Add the bacon and frankfurters and cook, stirring occasionally, for 5–6 minutes, until lightly browned. Remove from the pan and set aside. Add the bell pepper, celery and onion to the pan and cook, stirring occasionally, for 5–8 minutes, until crisp-tender. Add the olives and return the bacon and frankfurters to the pan. Stir in the rice. Mix well, add soy sauce to taste, and heat through. Season with salt, if necessary, remembering that the soy sauce is salty. Serve immediately.

Rice with rabbit

ARROZ CON CONEJO

- ¾ cup olive oil
- 1 small onion, chopped
- 1 clove garlic, chopped
- 1 tomato, chopped
- 1 sprig fresh parsley, chopped
- 14 ounces boned diced rabbit
- 2 artichokes,
  cut lengthwise into quarters
- pinch of ground cinnamon
- pinch of paprika
- 2½ cups long-grain rice
- salt

Serves 6

Heat the oil in a stovetop-safe casserole. Add the onion, garlic, tomato, and parsley and cook over low heat, stirring occasionally, for 10 minutes. Add the rabbit and artichokes, sprinkle with the cinnamon and paprika, cover, and cook, stirring occasionally, for 10 minutes, until the meat is browned. Pour in 4 cups water, add a pinch of salt, and bring to a boil. Add the rice, cover, and cook for 15–20 minutes, until the rice is tender and the liquid has been absorbed. Serve immediately straight from the casserole.

Rice with a crust
ARROZ CON COSTRA

- 9 ounces blood sausage (morcilla), or other sausage
- 9 ounces chicken, in parts
- 4 ounces chorizo sausage
- 2 ounces bacon
- ¼ cup garbanzo beans, soaked overnight in cold water and drained
- ¾ cup sunflower oil
- 1 cup long-grain rice
- 2 eggs, lightly beaten
- salt

Serves 4

Put the blood sausage, chicken, chorizo, bacon, and garbanzos in a large pan. Pour in 6 ¼ cups water and bring to a boil, then lower the heat, cover, and simmer for 1 ½ – 2 hours, until the meat and garbanzos are tender. Remove the pan from the heat. Remove all the meat and the garbanzos from the pan and reserve the stock. Let cool. Remove and discard any skin and bones and cut the meat into small pieces. Heat the oil in a shallow ovenproof casserole that can be used on the stove. Add the meat and garbanzos and cook over low heat, stirring occasionally, for 8–10 minutes, until lightly browned. Stir in the rice and cook, stirring constantly, for 2 minutes. Pour in 2 cups of the reserved stock, bring to a boil, cover, and cook for 15 minutes, until the rice is tender and almost all the liquid has been absorbed. Meanwhile, preheat the oven to 350°F. Remove the pan from the heat. Season the eggs with a pinch of salt and pour over the surface of the rice. Transfer to the oven and bake until the topping is golden brown. Serve immediately straight from the casserole.

Note: It is best to use a fairly shallow casserole to guarantee that this dish has a golden crust.

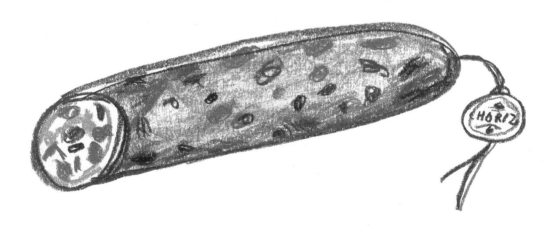

198

Curried rice
ARROZ AL CURRY

- 2 ½ cups long-grain rice
- 9 ounces chestnut mushrooms
  or other wild mushrooms,
  chopped
- ¼ cup (½ stick) butter
- juice of ½ lemon
- 2 tablespoons sunflower oil
- ½ teaspoon curry powder
- scant 1 cup drained canned peas
- 3 ½ ounces canned or bottled
  red bell peppers, drained and
  cut into ½-inch squares
- salt
- 2 sliced hard-cooked eggs
  or strips of fried bacon

Serves 6

Cook the rice in boiling water and rinse under cold running water as described in recipe 173. Drain well and set aside. Meanwhile, put the mushrooms into a pan with 1 tablespoon of the butter, a few drops of lemon juice, and a pinch of salt. Cover and cook over low heat, stirring occasionally, for 15 minutes. Melt the remaining butter with the oil in another pan. Stir in the rice, curry powder, the mushrooms with their cooking juices, peas, and bell peppers, season to taste with salt, and heat through, stirring constantly. Transfer the rice mixture to a warm serving dish and garnish with slices of hard-cooked egg or bacon strips. Serve immediately.

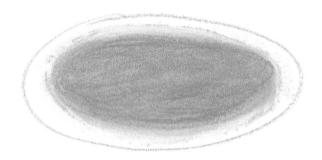

199

Chinese-style rice
ARROZ ESTILO CHINO

- 2 ½ cups long-grain rice
- 4–5 tablespoons peanut oil
- scant 1 ½ cups diced carrots
- 1 large green bell pepper,
  seeded and diced
- 4 cups bean sprouts,
  cut into short lengths
- 3 ½ ounces lean pork, diced
- 5 tablespoons soy sauce
- salt

Serves 6

Cook the rice in boiling water and rinse under cold running water as described in recipe 173. Drain well and set aside. Heat the oil in a large skillet. Add the carrot, bell pepper, and bean sprouts and stir-fry for 10 minutes. Add the pork and stir-fry for 5 minutes more, then stir in the rice. Pour in the soy sauce and season with salt, if necessary, remembering that the soy sauce is salty. Serve immediately.

Kidney bean, bacon, and red bell pepper rice

GUISO CON ARROZ, JUDÍAS ROJAS, BACON Y PIMIENTO

- Scant 1½ cups dried kidney beans, soaked overnight in cold water and drained
- 8–9 tablespoons olive oil
- 3½ ounces bacon, in strips
- 1 large red bell pepper, seeded and cut into 4 strips
- 2 onions, thinly sliced
- 1 clove garlic, halved and green shoot removed, if necessary
- pinch of ground cumin
- pinch of dried oregano
- 1 bay leaf
- 2½ cups long-grain rice
- salt

Serves 6

Put the beans in a pan, add water to cover, and bring to a boil. Boil vigorously for 15 minutes, then remove from the heat, and drain. Return the beans to the pan, add fresh cold water to cover, and bring to a boil over high heat. Lower the heat and simmer for 1½–2 hours, until tender. Alternatively, put the precooked beans in a pressure cooker, add water to cover, bring to high pressure, and cook for 25 minutes. In both cases, drain the beans and reserve the cooking liquid. Meanwhile, heat 4–5 tablespoons of the oil in a skillet. Add the bacon and cook, stirring occasionally, for 5–6 minutes, until lightly browned. Remove from the pan and set aside. Add the strips of bell pepper to the pan and cook, turning occasionally, for about 10 minutes, until tender. Remove the pan from the heat and, when cool enough to handle, remove the bell pepper and peel off the skin, then set aside. Reserve the oil in the pan. Heat the remaining oil in a large sauté pan. Add the onion and cook over low heat, stirring occasionally, for about 6 minutes, until softened and translucent. Add the garlic and cook, stirring occasionally, for 2 minutes more. Stir in the cumin and oregano, add the bay leaf, and season to taste with salt. Pour in 4 cups of the reserved cooking liquid and bring to a boil. Add the rice, beans, bacon, red bell pepper, and reserved oil. Cook, uncovered, over high heat until the liquid has been absorbed. Then lower the heat, cover, and cook for 6–8 minutes more, until the rice is tender and the grains are separated. Remove the pan from the heat and let stand, still covered, for 2 minutes, then serve.

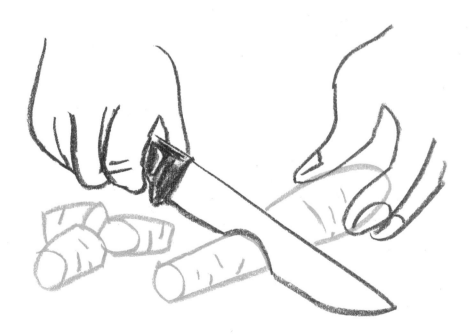

201

Simple paella

- 9 ounces monkfish tail
- 9 ounces raw shrimp, shells on
  and heads attached, if available
- scant 1 cup olive oil
- 1 small onion, chopped
- 2 tomatoes,
  peeled, seeded, and chopped
- 1 pound 2 ounces live
  cherrystone clams or
  2¼ pounds mussels
- 1 green bell pepper, seeded
  and cut into 1-inch squares
- 1 squid, cleaned (see page 468)
  and cut into thin strips or rings
- 3 cups long-grain rice
- 1 thick slice garlic
- 1 sprig fresh parsley
- pinch of saffron threads
- 2 tablespoons warm water
- 1 red bell pepper,
  seeded and cut into strips
- scant 1 cup drained canned peas
- ½ chorizo sausage,
  skinned and sliced
- salt
- lemon wedges

Serves 8

If necessary, remove and discard the gray membrane from the monkfish. Using a sharp knife, cut along either side of the backbone, remove the two fillets, cut into chunks, and set aside. Reserve the bone. Peel the shrimp and reserve the shells and heads, if attached. Set the shrimp aside. Put the monkfish bone and shrimp heads and shells into a pan. Pour in plenty of water, add a pinch of salt, and simmer for 15 minutes. Meanwhile, heat half the oil in a skillet. Add the onion and cook over low heat, stirring occasionally, for 5 minutes, until softened and translucent. Add the tomato and cook, stirring and breaking up the tomato with the side of the spoon, for 5 minutes more. Allow to cool slightly, then transfer the mixture to a food processor or blender and process to a purée. Scrape the purée into a paella pan or large, heavy skillet. If using the clams, scrub under cold running water. If using the mussels, and they are not pre-cleaned, scrape the shells with the blade of a knife and remove the "beards," then scrub under cold running water. Discard any shellfish with broken shells or any that do not shut immediately when sharply tapped. Put the shellfish into a pan, pour in ¼ cup water, and bring to a boil. Cover and cook over high heat for 3–6 minutes, until the shells have opened. Remove the pan from the heat and lift out the shellfish with a slotted spoon, reserving the cooking liquid. Remove and discard any shellfish that have not opened and the empty half shells. Set aside the clams or mussels on the half shell. Strain the reserved cooking liquid through a cheesecloth-lined strainer into a bowl. Strain the fish and shrimp stock into the same bowl. Add enough water to make 7½ cups, if necessary. Pour the stock into a pan and heat gently, but do not let boil. Pour the remaining oil into the paella pan. Add the green bell pepper and cook over medium heat, stirring occasionally, for 3–4 minutes. Add the squid, monkfish, and rice and cook, stirring constantly, for a few minutes, but do not let brown. Season with a pinch of salt and pour in the hot stock. Gently shake the pan to make sure that the liquid is evenly distributed. Pound the garlic, parsley, and saffron in a mortar with a little salt, or process in a mini-food processor. Mix in the warm water, and add to the pan. Gently shake the pan or stir with a spoon so the mixture is evenly incorporated. Stir in the shrimp. When about half the stock has been absorbed, arrange the red bell pepper strips, reserved shellfish, peas, and chorizo attractively in the pan. Continue to cook until the rice is tender and all the stock has been absorbed. (The paella usually takes a total of about 20 minutes from the time the stock is added, but this depends on the type of rice.) Spread out a dampened dishtowel on a work surface. Remove the paella pan from the heat, place it on the dishtowel, and let stand for 5 minutes. Serve the paella with lemon wedges hung over the side of the pan.

Note: Some people like to squeeze a little lemon juice over their paella once it has been served. Others prefer to add a few drops of lemon juice to the rice and stock during cooking, as the lemon helps to keep the rice grains separate.

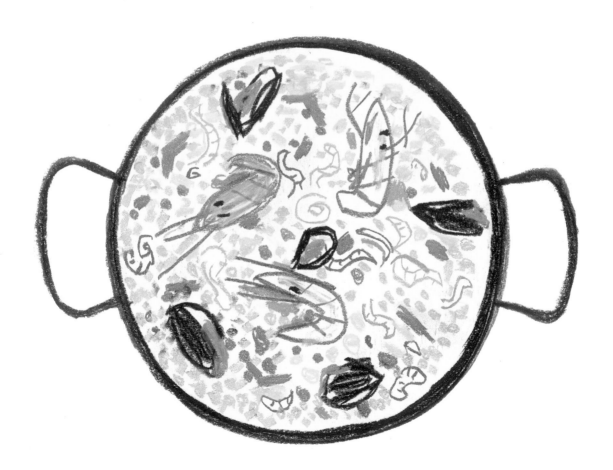

My paella

PAELLA A MI ESTILO

- 11 ounces raw shrimp, shells on
  and heads attached if available
- 2¼ pounds mussels or 1 pound
  2 ounces littleneck, steamer,
  or cherrystone clams
- ¾ cup olive oil
- 1 small onion, finely chopped
- 1 clove garlic, finely chopped
- 3 tablespoons tomato sauce
  or 1 large, ripe tomato, chopped
- 2 small squid, cleaned
  (see page 468) and cut into
  ¼-inch thick rings
- 2½ cups long-grain rice
- 3 sprigs fresh parsley
- pinch of saffron threads
- 2 chicken bouillon cubes
- scant 1 cup drained canned peas
- 1 red bell pepper,
  seeded and cut into strips
- salt
- lemon wedges

Serves 6–8

Peel the shrimp and reserve the shells and heads, if attached. Set the shrimp aside. Put the heads and shells into a pan, pour in plenty of water, and simmer for about 10 minutes. Remove the pan from the heat and strain the stock into a bowl. If using the mussels, and they have not been pre-cleaned, scrape the shells with the blade of a knife and remove the "beards," then scrub under cold running water. If using the clams, scrub under cold running water. Discard any shellfish with broken shells or any that do not shut immediately when sharply tapped. Put the shellfish in a pan or skillet, add ¼ cup water, cover and cook over high heat for 3–6 minutes, until the shells have opened. Lift out the shellfish with a slotted spoon, discarding any that remain closed. Reserve the cooking liquid. Remove nearly all the shellfish from their shells but leave a few in the shell or half shell for the garnish. Strain the reserved cooking liquid through a cheese-cloth-lined strainer into the shrimp stock. Add enough water to make 7½ cups, if necessary. Pour into a pan and heat gently, but do not let boil. Preheat the oven to 350°F. Pour just enough of the oil into a paella pan or large, heavy skillet with a metal handle to cover the base and heat it. Add the onion and garlic and cook over medium heat, stirring occasionally, for 7 minutes, until lightly browned. Add the tomato sauce or fresh tomato and cook, stirring constantly, for a few minutes. Reserve a few shrimp for the garnish and add the remainder to the pan with the squid rings and rice. Cook, stirring constantly, until the squid becomes opaque. Add the shelled mussels or clams. Season with a pinch of salt and pour in the hot stock. Gently shake the pan to make sure the liquid is evenly distributed. Pound the parsley with the saffron in a mortar, or process in a mini-food processor. Mix in 2 tablespoons water, and add to the paella pan. Crumble in the bouillon cubes. Gently shake the pan or stir with a wooden spoon. Add the peas to the paella and cook for a few minutes more. Garnish the paella with the strips of red bell pepper, the reserved shrimp, and the reserved shellfish in the shell. Transfer the pan to the oven and bake for about 25 minutes. Spread out a dampened dishtowel on a work surface. Remove the paella pan from the oven, place it on the dishtowel, and let stand for 5 minutes. Serve the paella with lemon wedges hung over the side of the pan.

203 Chicken paella

PAELLA DE POLLO

Additional ingredients:
- 1 skinless boneless chicken half

Serves 6–8

Make the paella as described in recipe 202, but first cut a skinless, boneless chicken half into bite-size pieces. Heat half the oil listed in the ingredients, in a skillet, add the chicken and cook, stirring occasionally, for about 10 minutes, until light golden brown. Remove with a slotted spoon and set aside. Proceed with the paella as described, adding the chicken at the same time as the shrimp.

204 Paella with stew ingredients

PAELLA CON TROPEZONES DE COCIDO

- 1 cup olive oil
- 1 small onion, chopped
- 1 large ripe tomato, seeded and chopped
- scant 1 cup cooked diced bacon
- 1 cooked chicken breast half, cut into bite-size pieces
- 1 cooked blood sausage (morcilla), sliced
- 1 cooked chorizo, sliced
- ½ cup cooked or canned garbanzo beans
- 3 cups long-grain rice
- 6¼ cups hot stock (homemade, canned or made with bouillon cubes)
- 1 thick slice garlic
- 1 sprig fresh parsley
- pinch of saffron threads
- 2 tablespoons warm water
- scant 1 cup drained canned peas
- 1 roasted or canned or bottled red bell pepper, seeded and cut into strips
- salt

Serves 6

Heat half the oil in a pan. Add the onion and cook over low heat, stirring occasionally, for about 5 minutes, until softened and translucent. Add the tomato and cook, stirring and breaking it up with the side of the spoon, for 5–10 minutes. Let cool slightly, then transfer the mixture to a food processor or blender and process to a purée. Scrape the purée into a paella pan or large, heavy skillet, add the remaining oil, and set over medium heat. Add the bacon, chicken, half the blood sausage, half the chorizo, and half the garbanzos. Stir in the rice and pour in the hot stock. Gently shake the pan to make sure that everything is evenly distributed. Pound the garlic, parsley, and saffron in a mortar with a little salt, or process in a mini-food processor. Mix in the warm water, then stir into the paella pan. Cook for 15 minutes, then add the peas, the remaining blood sausage, chorizo, and gar-banzos, and the strips of red pepper. Cook for 5 minutes more or until all the stock has been absorbed and the rice is tender. Spread out a dampened dishtowel on a work surface. Remove the paella pan from the heat, place it on the dishtowel, and let stand for 5 minutes. Serve immediately.

Note: This paella is designed to be made with leftover ingredients from a stew made the previous day, but if you haven't made a stew, you can still make the paella using cooked ingredients that you have to hand or that you buy from the store.

Salt cod paella

PAELLA DE BACALAO

- 12 ounces salt cod fillet
- all-purpose flour, for dusting
- generous 1 cup olive oil
- 2 cloves garlic
- 1 large onion, finely chopped
- 1 teaspoon paprika
- 1 pound 2 ounces ripe tomatoes,
  peeled, seeded, and chopped
- 3 cups long-grain rice
- 6¼ cups hot chicken stock
  (homemade, canned or
  made with bouillon cubes)
- pinch of saffron threads
- 2 tablespoons warm water
- scant 1 cup drained canned peas
- 1 teaspoon chopped
  fresh parsley
- 3½ ounces canned or bottled
  red peppers, drained, seeded,
  and cut into strips
- salt

Serves 6

Put the salt cod into a bowl, and add water to cover. Let soak for at least 12 hours or overnight, changing the water at least four times. (Each time you change the water rinse out the bowl as the salt tends to deposit on the base.) Drain the fish and pat dry, then cut into bite-size pieces. Roll the pieces in the flour, shaking off any excess. Heat ¾ cup of the oil in a skillet over high heat. Add the pieces of cod and cook, turning occasionally, until golden brown all over. Remove with a slotted spoon and set aside. Heat the remaining oil in a paella pan or large, heavy skillet. Meanwhile, finely chop one of the garlic cloves. Add the onion and chopped garlic to the pan and cook over low heat, stirring occasionally, for 5 minutes until softened and translucent. Stir in the paprika and tomato and cook, stirring and breaking up the tomato with the side of the spoon, for 10 minutes. Stir in the rice and cook, stirring constantly, for 1–2 minutes but do not let it brown. Add the cod, season with a pinch of salt, and pour in the hot stock. Pound the saffron with the remaining garlic clove and a pinch of salt in a mortar, or process in a mini-food processor. Mix in the warm water. Stir into the rice and gently shake the pan to make sure everything is evenly covered. Cook for 15 minutes, until all the stock is absorbed and the rice is beginning to dry a little, then add the peas and pars-ley, and place the strips of bell pepper on top to garnish. Cook for 5 min-utes more, until the rice is tender. Spread a dampened dishtowel on a work surface. Remove the paella pan from the heat, place it on the dishtowel, and let stand for 5 minutes. Serve immediately.

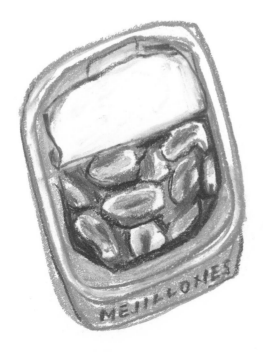

Canned fish paella

PAELLA DE PESCADOS DE LATA

- ¾ cup olive oil
- 1 onion, chopped
- small piece garlic, finely chopped
- 2 tomatoes,
  peeled, seeded, and chopped
- 2¾ ounces canned shrimp,
  drained
- 4 ounces canned clams, drained
- 3½ ounces canned tuna,
  drained and flaked
- 3 cups long-grain rice
- 7½ cups fish stock
  (homemade, canned or
  made with a bouillon cube)
- 2¾ ounces canned mussels
  or canned smoked mussels,
  drained
- pinch of saffron threads
- 2½ ounces canned sardines
  in oil, drained
- 1 canned or bottled red bell
  pepper, drained and cut into
  strips
- 1 sprig fresh parsley
- salt

Serves 6

Heat half the oil in a skillet. Add the onion and garlic and cook over low heat, stirring occasionally, for 5 minutes, until softened and translucent. Add the tomato and cook, stirring occasionally and breaking it up with the side of the spoon, for 5 minutes. Let cool slightly, then transfer the mixture to a food processor or blender and process until smooth. Pour into a paella pan or large heavy skillet. Add the remaining oil, the shrimp and half the clams, and cook over low heat for a few minutes, then add the tuna, and stir in the rice. Pour in the fish stock, add the mussels and the remaining clams, and bring to a boil. Add the saffron and cook for about 15–18 minutes, until the rice is tender and the stock has been absorbed. Season to taste with salt. Spread out a dampened dishtowel on a work surface. Remove the paella pan from the heat, place it on the dishtowel. Garnish the paella with the sardines, red bell pepper strips, and parsley, and let stand for 5 minutes before serving.

Note: Make this dish with any combination of canned fish that you like. Canned squid is a good choice if you can find it.

207

Rice with eggplant and zucchini

ARROZ CON BERENJENAS Y CALABACINES

- 2 tablespoons olive oil
- 2 onions, chopped
- 1 clove garlic, chopped
- 2 zucchini, diced
- 1 eggplant, diced
- 2 cups long-grain rice
- 5 cups boiling vegetable stock
  (homemade, canned or
  made with a bouillon cube)
- generous 1 grated cup
  Parmesan cheese
- 1 tablespoon chopped
  fresh parsley
- salt

Serves 6

Heat the oil in a paella pan or large, heavy skillet. Add the onion and garlic and cook over low heat, stirring occasionally, for 5 minutes until softened and translucent. Add the zucchini and eggplant and cook, stirring occasionally, for 5 minutes more. Stir in the rice and cook, stirring constantly, for 2 minutes, then pour in half the boiling stock. Cook until almost all the stock has been absorbed, then pour in the remaining stock, and cook until it has been absorbed and the rice is tender. This will take 15–20 minutes. Season with salt. Sprinkle the Parmesan and parsley over the rice and serve immediately.

208

Chicken risotto

RISOTTO DE POLLO

- 1 chicken, about 2¼ pounds
- 1 stalk celery
- 1 carrot
- 1 onion, plus 1 small onion, very finely chopped
- 7 tablespoons butter
- scant 1 cup dry white wine
- generous 1 cup risotto (arborio) rice
- ⅔ cup grated Parmesan cheese
- salt and pepper

Serves 6

Ask the butcher to bone the chicken and give you the bones. Dice the chicken meat. Put the chicken bones, celery, carrot, and whole onion into a pan, pour in 6¼ cups water, season with salt and pepper, and bring to a boil. Lower the heat and simmer for 30 minutes. Strain the stock and pour 2¼ cups into a clean pan. Return this to the heat, and bring to simmering point. Melt 5 tablepoons of the butter in another pan. Add the chopped onion and the chicken meat and cook over low heat, stirring frequently, for about 10 minutes, until lightly browned. Season with salt and pepper and pour in the wine. Simmer for 12–15 minutes, until the liquid has evaporated. Stir in the rice and cook, stirring constantly, for about 2 minutes, until translucent. Add a ladleful of the stock and cook, stirring constantly, until all the liquid has been absorbed. Continue adding the stock, a ladleful at a time, stirring constantly. Do not add more stock until the previous addition has been absorbed. When all the stock has been absorbed and the risotto is creamy—this will take about 20 minutes—remove the pan from the heat and stir in the remaining butter and the Parmesan. Cover and let stand for a few minutes before serving.

209

Baked rice
ARROZ AL HORNO

- 5 tablespoons olive oil
- 2 cloves garlic, chopped
- 9 ounces tomatoes, peeled, seeded, and finely chopped
- 1 pound 2 ounces potatoes
- 2½ cups long-grain rice
- salt

Serves 6

Preheat the oven to 400°F. Heat the oil in an ovenproof casserole that can be used on the stove. Add the garlic and cook, stirring frequently, for 2 minutes. Add the tomato and cook, stirring occasionally, for 8 minutes. Meanwhile, slice the potatoes. Add the potatoes to the casserole, season with salt, add the rice, and pour in 5 cups water. Bring to a boil, then cover, and transfer the casserole to the oven. Bake for about 20 minutes, until the rice is dry and lightly browned. Serve immediately straight from the casserole.

210

Rice with sherry

ARROZ AL JEREZ

- 5 tablespoons olive oil
- 5 ounces onion, finely chopped
- ¾ cup sherry
- 2½ cups long-grain rice
- 5 cups boiling chicken stock (homemade, canned or made with a bouillon cube)
- 2 tablespoons (¼ stick) butter, softened
- salt

Serves 4–6

Preheat the oven to 400°F. Heat the oil in an ovenproof casserole that can be used on the stove. Add the onion and cook over low heat, stirring occasionally, for 6–8 minutes, until beginning to brown. Stir in the sherry and rice, then pour in the boiling stock, and season with salt. Cover the casserole, transfer to the oven, and bake for about 20 minutes, until the rice is tender. Just before serving, stir in the butter until melted. Serve straight from the casserole.

Legumes

Tradition has it that soaking most dried beans for several hours or overnight makes them easier to digest and reduces the possibility of flatullence, as the water leeches out the indigestible substances they contain. Recent research has sparked debate on the topic of soaking, nevertheless I like to soak my beans.

Tricks
- It is important not to add salt to legumes before cooking them, as it will make them tough
- For the same reason, it is important to put them in a saucepan of cold water and cook them over low heat
- Cooking in hard water prolongs the cooking time. You can add a pinch of baking soda to counteract this, but it changes the flavor slightly and destroys the vitamin B
- Legumes are enhanced if you add an onion, carrot, bouquet garni, garlic clove, or other flavoring when they are cooking
- Do not discard the cooking water as mineral salts and other nutrients will be dissolved in it.

Garbanzo beans

Tricks

- When soaking garbanzos, add a pinch of baking soda. This helps soften them and improves their digestibility
- To avoid garbanzos becoming tough, do not add salt until they have been cooking for some time
- For tender results, add warm rather than cold water to garbanzos, and if it is necessary to top them up with stock during the cooking time heat it first.

211 Baked leftover stew

RESTO DE COCIDO EN FORMA DE BUDÍN

- **sunflower oil, for brushing**
- **bread crumbs, for sprinkling**
- **4–5 cups leftover stew**
- **3 eggs, separated**
- **1 quantity Classic Tomato Sauce (see recipe 73)**

Serves 6

Preheat the oven to 350°F. Brush a loaf pan with the oil and sprinkle with the bread crumbs, tapping out any excess. Process all the leftover stew briefly in a food processor or grind in a grinder. Lightly beat the egg yolks in a bowl, then stir them into the stew. Whisk the egg whites in a clean, dry bowl until they form soft peaks. Gently fold them into the mixture. Pour the mixture into the prepared pan. Place the pan in a roasting pan and pour in boiling water halfway up the sides of the loaf pan. Bake for 20–30 minutes, until set. Remove the pan from the roasting pan and turn the "loaf" out onto a serving dish. Serve immediately, offering the tomato sauce separately.

212

Dressed garbanzo beans

GARBANZOS ALIÑADOS

- 3 ¼ cups dried garbanzo beans
- pinch of baking soda
- 1 veal shank bone,
  preferably fatty
- 2 leeks, halved lengthwise
  and rinsed well
- 9 ounces carrots,
  halved lengthwise
- 3 tomatoes, sliced
- salt

  Dressing:
- 3 tablespoons white-wine
  vinegar
- 9 tablespoons sunflower oil
- 2 hard-cooked eggs, chopped
- 1 teaspoon very finely chopped
  fresh parsley
- 1 teaspoon chopped onion
  (optional)
- salt

Serves 6

Put the garbanzos in a bowl, pour in warm water to cover, and add the baking soda and a pinch of salt. Let soak for at least 12 hours, then drain, and rinse well. Put the garbanzos in a pan and pour in hot, but not boiling, water to cover. Add a pinch of salt, the veal bone, leeks and carrots and bring to a boil. Lower the heat to medium or medium-low and cook for 2–3 hours, until the garbanzos are tender. (The time depends on the type and age of the garbanzos and the softness of the water.) Drain the garbanzos, reserving 2 tablespoons of the cooking liquid. Spoon the garbanzos into a mound on a round serving dish. Arrange the tomato slices around them and put the carrots on top of them in the shape of a star. Top with one-fourth of the chopped hard-cooked eggs (see dressing ingredients). To make the dressing, whisk the vinegar with a pinch of salt in a bowl, then gradually whisk in the oil. Stir in the reserved cooking liquid, the remaining chopped hard-cooked eggs, the parsley, and the onion, if using. Pour into a sauceboat and serve with the garbanzos.

Note: The cooking liquid from the garbanzos is very good and can be used to cook rice, make soup, etc.

213

Fried garbanzo beans
GARBANZOS REFRITOS

- 2¼ cups dried garbanzo beans
- pinch of baking soda
- generous ½ cup lard or
  generous ⅓ cup butter
- 1 onion, finely chopped
- 3 ripe tomatoes,
  seeded and chopped
- 1 teaspoon paprika
- ½ cantimpalo chorizo
  (finger-sized dried pork
  sausage with garlic and paprika),
  skinned and thinly sliced
  or small piece of another
  precooked spicy sausage,
  thinly sliced
- salt

Serves 4

Put the garbanzos in a bowl, pour in warm water to cover, and add the baking soda and a pinch of salt. Let soak for at least 12 hours, then drain, and rinse well. Bring a pan of salted water to just below boiling point. Add the garbanzos, cover the pan and cook over medium heat for about 2 hours, until tender but not falling apart. (The time depends on the type and age of the garbanzos and the softness of the water.) Meanwhile, melt the lard or butter in a skillet. Add the onion and cook over low heat, stirring occasionally, for about 5 minutes, until softened and translucent. Add the tomato and cook, stirring and breaking it up with the side of a spoon, for 10 minutes. Stir in the paprika and chorizo, then remove the pan from the heat. Drain the garbanzos, add them to the skillet, and cook over high heat, stirring constantly, for 5 minutes. Serve immediately.

Note: This recipe can be made with garbanzo beans left over from a stew made the day before, in which case they will need to be heated for a little longer.

Poor man's garbanzo beans
GARBANZOS A LO POBRE

- 2¼ cups dried garbanzo beans
- pinch of baking soda
- 2 beef shank bones
- 1 ham bone
- 1 pound 2 ounces potatoes, diced
- 3–4 tablespoons olive oil
- 1 large onion, chopped
- 2 cloves garlic, finely chopped
- 1 tablespoon all-purpose flour
- 1 teaspoon paprika
- 5 tablespoons white wine
- 1½ tablespoons chopped fresh parsley
- salt

Serves 4

Put the garbanzos in a bowl, pour in warm water to cover, and add the baking soda and a pinch of salt. Let soak for at least 12 hours, then drain, and rinse well. Put the garbanzos in a large pan, pour in hot, but not boiling, water to cover, and add the beef bones, ham bone, and a pinch of salt. (Remember that the ham bone will probably be quite salty.) Cook for 1½ hours. (Alternatively, cook the garbanzos and bones in a pressure cooker on high for 25 minutes.) Add the potato and cook for 15–20 minutes more, until the potato is tender. Meanwhile, heat the oil in a skillet. Add the onion and cook over low heat, stirring occasionally, for about 6 minutes, until softened but not colored. Add the garlic, stir in the flour, and cook for 4 minutes more. Remove the pan from the heat and add the paprika, then return the pan to the heat. Pour in the wine, add about 1½ cups of the cooking liquid from the garbanzos, and cook for 5 minutes more. Meanwhile, remove the bones from the pan containing the garbanzos and drain off most of the remaining cooking liquid, depending on how soupy you like the dish. Add the onion and tomato mixture to the garbanzos and cook for 10 minutes. Taste and adjust the seasoning, sprinkle with the parsley, and serve.

Garbanzo bean stew with spinach

POTAJE CON ESPINACAS

- 2 ¼ cups dried garbanzo beans
- pinch of baking soda
- 7 ounces salt cod fillet
- ½ head garlic
- 1 bay leaf
- 2 small onions
- 2 ¼ pounds spinach,
  coarse stalks removed
- 6 tablespoons olive oil
- 1 large tomato,
  seeded and chopped
- 1 tablespoon all-purpose flour
- 1 teaspoon paprika
- 1 sprig fresh parsley
- salt

Serves 4

Put the garbanzos in a bowl, pour in warm water to cover, and add the baking soda and a pinch of salt. Let soak for at least 12 hours, then drain, and rinse well. Meanwhile, put the salt cod in a bowl, add cold water to cover, and let soak for at least 12 hours, changing the water three or four times. (Each time you change the water rinse out the bowl as salt tends to deposit on the base.) Put the garbanzos into a large pan and pour in hot, but not boiling, water to cover. Reserve a garlic clove and add the remainder of the head to the pan with the bay leaf and one of the onions. Cook over medium heat for 2 ¼–2 ½ hours. Drain the salt cod, add to the pan, and cook for 30 minutes more. Add the spinach and cook for 8 minutes more. Finely chop the remaining onion. Heat the oil in a skillet. Add the chopped onion and cook over low heat, stirring occasionally, for 10 minutes, until light golden brown. Add the tomato and cook, stirring and breaking it up with the side of the spoon, for 10 minutes more. Stir in the flour and cook, stirring constantly, for 2–3 minutes. Stir in the paprika and remove the pan from the heat. Let the mixture cool a little, then transfer to a food processor or blender, process to a purée, and stir into the garbanzos. Season to taste with salt. Pound the parsley in a mortar with the reserved garlic clove or process in a mini-food processor. Mix in 1 tablespoon of the cooking liquid from the garbanzos, then stir into the pan. Cook for 15–20 minutes and serve in a soup tureen.

Note: Some people like to add little Dumplings (see recipe 150) to this dish. Roll the dumplings in bread crumbs and fry in olive oil until golden brown all over. Add to the stew after adding the tomato and onion mixture.

Garbanzo bean stew with rice and potatoes

POTAJE CON ARROZ Y PATATAS

- **1 ¾ cups dried garbanzo beans**
- **pinch of baking soda**
- **2 tablespoons olive oil**
- **1 onion**
- **2 whole cloves**
- **1 ¾ cups diced potatoes**
- **1 ¼ cups long-grain rice**
- **1 clove garlic**
- **pinch of saffron threads**
- **1 sprig fresh parsley**
- **salt**

Serves 4

Put the garbanzos in a bowl, pour in warm water to cover and add the baking soda and a pinch of salt. Let soak for at least 12 hours, then drain, and rinse well. Preheat the oven to 400°F. Put the garbanzos in a pan, pour in hot, but not boiling, water to cover, and add the oil and a pinch of salt. Cook over medium heat for about 2 ½ hours, until the garbanzos are softening. (The time depends on the type and age of the garbanzos and the softness of the water.) Meanwhile, stud the onion with the cloves and roast in the oven until golden on the outside. Remove from the oven and add to the garbanzos along with the potato and cook for 15 minutes more. Add the rice and cook for another 20 minutes. Pound the garlic, saffron, parsley, and a pinch of salt in a mortar, or process in a mini-food processor. Mix in 2 tablespoons of the cooking liquid from the garbanzos, then add to the pan. Season to taste with salt and serve in a soup tureen.

217

Navy bean stew

JUDÍAS BLANCAS GUISADAS

- 3 ¾ cups dried navy beans,
  soaked for 3 hours or overnight
  in cold water and drained
- ½ head garlic, roasted
  (see Note)
- 1 bay leaf
- 2 small onions
- 1 chorizo sausage or Asturian
  blood sausage
- 4 tablespoons olive oil
- 1 tablespoon all-purpose flour
- 1 teaspoon paprika
- salt

Serves 6

Put the beans into a pan and pour in water to cover. Cover and bring to a boil, then remove the pan from the heat, and drain. Return the beans to the pan, pour in fresh cold water to cover, add the roasted garlic, bay leaf, on of the onions, and the chorizo or blood sausage, and cook for about 30 minutes over medium heat. Add 1 cup cold water, bring back to a boil, and simmer for 30 minutes more. Do this twice more at 30-minute intervals, then simmer for another 30 minutes (making a total cooking time of about 2 ½ hours). Chop the remaining onion. Heat the oil in a skillet. Add the chopped onion and cook over medium heat, stirring occasionally, for about 10 minutes, until lightly browned. Stir in the flour and cook, stirring constantly, for about 10 minutes, until lightly browned. Stir in the paprika and 3–4 table-spoons of the cooking liquid from the beans. Remove the pan from the heat and let cool a little, then transfer to a food processor or blender, process to a purée, and stir into the beans. Season to taste with salt. Remove the chorizo or blood sausage, cut into slices, and return to the pan. Remove and discard the bay leaf. Ladle into a soup tureen and serve immediately.

Notes: If the beans are less than a year old, they do not need to be soaked before cooking. To roast the garlic bulb, spear it with a fork and hold it in a gas flame, turning frequently. Alternatively, place on a sheet of aluminum foil, douse with olive oil and roast under a preheated broiler, turning frequently.

Navy bean salad

JUDÍAS BLANCAS EN ENSALADA

- 3 ¾ cups dried navy beans, soaked overnight in cold water and drained
- 1 small onion, halved, plus 1 tablespoon finely chopped onion
- 1 bay leaf
- 3 tablespoons white-wine vinegar
- 9 tablespoons sunflower oil
- 1 teaspoon chopped fresh parsley
- salt

Serves 6

Put the beans into a pan and pour in water to cover. Cover and bring to a boil, then remove the pan from the heat, and drain. Return the beans to the pan, pour in fresh cold water to cover, add the onion halves and bay leaf, and cook over medium heat for about 30 minutes. Add 1 cup cold water, bring back to a boil, and simmer for 30 minutes more. Do this twice more at 30-minute intervals, then simmer for another 30 minutes (making a total cooking time of about 2 ½ hours), until the beans are tender but not falling apart (the cooking time depends on the age of the beans). Remove the pan from the heat and drain. Remove and discard the bay leaf and onion halves and let the beans cool, then put them into a salad bowl. Whisk the vinegar with a pinch of salt in another bowl, then whisk in the oil. Pour the dressing over the beans, add the parsley and chopped onion, and toss lightly to mix. Garnish with tomato slices, if you like, and serve.

Navy beans with egg topping

JUDÍAS BLANCAS CON COSTRA

- 3¼ cups dried navy beans, soaked overnight in cold water and drained
- 1 bay leaf
- 1 onion, halved, plus 2 tablespoons finely chopped onion
- 4 tablespoons olive oil
- 2¼ pounds tomatoes, chopped
- 1 teaspoon sugar
- 2¼ cups drained canned peas
- 3 eggs, lightly beaten
- salt

Serves 6

Put the beans into a pan and pour in water to cover. Cover and bring to a boil, then remove the pan from the heat, and drain. Return the beans to the pan, pour in fresh cold water to cover, add the bay leaf and onion halves, and cook over medium heat for about 30 minutes. Add 1 cup cold water, bring back to a boil, and simmer for 30 minutes more. Do this twice more at 30-minute intervals, then simmer for another 30 minutes, until the beans are tender (making a total cook-ing time of about 2 ½ hours). Meanwhile, heat the oil in a skillet. Add the chopped onion and cook over low heat, stirring occasionally, for about 10 minutes, until lightly golden. Add the tomato and cook, stirring and breaking it up with the side of the spoon, for 15 minutes. Remove the pan from the heat and let cool slightly, then transfer the mixture to a food processor or blender, and process to a purée. Return the purée to the skillet, stir in the sugar, and season to taste with salt. Preheat the oven to 400°F. Drain the beans well and stir them into the tomato sauce with half the peas. Taste and adjust the seasoning, then pour the mixture into an ovenproof baking dish. Sprinkle the remaining peas on top, then pour the eggs over them. Bake for about 10 minutes, until the eggs have set. Serve immediately straight from the dish.

220

Navy beans with blood sausage
JUDÍAS BLANCAS GUISADA CON MORCILLAS

- 2 ¾ cups dried navy beans,
  soaked overnight in cold water
  and drained
- 1 small onion, peeled, plus
  1 large onion, finely chopped
- 6 tablespoons olive oil
- 1 bay leaf
- 2 cloves garlic, finely chopped
- 1 blood sausage (morcilla)
  or other sausage
- ¾ cup white wine
- 1 tablespoon white-wine vinegar
- 1 sprig fresh parsley
- salt and pepper

Serves 4

Put the beans into a pan and pour in water to cover. Bring to a boil, then remove the pan from the heat, and drain, reserving the cooking water. Return the beans to the pan, pour in fresh cold water to cover, add the small onion, 1 tablespoon of the oil, and the bay leaf, and bring back to a boil. Lower the heat and simmer for about 1 ½ hours, then drain. Heat the remaining oil in another pan. Add the chopped onion and garlic and cook over low heat, stirring occasionally, for 8–10 minutes, until lightly browned. Skin and chop the sausage, add to the pan and cook for 2–3 minutes. Add the beans, wine, vinegar, and parsley and pour in enough of the reserved cooking liquid to cover. Cover the pan and simmer gently for about 30 minutes, until the beans are tender. (The time depends on the age of the beans and the softness of the water.) Season to taste with salt and pepper, mix well, and simmer for about 5 minutes more. Remove and discard the parsley. Serve immediately.

221

Navy bean garnish
JUDÍAS BLANCAS DE ADORNO

- 1 ¾ cups dried navy beans,
  soaked for 3 hours in cold water
  and drained
- 1 bay leaf
- 1 small onion, halved
- 6 tablespoons (¾ stick) butter
- 1 teaspoon chopped
  fresh parsley
- salt

Serves 6

Put the beans into a pan and pour in water to cover. Cover and bring to a boil, then remove the pan from the heat, and drain. Return the beans to the pan, pour in fresh cold water to cover, add the bay leaf and onion halves, and cook over medium heat for about 30 minutes. Add 1 cup cold water, bring back to a boil, and simmer for 30 minutes more. Do this twice more at 30-minute intervals, then simmer for another 30 minutes (making a total cooking time of about 2 ½ hours). Drain the beans in a large colander. Melt the butter in a skillet and add the beans. Season to taste with salt and sprinkle with the parsley. Do not let the beans brown or they will become hard. These beans go well with roast leg of lamb.

White beans with sausages and bacon

JUDÍAS BLANCAS CON SALCHICHAS Y BACON

- 3 cups large dried white beans,
  such as lima beans, soaked for
  2 hours in cold water and drained
- 1 ham hock, about 9 ounces
- 2 bacon slices,
  about ¼ inch thick
- bouquet garni
  (1 sprig fresh parsley, 1 bay leaf,
  and 1 clove garlic tied together
  in cheesecloth)
- 3 tablespoons olive oil
- 6 fresh sausages
- 6 frankfurters
- 3 tablespoons butter
- 1 teaspoon chopped
  fresh parsley
- salt

Serves 6

Put the beans into a pan and pour in water to cover. Bring to a boil over low heat, then remove the pan from the heat, and drain. Return the beans to a clean pan and pour in fresh cold water to cover, then bring to a boil over low heat and cook for 15 minutes. Add 1 cup cold water, bring back to a boil, and simmer for 15 minutes more. Add another 1 cup cold water, bring back to a boil, and cook for 15 minutes more. Add the ham hock, bacon, and bouquet garni and cook for 1½ hours, until the beans are almost tender. (If necessary, add more cold water during the cooking to prevent the beans drying out.) Meanwhile, heat the oil in a skillet, add the fresh sausages, and cook over medium heat, turning occasionally, until browned all over and cooked through. (Prick the sausages first if they have artificial casings.) Season the beans to taste with salt, add the frankfurters, and cook for 10 minutes. Remove and discard the bouquet garni. Melt the butter in another pan and add the parsley. Using a slotted spoon, transfer the beans to the butter and parsley mixture and stir well. Cut the ham into six pieces and the bacon slices into three pieces each. Divide the beans among six warmed plates. Add a piece of ham, two pieces of bacon, a frankfurter, and a fried sausage to each and serve immediately.

Note: The cooking liquid from the beans is delicious. To make a soup, mix 2 tablespoons potato starch with 4 tablespoons water and add to the soup with 2 tablespoons butter, fresh parsley, and 1 egg yolk.

223

Bean stew

FABADA

• 2 ¾ cups dried Asturian beans
   or lima beans, soaked for
   3 hours or overnight in
   cold water and drained
• 1 large onion, cut into 4 pieces
• 2 cloves garlic
• ⅔ cup olive oil
• ½ pig's ear (optional)
• 1 pig's tail or pig's foot (optional)
• 1 teaspoon paprika
• 1 Serrano or other ham hock,
   about 3 ½ ounces
• 2 chorizo sausages
• 3 ½ ounces fatty bacon
• 2 Asturian blood sausages
• pinch of saffron threads
• salt

Serves 6

Put the beans into a pan and pour in cold water to cover. Bring to a boil over low heat, then remove the pan from the heat and drain. Return the beans to a clean pan, pour in fresh cold water to cover, and add the onion, garlic, oil, pig's ear and tail or foot, if using, and the paprika. Mix well and, if necessary, add more cold water to cover the contents of the pan. Bring to a boil over low heat and cook for 30 minutes. Add the ham hock and chorizos and cook for 30 minutes more. Add the bacon, and cook for another 30–60 minutes, until the beans are almost tender. Add the blood sausages and cook for 30 minutes more. Remove the ham hock, cut it into bite-sized pieces, and return the pieces to the pan. Crush the saffron in a mortar, or small bowl, and stir in 2 tablespoons of the cooking liquid, then stir into the stew. Season to taste with salt and serve.

Notes: It is not usual to serve the tail or the ear, although some people like them and leave them in the stew. If serving the ear, cut it into fine strips first. This bean stew is much better made the previous day and reheated. It is also usual to remove a ladleful of beans, make a purée with them, and then use the purée to thicken the stew.

Beans with clams

FABES CON ALMEJAS

- 2 ¾ cups dried Asturian beans or lima beans, soaked overnight in cold water and drained
- 3 tablespoons olive oil
- 1 clove garlic
- 1 bay leaf
- 1 small onion
- 3–4 sprigs fresh parsley, tied together with kitchen twine or thread
- pinch of saffron threads
- 3 tablespoons bread crumbs
- 14 ounces littleneck, steamer, or cherrystone clams
- dash of white-wine vinegar
- salt

Serves 4

Put the beans into a pan and pour in cold water to cover. Bring to a boil over low heat. Meanwhile, put the oil, garlic, bay leaf, whole onion, and parsley in another large pan and pour in a little cold water. When the beans come to a boil, remove the pan from the heat, and drain. Pour them into the pan with the parsley and add cold water to cover generously. Cover and cook over low heat for 1 ½ hours, adding more cold water if necessary. Crush the saffron in a mortar, or small bowl, and stir in 2 tablespoons of the cooking liquid from the beans, then stir into the pan. Sprinkle the bread crumbs over the mixture in the pan, cover and simmer gently over very low heat for 30 minutes more, until the beans are tender. (The total cooking time depends on the type and age of the beans and the softness of the water.) Meanwhile, wash the clams in cold water with a little salt and the vinegar. Discard any with broken shells or any that do not shut immediately when sharply tapped. Put them into a skillet or pan, add ¾ cup water, cover, and cook over high heat, shaking the pan occasionally, for 3–5 minutes, until the shells have opened. Remove the clams with a slotted spoon, reserving the cooking liquid. Discard any that remain shut. Remove the clams from their shells or, if you prefer, discard the empty half shells, and leave the clams on the half shell. Put the clams in a bowl and strain the reserved cooking liquid over them through a cheesecloth-lined strainer. Set aside. About 15 minutes before you're ready to serve, add the clams and their cooking liquid to the beans. Serve in a warm deep dish.

Pinto or kidney beans with red wine

JUDÍAS PINTAS O ENCARNADAS CON VINO TINTO

- 2 ¾ cups dried pinto or kidney beans, soaked overnight in cold water and drained
- 5 ounces fatty bacon in a single piece
- 1 veal shank bone
- 2 whole cloves
- 5 tablespoons olive oil
- 1 onion, finely chopped
- 2 cloves garlic, finely chopped
- 1 heaping tablespoon all-purpose flour
- 1 ¼ cups red wine
- salt

Serves 4

Put the beans into a pan and pour in water to cover. Bring to a boil, then remove the pan from the heat and drain. Return the beans to the pan, pour in fresh cold water to cover, and add the bacon, veal bone, and cloves. Bring to a boil, then lower the heat, and simmer for 1½ hours, until the beans are beginning to soften. (The time depends on the type and age of the beans and the softness of the water). Meanwhile, heat the oil in a skillet. Add the onion and garlic and cook over low heat, stirring occasionally, for 10 minutes, until beginning to brown, Stir in the flour and cook, stirring constantly, for 2–3 minutes, then gradually stir in the wine a little at a time. Stir the mixture into the beans and simmer for 30 minutes more. Season to taste with salt. Remove the bacon, cut into pieces, and return to the pan. Remove and discard the veal bone and cloves. Serve the beans in a warm deep dish.

Note: To reduce the cooking time, once the beans have come to a boil the first time, drain and transfer them to a pressure cooker with the bacon, veal bone, and cloves. Bring to high pressure and cook for 30 minutes, then remove the lid (once the pressure has reduced), and proceed as described above.

Pinto beans with rice

JUDÍAS PINTAS CON ARROZ

- 2 cups dried pinto beans, soaked overnight in cold water and drained
- 1 onion, cut into quarters
- 1 bay leaf
- 2 cloves garlic, peeled
- 2 cups long-grain rice
- 4 tablespoons olive oil
- 1 tablespoon all-purpose flour
- ½ teaspoon paprika
- 3 tablespoons butter
- salt

Serves 4

Put the beans into a pan and pour in enough water to cover. Cover and bring to a boil, then remove the pan from the heat, and drain. Return the beans to the pan, pour in fresh cold water to cover generously, and add half the onion, the bay leaf, and one of the garlic cloves, then cook over medium heat for about 30 minutes. Add 1 cup cold water, bring back to a boil, and simmer for 30 minutes more. Do this twice more at 30-minute intervals, then simmer for another 30–90 minutes (making a total cooking time of 2½–3½ hours). Meanwhile, cook the rice in boiling water and rinse under cold running water as described in recipe 173. Drain well and set aside. Chop the remaining onion and lightly crush the remaining garlic clove. Heat the oil in a skillet. Add the chopped onion and garlic and cook over low heat, stirring occasionally, for about 8 minutes, until beginning to brown. Stir in the flour and cook, stirring constantly, for about 10 minutes, until lightly browned. Stir in the paprika, followed immediately by 3–4 tablespoons of the cooking liquid from the beans. Stir the contents of the skillet into the beans and season to taste with salt. Melt the butter in another pan. Add the rice, season with salt, and heat through, stirring with a wooden spoon. Spoon the rice into a ring mold and turn out on a deep, round serving dish. Spoon the bean mixture into the center and serve immediately.

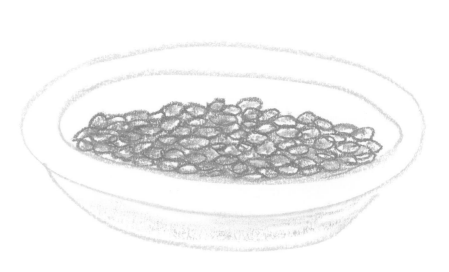

Lentils

Unlike other legumes, it is not necessary to soak lentils. Instead they can be precooked for 15 minutes. In fact, this is better than soaking, which can start fermentation, so making them more indigestible.

227

Lentil stew

LENTEJAS GUISADAS

- 1 onion, peeled
- ⅔ cup
- 2 ⅔ cups lentils
- 1 bay leaf
- 2 cloves garlic, unpeeled
- generous 1 cup olive oil
- 2 slices bread
- 1 ripe tomato,
  peeled, seeded, and chopped
- ½ teaspoon of paprika
- 1 sprig fresh parsley
- salt

Serves 6

Halve the onion and cut one half into pieces. Finely chop the other half. Put the lentils into a pan with the bay leaf, the pieces of onion, and one of the garlic cloves and pour in water to cover generously. Cover and bring to a boil, then lower the heat, and simmer for 1–2 hours, until the lentils are tender. (The cooking time depends on the type of lentil). Heat the oil in a skillet. Add the slices of bread and cook, turning occasionally, until crisp and evenly golden. Drain on paper towels and set aside. Drain off most of the oil, leaving just enough to cover the base of the skillet, and reheat. Add the chopped onion and cook over low heat, stirring occasionally, for about 8 minutes, until beginning to brown. Add the tomato and cook, stirring occasionally, for 10 minutes. Remove the pan from the heat, stir in the paprika, and add the mixture to the lentils. Peel the remaining garlic clove, then pound in a mortar with a pinch of salt and the parsley and fried bread, or process in a mini-food processor. Mix in 2–3 tablespoons of the cooking liquid from the lentils, then stir into the pan with the lentils. Season to taste with salt, and cook for 10 minutes more. Remove and discard the bay leaf and clove and serve immediately in a tureen.

228 Lentils with bacon and sausages

LENTEJAS CON TOCINO Y SALCHICHAS

- 1 small onion
- 2 whole cloves
- 2 ⅔ cups Puy lentils
- 1 bay leaf
- 1 carrot, cut into 4 pieces
- 2 cloves garlic, unpeeled
- 9 ounces bacon in a single piece
- 12 small sausages
- generous 1 cup olive oil
- salt

Serves 6

Stud the onion with the cloves. Put the lentils into a pan, add the onion, bay leaf, pieces of carrot, garlic cloves, and bacon, and pour in water to cover generously. Cover and bring to a boil, then lower the heat, and simmer for 1–1½ hours, until the lentils are tender. Drain the lentils, reserving the cooking liquid. Remove the onion, bay leaf, garlic, carrot, and bacon. Cut the bacon into small cubes and set aside. Prick the sausages if they have artificial casings. Heat the oil in a skillet. Add the sausages and cook, turning frequently, for about 5 minutes, until lightly browned and cooked through. Remove from the pan and keep warm. Drain off about half the oil from the skillet and reheat. Add the cubes of bacon and cook, stirring, for about 3 minutes, then add the lentils. Stir well and season to taste with salt. Put the lentils into a warm serving dish, place the sausages on top, and serve immediately.

Note: Some people prefer a liquid in the finished dish. If so, reserve and add some cooking liquid from the lentils to achieve the desired consistency. It's worth reserving the stock anyway, in case there are lentils left over. You can purée them in a food processor or blender and make a thick soup, garnishing it with croûtons or a little rice.

229 Lentil salad

LENTEJAS EN ENSALADA

- 1 small onion
- 2 whole cloves
- 2 ⅔ cups Puy lentils
- 1 bay leaf
- 1 carrot, cut into 4 pieces
- 2 cloves garlic, unpeeled
- olive oil
- white-wine vinegar
- salt

Serves 4–6

Proceed as described as in recipe 228, but do not use the bacon or sausages. When the lentils are cooked, drain them and remove the bay leaf, onion, garlic, and carrot. Put the lentils into a ceramic or glass salad bowl and dress with olive oil, vinegar, and a pinch of salt, mixing well. Serve warm or cold.

Note: The lentils can also be mixed with mayonnaise and garnished with drained, canned anchovy fillets and sliced tomatoes.

Potatoes

Origin and season

The potato originated in Peru and was introduced to Europe by the Spanish conquistadores. Pedro Cieza was the first to mention them in 1533. From Spain they traveled to the Netherlands and so to other parts of Europe. They are available all year around, although they have two seasons. New potatoes are in season from late fall to early summer and storage potatoes are in season from mid summer to spring. There are hundreds of varieties: some are better for frying, while others, with softer flesh, are better for mashing and soups

Selection

Potatoes should have no blemishes and should not show any signs of germination. It is especially important that they do not have green patches as this shows they contain a toxic substance. New potatoes should have a thin skin and be nice and firm.

Nutrition

Depending on how they are cooked, potatoes have 90 calories per 3 ½ ounces. They are easily digestible as they contain potassium, sugar, and starch. Potatoes are rich in vitamin C, although some of this is lost when they are cooked, and contain minerals. They are often recommended for those suffering from ulcers.

How to cook

Potatoes can be prepared many different ways to create economical and tasty dishes full of variety. A basic way to cook them (and the starting point for many recipes) is to wash and dry them without peeling; put them into a pan with enough cold water to cover generously, a dash of milk, and a pinch of salt; bring to a boil, then lower the heat to medium, and cook for about 30 minutes. The cooking time depends on the variety of potato. If the potatoes have to be peeled and cut into pieces before cooking, either because the recipe calls for it or to save time, the procedure should still be the same as above.

Tricks

- Do not leave mashed potatoes standing for long, as they lose 90–100 percent of their vitamins
- Be careful not to overcook potatoes to be used in salads
- To make potatoes easier to peel, put them into boiling water for 1–2 minutes first
- To prevent potatoes turning black after they have been peeled, leave them in a bowl of water
- Potatoes can be used to remove excess salt from a stew. Simply add a raw potato and leave it to cook for a few minutes in the stew before discarding it
- To keep potatoes looking white, add a little vinegar to the cooking water.

230

Mashed potato
PURÉ DE PATATAS

- 2½ pounds potatoes
- ¼ cup (½ stick) butter,
  cut into 2–3 pieces
- 1 cup hot milk
- salt

Serves 6

Cut any large potatoes into pieces. Put the potatoes in a large saucepan and add 1 teaspoon salt. Make sure that the water covers them completely. Bring to a boil, then lower the heat, and cook for 20–30 min-utes, until tender. Drain well. Put the butter in another pan over low heat. Add the potatoes and mash well. When the butter has been fully incorporated, stir with a wooden spoon and gradually stir in the hot milk. Season to taste with salt. Keep the mixture warm over low heat and serve as soon as possible.

Note: The quantity of milk used can easily be varied according to personal taste.

231

Mashed potato balls
BOLAS DE PURÉ DE PATATAS

- 2½ pounds potatoes
- 4 eggs
- 2 cups bread crumbs
- sunflower oil, for deep-frying
- salt

Serves 6

Cut any large potatoes into pieces. Put the potatoes into a large saucepan and add 1 teaspoon salt. Make sure the water covers them completely. Bring to a boil, then lower the heat, and cook for 20–30 minutes, until tender. Drain well and mash immediately. Beat two of the eggs in a bowl and stir them into the mixture. Season to taste with salt. Shape the mixture into small balls between the palms of your hands. Beat the remaining eggs in a shallow dish and pour the bread crumbs into another shallow dish. Roll the potato balls first in the beaten egg and then in the bread crumbs. Heat the oil in a deep-fryer or large saucepan to 350–375°F or until a cube of day-old bread browns in 30 seconds. Add the potato balls and cook until golden brown and crisp on the outside. Drain well and serve immediately.

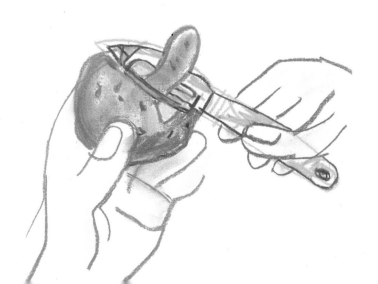

232

Mashed potato with chorizo, bacon, and paprika

PURÉ DE PATATAS CON CHORIZO, TOCINO Y PIMENTÓN (REVOLCONAS)

- 3¼ pounds potatoes
- 1 clove garlic, unpeeled
- 3 bay leaves
- ¾ cup olive oil
- 1 chorizo sausage, about 4 ounces, diced
- 4 ounces bacon, diced
- 1 teaspoon paprika
- salt
- triangles of fried bread (see recipe 130)

Serves 6

Cut any large potatoes into pieces. Put the potatoes into a large pan with plenty of cold water, a teaspoon of salt, the garlic, bay leaves, and 1 tablespoon of the oil. Bring to a boil, then lower the heat, and cook for about 20–30 minutes, until tender. Meanwhile, heat the remaining oil in a skillet. Add the chorizo and bacon and cook, stirring occasionally, for about 5 minutes, until lightly browned. Remove from the pan with a slotted spoon and set aside. Remove the skillet from the heat and stir in the paprika, then return the chorizo and the bacon to the pan, and keep warm over low heat. Drain the potato and remove and discard the garlic and bay leaves. Pour the mixture into a warm large serving bowl, add the contents of the skillet, including the oil, and stir well. Serve immediately, garnished with triangles of fried bread.

233

Potato croquettes with salt cod

CROQUETAS DE PURÉ DE PATATAS CON BACALAO

- 9 ounces salt cod fillet
- 3¼ pounds red-skinned potatoes, unpeeled
- 2 eggs, separated
- sunflower oil, for deep-frying
- 1 clove garlic (optional)
- salt
- 2 deep-fried parsley sprigs (see recipe 918) or Classic Tomato Sauce (see recipe 73)

Serves 6

If the salt cod is not too dry, you can use it straightaway. Otherwise, put in a bowl, add water to cover, and let soak for several hours, changing the water three or four times. (Each time you change the water, rinse out the bowl as the salt tends to deposit on the bottom.) Drain, then put the cod and potatoes into a pan. Add cold water to cover and bring to a boil. Lower the heat, and cook for 20–30 minutes, until the potatoes are tender. Remove the fish and drain. Drain, peel, and mash the potatoes before they cool. Remove any skin and bones from the cod and flake the flesh or process in a food processor or blender. Mix the fish with the mashed potato and beat in the egg yolks. If using the garlic, heat 1 tablespoon of the oil in a small skillet. Add the garlic and cook for a few minutes, until just beginning to color. Remove the garlic from the pan and crush with a pinch of salt in a mortar, or process in a mini-food processor, then add to the mixture. Whisk the egg whites with a pinch of salt in a clean, dry bowl until they form soft peaks. Fold into the potato mixture. Shape the mixture into croquettes with damped hands. Heat the remaining oil in a deep-fryer or deep saucepan to 350–375°F or until a cube of day-old bread browns in 30 seconds. Add the croquettes, in batches of six or eight, and cook until golden brown. Drain well and serve immediately with the parsley sprigs or the tomato sauce offered separately in a sauceboat.

234

Potatoes baked in béchamel sauce

PATATAS ASADAS AL HORNO CON BECHAMEL

- 2½ pounds potatoes, unpeeled
- 1 clove garlic
- 3 tablespoons butter
- 1½ tablespoons olive oil
- 1½ tablespoons all-purpose flour
- 4 cups milk
- ½ teaspoon meat extract or Maggi Seasoning
- ¾ cup grated gruyere cheese
- salt

Serves 6

Put the potatoes into a large pan of cold water and add 1 teaspoon salt. Make sure the water covers them completely. Bring to a boil, lower the heat, and cook for about 20–30 minutes, until tender but not falling apart. Drain, peel, and slice thinly. Rub the garlic clove around the inside of an ovenproof baking dish and lay half the potato slices in the dish. Preheat the oven to 400°F. To make a béchamel sauce, melt the butter with the oil in a pan. Stir in the flour and cook, stirring constantly, for 2 minutes. Gradually stir in the milk and season lightly with salt (bearing in mind that the cheese and the meat extract will both be salty). Cook, stirring constantly, for about 4 minutes, until thickened, then stir in the meat extract or Maggi Seasoning. Pour half the sauce over the potatoes in the dish and top with half the gruyere. Add the remaining potato slices, pour in the rest of the sauce, and sprinkle with the remaining gruyere. Bake for about 15 minutes, until the topping is golden brown. Serve immediately straight from the dish.

235

Potato fritters with grated cheese or nutmeg

BUÑUELOS DE PURÉ DE PATATAS EMPANADOS, CON QUESO RALLADO O NUEZ MOSCADA

- 3¼ pounds potatoes, unpeeled
- 1½ tablespoons butter
- 4 tablespoons warm milk
- scant 1 cup grated gruyere cheese or a pinch of freshly grated nutmeg
- 4 eggs
- 1 egg white
- 1½–2 cups bread crumbs
- sunflower oil, for deep-frying
- salt
- 1 quantity Classic Tomato Sauce (see recipe 73)

Serves 6

Put the potatoes into a pan of cold water and add 1 teaspoon salt. Make sure that the water covers them completely. Bring to a boil, lower the heat, and cook for about 20 minutes if they are new potatoes or 30 minutes if not. Drain, peel, and mash while still hot. Stir in the butter, warm milk, and gruyere or nutmeg. Separate three of the eggs and beat the yolks with the remaining egg. Add to the potatoes, mix well with a wooden spoon, and season to taste with salt. Stiffly whisk all the egg whites in a clean, dry bowl and fold them into the mixture. Shape the mixture into 2-inch square fritters. Pour the bread crumbs into a shallow dish and gently roll the fritters in them to coat. Heat the oil in a deep-fryer or deep saucepan to 350–375°F or until a cube of day-old bread browns in 30 seconds. Add the fritters, in batches, and cook until golden brown. Drain well and keep warm until all the potato fritters are cooked. Serve immediately, offering the tomato sauce separately.

Important potatoes
PATATAS A LA IMPORTANCIA

- 2¼ pounds potatoes,
  cut into ¼-inch slices
- ¾–1 cup all-purpose flour
- 4 eggs
- sunflower oil, for deep-frying
- 1 clove garlic
- pinch of saffron threads
- 1 onion, very finely chopped
- 1 tablespoon chopped
  fresh parsley
- salt

Serves 6

Season the potato slices with salt. Reserve 1 tablespoon of the flour and pour the remainder into a shallow dish. Lightly beat the eggs in another shallow dish. Dip the potato slices first in the flour and then in the beaten egg. Heat the oil in a deep-fryer or deep saucepan to 350–375°F or until a cube of day-old bread browns in 30 seconds. Add the slices of potato, four at a time, and cook until golden brown. Remove with a slotted spoon and drain on paper towels. Put them into an ovenproof casserole that can be used on the stove, arranging them in loosely packed layers. Pound the garlic with a pinch of salt in a mortar and stir in the saffron, or process in a mini-food processor. Add a little water, and pound or process again. Transfer 3 tablespoons of the oil to a clean skillet and heat. Add the onion and cook over low heat, stirring occasionally, for 5 minutes, until softened. Stir in the reserved flour, then add the contents of the mortar or processor, 4 cups water, and a pinch of salt. Strain this mixture over the potatoes, sprinkle with the parsley, and simmer over low heat for 30 minutes. Halfway through the cooking time, preheat the oven to 400°F. When the cooking time is up, transfer the casserole to the oven and bake for 10 minutes. Serve immediately straight from the casserole.

237

Potatoes with chorizo
PATATAS CON CHORIZO

- 2 tablespoons olive oil
- 3 cloves garlic, lightly crushed
- 2 teaspoons paprika
- 1 small onion
- 1 bay leaf
- 6 black peppercorns
- 6 pieces of chorizo sausage
  or other sausage (see Note)
- 3¼ pounds potatoes
- salt

Serves 6

Heat the oil in a skillet. Add the garlic and cook, stirring occasionally, for a few minutes, until beginning to brown. Remove the pan from the heat and stir in the paprika, then pour the contents of the pan into a stove-top safe casserole. Pour in 6¼ cups water, add the onion, bay leaf, peppercorns, and chorizo, and bring to a boil. Lower the heat, cover, and simmer for 1 hour. Insert a knife a little way into each potato and twist slightly as you pull it out to split the potato. Add the potatoes to the casserole. If there is not enough liquid just to cover the potatoes, add a little water. Season to taste with salt, re-cover the casserole, and simmer for 45 minutes. The potatoes may fall apart slightly but this does not matter. Remove the casserole from the heat and let stand for 5 minutes before serving.

Note: This dish is best with the long thin cooking chorizo; the type used for stews rather than the kind for slicing and eating raw. The pieces (one per serving) should each be about 1½ inches long.

238

Potato gratin
PURÉ DE PATATAS AL GRATÉN

- **2 ¼ pounds potatoes, cut into large pieces**
- **7 tablespoons butter, plus extra for greasing**
- **1 cup hot milk**
- **scant 1 cup grated cheese, such as Cheddar or gruyere**
- **2 eggs, separated**
- **2 egg whites**
- **salt**

Serves 6

Put the potato into a pan, pour in water to cover, and add 1 teaspoon salt. Bring to a boil, lower the heat, and cook for 20–30 minutes, until tender. Preheat the oven to 400°F. Grease a gratin dish or ovenproof baking dish with butter. Drain and mash the potatoes while they are still hot, then stir in the butter, hot milk, ¾ cup of the cheese, and the egg yolks. Stiffly whisk all the egg whites in a clean, dry bowl and fold into the mixture. Spoon the mixture into the prepared baking dish, sprinkle with the remaining cheese, and use a tablespoon to make a pattern on the top. Bake for about 30 minutes, until the top is golden. Serve immediately straight from the dish.

239

Tuna, mayonnaise, and potato roll
BRAZO DE GITANO DE PURÉ DE PATATAS, ATÚN Y MAYONESA

- **3 ½ pounds potatoes**
- **¼ cup (½ stick) butter**
- **¾ cup hot milk**
- **9 ounces canned tuna, drained**
- **3 firm tomatoes**
- **½ cup black olives**
- **salt**
- **lettuce leaves**

Mayonnaise (or use good-quality bottled):
- **2 eggs**
- **juice of ½ lemon**
- **scant 2 cups sunflower oil**
- **salt**

Serves 6

Make the mayonnaise as described in recipe 106, cover, and let stand in the refrigerator. Boil and mash the potatoes with the butter and hot milk as described in recipe 230. Flake the tuna and mix it with 3–4 tablespoons of the mayonnaise. Peel, seed, and dice one of the tomatoes. Slice the remainder. Soak a clean dishtowel in hot water and wring it out well. Spread it out on a surface and put the mashed potato on it. Use a large spoon to spread out the potato until it is about ½ inch thick. Spoon the tuna and mayonnaise mixture in a strip along the middle, together with the diced tomato. Using the dishtowel to help, roll up the mashed potato like a jellyroll. Spread some of the mayonnaise on top of the roll and garnish with the tomato slices, olives, and lettuce leaves. Chill in the refrigerator for at least 1 hour and serve, with the remaining mayonnaise offered separately.

Note: You can make this roll with cooked ground beef or cooked peeled shrimp instead of canned tuna.

240

Fish and potato roll with tomato sauce
BRAZO DE GITANO DE PURÉ DE PATATAS, PESCADO Y SALSA DE TOMATE

- 2½ pounds potatoes
- ¼ cup (½ stick) butter
- generous 1 cup hot milk
- 1 pound 2 ounces firm white
  fish fillets, such as monkfish
  or grouper
- 2 tablespoons white wine
- ½ small onion
- 1 bay leaf
- pinch of freshly grated nutmeg
- salt
- black or green olives (optional)
- 1 quantity Classic Tomato Sauce
  (see recipe 73)

Serves 6

Boil and mash the potatoes with the butter and hot milk as described in recipe 230. Meanwhile, put the fish in a pan, pour in cold water to cover, and add the wine, onion, bay leaf, and a pinch of salt. Cover and bring to a boil, then remove the pan from the heat, and let stand, still covered, for 5 minutes. Lift out the fish with a slotted spatula and remove and discard any skin and bones. Flake the fish and mix with 3 tablespoons of the tomato sauce and the nutmeg. Preheat the oven to 350°F. Soak a clean dishtowel in hot water and wring it out well. Spread it out on a work surface and put the mashed potato on it. Make the potato and fish roll as described in recipe 239, working as quickly as possible to prevent the ingredients getting too cold. Place the roll in an ovenproof baking dish, pour the tomato sauce over it, and bake for about 5 minutes, until heated through. Serve immediately, garnished with olives, if you like. If there is any tomato sauce left over, serve it in a sauceboat.

241

Mashed potato with eggs
PURÉ DE PATATAS CON HUEVOS

- 2¼ pounds potatoes
- 5 tablespoons butter
- 1 cup hot milk
- scant 1 cup grated cheese,
  such as Cheddar or gruyere
- 6 eggs
- salt

Serves 6

Boil and mash the potatoes with 4 tablespoons of the butter and the hot milk as described in recipe 230. Stir in ¾ cup of the cheese and season with salt if necessary. Preheat the oven to 400°F. Spoon the mixture into an ovenproof baking dish and make six hollows with the back of a spoon. Crack an egg into each one, sprinkle with a little salt, and add a small pat of the remaining butter. Sprinkle the remaining cheese over the top and bake for 5–10 minutes, until the egg whites are set. Serve immediately, straight from the dish.

242

French fries

PATATAS FRITAS

- **2¼ pounds potatoes, preferably yellow-fleshed**
- **sunflower oil, for deep-frying**
- **salt**

Serves 6

Cut the potatoes into ¾-inch wide strips. Rinse well and let soak in cold water for 30 minutes to remove the starch, then pat dry. Put them in a dishtowel, add a little salt, gather up the edges of the dishtowel, and shake to make sure the salt is evenly distributed. Heat the oil in a deep-fryer or deep saucepan to 300–325°F or until a cube of day-old bread browns in 45 seconds. Add the potato slices, in batches, and cook until they are beginning to color, then remove from the oil, and drain well. When all the potatoes have been cooked at this temperature, heat the oil to 350–375°F or until a cube of day-old bread browns in 30 seconds. Add the fries, in batches, and cook until they are golden brown. Remove from the oil, drain and keep warm until all the batches are cooked. Sprinkle with salt and serve immediately.

Note: Crisps, straw potatoes and other deep-fried potatoes are prepared in the same way as French fries, but without soaking them in water for so long. After soaking, pat dry, and fry only once until they are golden brown in oil heated to 350–375°F.

243

Straw potatoes with scrambled eggs and salt cod

REVUELTO DE PATATAS PAJA, HUEVOS Y BACALAO

- **9 ounces salt cod fillet**
- **3¼ pounds potatoes**
- **sunflower oil, for deep-frying**
- **5 eggs, beaten**
- **salt**

Serves 4

Put the salt cod in a bowl, add water to cover, and let soak for 8 hours, changing the water at least three times. (Each time you change the water rinse out the bowl as the salt tends to deposit on the bottom.) Drain the fish, put into a pan, and pour in water to cover. Bring to a boil, then remove the pan from the heat. Let stand until the water is only just warm. Lift out the fish with a fish slice, remove and discard any skin and bones and flake the flesh. Cut the potatoes into thin julienne strips. This is most easily done with a mandoline. Heat the oil in a deep-fryer or deep saucepan to 350–375°F or until a cube of day-old bread browns in 30 seconds. Add the potato strips, in batches, and cook for about 2 minutes, until golden brown. Remove from the oil and drain. Transfer 1–2 tablespoons of the oil to a large skillet and reheat. Add the eggs and cook over a low heat, stirring with a fork, until they are beginning to set. Add the straw potatoes and flaked cod, mix well, season with salt, and cook until the eggs are set but not dry. Serve immediately.

244

Diced potatoes with scrambled eggs and peas

REVUELTO DE PATATAS EN CUADRADITOS, HUEVOS Y GUISANTES

- **3¼ pounds potatoes, cut into ½-inch cubes**
- **sunflower oil, for deep-frying**
- **6 eggs, beaten**
- **2¼ cups drained canned peas**
- **salt**

Serves 6

Season the potato lightly with salt. Heat the oil in a deep-fryer or deep saucepan to 350–375°F or until a cube of day-old bread browns in 30 seconds. Add the potato, in batches, and cook for 3–5 minutes, until golden brown. Remove from the oil and drain. Transfer 1–2 tablespoons of the oil to a large skillet set over low heat and add the potato cubes. Season the eggs with salt, pour into the pan on top of the potatoes, and add the peas. Increase the heat to high and cook, stirring constantly, for about 5 minutes, until the eggs are set but not dry. Transfer the scrambled eggs to a warm serving dish and serve immediately.

Note: This dish can be made with asparagus tips instead of peas.

245

Potatoes baked with salt cod and cream

PATATAS CON BACALAO Y NATA AL HORNO

- **1 pound 2 ounces thick salt cod fillet**
- **2¼ pounds large potatoes, unpeeled**
- **7 ounces onions, sliced**
- **1½ cups heavy cream**
- **margarine, for greasing**
- **salt**

Serves 4

Put the salt cod in a bowl, add cold water to cover, and let soak for 8 hours, changing the water three or four times. (Each time you change the water rinse out the bowl as the salt tends to deposit on the bot-tom.) Put the potatoes into a large pan of water and add 1 teaspoon salt. Make sure the water covers them completely. Bring to a boil, lower the heat, and cook for 20–30 minutes, until tender but not falling apart. Drain well and let cool. Drain the fish, put into a pan, and pour in water to cover. Bring to a boil, then remove the pan from the heat. Let cool until the water is only just warm. Lift out the fish with a slotted spatula, remove and discard any skin and bones, and flake the flesh. Preheat the oven to 350°F. Grease an ovenproof baking dish with margarine.Peel and slice the potatoes. Place a third of the potato slices in the prepared baking dish and cover with half the salt cod, lightly seasoning each layer with salt. Make another layer with half the remaining potato slices. Add the onion in one layer, then add a layer of the remaining salt cod, and top with the remaining potato slices, lightly seasoning each layer with salt. Use very thin slices for the top layer if possible. Pour the cream over the top and bake for about 45 minutes, then increase the oven temperature to broil and put the dish under the broiler for a few minutes, until the top is golden brown. Serve immediately, straight from the dish.

Potatoes with milk cap mushrooms

PATATAS CON NÍSCALOS

- 1 pound 2 ounces milk cap mushrooms or other wild mushrooms, cut into medium-size pieces
- 4 tablespoons olive oil
- 1 large onion, finely chopped
- 3¼ pounds potatoes, diced
- 1 tablespoon all-purpose flour
- 1 teaspoon paprika
- 1 bay leaf
- ¾ cup white wine
- salt and pepper

Serves 4

Put the milk cap mushrooms in a pan, without added oil, and cook over low heat until they have released all their juices. Remove the mushrooms and discard the juices. (You can omit this step if you are using other wild mushrooms.) Heat the oil in a pan. Add the onion and cook over low heat, stirring occasionally, for 5 minutes, until softened and translucent. Add the potato and mushrooms and cook, stirring constantly, for 2–3 minutes. Stir in the flour and cook, stirring constantly, for 2–3 minutes, then add the paprika and bay leaf. Gradually stir in the wine and 3 cups water. Season with salt and pepper to taste and bring to a boil. Lower the heat and simmer for about 45 minutes, until the potato is tender. Remove the bay leaf. Serve immediately in a soup tureen or deep dish.

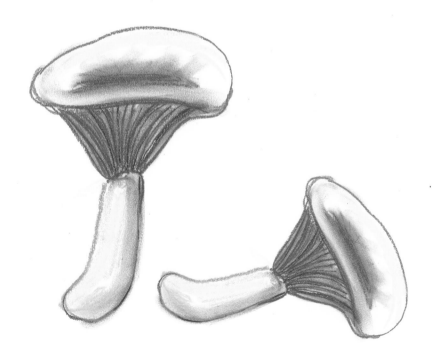

Potatoes with clams

PATATAS GUISADAS CON CHIRLAS

- 9 ounces cherrystone clams
- 6 tablespoons olive oil
- 1 onion, finely chopped
- 2 ripe tomatoes,
  peeled, seeded, and chopped
- 3¼ pounds potatoes,
  cut into pieces
- 1 tablespoon all-purpose flour
- 1 clove garlic
- 1 sprig fresh parsley
- pinch of saffron threads
- salt

Serves 4–6

Wash the clams in salted water, changing the water twice. Discard any with broken shells or any that do not shut immediately when sharply tapped. Put them in a pan, pour in ¼ cup water, and add a pinch of salt. Cover and cook over high heat for 3–5 minutes, until the shells have opened. Remove the pan from the heat and lift out the clams with a slotted spoon. Discard any clams that remain shut. Strain the cooking liquid into a bowl through a cheesecloth-lined strainer and reserve. Remove the clams from their shells and add them to the bowl. Heat the oil in a small skillet. Add the onion and cook, stirring occasionally, for 3 minutes, then add the tomato, and cook, stirring occasionally, for 8 minutes more. Transfer the onion and tomato mixture to a larger pan and set over low heat. Add the potatoes and stir in the flour. Pound the garlic in a mortar with a pinch of salt, and the parsley, and saffron, or process in a mini-food processor. Mix in 2–3 tablespoons of the reserved cooking liquid from the clams, then pour into the pan with the potato. Add the clams and their cooking liquid and pour in enough water to generously cover the potatoes. Bring to a boil, then lower the heat, and cook for about 20–30 minutes, until the potato is tender. Serve immediately in a soup tureen.

248

Potatoes with green bell peppers

PATATAS GUISADAS CON PIMIENTOS VERDES

- 6 tablespoons olive oil
- 1 onion, finely chopped
- 2–3 green bell peppers,
  seeded and diced
- 2 ripe tomatoes,
  peeled, seeded, and chopped
- 3¼ pounds potatoes,
  cut into pieces
- 1 tablespoon all-purpose flour
- 1 clove garlic
- 1 sprig fresh parsley
- pinch of saffron threads
- salt

Serves 4–6

Heat the oil in a small skillet. Add the onion and cook, stirring occasionally, for 3 minutes, then add the bell pepper and tomato, and cook, stirring occasionally, for 8 minutes more. Transfer the mixture to a larger pan and set over low heat. Add the potatoes and stir in the flour. Pound the garlic in a mortar with a pinch of salt, and the parsley, and saffron, or process in a mini-food processor. Mix in 2–3 tablespoons water, then pour into the pan with the potato. Pour in enough water to generously cover the potatoes. Bring to a boil, then lower the heat, and cook for about 20–30 minutes, until the potato is tender. Serve immediately in a soup tureen.

Widow's potatoes

PATATAS GUISADAS VIUDAS

- **6 tablespoons olive oil**
- **1 large onion, finely chopped**
- **3¼ pounds red-skinned potatoes, cut into medium-size pieces**
- **1 teaspoon paprika**
- **1 chicken bouillon cube**
- **pinch of saffron threads**
- **1 tablespoon chopped fresh parsley**
- **salt**

Serves 6

Heat the oil in a pan. Add the onion and cook over medium heat, stirring occasionally, for 4–6 minutes, until beginning to brown. Add the potato and cook, stirring frequently, for 5 minutes, then stir in the paprika. Cook, stirring constantly, for 2 minutes more, then pour in water to cover—about 4 cups—crumble in the bouillon cube, and sea-son lightly with salt. Crush the saffron in a mortar, or small bowl, and stir in 2–3 tablespoons water, then pour into the pan with the potato, and mix well. Cook over medium heat for about 20–30 minutes, until the potato is tender. Sprinkle with the parsley, stir, and serve immediately in a soup tureen.

250

Gratin potatoes with onions and cream
PATATAS GRATINADAS CON CEBOLLA Y NATA

- 2 ½ pounds potatoes, unpeeled
- 3 tablespoons olive oil
- 3 large onions, sliced
- butter, for greasing
- ¾ cup grated cheese,
  such as Cheddar or gruyere
- 1 cup light cream
- salt

Serves 6

Put the potatoes into a large pan of cold water and add 1 teaspoon salt. Make sure the water covers them completely. Bring to a boil, lower the heat and cook for 20–30 minutes until tender. Drain, peel, and slice thinly. Heat the oil in a pan. Add the onion and cook over low heat, stirring occasionally, for about 10 minutes, until beginning to brown. Remove from the heat and set aside. Preheat the oven to 350°F. Grease a deep ovenproof baking dish with butter and lay half the potato slices in it. Cover with half the onion, sprinkle with half the cheese and season lightly with salt. Add the remaining potatoes and top with the remaining onion. Season lightly and pour the cream over the top of the layers, shaking the dish gently to make sure the cream flows down between the potato slices. Sprinkle the remaining cheese on top. Bake for about 20 minutes, then increase the oven temperature to broil and put the dish under the broiler for a few minutes, until the top is golden brown. Serve immediately, straight from the dish.

251

Potatoes with tomato sauce and béchamel
PATATAS CON SALSA DE TOMATE Y BECHAMEL

- sunflower oil, for deep-frying
- 3 ¼ pounds potatoes, sliced
- 1 cup Classic Tomato Sauce
  (see recipe 73)
- 2 tablespoons butter
  or margarine
- 2 tablespoons olive oil
- 1 heaping tablespoon
  all-purpose flour
- scant 2 cups milk
- 1 ½ tablespoons butter
- salt

Serves 6

Heat the sunflower oil in a deep-fryer or deep saucepan to 350–375°F or until a cube of day-old bread browns in 30 seconds. Add the potato slices, in batches, and cook until golden brown. Remove with a slotted spoon and drain on paper towels. Place half the potato slices in a deep, ovenproof baking dish and pour in half the tomato sauce to cover and sprinkle with salt. Add the remaining potato and cover them with the rest of the tomato sauce. Preheat the oven to 400°F. Make the béchamel sauce: Melt the butter or margarine with the oil in a pan. Stir in the flour and cook, stirring constantly, for 2–3 minutes, then remove the pan from the heat. Gradually stir in the milk, a little at a time. Return the pan to the heat and cook, stirring constantly, for 8–10 minutes. Pour the sauce into the baking dish with the potatoes. Dot the butter on top and bake for about 15 minutes. Serve immediately, straight from the dish.

252 Fried potato stew

PATATAS REHOGADAS Y GUISADAS

- sunflower oil, for deep-frying
- 3¼ pounds potatoes,
  thinly sliced
- 2 cloves garlic
- 1 sprig fresh parsley
- ½ teaspoon paprika
- 1 chicken bouillon cube
- ¾ cup white wine
- salt

Serves 6

Heat the oil in a deep-fryer or deep saucepan to 350–375°F or until a cube of day-old bread browns in 30 seconds. Add the potato, in batches, and cook until golden brown. Remove with a slotted spoon and drain on paper towels. Put the potato slices into a pan. Crush the garlic with a pinch of salt in a mortar, or process in a mini-food processor, then add the parsley and paprika. Stir in 2 tablespoons water, add the mixture to the potatoes and mix well with a wooden spoon. Add 5 cups water, the bouillon cube, and wine and season to taste with salt. Bring to a boil, then lower the heat, and cook for 10–15 minutes. Serve immediately, in a warm deep serving dish.

253 Coated potato casserole

PATATAS REBOZADAS Y GUISADAS

- 1¼ cups all-purpose flour
- 4 eggs
- 3¼ pounds potatoes,
  cut into ¼-inch thick slices
- sunflower oil, for deep-frying
- 1 clove garlic
- pinch of saffron threads
- 1 small onion, finely chopped
- 1 tablespoon chopped
  fresh parsley
- salt

Serves 4–6

Set aside 1 tablespoon of the flour and pour the remainder into a shallow dish. Beat the eggs in another shallow dish. Season the potato slices with salt and dip them first in the flour and then in the beaten egg. Heat the oil in a deep-fryer or deep saucepan to 350–375°F or until a cube of day-old bread browns in 30 seconds. Add the slices of potato, four at a time, and cook until golden brown. Remove with a slotted spoon and drain on paper towels. When all the slices are cooked, put them into an ovenproof casserole that can be used on the stove, arranging them in loosely packed layers. Crush the garlic in a mortar with a little salt and the saffron, or process in a mini-food processor. Stir in 2 tablespoons water. Transfer 3 tablespoons of the oil to a pan. Add the onion and cook over low heat, stirring occasionally, for 8–10 minutes, until golden brown. Stir in the reserved flour and cook, stirring constantly, for 2–3 minutes, then add the contents of the mortar or processor and 4 cups water. Season to taste with salt. Pour the mixture through a large colander over the potatoes. Sprinkle the parsley over the top and simmer gently for 30 minutes. Preheat the oven to 350°F. Transfer the casserole to the oven and bake for 10 minutes. Serve immediately, straight from the casserole.

254

Potatoes with milk and eggs
PATATAS CON LECHE Y HUEVOS

- **sunflower oil, for deep-frying**
- **2½ pounds potatoes, sliced**
- **3 eggs**
- **scant 1 cup grated gruyere cheese**
- **3 cups milk**
- **salt**

Serves 6

Heat the oil in a deep-fryer or deep saucepan to 300–325°F or until a cube of day-old bread browns in 45 seconds. Season the potato slices with salt and cook, in batches, until just beginning to color. Remove with a slotted spoon and drain on paper towels. Put the potato slices into a deep ovenproof baking dish. Preheat the oven to 350°F. Beat the eggs with a pinch of salt in a bowl. Stir in ¾ cup of the gruyere, then gradually whisk in the milk, a little at a time. Pour the mixture over the potatoes and mix gently with a fork. Sprinkle the remaining gruyere over the top. Bake for 20 minutes, stirring occasionally with a fork. If the potatoes seem to be drying out during the cooking time, add a little more milk to the baking dish. Increase the oven temperature to broil and brown the top under the broiler for about 10 minutes.Serve immediately.

255

Potatoes with tomato, onion, and aromatic herbs
PATATAS CON TOMATES, CEBOLLAS Y HIERBAS AROMÁTICAS, AL HORNO

- **3¼ pounds potatoes, unpeeled**
- **¾ cup olive oil**
- **1 large onion, sliced and pushed out into rings**
- **4 large, ripe tomatoes, sliced**
- **½ teaspoon chopped fresh aromatic herbs (parsley, thyme or oregano) or**
- **2 sprigs fresh thyme**
- **¾ cup grated gruyere cheese**
- **salt**

Serves 6

Put the potatoes into a large pan of cold water and add 1 teaspoon salt. Make sure that the water covers them completely. Bring to a boil, then lower the heat, and cook for about 20–30 minutes, until tender, but not falling apart. Drain well, peel and cut into ½-inch thick slices. Preheat the oven to 350°F. Pour a thin layer of oil into an ovenproof baking dish. Put half the potato slices into the dish and top with half the onion rings. Next, make a layer with half the tomato slices, then season lightly with salt, and add half the aromatic herbs or one of the thyme sprigs. Sprinkle with half the gruyere. Repeat the layers of potato, onion, tomato, and herbs. Pour the remaining oil over the dish and sprinkle with the rest of the gruyere. Bake for about 45 minutes, until the tomato slices have softened and browned. Serve the potatoes immediately, straight from the dish.

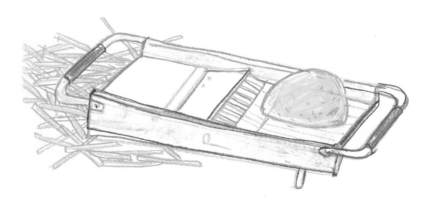

Potatoes baked in tomato sauce

PATATAS AL HORNO CON SALSA DE TOMATE

- 1 quantity Classic Tomato Sauce
  (see recipe 73)
- 2¼ cups sunflower oil
- 3¼ pounds potatoes,
  thinly sliced
- scant 1 cup diced bacon
- ½ cup grated cheese,
  such as Cheddar or gruyere
- 2 tablespoons (¼ stick) butter
- salt

Serves 6

Process the tomato sauce to a purée in a food processor or blender and set aside. Heat the oil in a skillet. Add the potato slices, in batches, and cook until light golden brown. Remove with a slotted spoon and drain on paper towels. Add the bacon to the pan and cook until lightly browned, then drain well, and set aside. Preheat the oven to 325°F. Layer the potato slices, bacon, and tomato sauce in a deep ovenproof baking dish, seasoning each layer with salt. Sprinkle the cheese on top and dot with the butter. Bake for about 1 hour, until golden and bubbling. Serve immediately, straight from the dish.

Potatoes served with a spicy sauce

PATATAS BRAVAS

- 12 small potatoes, unpeeled
- 2 tablespoons olive oil
- 1 tablespoon white-wine vinegar
- pinch of hot paprika
- 1 clove garlic, finely chopped
- 1 teaspoon chili powder or
  Worcestershire sauce
- salt

Serves 4

Bring a large pan of salted water to a boil. Add the potatoes and cook for 20–25 minutes, until tender but not falling apart. Drain and let cool, then peel, and slice or dice. Transfer to a plate or tray. Combine the oil, vinegar, paprika, garlic, and the chili powder or Worcestershire sauce in a bowl. Pour the mixture over the potatoes and serve them as an appetizer.

Potatoes stuffed with ham

PATATAS RELLENAS DE JAMÓN

- 6 large potatoes,
  about 7 ounces each, unpeeled
- 6 tablespoons (¾ stick) butter
- scant 1 cup finely chopped
  Serrano ham or prosciutto
- salt

Serves 6

Preheat the oven to 350°F. Wash and dry the potatoes. Bake for 1–1½ hours, until soft. Remove the potatoes from the oven and cut in half widthwise. Do not switch off the oven. Using a teaspoon, scoop out the flesh into a bowl without piercing the skins. Lightly season each skin with salt and divide half the butter among them. Mash the potato flesh with a fork, lightly season with salt, and mix in the ham. Fill the skins with the mixture and place in a single, fairly tight-fitting layer in an ovenproof baking dish. Dot the remaining butter over them and bake for 10 minutes more. Serve immediately.

259

Potatoes with bell peppers

PATATAS CON PIMIENTOS

- 1 large red bell pepper
- 6 large potatoes,
  about 7oz each, unpeeled
- scant 2 cups sunflower oil
- 4 large green bell peppers,
  seeded and cut into
  large squares
- 2 hard-cooked eggs,
  coarsely chopped
- salt

Serves 6

Preheat the oven to 350°F. Put the red bell pepper on a baking sheet and roast, turning occasionally, for 10–20 minutes, until the skin is blistered and charred. Remove from the oven, place in a bowl, and cover with a dishtowel or paper towels. When the bell pepper is cool enough to handle, peel off the skin, remove the stalk and seeds, and cut the flesh into strips. Season with salt and set aside. Put the potatoes into a large pan of cold water and add 1 teaspoon salt. Make sure the water covers them completely. Bring to a boil, then lower the heat, and cook for 20–30 minutes, until tender but not falling apart. Drain well. Meanwhile, heat the oil in a deep skillet. Add the green bell pepper and some salt, cover, and cook over medium heat for 15–20 minutes, until tender. Remove with a slotted spoon and drain. Preheat the oven to 400°F. Transfer 3 tablespoons of the oil from the skillet to an ovenproof baking dish. Peel the potatoes, cut a segment out of the top and cut a slice off the base of each one so that they will stand up. Put them in a single layer in the dish. Season lightly with salt and spoon a little of the oil from the skillet onto each one. Place a little hard-cooked egg and a few strips of red bell pepper in the cavity in the top of each potato. Put the green bell peppers around the edge of the dish and spoon a little more of the oil from the skillet over the potatoes. Bake for about 10 minutes, until heated through, then serve.

260

Twice cooked potatoes

PATATAS COCIDAS Y REHOGADAS

- 1 pound 10 ounces red-skinned
  or new potatoes, unpeeled
- 1 tablespoon milk
- 2 ounces of lard or ¼ cup
  (½ stick) butter
- 4 tablespoons sunflower oil
- 1 tablespoon chopped
  fresh parsley
- salt

Serves 4

Put the potatoes into a large pan of cold water and add the milk and 1 teaspoon salt. Make sure that the liquid covers them completely. Bring to a boil, then lower the heat to medium, and cook for 20–30 minutes, until tender but not falling apart. Drain well, then peel, and cut into pieces. Melt the lard or butter with the oil in a skillet over high heat. Add the potato and cook, shaking the pan frequently, until all the pieces of potato are golden brown. Remove with a slotted spoon, season to taste with salt, sprinkle with the parsley, and serve immediately.

Note: These potatoes can be served with all kinds of dishes.

Potatoes with chorizo and bacon
PATATAS CON CHORIZO Y BACON

- **4 tablespoons lard or**
  3 tablespoons butter
- **5 tablespoons sunflower oil**
- **2 ounces chorizo sausage,**
  peeled and thinly sliced
- **3½ ounces thickly sliced bacon,**
  cut into ½-inch wide strips
- **3¼ pounds small potatoes,**
  preferably new potatoes
- **1 tablespoon chopped**
  fresh parsley
- **1 clove garlic, finely chopped**
- **salt**

Serves 4

Melt the lard or butter with the oil in a pan or large skillet. (It needs to be big enough to hold the potatoes in a single layer.) Add the chorizo and bacon and cook over medium heat, stirring constantly, for a few minutes, then add the potatoes. Season with salt and cook over low heat, shaking the pan occasionally, for 45–60 minutes, until the potatoes are evenly browned. Just before serving, sprinkle with the parsley and garlic and stir for a few minutes more. Transfer to a warm serving dish and serve immediately.

Note: Some types of chorizo become hard with prolonged cooking. To prevent this, cook the slices with the bacon, then remove and set aside. About 10 minutes before serving, return the slices of chorizo to the pan.

Potatoes with sausages
PATATAS CON SALCHICHAS

- **12 small or new potatoes,**
  about 2 ounces each
- **12 small sausages**
- **4 tablespoons olive oil**
- **1 tablespoon chopped**
  fresh parsley
- **2 cloves garlic, finely chopped**
- **salt**

Makes 12

Preheat the oven to 400°F. Using an apple corer or a small sharp knife, make a hole through the center of each potato. Place a sausage in each one. Reserve the cut-out pieces of potato. Put the oil into a roasting pan and add the sausage-filled potatoes. Put the reserved potato pieces in the pan, lightly season with salt, and sprinkle with half the parsley and half the garlic. Roast for 15 minutes, then turn the potatoes over, season with salt, sprinkle with the remaining parsley and remaining garlic, and baste with the oil. Return the pan to the oven and roast, turning and basting three or four more times, for about 30 minutes. Serve immediately in a warm serving dish.

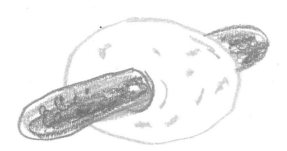

263

Roasted potatoes with Roquefort

PATATAS ASADAS CON ROQUEFORT

• 9 large potatoes, about
  3½ ounces each, unpeeled
• 2 tablespoons (¼ stick) butter
• 2 ounces Roquefort cheese
• 1 egg, beaten
• pinch of fresh grated nutmeg
• scant 2 cups hot milk
• salt

Serves 4

Preheat the oven to 350°F. Wash and dry the potatoes, then bake for about 1 hour, until tender. Remove from the oven, cut in half lengthwise, and scoop out the flesh into a bowl using a teaspoon, without piercing the skins. Put the flesh in a food processor or blender and process briefly. Transfer to a bowl, beat in the butter, Roquefort, egg, and nutmeg, and season with salt. Finally, stir in enough hot milk to make a thick mixture. Fill the potato skins with the mixture. Increase the oven temperature to broil and put the shells under the broiler and cook for about 15 minutes, until golden brown. Serve immediately.

Note: If you like, separate the egg, then add the yolk to the potato mixture with the other ingredients. Whisk the egg white in a clean, dry bowl until it forms soft peaks and then fold it in.

264

American baked potatoes

PATATAS ASADAS A LA AMERICANA

• 4 large potatoes, unpeeled
• 1 clove garlic
• 2 tablespoons olive oil

Serves 4

Preheat the oven to 325°F. Wash and dry the potatoes. Rub the garlic over the outside of each potato, then rub with the oil. Do this with your fingers as if giving the potatoes a massage. Lightly prick the skins with a fork three or four times in different places. Wrap each potato in aluminum foil and bake for 10 minutes. Increase the oven temperature to 425°F and bake for 50 minutes more. Serve the potatoes immediately, with their foil half opened just at the point where the two ends of foil meets.

Notes: This recipe requires top-quality potatoes. Allow 1 large potato per serving and serve as an accompaniment to broiled steak or chops. You can cut open each potato with a knife and insert a pat of butter just before serving.

Potato patty to accompany cold meats and meat dishes

TORTA DE PATATAS PARA ACOMPAÑAR FIAMBRES Y CARNES

- 1 pound 10 ounces potatoes, unpeeled
- 3–4 tablespoons olive oil
- ¼ cup (½ stick) butter or ⅓ cup lard
- onion and bacon (optional – see Note), finely chopped
- salt

Serves 4

Put the potatoes into a large pan of cold water and add 1 teaspoon salt. Make sure that the water covers them completely. Bring to a boil, then lower the heat to medium, and cook for 20–30 minutes, until tender but not falling apart. Drain well and let cool. (You can prepare the potatoes to this stage the day before they are required). Peel the potatoes and push them through a ricer or cut them into thin julienne strips with a mandoline. Heat the oil in a skillet. Add the potato, shape it into a patty, without flattening too much, and cook for about 10 minutes, until the underside is lightly browned. Turn the patty over by inverting onto a plate and then sliding it back into the pan. Cook for about 10 minutes, until the second side is lightly browned. Invert the patty onto the pan lid or plate again and drain the oil from the pan. Melt half the butter or lard in the skillet, add the potato patty, and cook for about 5 minutes, then turn it, and cook for 5 minutes more, until browned and crusty. Transfer to a warm serving dish and cut into triangles. It can be served with all kinds of dishes.

Note: If you want to add the onion, cook it in the skillet over low heat, stirring occasionally, for 5 minutes before adding the potato. If you want to add the bacon, cook it in the skillet for a few minutes before adding the potato. Both onion and bacon provide additional flavor.

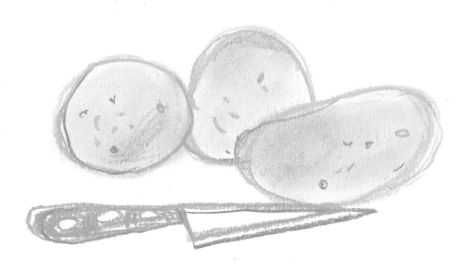

266

Potato salad with tuna and hard-cooked egg
PATATAS EN ENSALADILLA CON ATÚN Y HUEVO DURO

- 2½ pounds potatoes, unpeeled
- 2 tablespoons milk
- 8 ounces canned tuna in oil, drained and broken into chunks
- 3 hard-cooked eggs, sliced
- 3 tablespoons white-wine vinegar
- 6 tablespoons sunflower oil
- 1 scallion, finely chopped
- 1 teaspoon chopped fresh parsley
- salt

Serves 6

Put the potatoes into a large pan of cold water and add the milk and a generous pinch of salt. Make sure that the liquid covers them completely. Bring to a boil, then lower the heat to medium, and cook for 20–30 minutes, until tender but not falling apart. Drain well, peel, and cut into slices. Put the slices into a bowl, alternating with the tuna and hard-cooked eggs. Whisk the vinegar with a little salt using a fork, then pour over the potatoes. Pour the oil over the salad and add the scallion and parsley. Toss lightly to avoid breaking up the potatoes or eggs and let stand until almost cold before serving.

267

Potato and tuna salad
ENSALADA DE PATATAS CON ATÚN

- 8 ounces canned tuna in oil, drained
- juice of 1 lemon
- 4 large potatoes
- 2 tablespoons white-wine vinegar
- 4 tablespoons olive oil
- 4–6 lettuce leaves
- 12 olives
- 2 hard-cooked eggs, cut into quarters
- salt

Serves 4

Coarsely flake the tuna into a bowl and pour the lemon juice over it. Cook the potatoes as described on page 196. Drain, peel, and slice, then put the slices in another bowl. Whisk the vinegar with a pinch of salt, then whisk in the oil with a fork. Pour half the vinaigrette over the potatoes.Make a bed of lettuce leaves in a salad bowl. Mix the tuna with the remaining potato and spoon into the salad bowl. Add the olives, pour the remaining vinaigrette over the salad, and garnish with the hard-cooked eggs.

Potatoes with mayonnaise, tomatoes, and anchovies

PATATAS CON MAYONESA, TOMATES Y ANCHOAS

- 1 quantity Classic Mayonnaise
  (see recipe 105)
- 2¼ pounds potatoes, unpeeled
- 2 tablespoons capers, rinsed,
  drained and chopped
- 2 tablespoons milk
- 1 cucumber,
  peeled and thinly sliced
- 3 firm tomatoes, sliced
- 1 canned or bottled red bell
  pepper, drained and sliced
- 1 hard-cooked egg, sliced
- 2 ounces canned anchovies
  in oil, drained
- scant 1 cup pitted olives
- salt

Serves 6

Divide the mayonnaise equally between two bowls and stir the capers into one bowl, then set both bowls aside in the refrigerator. Put the potatoes into a large pan of cold water and add the milk and 1 teaspoon salt. Make sure that the liquid covers them completely. Bring to a boil, then lower the heat to medium, and cook for about 20–30 minutes, until tender but not falling apart. Drain well and let cool slightly, then peel, and slice. Meanwhile, spread out the cucumber slices on a plate, sprinkle with a little salt, and let stand until they have released some of their water. Drain and pat dry with paper towels. Combine the caper mayonnaise, potatoes, and cucumber in a bowl, then spoon the mixture onto a serving dish, mounding it up into a dome. Cover with the remaining mayonnaise and garnish with the tomatoes, red bell pepper, hard-cooked egg, anchovies, and olives. Chill in the refrigerator for at least 1 hour before serving.

Pasta

How to cook

Pasta is one of the most versatile ingredients in any mediterranean cook's kitchen. However, it needs careful cooking to prevent its becoming soggy or remaining too hard. The cooking time depends on the brand of pasta and personal taste. Italians prefer their pasta al dente—only just tender rather than well done, for example.

Macaroni: Allow 2–2 ½ ounces dried pasta per person. Bring a large pan of salted water to a boil, add the macaroni, and cook uncovered. When the water comes back to a boil, lower the heat slightly but make sure the water is still boiling and cook for 10–12 minutes. Drain the macaroni in a large colander and refresh under cold running water. The pasta is now ready to use.

Tagliatelle and spaghetti: These are cooked in the same way as macaroni but are not refreshed under running water. It is important, therefore, to calculate exactly when you are going to serve the pasta so it is not left standing in hot water for longer than necessary as this will make it slimy. Serve tagliatelle and spaghetti on warm plates.

Cannelloni: Pasta tubes that do not need precooking are now widely available. Just leave them to soak in cold water for 1 hour to allow the pasta to soften or follow the instructions on the package. If using cannelloni that requires precooking, treat it in the same way as macaroni but do not refresh under running water. When it is tender, remove it from the water very carefully to avoid breaking it and drain on a clean dishtowel until required.

Note: Some people add a teaspoon of sunflower or olive oil to the cooking water to prevent the pasta sticking.

269

Pasta dough

PASTA DE LOS ESPAGUETIS

- 4½ cups all-purpose flour, plus extra for dusting
- 3 eggs
- salt

Serves 6

Put half the flour into a bowl and make a well in the center. Add the eggs, a little water, and a pinch of salt. Mix with your hands and knead the dough well, adding the rest of the flour a little at a time. Shape it into a ball, then throw it onto a surface quite hard and from quite high, eight or ten times. Roll out the dough on a lightly floured surface and let dry for about 30 minutes. Roll it again, without pressing down, and cut into strips ¼ inch wide, or wider if preferred. Dangle the pasta over the edge or your work suface to stretch the strips, then cook them the same way as dried pasta, but for a much shorter time. The pasta keeps for up to a week as long as it has dried completely before it is stored.

270

Macaroni with chorizo and tomato

MACARRONES CON CHORIZO Y TOMATE

- 12 ounces (about ¾ box) macaroni
- 3 tablespoons olive oil
- 1 onion, chopped
- 2¼ pounds ripe tomatoes, seeded and chopped
- 1 teaspoon sugar
- scant 1 cup grated gruyere or Parmesan cheese
- 3½ ounces chorizo sausage, skinned and chopped
- 2 tablespoons (¼ stick) butter
- salt

Serves 6

Cook the macaroni as described on page 221, refresh under cold running water, drain and set aside. Make a tomato sauce with the oil, onion, tomatoes, and sugar as described in recipe 73. Preheat the oven to 350°F. Reserve 2–3 tablespoons of the tomato sauce and mix the remainder with the macaroni. Stir in half the cheese and pour the mixture into a deep ovenproof baking dish. Sprinkle the chorizo over the pasta and push the pieces down into the dish to prevent them drying out during cooking. Pour the reserved tomato sauce over the top and sprinkle with the remaining cheese. Dot the top with the butter and bake for 15–30 minutes, until golden brown and bubbling. Serve immediately.

American macaroni

MACARRONES A LA AMERICANA

- **12 ounces (about ¾ box) macaroni**
- **12 fl oz canned condensed cream of mushroom soup**
- **scant 2 cups milk**
- **1 teaspoon curry powder**
- **½ cup grated gruyere or Parmesan cheese**
- **2 tablespoons (¼ stick) butter**
- **salt**

Serves 4

Preheat the oven to 350°F. Cook the macaroni as described on page 221, refresh under cold running water, drain and set aside. Pour the soup and milk into a pan and heat gently. Add the macaroni and sprinkle in the curry powder. Mix well and pour into a deep ovenproof baking dish. Sprinkle with the cheese and dot with the butter. Bake for about 15–20 minutes until golden brown and bubbling. Serve immediately.

272

Macaroni with mayonnaise and tuna
MACARRONES Y CODITOS CON MAYONESA Y ATÚN

- 2 ¾ cups macaroni
- 1 quantity Thick Mayonnaise
  (see recipe 106)
- 3 ½ ounces canned tuna in oil
  or water, drained
- 1 pound 2 ounces firm tomatoes
- 6 stuffed olives
- 1 hard-cooked egg,
  finely chopped
- salt

Serves 4

Cook the macaroni as described on page 221. Refresh under cold running water, then drain. Combine the cold macaroni, half the mayonnaise, and the tuna in a bowl and arrange the mixture in the center of a serving dish. Garnish the edge of the dish with tomato slices topped with a little of the remaining mayonnaise and the olives. Sprinkle the hard-cooked egg over the pasta. Chill in the refrigerator for 30 minutes before serving.

273

Macaroni with mayonnaise and gruyere
MACARRONES Y CODITOS CON MAYONESA Y QUESO

- 12 ounces (about ¾ box)
  macaroni
- 1 quantity Thick Mayonnaise
  (see recipe 106)
- 2 tablespoons (¼ stick) butter
- ¾ cup grated gruyere cheese

Serves 4

Cook the macaroni as described on page 221. Refresh under cold running water, then drain. Preheat the broiler. Put the macaroni, butter, and gruyere into a saucepan and heat gently, stirring constantly. Remove the pan from the heat and add about one-third of the mayonnaise, mix well, and pour the mixture into an overnproof baking dish. Pour the remaining mayonnaise over the top and cook under the broiler until the mayonnaise has set. Serve immediately straight from the dish.

Note: Sometimes it is necessary to tilt the dish and spoon off any oil that the mayonnaise has released during cooking.

Macaroni with spinach

MACARRONES CON ESPINACAS

- 3 ¼ pounds spinach,
  coarse stalks removed
- 12 ounces (about ¾ box)
  macaroni
- 6 tablespoons (¾ stick) butter
- 1 tablespoon sunflower oil
- 1 tablespoon all-purpose flour
- 1 cup milk
- scant ¾ cup grated gruyere
  or Parmesan cheese
- salt

Serves 4

Add the spinach to a large pan of boiling salted water. Bring back to a boil, lower the heat, and cook for about 10 minutes. Drain well, pressing down with the back of a spoon to squeeze out all the water. Coarsely chop the leaves. Cook the macaroni as described on page 221. Refresh under cold running water, then drain and set aside. Meanwhile, make a béchamel sauce. Melt 2 tablespoons of the butter with the oil in a pan. Stir in the flour and cook, stirring constantly, for 2–3 minutes, but do not let the flour brown. Gradually stir in the milk, a little at a time, and season with salt. Cook over low heat, stirring constantly, for 5 minutes. Preheat the oven to 350°F.Melt 3 table-spoons of the remaining butter in another pan, add the spinach, and toss well to coat. Spoon the spinach into a deep ovenproof baking dish, spreading it out evenly. Mix the macaroni with half the cheese, then pour the mixture over the spinach. Pour the béchamel sauce on top, sprinkle with the remaining cheese, and dot with the rest of the butter. Bake for about 15–20 minutes, until golden brown and bubbling. Serve immediately.

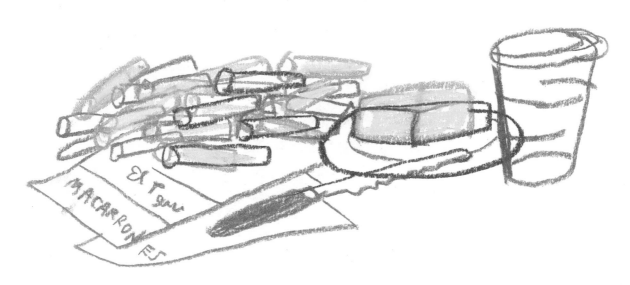

Macaroni with curried mussels

MACARRONES CON MEJILLONES AL CURRY

- 2¼ pounds mussels
- 5 tablespoons white wine
- 1 stalk celery, chopped (optional)
- 12 ounces (about ¾ box) macaroni
- 2 tablespoons (¼ stick) butter
- 2 tablespoons sunflower oil
- 1 large shallot or 1 small onion, very finely chopped
- 1 teaspoon curry powder
- 1½ tablespoons all-purpose flour
- 2¼ cups milk
- scant 1 cup grated cheese, such as Cheddar or gruyere
- 1 teaspoon finely chopped fresh parsley
- salt

Serves 4

If your mussels have not been pre-scrubbed, scrape their shells with the blade of a knife and remove the "beards," then scrub under cold running water. Discard any mussels with broken shells or any that do not shut immediately when sharply tapped. Put them into a large pan with the wine, celery, if using, and a pinch of salt. Cover and cook over medium heat, shaking the pan occasionally, for 4–5 minutes, until the shells have opened. Remove the mussels with a slotted spoon and reserve the cooking liquid. Discard any mussels that remain closed. Remove the mussels from their shells and if they are very big, cut them into two or three pieces with kitchen scissors. Strain the reserved cooking liquid into a bowl through a cheese-cloth-lined strainer. Cook the macaroni as described on page 221. Meanwhile, make the sauce. Melt half the butter with the oil in a skillet. Add the shallot or onion and cook over low heat, stirring occasionally, for about 5 minutes, until softened but not brown. Stir in the curry powder and flour and cook, stirring constantly, for 2 minutes, then gradually stir in the milk and the reserved cooking liquid. Cook, stirring constantly, for 5–10 minutes, until thickened. Preheat the broiler. Drain the macaroni and put it into an ovenproof baking dish. Add the mussels and stir in half the cheese and the parsley. Pour the sauce over the top, sprinkle with the remaining cheese and dot with the rest of the butter. Cook under the broiler for 10–15 minutes, until golden brown and bubbling. Serve immediately.

276

Macaroni with canned tuna
MACARRONES CON ATÚN DE LATA

- 12 ounces (about ¾ box) macaroni
- 4 tablespoons sunflower oil
- 1 onion, finely chopped
- 1 clove garlic, finely chopped
- 14 ounces ripe tomatoes, peeled, seeded, and chopped
- 5 tablespoons white wine
- ½ teaspoon sugar
- pinch of aromatic herbs
- 2 tablespoons (¼ stick) butter
- ½ cup grated gruyere cheese
- 5 ounces canned tuna, drained and flaked
- salt

Serves 4–5

Cook the macaroni as described on page 221. Refresh under cold running water, drain and set aside. Heat the oil in a pan. Add the onion and garlic and cook over low heat, stirring occasionally, for about 5 minutes, until softened and translucent. Add the tomato and cook, stirring and breaking it up with the side of the spoon, for a few minutes, then add the wine, sugar, herbs, and a pinch of salt. Cook, stirring occasionally, for 15 minutes, then add the macaroni, butter, gruyere, and tuna. Mix well and serve hot.

277

Macaroni with bacon and peas
CODITOS CON BACON Y GUISANTES

- 2¾ cups elbow macaroni
- 2 tablespoons sunflower oil
- 1 large onion, finely chopped
- 2¼ pounds ripe tomatoes, seeded and coarsely chopped
- 1 teaspoon sugar
- 9 ounces canned peas, drained
- ¾ cup grated gruyere cheese
- 12 thin smoked bacon slices
- salt

Serves 4–5

Cook the macaroni as described on page 221. Refresh under cold running water, drain and set aside. Heat the oil in a skillet. Add the onion and cook over low heat, stirring occasionally, for about 8 minutes, until beginning to brown. Add the tomato and cook, stirring occasionally and breaking it up with the side of the spoon, for about 10 minutes. Let cool slightly, then transfer the mixture to a food processor or blender and process to a purée. Add the sugar and season to taste with salt. Preheat the oven to 350°F. Combine the macaroni, tomato sauce, peas, and all but 2 tablespoons of the gruyere in an ovenproof baking dish. Sprinkle the remaining gruyere on top and bake for a few minutes, until the cheese has melted. Meanwhile, roll up the bacon slices, and secure with wooden toothpicks. Cook in a heavy or non-stick skillet, turning frequently, for 5–10 minutes, until lightly browned and cooked through. Remove and discard the toothpicks, place the bacon rolls on top of the pasta, and serve immediately.

278

Tagliatelle with shrimp and pistachio nuts

CINTAS CON GAMBAS Y PISTACHOS

- 7 ounces raw shrimp, shells and heads attached, if available
- 2 zucchini
- 5 tablespoons olive oil
- 2 shallots, finely chopped
- ½ cup shelled pistachio nuts
- pinch of dried oregano
- 14 ounces fresh tagliatelle
- 1 tablespoon chopped fresh basil
- salt and pepper

Serves 4

Peel the shrimp, reserving the shells and heads, if attached. Put the heads and shells into a pan, pour in 8 ¾ cups water, and bring to a boil. Lower the heat and simmer for 15 minutes. Meanwhile, slice the zucchini lengthwise into thin strips with a vegetable peeler. Season with salt and pepper. Heat half the oil in a skillet. Add the shallots and cook over low heat, stirring occasionally, for 5 minutes, until softened and translucent. Add the zucchini and cook, stirring occasionally, for 5 minutes. Add the shrimp, pistachio nuts, and oregano and cook, stirring occasionally, for 3–5 minutes, until the shrimp are opaque. Strain the shrimp shell stock into a clean pan, add a pinch of salt, and bring to a boil. Add the tagliatelle and cook for 3–4 minutes, until tender, but still firm to the bite. Drain, add to the skillet, and toss with the sauce. Add the remaining oil and the basil and toss lightly again. Serve immediately.

279

Pasta with bell peppers and ham

PASTA CON PIMIENTOS Y JAMÓN

- 2 large red bell peppers
- 7 ounces Serrano ham or prosciutto, thinly sliced
- 3 tablespoons olive oil
- 3 red onions, sliced
- 2 tablespoons capers, rinsed and drained
- 4 tablespoons chopped fresh basil
- 14 ounces tagliatelle
- salt and pepper

Serves 4

Preheat the oven to 400°F or preheat the broiler. Put the bell peppers on a baking sheet and place in the oven or under the broiler and cook, turning frequently, for about 25 minutes, until charred and blistered. Transfer to a cutting board, cover with a dishtowel, and let cool, then peel off the skins. Halve lengthwise, remove and discard the seeds, and cut the flesh into thick strips. Cut the ham into strips. Heat the oil in a skillet. Add the onion and cook over low heat, stirring occasionally, for about 5 minutes, until softened and translucent. Remove the pan from the heat, stir in the pepper strips, ham, capers, and basil, season with salt and pepper, and pour into a bowl. Bring a large pan of salted water to a boil. Add the tagliatelle, bring back to a boil, and cook for 8–10 minutes, until tender but still firm to the bite. Drain well and toss with the mixture in the bowl. Serve warm or cold.

Note: For a contrast of textures, cook the ham in a skillet until crisp.

Seafood noodles

FIDEOS CON MARISCOS (FIDEUÁ)

- 11 ounces raw shrimp, shells on and heads attached, if available
- 14 ounces monkfish
- ¾ cup olive oil
- 6 small langoustines
- 4 tomatoes, peeled, seeded, and diced
- 2 cloves garlic, crushed
- 1 teaspoon paprika
- pinch of saffron powder
- 1 pound 2 ounces very fine noodles
- salt

Serves 6

Peel the shrimp, reserving the shells and heads, if attached. Set the shrimp aside. Cut along either side of the monkfish bone, set the fillets aside, and reserve the bone. Pour 7 ½ cups water into a pan, add a pinch of salt, the shrimp heads and shells, and the monkfish bone, and bring to a boil. Lower the heat and simmer for 20 minutes. Meanwhile, cut the monkfish fillets into ¾-inch cubes. Remove the pan from the heat, let cool slightly, then strain the stock into a bowl and set aside. Heat the oil in an ovenproof earthenware baking pan, paella pan or large ovenproof skillet that can be used on the stove. Add the langoustines and cook for a few minutes, then add the shrimp and monkfish. Cook for a few minutes more, then transfer to a plate, and set aside. Add the tomato and garlic to the paella pan and cook, stirring occasionally, for 5 minutes. Stir in the paprika and saffron and cook, stirring occasionally, for 8–10 minutes. Preheat the oven to 350°F. Add the noodles to the paella pan, stir with a wooden spoon and pour in 6 ¼ cups of the reserved stock. Cook over high heat for 12 minutes, add the seafood, placing it carefully around the dish, and cook for 3 minutes more. Transfer to the oven and bake for about 5 minutes, until the top is lightly colored. Serve immediately straight from the dish.

Note: You can substitute mussels for the langoustines. They are less expensive but are also very tasty. If you are substituting mussels for langoustines, use their strained cooking liquid instead of the fish stock and shell them before adding them to the dish.

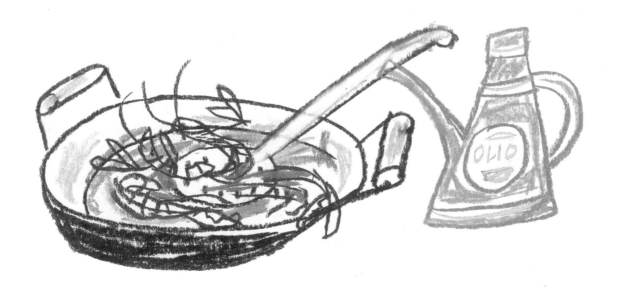

281

Noodles with crayfish

TALLARINES CON CANGREJOS

- 24 live crayfish, or thawed
  frozen crayfish
- 1½ teaspoons sea salt
- 9 ounces fresh noodles
- 1 cup light cream
- 6 sprigs fresh parsley, chopped
- salt and pepper

  Stock:
- 2 carrots
- 1 onion
- 6 black peppercorns
- 1 bay leaf
- 1 sprig fresh parsley
- 1 sprig fresh thyme
- 1 tablespoon olive oil
- salt

  Serves 4

Put all the stock ingredients into a pan, pour in 8 ¾ cups water, and bring to a boil over high heat. Meanwhile, wash the crayfish in plenty of cold water. When the stock is boiling vigorously, add the crayfish, bring back to a boil, and cook for 4–6 minutes, depending on their size. Remove from the pan, twist off the heads and remove the shells. (The edible meat is in the tail). Flake the flesh. Pour 13 cups water into a large pan and bring to a boil. Add the salt and noodles, stir with a fork to prevent the noodles from sticking, bring back to a boil, and cook for a few minutes, until tender but still firm to the bite. Drain well. Meanwhile, gently heat the cream in another large pan, but do not let it boil. Stir in the crayfish meat and cook, stirring constantly, for 1 minute, to heat through. Add the noodles and toss over low heat. Serve immediately, seasoned with pepper and sprinkled with the parsley.

282

Noodles with walnuts and truffles

TALLARINES CON NUECES Y TRUFA

- 1 truffle, about 1½ ounces
- 1 egg yolk, lightly beaten
- ⅔ cup mascarpone cheese
- 14 ounces fresh noodles
- 12 walnuts,
  shelled, peeled, and chopped
- ⅓–½ cup grated
  Parmesan cheese
- salt and pepper

  Serves 4

Clean the truffle with a small brush and a damp cloth. Stir the egg yolk into the mascarpone with a wooden spoon. Season with salt and pepper. Bring a large pan of salted water to a boil. Add the noodles, bring back to a boil, and cook for a few minutes, until tender but still firm to the bite. Drain the noodles and toss with the mascarpone mixture. Sprinkle with the walnuts and Parmesan to taste, and grate a little truffle to taste over the top. Alternatively, sprinkle the noodles with very thinly sliced truffle.

Note: For a delicious variation, crush the walnuts until they are reduced to a paste, then season them with salt and pepper, and add a pinch of freshly grated nutmeg and a pinch of ground cinnamon. Stir in a little oil and mix the paste in with the drained noodles before continuing as above.

283

Spaghetti alla carbonara

ESPAGUETIS A LA ITALIANA CON BACON Y HUEVOS

- 12 ounces (about ¾ box)
  spaghetti
- ½ cup olive oil
- 5 ounces bacon,
  cut into ½-inch pieces
- 6 tablespoons (¾ stick) butter
- 4 eggs, beaten
- small pinch of aromatic herbs
- 1 cup grated Parmesan cheese
- salt

Serves 4

Cook the spaghetti as described on page 221. Meanwhile, heat the oil in a skillet. Add the bacon and cook, stirring occasionally, for about 5 minutes, until tender and cooked through. Remove from the pan and drain on paper towels. Drain the spaghetti in a large colander and cover with a clean dishtowel to prevent it getting cold. Melt the butter in another large pan. Remove the pan from the heat, then add the bacon and eggs, followed immediately by the spaghetti, aromatic herbs, and Parmesan. Stir well, then transfer to a warm serving dish and serve immediately.

Spaghetti with peas and clams

ESPAGUETIS CON GUISANTES Y ALMEJAS

- **12 ounces (about ¾ box) spaghetti**
- **1 pound 2 ounces clams**
- **5 tablespoons white wine**
- **1 shallot, finely chopped**
- **¼ cup (½ stick) butter**
- **scant 1 cup drained canned peas**
- **1 cup grated Parmesan cheese**
- **salt**

Serves 4

Cook the spaghetti as described on page 221. Meanwhile, wash the clams in salted water. Discard any with broken shells or any that do not shut immediately when sharply tapped. Put them into a pan, pour in the wine, and add the shallot. Cover and cook over high heat, shaking the pan occasionally, for 3–5 minutes, until the shells have opened. Remove the pan from the heat. Remove the clams with a slotted spoon and reserve the cooking liquid. Discard any that remain closed. Remove the clams from their shells and set aside. Strain the cooking liquid into a bowl through a cheesecloth-lined strainer. Drain the spaghetti. Melt the butter in another large pan. Add the spaghetti, clams, peas, reserved cooking liquid, and Parmesan. Mix well and heat through briefly, then transfer to warm serving dish. Serve immediately.

285

Spaghetti with clams and porcini
ESPAGUETIS CON ALMEJAS Y SETAS

- 1½ small onions
- 1 hake or other white fish head, gills removed
- 3 cloves garlic
- 1 sprig fresh parsley
- ½ cup dried porcini or 1 ounce fresh
- 9 ounces clams
- 4 tablespoons olive oil
- 9 ounces raw shrimp, peeled
- 14 ounces canned chopped tomatoes
- pinch of saffron threads
- 12 ounces spaghetti
- salt

Serves 4

Cut the half onion into wedges and finely chop the whole onion. Put the fish head into a pan with the onion wedges, one of the garlic cloves, and the parsley. Pour in water to cover and bring to a boil, then lower the heat, and simmer for about 30 minutes. Meanwhile, if using dried porcini put them into a small bowl and pour in warm water to cover. Set aside to soak. Finely chop the remaining garlic. Scrub the clams under cold running water. Discard any with damaged shells or any that do not shut immediately when sharply tapped. Heat the oil in a pan. Add the chopped garlic and the chopped onion and cook over low heat, stirring occasionally, for 8 minutes, until beginning to brown. Add the shrimp, clams, and ¼ cup water, cover, and cook for 10 minutes. Discard any clams that remain closed. Meanwhile, drain the dried porcini, if using. Chop the porcini (dried or fresh). Add the porcini and the tomato to the pan, and cook for 5 minutes more. Strain the fish stock into a clean pan, add the saffron and a pinch of salt, and bring to a boil. Add the spaghetti, bring back to a boil, and cook for 10–12 minutes, until tender but still firm to the bite. Drain and add to the sauce. Toss to coat and serve immediately.

286

Spaghetti with peas and porcini
ESPAGUETIS CON GUISANTES Y SETAS

- 12 ounces spaghetti
- ½ cup (1 stick) butter
- 1 cup dried porcini or 2 ounces fresh
- 3½ ounces drained canned peas
- 3 ounces Parmesan cheese, grated
- salt

Serves 4

If you are using dried porcini, soak them as described in recipe 285, drain and slice. Cook the spaghetti as described on page 221. Melt the butter in a skillet, add the mushrooms and cook until softened. Drain the spaghetti well and add it and the peas to the skillet and toss. Sprinkle with the cheese and serve immediately. This is a dish with a very distinctive taste but it is also delicious.

287

Spaghetti with zucchini

ESPAGUETIS CON CALABACINES

- 1 pound 2 ounces zucchini,
  cut into thick sticks
- 12 ounces spaghetti
- 3 tablespoons olive oil
- 1 onion, finely chopped
- juice of ½ lemon
- generous 1 cup heavy cream
- ¾ cup grated cheese,
  such as Cheddar or gruyere
- salt

Serves 4

Cook the zucchini in plenty of salted boiling water for 2 minutes, then drain, and refresh under cold running water. Set aside in a clean dishtowel to dry. Cook the spaghetti as descibed on page 221. Meanwhile, heat the oil in a skillet. Add the zucchini and onion and cook over low heat, stirring occasionally, for 8–10 minutes. Stir in the lemon juice. Drain the spaghetti well and add it to the pan. Stir in the cream, season to taste with salt, and serve immediately, offering the cheese separately.

288

Spaghetti Bolognese

ESPAGUETIS CON SALSA BOLOÑESA

- 12 ounces (about ¾ box)
  spaghetti
- salt

Bolognese sauce:
- 2 tablespoons olive oil
- ⅓ cup finely chopped bacon
- 1¼ cups ground beef
- 1 large onion, finely chopped
- 1 carrot, finely chopped
- 1–2 stalks celery, finely chopped
- pinch of ground cloves
- 6 tablespoons canned
  tomato pueée
- 2 tablespoons white wine
- generous 1 cup light cream
- 1 cup grated Parmesan cheese
- salt

Serves 6

Make the Bolognese sauce. Heat the oil in a pan. Add the bacon and cook over low heat, stirring occasionally, for 4 minutes. Add the ground beef, onion, carrot, celery, and cloves, season with salt, and cook, stirring frequently, for 10 minutes. Stir in the tomatoes and wine, cover, and simmer for 10 minutes. Meanwhile, cook the spaghetti as described on page 221. Drain well and stir into the sauce along with the cream and Parmesan. Serve immediately.

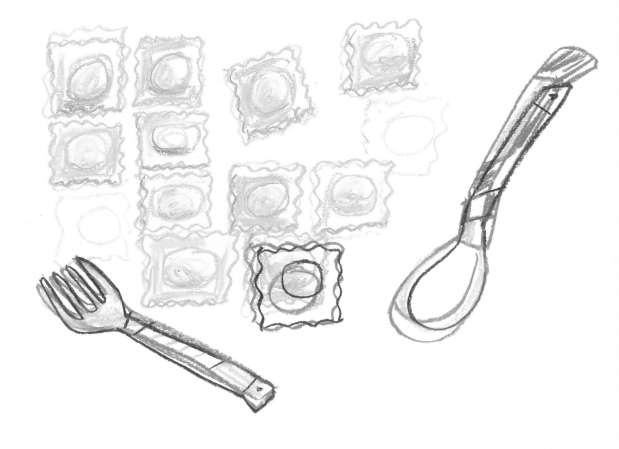

289

Ravioli

RAVIOLIS

Make the pasta dough as described in recipe 269, shape into a ball, and let rest for 2 hours. Cut it in half and roll it out into two very thin squares. Place small heaps of the prepared filling (see the following recipes) onto one of the squares, spacing them 1 inch apart. Brush the spaces in between the mounds of filling with water and brush the second dough square with water. Place the second square, damp side down, on top of the first square. Use a fluted pasta wheel to cut between the ravioli, pressing down hard to make sure the edges stick together. Bring a large pan of salted water to a boil. Add the ravioli, in batches, and bring back to a boil, then lower the heat, and cook for about 20 minutes, until tender. Drain and refresh under cold running water to prevent the ravioli sticking. The ravioli are now ready to be mixed with a sauce and baked. Cook them as soon as they are ready to prevent them drying out.

Note: Ready-made ravioli are widely available, in which case you need only to cook them, make the sauce, and then bake them—an easier and quicker process.

290

Fillings for ravioli (first version)
RELLENOS PARA RAVIOLIS

- 1 pound 2 ounces spinach, coarse stalks removed
- 2 ounces bread, crusts removed
- 5 tablespoons hot milk
- 3 tablespoons olive oil
- 1 tablespoon finely chopped onion
- 1¼ cups bulk sausage
- 1 tablespoon sherry
- 1 egg, lightly beaten
- salt

Makes about 35

Cook the spinach in salted boiling water for about 10 minutes. Drain it well, pressing down with the back of a spoon to squeeze out all the water. Finely chop the leaves. Put the bread in a bowl, add the hot milk, and let soak. Heat the oil in a skillet. Add the onion and cook over low heat, stirring occasionally, for about 10 minutes, until lightly browned. Stir in the bulk sausage. Remove the pan from the heat and put the meat and onion mixture into a bowl. Gently squeeze out the bread and add it to the bowl along with the sherry, egg, and a pinch of salt. Mix well with a wooden spoon, then add the spinach. Let the mixture cool completely before using it to fill the ravioli.

291

Fillings for ravioli (second version)
RELLENOS PARA RAVIOLIS

- 1 pound 2 ounces spinach, coarse stalks removed
- 3 tablespoons olive oil
- 2 leeks, halved lengthwise, and cut into 1-inch lengths, and rinsed well
- 5 ounces lean beef, diced
- 1¾ cups bread crumbs
- ½ cup grated gruyere or Parmesan cheese
- 1 egg, lightly beaten
- 1 tablespoon sherry
- salt

Makes about 35

Cook the spinach in salted boiling water for about 10 minutes. Drain it well, pressing down with the back of a spoon to squeeze out all the water. Finely chop the leaves. Heat the oil in a skillet. Add the leek and cook over low heat, stirring occasionally, for 10 minutes. Add the beef, cover, and cook over low heat, stirring occasionally, for 15–20 minutes. Process the meat mixture and spinach in a food processor or grind with a meat grinder. Put the resulting mixture into a bowl with the bread crumbs, cheese, egg, sherry, and a pinch of salt. Stir well until the mixture comes together. Leave the mixture to cool completely before using it to fill the ravioli.

292

Tomato sauce for ravioli

SALSA DE TOMATE PARA RAVIOLIS

- 3 tablespoons sunflower oil
- ¼ cup chopped onion
- 3¼ pounds ripe tomatoes, seeded and diced
- 1 teaspoon sugar
- 1 cup grated Parmesan or gruyere cheese
- 2 tablespoons (¼ stick) butter
- salt

Serves 4

Heat the oil in a skillet. Add the onion and cook over low heat, stirring occasionally, for about 5 minutes, until softened. Add the tomato and cook, breaking it up with the edge of a slotted spoon, for 10 minutes. Let cool slightly, then transfer to a food processor or blender and process to a purée. Add the sugar and a pinch of salt. Preheat the oven to 400°F. Spoon a little of the sauce into an ovenproof baking dish and sprinkle with half the cheese. Place the ravioli on top and pour the remaining tomato sauce over them. Sprinkle with the remaining cheese and dot with the butter. Bake for 20–30 minutes, until golden brown.

293

Béchamel sauce for ravioli

SALSAS BECHAMEL PARA RAVIOLIS

- ¼ cup (½ stick) butter
- 2 tablespoons olive oil
- 1 tablespoon all-purpose flour
- 2¼ cups milk
- 2 teaspoons tomato paste
- ½ cup grated gruyere cheese
- salt

Serves 4

Melt half the butter with the oil in a pan. Stir in the flour and cook, stirring constantly, for 2 minutes. Gradually stir in the milk, a little at a time. Season with salt and cook, stirring constantly, for 6 minutes. Stir in the tomato paste. Preheat the oven to 400°F. Place the ravioli in an ovenproof baking dish and pour the béchamel sauce over them. Sprinkle with the cheese and dot with the remaining butter. Bake for 20–30 minutes, until the cheese has melted.

Porcini ravioli in leek sauce

RAVIOLI DE SETAS CON SALSA DE PUERROS

- 2 ¾ cups all-purpose flour,
  plus extra for dusting
- 1 teaspoon salt
- 3 eggs, lightly beaten
- 2 chicken bouillon cubes

Filling:
- 2 tablespoons (¼ stick) butter
- 1 shallot, chopped
- 1 clove garlic, crushed
- 1 pound 2 ounces porcini
  mushrooms, finely chopped
- juice of 1 lemon
- salt and pepper

Sauce:
- 1 ounce butter
- 1 pound 2 ounces leeks,
  halved lengthwise, chopped
  and rinsed well
- 4 tablespoons chicken stock
  (homemade, canned or
  made with a bouillon cube)
- scant ½ cup light cream
- salt and pepper

Serves 4–6

Sift the flour and salt onto a work surface and make a well in the center. Break the eggs into the well and gradually incorporate the dry ingredients to make a smooth dough. If the dough is too sticky, add a little more flour. Cover and let rest while preparing the filling. Melt the butter in a large skillet. Add the shallot and garlic and cook over low heat, stirring occasionally, for 5 minutes, until softened. Add the porcini and lemon juice and season to taste with salt and pepper. Cover and simmer gently for 10 minutes, until the liquid has evaporated, then remove from the heat, and let cool. Roll out the dough on a lightly floured surface. Fill, and cut out ravioli as described in recipe 289. To make the sauce, melt the butter in a skillet. Add the leek and cook over low heat, stirring occasionally, for 5 minutes, until softened. Add the stock and simmer for 10 minutes more, until tender. Let cool slightly, then transfer to a food processor or blender, add the cream, and process until smooth. Strain into a clean pan and reheat gently. Season to taste with salt and pepper and, if necessary, add a little more stock. Bring a large pan of water to a boil and crumble in the bouillon cubes. Add the ravioli, in batches, bring back to a boil, and cook for 4 minutes, until tender but still firm to the bite. Drain and serve immediately with the sauce.

Note: Test the edge of one of the ravioli before draining. As it is thicker there it takes longer to cook. The ravioli may also be served with a mustard and cream sauce.

295

Duck and foie gras ravioli with sauce

RAVIOLIS DE PATO Y FOIE CON SALSA

- 3½ cups all-purpose flour,
  plus extra for dusting
- 3 extra large eggs
- 1 teaspoon olive oil
- salt

Filling:
- 11 ounces cooked duck fillet
- 3½ ounces head cheese,
  in a single piece (optional)
- 3½ ounces cooked duck
  foie gras, chopped
- 4 tablespoons chopped
  fresh parsley
- pinch of freshly grated nutmeg
- 1¼ teaspoons finely
  chopped onion
- 1 teaspoon finely chopped
  pickled gherkin
- 1 teaspoon capers,
  rinsed and drained
- ¼ cup balsamic vinegar
- ¼ cup walnut oil
- 1 teaspoon strong mustard
- salt and pepper

Serves 4

Sift the flour and a pinch of salt onto a work surface and make a well in the center. Break the eggs into the well and add 2 tablespoons water and the olive oil. Gradually incorporate the dry ingredients to make a smooth dough. Cover and let rest for 1 hour. Heat the duck fillet in the microwave. Cut off the meat and chop. Heat the head cheese in the microwave, drain off the fat into a bowl, and reserve. Chop the meat. Combine the duck meat, head cheese, foie gras, parsley, nutmeg, onion, gherkin, and capers in a bowl and stir in the reserved fat. Season with pepper. Roll out the dough on a lightly floured surface. Fill, and cut out ravioli as described in recipe 289. Bring a large pan of salted water to a boil. Add the ravioli, bring back to a boil, and cook for 5 minutes, until tender but still firm to the bite. Meanwhile, whisk together the balsamic vinegar, walnut oil, and mustard in a bowl. Drain the ravioli, put in a warm serving dish, and pour the dressing over them. Serve immediately.

Note: If you do not use the optional head cheese, increase the amount of duck breast meat by 3½ ounces. This filling is also delicious in cannelloni. Serve the cannelloni on a bed of chopped mushrooms and finely chopped onion lightly cooked in a little butter. It will make them more succulent.

296

Gnocchi

ÑOQUIS

- 6¼ cups milk
- scant 2 cups semolina flour
- 7 tablespoons butter
- ⅔ cup grated Parmesan
  or gruyere cheese,
- 4 egg yolks
- salt

  Béchamel sauce:
- 2 tablespoons (¼ stick) butter
- 1 tablespoon olive oil
- 1 tablespoon all-purpose flour
- 1¼ cups milk
- generous ½ cup white wine
- pinch of freshly grated nutmeg
  (optional)
- salt
  Serves 6

Bring the milk just to a boil in a pan. Sprinkle in the semolina flour and cook, stirring constantly, for 5 minutes. Stir in the butter and cheese. Remove the pan from the heat and stir in the egg yolks, one at a time. Season to taste with salt and let cool. Shape the cooled mixture into little balls about the size of walnuts and place them in an ovenproof baking dish that can be used on the stove. Preheat the broiler. Make the béchamel sauce: melt the butter with the oil in a pan. Stir in the flour and cook, stirring constantly, for 2 minutes. Gradually stir in the milk and then the wine, season with salt, and add the nutmeg, if using. Cook over low heat, stirring constantly, for 10 minutes. Pour the sauce over the gnocchi and broil lightly before serving.

Cannelloni

CANELONES DE CARNE

- 12 cannelloni or manicotti tubes
  or 12 sheets of egg pasta,
  6 x 3 inches
- scant 1 cup grated
- gruyere cheese
- 2 tablespoons (¼ stick) butter
- ¾ quantity Classic Tomato
  Sauce (see recipe 73)

Filling:
- 2 tablespoons olive oil
- 1 small onion, finely chopped
- 5 ounces ground beef
- 1 cooked chicken breast half and
  1 cooked lamb's brain or
  2 cooked boneless chicken
  breast halves
- 1 ounce foie gras pate

Béchamel sauce:
- 2 tablespoons (¼ stick) butter
- 2 tablespoons sunflower oil
- 2 tablespoons all-purpose flour
- 3 cups milk or half milk
  half stock
- salt

Makes 12 cannelloni

The filling for cannelloni can be made in several ways, some more expensive than others. The base is always meat—ground beef, veal, or even better, pork. This can be mixed with various other ingredients such as fried chicken livers; ground cooked chicken; a cooked lamb's brain; foie gras; Serrano, Smithfield, or other dry-cured ham or prosciutto; and bulk sausage. The idea is to mix the meat with one or more ingredients that add flavor but do not overpower it. Another delicious alternative is to cook a small finely chopped onion with a little chopped tomato to make a paste. If using cannelloni tubes, prepare according to the instructions on the package. The type that does not require precooking is the easiest to use. To make the dish a little simpler, you could use good-quality bottled tomato sauce, if you like, instead of making the sauce, but it should be quite thick. To make the filling, heat the oil in a small skillet. Add the onion and cook over low heat, stirring occasionally, for about 5 minutes, until softened and translucent. Stir in 2 tablespoons of the tomato sauce and remove from the heat. Mix the onion with all the other filling ingredients in a bowl. Drain the cannelloni tubes, if necessary. Fill the tubes using a teaspoon or divide the filling among the pasta sheets and roll them up. Put them into an ovenproof baking dish. Preheat the oven to 400°F. Make a thin béchamel sauce as described in recipe 77 and stir in the remaining tomato sauce. (You can omit the tomato sauce, if you like.) Strain the sauce over the cannelloni through a coarse strainer. (This is not necessary if the tomato sauce has been omitted.) Sprinkle the gruyere over the top and dot with the butter. Bake for about 20 minutes, until the topping is golden brown. Remove the dish from the oven, and let stand for about 5 minutes before serving.

Fried cannelloni

CANELONES FRITOS

- 1¾ cups all-purpose flour
- 1 egg
- 1 bottle of beer,
  at room temperature
- 4 cups olive oil
- 12 filled cannelloni or manicotti
  (see recipe 297)
- salt
- 1 quantity Classic Tomato Sauce
  (see recipe 73)

Serves 4

Sift the flour into a bowl and sprinkle in a pinch of salt. Add the egg and mix lightly, then gradually stir in the beer, a little at a time, until the batter has the consistency of a thick béchamel. Heat the oil in a skillet. Dip the filled cannelloni, one at a time, into the beer batter to coat, then place into the hot oil, seam sides down. Cook until golden brown, then remove with a skimmer or slotted spoon. Drain well, and keep warm while cooking the remaining cannelloni. Serve the fried cannelloni plain or with tomato sauce offered separately.

299 Tuna, egg, and mushroom cannelloni

CANELONES DE ATÚN, HUEVOS DUROS Y CHAMPIÑONES

- **12 cannelloni or manicotti tubes or 12 sheets of egg pasta, 6 x 3 inches**
- **3½ ounces cremini mushrooms, chopped**
- **1½ tablespoons butter**
- **juice of ½ lemon**
- **3 tablespoons olive oil**
- **7 ounces onions, finely chopped**
- **1 quantity Classic Tomato Sauce (see recipe 73)**
- **9 ounces canned tuna in oil or brine, drained and flaked**
- **2 hard-cooked eggs, chopped**
- **½ cup grated gruyere cheese**
- **salt**

Béchamel sauce:
- **2 tablespoons (¼ stick) butter**
- **2 tablespoons sunflower oil**
- **2 tablespoons all-purpose flour**
- **2¼ cups milk or half milk half stock**

Serves 6

If using the cannelloni tubes, prepare them according to the instructions on the package. Put the mushrooms into a pan with the butter and the lemon juice. Cover and cook over low heat for about 10 minutes. Heat the oil in a skillet. Add the onion and cook over low heat, stirring occasionally, for about 5 minutes, until softened but not browned. Remove the pan from the heat and stir in 2 tablespoons of the tomato sauce, the tuna, mushrooms, and hard-cooked eggs. Season to taste with salt. Drain the cannelloni tubes, if necessary. Fill the tubes using a teaspoon or divide the filling among the pasta sheets and roll them up. Put them into an ovenproof baking dish. Preheat the oven to 400°F. Make the béchamel sauce as described in recipe 77 and stir in 3–4 tablespoons of the tomato sauce to turn it pink. Pour the béchamel sauce over the cannelloni, sprinkle with the gruyere, and dot with the butter. Bake for about 20 minutes, until the topping is golden brown. Remove the dish from the oven and let stand for 5 minutes before serving.

Note: You can use fresh or leftover cooked fish instead of tuna. If using fresh fish, poach it first.

300

Cannelloni with leftover ragout
CANELONES CON UN RESTO DE RAGOÛT

- 12 cannelloni or manicotti tubes
  or 12 sheets of egg pasta,
  6 x 3 inches
- 9 ounces leftover ragout
- 1 quantity Classic Béchamel
  Sauce (see recipe 77)
- scant 1 cup grated
  gruyere cheese
- 1 tablespoon butter

Serves 6

Cannelloni made with leftover ragout (or meat stew) are delicious and original. Grind the meat, carrots, and onion and use this to fill the cannelloni. Put the leftover ragout into an ovenproof baking dish and place the filled cannelloni on top. Spoon some of the meat sauce over them. Pour the béchamel sauce over the cannelloni. Sprinkle with gruyere, dot with butter, and bake until golden brown. Serve straight from the dish.

301

Spinach cannelloni with hard-cooked egg
CANELONES DE ESPINACAS Y HUEVOS DUROS

- 12 cannelloni or manicotti tubes
  or 12 sheets of egg pasta,
  6 x 3 inches
- 3¼ pounds spinach,
  coarse stalks removed
- 6 tablespoons (¾ stick) butter
- 3 hard-cooked eggs, chopped
- 1 cup grated gruyere cheese
- salt

Béchamel sauce:
- 2 tablespoons (¼ stick) butter
- 2 tablespoons sunflower oil
- 2 tablespoons all-purpose flour
- 2¼ cups milk or half milk
  half stock

Serves 6

If using the cannelloni tubes, prepare them according to the instructions on the package. Cook the spinach in salted boiling water for about 10 minutes. Drain well, pressing down with the back of a spoon to squeeze out all the water, then finely chop the leaves. Melt 4 tablespoons of the butter in a skillet and stir in the spinach. Remove the pan from the heat and add the hard-cooked eggs and half the gruyere. Drain the cannelloni tubes, if necessary. Fill the tubes using a teaspoon or divide the filling among the pasta sheets and roll them up. Put them into an ovenproof baking dish. Preheat the oven to 400°F. Make the béchamel sauce as described in recipe 77 and pour it over the cannelloni. Sprinkle with the remaining cheese and dot with the remaining butter. Bake for 15–30 minutes, until the topping is golden brown. Remove the dish from the oven and let stand for about 5 minutes before serving.

Salmon lasagna with ratatouille

LASAÑA DE SALMÓN CON PISTO

- **12–14 ounces lasagna**
- **1 pound 10 ounces thin salmon fillets**
- **1½ cups thick fish stock (homemade or bottled) or white wine**

Ratatouille:
- **7 tablespoons olive oil**
- **2 large onions, chopped**
- **4½ pounds zucchini, peeled, halved, seeded, and diced**
- **2¼ pounds ripe tomatoes, peeled and chopped**
- **1 teaspoon sugar**
- **2 green bell peppers, diced**
- **salt**

Serves 6

Make the ratatouille. Heat 3 tablespoons of the oil in a pan. Add the onion and cook, stirring occasionally, for 5 minutes, until soft and translucent. Add the zucchini and cook, stirring occasionally, for 10 minutes more, until lightly browned. Meanwhile, heat 2 tablespoons of the remaining oil in a skillet. Add the tomato and cook, stirring occasionally and breaking it up with the side of the spoon for 10 minutes. Let cool slightly, then transfer to a food processor or blender and process to a purée. Stir in the sugar, season with salt, and stir into the zucchini. Simmer gently for 20 minutes. Meanwhile, heat the remaining oil in another skillet. Add the bell pepper, cover the skillet, and cook over low heat, stirring occasionally, for 20 minutes. Add to the zucchini and tomato mixture and stir well. Cook the sheets of lasagna according to the instructions on the package. Put the salmon into a fish kettle or large shallow pan. Add the stock and bring just to a boil. Lower the heat and poach for about 10 minutes, until cooked through. Lift out carefully. Make a layer of salmon in a deep ovenproof baking dish, then add a layer of ratatouille, and then one of lasagna. Continue until all your ingredients are used. Serve immediately.

Lasagna

LASAÑA

- olive oil, for brushing
- 12–14 ounces lasagna
- 1 cup grated Parmesan cheese
- 1 tablespoon butter

Béchamel sauce:
- ¼ cup (½ stick) butter
- ½ cup all-purpose flour
- 2¼ cups milk
- pinch of freshly grated nutmeg
- salt and pepper

Filling:
- 2 tablespoons olive oil
- ½ cup bulk sausage
- ⅓ cup chopped ham
- ½ onion, chopped
- ½ carrot, chopped
- ½ stalk celery, chopped
- 1 clove garlic, chopped
- 5 ounces ground beef
- 5 tablespoons red wine
- 11 ounces ripe tomatoes, peeled and chopped
- 1 bay leaf
- pinch of ground cloves
- salt and pepper

Serves 4

Make the filling. Heat the oil in a skillet. Add the bulk sausage and cook over low heat, stirring frequently, for a few minutes, until lightly browned. Add the ham, onion, carrot, celery, and garlic and cook, stirring occasionally, for 5 minutes. Add the ground beef and cook, breaking it up with a wooden spoon, for 5–8 minutes, until browned. Increase the heat to medium, pour in the wine, and cook until it has almost evaporated, then add the tomato, bay leaf, and cloves, and season with salt and pepper. Lower the heat, cover, and simmer for 40 minutes. Remove and discard the bay leaf. Make the béchamel sauce as described in recipe 77. Season to taste with salt and pepper, and stir in the nutmeg. Preheat the oven to 400°F. Brush the base of an ovenproof baking dish with oil. Prepare the lasagna according to the instructions on the package. Spoon some of the filling into the prepared baking dish to cover the base and top with a layer of béchamel sauce. Cover with a layer of lasagna sheets and sprinkle with some of the Parmesan. Continue making layers in this way until all the ingredients are used up, ending with a layer of béchamel sauce sprinkled with Parmesan. Dot with the butter and bake for 40 minutes. Remove from the oven and let stand for 5 minutes before serving.

Note: The pasta for the lasagna can be made using 3¼ cups all-purpose flour, 4 eggs, and salt (see recipe 269). Roll out and cut into rectangles. Cook in salted boiling water for a few minutes, then refresh in cold water, and spread out on a dishtowel to dry.

VEGETABLES AND MUSHROOMS

Vegetables

Sorrel

Origin and season

Sorrel comes from Africa. For a long time it was not very popular because it was considered too sour. Nowadays, cooks use it to give an original touch to their dishes. It can be found in markets from early spring to early fall.

Selection

Choose the variety with thin arrow-shaped leaves, sometimes known as herb patience or sorrel dock. The leaves should look fresh with no blemishes.

Nutrition

Sorrel contains about 25 calories per 3 ½ ounces and lots of vitamin C, but the leaves also contain oxalic acid which should not be consumed by people with nephritic colic, asthma, arthritis, or liver complaints.

Tricks

- If sorrel is to be puréed, mix it with lettuce to reduce the acidity
- Sorrel goes very well with chicken
- An infusion of sorrel is wonderful for removing rust stains.

304

French-style sorrel
ACEDER AS A LA FRANCESA

- **4½ pounds sorrel, stalks removed**
- **¼ cup (½ stick) butter**
- **1 tablespoon all-purpose flour**
- **2¼ cups milk**
- **2 egg yolks**
- **salt**

Serves 6

Pour 3–4½ quarts water into a pan and add 1 tablespoon salt. Add the sorrel, bring to a boil over high heat, and cook for 10 minutes. Drain well and chop finely. Melt the butter in a pan. Stir in the flour and cook, stirring constantly, for 2 minutes. Gradually stir in the milk, a little at a time, and cook, stirring constantly, for 4 minutes. Lightly season with salt, then add the sorrel, and stir well to mix. Cover and simmer over low heat, stirring occasionally, for 10 minutes. Lightly beat the egg yolks in a bowl, stir in a little of the sorrel mixture to prevent them curdling, then stir the eggs into the pan. Season to taste with a little salt. This dish should be served as an accompaniment to eggs or meat.

305

Fried sorrel
ACEDERAS REHOGADAS

- **4½ pounds sorrel, stalks removed**
- **6 tablespoons olive oil**
- **2 cloves garlic, lightly crushed**
- **1½ tablespoons white-wine vinegar**
- **salt**

Serves 6

Pour 3–4½ quarts water into a pan and add 1 tablespoon salt. Add the sorrel, bring to a boil over high heat, and cook for 10 minutes. Drain well and chop. Heat the oil in a pan. Add the garlic and cook for a few minutes, until lightly browned. Remove and discard the garlic, add the sorrel to the pan, and cook, stirring frequently, until wilted. Remove the pan from the heat and pour the vinegar over the leaves. Reheat gently and serve.

Marinated Swiss chard

ACELGAS EN ESCABECHE

- 3 ¼ pounds Swiss chard, finely chopped
- sunflower oil, for deep-frying
- 4 cloves garlic
- 3 bay leaves
- 3 tablespoons white-wine vinegar
- salt

Dough:
- 5 tablespoons all-purpose flour
- salt

Serves 6

Put the Swiss chard into a pan, pour in water to cover, and add a pinch of salt. Bring to a boil, then lower the heat, and simmer for about 20 minutes, until tender. Drain well and, if necessary, chop more finely with a mezzaluna. Make the dough. Sift the flour with a pinch of salt into a bowl and stir in about 1 cup water to make a dough. Mix the dough with the Swiss chard. Heat the oil in a deep-fryer or deep skillet to 350–375°F or until a cube of day-old bread browns in 30 seconds. Using a tablespoon, take small mounds of the Swiss chard mixture, add them to the pan, in batches of four, and cook for 3–4 minutes, until golden. Remove with a slotted spoon and drain on paper towels, then transfer to a deep serving dish, and keep warm. Prepare the marinade. Transfer 6 tablespoons of the oil to a small skillet and heat. Add the garlic and cook for a few minutes until lightly browned. Add the bay leaves, and cook for a few minutes more. Remove the pan from the heat and add 1 ½ cups water, taking care that the oil does not splatter, and the vinegar. Return the pan to the heat, bring to a boil, and simmer for 3–4 minutes. Remove and discard the garlic and bay leaves and pour the marinade over the Swiss chard. Let stand for 5 minutes before serving to allow the Swiss chard to absorb the flavor of the marinade.

Note: This dish may also be served cold. Let the Swiss chard cool and prepare the marinade in advance to let it cool.

307

Fried Swiss chard with croûtons, meat juices, and vinegar

ACELGAS REHOGADAS, CON CUSCURROS DE PAN, JUGO DE CARNE Y VINAGRE

- 3 ¼ pounds Swiss chard, finely chopped
- 1 cup olive oil
- 2 ounces white bread, crusts removed, cut into small cubes
- 1 cup meat cooking juices or beef stock (homemade, canned or made with a bouillon cube)
- 1 tablespoon white-wine vinegar
- salt

Serves 4–6

Put the Swiss chard into a pan, pour in water to cover, and add a pinch of salt. Bring to a boil, then lower the heat, and simmer for about 20 minutes, until tender. Drain well. Heat the oil in a pan. Add the cubes of bread and cook, stirring frequently, until golden brown all over. Remove from the pan and set aside. Put the Swiss chard into a large skillet, pour the meat sauce over the top, and cook, stirring with a wooden spoon, for 5 minutes. Stir in the croûtons and vinegar, heat through for a few minutes more, and serve.

308

Swiss chard with tomatoes

ACELGAS CON TOMATE

- 4 pounds Swiss chard, finely chopped
- 3 tablespoons sunflower oil
- 1 onion, chopped
- 2 ¼ pounds very ripe tomatoes, seeded and chopped
- 1 teaspoon sugar
- pinch of aromatic herbs
- salt

Serves 4–6

Put the Swiss chard into a pan, pour in water to cover, and add a pinch of salt. Bring to a boil, then lower the heat, and simmer for about 20 minutes, until tender. Drain well. Heat the oil in a skillet. Add the onion and cook over low heat, stirring occasionally, for about 5 minutes, until softened and translucent. Add the tomato and cook, stirring occasionally and breaking up the tomato with the side of the spoon, for 20 minutes. Stir in the sugar, a pinch of salt, and the Swiss chard. Add the herbs and cook for 3 minutes. Serve immediately.

309

Deep-fried Swiss chard ribs

PENCAS DE ACELGAS REBOZADAS

- 3 ¼ pounds Swiss chard
- ¾ cup all-purpose flour
- 2 eggs, lightly beaten
- sunflower oil, for deep-frying
- salt

Serves 4–6

Cut out the ribs of the Swiss chard and cut them into 1-inch long pieces. Put them into a pan, pour in water to cover, and add a pinch of salt. Bring to a boil, then lower the heat, and simmer for about 35 minutes, until tender. Drain well. Heat the oil in a deep-fryer or deep saucepan until a cube of day-old bread browns in 30 seconds. Roll each piece of Swiss chard rib in the flour, shaking off any excess, then dip into the eggs. Carefully add to the oil and cook until golden.

310

- 5 ½ pounds Swiss chard
- 6 tablespoons olive oil
- 1 large onion, chopped
- 9 ounces carrots, sliced
- 2 ¼ pounds very ripe tomatoes, peeled, seeded, and coarsely chopped
- ¾ cup white wine
- 1 bay leaf
- 1 sprig fresh thyme
- 1 sprig fresh parsley
- 1 teaspoon sugar
- 1 clove garlic, finely chopped
- ½ cup grated gruyere cheese
- salt

Serves 6

Baked Swiss chard ribs with Spanish sauce

PENCAS DE ACELGAS AL HORNO CON SALSA ESPAÑOLA

Cut out the ribs of the Swiss chard and cut them into 1-inch long pieces. Put them into a pan, pour in water to cover, and add a pinch of salt. Bring to a boil, then lower the heat, and simmer for 20 minutes. Drain well. Heat the oil in a large skillet. Add the onion and cook over low heat, stirring occasionally, for about 5 minutes, until softened and translucent. Add the carrot and cook, stirring frequently, for 10 minutes more. Add the tomato and cook, stirring occasionally, for 8 minutes, then add the wine, bay leaf, thyme, parsley, sugar, and garlic. Season with salt and pour in 2 ¼ cups water. Cook over medium heat for 1 hour. Remove and discard the bay leaf, thyme, and parsley. Preheat the oven to 400°F. Let the tomato mixture cool a little, then transfer the mixture to a food processor or blender and process to a purée. Put half the Swiss chard ribs into an ovenproof baking dish and spoon a little of the sauce over them. Add the remaining ribs and pour the remaining sauce over them. Sprinkle with the gruyere and bake for about 15 minutes, until the cheese has melted. Serve immediately straight from the dish.

311

- 5 ½ pounds Swiss chard
- 2 teaspoons chopped fresh parsley
- 3 cloves garlic, finely chopped
- 4 tablespoons sunflower oil
- 3 tablespoons bread crumbs
- 2 tablespoons (¼ stick) butter
- salt

Serves 6

Baked Swiss chard ribs with garlic and parsley

PENCAS DE ACELGAS AL HORNO CON AJO Y PEREJIL

Cut out the ribs of the Swiss chard and cut them into 1 ½-inch long pieces. Put them into a pan, pour in water to cover, and add a pinch of salt. Bring to a boil, then lower the heat, and simmer for about 35 minutes, until tender. Drain well. Preheat the oven to 400°F. Lay the Swiss chard ribs in an ovenproof baking dish and top with the parsley, garlic, and oil. Sprinkle with the bread crumbs and dot with the butter. Bake for 10–15 minutes. Serve immediately.

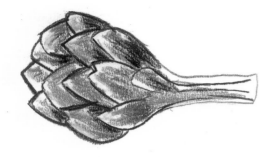

312

Artichokes in vinaigrette
ALCACHOFAS EN VINAGRETA

- 1 lemon, halved
- 12 globe artichokes
- 3 tablespoons white-wine vinegar
- 9 tablespoons sunflower oil
- 1 tablespoon chopped fresh parsley
- salt

Serves 6

Squeeze the juice from one lemon half and add the juice to a large bowl of water. Break off the artichoke stalks and remove the coarse outer leaves. Cut off the tips of the remaining leaves. Cut the artichokes in half lengthwise, and remove and discard the chokes. Rub the artichokes with the remaining lemon half and place in the acidulated water. Bring a large pan of salted water to a boil. Add the artichokes and bring back to a boil, then lower the heat, cover, and simmer for about 25 minutes, until tender. (Test by gently pulling a leaf; it should come away easily.) Drain well, turning the artichokes upside down and pressing down gently. Place the artichokes in a dish, cut side up. Whisk the vinegar with a pinch of salt in a bowl, then whisk in the oil. Pour the vinaigrette over the artichokes, sprinkle with the parsley, and serve.

313

Artichokes in sauce
ALCACHOFAS EN SALSA

- 1 lemon, halved
- 3¼–4½ pounds small young globe artichokes
- 2 heaping tablespoons bread crumbs
- 2 tablespoons olive oil
- 1 teaspoon chopped fresh parsley
- 2 cloves garlic, finely chopped
- salt

Serves 6

Squeeze the juice from one lemon half and add the juice to a large bowl of water. Cut off and reserve one slice from the other half. Remove the coarse outer leaves from the artichokes and cut off the tips of the remaining leaves. Cut the artichokes into halves or quarters lengthwise and remove and discard the choke. Rub the artichokes with the remaining lemon half and place in the acidulated water. When all the artichokes have been prepared, drain them and put into a pan, which should be deep and not too wide. Add the reserved lemon slice, bread crumbs, oil, parsley, and garlic. Pour in just enough water to cover, add a pinch of salt, and mix well. Bring to a boil over high heat, then lower the heat to medium, cover, and cook for about 45 minutes, until tender. (Test by gently pulling a leaf; it should come away easily.) Serve immediately.

314

Fried artichokes in sauce
ALCACHOFAS REBOZADAS Y EN SALSA

- 1 lemon, halved
- 12 globe artichokes
- 1 tablespoon all-purpose flour, plus extra for dusting
- 2 ¼ cups sunflower oil
- 3 tablespoons olive oil
- 2 onions, finely chopped
- generous ½ cup finely chopped Serrano ham or prosciutto
- salt

Serves 6

Squeeze the juice from one lemon half and add the juice to a large bowl of water. Break off the artichoke stalks and remove the coarse outer leaves. Cut off the tips of the remaining leaves. Open out the centres of the artichokes, and remove the chokes. Rub the artichokes with the remaining lemon half and place in the acidulated water. Bring a large pan of salted water to a boil. Add the artichokes and bring back to a boil, then lower the heat, cover, and cook for about 35 minutes, until tender. (Test by gently pulling a leaf; it should come away easily.) Drain well, turning the artichokes upside down and pressing gently. Reserve 3 cups of the cooking liquid. Cut the artichokes in half lengthwise. Dust with flour and shake off any excess. Heat the sunflower oil in a skillet. Add the artichokes and cook until golden brown. Remove with a slotted spoon, drain well, and put into a stovetop-safe casserole. Heat the olive oil in another skillet. Add the onion and cook over low heat, stirring occasionally, for about 8 minutes, until lightly browned. Stir in the flour and cook, stirring constantly, for 2 minutes, then gradually stir in the reserved cooking liquid. Cook, stirring constantly, for 5 minutes, then add the ham. Season to taste with salt and pour the sauce over the artichokes. Bring to a boil, lower the heat, and simmer for 10–15 minutes. Serve immediately straight from the dish.

315

Baked artichokes
ALCACHOFAS AL HORNO

- 1 lemon, halved
- 12 globe artichokes
- 2 ½ tablespoons lard (optional)
- 4 tablespoons white wine
- sunflower oil, for drizzling
- 2 teaspoons finely chopped fresh parsley
- ½ cup bread crumbs
- salt

Serves 6

Squeeze the juice from one lemon half and add the juice to a large bowl of water. Break off the artichoke stalks and remove the coarse outer leaves. Cut off the tips of the remaining leaves. Cut the artichokes in half lengthwise and remove and discard the chokes. Rub the artichokes with the remaining lemon half and place in the acidulated water. Bring a large pan of salted water to a boil. Add the artichokes and bring back to a boil, then lower the heat, cover, and cook for 30–60 minutes, until tender. (Test by gently pulling a leaf; it should come away easily.) Preheat the oven to 350°F. Cut the lard, if using, into three pieces and put it into an ovenproof baking dish with the white wine. Remove the artichokes from the pan and place them cut side uppermost in the dish without draining them. Drizzle a little oil over each artichoke and sprinkle with the parsley and bread crumbs. Bake for 15 minutes and serve straight from the dish.

316

Artichokes stuffed with Serrano ham

ALCACHOFAS RELLENAS DE JAMÓN SERRANO

• 1 lemon, halved
• 12 globe artichokes
• scant 1 cup finely chopped
  Serrano ham or prosciutto
• 2 ½ tablespoons bread crumbs
• 1 tablespoon white wine
• 1 tablespoon chopped
  fresh parsley
• 1 clove garlic (optional),
  finely chopped
• 1 chicken bouillon cube
• 2 tablespoons sunflower oil
• salt

Serves 6

Squeeze the juice from one lemon half and add the juice to a large bowl of water. Break off the artichoke stalks and remove the coarse outer leaves. Cut off the tips of the remaining leaves. Open out the centers of the artichokes and remove the chokes. Rub the artichokes with the remaining lemon half and place in the acidulated water. Combine the ham, 1 ½ tablespoons of the bread crumbs, the wine, parsley, and garlic, if using, in a bowl. Drain the artichokes and fill with the ham mixture. Put the artichokes filling uppermost into a pan just large enough to hold them in a single layer. Pour in water to cover. Crumble the bouillon cube and dissolve it in a little water, then add it to the pan. Sprinkle the remaining bread crumbs and the oil over the artichokes. Bring to a boil, lower the heat, cover, and simmer for 30 minutes. Season with salt if necessary (bearing in mind that the ham and bouillon cube are both salty). Re-cover the pan and cook for 30 minutes more, until the liquid has reduced to a sauce and the artichokes are tender. Serve the artichokes in a dish with a little sauce in the base.

317

Artichoke and ham gratin

ALCACHOFAS AL HORNO CON JAMÓN Y BECHAMEL

• 1 lemon, halved
• 12 globe artichokes
• strip of thinly pared lemon rind
• scant 1 cup diced ham
• 2 tablespoons (¼ stick) butter
• 2 tablespoons sunflower oil
• 2 tablespoons all-purpose flour
• 2 ¼ cups milk
• ⅔ cup grated gruyere cheese
• salt

Serves 6

Squeeze the juice from one lemon half and add the juice to a large bowl of water. Break off the artichoke stalks and remove the coarse outer leaves. Cut off the tips of the remaining leaves. Open out the centers of the artichokes and remove the chokes. Rub the artichokes with the remaining lemon half and place in the acidulated water. Bring a large pan of salted water to a boil. Add the lemon rind and artichokes and bring back to a boil, then lower the heat, cover, and simmer for 30–60 minutes, until tender. (Test by gently pulling a leaf; it should come away easily.) Drain well, turning the artichokes upside down and pressing gently. Put the artichokes, cut side uppermost, into an ovenproof baking dish that can be used on the stove. Fill them with the ham. Preheat the broiler. Melt the butter with the oil in a pan. Stir in the flour and cook, stirring constantly, for 2 minutes. Gradually stir in the milk, a little at a time. Cook, stirring constantly, for 6 minutes. Season with salt and pour the sauce over the artichokes, covering them completely. Sprinkle with the gruyere and cook under the broiler for about 10 minutes, until the topping is golden brown. Serve immediately straight from the dish.

318

Artichoke hearts with foie gras and béchamel sauce

FONDOS DE ALCACHOFAS CON FOIE-GRAS Y BECHAMEL

• 1 lemon, halved
• 12 large globe artichokes
• 7 ounces canned foie gras
• 2 tablespoons (¼ stick) butter
• 2 tablespoons sunflower oil
• 2 heaping tablespoons
  all-purpose flour
• 3 cups milk
• ⅔ cup grated gruyere cheese
• salt

Serves 6

Squeeze the juice from one lemon half and add the juice to a large bowl of water. Break off the artichoke stalks and remove the coarse outer leaves. Cut off the remaining leaves at the base. Rub the artichoke hearts with the remaining lemon half and place in the acidulated water. Bring a large pan of salted water to a boil. Add the artichoke hearts and cook for 20 minutes. (They should not be fully cooked as they will finish cooking in the oven.) Lift the artichoke hearts out of the water with a slotted spoon and turn them upside down to drain. Remove the chokes with a teaspoon and discard. Fill each artichoke heart with foie gras and put them, filling uppermost, in a single layer in an ovenproof baking dish that can be used on the stove. Preheat the broiler. Melt the butter with the oil in a pan. Stir in the flour and cook, stirring constantly, for 2 minutes, then gradually stir in the milk, a little at a time. Season with salt and cook, stirring constantly, for 10 minutes. Pour the béchamel sauce over the artichoke hearts and sprinkle with the gruyere. Cook under the broiler until golden and bubbling. Serve immediately straight from the dish.

319

Fried artichokes

ALCACHOFAS REHOGADAS

• 1 lemon, halved
• 3¼–4½ pounds small
  young artichokes
• 2½ tablespoons lard (optional)
• 2–4 tablespoons sunflower oil
• scant 1 cup diced Serrano ham
  or prosciutto
• 1 tablespoon chopped
  fresh parsley
• salt

Serves 6

Squeeze the juice from one lemon half and add the juice to a large bowl of water. Break off the artichoke stalks and remove the coarse outer leaves. Cut off the tips of the remaining leaves. Cut the artichokes in half lengthwise and remove and discard the chokes. Rub the artichokes with the remaining lemon half and place in the acidulated water. Bring a large pan of salted water to a boil. Add the artichokes and bring back to a boil, then lower the heat, cover, and simmer for about 25 minutes, until tender. (Test by gently pulling a leaf; it should come away easily.) Drain well, turning the artichokes upside down and pressing gently. Melt the lard, if using, with 2 tablespoons of the oil in a pan. If you're not using lard, add 2 tablespoons more oil and heat. Add the ham and artichokes and cook gently, stirring occasionally, for 8 minutes. Sprinkle with the parsley and serve immediately.

320

Deep-fried artichokes
ALCACHOFAS REBOZADAS

- 1 lemon, halved
- 12 small globe artichokes
- ½ cup all-purpose flour
- 2–3 eggs
- sunflower oil, for deep-frying
- salt

Serves 6

Squeeze the juice from one lemon half and add the juice to a large bowl of water. Break off the artichoke stalks and remove the coarse outer leaves. Cut off the tips of the remaining leaves. Cut the artichokes in half lengthwise, or into quarters if they are large, and remove and discard the chokes. Rub the artichokes with the remaining lemon half, then place in the acidulated water Bring a large pan of salted water to a boil. Add the artichokes and bring back to a boil, then lower the heat, cover, and simmer for about 25 minutes, until tender. (Test by gently pulling a leaf; it should come away easily.) Drain well, turning the artichokes upside down and pressing gently. Pour the flour into a shallow dish. Lightly beat the eggs in another shallow dish. Roll the artichokes in the flour, shaking off any excess, and then dip each one into the beaten eggs. Heat the oil in a deep-fryer or deep saucepan to 350–375°F or until a cube of day-old bread browns in 30 seconds. Add the artichokes, in batches if necessary, and cook until golden brown. Drain well and serve immediately, either on their own or as an accompaniment to meat.

321

Celery hearts with béchamel sauce
APIO CON BECHAMEL

- 6 small or 3 large bunches
  of celery
- 3 tablespoons butter
- 2 tablespoons sunflower oil
- 3 tablespoons all-purpose flour
- 3 cups milk
- ⅔ cup grated gruyere or
  Parmesan cheese
- salt

Serves 6

Cut large bunches of celery in half. Cut the celery into pieces about 6 inches long. Remove the outside stalks, leaving just the hearts. Rinse thoroughly. Bring a large pan of salted water to a boil. Add the celery hearts, cover, and cook for 10 minutes. Remove with a skimmer or slotted spoon and let drain. Preheat the oven to 350°F. Melt the butter with the oil in a pan. Stir in the flour and cook, stirring constantly, for 2 minutes, then gradually stir in the milk, a little at a time. Cook, stirring constantly, for 3–4 minutes and season with salt. Put the celery hearts into an ovenproof baking dish and pour in the béchamel sauce to cover. Sprinkle with the cheese and bake for about 15 minutes, until the topping is golden brown. Serve immediately straight from the dish.

Braised celery hearts

APIO EN SU JUGO

- **6 small or 3 large bunches of celery**
- **3 thin bacon slices, diced**
- **1 tablespoon olive oil**
- **1 small onion, sliced**
- **2 carrots, sliced**
- **1 tablespoon all-purpose flour**
- **¾ cup white wine**
- **1 tablespoon tomato paste or 2 tablespoons thick tomato sauce**
- **¼ teaspoon meat extract or Maggi Seasoning**
- **salt**

Serves 6

Cut large bunches of celery in half. Cut the celery into pieces about 6 inches long. Remove the outside stalks, leaving just the hearts. Rinse thoroughly. Bring a large pan of salted water to a boil. Add the celery hearts, cover, and cook for 10 minutes. Remove with a skimmer or slotted spoon and let drain. Put the bacon into another large pan and cook over low heat for a few minutes, until the fat runs. Add the oil and heat, then add the onion and carrot, and cook, stirring occasionally, for 5 minutes. Stir in the flour and cook, stirring constantly, for 5 minutes more. Add the celery hearts and pour in the wine and generous 1 cup water. Cover and simmer for about 1 hour, until the celery hearts are tender. Remove the celery hearts with a skimmer or slotted spoon and keep warm. Transfer the sauce to a food processor or blender and process to a purée. Add the tomato paste or tomato sauce and the meat extract or Maggi Seasoning and process briefly again to mix. If the sauce is too thick, add a little water. Return the sauce to a clean pan and bring to a boil, then pour over the celery hearts, and serve immediately.

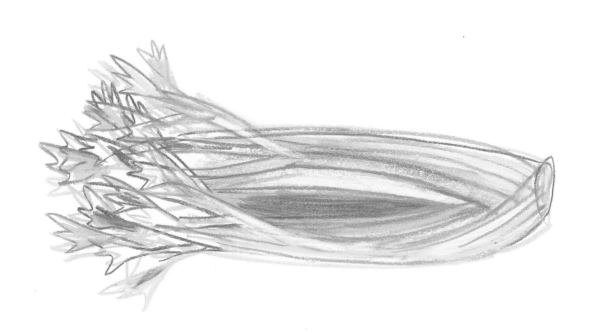

323 Celery hearts with butter and grated cheese

APIO CON MANTEQUILLA Y QUESO RALLADO

- **6 small or 3 large bunches of celery**
- **⅔ cup butter**
- **scant 1 cup grated gruyere cheese**
- **salt**

Serves 6

Cut large bunches of celery in half. Cut the celery stalks into pieces about 6 inches long. Remove the outside stalks, leaving just the hearts. Rinse thoroughly. Bring a large pan of salted water to a boil. Add the celery hearts, cover, and cook for 1 hour, until tender. Remove with a skimmer or slotted spoon and set aside to drain. Preheat the oven to 350°F. Put the celery hearts into an ovenproof baking dish, dot with the butter, and sprinkle with the gruyere. Bake for about 15 minutes, until golden brown. Serve the celery hearts immediately, straight from the dish.

324 Preparing raw celery for salads

PREPARACIÓN DEL APIO CRUDO PARA MEZCLAR CON ENSALADA

- **1 quantity escarole or lettuce salad**
- **6 tender, very white stalks celery**

Serves 3

Celery has a wonderful flavor that goes well with escarole and lettuce. Prepare your favourite salad. Rinse the celery well, then cut each stalk into pieces 1 inch long. Cut each piece lengthwise into three without cutting all the way down. Add the little celery "flowers" to the salad.

325 Eggplants with garlic

BERENJENAS AL AJO

- **6 eggplants**
- **¾ cup olive oil**
- **2 tablespoons chopped fresh parsley**
- **3 cloves garlic, finely chopped**
- **¾ cup bread crumbs**
- **salt**

Serves 6

Cut the eggplants in half lengthwise, sprinkle with a little salt, and put in a colander, cut side down, for about 1 hour to draw out some of their juices. Rinse well and pat dry. Heat three-quarters of the oil in a large skillet. Add the eggplant, cut sides down in a single layer. Cook over medium heat for 30 minutes, until soft. Preheat the oven to 400°F. Put the eggplants, cut sides up, side by side in an ovenproof baking dish. Combine the parsley and garlic and sprinkle over the eggplants. Sprinkle with the bread crumbs and drizzle with the remaining oil. Bake for about 10 minutes, until golden brown. Serve immediately straight from the dish.

326

Eggplants au gratin with sauce

BERENJENAS EN SALSA AL GRATÉN

• 7 large eggplants

• sunflower oil, for deep-frying

• 2 chicken bouillon cubes

• 4 cups hot water

• 2 tablespoons (¼ stick) butter

• 2 tablespoons all-purpose flour

• ½ cup grated gruyere cheese

• salt

Serves 6

Peel the eggplants and cut into ¼-inch thick slices. Put them into a deep dish or a bowl, sprinkling each layer with salt. Let stand for about 1 hour to draw out some of their juices. Rinse well and pat dry. Heat the oil in a deep-fryer or deep saucepan to 350–375°F or until a cube of day-old bread browns in 30 seconds. Add the eggplants, in batches, and cook until golden brown. Remove with a slotted spoon and drain well. Preheat the broiler. Dissolve the bouillon cubes in the hot water. Melt the butter with 1 tablespoon oil in a pan. Stir in the flour and cook, stirring constantly, for 2 minutes. Gradually stir in the stock, a little at a time. Cook, stirring constantly, for 8 minutes. Put half the eggplant slices into a deep ovenproof baking dish and pour in half the sauce. Add the remaining slices and pour in the remaining sauce. Sprinkle with the gruyere and cook under a hot broiler for about 10 minutes, until golden. Serve immediately from the dish.

327 Eggplants stuffed with mushrooms and béchamel sauce

BERENJENAS RELLENAS CON CHAMPIÑON Y BECHAMEL

- 6 eggplants
- 2 ¾ cups chopped mushrooms
- 2 tablespoons (¼ stick) butter
- juice of 1 lemon
- 5 tablespoons olive oil
- 1 onion, finely chopped
- 1 heaping tablespoon
  all-purpose flour
- 1 cup milk
- 1 egg yolk
- ¾ cup grated gruyere cheese
- salt

Serves 6

Cut the eggplants in half lengthwise. Remove and discard the seeds and scoop out the flesh with a teaspoon without piercing the skins. Dice the flesh and sprinkle with salt. Sprinkle the inside of the eggplant skins with salt. Let stand for 1 hour to draw out some of their juices. Rinse well and pat dry. Preheat the oven to 350°F. Put the mushrooms, 1½ tablespoons of the butter, and a few drops of the lemon juice into a pan and cook over low heat, stirring occasionally, for 6 minutes. Put the eggplant skins cut sides up in a single layer in an ovenproof baking dish and add a little of the oil to each, then bake for about 25 minutes while you prepare the filling. Melt the remaining butter with the remaining oil in a pan. Add the onion and cook over low heat, stirring occasionally, for 5 minutes, until softened and translucent. Add the diced eggplant and cook, stirring constantly, for 8 minutes, then add the mushrooms. Stir in the flour and cook, stirring constantly, for 2 minutes. Gradually stir in the milk, a little at a time. Cook over low heat, stirring constantly, for 10 minutes, adding a little more milk if the mixture is too thick. Beat together the remaining lemon juice and the egg yolk in a bowl, then stir in a little of the eggplant-mushroom béchamel sauce to prevent the yolk curdling. Stir the mixture into the pan. Fill the eggplant skins with the mixture, sprinkle with the gruyere, return the dish to the oven, and bake until the cheese has melted. Serve immediately straight from the dish.

Note: The mushrooms can be replaced with chopped Serrano ham or prosciutto.

328

Baked eggplants and tomatoes with grated cheese
BERENJENAS Y TOMATES AL HORNO, CON QUESO RALLADO

- 4 large eggplants
- sunflower oil, for deep-frying
- 1 heaping tablespoon
  all-purpose flour,
  plus extra for dusting
- 2–3 large tomatoes, thinly sliced
- ¼ cup margarine
- scant 2 cups milk
- ⅓ cup grated gruyere cheese
- salt

Serves 4

Peel and slice the eggplants. Heat the oil in a deep-fryer or deep saucepan to 350–375°F or until a cube of day-old bread browns in 30 seconds. Dust the eggplant slices with flour and cook them, in batches, in the hot oil. Remove with a slotted spoon and drain well. Put the tomato slices on a plate, sprinkle each layer with a little salt and let stand to draw out some of their juices. Preheat the oven 400°F. Arrange the eggplant and tomato slices in an overlapping pattern in a round ovenproof baking dish, putting one slice of tomato after every three slices of eggplant until all the tomatoes and eggplants are used up. Make a thin béchamel sauce with half the margarine, the reserved oil, the flour, and milk as described in recipe 77. Lightly season the eggplant and tomato slices with salt and pour the béchamel sauce over them. Sprinkle with the gruyere, dot with the remaining margarine, and bake for about 15 minutes, until golden. Serve immediately straight from the dish.

329

Eggplants stuffed with rice
BERENJENAS RELLENAS DE ARROZ

- 6 eggplants
- 6 tablespoons olive oil
- 6 tablespoons long-grain rice
- 2 tablespoons bread crumbs
- ¼ cup (½ stick) butter
- salt

Tomato sauce:
- 2 tablespoons olive oil
- 1 small onion, chopped
- 1 pound 2 ounces very ripe
  tomatoes, seeded and chopped
- 1 teaspoon sugar
- salt

Serves 6

Preheat the oven to 350°F. Make a very concentrated tomato sauce as described in recipe 73. Cut the eggplants in half lengthwise, slash the flesh, season lightly with salt, and put them into an ovenproof baking dish. Pour the oil over them and roast for 30 minutes, until the flesh is soft. Meanwhile, bring a large pan of unsalted water to a boil. Add the rice, stir with a wooden spoon to prevent the grains from clumping together, and cook over high heat for 12–18 minutes, until tender. (The cooking time depends on the type of rice.) Drain the rice in a large fine mesh sieve and rinse well under cold running water, stirring to make sure that it is well washed. Drain well again and season lightly with salt while it is still in the sieve. Remove the eggplants from the oven but do not switch off the oven. Let cool slightly, then scoop out the flesh with a teaspoon without piercing the skins. Remove and discard the seeds, then chop the flesh. Combine the eggplant flesh, rice, and tomato sauce in a bowl and divide the mixture among the eggplant skins. Sprinkle with the bread crumbs and dot with the butter. Return to the oven and cook for 25 minutes, until golden. Serve immediately straight from the dish.

330

Eggplants stuffed with meat

BERENJENAS RELLENAS DE CARNE

- 6 eggplants
- 1½ tablespoons sunflower oil
- 1¾ cups ground beef or other leftover meat or scant 1 cup chopped Serrano ham or prosciutto
- 1 egg, lightly beaten
- 4 tablespoons bread crumbs
- 2 cloves garlic, chopped
- 1 sprig fresh parsley, chopped
- salt

Serves 6

Preheat the oven to 350°F. Cut the eggplants in half lengthwise and slash the flesh. Lightly season with salt, place in a roasting pan, and drizzle with the oil. Roast for 30 minutes, until soft. Remove the eggplants from the oven but do not switch off the oven. Let cool slightly, then scoop out the flesh with a teaspoon without piercing the skins. Remove and discard the seeds. Chop the flesh, mix with the meat, egg, half the bread crumbs, the garlic, and parsley, and season with salt. Divide the mixture among the eggplant skins. Sprinkle with the remaining bread crumbs and drizzle with the remaining oil. Return to the oven and bake for about 35 minutes, then increase the oven temperature to broil and put the dish under the broiler for about 10 minutes more. Serve immediately straight from the dish.

331

Eggplant omelets

BERENJENAS EN TORTILLA

- 3 eggplants
- 4 tablespoons olive oil
- 1 onion, finely chopped
- 2 tablespoons all-purpose flour
- 2¼ cups milk
- ⅔–¾ cups sunflower oil
- 6 eggs
- ¾ cup grated gruyere cheese
- 1 quantity Classic Tomato Sauce (see recipe 73)
- salt

Serves 4–6

Peel the eggplants and coarsely chop the flesh, then shred it in a food processor or put through a meat grinder. Heat the olive oil in a large skillet. Add the onion and eggplant and cook over low heat, stirring occasionally, for 10 minutes. Stir in the flour and cook, stirring constantly, for 2 minutes. Gradually stir in the milk, a little at a time. Cook, stirring constantly, for 10 minutes, season with salt, and remove the pan from the heat. Preheat the broiler. Heat a little of the sunflower oil in another skillet. Beat one of the eggs with a pinch of salt in a bowl. Pour half the egg mixture into the skillet and cook until just beginning to set. Put a little of the eggplant mixture in the middle of the omelet, flip it over, and slide it out of the pan into an ovenproof baking dish. Continue to make more little omelets in the same way until the eggs and filling have been used up. Pour the tomato sauce over the omelets, sprinkle with the gruyere, and cook under the broiler for 5–10 minutes, until golden and bubbling. Serve immediately straight from the dish.

Note: You can cover the omelets with Classic Béchamel Sauce (see recipe 77), made with milk or a mixture of equal parts milk and stock, instead of tomato sauce.

332

Eggplants cooked in tomato sauce
BERENJENAS COCIDAS CON SALSA DE TOMATE

- 4½ pounds eggplants
- ¾ cup olive oil
- 2 large onions, finely chopped
- 3¼ pounds ripe tomatoes, seeded and chopped
- 1 teaspoon sugar
- salt

Serves 6

Peel and dice the eggplants and put them into a pan. Pour in water to cover, add a pinch of salt, and cook for 15 minutes. Drain in a large colander. Heat the oil in a large skillet. Add the onion and cook over low heat, stirring occasionally, for about 8 minutes, until lightly browned. Add the tomato, increase the heat to medium, and cook, stirring occasionally and breaking up the tomato with the side of the spoon, for about 10 minutes. Let cool slightly, then transfer to a food processor or blender and process to a purée. Return to the pan, stir in the sugar, and add the diced eggplant. Season to taste with salt and cook over low heat for about 10 minutes. Serve immediately.

333

Eggplant garnish
BERENJENAS ESTILO SETAS

- 1 pound 10 ounces eggplants
- 2¼ cups sunflower oil
- 1 clove garlic, chopped
- 1 tablespoon chopped fresh parsley
- salt

Serves 4

Peel the eggplants and cut into slices about ¾ inch thick. Scoop out the seeds if you like. Put the slices into a colander, sprinkling each layer with salt, and let stand for about 1 hour to draw out some of their juices. Rinse thoroughly and pat dry. Heat the oil in one very large or two skillets. Add the eggplant slices, packing them in tightly. Cover and cook over low heat for about 20 minutes, until soft. Drain off nearly all the oil, leaving just enough to prevent the eggplant from sticking. Sprinkle the garlic and parsley over the eggplant and season lightly with salt. Increase the heat to medium and cook for a few minutes, shaking the pan. Serve immediately.

Note: This recipe is intended to be used as a garnish for a meat dish. To serve as a vegetable dish, allow 5 ½ pounds eggplants for serving six people.

334 Fried eggplant garnish

BERENJENAS FRITAS DE ADORNO

- 1 pound 10 ounces eggplants
- ½ cup all-purpose flour
- sunflower oil, for deep-frying
- salt

Serves 4

Peel the eggplants and thinly slice lengthwise. Scoop out the seeds if you like. Put the slices into a colander, sprinkling each layer with salt, and let stand for about 1 hour to draw out some of their juices. Rinse thoroughly and pat dry. Pour the flour into a shallow dish. Dip the slices in the flour to coat, shaking off any excess. Heat the oil in a deep-fryer or deep saucepan to 350–375°F or until a cube of day-old bread browns in 30 seconds. Add the eggplant slices, in batches, and cook until golden brown and crisp. Drain well and keep warm while you cook the other batches. Sprinkle with a little fine salt and serve.

Note: This recipe is a garnish for a meat dish. To serve as a vegetable dish, allow 5 ½ pounds eggplants for six people.

335 Watercress salad

BERROS EN ENSALADA

- 1 bunch of watercress
- 1 quantity vinaigrette
  (see recipe 98)

Serves 2–4

Remove and discard the long stalks, wash the leaves well, and pat or spin dry. Toss lightly with a vinaigrette (see recipe 98).

336 Fantasy salad

ENSALADA FANTASÍA

- 1 bunch of watercress
- 1 avocado
- 3 ½ ounces potatoes
- 2 apples
- 1 quantity Classic Mayonnaise
  (see recipe 105)

Serves 2–4

Boil and slice the potatoes. Remove and discard the long stalks of the watercress. Wash the leaves well and pat or spin dry. Place in a salad bowl. Peel and cut the avocado into wedges. Peel, core and dice the apples. Add to the watercress along with the potato and avocado Toss gently with the mayonnaise.

337 Watercress as garnish

BERROS PARA ADORNO

- 1 bunch of watercress

Serves 2–4

Remove and discard the longest stalks. Wash the watercress, drain and tie into bunches with chives or pieces of kitchen twine.

338

Potatoes with borage
PATATAS CON BORRAJAS

- 2 bunches fresh borage
- 2¼ pounds potatoes,
  cut into walnut-size pieces
- 4 tablespoons olive oil
- 1 onion, finely chopped
- 1 large or 2 small cloves garlic,
  finely chopped
- 1 teaspoon paprika
- salt

Serves 4

Scrape off the hairs from the borage stalks and cut the stalks into 1-inch lengths. Put the borage and potato into a pan, pour in water to cover, add a pinch of salt, and bring to a boil. Lower the heat and cook for about 25 minutes, until the potatoes are tender. Heat the oil in a large skillet. Add the onion and garlic and cook over low heat, stirring occasionally, for about 6 minutes, until the onion is softened and translucent. Remove the pan from the heat and sprinkle in the paprika. Drain the potatoes and borage and add to the skillet. Return the pan to the heat and cook, stirring occasionally, for 5 minutes. Serve immediately.

339

Fried zucchini garnish
CALABACINES FRITOS

- 3 tablespoons all-purpose flour
- generous 1 cup beer
- 1 pounds 10 ounces zucchini
- sunflower oil, for deep-frying
- salt

Serves 6.

Sift the flour into a bowl and gradually stir in the beer, a little at a time, until the batter has the consistency of a thick custard. Lightly season with salt and let stand for 30 minutes. Meanwhile, peel and thinly slice the zucchini. Heat the oil in a deep-fryer or deep saucepan to 350–375°F or until a cube of day-old bread browns in 30 seconds. One at a time, dip the zucchini slices into the batter, and add to the hot oil in batches. Cook until golden brown, then remove with a slotted spoon and drain well. Serve immediately.

340

Fried coated zucchini
CALABACINES REBOZADOS Y FRITOS

- 3¼ pounds fairly large zucchini,
  peeled and thinly sliced
- ½ cup all-purpose flour
- 4 eggs
- sunflower oil, for deep-frying
- 1 teaspoon chopped
  fresh parsley
- salt

Serves 6

Put the zucchini slices in a colander, sprinkling each layer with salt, and let stand for at least 1 hour to draw out some of their juices. Rinse thoroughly and pat dry. Pour the flour into a shallow dish. Lightly beat the eggs in another shallow dish. Heat the oil in a deep-fryer or deep saucepan to 350–375°F or until a cube of day-old bread browns in 30 seconds. Dip the zucchini slices first in the flour, shaking off any excess, then the beaten egg. Add to the hot oil, in batches, and cook until golden brown. Remove with a slotted spoon and drain well, then keep warm while cooking the remaining batches. Serve immediately, sprinkled with the parsley.

Fried zucchini with bacon

CALABACINES FRITOS Y BACON

• 2½ pounds zucchini,
  peeled and cut into¼-inch slices
• ½ cup all-purpose flour
• sunflower oil, for deep-frying
• 6 thin bacon slices
• 1 large onion, finely chopped
• 2 cloves garlic, finely chopped
• salt

Serves 6

Preheat the oven to 325°F. Season the zucchini slices with salt. Pour the flour into a shallow dish. Heat the oil in a deep-fryer or deep saucepan to 350–375°F or until a cube of day-old bread browns in 30 seconds. One at a time, dip the zucchini slices in the flour, shaking off the excess, add to the hot oil in batches, and cook until golden brown. Remove with a slotted spoon and drain well, then arrange in a spiral in a round ovenproof baking dish. Keep warm in the oven. Add the bacon to the oil and cook until crisp and golden brown. Drain well and keep warm in the oven. Transfer 5 tablespoons of the oil into another skillet and heat it. Add the onion and garlic and cook over medium heat, stirring occasionally, for 5–6 minutes, until the onion is beginning to brown.Increase the oven temperature to 450°F. Pour the onion mixture over the zucchini slices and place the bacon on top. Return the baking dish to the oven for 4 minutes. Serve immediately straight from the dish.

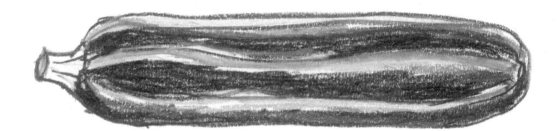

342

Zucchini stuffed with shrimp
CALABACINES RELLENOS DE GAMBAS

- 4 zucchini
- ½ tablespoon butter,
  plus extra for greasing
- 2 shallots, chopped
- generous 1 cup white wine
- 2¼ pounds raw shrimp, peeled
- 4 sprigs fresh tarragon
- 1¼ cups light cream
- 2 tablespoons mustard
- salt and pepper

Serves 4

Working on one zucchini at a time, peel off narrow strips of skin lengthwise, leaving wider strips intact in between to create a striped effect. Cut each zucchini into three pieces and scoop out and discard some of the flesh. Steam for 10 minutes. Preheat the oven to 350°F degrees. Grease an ovenproof baking dish with butter. Melt the remaining butter in a skillet. Add the shallots and cook over low heat, stirring occasionally, for 5 minutes. Pour in the wine and cook for 5 minutes more. Add the shrimp and three of the tarragon sprigs, season with salt and pepper, and cook for a few minutes until the prawns are opaque. Remove them from the pan and keep warm. Stir the cream and mustard into the pan and simmer for 10 minutes. Mean-while, chop the remaining tarragon. Put the pieces of zucchini into the prepared baking dish and bake for 10 minutes. Add the shrimp to the cream sauce and remove the pan from the heat. Remove the tarragon sprigs and stir in the chopped tarragon. Fill the zucchini with the shrimp and pour the sauce over them.

343

Zucchini stuffed with mussels
CALABACINES RELLENOS DE MEJILLONES

- 2½ pounds mussels
- generous 1 cup white wine
- 4 zucchini
- ½ tablespoon butter,
  plus extra for greasing
- 2 shallots, chopped
- 4 sprigs fresh tarragon
- 1¼ cups light cream
- 2 tablespoons mustard
- salt and pepper

Serves 4

Discard any mussels with broken shells or any that do not shut immediately when sharply tapped. Cook the mussels with the wine in pan over high heat for 3–5 minutes, until they open. Discard any that remain closed, remove the mussels from their shells and strain the cooking liquid through a fine muslin-covered sieve into a bowl. Working on one zucchini at a time, peel off narrow strips of skin lengthwise, leaving wider strips intact in between to create a striped effect. Cut each zucchini into three pieces and scoop out and discard some of the flesh. Steam for 10 minutes. Preheat the oven to 350°F degrees. Grease an ovenproof baking dish with butter. Melt the remaining butter in a skillet. Add the shallots and cook over low heat, stirring occasionally, for 5 minutes. Add the cooking liquid from the mussels, and 3 of the tarragon sprigs, season with salt and pepper and cook for a few minutes. Stir in the cream and mustard and simmer for 10 minutes. Meanwhile, chop the remaining tarragon. Put the pieces of courgette into the prepared baking dish and bake for 10 minutes. Remove the tarragon and stir in the chopped tarragon and the mussels. Fill the courgettes with the prawns and pour the sauce over.

344

Zucchini with mashed potato
CALABACINES CON PURÉ DE PATATAS

- 3¼–4½ pounds zucchini, peeled and cut into ¼-inch thick slices
- generous 1 cup sunflower oil
- 3½ ounces dried instant mashed potato
- 1½ tablespoons butter
- generous 1 cup milk
- 1 egg, separated
- 1 egg white
- ¼ cup grated gruyere cheese
- salt

Serves 4

Put the zucchini slices into a colander, sprinkling each layer with salt, and let stand for at least 1 hour to draw out some of their juices. Rinse thoroughly and pat dry. Heat the oil in a skillet. Add the zucchini, in batches, and cook until light golden brown. Remove with a slotted spoon and set aside.Preheat the oven to 400°F. Make the mashed potato in a pan according to the instructions on the package, using the instant mashed potato, generous 1 cup water, the butter, milk, and a pinch of salt. It should be quite thick. Remove the pan from the heat and beat in the egg yolk. Whisk the egg whites in a clean, dry bowl until they form firm peaks, then fold into the potato. Put half the zucchini into an ovenproof baking dish in an even layer and cover with the mashed potato. Top with the remaining zucchini, sprinkle with the gruyere, and bake for 5 minutes, until golden brown. Serve immediately.

345

Zucchini ratatouille
PISTO DE CALABACÍN

- 4½ pounds zucchini
- 5–7 tablespoons olive oil
- 9 ounces onions, chopped
- 2¼ pounds ripe tomatoes, peeled and chopped
- 1 teaspoon sugar
- 2 green bell peppers, seeded and diced (optional)
- salt

Serves 6

Peel and dice the zucchini, removing the seeds. Heat 3 tablespoons of the oil in a pan. Add the onion and cook over low heat, stirring occasionally, for about 5 minutes, until softened and translucent. Add the zucchini and cook, stirring occasionally, for 5 minutes more, until lightly browned. Heat 2 tablespoons of the remaining oil in a skillet. Add the tomato and cook over low heat, stirring occasionally and breaking it up with the side of the spoon, for 10 minutes. Let cool slightly, then transfer to a food processor or blender and process to a purée. Season with salt, add the sugar, and process briefly again, then pour the mixture over the zucchini, and stir well. Cook over low heat for 25 minutes more, adding a little water if the mixture is becoming too thick. If using the bell peppers, heat 2 tablespoons oil in a small skillet. Add the bell peppers, cover, and cook over low heat, stirring occasionally, for about 25 minutes. Stir them into the zucchini just before serving. Serve in a warm deep dish.

Note: This dish can be made in advance and reheated. You can also process the ratatouille in a food processor or blender once it is cooked, then just before serving, add 3 beaten eggs. Serve garnished with triangles of fried bread (see recipe 130).

Zucchini ratatouille with potatoes

PISTO DE CALABACÍN CON PATATAS

- 5 tablespoons olive oil
- 9 ounces onions, finely chopped
- 2¼ pounds very ripe tomatoes, peeled, seeded, and chopped
- 2 green bell peppers, seeded and diced
- sunflower oil, for deep-frying
- 7 ounces potatoes, thinly sliced
- 2¼ pounds zucchini
- 1 teaspoon sugar
- 1 egg, lightly beaten
- salt

Serves 6

Heat 3 tablespoons of the olive oil in a skillet. Add the onion and cook over low heat, stirring occasionally, for about 5 minutes, until softened and translucent. Add the tomato, increase the heat to medium, and cook, stirring occasionally and breaking up the tomato with the side of the spoon, for 15 minutes more. Heat the remaining olive oil in a small skillet. Add the bell pepper, cover, and cook over low heat, stirring occasionally, for 25 minutes. Heat the sunflower oil in a deep-fryer or saucepan to 350–375°F or until a cube of day-old bread browns in 30 seconds. Add the potato slices and cook for 5–10 minutes, until golden brown. Remove with a slotted spoon and drain well. Peel the zucchini, cut them in half lengthwise, and remove the seeds, then slice thinly. Put into a pan, pour in just enough water to cover, and bring to a boil. Lower the heat and simmer for 5 minutes, then drain well. Stir the sugar into the onion and tomato mixture. Using a slotted spoon, transfer the bell pepper to the onion and tomato mixture, then add the potato and zucchini. Season to taste with salt and cook, stirring constantly, for 5 minutes. Just before serving, stir the egg into the warm ratatouille.

Note: This dish can be made in advance and reheated, but do not add the egg until just before serving.

347

Zucchini ratatouille with rice

PISTO DE CALABACÍN CON ARROZ

- 4 tablespoons long-grain rice
- 4 tablespoons olive oil
- 1 large onion, chopped
- 1 clove garlic, finely chopped
- 14 ripe tomatoes,
  peeled, seeded, and chopped
- 3¼ pounds zucchini, diced
- salt

Serves 6

Bring a large pan of water to a boil. Add the rice, bring back to a boil, then lower the heat, and cook for about 15–18 minutes, until tender. Drain well in a large colander, rinse under cold running water, and drain well again. Heat the oil in a skillet. Add the onion and garlic and cook over low heat, stirring occasionally, for 2 minutes. Add the tomato and cook, stirring occasionally, for 5 minutes more, then add the zucchini. Season with salt, cover, and simmer, stirring frequently, for 35 minutes. Stir in the rice, then heat through gently, and serve immediately.

Note: This dish can be made in advance and reheated, but do not stir in the rice until just before serving.

348

Ratatouille

PISTO ESTILO FRANCÉS

- ⅔ cup olive oil
- 11 ounces onions, finely chopped
- 3 eggplants, peeled and cut into
  ¾-inch cubes
- 2 green bell peppers,
  seeded and diced
- 4 zucchini, peeled and diced
- 1 pound 2 ounces very ripe
  tomatoes, peeled, seeded,
  and chopped
- 2 cloves garlic
- salt

Serves 6

Heat the oil in a large, deep skillet. Add the onion and cook over low heat, stirring occasionally, for 10 minutes. Add the eggplant and cook, stirring occasionally, for 10 minutes more. Add the bell pepper and cook, stirring occasionally, for another 10 minutes. Stir in the zucchini and tomato, add the garlic, and season with salt. Cover and simmer over low heat for 1 hour. If the ratatouille is very runny, remove the lid for the last 10 minutes to let some of the liquid evaporate. Remove and discard the garlic before serving. Serve immediately.

Note: This dish can be prepared in advance and reheated.

349

Zucchini ratatouille with tuna
PISTO DE CALABACÍN CON ATÚN

- ½ cup olive oil
- 3¼ pounds zucchini,
  peeled and coarsely chopped
- 1 green bell pepper,
  seeded and diced
- 2 large onions, chopped
- 1 pound 10 ounces tomatoes,
  peeled, seeded, and chopped
- 7 ounces canned tuna,
  drained and flaked
- salt

Serves 6

Heat 4 tablespoons of the oil in a large skillet. Add the zucchini and cook, stirring frequently, for 2–3 minutes, then add 3 tablespoons water, and simmer for about 15 minutes, until soft. Heat 3 table-spoons of the remaining oil in another skillet. Add the bell pepper and cook over medium heat, stirring occasionally, for about 15 minutes, until soft. Remove from the pan and set aside. Add the onion to the pan and cook over low heat, stirring occasionally, for about 10 minutes, until beginning to brown. Add the tomato and cook, stirring occasionally and breaking it up with the side of the spoon, for 15–20 minutes, until it forms a thick sauce. Transfer the mixture to the pan of zucchini, stir in the bell pepper, and cook, stirring occasionally, for 10 minutes. Stir in the tuna, heat through, and serve.

Note: This dish can be made in advance and reheated, but do not add the tuna until just before serving.

350

Zucchini with tomato sauce au gratin
CALABACINES CON SALSA DE TOMATE AL GRATÉN

- 4½ pounds large zucchini,
  peeled and sliced lengthwise
- 1½ tablespoons butter,
  plus extra for greasing
- 1¼ cups grated gruyere cheese
- 1 quantity Classic Tomato Sauce
  (see recipe 73)
- salt

Serves 6

Bring a large pan of salted water to a boil. Add the zucchini slices nd cook for 5 minutes. Drain well and set aside in a colander to drain completely. Preheat the oven to 350°F. Grease an ovenproof baking dish with butter. Layer the zucchini slices in the prepared baking dish, sprinkling a little of the gruyere between each layer. Pour in the tomato sauce, sprinkle with the remaining grated cheese, and dot with the butter. Bake for 15–20 minutes, until golden brown. Serve immediately straight from the dish.

351

Zucchini with béchamel sauce
CALABACINES CON BECHAMEL

- 4½ pounds zucchini,
  peeled and cut into ¼-inch slices
- 2 tablespoons (¼ stick) butter
- 2 tablespoons sunflower oil
- 2 heaping tablespoons
  all-purpose flour
- 2¼ cups milk
- ¾ cup grated gruyere cheese
- salt

Serves 6

Put the zucchini into a pan, pour in water to cover, and add a pinch of salt. Bring to a boil, then remove the pan from the heat, and drain well. Place the slices in an ovenproof baking dish. Preheat the oven to 400°F. To make the béchamel sauce, melt the butter with the oil in another pan. Stir in the flour and cook, stirring constantly, for 2 minutes. Gradually stir in the milk, a little at a time. Lightly season with salt and cook, stirring constantly, for 10 minutes. Pour the sauce over the zucchini, sprinkle with the gruyere, and bake for about 10–15 minutes, until golden brown. Serve immediately, straight from the dish.

352

Broiled zucchini with cheese
CALABACINES GRATINADOS CON QUESO

- 4½ pounds zucchini, peeled
  and cut into ¼-inch thick slices
- scant 1 cup grated gruyere cheese
- pinch of freshly grated nutmeg
  (optional)
- 3–4 tablespoons bread crumbs
- ¼ cup (½ stick) butter
- salt

Serves 6

Preheat the oven to 400°F. Bring a large pan of salted water to a boil. Add the zucchini and cook for 5 minutes, until tender. Drain well. Place a layer of zucchini slices in a deep ovenproof baking dish, sprinkling a little gruyere and nutmeg, if using, over the top. Continue in this way until all the zucchini slices are used. Sprinkle the remaining cheese on top, then sprinkle with the bread crumbs, and dot with the butter. Bake for 15–20 minutes, until golden brown. Serve immediately straight from the dish.

353

- 6 zucchini, halved lengthwise
- scant 2 cups chopped,
  Smithfield, prosciutto or
  other dry-cured ham
- 3 tomatoes,
  peeled, seeded, and chopped
- 1 teaspoon chopped
  fresh tarragon
- 2–3 tablespoons olive oil
- 3 tablespoons bread crumbs
- salt

Serves 6

Zucchini stuffed with ham and tomatoes
CALABACINES RELLENOS CON JAMÓN DE YORK Y TOMATES

Bring a large pan of salted water to a boil. Add the zucchini, bring back to a boil, and cook for 10 minutes. Remove the zucchini and let drain on a dishtowel. When cool enough to handle, scoop out the flesh with a teaspoon without piercing the skins. Chop the flesh. Preheat the oven to 400°F. Combine the ham, tomato, zucchini flesh, and tarragon in a bowl and season to taste with salt. Spoon the mixture into the zucchini skins. Put just enough of the oil into an ovenproof baking dish to cover the base, then place the filled zucchini in the dish side by side, filling uppermost. Sprinkle with the bread crumbs, drizzle with the remaining oil, and bake for about 15 minutes, until lightly browned. Serve immediately straight from the dish.

354

- ½ cup olive oil
- 2¼ pounds onions,
  cut into ½-inch wedges
- 9 ounces green bell peppers,
  seeded and cut into thin strips
- 2¼ pounds very ripe tomatoes,
  peeled, seeded, and chopped
- 1–2 cloves garlic (optional),
  finely chopped
- salt

Serves 4–6

Piperade
PIPERADA

Heat the oil in large, deep skillet. Add the onion and cook over low heat, stirring occasionally, for 10 minutes. Add the bell pepper and cook for 5 minutes more. Add the tomato, season with salt, and simmer over low heat, stirring occasionally, for 1½ hours. If using the garlic, heat 2 tablespoons olive oil in a small skillet. Add the garlic and cook over low heat, stirring frequently, for a few minutes, until lightly browned. Remove from the heat and add to the vegetables just before the end of the cooking time.

Note: Piperade is a stew-like dish that originated in the Basque region of France.

Pumpkin

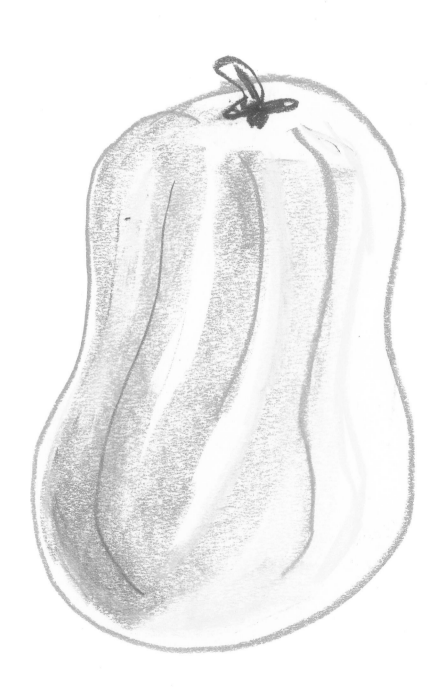

Origin and season

The exact origin of calabaza (or West Indian pumpkin) is not known but it is a favourite throughout the Caribbean and Central and South America. It is at its best in the fall. If you can't find this winter squash, butternut squash is a good alternative. The custom of carving pumpkin lanterns at Halloween is popular in many countries, most notably the United States, where pumpkin soup and pumpkin pie also feature as part of the traditional Thanksgiving meal.

Selection

As pumpkins can grow extremely large, they are often sold in pieces. Their skin might be green or orange, but their flesh should have a good orange color with no signs of mold.

Nutrition

Pumpkins contain a lot of water and so are easy to digest. They contain about 20 calories per 3 ½ ounces.

Trick

• To extract the maximum flavor, cut the flesh into cubes and cook them in a little water with a few slices of potato and a finely chopped onion. Purée in a food processor or blender, and season well with pepper. Serve the soup in a hollowed-out pumpkin "shell."

355

Fried pumpkin

CALABAZA REHOGADA

- 4 leeks, cut into 1-inch lengths, and rinsed well
- 3 ¼ pounds West Indian pumpkin (calabaza) or butternut squash, peeled, seeded, and cubed
- 1 cup olive oil
- 3–4 slices of bread, crusts removed, cubed
- 3 cloves garlic, lightly crushed
- salt

Serves 4

Bring a large saucepan of salted water to a boil. Add the leek and cook over medium heat for 20 minutes. Add the pumpkin and cook for about 25 minutes, until the pumpkin is tender. (Test by piercing with a fork.) Drain off the water, cover the pan, and set aside. Heat the oil in a large skillet. Add the bread and cook, stirring frequently, until evenly browned. Remove with a slotted spoon and drain on paper towels. Pour off most of the oil, leaving just enough to cover the base of the pan, and return the pan to the heat. Add the garlic and cook for a few minutes until well browned, then remove and discard. Add the pumpkin, leek, and croûtons to the pan and cook over low heat for 5 minutes. Serve immediately.

Pumpkin purée gratin

PURÉ DE CALABAZA GRATINADO

- ½ cup olive oil
- 3¼ pounds West Indian pumpkin (calabaza) or butternut squash, peeled, seeded, and cubed
- 2 tablespoons (¼ stick) butter
- 2 heaping tablespoons all-purpose flour
- 2¼ cups milk
- pinch of freshly grated nutmeg
- 3 eggs, lightly beaten
- scant 1 cup grated gruyere cheese
- salt

Serves 4–6

Heat 6 tablespoons of the oil in a pan. Add the pumpkin and cook over low heat, stirring occasionally, for 10–15 minutes, until tender. (Test by piercing with a fork.) Transfer to a food processor or blender and process to a purée, then scrape into a bowl. Preheat the oven to 350°F. Melt the butter with the remaining oil in another pan. Stir in the flour and cook, stirring constantly, for 2 minutes. Gradually stir in the milk, a little at a time. Add the nutmeg, season with salt, and cook, stirring constantly, for 10 minutes. Stir the sauce into the pumpkin purée, then beat in the eggs. Pour the mixture into an ovenproof baking dish, sprinkle with the gruyere, and bake for about 15 minutes, until golden. Serve immediately straight from the dish.

Cardoons

Origin and season

This tall plant, resembling celery in appearance, comes from the Mediterranean islands of Sicily, the Balearics, and Sardinia. It is from the same family as the globe artichoke. It is popular in southern Europe and North Africa. It is at its best in the early winter.

Selection

Choose light-colored cardoons and allow quite a lot per serving— about 14 ounces—as only the inner ribs and heart are edible.

Nutrition

Cardoons consist of about 90 percent water and contain approximately 40 calories per 3 ½ ounces. The plant is said to have calming properties and is therefore used in some herbal teas.

How to cook

Trim the base. Remove and discard the hard outer stalks. Pull off the inedible strings. Remove the inner stalks, one at a time, rub with ½ lemon, and cut into pieces about 1½ inches long. Cut the heart into quarters. Put the pieces of cardoon into a large bowl of water mixed with lemon juice. Put 1 tablespoon all-purpose flour into a bowl and mix to a paste with water. Pour this into a pan, pour in plenty of water (enough to cover the cardoon once it has been added to the pan), and add a pinch of salt. Partially cover the pan and bring to a boil. Add the cardoon and cook over medium heat for 1–1½ hours, until tender. Drain well, then cook as preferred.

357

Cardoon with paprika sauce
CARDO CON SALSA DE PIMENTÓN

- 1 cardoon
- 1 lemon
- 2½ tablespoons all-purpose flour
- 3 tablespoons olive oil
- 1 onion, finely chopped
- 1 teaspoon paprika
- salt

Serves 4

Prepare and precook the cardoon, using the lemon and 1 tablespoon of the flour, as described on page 285. Drain well, reserving the cooking liquid. Heat the oil in a skillet. Add the onion and cook over low heat, stirring occasionally, for 8–10 minutes, until golden brown. Stir in the remaining flour and cook, stirring constantly, for 2 minutes. Stir in the paprika, then gradually stir in scant 2 cups of the reserved cooking liquid. Bring to a boil, stirring constantly. Pour the mixture into a large pan. If you prefer to remove the onion, strain through a coarse strainer. Add the cardoon and simmer over low heat for 10 minutes. Serve immediately.

358

Cardoon in milk sauce with saffron and cinnamon
CARDO EN SALSA DE LECHE CON AZAFRÁN Y CANELA

- 1 cardoon
- ½ lemon, peeled and coarsely chopped
- ¾ cup olive oil
- 2 cloves garlic
- 2 tablespoons all-purpose flour
- 2¼ cups milk
- ½ teaspoon ground cinnamon
- pinch of saffron threads
- 2 slices of fried bread, (see recipe 130) broken into pieces
- 2 tablespoons chopped fresh parsley
- salt and pepper

Serves 4

Prepare the cardoon as described on page 285, but do not precook. Put the pieces of cardoon into a pressure cooker, pour in water to cover, and add the lemon and a pinch of salt. Bring to high pressure and cook for 35 minutes (longer for a large cardoon, shorter for a small one). Remove from the heat and leave covered until the pressure has reduced, then remove the cardoon with a slotted spoon, reserving the cooking liquid. Heat the oil in a pan. Add one of the garlic cloves and cook for a few minutes, until browned. Stir in the flour and cook, stirring constantly, for 2 minutes. Remove and discard the garlic. Add the cardoon to the pan, stir in the milk, and add 1 cup of the reserved cooking liquid. Sprinkle in the cinnamon and season to taste with salt and pepper. Cover and simmer over low heat for 30 minutes. Cut the remaining garlic into four pieces and pound in a mortar with the saffron and fried bread, or process in a mini-food processor. Stir the mixture into the pan, re-cover, and simmer gently for 10 minutes more. Serve immediately, garnished with the parsley.

359

Cardoon gratin

CARDO AL GRATÉN CON QUESO Y MANTEQUILLA

- 1 cardoon
- 1 lemon
- 1 tablespoon all-purpose flour
- 2 tablespoons sunflower oil
- scant 1 cup grated
  gruyere cheese
- ¼ cup (½ stick) butter
- salt

Serves 4

Prepare and precook the cardoon, using the lemon and flour, as described on page 285. Drain well. Preheat the broiler. Pour the oil into an ovenproof baking dish, add the cardoon, sprinkle with the gruyere, and dot with the butter. Cook under the broiler for 5 minutes, or until golden brown. Serve immediately straight from the dish.

360

Cardoons with red bell pepper and anchovies

CARDOS CON PIMIENTOS Y ANCHOAS

- 2¼ pounds cardoons
- 1 lemon
- 2 tablespoons all-purpose flour
- 2 tablespoons olive oil
- 3 cloves garlic
- 3 canned anchovy fillets, drained
- 3 tablespoons chopped
  fresh parsley
- 1 red bell pepper,
  seeded and sliced
- 1 bouquet garni (1 sprig fresh
  parsley and 1 bay leaf tied
  together in cheesecloth)
- salt and pepper

Serves 4

Prepare and precook the cardoons, using the lemon and 1 tablespoon of the flour, as described on page 285. Drain well, reserving the cooking liquid. Heat the oil in a pan. Stir in the remaining flour and cook, stirring constantly, for 2 minutes. Add the bell pepper and bouquet garni. Gradually stir in 1½ cups of the reserved cooking liquid, a little at a time. Season to taste with salt and pepper and cook over low heat, stirring constantly, for 5 minutes. Pound the garlic with the anchovies in a mortar, or process in a mini-food processor, then stir into the sauce, together with the parsley. Mix well and serve the cardoons with the sauce poured over them.

361 Cardoon in garlic and vinegar sauce
CARDO EN SALSA CON AJO Y VINAGRE

• 1 cardoon
• 1 lemon
• 2 tablespoons all-purpose flour
• 5 tablespoons olive oil
• 1 onion, finely chopped
• 1 clove garlic
• 1 sprig fresh parsley
• 1 slice of fried bread
• pinch of ground cumin or pepper
• 1 tablespoon white-wine vinegar
• salt
Serves 4

Prepare and precook the cardoon, using the lemon and 1 tablespoon of the flour, as described on page 285. Drain well, reserving the cooking liquid. Heat the oil in a pan. Add the onion and cook over low heat, stirring occasionally, for about 10 minutes, until lightly browned. Put the garlic, parsley, fried bread, cumin or pepper, and a pinch of salt into a mortar and pound with a pestle, or process in a mini-food processor, then pour the mixture into the pan. Stir in the remaining flour and cook, stirring constantly, for 2 minutes. Stir in the vinegar and some of the reserved cooking liquid. Add the cardoon and pour in enough of the remaining reserved cooking liquid to just cover. Season to taste with salt and simmer for 10 minutes. Serve immediately.

362 Cardoon in vinaigrette
CARDO EN VINAGRETA

• 1 cardoon
• 1 lemon
• 1 tablespoon all-purpose flour
• 3 tablespoons wine vinegar
• 9 tablespoons sunflower oil
• 1 sprig fresh parsley
• 1 hard-cooked egg (optional)
• salt
Serves 4

Prepare and precook the cardoon, using the lemon and flour, as described on page 285. Drain well and put into a deep dish or bowl. Make a vinaigrette with the vinegar, oil, and salt as described in recipe 98, and pour it over the cardoon. Finely chop the parsley and chop the hard-cooked egg, if using, and sprinkle over the cardoon. Serve immediately.

Note: This dish is usually served hot but it is also very good cold.

363 Baby cardoons
CARDILLOS

• 1 pound 2 ounces baby cardoons
• 2 tablespoons sunflower oil
• 2 tablespoons olive oil
• 1 tablespoon white-wine vinegar
• 1 tablespoon bread crumbs
• 4 sprigs chopped fresh parsley
• 1 clove garlic, finely chopped
• salt
Serves 4

Clean off any earth and pull off the strings, leaving the baby cardoons attached. Cook them in salted boiling water for about 20 minutes, until tender. Drain well. Heat the sunflower oil in a skillet and cook the cardoons over medium heat until lightly browned. Remove from the pan with a slotted spoon and drain. Make a vinaigrette with the oil, vinegar and salt as described in recipe 98. Add the bread crumbs, parsley, and garlic. Serve the baby cardoons with the vinaigrette. These vegetables are usually served with stew.

Onion

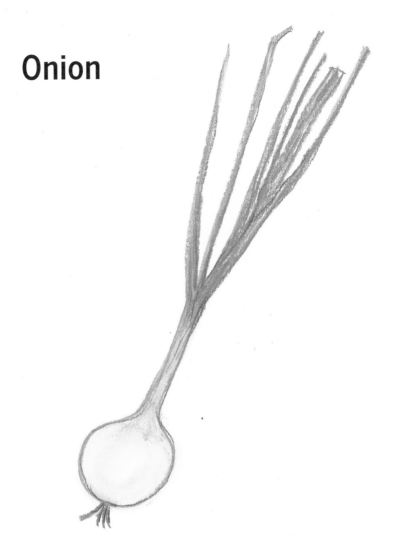

Origin and season

Believed to be one of the oldest vegetables, onions come from Persia (modern Iran). They were popular with the ancient Greeks and the Romans. They are widely grown in Europe, Asia, and America and opinion is unanimous on their medicinal, nutritional, gastronomic, and even meteorological virtues. Although there are many members of the onion family, there are two main types of true onion: the scallion with a small white bulb and green top and the winter onion with a dry, brownish skin, also known as yellow onion. There are many other varieties such as red, white, and sweet Bermuda and Vidalia onions.

Selection

Winter onions should be firm with no signs of germination. The green part of scallions should give off a pungent smell. If you buy them in bunches, make sure the ones on the inside of the bunch are not soft or going rotten.

Nutrition

Onions contain 40 calories per 3 ½ ounces. Eaten raw, they are an excellent diuretic and have antiseptic properties. They are rich in vitamin C. A glass of onion juice each morning is an excellent protection against infections, as well as being a good tonic.

Tricks

- If eating raw onions results in bad breath, chew a few coffee beans
- If you use only part of an onion for a recipe, it is not advisable to keep the remainder as it may be harmful to health
- To avoid crying when peeling onions, wear sunglasses or put the onions into the freezer for 15 minutes first
- To reduce pungency, marinate onions in lemon juice for 2 hours
- It is not advisable to use winter onions once they have germinated, although the green sprouts can be used for salads and omelets.

364

Battered onion garnish

CEBOLLAS REBOZADAS Y FRITAS PARA ADORNO

- 1¼ cups all-purpose flour
- 1 egg, separated
- sunflower oil, for deep-frying
- 1 bottle of beer (1⅓ cups)
- 2 large onions,
  sliced and pushed out into rings
- salt

First version

Sift the flour with a pinch of salt into a bowl. Add the egg yolk and 1 tablespoon of the oil and mix well. Gradually stir in the beer, a little at a time, until the batter has the consistency of thick custard. Whisk the egg white with a pinch of salt in a clean, dry bowl until soft peaks form, then gently fold it into the batter. Heat the remaining oil in a deep-fryer or deep saucepan to 350–375°F or until a cube of day-old bread browns in 30 seconds. Dip the onion rings, one at a time, into the batter, add to the hot oil, and cook, in batches, until golden brown. Do not cook too many at once. Remove the onion rings from the pan and drain well. Serve hot, as a garnish alongside roasted or broiled meat.

- 4 tablespoons all-purpose flour
- generous 1 cup club soda
- 1 tablespoon chopped
  fresh parsley
- 2 large onions, sliced
  and pushed out into rings
- sunflower oil, for deep-frying
- salt

Second version

Sift the flour with a pinch of salt into a bowl and gradually stir in the club soda, a little at a time, until the batter has the consistency of thick custard. Sprinkle in the parsley. Dip the onion rings in the batter and cook in the hot oil as described in the previous recipe.

365

Onion purée
CEBOLLAS EN PURE

- **4 tablespoons olive oil**
- **4½ pounds onions,**
  cut into ½-inch thick slices
- **2 tablespoons all-purpose flour**
- **1 teaspoon sugar**
- **5 tablespoons white wine**
- **salt**

Serves 4

Heat the oil in a large, heavy pan, preferably a Dutch oven. Add the onion and cook over very low heat, stirring occasionally, for 30–45 minutes, until very soft. Sprinkle in the flour and sugar and stir in the wine. Season with salt, mix well, cover, and cook on very low heat for about 2 hours.

Note: This dish can be made in advance and reheated. In fact, it is even better that way.

366

Onions stuffed with meat
CEBOLLAS RELLENAS DE CARNE

- **12 onions, 3–3½ ounces each**
- **1 thick slice of bread,**
  crusts removed
- **¾ cup hot milk**
- **2½ cups mixed ground pork and**
  beef or 2½ cups ground beef
- **1 teaspoon chopped**
  fresh parsley
- **½ clove garlic, finely chopped**
- **1 tablespoon white wine**
- **2 eggs, lightly beaten**
- **1 cup sunflower oil**
- **¾ cup all-purpose flour**
- **2 tablespoons olive oil**
- **1 beef bouillon cube**
- **salt**

Serves 6

Peel the onions and, using a thin sharp knife, make a circular cut around the top and cut a slice off the base of each so that it stands up. Bring a large saucepan of salted water to a boil, add the onions, and cook for 15 minutes. Remove the onions with a slotted spoon and reserve the cooking liquid. Meanwhile, tear the bread into pieces and place in a bowl. Pour in the hot milk and let soak. Put the ground meat into a bowl and add the soaked bread, drained if necessary, the parsley, garlic, wine, three-quarters of the beaten eggs, and a pinch of salt. Mix well. Cut into the onions where the circular cut was made in the tops and scoop out the centers. Fill the cavities with the meat mixture. Heat the sunflower oil in a deep skillet. Brush the surface of the filling in each onion with the remaining beaten egg and then dust the whole onion with some of the flour. Add the onions to the pan, in batches, and cook until evenly browned. Preheat the oven to 350°F. Heat the olive oil in an ovenproof casserole that can be used on the stove. Arrange the onions in the casserole, side by side and filling uppermost, in a single layer. Dissolve the bouillon cube in a bowl with the reserved cooking liquid and pour enough into the casserole to come halfway up the onions. Transfer to the oven and bake, basting occasionally, for about 30 minutes, until tender and browned. (Test by piercing with a skewer or the tip of sharp knife.) Serve immediately straight from the casserole.

Shallots

Shallots are small, elongated members of the onion family with a less acerbic flavor than onions. They have brown or red skins and often consist of two or more "cloves." Grelots are small, flat French onions that are not always easy to obtain.

How to cook

Peel the shallots and place them in a single layer into a pan. Pour in water to cover generously and add a pat of butter (allow 1 ½ table-spoons butter for every 9 ounces shallots or grelots), a pinch of salt, and a few drops of lemon juice. Cover and cook over medium heat for about 30 minutes, until tender. (Test by piercing with a skewer or the tip of a sharp knife.)

How to glaze

Preheat the oven to 350°F. Peel the shallots or grelots and place them in a single layer in an ovenproof baking dish. Pour in warm or cold water to cover and add a pat of butter, a pinch of salt, and 1 teaspoon sugar. Cut a disk of parchment paper that will just fit in the dish and position it so that it almost touches the shallots or greylots. Bake until all the liquid has evaporated and the shallots or grelots are shiny and tender. (Test by piercing with a skewer or the tip of a sharp knife.) Use to garnish any dish.

367

Shallots with béchamel sauce
CEBOLLITAS FRANCESAS CON BECHAMEL

- 12–18 shallots
- 5 tablespoons butter
- dash of lemon juice
- 2 tablespoons olive oil
- 2 tablespoons all-purpose flour
- 2¼ cups milk
- 1½ teaspoons tomato paste
- ½ cup grated gruyere cheese
- salt

Serves 4

Prepare and cook the shallots, using 3 tablespoons of the butter and the lemon juice, as described on page 294. Drain well. Melt the remaining butter with the oil in a pan. Stir in the flour and cook, stirring constantly, for 2 minutes. Gradually stir in the milk, a little at a time, then cook, stirring constantly, for 8 minutes. Remove the pan from the heat and stir in the tomato paste. Season to taste with salt. Preheat the oven to 350°F. Place the shallots in a single layer in an ovenproof baking dish and pour the béchamel sauce over them. Sprinkle with the gruyere and bake for 10–15 minutes, until the cheese has melted. Serve immediately straight from the dish.

368

Celery root
APIO-RÁBANO

- 4 celery root
- 1 quantity Classic Mayonnaise
  (see recipe 105)
- 2 tablespoons mustard
- salt
- pepper

Serves 4

Peel the celery root, cut in half, and put into a pan. Pour in water to cover, add a pinch of salt, and bring to a boil. Lower the heat and cook for 30 minutes. Drain and let cool, then cut into strips like straw potatoes. Mix with the mayonnaise, and add the mustard, and pepper to taste. Let stand for at least 30 minutes before serving to let the flavors mingle.

Note: Instead of boiling the celery root, some people prefer to grate and lightly blanch it, before mixing it with the mayonnaise.

Brussels sprouts

Origin and season

As their name suggests, Brussels sprouts were cultivated in Flanders, now Belgium, in the fifteenth century, although the Belgians claim that they were introduced into their country by the Romans. They are in season from mid fall to early spring.

Selection

They should be completely closed with no yellowing leaves. Try to select sprouts that are more or less the same size so that they need the same cooking time.

Nutrition

They contain vitamin C and are rich in minerals.

How to cook

Brussels sprouts should be very green with tightly wrapped leaves and as uniform in size as possible. Remove any limp or coarse leaves and trim the stems. Wash thoroughly in plenty of water with some vinegar or lemon juice added to remove any bugs. Bring a pan of salted water to a boil, add a handful of sprouts, and cover the pan. Continue adding them handful by handful and re-covering the pan to prevent the temperature of the water dropping below boiling point. When all the sprouts have been added, remove the lid so that they stay green. Some people like to add a pinch of baking soda to keep the sprouts bright green, but this is not recommended, as it makes them soft and they already need to be watched carefully while cooking to make sure they do not begin to disintegrate. The cooking time depends on size and freshness but it will be 20–25 minutes. Drain the sprouts well and refresh under cold running water, taking care they do not start to fall apart. They are then ready to be used. Frozen Brussels sprouts are also available. Add the frozen Brussels sprouts to boiling water and cook until just tender, or steam in the microwave with just a little water for 2–4 minutes until just tender. Then add them to your recipe.

369

Fried Brussels sprouts

COLES DE BRUSELAS REHOGADAS

- 2½–3¼ pounds
  Brussels sprouts
- 7 tablespoons butter
  or ¾ cup olive oil
- 2 cloves garlic (optional),
  lightly crushed
- 2 tablespoons white-wine
  vinegar or 1 teaspoon
  Dijon mustard
- salt and pepper

Serves 4–6

Prepare and cook the sprouts as described on page 296, then drain, and refresh under cold running water. If using the butter, melt half in a large skillet. Add the sprouts and cook over medium-low heat, occasionally stirring gently, for about 5 minutes, until lightly browned. Meanwhile, melt the remaining butter in a small pan. Season the sprouts to taste with salt and pour the melted butter over them just before serving. If using the oil instead of butter, heat the oil with the garlic in a skillet for a few minutes, until the garlic has browned. Remove and discard the garlic and add the sprouts to the pan. Cook for about 5 minutes until lightly browned. Season with pepper and pour the vinegar over them. Alternatively, do not season with pepper and stir in the mustard.

370

Brussels sprouts with béchamel sauce

COLES DE BRUSELAS CON BECHAMEL

- 2½–3¼ pounds Brussels
  sprouts
- 2 tablespoons (¼ stick) butter
- 2 tablespoons olive oil
- 2 tablespoons all-purpose flour
- 2¼ cups milk
- 1 teaspoon chopped
  fresh parsley
- salt

Serves 4–6

Prepare and cook the sprouts as described on page 296, then drain, and refresh under cold running water. Melt the butter with the oil in a skillet. Stir in the flour and cook, stirring constantly, for 2 minutes. Gradually stir in the milk, a little at a time. Season with salt and cook, stirring constantly, for about 8 minutes. Carefully add the sprouts, stirring just enough to make sure that they are coated with sauce. Transfer to a vegetable dish, sprinkle with the parsley, and serve immediately.

Note: The béchamel sauce can be made with half milk and half stock.

371

- 2½–3¼ pounds Brussels sprouts
- 1 quantity Classic Béchamel Sauce (see recipe 77)
- ¾ cup grated gruyere cheese

Brussels sprouts au gratin
COLES DE BRUSELAS GRATINADAS

Prepare and cook the Brussels sprouts as described on page 296. Preheat the oven to 350°F. Transfer the sprouts and béchamel sauce to an ovenproof baking dish and sprinkle with the cheese. Bake for 10–15 minutes, until the cheese has melted. Serve immediately straight from the dish.

Cauliflower

Origin and season
The cauliflower is known to have been cultivated in Europe since the Middle Ages but there is dispute over its country of origin. It is available almost all year around, although it is at it best from midwinter to late spring. It is most abundant early fall to the middle of winter.

Selection
Always buy cauliflower with its leaves still attached, even if they have been trimmed. Although the leaves are not eaten, they are a good indication of freshness. The head should be crisp, very white, and tightly packed. Remember when buying cauliflower that you will lose half the weight during its preparation.

Nutrition
Cauliflower is very rich in vitamin C, possibly richer than orange juice as long as it is eaten raw. The slightly unpleasant smell produced when it is cooking is because of the magnesium and potassium it contains, but there are tricks to avoid this, such as placing a slice of bread soaked in a little milk on top of the cauliflower or adding 2 bay leaves to the pan during cooking.

How to cook

Separate the flowerets, or if the cauliflower is to be cooked whole, cut out as much of the stalk as possible. If cooking flowerets, peel the stalks a little so that they become tender when cooked. Rinse the flowerets in cold water mixed with the juice of ½ lemon. Bring a large pan of salted water to a boil. Add the flowerets and a little milk and cook, uncovered, for about 20 minutes, until tender. Drain well, taking care not to break up the flowerets, then refresh under cold running water. Pour onto a clean dishtowel to drain. Cook a whole cauliflower in the same way, taking care when draining not to damage the flowerets.

372

Coated cauliflower
COLIFLOR REBOZADA

- 1 small cauliflower,
  about 2¼ pounds,
  separated into small flowerets
- juice of ½ lemon
- a little milk, for cooking
- sunflower oil, for deep-frying
- ½ cup all-purpose flour
- 2 eggs, lightly beaten
- salt

Serves 6

Prepare and cook the cauliflower as described on page 299, then refresh under cold running water, and drain on a clean dishtowel. Heat the oil in a deep-fryer or deep saucepan to 350–375°F or until a cube of day-old bread browns in 30 seconds. Dip each floweret in the flour, shaking off any excess, and then in the beaten egg. Add to the hot oil and cook for a few minutes, until golden brown. Do not add too many at a time. Remove with a slotted spoon. Drain well and serve immediately. This is delicious served as an accompaniment to meat.

373

Cauliflower fritters
BUÑUELOS DE COLIFLOR

- 1 cauliflower, about 3¼ pounds,
  separated into flowerets
- juice of ½ lemon
- a little milk, for cooking
- sunflower oil, for deep-frying
- lemon slices and fresh
  parsley sprigs
- salt

Batter:
- 2¼ cups all-purpose flour
- 3 tablespoons white wine
- 3 tablespoons sunflower oil
- scant 1 cup milk
- 1 teaspoon rapid-rise active
  dry yeast
- salt

Serves 6

Prepare and cook the cauliflower as described on page 299, then refresh under cold running water, and drain on a clean dishtowel. Make the batter. Sift the flour with a pinch of salt into a bowl and make a well in the center. Pour the wine and oil into the well and stir in the flour. Gradually stir in the milk, a little at a time. When the batter is smooth, cover and let stand for 30 minutes. When you are ready to cook, stir in the yeast. Heat the oil in a deep-fryer or deep saucepan to 350–375°F or until a cube of day-old bread browns in 30 seconds. One at a time, dip the flowerets into the batter, add to the hot oil, and cook for about 5 minutes, until golden brown. Do not add too many at a time. Remove with a slotted spoon, drain well, and keep warm. When all the flowerets have been fried, pile them into the middle of a round dish and garnish with the lemon slices and parsley. Serve the fritters immediately.

Note: This can be served with Classic Tomato Sauce (see recipe 73).

374

Cauliflower in caper and paprika sauce

COLIFLOR CON SALSA DE ALCAPARRAS Y PIMENTÓN

- 1 cauliflower, about 3¼ pounds, separated into flowerets
- juice of ½ lemon
- 2¼ cups milk, plus a little to cook the cauliflower
- 6 tablespoons (¾ stick) butter
- 3 tablespoons olive oil
- 1 onion, chopped
- 1 clove garlic
- 1 bay leaf
- 2 tablespoons all-purpose flour
- 2¼ cups chicken stock (homemade, canned or made with a bouillon cube)
- ½ teaspoon paprika
- 2 tablespoons white-wine vinegar
- 3 tablespoons capers, rinsed and drained
- 3 tablespoons bread crumbs
- salt

Serves 6

Prepare and cook the cauliflower as described on page 299, then refresh under cold running water, and drain on a clean dishtowel. Melt 2 tablespoons of the butter with the oil in a pan. Add the onion and cook over low heat, stirring occasionally, for about 5 minutes until softened. Add the garlic and bay leaf and cook for a few minutes more, then remove the pan from the heat. Stir the flour into the stock. Stir the paprika into the onion, immediately add the flour and stock mixture, and stir in the milk. Pour in the vinegar, return the pan to the heat, and cook gently, stirring constantly, for 5–6 minutes. Season to taste with salt. Preheat the oven to 350°F. Pour a little of the sauce into an ovenproof baking dish and sprinkle half the capers over the base of the dish. Add the flowerets, pour the remaining sauce over them, and sprinkle with the remaining capers. Sprinkle the bread crumbs over the dish and dot with the remaining butter. Bake for 10–15 minutes, until lightly browned. Remove and discard the bay leaf and garlic. Serve immediately straight from the dish.

375

Cold cauliflower with mayonnaise

COLIFLOR FRÍA CON MAYONESA

- 1 cauliflower, about 3¼ pounds, separated into flowerets
- juice of ½ lemon
- a little milk, for cooking
- 1 quantity Thick Mayonnaise (see recipe 106)
- 2 hard-cooked eggs
- salt

Serves 6

Prepare and cook the cauliflower as described on page 299, then refresh under cold running water, and drain on a clean dishtowel. Put the flowerets into a round dish and spoon the mayonnaise over them to cover completely. Chop one of the hard-cooked eggs and sprinkle it over the flowerets. Slice the other egg and arrange it around the edge of the dish. Serve cold.

376

Cauliflower pie
BUDÍN DE COLIFLOR

- 1 cauliflower, about 1½ pounds,
  separated into flowerets
- juice of ½ lemon
- 2¼ cups milk, plus a little
  to cook the cauliflower
- 2½ tablespoons butter
  or margarine, plus extra
  for greasing
- 2 tablespoons sunflower oil
- 3 tablespoons all-purpose flour
- pinch of freshly grated nutmeg
- 4 eggs
- scant 1 cup grated gruyere
- 1 quantity Classic Tomato Sauce
  (see recipe 73)
- salt

Serves 6

Prepare and cook the cauliflower as described on page 299, then refresh under cold running water, and drain on a clean dishtowel. Transfer to a bowl and mash with a fork. Preheat the oven to 325°F. Grease a 7 ½-inch tart pan with butter or margarine. Melt the remaining butter or margarine with the oil in a pan. Stir in the flour and cook, stirring constantly, for 2 minutes. Gradually stir in the milk, a little at a time. Add the nutmeg, season with salt, and cook, stirring constantly, for 8 minutes. Remove the pan from the heat. Beat two of the eggs, then beat them into the béchamel sauce. Repeat with the remaining eggs. Stir in the gruyere and when thoroughly incorporated, add the cauliflower. Pour the mixture into the prepared pan and place the tin in a roasting pan. Pour in boiling water to come about halfway up the sides and bake for about 1 hour, until set. To serve, run a round-bladed knife around the edge of the tart pan and turn the pie out onto a round serving dish. Pour the warmed tomato sauce over it and serve immediately.

377

Cauliflower with béchamel sauce
COLIFLOR CON BECHAMEL

- 1 cauliflower, about 3¼ pounds,
  separated into flowerets
- juice of ½ lemon
- 2¼ cups milk, plus a little
  to cook the cauliflower
- 2 tablespoons (¼ stick) butter
- 2 tablespoons sunflower oil
- 2 tablespoons all-purpose flour
- ¾ cup grated gruyere cheese
- salt

Serves 6

Prepare and cook the cauliflower as described on page 299, then refresh under cold running water, and drain on a clean dishtowel. Put the flowerets into an ovenproof baking dish. Preheat the oven to 350°F. Melt the butter with the oil in a pan. Stir in the flour and cook, stirring constantly, for 2 minutes. Gradually stir in the milk, a little at a time. Season with salt and cook, stirring constantly, for 10 minutes, then pour the sauce over the flowerets. Sprinkle with the gruyere and bake for 10–15 minutes, until golden brown. Serve immediately straight from the dish.

Note: For a tasty variation, when the cheese begins to melt, push generous ½ cup peeled almonds or pine nuts into the cauliflower so half of each nut protrudes. Return the dish to the oven and bake for a few more minutes, taking care the nuts do not brown too much.

378

Baked cauliflower with butter, lemon, parsley, and hard-cooked egg

COLIFLOR AL HORNO CON MANTEQUILLA, LIMÓN, PEREJIL Y HUEVO DURO

- 1 cauliflower, about 3¼ pounds
- juice of 2 lemons
- a little milk, for cooking
- ⅔ cup butter
- 1 tablespoon chopped fresh parsley
- 1 hard-cooked egg, finely chopped
- salt

Serves 6

Preheat the oven to 350°F. Prepare and cook the cauliflower, without separating it into flowerets, as described on page 299 and using the juice of half of one of the lemons, then refresh under cold running water, and drain on a clean dishtowel. Put the cauliflower into a deep ovenproof baking dish. Dot the butter all over the cauliflower and pour the remaining lemon juice over it. Bake, basting occasionally, for 15–20 minutes, until lightly browned. Remove the dish from the oven, sprinkle with the parsley and hard-cooked egg, and serve immediately.

Note: You could sprinkle grated cheese over the cauliflower, but in this case, pour the juice of only 1 lemon into the dish. (You will require the juice of 1½ lemons in total because the cauliflower should be washed in acidulated water as described on page 299.) Use slightly less butter and omit the parsley and egg.

379

Cauliflower in toasted butter and bread crumb sauce

COLIFLOR COCIDA CON SALSA DE MANTEQUILLA TOSTADA Y PAN RALLADO

- 1 cauliflower, about 3¼ pounds, separated into large flowerets
- juice of 1 lemon
- a little milk, for cooking
- scant 1 cup butter
- 3 tablespoons bread crumbs
- salt

Serves 6

Prepare and cook the cauliflower as described on page 299 and using the juice of half of the lemon, then drain, and keep warm. Melt the butter in a pan and cook over low heat until browned, then remove the pan from the heat, and add the remaining lemon juice. Return the pan to the heat and stir in the bread crumbs, but do not let the sauce brown any further. Pour the sauce over the flowerets and serve.

380

- 12 heads endive, trimmed
- 7 tablespoons butter
- 2/3 cup grated gruyere cheese
- salt

Serves 6

Endive gratin
ENDIVIAS AL GRATÉN

Put the endive heads into a pan, pour in enough water to cover, and add a pinch of salt. Bring to a boil and, at the same time, bring another pan with the same amount of salted water to a boil. When the water in both pans is boiling, use a slotted spoon to transfer the endive to the second pan. This step helps prevent the endive becoming bitter. Bring the water back to a boil and cook for about 20 minutes, until tender. Meanwhile, preheat the oven to 350°F. Drain the endive well and put into an ovenproof baking dish. Dot with the butter, sprinkle with the gruyere, and bake for about 10–15 minutes, until the cheese has melted and the top has browned. Serve immediately straight from the dish.

381

- 12 heads endive, trimmed
- 2 tablespoons (¼ stick) butter
- 2 tablespoons sunflower oil
- 2 tablespoons all-purpose flour
- 2¼ cups milk
- scant 1 cup grated gruyere cheese
- salt

Serves 6

Endive in béchamel sauce
ENDIVIAS CON BECHAMEL

Cook the endive heads in salted boiling water, using two pans as described in recipe 380. Drain well and put into an ovenproof baking dish. Preheat the oven to 350°F. Melt the butter with the oil in a pan. Add the flour and cook, stirring constantly, for 2 minutes. Gradually stir in the milk, a little at a time, and bring to a boil, stirring constantly. Season with salt and simmer over medium heat, stirring constantly, for 8–10 minutes. Pour over the endive. Sprinkle with the gruyere and bake for 10–15 minutes, until golden brown. Serve immediately straight from the dish.

Endive with ham and béchamel sauce

ENDIVIAS CON JAMÓN DE YORK Y BECHAMEL

- 12 heads endive, trimmed
- 12 thin slices Smithfield or Black Forest ham, prosciutto or other dry-cured ham
- 2 tablespoons (¼ stick) butter
- 2 tablespoons sunflower oil
- 2 tablespoons all-purpose flour
- 2¼ cups milk
- scant 1 cup grated gruyere cheese
- salt

Serves 6

Follow the method for recipe 381, but before putting the endive heads into an ovenproof baking dish, wrap each in one of the slices of ham. Pour in the béchamel sauce, sprinkle with the gruyere, and cook under a preheated broiler, until golden brown.

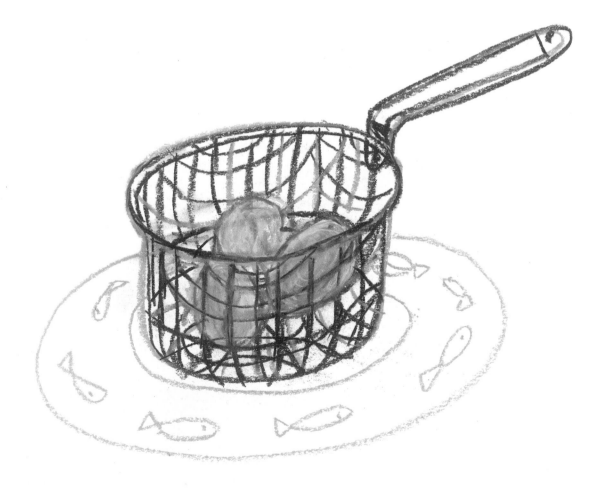

383

Braised endive
ENDIVIAS AL JUGO

- 12 heads endive, trimmed
- 2 tablespoons (¼ stick) butter
- 2 tablespoons sunflower oil
- 1 tablespoon all-purpose flour
- generous 1 cup veal or beef stock (homemade, canned or made with a bouillon cube)
- 1 veal shank bone
- pinch of freshly grated nutmeg
- salt

Serves 6

Cook the endive heads in salted boiling water, using two pans as described in recipe 380, but for only 15 minutes in the second pan. Drain well. Melt the butter with the oil in a pan. Stir in the flour and cook, stirring constantly, for 2 minutes. Gradually stir in the stock, a little at a time. Add the veal bone and endive and sprinkle with the nutmeg. Cook for 10–12 minutes, then remove the veal bone and transfer the endive and sauce to a warm serving dish.

Note: This dish can be made in advance. Cook the endive for just 5 minutes in the sauce and then 5 minutes more when reheat-ing.

384

Endive salad
ENDIVIAS EN ENSALADA

- 6 heads endive
- 1 quantity Vinaigrette (see recipe 98)

Serves 4–6

Trim the endive heads, separate the leaves, and cut them in half lengthwise. Wash them well under cold running water, but do not let soak as this makes them bitter. Pat dry, put into a bowl, and dress with the vinaigrette. Serve the salad quite soon after adding the dressing or it will become soggy.

385

Grapefruit salad with apples and endives
ENESALADA DE POMELO CO MANZANA Y ENDIVIAS

- 1 pink grapefruit
- 1 apple
- juice of ½ lemon
- 2 heads endive, cut into thin strips
- 3½ ounces Roquefort cheese, crumbled
- 2 tablespoons olive oil
- juice of 1 lemon
- 2 tablespoons plain yogurt
- fresh mint leaves
- salt and pepper

Serves 4

Peel the grapefruit with a sharp knife, removing all traces of pith. Cut out the segments from the membranes and cut them into pieces. Peel, core, and dice the apple and toss with half the lemon juice. Put the grapefruit, apple, and endive into a salad bowl and mix well. Prepare the sauce by mashing the cheese with the oil in a bowl, then stir in the lemon juice, and season to taste with salt and pepper. Gradually stir in the yogurt, a little at a time. Add the sauce to the salad and chill well before serving, garnished with the mint leaves.

Note: If the flavor of the Roquefort is too strong, it can be replaced with soft, unripened cheese, such as ricotta. The grapefruit can be replaced with orange, in which case cut the apple into thick slices and leave the skin on to give the salad more color.

386

- **11 ounces escarole leaves**
- **1 quantity Vinaigrette (see recipe 98)**
- **1 clove garlic (optional)**

Serves 4

Escarole salad
ENSALADA DE ESCAROLA

Separate the escarole leaves, discarding all but the pale inner leaves, and wash, then pat dry. If the leaves are long, cut them into two or three pieces. Put into a bowl and dress with the vinaigrette. Serve the salad quite soon after adding the dressing or it will become soggy. If you like, you can rub the inside of the salad bowl with a peeled garlic clove before adding the leaves.

Note: Peeled, diced tomato may be mixed into the salad. Chopped celery may also be added.

Asparagus

Origin and season
Asparagus was known to the ancient Egyptians, regarded as an aphrodisiac by the Greeks, and cultivated by the Romans. Since then, however, although wild asparagus grows in central and southern Europe and in North Africa there is little mention of it being eaten until the seventeenth and eighteenth centuries. It is widely cultivated under glass from at the end of winter and the beginning of spring. Green asparagus can be thin, medium, or fat, while white asparagus is usually fat. Wild asparagus is hard to find and then is available only in small quantities. It tends to be bitter.

Selection
The spears should be straight and even in color. If you snap off the end, a little moisture should appear. The yellower the spears are, the older they are and the more likely they are too woody. Choose asparagus spears of a uniform length so that they will cook in the same amount of time. When sold in bunches, they will have been selected with this in mind. It is not a good idea to buy spears that are too long. The best time for asparagus is middle to late spring.

Nutrition

Asparagus does not have a high nutritional value, as it consists of 92 percent water and has only 15 calories per 3½ ounces. It contains vitamins and is a good source of the minerals potassium, iron, and calcium. It also contains a substance that can irritate the renal system, so it should be avoided by people with kidney problems. It is good for cleansing the system. Asparagus is a good convalescent food and may be helpful for those suffering from treating anemia, rheumatism, some types of eczema, palpitations, and diabetes.

How to prepare and cook

Allow 3¼–4½ pounds to serve four. Try to buy asparagus spears that are the same thickness. Peel them from the tip to the base, if necessary, then cut them all to the same length (about 10 inches). Make sure you cut off the woody ends. As they are cut put them into cold water. Bring a large pan of salted water to a boil. Add the asparagus, submerging it completely and with all the tips pointing in the same direction so that they will not break when lifted out. Cover the pan, bring back to a boil, and cook for about 10 minutes for medium asparagus or 20 minutes for fat asparagus. In both cases, check that the spears are cooked by piercing one with the tip of a sharp knife. You can also buy a special asparagus pan which is tall enough to allow the spears to stand up, so that the stems cook in water while the tips are gently steamed.

Tricks

- If you're not ready to serve the asparagus immediately, leave it in its cooking water for up to 1 hour. If you need to keep it longer, drain it well, put a doubled paper towel in a dish, put the asparagus on the paper towel, and cover the dish with aluminum foil
- Asparagus may be served hot or cold
- Asparagus can be served with various sauces: melted butter with chopped fresh parsley; all kinds of mayonnaise (see recipes 105–111); vinaigrette with chopped hard-cooked egg, etc. (see recipes 98–101).

387

Ham with asparagus

JAMÓN CON ESPÁRRAGOS

- 4½ pounds green asparagus, trimmed
- 6 slices ham
- 1½ tablespoons butter
- 1 tablespoon sunflower oil
- 1 tablespoon all-purpose flour
- scant 2 cups milk
- ½ cup grated gruyere cheese
- salt

Serves 6

Bring a large pan of salted water to a boil. Add the asparagus, cover, and cook for 10–20 minutes, until tender but not falling apart. Carefully lift out the spears and drain on a folded dishtowel. Divide the spears into six portions and wrap each portion in a slice of ham, leaving the tips sticking out. Put into an ovenproof baking dish in a single layer. Preheat the oven to 350°F. Melt the butter with the oil in a pan. Stir in the flour and cook, stirring constantly, for 2 minutes. Gradually stir in the milk, a little at a time. Season with salt and cook, stirring constantly, for 4 minutes. Remove the pan from the heat and pour the sauce over the rolls of ham, but do not cover the asparagus tips. Sprinkle with the gruyere and bake for 10–15 minutes, until golden brown. Serve immediately straight from the dish.

388

Asparagus with peas
PUNTAS DE ESPÁRRAGOS CON GUISANTES

- 3 tablespoons sunflower oil
- 1 scallion, chopped
- 3 ¼ pounds peas, shelled
- 1 teaspoon sugar
- generous ½ cup finely chopped Serrano ham or prosciutto
- 4 ½ pounds thin asparagus, trimmed
- 1 hard-cooked egg, sliced or chopped
- salt

Serves 6

Heat the oil in a pan. Add the scallions and cook over low heat, stirring occasionally, for 3–4 minutes, but do not let them brown. Add the peas and cook, stirring constantly, for a few minutes. Pour in generous 1 cup water, stir in the sugar, cover the pan, and simmer for 15 minutes. Add the ham and cook for 20 minutes more, until the peas are tender. Season to taste with salt. Meanwhile, cut the asparagus into 1-inch lengths. Bring a large pan of salted water to a boil. Add the asparagus, cover, and cook for about 10 minutes, until tender but not falling apart. Drain well and combine with the peas and ham in a warm deep serving dish. Garnish with the hard-cooked egg and serve immediately.

389

Scrambled eggs with asparagus and potatoes
PUNTAS DE ESPÁRRAGOS REVUELTAS CON PATATAS Y HUEVOS

- 4 ½ pounds asparagus, trimmed
- sunflower oil, for deep-frying
- 2 ¼ pounds potatoes, diced
- 6 eggs, lightly beaten
- salt

Serves 6

Cut the asparagus into 1-inch lengths. Bring a large pan of salted water to a boil, add the asparagus, cover, and cook for 10–20 minutes, until tender but not falling apart. Drain well. Heat the oil in a deep skillet to 350–375°F or until a cube of day-old bread browns in 30 seconds. Add the potato and cook for 5–8 minutes, until evenly browned. Remove with a slotted spoon, drain well, lightly season with salt, and set aside. Drain off almost all the oil from the skillet, leaving just a thin layer on the base, and reheat. Add the asparagus. Season the eggs with salt and then pour into the skillet. Cook, stirring frequently with a fork, for a few minutes, until the eggs are creamy. Remove the pan from the heat and let the eggs set a little more, then add the potato. Stir well, and if necessary return the mixture to the heat to be sure the eggs are cooked through. Turn the mixture out onto a warm serving dish and serve immediately.

390

Green asparagus with sauce

ESPÁRRAGOS VERDES EN SALSA

- 4 tablespoons olive oil
- 2 slices of bread, crusts removed
- 1 clove garlic
- 1 sprig fresh parsley
- 4½ pounds green asparagus, trimmed
- 1 tablespoon white-wine vinegar
- ½ teaspoon paprika
- 2 eggs, lightly beaten
- salt

Serves 4

Heat the oil in a skillet. Add the bread, garlic, and parsley and cook, turning the bread occasionally, for a few minutes until golden brown on both sides. Transfer the bread, garlic, and parsley to a mortar and pound with a pestle, or process in a food processor. Cut the asparagus into 1-inch lengths. Add to the pan with the vinegar and cook for 5 minutes. Stir in the paprika, pour in just enough water to cover the asparagus, add the contents of the mortar or processor, and season. Simmer for about 20 minutes, until the asparagus is tender. Just before serving, stir in the eggs and heat through. Serve immeditely.

391

Fried green asparagus with garlic, vinegar, and paprika

ESPÁRRAGOS VERDES REHOGADOS CON AJO, VINAGRE Y PIMENTÓN

- 4½ pounds green asparagus, trimmed
- 6 tablespoons olive oil
- 3 slices of bread, crusts removed
- 2 cloves garlic
- ½ teaspoon paprika
- scant 2 cups hot water
- 3 tablespoons white-wine vinegar
- 1 teaspoon chopped fresh parsley
- salt

Serves 6

Cut the asparagus into 1½-inch lengths. Heat the oil in a skillet. Add the bread and cook, turning occasionally, for a few minutes, until golden brown on both sides. Remove from the pan and set aside. Add the garlic to the pan and cook, stirring frequently, for a few minutes, until golden brown. Transfer to a mortar, add the fried bread, and pound with a pestle, or process in a food processor. Pour the oil from the skillet into a saucepan and heat. Add the asparagus and cook for 2–3 minutes. Remove the pan from the heat and stir in the paprika, then pour in the hot water. Return the pan to medium heat, cover, and cook, shaking the pan occasionally, for 1 hour. Add the vinegar and a little of the asparagus cooking liquid to the mixture in the mortar or processor and mix well, then stir into the pan containing the asparagus. Season with salt and cook for 5 minutes more. Sprinkle with the parsley and serve immediately.

Wild asparagus omelet

ESPÁRRAGOS TRIGUEROS PARA TORTILLA

- **1 bunch wild asparagus, trimmed**
- **4 eggs, lightly beaten**
- **3 tablespoons olive oil**
- **salt**

Serves 2

Cut the asparagus into 1-inch lengths. Put into a pan, add water to cover, and bring to a boil. At the same time, bring another pan of lightly salted water to a boil. When the asparagus has been boiling for 3 minutes, transfer it to the second pan, using a slotted spoon. Cook for 10 minutes more, until tender. Drain well. Lightly beat the eggs with a pinch of salt in a bowl, then add the asparagus. Heat the oil in a skillet. Pour in the egg and asparagus mixture and cook until the underside has set and is golden brown. Turn the omelet by inverting it onto a plate and then carefully sliding it back into the pan, and cook until the second side is golden brown. Serve immediately.

Note: This recipe can be used for cultivated asparagus; just modify the cooking time so that the asparagus gets tender.

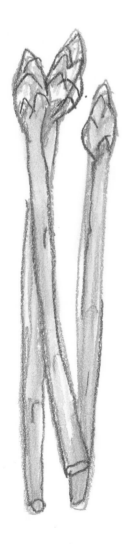

Spinach

Origin and season
Of Persian origin, spinach was introduced to Europe by the Arabs at the end of the Middle Ages. For a long time, it was considered to be a plant that invigorated the body owing to its high iron content. Fresh spinach has two seasons: late winter to late spring and mid to late fall.

Selection
The leaves should have a uniform green color, which may be dark or light depending on the variety. Choose the larger leaves for cooking and the smaller, more tender leaves for salads.

Nutrition
Spinach is a vegetable with a relatively low nutritional value and contains about 18 calories per 3 ½ ounces. It contains vitamins A, B, and C, as well as iron, calcium, phosphorus, and cobalt. It is not as rich in iron as was once thought. It is not recommended for people with rheumatism, arthritis, or nephritic colic. However, it is good for children who suffer from anemia.

How to prepare and cook

Most recipes require spinach to be precooked. To do this, remove and discard the coarse stalks and wash the spinach in several changes of water. Drain slightly, then put into a pan with just the water clinging to its leaves. Add a pinch of salt and cook, stirring occasionally, for 8–10 minutes. Drain well, pressing out as much liquid as you possibly can with the back of a spoon. Allow 5½–6½ pounds spinach for 6 servings.

393

Spinach with béchamel sauce
ESPINACAS CON BECHAMEL

- 6½ pounds spinach,
  coarse stalks removed
- 2 tablespoons (¼ stick) butter
- 2 tablespoons sunflower oil
- 1 tablespoon all-purpose flour
- generous 1 cup milk
- 3 slices of bread,
  cut into triangles and fried
  (see recipe 130)
- 2 hard-cooked eggs, sliced
- salt

Serves 6

Cook the spinach as described above. Drain well and chop finely. Melt the butter with the oil in a skillet. Stir in the flour and cook, stirring constantly, for 2 minutes. Gradually stir in the milk, a little at a time. Cook, stirring constantly, for 8 minutes. Lightly season with salt and add the spinach, in three or four batches, stirring well to prevent it sticking to the pan. Transfer to a warm serving dish and garnish with the triangles of fried bread around the edge and the slices of hard-cooked egg on top. Serve immediately.

Note: Add slightly less milk if you prefer thicker creamed spinach; or slightly more if you prefer it thinner.

394

Scrambled eggs with spinach and shrimp
REVUELTO DE ESPINACAS, GAMBAS Y HUEVOS

- 2¼ pounds spinach,
  coarse stalks removed
- pinch of baking soda
- 4 tablespoons butter or
  5 tablespoons sunflower oil
- 11 ounces raw shrimp, peeled
- 8 eggs, lightly beaten
- salt

Serves 6

Cook the spinach as described above, adding baking soda to preserve the green color. Drain well and chop finely. Heat the butter or oil in a skillet. Add the shrimp and cook over medium heat, stirring occasionally, for 2 minutes. Stir in the spinach and cook, stirring constantly, for 3 minutes. Season the beaten eggs with salt, pour into the pan, and cook, stirring frequently, for a few minutes, until the eggs begin to set. Turn the mixture out onto a warm serving dish and serve immediately, garnished with triangles of fried bread (see recipe 130), if you like.

395

Spinach, cream and asparagus vol-au-vent
VOL-AU-VENT DE ESPINACAS CON NATA Y PUNTAS DE ESPÁRRAGOS

- **4½ pounds spinach,**
  coarse stalks removed
- **¾ cup light cream**
- **1 vol-au-vent case, 6–8 inches**
  in diameter, cooked
- **14 ounces canned asparagus**
  tips, drained
- **3 tablespoons butter**
- **salt**

Serves 6

Preheat the oven to 325°F. Cook the spinach as described on page 315. Drain and chop finely. Melt the butter in a skillet. Stir in the spinach and then add the cream. Mix well. Place the vol-au-vent case on a cookie sheet. Remove the pan from the heat and spoon the spinach mixture into the vol-au-vent case. Insert the asparagus spears into the spinach mixture in a circle. Put the pastry lid on the vol-au-vent case and heat through in the oven for 15–20 minutes, until warm. Serve immediately.

Note: You can also make this dish with a double-crust piecrust,

396

Spinach and potato stew
ESPINACAS Y PATATAS GUISADAS

- **3¼ pounds spinach,**
  coarse stalks removed
- **4 tablespoons olive oil**
- **2 cloves garlic**
- **1 onion, chopped**
- **pinch of saffron threads**
- **2 slices of fried bread**
  (see recipe 130)
- **5 waxy potatoes,**
  cut into small pieces
- **salt**

Serves 6

Cook the spinach as described on page 315 for just 5 minutes. Drain well, reserving a little of the cooking liquid, and chop. Heat the oil in a stovetop safe earthenware pot. Add the garlic cloves and cook, stirring occasionally, for a few minutes, until lightly browned, then remove from the pan, and reserve. Add the onion and cook over low heat, stirring occasionally, for about 5 minutes, until softened and translucent. Add the spinach and pour in water to cover. Put the saffron, reserved garlic, and the fried bread in a mortar and pound with a pestle, or process in a food processor. Mix in the reserved cooking liquid and pour into the pan. Add the potatoes, season to taste, cover, and cook over medium heat for about 30 minutes, until the potatoes are tender. Serve straight from the pot or transfer to a warm deep serving dish. Ladle into soup plates and eat with spoons.

397

Spinach garnish
ESPINACAS DE ADORNO

- **3½ pounds spinach,**
  coarse stalks removed
- **¼ cup (½ stick) butter**

Serves 6

Prepare and cook the spinach as described on page 315. Drain well, and chop. Melt the butter in a skillet, add the spinach, and cook, stirring occasionally, for 3–5 minutes. Serve with meat or fish.

Note: You can put this into an ovenproof baking dish with fish or as a base for macaroni (see page 221). Cover with béchamel sauce (see recipe 77) sprinkle with grated cheese, and bake in the oven.

Peas

Origin and season

Peas have been known since ancient times and were already growing wild several thousand years BC. The ancient Egyptians, Greeks and Romans grew them, although the cultivated variety originated in China. Their season is from late spring to early summer.

Selection

Peas must be very fresh, otherwise they will be starchy and hard. The pods should not show any discoloration. Bear in mind that peas can be bought frozen and canned and that both are good-quality products. You should check the amount of sugar that has been added during processing; in the case of canned peas this should not be more than 5 per cent.

Nutrition

Fresh peas have about 80 calories per 100 g/3 ½ oz, and contain starch and sucrose (so they may not be suitable for diabetics) and cellulose.

Tricks

- Do not wash peas when preparing them. To enhance their flavour, add fresh mint leaves to the cooking water
- Peas can be frozen after shelling and freeze quite well. To cook, put them straight into boiling water
- Do not cover the pan when cooking, and add a little bicarbonate of soda to preserve a good green colour
- Do not forget to add a little sugar when cooking peas, as this makes them more tender
- Rinse drained canned peas with warm water to remove the metallic taste and pour lemon juice over them

398 Simple peas

GUISANTES SENCILLOS

- 3 tablespoons sunflower oil
- 2 scallions, chopped
- 5½–6½ pounds peas, shelled
- 1 teaspoon sugar
- 3½ ounces Serrano ham or prosciutto, finely chopped
- salt

Serves 6

Heat the oil in a pan. Add the scallions and cook over low heat, stirring occasionally, for 3–4 minutes, but do not let them brown. Add the peas and cook, stirring constantly, for a few minutes. Pour in generous 1 cup water, stir in the sugar, cover the pan, and simmer for 15 minutes. Add the ham and cook for 20 minutes more, until the peas are tender. Season to taste with salt and serve immediately.

399 Peas and carrots

GUISANTES Y ZANAHORIAS

- 3¼ pounds peas, shelled and pods reserved
- 1¼ cups sunflower oil
- 1 scallion, finely chopped
- 4 cups diced carrots, preferably baby
- 2 tablespoons (¼ stick) butter
- 6 thin slices bacon
- salt

Serves 6

Tie a couple of handfuls of the reserved pea pods together with kitchen string or tie them in a piece of cheesecloth. Heat 3 table-spoons of the oil in a pan. Add the scallion and cook over low heat, stirring occasionally, for about 3 minutes, but do not let it brown. Add the carrot and pour in 2¼ cups water. Simmer for 15 minutes, then add the peas and tied pods, season with salt, and cook for 20 minutes more, until the vegetables are tender. Just before serving, remove and discard the pea pods and use the lid of the pan to drain off nearly all the water. Stir in the butter until it melts. Meanwhile, heat the remaining oil in a skillet. Add the bacon and cook for 2–4 minutes on each side, until lightly browned. Serve the vegetables in a warm vegetable dish, garnished with the bacon.

Fava beans

Origin and season

Fava beans originated Persia (modern Iran). In the past they were regarded as a symbol of the migration of souls and did not have a very good reputation. Some believed they caused infertility, while others considered them a powerful aphrodisiac. This was why eating fava beans was forbidden in convents in the Middle Ages. The best time for fresh beans is from late spring to early summer, when they are small and tender.

Selection

Fava beans should not have any discoloration and they should be firm and flawless.

Nutrition

Fresh beans have 36 calories per 3 ½ ounces and some vitamins and minerals. Dried beans have more calories—250 per 3 ½ ounces. They are also high in fiber, which may have a laxative effect and can cause gas. Consuming them in large quantities outside a well-balanced diet can result in anemia.

Tricks

• Very young beans can be cooked in their skins, but older beans should be peeled
• To eat them in the pod, trim the ends and pull them to remove any stringy parts there might be, just like a string bean.

400

Fava beans with eggs

HABAS CON HUEVOS

- 4½ pounds fresh baby
  fava beans
- pinch of baking soda
- 6 tablespoons olive oil
- 1 onion, very finely chopped
- generous finely chopped ½ cup
  Serrano ham or prosciutto
- 3 eggs, lightly beaten
- salt

Serves 6

Fresh baby fava beans can be eaten in their pods. Trim the ends and pull off any strings from the sides. Cut the pods into little squares around the beans. Wash and drain thoroughly. Bring a large pan of salted water to a boil. Add the beans and the baking soda. Cook, uncovered, for 1 hour. Meanwhile, heat the oil in a skillet. Add the onion and cook over low heat, stirring occasionally, for about 5 minutes, until softened and translucent. Add the ham and cook, stirring frequently, for 3 minutes more. Drain the beans and add them to the pan. Lightly season the eggs with salt and pour them into the pan. Cook, stirring constantly, until the eggs start to set around the beans. Serve immediately.

401

Sautéed fava beans with ham

HABAS SALTEADAS CON JAMÓN

- 4½ pounds baby fava beans
- 6 tablespoons olive oil
- 2 cloves garlic, chopped
- 2 sprigs chopped fresh parsley
- generous ½ cup finely chopped
  Serrano ham or prosciutto
- salt

Serves 6

Fresh baby fava beans can be eaten in their pods. Trim the ends and pull off any strings from the sides. Cut the pods into little squares around the beans. Wash and drain thoroughly. Heat the oil in a pan. Add the beans, sprinkle in the garlic and parsley, and season with salt. Cook, uncovered, over low heat, shaking the pan occasionally, for 15 minutes. Add the ham and 5 tablespoons water and cook for 30–45 minutes, until the beans are tender. Serve immediately.

402

Fava beans with blood sausage

HABAS CON MORCILLA

- 5¼ cups shelled fresh
  or frozen fava beans
- 1 tablespoon olive oil
- 1 small onion, chopped
- 11 ounces blood sausage
  (morcilla) or other sausage,
  skinned and cut into small
  pieces
- salt

Serves 6

If using frozen fava beans, cook them according to the instructions on the package. If using fresh fava beans, pop them out of their skins by squeezing them between your thumb and index finger. Bring a large pan of salted water to a boil. Add the beans and cook, uncovered, for about 1 hour, until tender. Meanwhile, heat the oil in a skillet. Add the onion and cook over low heat, stirring occasionally, for about 7 minutes, but do not let brown. Drain the beans, add to the onion and cook over very low heat for 6 minutes. Meanwhile, heat another skillet. Add the sausage and cook, stirring occasionally, for 5–8 minutes. Add to the beans and cook, stirring occasionally, for another 10 minutes. Serve immediately.

403

Fava beans with milk and egg yolks
HABAS CON LECHE Y YEMAS

- 8 ¾ pounds fresh fava beans, shelled
- small pinch of baking soda
- 2 tablespoons (¼ stick) butter
- 2 tablespoons olive oil
- 1 teaspoon chopped fresh parsley
- 1 tablespoon all-purpose flour
- scant 2 cups milk
- 2 egg yolks, lightly beaten
- salt

Serves 6

Pop the fava beans out of their skins by squeezing them between your thumb and index finger. Bring a large pan of salted water to a boil. Add the baking soda and the beans and cook, uncovered, for 20 minutes. Melt the butter with the oil in a pan. Using a slotted spoon, transfer the beans to the pan of melted butter. Sprinkle with the parsley and flour, and cook, stirring constantly, for 2 minutes. Gradually stir in the milk, a little at a time. Simmer over low heat for 10 minutes more, until the beans are tender. Stir a little of the sauce from the beans into the egg yolks to prevent them curdling, then stir into the beans. Serve immediately.

404

Fava beans in sauce
HABAS EN SALSA

- 4 ½ pounds fresh baby fava beans
- pinch of baking soda
- 6 tablespoons olive oil
- 1 onion, chopped
- 2 tablespoons all-purpose flour
- generous ½ cup chopped Serrano ham or prosciutto
- ¾ cup white wine
- salt

Serves 4

Fresh baby fava beans can be eaten in their pods. Trim the ends and pull off any strings from the sides. Cut the pods into little squares around the beans. Wash and drain thoroughly. Bring a large pan of salted water to a boil. Add the baking soda and the beans. Cook, uncovered, for 35 minutes, until tender. Just before the beans are ready, prepare the sauce. Heat the oil in a skillet. Add the onion and cook over low heat, stirring occasionally, for about 6 minutes, until softened but not browned. Stir in the flour and cook, stirring constantly, for 5 minutes more. Add the ham and cook for a few minutes, then pour in the wine. Drain the beans, reserving the cooking liquid. Pour the sauce into a saucepan and add the beans. Stir well and add just enough of the reserved cooking liquid to cover. Cook, uncovered, over low heat for 10 minutes. Serve immediately.

405

- 8 ¾ pounds fresh fava beans, shelled
- scant pinch of baking soda
- 4 tablespoons olive oil
- 2 slices of bread, crusts removed
- 1 clove garlic
- 1 small onion, chopped
- 1 teaspoon paprika
- 1 small lettuce, shredded
- 1 tablespoon white-wine vinegar
- salt

Serves 6

Stewed fava beans

HABAS GUISADAS

Pop the fava beans out of their skins by squeezing them between your thumb and index finger. Bring a large pan of salted water to a boil. Add the beans and the baking soda and cook, uncovered, for 15 minutes. Drain well. Heat the oil in a skillet. Add the bread and garlic and cook, turning occasionally, for a few minutes until evenly browned. Remove the bread and garlic from the pan and pound in a mortar, or process in a food processor. Add the onion to the skillet and cook over low heat, stirring occasionally, for about 6 minutes, until softened but not browned. Remove the pan from the heat and stir in the paprika, then immediately add the lettuce and beans, and stir well. Stir the vinegar into the mixture in the mortar or processor, then add to the skillet. Season and, if necessary, add 3–4 tablespoons water. Simmer gently for about 15 minutes, until the beans are tender, adding a little hot water if necessary. Serve immediately.

406

- 2 ¼ pounds baby fava beans
- pinch of baking soda
- ½ cup all-purpose flour
- sunflower oil, for deep-frying

Serves 4–6

Fried fava bean garnish

HABAS FRITAS DE ADORNO

Baby fava beans can be eaten in their pods. Trim the ends and pull off any strings from the sides. Cut the pods into little squares around the beans. Wash and dry thoroughly. Bring a large saucepan of salted water to a boil. Add the beans and the baking soda and cook, uncovered, for 1 hour. Drain well. Heat the oil in a deep-fryer or deep saucepan to 350°F, or until a cube of day-old bread browns in 30 seconds. Coat the beans in the flour and cook them, in batches, for 6 minutes, until lightly browned. Serve as a garnish with meat.

Fennel

Origin and season

Fennel comes from southern Europe. The ancient Egyptians and Greeks used it as medicine but it was the Italians who first used it as a foodstuff in the Middle Ages. There are two types: wild fennel is used mostly for producing alcohol, while the cultivated variety has a mild flavor and may be eaten raw or cooked. The season is from late fall to late spring.

Selection

The bulb should feel heavy in the hand and look smooth with no imperfections or discoloration. The best bulbs are small with tightly packed leaves.

Nutrition

Fennel has few calories—25 per 3 ½ ounces. It contains calcium, iron, and small quantities of vitamins A and C. It also contains an aromatic oil. Eating fennel is said by some to help lactation.

Tricks

- A few fennel leaves can be added to a filling or stuffing to create a very special flavor. They can also be combined with herbs such as tarragon to give more aroma to chicken, whether cooked in the oven or in a pan.
- Fennel has a special affinity with fish
- Allow half a fennel bulb per serving. A whole bulb will take about 15 minutes to cook.

Green beans

Origin and season

It is believed they were brought to Europe from South America by Christopher Columbus. It is said that Charles Darwin use to play the trombone to his green beans to encourage them to grow. They are available all year round although the best time to eat them is from late spring to fall, when they are at their most succulent.

Selection

When they are very fresh they look shiny. It is best to choose small beans. To check for freshness, snap the end off one of them; it should break off cleanly, without any stringy part, and should look juicy.

Nutrition

Beans contain high levels of vitamin C, potassium, calcium, and iron and have only 35 calories per 3½ ounces. According to some research, they have an invigorating effect on the heart. Tender green beans are recommended for everyone and are ideal for those on a weight loss program as part of a balanced diet.

How to cook

If the beans are large, cut them into smaller pieces. Bring a large pan of salted water to a boil. Add the beans, bring back to boil, and cook, uncovered, for 10–12 minutes, until tender, then refresh in cold water. Drain immediately and pat dry. Alternatively, steam the beans for 12 minutes.

Tricks

- You can add a little baking soda to cooking water to preserve the good green color of beans
- Remember that frozen beans will never be so small as fresh beans, as the smaller varieties do not freeze well.

407

Green beans sautéed in butter, parsley, and lemon
JUDÍAS VERDES SALTEADAS CON MANTEQUILLA, PEREJIL Y LIMÓN

- 2 ¼ pounds green beans, trimmed
- 7 tablespoons butter
- 1 heaping tablespoon chopped fresh parsley
- juice of 1 lemon
- salt

Serves 4–6

Prepare, cook and refresh the beans as described on page 325. Melt the butter in a pan or skillet and add the beans just before it is completely melted. Cook gently for several minutes and just before serving sprinkle with the parsley and add the lemon juice. Serve immediately.

408

Green beans fried in oil with garlic
JUDÍAS VERDES REHOGADAS SÓLO CON ACEITE Y AJOS

- 3 ¼ pounds green beans, trimmed
- 5 tablespoons sunflower oil
- 2 cloves garlic, lightly crushed
- salt

Serves 6

Prepare, cook, and refresh the beans as descibed on page 325. Heat the oil in a skillet. Add the garlic and cook for a few minutes, until lightly browned. Remove and discard the garlic. Add the beans to the pan and cook briefly, taking care that they neither disintegrate nor burn. Serve immediately.

409

Green beans fried with bacon
JUDÍAS VERDES REHOGADAS CON TOCINO

- 3 ¼ pounds green beans, trimmed
- 3 tablespoons sunflower oil
- 1 onion, thinly sliced
- scant 1 cup chopped bacon or Serrano ham or prosciutto
- 1 tablespoon chopped fresh parsley
- salt

Serves 6

Prepare, cook, and refresh the beans as descibed on page 325. Heat the oil in a skillet. Add the onion and cook over low heat, stirring occasionally, for about 5 minutes, until softened. Add the bacon or ham and cook, stirring frequently, for 5 minutes more. Add the beans and cook for 5–10 minutes, until heated through. Season to taste with salt and sprinkle with the parsley. Serve immediately.

410

Green bean salad with foie gras

ENSALADA DE JUDIAS VERDES CON FOIE-GRAS

- 1 pound 2 ounces green beans, trimmed
- 3½ ounces mushrooms
- juice of ½ lemon
- 2 cooked or canned artichoke hearts, drained and thickly sliced
- 7 ounces cooked or canned foie gras, diced
- 1 truffle, cut into julienne strips
- 3 tablespoons olive oil
- salt and pepper

Serves 4

Prepare and cook the beans as descibed on page 325, but cook them for only 10 minutes, until tender but still crisp. Refresh in cold water, drain immediately and pat dry. Separate the mushroom stalks from the caps (keep the stalks for soup) and thickly slice the caps. Sprinkle with the lemon juice. Put the artichoke hearts onto plates and add the beans and slices of mushroom. Place the foie gras and truffle on top, drizzle with the olive oil, season with salt and pepper, and serve.

411

Green beans with tomato sauce

JUDÍAS VERDES CON SALSA DE TOMATE

- 3¼ pounds green beans, trimmed
- 1 tablespoon chopped fresh parsley
- salt

Tomato sauce:
- 3 tablespoons sunflower oil
- 1 onion, finely chopped
- 1 pound 10 ounces very ripe tomatoes, peeled, seeded, and chopped
- 1 teaspoon sugar

Serves 6

Make the tomato sauce as descibed in recipe 73 and process to a purée in a food processor or blender. Prepare and cook the beans as descibed on page 325, but cook them for only 10 minutes. Drain well and return to the pan; do not refresh under cold running water. Add the tomato sauce and cook over low heat, uncovered, for 10 minutes, until the beans are tender.Sprinkle with the parsley and serve.

412

- 3¼ pounds green beans, trimmed
- 6 tablespoons olive oil
- 1 heaping tablespoon all-purpose flour
- 2 egg yolks
- 1 tablespoon white-wine vinegar
- salt

Serves 6

Green beans with vinegar and egg yolk sauce

JUDÍAS VERDES CON SALSA DE VINAGRE Y YEMAS

If the beans are long and wide, cut them in half lengthwise and widthwise. Heat the oil in a pan. Add the beans and cook, stirring occasionally, for about 5 minutes. Stir in the flour and cook, stirring constantly, for 2 minutes. Stir in cold water to cover. Season with salt and cook, uncovered, over low heat for 15–20 minutes, until tender. Lightly beat the egg yolks with the vinegar in a bowl, then gradually whisk in a few spoonfuls of the sauce from the beans. Remove the pan from the heat and stir the egg mixture into the beans to heat through. Serve immediately.

413

- 3¼ pounds green beans, trimmed
- 2 tablespoons white-wine vinegar
- 6 tablespoons sunflower oil
- 1 tablespoon chopped shallot (optional)
- 1 teaspoon chopped fresh parsley
- 2 large firm tomatoes, sliced
- salt

Serves 6

Green beans in vinaigrette

JUDÍAS VERDES CON VINAGRETA

Prepare, cook, and refresh the beans as descibed on page 325. Make a vinaigrette with the vinegar, oil, and salt as descibed in recipe 98. Put the beans in a serving dish and sprinkle with the shallot, if using, and the parsley. Pour the vinaigrette over the beans and toss to mix. Lightly season the tomato slices and use to garnish the beans.

414 Coated green beans

JUDÍAS VERDES REBOZADAS

- 1 pound 5 ounces young
  green beans
- 2¼ cups sunflower oil
- ½ cup all-purpose flour
- 1–2 eggs
- 2 slices of fried bread
  (see recipe 130)
- 1 large clove garlic
- 3–4 sprigs fresh parsley
- 3 tablespoons white-wine
  vinegar
- salt

Serves 4

Look for beans that do not have any strings. Cook them in salted boiling water for 8–12 minutes, until tender. Alternatively, steam them in a pressure cooker for 6 minutes. Drain well and pat dry. Heat the oil in a deep-fryer or deep saucepan to 350–375°F or until a cube of day-old bread browns in 30 seconds. Beat the eggs in a shallow dish and pour the flour into another shallow dish. One at a time, dip the beans first in the flour and then in the egg. Add them to the oil, in batches, and cook until golden. Drain well and put them into a deep serving dish. Pound the fried bread, garlic clove, and parsley in a mortar, or process in a food processor. Mix in the vinegar and generous 1 cup of the oil used to fry the beans. Mix well, pour over the beans, and let stand for 15 minutes before serving.

415 Green beans with mayonnaise

JUDÍAS VERDES CON MAYONESA

- 3¼ pounds green beans,
  trimmed
- 1–2 tomatoes, sliced
- salt

Mayonnaise:
- 2 eggs
- juice of 1 small lemon
- 2¼ cups sunflower oil
- salt and pepper

Serves 6

Make the mayonnaise, using a food processor or blender as described in recipe 105, second part. Prepare, cook, and refresh the beans as descibed on page 325. Put into a serving dish while still warm or let cool completely. Cover them with the mayonnaise and garnish with the tomato slices.

Lettuce

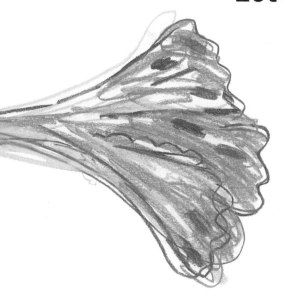

Origin and season

The precise origins of lettuce are not known but the ancient Greeks are known to have liked it and attributed therapeutic qualities to it, such as combating insomnia and easing coughs. Lettuce contains a milky-looking substance in its fibers which have a soporific effect (the origin of the word lettuce is lactua meaning milk). In the Middle Ages, priests were recommended to eat lettuce in order to diminish their interest in the opposite sex. Although it is available all year around, the best time for lettuce is spring.

Selection

The stalk should be white and surrounded by firm leaves without any marks. There may be traces of pesticide on the outer leaves so it is advisable to remove them and wash the lettuce in water mixed with lemon juice or vinegar.

Nutrition

Lettuce has only 20 calories per 3 ½ ounces. When fresh it provides vitamins A, C and E, and calcium, iron, potassium and magnesium.

Tricks

• To keep lettuce as fresh as possible in the refrigerator, wrap it in a dishtowel or put it in a plastic bag
• Toss lettuce in a dressing only just before serving to prevent it becoming limp.

416

- 2 Romaine or other lettuce
  hearts, washed and trimmed
- 6 tablespoons olive oil
- 1 tablespoon all-purpose flour
- ¾ cup white wine
- 1 tablespoon meat extract
  or Maggi Seasoning
- salt

Serves 4

Lettuces in jus

LECHUGAS AL JUGO

Tie each lettuce heart into shape with fine kitchen string to prevent them opening during cooking. Heat the oil in a pan. Add the lettuces in a single layer and cook, turning occasionally, for 3 minutes. Sprinkle the flour over them and add the wine, 1 ½ cups water, and a pinch of salt (remember that the meat extract will be salty). Cover and cook over low heat for 15 minutes. Put the lettuces on a warm serving dish and remove and discard the string. Stir the meat extract or Maggi Seasoning into the pan, pour the cooking juices over the lettuces, and serve immediately.

417

- 4 tablespoons olive oil
- 1 large onion,
  cut into thin wedges
- 6 Romaine or other lettuce
  hearts, washed and trimmed
  if necessary
- 3 tomatoes, peeled, seeded,
  and cut into quarters
- ¾ cup white wine
- ½ teaspoon meat extract
  or Maggi Seasoning
- salt

Serves 6

Braised lettuces

LECHUGAS GUISADAS

Heat the oil in a large skillet. Spread out the onion wedges over the base of the pan and top with the lettuce hearts in a single layer. Place the tomato quarters among the lettuces. Lightly season with salt (remember that the meat extract will be salty). Add the wine, cover, and cook over low heat for 5 minutes. Gradually add 2 cups water, a little at a time, and cook for 15 minutes, until tender. (Check by piercing the stalks with a skewer or the tip of a sharp knife.) Transfer the lettuce hearts to a long dish. Stir the meat extract or Maggi Seasoning into the pan, pour the sauce over the lettuces, and serve.

Note: This dish can be made in advance and reheated. Do not add the meat extract or Maggi Seasoning until just before serving.

Stuffed lettuces

LECHUGAS RELLENOS

- **4 small heads Bibb or Boston lettuce**
- **3 tablespoons butter**
- **1 onion, very finely chopped**
- **1¾ cups chopped leftover roasted meat**
- **scant ½ cup chopped ham**
- **1 egg, lightly beaten**
- **2 tablespoons bread crumbs**
- **2 ounces thinly sliced bacon**
- **generous 1 cup chicken stock (homemade, canned or made with a bouillon cube)**
- **salt and pepper**

Serves 4

Remove and discard the outer lettuce leaves and cut out as much of the stalk as possible while keeping the lettuces whole. Bring a large pan of salted water to a boil. Add the lettuce heads, keeping them whole, bring back to a boil, and cook for 2 minutes. Remove from the pan and drain well. Melt 2 tablespoons of the butter in a skillet. Add the onion and cook over low heat, stirring occasionally, for 5 minutes, until softened. Transfer to a bowl, add the meat, ham, egg, and bread crumbs, and mix well. Season with salt and pepper and then use the mixture to fill the lettuce heads. Tie them in shape with fine kitchen string to prevent them from opening during cooking. Line an ovenproof baking dish with the bacon, add the lettuce heads, and dot with the remaining butter. Pour in the stock and bake for 30 minutes. Serve immediately.

Red cabbage

Trick

• To preserve the color of red cabbage, add a tablespoon of vinegar to the cooking water.

419

Red cabbage with apple and red wine

LOMBARDA CON MANZANAS Y VINO TINTO

• 5 tablespoons olive oil
• 16¼ cups shredded red cabbage (about 1¾ pounds)
• 9 ounces onions, thinly sliced
• generous pinch of aromatic herbs
• 2 cloves garlic, finely chopped
• 2 tart apples, such as Granny Smith or Fuji, peeled, cored, and thinly sliced
• 2 tablespoons red-wine vinegar
• 2¼ cups red wine
• 5 tablespoons boiling water
• salt

Serves 6

Preheat the oven to 325°F. Heat the oil in an ovenproof casserole that can be used on the stove. Add the cabbage and cook, stirring constantly, until it is well coated with the oil, then cover, and cook over medium heat for 10 minutes. Transfer two-thirds of the cabbage to a plate, leaving a third as a layer in the base of the pan. Put half the onion on top of the layer of cabbage, season with salt, add half the aromatic herbs, and sprinkle with half the garlic. Top with half the apples. Make another layer of cabbage, then herbs, then garlic, then apple, finishing with the remaining cabbage. Pour the vinegar, wine, and boiling water into the casserole, cover, transfer to the oven, and cook for about 2 hours, until the cabbage is tender. Serve immediately straight from the casserole.

420

Red cabbage with apple

LOMBARDA CON MANZANA

• 3½ ounces onions, finely chopped
• 2 tablespoons (¼ stick) butter
• 8 cups shredded red cabbage (about 1¼ pounds)
• ¾ cup red wine
• 1 teaspoon vinegar
• 1 pound 2 ounces tart apples, such as Granny Smith or Fuji, peeled, cored, and sliced
• salt and pepper

Serves 4

Put the onions into a large microwave-safe dish, add the butter, cover, and microwave on full power for 2 minutes. Add the cabbage, wine, and vinegar, cover, and microwave for 3 minutes more. Add the apples and mix well, season with salt and pepper, cover, and microwave for 3 minutes. Taste and adjust the seasoning, if necessary, re-cover the dish, and cook for 2 minutes more. Check how tender the cabbage is and, if necessary, microwave for another 2 minutes, then check again. Add a little hot water if necessary.

421

Red cabbage with red wine and onion
LOMBARDA CON VINO TINTO Y CEBOLLA

- 5 tablespoons olive oil
- 1 red cabbage,
  about 3¼ pounds, shredded
- 9 ounces onions, thinly sliced
- 2 tablespoons red-wine vinegar
- 2¼ cups red wine
- 1 tablespoon all-purpose flour
- salt and pepper

Serves 6

Heat the oil in a heavy-based casserole that can be used on the stove or Dutch oven. Add the cabbage and cook over low heat, stirring constantly, until it is well coated with the oil. Cover the casserole, increase the heat to medium, and cook for 10 minutes. Transfer two-thirds of the cabbage to a plate, leaving a third as a layer in the base of the casserole. Make a layer of onion on top of the cabbage and cover with another layer of cabbage. Continue making layers in this way until the onions and cabbage are used up. Pour in the vinegar and wine, sprinkle in the flour, and season with salt and pepper. Cover and cook over low heat for about 2 hours, until the cabbage is tender and there is no liquid left in the base of the casserole. Serve the cabbage immediately.

Note: This dish can be made in advance and reheated. It can also be cooked in a preheated oven at 325°F for 2 hours. It is delicious as an accompaniment to roasted meat, pork chops, and game.

422

Red cabbage salad

ENSALADA DE LOMBARDA

- **2 red cabbages,**
  about 1 pounds 2 ounces each
- **salt**

Vinaigrette:
- **2 tablespoons red wine vinegar**
- **6 tablespoons olive oil**
- **salt and pepper**

Serves 6

Remove and discard the tough outer leaves of the cabbages. Separate the leaves and cut out the stalks. Shred the leaves, wash in plenty of cold water, and drain well. Bring a large pan of salted water to a boil. Add the cabbage, pushing it down with a spoon so that it is covered by the water. Cook for 5 minutes, then drain well in a large colander and let stand until just warm. Meanwhile, make the vinaigrette. Whisk together the vinegar and oil and season to taste with salt and pepper. Put the cabbage into a serving dish and dress with the vinaigrette. Serve warm or cold

Turnips

Origin and season

The precise origin of turnips is not known but it is believed that prehistoric man ate them. The ancient Greeks liked them very much and used them medicinally as well as for food. They were eaten in large quantities in the Middle Ages, but nowadays they are less popular. Turnip is a winter vegetable, although it also grows in spring and fall. It may be round or long.

Selection

Whether round or long, a turnip should feel heavy in the hand and be firm to the touch. Soft turnips will be fibrous. When a turnip is cut, a drop of liquid should appear. If it has a noticeable smell, the turnip will be hot. Do not buy turnips with any blemishes.

Nutrition

Turnips contain a lot of water and have about 28 calories per 3 ½ ounces. They contain vitamins A and B, and calcium and potassium. Taken as a syrup, they are recommended to combat coughs. They are quite hard to digest. According to the sixteenth-century scholar, Sir Thomas Elyot, "They increase the seduction of man and increase his carnal appetite".

How to prepare and cook

Most recipes require turnips to be washed and peeled. Cut them in half lengthwise or into medium slices, even when they are small. Bring a large pan of salted water to a boil, add the turnips, making sure they are covered, and cook for 10 minutes. Drain well before using.

Tricks

- Never peel turnips in advance, as they will oxidize and may cause intestinal problems
- Very young and tender turnips do not need to be peeled— simply scraping them with the tip of a knife is enough
- The leaves can be added to a stock to give it a delightful flavor.

423

Turnips with béchamel sauce and egg yolks

NABOS CON BECHAMEL Y YEMAS

- 4 ½ pounds young turnips
- 2 tablespoons (¼ stick) butter
- 2 tablespoons sunflower oil
- 2 tablespoons all-purpose flour
- scant 2 cups milk
- pinch of grated nutmeg
- 2 egg yolks
- salt

Serves 6

Prepare and cook the turnips as described on page 336. Melt the butter and oil in a pan. Stir in the flour and cook, stirring constantly, for 2 minutes. Gradually stir in the milk, a little at a time. Cook, stirring constantly, for 5 minutes. Season. Add the turnips and nutmeg, mix well, and cook, stirring occasionally, for about 25 minutes, until the turnips are tender. (Test by piercing one with a skewer or the tip of a sharp knife). Lightly beat the egg yolks in a bowl and stir in a little sauce to prevent them from curdling, then stir into the pan. Serve immediately.

424

Turnip gratin

NABOS CON BECHAMEL Y QUESO RALLADO, GRATINADOS

- 4 ½ pounds turnips, sliced
- 3 tablespoons butter
- 2 tablespoons sunflower oil
- 3 tablespoons all-purpose flour
- 3 cups milk
- ½ teaspoon meat extract
- ¾ grated cup gruyere cheese
- salt

Serves 6

Prepare and cook the turnips as described on page 336. Preheat the oven to 400°F. Melt the butter with the oil in a pan. Stir in the flour and cook, stirring constantly, for 2 minutes. Gradually stir in the milk, a little at a time. Cook, stirring constantly, for 5 minutes. Stir in the meat extract or some Maggi Seasoning and season to taste with salt. Put the turnip slices into an ovenproof baking dish, pour the sauce over them, and sprinkle with the gruyere. Bake for 10–15 minutes, until golden brown. Serve immediately.

425

Turnips with carrots

NABOS CON ZANAHORIAS

- 1 pound 10 ounces carrots, peeled
- 1 pound 10 ounces turnips, peeled
- 6 tablespoons olive oil
- 1 large onion, finely chopped
- 1 tablespoon all-purpose flour
- 1 teaspoon sugar
- salt

Serves 6

Cut the carrots and the turnips lengthwise into halves or quarters, depending on their thickness. Heat the oil in a pan. Add the onion and cook over low heat, stirring occasionally, for about 6 minutes, until softened and translucent. Add the carrots and turnips. Stir in the flour, then add the sugar and a pinch of salt. Mix well and add just enough water to cover. Cook over medium heat for about 30 minutes, until the vegetable are tender. Transfer the vegetables and sauce to a warm dish and serve immediately.

426

Turnips in cider
NABOS A LA SIDRA

- **2¼ pounds small turnips**
- **⅔ cup hard cider**
- **⅓ cup lard or ¼ cup butter**
- **generous 1 cup hot chicken stock (homemade, canned or made with a bouillon cube)**
- **1 bouquet garni (1 sprig fresh parsley, 1 bay leaf, and 1 clove garlic tied in cheesecloth)**
- **salt and pepper**
- **chopped fresh parsley (optional)**

Serves 6

Bring a large pan of salted water to a boil. Add the turnips and cook for 5 minutes. Drain well. Heat the hard cider in another pan and cook until it has reduced by half, then remove the pan from the heat. Melt the lard or butter in a heavy pan or Dutch oven. Add the turnips and cook over low heat, stirring occasionally, for about 5 minutes, until lightly browned. Pour in the hard cider and stock, add the bouquet garni, and season to taste with salt and pepper. Cover and simmer over very low heat for 30 minutes. Remove the bouquet garni. Serve immediately, garnished with chopped parsley if you like.

427

Glazed turnips
NABOS GLASEADOS

- **2¼ pounds turnips, sliced**
- **5 tablespoons butter**
- **1 teaspoon sugar**
- **salt**

Serves 6

Put the turnip into a pan, pour in just enough water to cover, and add the butter, sugar, and a pinch of salt. Cook over medium-low heat for 20 minutes, until the water has evaporated. Serve immediately as an accompaniment to meat.

Cucumber

Origin and season

Cucumbers have grown wild in the foothills of the Himalayas for 6,000 years and, although nobody really knows how, they appeared in ancient Egypt, where they were a favorite vegetable of the pharaohs. The celebrated Roman gourmet Apicius invented a recipe based on cucumber with honey, oil, and eggs. The best cucumbers are available from early summer to early fall, as this is usually the period of least rain and the cucumbers have lots of flavor and are not bitter. However, the season is from mid spring to mid fall.

Selection

Choose firm cucumbers without any blemishes. The skin should be shiny and smooth except in the case of ridged cucumbers which have a naturally knobby skin. Try to find cucumbers that are not too fat as they will have fewer seeds.

Nutrition

Cucumbers contain about 15 calories per 3 ½ ounces. A light food, they are a source of minerals and vitamins but are difficult to digest. The skin contains a bitter laxative substance that could cause irritation to the intestinal wall, so it is advisable to peel cucumbers before eating them.

Tricks

- Peel cucumbers from head to tail in order to avoid the bitterness that can sometimes be given off
- To draw out some of their water, slice cucumbers, then sprinkle with salt, and let stand. Alternatively, put the slices in a dishtowel and twist it, pressing hard, so that the water is released and the cucumber is ready to be seasoned
- Cucumber makes a good face mask for oily skin to help close the pores. Process the flesh in a food processor with a pot of plain yogurt. Leave the mask on for about 10 minutes and rinse off with water.

428

Cucumbers for salads

PEPINOS PARA ENSALADA

- 4 cucumbers
- 1 quantity Vinaigrette (see recipe 98)
- 1 tablespoon chopped fresh parsley (optional)

Serves 4–6

Choose cucumbers that are very green and firm. Peel and thinly slice, then sprinkle with salt, and let stand for at least 2 hours. Rinse well and pat dry, then put the slices on a plate and sprinkle with the vinaigrette and chopped parsley, if using. Chill in the refrigerator until ready to serve. The slices can be served alone or mixed with tomatoes and bell peppers.

429

Cucumber boats with salad

BARCAS DE PEPINOS CON ENSALADILLA

- 6 cucumbers
- 1 small onion, chopped
- 2 cloves garlic, chopped
- 9 ounces raw shrimp, shells on
- 3 firm tomatoes, diced
- 1 small green bell pepper or 1 small canned or bottled red bell pepper, drained and diced
- 2 hard-cooked egg

Mayonnaise:
- 1 egg
- juice of 1 lemon
- 1 cup sunflower oil
- salt

Serves 6

Halve the cucumbers lengthwise. Sprinkle with salt and let stand, cut side down, for 30 minutes. Meanwhile, make the mayonnaise as described in recipe 105. Using the tip of a knife, scrape out the seeds and remove the centers from the cucumbers so that they resemble little boats. Chop the scooped-out flesh and reserve. Sprinkle the onion and garlic into the cucumbers, put them in a dish, cover with aluminum foil, and chill in the refrigerator for 1 hour. Meanwhile, put the shrimp into a pan, pour in water to cover, and add a pinch of salt. Bring to a boil, then drain, and peel. Combine the tomato, bell pepper, reserved cucumber flesh, shrimp, and mayonnaise in a bowl and divide among the cucumber boats. Finely chop the hard-cooked eggs and sprinkle over the boats. Cover with aluminum foil again and chill in the refrigerator for another hour before serving.

Stuffed cucumbers

PEPINOS RELLENOS

- 6½ tablespoons butter,
  plus extra for greasing
- 2¼ pounds cucumbers,
  cut into 1½-inch lengths
- 3½ ounces mushrooms
- juice of ½ lemon
- scant 1 cup coarsely
  chopped ham
- 1 tablespoon chopped
  fresh parsley
- 2 tablespoons bread crumbs
- salt and pepper

Tomato sauce:
- 3 tablespoons sunflower oil
- 1 small onion, chopped
- 2¼ pounds very ripe tomatoes,
  peeled, seeded, and chopped
- 1 bouquet garni (1 sprig fresh
  parsley, 1 clove garlic, and 1 bay
  leaf tied in cheesecloth)
- 3 tablespoons dry white wine
- 1 teaspoon sugar
- salt

Serves 6

Preheat the oven to 350°F. Grease an ovenproof baking dish with butter. Scoop out the cucumber seeds with a teaspoon and put the pieces of cucumber into the prepared baking dish. Remove and discard the mushroom stalks, cut the caps into large pieces, place in a bowl, and sprinkle with lemon juice. Stir in the ham. Melt 2 tablespoons of the butter in a pan. Add the mushroom mixture and cook over low heat, stirring occasionally, for 5 minutes. Season with salt and pepper and stir in the parsley and bread crumbs. Remove the pan from the heat. Season the pieces of cucumber with salt and pepper and fill them with the mushroom mixture. Dot with the remaining butter, cover the dish with aluminum foil, and bake for 40 minutes, until the cucumbers are tender but still crunchy. Meanwhile, make the tomato sauce. Heat the oil in a skillet. Add the onion and cook over low heat, stirring occasionally, for about 7 minutes, until beginning to brown. Add the tomato, bouquet garni, and wine and cook, stirring occasionally and breaking up the tomato with the side of the spoon, for 15 minutes. Remove and discard the bouquet garni, let the sauce cool a little, then process in a food processor or blender. Stir in the sugar and season to taste with salt. Serve the stuffed cucumbers with the hot tomato sauce offered separately.

Bell peppers

Origin and season

Bell peppers come from the Americas and were taken to Europe by Christopher Columbus. They are available all year around.

Selection

The skin should be smooth and shiny, without any blemishes and with a distinct color. Allow about 9 ounces per person.

Nutrition

Bell peppers contain about 30 calories per 3 ½ ounces. They are a rich source of vitamin C. They are difficult to digest when eaten raw but present no problems when cooked. In small quantities they stimulate the appetite. The skin irritates the intestine and is hard to digest, so it is advisable to peel bell peppers before eating them. (see below).

Tricks

• To peel bell peppers easily, put them into an oven preheated to 350°F or under a preheated broiler for about 10 minutes, turning them once. Alternatively, spear them on a long-handled fork and hold them directly in a flame. When they have been roasted, wrap them in a dishtowel or sheet of newspaper, put them into a plastic or brown paper bag and tie the top, or place in a bowl and cover with crumpled paper towels. Let cool, then peel off the skins

• Bell peppers freeze perfectly, but their smell can contaminate other food, so freeze them in a closed container or a sealed freezer bag.

431

Red bell peppers with hard-cooked eggs

PIMIENTOS ROJOS CON HUEVOS DUROS

- 2 ¼ ounces red bell peppers
- 1 quantity Vinaigrette
  (see recipe 98)
- 2 hard-cooked eggs, sliced

Serves 6

Roast and peel red bell peppers as described on page 342, then remove and discard the seeds, and cut the flesh into strips. Put into a dish, add the vinaigrette, and let marinate for 30 minutes. Drain slightly and serve with the slices of hard-cooked egg.

432

Fried green bell pepper garnish

PIMIENTOS VERDES FRITOS, PARA ADORNAR LA CARNE

- 2 ¼ pounds green bell peppers
- 1 ½ cups olive oil
- salt

Serves 6

Cut out the stalks and remove the seeds from the bell peppers. If they are large, cut them into strips or rings. If they are small, cut them in half lengthwise or even leave them whole. Season the insides of the bell peppers with salt. Heat the oil with 2 tablespoons water in a deep skillet. Add the bell peppers, season with salt, cover, and cook over low heat for about 10 minutes, until tender. Drain off the oil and serve as a garnish for a meat dish.

Green bell peppers stuffed with meat
PIMIENTOS VERDES RELLENOS DE CARNE

- 12 green bell peppers
- 2¼ cups sunflower oil

Filling:
- 2¾ cups mixed ground pork and beef
- scan 1 cup ground Serrano ham or prosciutto
- 1 slice of bread, crusts removed and soaked in hot milk
- 1 clove garlic, finely chopped
- 1 teaspoon chopped fresh parsley
- 1 egg, lightly beaten
- 1 tablespoon white wine
- salt

Sauce:
- 1 large onion, chopped
- 1 large ripe tomato, seeded and cut into quarters
- 2 carrots, sliced
- 1 tablespoon all-purpose flour
- ¾ cup white wine
- salt

Serves 6

Cut out the stalks and remove the seeds from the peppers. Make the filling. If you are grinding the meat yourself, grind the ham at the same time. Otherwise, thoroughly mix the meat and ham together in a bowl. Gently squeeze out the bread, if necessary, and add it to the bowl with the garlic, parsley, egg, and wine. Season with salt and mix well. Fill the bell peppers with the meat mixture, using a teaspoon, and secure with wooden toothpicks. Heat the oil with 2 tablespoons water in a deep skillet. Add the bell peppers, three at a time, and cook over low heat for 10 minutes. Using a slotted spoon, transfer the cooked bell peppers to a clean pan, arranging them in a single layer. Drain all but about 5 tablespoons of the oil from the skillet and reheat. Add the onion and cook over low heat, stirring occasionally, for about 10 minutes, until browned. Add the tomato and carrot and cook, stirring occasionally, for 5 minutes more. Stir in the flour and cook, stirring constantly, for 2 minutes, then stir in the wine and 4 cups water. Simmer for 15 minutes. Let cool slightly, then transfer to a food processor or blender, process until smooth, and pour into the pan of bell peppers. Season with salt and cook over low heat, stirring occasionally, for 15 minutes. If the sauce is too thick, add a little hot water. Serve in a warm deep dish.

Note: This dish can be made in advance and it is quite delicious when it is reheated.

434 Bell peppers stuffed with meat and rice

PIMIENTOS RELLENOS DE CARNE PICADA Y ARROZ CRUDO

- **6 round green bell peppers**
- **6 tablespoons long-grain rice**
- **3¼ cups ground beef**
- **½ clove garlic, finely chopped**
- **1 tablespoons finely chopped fresh parsley**
- **¾ cup sunflower oil**
- **¼ cup all-purpose flour**
- **1 egg, lightly beaten**
- **salt**

Sauce:
- **1 onion, chopped**
- **1 tablespoon all-purpose flour**
- **pinch of saffron threads**
- **1 beef bouillon cube**
- **salt**

Serves 6

Cut out the stalks and remove the seeds from the bell peppers. Season the insides of the bell peppers with salt. Put 1 tablespoon of the rice into each one. Combine the beef, garlic, and parsley in a bowl and season with salt. Using a teaspoon, divide the mixture among the bell peppers. Heat the oil in a deep skillet. Coat the opening of the bell peppers first with the flour and then with the beaten egg. Add the bell peppers to the skillet, cut sides down, and cook until the egg has set. Lay the bell peppers on their sides and cook, turning occasionally, for 5 minutes. You may need to do this in two batches to allow sufficient room. Transfer the cooked bell peppers to a clean pan. Make the sauce. Drain of all but 4 tablespoons of the oil from the skillet and reheat. Add the onion and cook over low heat, stirring occasionally, for about 7 minutes, until beginning to brown. Stir in the flour and cook, stirring constantly, for 2 minutes. Lightly season with salt, add the saffron, and pour in 2¼ cups water. Cook, stirring constantly, for 3 minutes, then strain into the pan of bell peppers. Crumble the bouillon cube into a little water, then add it to the pan. Pour in enough water to half cover the bell peppers, cover, and cook over low heat for about 30 minutes, until tender. Serve the peppers immediately with their sauce or let cool, then reheat just before serving.

435 Bell peppers stuffed with quail

PIMIENTOS RELLENOS DE CODORNICES

- **5 tablespoons olive oil**
- **6–12 boneless quail**
- **6 slices of bacon**
- **6–12 large bell peppers**
- **¼ cup (½ stick) butter**
- **salt**

Sauce:
- **1 onion, finely chopped**
- **20 grapes, peeled and seeded**
- **5 tablespoons red wine**
- **5 tablespoons white wine**
- **a little meat sauce**
- **1 bay leaf**

Serves 6

Preheat the oven to 400°F. Heat the oil in a skillet. Add the quail and cook over low heat, turning occasionally, for a few minutes, but do not let them brown. Remove the quail from the pan and reserve the oil. Lightly season the quail with salt and put a slice of bacon into the cavity of each one. Cut out the stalks and remove the seeds from the bell peppers. Put each quail into a bell pepper and add a little butter. Put into an ovenproof baking dish and bake for about 1 hour. Meanwhile, make the sauce. Reheat the oil in the skillet. Add the onion and cook over low heat, stirring occasionally, for 5 minutes, until softened. Add the grapes, red and white wine, meat sauce, and bay leaf, season to taste with salt, and cook for 10 minutes. Remove and discard the bay leaf. Serve the quail in the bell peppers and offer the sauce separately.

Leek

Origin and season

The origin of leeks is unknown, although it is certain that they have been grown for a very long time. The ancient Egyptians liked them, so much so that the pharaoh used to give his soldiers bunches of leeks instead of gold. The Greeks used them to combat infertility and the Roman emperor Nero ate great quantities of them to clear his voice. They are available nearly all year around, but their best season is from mid-fall to mid-spring.

Selection

Leeks should be straight, white, and not too fat, with shiny green leaves. Allow about 5 ounces per serving.

Nutrition

Leeks contain about 40 calories per 3 ½ ounces. They provide the minerals potassium and magnesium and contain a lot of water, so they have diuretic and laxative properties. Although they contain sugars, these are easily assimilated by the body. They are wonderful for the skin and hair. Leek skin should be eaten, as this is where nearly all the nutritional value is concentrated. The green part is where most of the vitamins are.

Tricks

- Always remove the roots and dark green outer leaves, and wash leeks under cold running water to remove any earth that may be trapped between the leaves
- Give leeks an original touch by preparing them with honey or brown sugar. Cook them in butter and when they are beginning to brown, add a spoonful of honey and cook until golden and glazed. Finally, add a dash of vinegar for sharpness. Serve the leeks with this sauce poured over them.

436

Leeks with vinaigrette or mayonnaise
PUERROS CON VINAGRETA O CON MAYONESA

- 2–3 leeks per serving,
  trimmed and rinsed well
- salt

Serves 6

Bring a pan of salted water to a boil. Add the leeks and cook for about 15 minutes, until tender. Drain and serve warm. They may be served with a vinaigrette (see recipe 98), capers and canned anchovy fillets, or with Classic Mayonnaise (see recipe 105).

437

Leeks au gratin
PUERROS GRATINADOS

- 12–18 leeks,
  trimmedand rinsed well
- 3 tablespoons olive oil
- 2 thick slices bacon,
  cut into strips
- ¾ grated cup gruyere cheese
- 2 tablespoons (¼ stick) butter
- salt

Serves 6

Bring a pan of salted water to a boil. Add the leeks and cook for about 15 minutes, until tender. Preheat the oven to 400°F. Drain the leeks well and put them into an ovenproof baking dish. Heat the oil in a skillet. Add the bacon and cook over medium heat, stirring occasionally, for about 5 minutes, until lightly browned. Remove from the pan, drain and add to the baking dish. Sprinkle with the gruyere and dot with the butter. Bake for 10–15 minutes, until golden brown. Serve immediately straight from the dish.

438

Leeks with béchamel sauce
PUERROS CON BECHAMEL

- 12 large leeks,
  trimmed and rinsed well
- 2 tablespoons (¼ stick) butter
- 2 tablespoons sunflower oil
- 1 heaping tablespoon
  all-purpose flour
- 2 ¼ cups milk
- 1 tablespoon tomato paste
- ¾ cup grated gruyere cheese
- 2 tablespoons chopped
  fresh parsley
- salt

Serves 6

Bring a pan of salted water to a boil. Add the leeks and cook for about 15 minutes, until tender. Drain well. Preheat the oven to 400°F. Melt the butter with the oil in a pan. Stir in the flour and cook, stirring constantly, for 2 minutes. Gradually stir in the milk, a little at a time. Cook, stirring constantly, for 10 minutes, then lightly season with salt, and stir in the tomato paste. Put the leeks into an ovenproof baking dish and pour the béchamel sauce over them. Sprinkle with the gruyere and bake for 10–15 minutes, until golden brown. Sprinkle the parsley on top in two lines and serve immediately.

439

Curried leeks

PUERROS AL CURRY

- 12 large leeks,
  trimmed and rinsed well
- 2 tablespoons (¼ stick) butter
- 2 tablespoons sunflower oil
- 1 tablespoon all-purpose flour
- 2¼ cups milk
- ½ teaspoon curry powder
- ¾ cup grated gruyere cheese
- 2 tablespoons chopped
  fresh parsley
- salt

Serves 6

Bring a pan of salted water to a boil. Add the leeks and cook for about 15 minutes, until tender. Drain well. Preheat the oven to 400°F. Melt the butter with the oil in a pan. Stir in the flour and cook, stirring constantly, for 2 minutes. Gradually stir in the milk, a little at a time. Cook, stirring constantly, for 10 minutes, then lightly season with salt, and stir in the curry powder. Put the leeks into an ovenproof baking dish and pour the béchamel sauce over them. Sprinkle with the gruyere and bake for 10–15 minutes, until golden brown. Sprinkle the parsley on top in two lines and serve immediately.

440

Leek tart with rice

TARTA DE PUERROS CON ARROZ

- 3 tablespoons olive oil,
  plus extra for brushing
- 4 leeks,
  trimmed, sliced and rinsed well
- 2 large onions, finely chopped
- 1 bay leaf
- ½ teaspoon dried thyme
- ⅔ cup white wine
- 3 eggs
- 1¼ cups milk
- ½ cup grated gruyere cheese
- generous 1 cup long-grain rice,
  cooked

Sauce:
- 1 large red bell pepper, roasted
  and peeled (see page 342)
- ½ chicken bouillon cube
- ⅔ cup warm water
- 4 tablespoons light cream
- salt and pepper

Serves 6

Preheat the oven to 350°F. Brush an ovenproof baking dish with oil. Heat the oil in a pan. Add the leek, onion, bay leaf, and thyme and cook over low heat, stirring occasionally, for 5 minutes, until softened and translucent. Pour in the wine, cover, and simmer for 12 minutes. Beat the eggs in a bowl, then stir in the milk and gruyere. Mix the leek and onion with the cooked rice in another bowl and add the egg mixture. Spoon into the prepared dish and bake for 30 minutes. Meanwhile, make the sauce. Remove and discard the seeds from the bell pepper and coarsely chop the flesh. Dissolve the bouillon cube in the warm water. Put the bell pepper and stock into a food processor or blender and process to a purée, then pour into a pan, and bring to a boil. Simmer for 2 minutes. Stir in the cream and heat through but do not let boil. Season to taste with salt and pepper. Turn the leek tart out onto a plate and serve immediately, offering the sauce separately.

Radish

Origin and season

Radishes are a very old vegetable, although it is difficult to determine their exact origin. The ancient Greeks ate radishes to prevent gallstones and stop hemorrhaging. Radishes can be found all year around. Early spring ones are the hottest. The best time for radishes is from the late spring to early fall.

Selection

Radishes should be smooth and not too fat, with very shiny green leaves (if attached). They lose their crispness and the leaves wilt within 48 hours of harvesting. Be careful when buying bunches without leaves, as this could indicate that the radishes are already deteriorating; be sure the radishes are firm to the touch.

Nutrition

Radishes contain about 20 calories per 3 ½ ounces. Though difficult to digest, they are rich in iron and vitamins B and C and often form part of a balanced weight-loss diet.

Tricks

- If the pink radishes are very fresh, they do not need to be peeled, but they should be washed in plenty of water and thoroughly dried
- Do not discard the leaves; you can add them to a vegetable soup for extra flavor
- The best way to keep radishes is with the stalks and leaves in water, but do not submerge the radish.

441

Orange and radish salad

ENSALADA DE NARANJAS Y RABANOS

- 2 bunches radishes, trimmed
- 1 tablespoon confectioner's sugar
- 6 tablespoons lemon juice
- 6 oranges
- ½ cup shelled walnuts, sliced
- salt and pepper

Serves 4

Coarsely grate the radishes into a bowl. Add the sugar, a pinch of salt, a pinch of pepper, and the lemon juice. Cut the rinds off the oranges with a sharp knife, removing all traces of the bitter pith. Thinly slice the flesh. Mix the oranges and radishes together and garnish with the walnuts. Chill in the refrigerator before serving.

442

Radish salad

ENSALADA CON RABANOS

- 5 ounces mixed salad greens
- ½ bunch radishes,
  trimmed and sliced
- salt and pepper

Dressing:
- ⅔ cup plain yogurt
- 1 tablespoon lemon juice
- 1 tablespoon chopped
  fresh chives

Serves 4

Put the salad greens and radishes into a salad bowl. Combine all the dressing ingredients and pour over the salad. Season to taste with salt and pepper and toss lightly. Chill in the refrigerator for 1 hour before serving.

Notes: Wash the salad greens but do not let them soak for too long, as they will lose their vitamins. Give a salad a personal touch by adding fresh herbs, such as parsley, chives, mint, or basil. Diced apple is also a very tasty addition. A little mustard or a pinch of herbs can be added to the yogurt dressing.

Beet

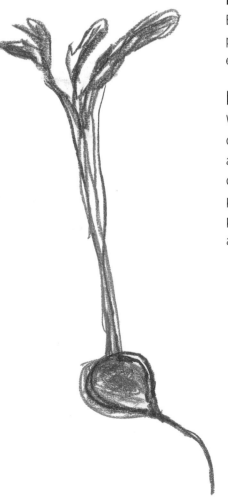

Origin and season

Beets come from North Africa. The ancient Greeks valued them for their therapeutic properties, principally to combat stomach problems. As well as the root itself, the tender greens can also be eaten as a vegetable. Beets are available all year around.

Selection

Although there are various types of beet, the most common is the red one. It can be bought raw, but does take a long time to cook. Ready-cooked beets are also available. A good rule when buying cooked beets is that the tastiest ones are those that look least attractive. A dull, wrinkled appearance means they have been cooked in the oven, while shiny smooth beets have been cooked in water or steamed and will have less flavor.

Nutrition

Beets contain about 42 calories per 3 ½ ounces and are rich in potassium and sugar. They can be difficult to digest so should be eaten in moderation.

How to cook

Wash beets whole with the skin and leaves intact. Do not cut these off as the beets will loose their lovely red color. Put the beets into a pan with plenty of cold water and a pinch of salt. Bring to a boil and cook over medium heat for about 1 ½ hours, until tender. Check by piercing with a skewer or the tip of a sharp knife. Remove from the pan and let cool. Peel, then slice or dice, and dress with oil, vinegar, and salt.

443

443 ## Stuffed beets

REMOLACHAS RELLENAS

- **4 cooked beets**
- **2 hard-cooked eggs, halved**
- **½ cup long-grain rice, cooked**
- **1 apple, peeled, cored, and diced**
- **½ small onion, finely chopped**
- **1 tablespoon chopped**
  fresh parsley
- **1 tablespoon red-wine vinegar**
- **3 tablespoons olive oil**
- **salt and pepper**

Serves 4

Peel the beets and cut a slice like a little hat off the top of each one. Hollow out the centers, taking care not to break the "shells." Dice the scooped-out flesh and set aside. Scoop the yolks out of the hard-cooked eggs and set aside. Finely chop the whites. Combine the diced beet, egg whites, rice, apple, onion, and parsley in a bowl. Whisk together the vinegar and oil in another bowl, stir in the egg yolks, and season with salt and pepper, then pour over the beet and rice mixture. Season to taste with salt and pepper and use the mixture to fill the beet shells. Store in the refrigerator until ready to serve.

Cabbage

Origin and season
Cabbage is one of the oldest European vegetables and has grown naturally for 6,000 years in places such as the Balearic Islands and Sardinia. The ancient Romans used it as a remedy for melancholy. It is a winter vegetable with a season from the end of fall until the middle of spring. There are two main types, one from Milan and the one called Savoy. There are several varieties of cabbage, including green, white, and red. Both white and red cabbages have smooth, firm, tightly packed leaves. Savoy cabbage has slightly looser crimped leaves and needs less cooking than other varieties. Winter cabbages are rounded, while spring cabbages are pointed.

Selection
A cabbage should feel heavy in the hand and the leaves should be well established. When calculating quantities remember that cabbage reduces by about half during cooking.

Nutrition

Cabbage is one of the richest vegetable sources of vitamins and minerals. It contains as much vitamin C as lemon juice and is rich in calcium, magnesium, and sulfur. It has only 25 calories per 3 ½ ounces when eaten raw and 15 calories per 3 ½ ounces when cooked. The leaves are thought by some to be helpful for those with bronchitis and rheumatism. Unfortunately, cabbage fibers contain a substance that ferments in the intestine and can produce gas.

Tricks

- Cooking cabbage in two stages will prevent it causing gas
- To avoid the unpleasant smell of cooking cabbage, put a piece of bread in the water. If this still doesn't help, be patient; studies are currently being carried out to produce a variety that does not have this characteristic odor
- Remove the cabbage from leftover cabbage soup, otherwise it will turn the soup sour
- To retain the vitamins and minerals in cabbage do not leave it soaking for too long and try to eat it raw in salads.

444

Cabbage with mayonnaise

REPOLLO CON MAYONESA

- 4 ½ pounds cabbage
- 4 boiled new potatoes, cut into
  2–4 pieces, or tomato slices
- salt

  Mayonnaise:
- 2 eggs
- juice of 1 lemon or 4 tablespoons
  white-wine vinegar
- 3 cups sunflower oil
- salt

  Serves 6

Remove and discard the tough outer leaves of the cabbage. Cut into quarters and remove the core, then slice the leaves into ¾-inch strips. Wash well. Bring a large pan of salted water to a boil. Add the cabbage, pushing it down into the water with a spoon. Bring back to a boil, cover, and simmer for about 30 minutes, until tender. Meanwhile, make the mayonnaise as described in recipe 105. Drain the cabbage well. If the cabbage is to be served cold or just warm, garnish it with slices of tomato and then cover with the mayonnaise. If it is to be served hot, put it into a warm round or oval dish and garnish with the potato. Cover with the mayonnaise and serve straight away. An alternative is to heat some oil in a skillet. Add 1–2 garlic cloves and cook for a few minutes, until lightly browned. Remove and discard the garlic, add the cabbage to the pan, and cook, stirring frequently, for a few minutes. Remove from the pan, drain well, and place in an ovenproof baking dish. Spoon the mayonnaise over the cabbage and bake in a preheated oven, 400°F, for about 10 minutes, until browned.

445

Cabbage in jus

REPOLLO AL JUGO

- **4½ pounds Savoy cabbage**
- **scant ½ cup lard or generous ⅓ cup butter**
- **5 ounces bacon, thinly sliced**
- **1 onion, thinly sliced and pushed out into rings**
- **2 carrots, thinly sliced**
- **2¼ cups chicken stock (homemade, canned or made with a bouillon cube)**
- **2 bay leaves**
- **salt**

Serves 6

Prepare and cook the cabbage as described in recipe 444. Drain well. Melt the lard or butter in a pan. Add the bacon and cook over medium heat, stirring occasionally, for about 5 minutes, until browned. Remove from the pan and set aside. Add the onion to the pan and cook over low heat, stirring occasionally, for about 5 minutes, until softened and translucent. Add the cabbage, carrot, and half the bacon and mix well. Pour the stock over the mixture and add the remaining bacon and the bay leaves. Cover and simmer over low heat, stirring occasionally, for 1½ hours. Serve immediately.

446

Cabbage pie with tomato sauce

BUDÍN DE REPOLLO CON SALSA DE TOMATE

- **1 quantity fresh Tomato Sauce (see recipe 73)**
- **3¼ pounds Savoy cabbage**
- **3 tablespoons butter, plus extra for greasing**
- **generous ½ cup finely chopped Serrano ham or prosciutto**
- **3 eggs**
- **3 tablespoons milk**
- **salt**

Serves 6

Process the tomato sauce in a food processor or blender and set aside. Prepare and cook the cabbage as described in recipe 444. Drain well. Preheat the oven to 325°F. Grease an ovenproof baking dish with butter. Melt the butter in a skillet. Add the cabbage and ham and cook over medium heat, stirring frequently, for 5 minutes. Remove the pan from the heat. Beat the eggs with the milk in a bowl, then stir into the cabbage mixture. Spoon the mixture into the prepared baking dish, then place the dish in a roasting pan, and pour in boiling water to come about halfway up the sides. Transfer to the oven and bake for about 1 hour, until set. Turn off the oven, open the door, and let the pie stand for 8 minutes. Meanwhile, reheat the tomato sauce. Turn out the pie onto a warm serving dish and pour the tomato sauce over it. Serve immediately.

447

Cabbage pie
PASTEL DE REPOLLO

- 2¼ pounds cabbage
- 2 tablespoons olive oil,
  plus extra for brushing
- 1 pound 10 ounces bulk sausage
- 3 eggs, lightly beaten
- 2 tablespoons of milk
- generous ½ cup chopped
  Serrano ham or prosciutto
- 12 ounces thinly sliced bacon

Serves 6

Prepare and cook the cabbage as described in recipe 444. Drain well. Preheat the oven to 325°F. Brush an ovenproof baking dish with oil. Combine the bulk sausage and eggs in a bowl, then add the milk. Heat the oil in a skillet. Add the cabbage and ham and cook over medium heat, stirring occasionally, for about 5 minutes, until lightly browned. Remove the pan from the heat. Line the prepared baking dish with the some of the bacon. Add a layer of the sausage mixture, then a layer of cabbage and ham. Continue making layers in this way until all the ingredients are used up, ending with a layer of bacon. Put the dish into a roasting pan and pour in boiling water to come about halfway up the sides. Bake for 1½ hours, until set. Remove the dish from the oven, cover with aluminum foil, put a weight on top, and let cool. Refrigerate until ready to serve. This dish is best eaten the following day.

448

Fried cabbage garnish
HOJAS DE REPOLLO FRITAS (PARA ADORNO DE LA CARNE)

- 1 cabbage, about 2¼ pounds
- sunflower oil, for deep-frying
- ½ cup all-purpose flour
- salt

Serves 6

Cut out the core and carefully separate the cabbage leaves without breaking them. Bring a large pan of salted water to a boil. Add the cabbage leaves, gently pushing them down into the water with a spoon. Bring back to a boil, cover, and simmer for about 30 minutes, until tender. Carefully remove the leaves from the pan, drain, and place them on a clean dishtowel to dry. Heat the oil in a deep-fryer or deep saucepan to 350–375°F or until a cube of day-old bread browns in 30 seconds. Meanwhile, fold in the two outside edges of each cabbage leaf and roll the leaf up so that it is about the size of a large croquette with straight ends. Coat in the flour and add to the hot oil, in batches of four. Cook for a few minutes, until golden brown. Drain well and use to garnish meat. These rolls go very well with stews, casseroles, and meat cooked in a sauce.

449

Cabbage leaves stuffed with ham in béchamel sauce

HOJAS DE REPOLLO RELLENAS DE JAMÓN DE YORK CON BECHAMEL

- 1 cabbage, about 2¼ pounds
- 1 cup finely chopped cooked
  meat or Smithfield, Black Forest
  Ham, prosciutto, or other
  dry-cured ham
- 2 tablespoons (¼ stick) butter
- 2 tablespoons sunflower oil
- 2 tablespoons all-purpose flour
- 2¼ cups milk
- ¾ cup grated gruyere cheese
- salt

Serves 6

Prepare and cook the cabbage leaves as described in recipe 448. Carefully remove the leaves from the pan, drain, and place on a clean dishtowel to dry. Divide the meat or ham among the leaves and roll each leaf up like cannelloni. Put the rolls into an ovenproof baking dish in a single layer. Preheat the oven to 400°F. Melt the butter with the oil in a pan. Stir in the flour and cook, stirring constantly, for 2 minutes. Gradually stir in the milk, a little at a time. Cook, stirring constantly, for 10 minutes. Season with salt then pour the sauce over the cabbage rolls. Sprinkle the gruyere over the top and bake for 10–15 minutes, until golden brown. Serve immediately straight from the dish.

Note: The béchamel sauce can also be made by using half milk and half stock.

450

Snow peas

TIRABEQUES

- 5 tablespoons olive oil
- 1 onion, chopped
- generous ½ cup diced bacon
- 3¼–4½ pounds snow peas,
  trimmed
- 2 tablespoons all-purpose flour
- 4 cups chicken stock
  (homemade, canned or
  made with a bouillon cube)
- 2 egg yolks
- salt

Serves 6

Heat the oil in a pan. Add the onion and cook over low heat, stirring occasionally, for about 5 minutes, until softened and translucent. Add the bacon and cook, stirring occasionally, for 5 minutes more. Add the snow peas, increase the heat to high, cover, and cook, shaking the pan occasionally, for 10 minutes. Season with salt and stir in the flour. Cook, stirring constantly, for 2 minutes, then stir in the stock. Bring to a boil, lower the heat, cover, and simmer for 30 minutes. Lightly beat the egg yolks in a bowl and stir in a little of the cooking liquid from the snow peas to prevent them curdling, then stir into the pan. Serve immediately.

Note: If there is too much liquid in the pan containing the snow peas, remove some before adding the egg yolks.

Tomatoes

Origin and season

Tomatoes, which are actually a fruit rather than a vegetable, come from Peru and Mexico and were taken to Europe by the conquistadores of the sixteenth century. In some countries, such as pre-revolutionary France, they were considered to be inedible as they are part of the nightshade family. Nowadays, tomatoes are among the most commonly eaten fruits. They are available all year-round but the best time for them is early fall when they have had all the sun they need.

Selection

Tomatoes are best bought fully ripe. They should be firm to the touch and the skin should be smooth and without blemishes. Green tomatoes are indigestible; let them ripen by wrapping them in newspaper and leaving them to ripen in a dark place.

Nutrition

Tomatoes have about 20 calories per 3½ ounces. They stimulate the appetite and are rich in vitamins A, B, and C. They also contain iron and magnesium. Their high level of acidity can cause stomach problems for some people.

Tricks

- There are two ways to peel tomatoes. Put them in a heatproof bowl and pour in boiling water to cover. Leave for 3 seconds, then drain, peel off the skins, and refresh in cold water. Alternatively, run the blunt edge of a knife blade over the tomato, pressing quite hard, then peel off the skin with the sharp edge
- To store leftover tomato paste, cover it with a layer of oil
- To reduce the acidity of a tomato sauce, add a pinch of sugar
- When making a tomato sauce, give it a different touch by adding a few fresh basil leaves at the last minute
- Raw tomatoes do not freeze well but tomato sauce can be frozen successfully
- The best way to keep tomatoes is to stand them on their bases without touching each other.

451

Tomatoes stuffed with meat

TOMATES RELLENOS DE CARNE

- **12 tomatoes**
- **2 ¾ cups mixed ground pork and beef**
- **1 egg, lightly beaten**
- **1 clove garlic, finely chopped**
- **1 teaspoon chopped fresh parsley**
- **2 heaping tablespoons bread crumbs**
- **2 tablespoons olive oil**
- **salt**

Serves 4–6

Core the tomatoes with the tip of a knife and scoop out the seeds and flesh with a teaspoon. Sprinkle a little salt in the cavities and let drain, upside down, for about 1 hour. Preheat the oven to 350°F. Combine the ground meat, egg, garlic, parsley, and bread crumbs in a bowl and season with salt. Using a teaspoon, fill the tomatoes with the mixture, leaving some of it protruding. Pour the oil over the base of an ovenproof baking dish and place the tomatoes in the dish in a single layer. Bake for about 1 hour until cooked through and tender. Serve immediately straight from the dish.

452

Tomatoes stuffed with béchamel sauce and grated cheese

TOMATES RELLENOS DE BECHAMEL Y QUESO RALLADO

- 12 ripe tomatoes
- 5 tablespoons olive oil
- 2 tablespoons (¼ stick) butter
- 2 tablespoons sunflower oil
- 2 tablespoons all-purpose flour
- 2¼ cups milk
- scant 1 cup grated gruyere cheese
- 2 eggs, separated
- salt

Serves 4–6

Core the tomatoes with the tip of a knife and scoop out the seeds and flesh with a teaspoon. Sprinkle a little salt in the cavities and let drain, upside down, for about 1 hour. Preheat the oven to 350°F. Put the tomatoes into an ovenproof baking dish and divide the olive oil among the cavities. Bake for about 20 minutes. Meanwhile, make the béchamel sauce by melting the butter with the sunflower oil in a pan. Stir in the flour and cook, stirring constantly, for 2 minutes. Gradually stir in the milk, a little at a time. Cook, stirring constantly, for 10 minutes. Lightly season the sauce with salt, remove the pan from the heat, and stir in half the gruyere and the egg yolks. (Take care that the sauce is not too hot or the egg yolks will curdle.) Whisk the egg whites in a clean, dry bowl until they form soft peaks, add a little salt, and fold the whites into the sauce. Fill the tomatoes with the sauce, sprinkle with the remaining cheese, return to the oven, and bake for 10–15 minutes, until golden brown. Serve immediately straight from the dish.

453

Baked tomatoes with parsley and garlic

TOMATES AL HORNO CON PEREJIL Y AJO PICADO

- 6 large ripe tomatoes, halved widthwise
- 1 tablespoon chopped fresh parsley
- 1½ teaspoons chopped garlic
- 6 tablespoons bread crumbs
- 6 tablespoons olive oil
- salt

Serves 6

Core the tomatoes with the tip of a knife, scoop out the seeds, and sprinkle the insides of the "shells" with salt. Let the tomato halves drain, upside down, for 1 hour. Preheat the oven to 350°F. Put the tomatoes into an ovenproof baking dish, cut sides up and in a single layer. Divide the parsley and garlic among them and sprinkle with the bread crumbs. Drizzle the oil over the tomatoes and bake for about 1 hour, until the flesh is well roasted and soft. Serve immediately straight from the dish.

Note: Smaller tomatoes that have been prepared in this way make a good accompaniment to meat dishes.

Tomatoes filled with Russian salad

TOMATES RELLENOS DE ENSALADILLA RUSA

- **6 large tomatoes**
- **11 ounces Russian Salad (see recipe 21)**
- **lettuce leaves**

Serves 4–6

Core the tomatoes with the tip of a knife and scoop out the seeds and some of the flesh with a teaspoon. Sprinkle a little salt in the cavities and let drain, upside down, for about 1 hour. Fill the tomatoes with the Russian Salad and chill in the refrigerator for at least 1 hour. Just before serving, garnish with the lettuce.

Notes: This dish can be served as an appetizer in summer. In Spain you can buy ready-made Russian salad. Alternatively, to save time buy cans of ready prepared vegetables that can be mixed with Classic Mayonnaise (see recipe 105).

455 Tomatoes filled with sardines, green bell peppers, and olives

TOMATES RELLENOS DE SARDINAS EN ACEITE, PIMIENTOS VERDES Y ACEITUNAS

- **12 tomatoes**
- **3 tablespoons olive oil**
- **2 green bell peppers,**
  seeded and diced
- **9 large canned sardines in oil,**
  drained
- **scant 1 cup pimiento-stuffed**
  olives, halved
- **lettuce leaves**
- **salt**

Vinaigrette:
- **1 tablespoon white-wine vinegar**
- **3 tablespoons sunflower oil**
- **½ teaspoon mustard**
- **1 teaspoon chopped**
  fresh parsley
- **salt**

Serves 6

Core the tomatoes with the tip of a knife and scoop out the seeds and some of the flesh with a teaspoon. Sprinkle a little salt in the cavities and let drain, upside down, for about 1 hour. Heat the oil in a skillet. Add the bell pepper, cover, and cook over low heat, shaking the pan occasionally, for 10 minutes. Just before the end of the cooking time, lightly season with salt.Meanwhile, make the vinaigrette as described in recipe 98. Remove the skin and bones from the sardines and flake the flesh into a bowl with a fork. Add the pepper and vinaigrette, mix well, and divide the mixture among the tomatoes. Chill in the refrigerator for 2 hours, then top with the olives and garnish with the lettuce leaves, and serve.

456 Fried tomato slices

RODAJAS DE TOMATE EMPANADAS Y FRITAS

- **6 large ripe, fleshy tomatoes**
- **6 tablespoons bread crumbs**
- **1 egg, lightly beaten**
- **vegetable oil, for frying**
- **salt**

Serves 4

Thickly slice some fleshy tomatoes, sprinkle with salt on both sides, and let drain for 30 minutes. Pat dry and dip in bread crumbs, then in beaten egg, and finally in bread crumbs again. Fry on both sides in plenty of hot oil. Serve immediately. These slices make an attractive garnish for meat and some fish dishes.

457 Tomato sorbet

TOMATE EN SORBETE

- 3 ¼ pounds very ripe tomatoes,
  peeled, seeded and chopped
- 1 small onion, chopped
- 1 sprig fresh mint
- 1 sprig fresh basil
- 1 sprig fresh marjoram
- 1 tablespoon tomato paste
- juice of 2 lemons
- 2 tablespoons brown sugar
- slices of lemon

Serves 4–6

Put the tomato, onion, mint, basil, and marjoram into a pan and cook over low heat, stirring occasionally, for 30 minutes. Remove and discard the herbs, let cool slightly, then process in a food processor or blender, and pour into a freezer-proof container. Stir in the tomato paste, lemon juice, and sugar and let cool. Stand the container on a tray of ice in the freezer for at least 4 hours. Just before serving, take the sorbet out of the freezer, beat gently to break the ice, and serve in glasses, garnished with slices of lemon. Serve the sorbet at the beginning of a meal.

458 Preserved tomatoes

- 2 ¼ pounds small tomatoes
  (the greener the better)
- 1 tablespoon black peppercorns
- 2 onions, chopped
- 1 tablespoon sugar
- 3 cups strong vinegar
- 1 sprig fresh tarragon
- 1 sprig fresh fennel
- 1 tablespoon wholegrain mustard
- salt

Serves 6

TOMATITOS EN CONSERVA

Put the tomatoes into a large saucepan of boiling water for 1 minute, then drain. Put them into a sterilized glass pickling jar, add the peppercorns, onion, sugar, and a pinch of salt. Bring the vinegar to a boil in a small pan and simmer for 10 minutes. When the tomatoes have cooled, pour the vinegar over them. Close the lid and let marinate for 24 hours. Add the tarragon, fennel, and mustard, seal the jar so that it is airtight, and leave for 2 months before using.

Carrots

Origin and season

Carrots have been grown for more than 5,000 years. Until the Renaissance they were considered a medicinal rather than a culinary plant, and up to the middle of the nineteenth century they were beige in color; their now familiar orange color is the result of cross-breeding. The best time for carrots is spring and early summer, when they are smaller in size and have almost no skin. At this time of year they are very tender and can be eaten raw. Thicker carrots appear in winter and are ideal for stews.

Selection

In spring the best carrots are small and shiny with fresh green feathery tops. The larger winter carrots should not have any cracks as they will have a hard, yellow part in the middle that has to be removed before the carrots can be eaten. In general, the more orange the carrot, the sweeter and more tender it will be. It is better to buy carrots loose, rather than in plastic bags; if they are not well ventilated, dampness forms and causes mold. If the carrots are served as an accompaniment allow 5 ounces per serving.

Nutrition

Many virtues have been attributed to carrots, including giving the skin a good color, improving the eyesight, and helping to maintain good humor. They contain 26 calories per 3½ ounces and are a rich source of vitamins A, B, C, and E. They also contain carotene, pro-vitamin A that the body converts into retinol, and the minerals potassium, iron, calcium, and zinc.

Tricks

- To retain vitamins and minerals, scrape carrots with a knife rather than peeling them
- Cook carrots in salted boiling water with a pinch of sugar for 10–15 minutes
- If they are to be steamed, dice them first
- Wetting your hand before peeling carrots will prevent any trace of color being left on your skin.

459

Carrots in sauce
ZANAHORIAS EN SALSA

- 6 tablespoons olive oil
- 1 onion, finely chopped
- 3¼ pounds carrots, cut into ¼-inch thick slices
- 1 tablespoon all-purpose flour
- ¾ cup white wine
- 1 teaspoon chopped fresh parsley
- salt

Serves 6

Heat the oil in a pan. Add the onion and cook over medium heat, stirring occasionally, for 6 minutes, until soft and translucent. Add the carrot and cook, stirring occasionally, for 5 minutes more. Stir in the flour and cook, stirring constantly, for 5 minutes, then add the wine, season with salt, and pour in water to cover. Cook over medium heat, stirring occasionally, for 30–60 minutes, depending on the variety and freshness of the carrots. Serve in a warm deep dish, garnished with the parsley.

460

Carrot salad appetizer
ZANAHORIAS EN ENSALADA PARA ENTREMESES

- 1 pound 10 ounces carrots
- ¼ cup butter
- 1 quantity Vinaigrette (see recipe 98)

Serves 6

Scrape the carrots with a knife, then wash, and dry them. Cut into small thin sticks with a mandoline, like straw potatoes. Dress the carrot sticks with the vinaigrette and serve as an appetizer with tomatoes, lettuce, and beet.

Note: Carrots are delicious and very healthy when mixed with escarole in salads. Use only the freshest and most tender carrots available.

Glazed carrots

ZANAHORIAS GLASEADAS

- 1 pound 2 ounces tender carrots
- ¼ cup (½ stick) butter
- 1 heaping teaspoon sugar
- salt

Serves 4

If the carrots are small, leave them whole, otherwise halve them lengthwise. Put into a pan, pour in 2¼ cups water, and add the butter, sugar, and a generous pinch of salt. Cut a disk of parchment paper slightly larger than the diameter of the pan and position it in the pan so that it nearly touches the carrots. Cook over high heat until all the water has evaporated. Serve immediately as a garnish to meat dishes.

Mixed vegetable dishes

462

Vegetable stew

MENESTRA DE VERDURAS VERDES

- 1 lemon, halved
- 4 tablespoons olive oil
- 3 shallots, chopped
- scant 1 cup chopped
  Serrano ham or prosciutto
- 1 tablespoon all-purpose flour
- 1 small lettuce, shredded
- 1 pound 2 ounces green beans,
  trimmed
- 2¼ pounds peas, shelled
- 2 tablespoons white wine
- salt

Serves 6

Remove and discard the tough outer leaves of the artichokes and cut off the tops of the remaining leaves. Cut the artichokes lengthwise into halves or quarters, depending on their size, and remove the chokes with a teaspoon. Rub the artichokes all over with the lemon halves to prevent them turning black. Heat the oil in a pan. Add the shallots and cook over low heat, stirring occasionally, for about 8 minutes, until beginning to brown. Add the ham and cook for 3 minutes, then stir in the flour, and add the lettuce, artichokes, beans, and peas. Cook, stirring occasionally, for 5 minutes more, then pour in the wine, and season with salt. Stir well and add enough water to just cover the vegetables. Cover the pan and simmer, stirring occasionally, for about 45 minutes. Add a little more water during cooking, if necessary. Serve immediately, garnished with slices of hard-cooked egg, if you like.

Note: You can add fava beans to the stew.

463

Classic vegetable soup

MENESTRA DE VERDURAS CORRIENTE

- 4 tablespoons olive oil
- 1 small onion, finely chopped
- generous ½ cup diced
  Serrano ham or prosciutto
- 6 lettuce leaves, shredded
- 1 tablespoon all-purpose flour
- 2¾ cups diced carrots
- 1 pound 10 ounces small
  young globe artichokes
- 1 lemon, halved
- 2 turnips, diced
- 1 pound 2 ounces green beans,
  trimmed and cut into short
  lengths
- 2¼ pounds peas, shelled
- salt

Serves 6

Heat the oil in a pan. Add the onion and cook over low heat, stirring occasionally, for about 5 minutes, until softened and translucent. Add the ham and lettuce and cook for a few minutes, then stir in the flour. Add the carrot and pour in enough water to cover. Simmer gently for 10–15 minutes. Meanwhile, remove and discard the tough outer leaves of the artichokes and cut off the tops of the remaining leaves. Cut the artichokes lengthwise into halves or quarters, depending on their size, and remove the chokes with a teaspoon. Rub the artichokes all over with the lemon halves to prevent them turning black. Add the artichokes, turnips, beans, peas, and a pinch of salt to the pan. (If you're unsure about how tender the artichokes are, cook them separately and add them to the soup later.) Simmer over low heat, stirring occasionally, for 30–45 minutes, until the vegetable are tender but not falling apart. If the soup is too liquid, remove some of the stock before serving. Garnish with slices of hard-cooked egg, if you like.

Note: This is a very flexible recipe; you can use different vegetables, depending on the time of year.

464

Vegetable pie
BUDÍN DE VERDURAS

- 3¼ pounds spinach or
  2¼ pounds Swiss chard
- 11 ounces carrots, thinly sliced
- 1 pound 10 ounces peas, shelled
- ¼ cup (½ stick) butter,
  plus extra for greasing
- 2 eggs
- 3 tablespoons milk
- salt

Sauce:
- 1½ tablespoons butter
- 2 tablespoons olive oil
- 1½ tablespoons all-purpose
  flour
- 2¼ cups milk
- 1 tablespoon tomato paste
- salt

Serves 6

Cook the vegetables in separate pans. If using the spinach, remove the coarse stalks, put the leaves into a pan with just the water clinging to them after washing, and cook for 8–10 minutes. Drain well, pressing out as much liquid as possible with the back of a spoon, then chop. If using the Swiss chard, chop it and put it into a pan. Pour in water to cover, and add a pinch of salt. Bring to a boil, lower the heat, and simmer for about 20 minutes, until tender. Drain well. Cook the carrot in a pan of salted boiling water for 10–15 minutes, until tender. Drain well, reserve a few slices and chop the remainder. Cook the peas in a pan of salted boiling water for 20–30 minutes, until tender. Drain well. Preheat the oven to 350°F. Grease a cake pan with butter. Cut out a piece of waxed paper to fit the base of the pan and grease with butter, then place in the pan. Arrange the reserved carrot slices and some peas in a decorative pattern on the paper. Melt the butter in a large skillet. Add the spinach or Swiss chard, carrot, and peas and cook, stirring occasionally, for 5 minutes. Lightly beat the eggs with the milk in a bowl and pour into the pan. Transfer the vegetable mixture to the prepared pan and press down gently to remove any air bubbles. Put the pan into a roasting pan and pour in boiling water to come about halfway up the sides. Bake for about 1 hour, until set. Meanwhile, make the sauce. Melt the butter with the oil in a pan. Stir in the flour and cook, stirring constantly, for 2 minutes. Gradually stir in the milk, a little at a time. Season with salt and cook, stirring constantly, for 10–15 minutes, until thickened. Stir in the tomato paste. When the pie is cooked, turn off the oven and open the door. Let the pie stand for 5–8 minutes. Run a round-bladed knife around the edge of the pie, then turn out on to a warm serving dish. Remove the paper and pour the sauce over the pie. Serve immediately.

Note: The vegetables can be varied according to the season.

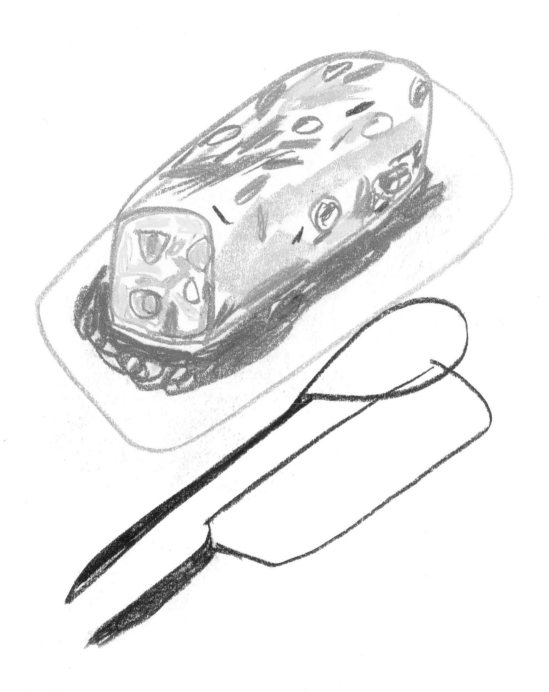

465

Vegetable tart
FLAN DE VERDURAS

- 6½ cups shelled or frozen peas
- 1 pound 2 ounces green beans, trimmed and cut into ¾-inch lengths
- 1 pound 2 ounces carrots, sliced
- 11 ounces turnips, diced
- margarine, for greasing
- 4–5 eggs
- ¾ cup milk
- salt
- 1 quantity Béchamel Sauce with Tomato (see recipe 78) or Classic Béchamel Sauce (see recipe 77) with ½ teaspoon curry powder

Serves 6

Cook the vegetables in separate pans. Cook the peas in salted boiling water for 20–30 minutes, until tender or according to the instructions on the package. Drain well. Cook the green beans in salted boiling water for 12–15 minutes, until tender, then drain well. Cook the carrot in salted boiling water for 10–15 minutes, until tender, then drain well. Cook the turnip in salted boiling water for 10 minutes, then drain well. This can be done in advance or even the night before. Preheat the oven to 350°F. Line the base of a tart pan with aluminum foil and generously grease the whole pan, including the foil, with margarine. Put the carrots in the base of the pan, put the green beans on top, then the turnips, and, finally, the peas. Lightly beat the eggs with the milk in a bowl. Lightly season with salt and carefully pour over the vegetables. Gently move the vegetables slightly to make sure that the egg mixture penetrates. Put the pan into a roasting pan and pour in hot water to come about halfway up the sides. Bake for 1 hour, until set. Remove from the oven and let stand for about 5 minutes. Run a round-bladed knife around the edge of the flan, then turn out onto a warm serving dish. Pour the sauce over the tart or serve separately in a sauceboat.

466

Eggplant, zucchini, tomato, and bell pepper medley
REVUELTO DE BERENJENAS, CALABACINES, TOMATES Y PIMIENTOS

- 6 tablespoons olive oil
- 1 onion, chopped
- 1 pound 10 ounces tomatoes, peeled, seeded, and chopped
- 3 large zucchini, peeled and cut into large pieces
- 3 large eggplants, peeled and cut into large pieces
- 1 green bell pepper, seeded and cut into thin strips
- 1 tablespoon all-purpose flour
- 1–3 tablespoons leftover meat sauce or 1 chicken bouillon cube
- salt

Serves 6

Heat the oil in a pan. Add the onion and cook over low heat, stirring occasionally, for 10 minutes, until lightly browned. Add the tomato and cook, stirring occasionally, for 8 minutes more. Add the zucchini, eggplants, and bell pepper, season with salt, and cook, stirring occasionally, for 10 minutes. Stir in the flour and add the meat sauce or the bouillon cube dissolved in a little water. Mix well and cook over medium heat, stirring occasionally, for 30–40 minutes, until all the vegetables are tender. Serve in a warm deep dish.

Note: This dish can be made earlier and reheated before serving.

467

Stuffed mixed vegetables
RELLENO DE VERDURAS VARIADAS

- 2 zucchini, halved
- 4 tomatoes, cored
- 4 potatoes
- 4 small onions
- 4 small red or green bell peppers
- ½–¾ cup all-purpose flour
- 2¼ cups sunflower oil

Stuffing:
- 1 thick slice bread, crusts removed
- 3–4 tablespoons warm milk
- 1 clove garlic
- 1 sprig fresh parsley
- 2¼ cups mixed ground pork and beef
- 2 eggs, lightly beaten
- 1 tablespoon white wine
- salt

Sauce:
- 6 tablespoons sunflower oil
- 1 large onion, chopped
- 1 heaping tablespoon all-purpose flour
- 2 carrots, thinly sliced
- ¾ cup white wine
- salt

Serves 6–8

Prepare the stuffing. Put the bread into a bowl and add the milk, then let soak for 10 minutes. Pound the garlic with a pinch of salt and the parsley in a mortar, or process in a mini-food processor. Combine the meat, bread, squeezed out if necessary, eggs, wine, and garlic mixture in a bowl. Mix as if making meatballs. Using a sharp knife or an apple corer, make a cavity about the size of a walnut in the center of the zucchini halves, tomatoes, potatoes, and onions. Fill the cavities with a little of the stuffing. Cut out the stalk from the peppers and remove the seeds, then fill with the stuffing. Dust all the stuffed vegetables with the flour. Heat the oil in a deep skillet. Add the stuffed vegetables, one at a time, and cook until browned all over. Remove with a slotted spoon and, with the exception of the tomatoes, place in a single layer in another large pan. Set the tomatoes aside on a plate. Make the sauce. Heat the oil in a skillet. Add the onion and cook over low heat, stirring occasionally, for about 10 minutes, until lightly browned. Stir in the flour and cook, stirring constantly, for 3–5 minutes, until lightly browned. Add the carrots, pour in the wine and 6¼ cups water, and simmer for 15 minutes. Let cool slightly, then process in a food processor or blender, season with salt, and pour it into the pan of stuffed vegetables. Cook over low heat for 45 minutes, then add the tomatoes, and cook for 15 minutes more. Remove from the heat and let stand for 5 minutes before serving.

Note: This dish can be made earlier and reheated before serving.

468

Ratatouille with squid in julienne strips
PISTO CON JULIANA DE CALAMARES

- ²/₃ cup olive oil
- 2 large onions, finely chopped
- 3 eggplants, peeled and diced
- 2 green bell peppers,
  seeded and cut into pieces
- 4 zucchini, diced
- 1 pound 2 ounces ripe tomatoes,
  peeled, seeded, and chopped
- 2 cloves garlic, finely chopped
- 4 squid, cleaned and cut into
  thin strips (see page 468)
- salt

Serves 4

Reserve 2 tablespoons of the oil and heat the remainder in a large skillet. Add the onion and cook over low heat, stirring occasionally, for 5 minutes, until softened and translucent. Add the eggplant and cook, stirring occasionally, for 10 minutes. Add the bell pepper and cook, stirring occasionally, for 10 minutes more. Add the zucchini, tomato, and garlic and season with salt. Cover and simmer gently for 1 hour. Heat the reserved oil in another skillet. Add the strips of squid and cook over high heat, stirring constantly, for 2–3 minutes, until lightly colored. Remove the pan from the heat. If the ratatouille has too much liquid, drain some off, then put the strips of squid on top, and serve.

Note: The strips of squid can be coated in flour before being fried. Instead of adding chopped garlic to the ratatouille, crush the cloves and mix with 4 tablespoons olive oil, then pour this over the served dish. In this case, use only 4 tablespoons oil to cook the vegetables.

469

Manchegan ratatouille
PISTO MANCHEGO

- ²/₃ cup olive oil
- 1¾ cups diced chorizo sausage
- generous 1 cup diced ham
- 2¼ pounds onions, chopped
- 2¼ pounds green bell peppers,
  seeded and diced
- 2¼ pounds zucchini, diced
- 2¼ pounds ripe tomatoes,
  peeled and chopped
- croûtons
- salt

Serves 10

Heat the oil in a pan. Add the chorizo and ham and cook over low heat, stirring occasionally, for 5 minutes. Remove with a slotted spoon and set aside. Add the onion and bell pepper to the pan and cook, stirring occasionally, for 10 minutes. Add the zucchini and tomato, mix well, cover, and simmer gently for 30 minutes. Season to taste with salt, add the chorizo and ham, and heat through for a few minutes. Serve immediately with the croûtons.

Note: This recipe comes from the Spanish region of La Mancha.

Mushrooms and truffles

Cultivated mushrooms

Origin and season

Mushrooms have been cultivated since the time of Napoleon. They are available all year-round but the best season for them is the fall.

Selection

There should be no cracks or holes in the caps which should feel firm to the touch. Avoid mushrooms with blemishes on the caps. The cap and stalk should be firmly attached; if they separate too easily, it is a sign of poor quality.

Nutrition

Mushrooms have very few calories—35 per 3 ½ ounces. They are rich in vitamin C and phosphorous.

Tricks

• If they are cleaned with fresh water and lemon juice and then wrapped in a dishtowel, mushrooms will last for several days in good condition in the refrigerator. Do not let them come into contact with metal as it will turn them black.

Wild mushrooms

Origin and season

The term wild mushrooms includes all the types of mushrooms that grow naturally in the wild, even though some varieties are now cultivated. These are sometimes called "exotic" mushrooms. Some, such as milk cap mushrooms, appear in the fall, while others, such as morels, in spring. Porcinis, also known by their French name ceps, are especially highly prized fall mushrooms, but are available dried throughout the year.

Selection

The fresher wild mushrooms are, the better. However, do not pick them unless you are absolutely certain you can identify them properly. Some poisonous mushrooms look very similar to edible ones. If in any doubt, it is better to buy them at a grocer's.

Nutrition

In general, mushrooms have few calories: 25–50 per 3 ½ ounces. They are rich in proteins.

Tricks

• Always wash wild mushrooms very carefully as they may contain small bugs and a lot of earth. It is best to wash them in water with a dash of vinegar

• Although canned wild mushrooms are available all year-round they do not have half the flavor of fresh ones

• Dried mushrooms are available all year, and are a good choice if fresh are not available. They must be reconstituted in liquid. They tend to be strongly flavored so only small quantities are needed.

How to prepare mushrooms for a sauce

Choose the freshest white mushrooms. If they are large, separate the stalks from the caps. Trim the stalks and cut them widthwise into two or three pieces. Wash the caps and brush with a fine brush to remove any traces of earth, then cut them into two or four pieces, and put into cool water with a few drops of lemon juice. Wash well and drain immediately. Put a pat of butter (about 1½ tablespoons butter to 9 ounces mushrooms), a pinch of salt, and the juice of ½ lemon into a pan. Cover and cook over medium heat, shaking the pan occasionally, for about 6 minutes. The mushrooms are then ready to be made into a sauce. They can also be cut into thin slices for use in sauces to accompany meat, and for omelets.

470

Garlic mushrooms

CHAMPIÑONES AL AJILLO

- **9 tablespoons sunflower oil**
- **3¼ pounds white mushrooms**
- **3 cloves garlic, chopped**
- **2 tablespoons chopped fresh parsley**
- **salt**

Serves 6

Preheat the oven to 350°F. Divide the oil and mushrooms among six stovetop-safe earthenware ramekins or other individual cooking dishes. (If you don't have individual dishes, just cook the ingredients all together in a skillet and divide between six serving dishes or ramekins when you are done.) Add some salt, and garlic to each and cook for 5 minutes. Increase the temperature to high and cook, shaking the dishes occasionally, for 5 minutes more. Sprinkle the parsley over the mushrooms and serve immediately.

471

Mushrooms in béchamel sauce

CHAMPIÑONES CON BECHAMEL

- 2¼ pounds mushrooms
- ¼ cup (½ stick) butter
- juice of ½ lemon
- 2 tablespoons sunflower oil
- 3 tablespoons all-purpose flour
- 3 cups milk
- 2 egg yolks, lightly beaten
- 2 tablespoons chopped
  fresh parsley
- 6 triangles of fried bread
  (see recipe 130)
- salt and pepper

Serves 6

If the mushrooms are small, leave them whole, otherwise cut the caps and stalks into large pieces. Put them into a pan with half the butter and the lemon juice. Cook, shaking the pan occasionally, for 6 minutes, then remove from the heat, and set aside. Make the béchamel sauce. Melt the remaining butter with the oil in another pan. Stir in the flour and cook, stirring constantly, for 2 minutes. Gradually stir in the milk, a little at a time. Cook, stirring constantly, for 10–12 minutes. Stir a little of the sauce into the egg yolks to prevent them curdling, then stir into the pan of sauce. Season to taste and remove the pan from the heat. Drain the mushrooms and stir them into the béchamel sauce. Serve in warm individual dishes, sprinkled with the parsley and garnished with the triangles of fried bread if you like.

Note: This mixture can be used to fill small individual puff pastry shells or a large pastry shell.

472

Mushroom appetizer

CHAMPIÑONES PARA ENTREMESES

- 5 tablespoons olive oil
- 1 onion, chopped
- 2 small carrots, diced
- 2 cloves garlic, peeled
- generous 1 cup white wine
- 2 sprigs fresh parsley
- 1 bay leaf
- 1 pound 10 ounces
  white mushrooms
- 2 ripe tomatoes,
  peeled, seeded, and chopped
- 1 tablespoon chopped
  fresh parsley
- salt and pepper

Serves 4

Heat 3 tablespoons of the oil in a pan. Add the onion, carrot, and garlic and cook over low heat, stirring occasionally, for 5 minutes. Pour in the wine, add the parsley sprigs and bay leaf, season with salt and pepper, and cook for 5 minutes more. Add the mushrooms and tomato and cook for 5 minutes. Remove and discard the parsley sprigs, bay leaf, and garlic. Pour the mixture into a warm serving dish, drizzle with the remaining oil, and sprinkle with the chopped parsley. Mix well and chill in the refrigerator before serving.

473

Stuffed mushrooms

CHAMPIÑONES RELLENOS DE UN PICADITO CON CHALOTA

- **4 large flat cap mushrooms**
- **2 shallots, chopped**
- **2 tablespoons olive oil**
- **juice of ½ lemon**
- **salt**

Serves 4

Use large flat-cap mushrooms for stuffing. Separate the caps and stalks, and chop the stalks. Heat the oil in a small skillet. Add the stalks and shallots and cook over low heat, stirring occasionally, for about 5 minutes. Season with salt, stir in a few drops of the lemon juice, and cook for 5–8 minutes more. Divide the filling among the mushroom caps and then bake as in recipe 470.

474

Mushroom brochettes

BROCHETAS DE CHAMPIÑONES

- **1 pound 2 ounces white mushrooms**
- **9 ounces bacon, in thick slices, if available**
- **7 tablespoons olive oil**
- **½ teaspoon fresh rosemary leaves**
- **salt and pepper**

Serves 4

Preheat the broiler. Separate the caps and stalks of the mushrooms (the stalks can be kept to make soup). Cut the bacon into strips about ½ inch wide. Put the oil into a bowl, add the rosemary, and season with salt and pepper. Mix well. Thread the mushroom caps onto skewers, alternating with pieces of bacon. Brush the brochettes with the oil mixture. Cook under the broiler, turning and brushing with more oil occasionally, for about 15 minutes, until cooked through and tender. Serve immediately.

Note: The brochettes can also be cooked on a grill set to medium.

475

Mushrooms with rosemary

CHAMPIÑONES AL ROMERO

- **1 pound 2 ounces large mushrooms**
- **juice of ½ lemon**
- **¼ cup (½ stick) butter**
- **generous ½ cup very finely chopped Serrano ham or prosciutto (optional)**
- **2 sprigs fresh rosemary, leaves removed and chopped**
- **salt and pepper**

Serves 4

Separate the mushroom stalks and caps. Sprinkle the caps with lemon juice and chop the stalks. Melt ½ tablespoon of the butter in a skillet or pan. Add the stalks and cook, stirring occasionally, for 6–7 minutes. If using the ham, add it to the pan after about 3 minutes and cook with the mushroom stalks. Season with salt and pepper, remove the mixture from the pan, and set aside. Put the mushroom caps into a skillet, gill sides up. Season with salt and pepper, cover, and cook over low heat for 1 minute. Drain off and reserve the liquid released by the mushrooms, return the pan to the heat, and cook for 10 minutes more, until tender. (Check by piercing a mushroom with the tip of a knife—it should penetrate but the mushroom should feel firm.) Fill the caps with the chopped mixture. Mix the rosemary with the remaining butter, put it in a pan with the reserved cooking juices, and cook over low heat, stirring vigorously with a wooden spoon or whisk. Pour the rosemary sauce over the mushrooms and serve immediately.

476

Raw mushroom salad

ENSALADA DE CHAMPIÑONES CRUDOS

- **1 pound 10 ounces mushrooms**
- **6 tablespoons sunflower oil**
- **juice of 1 lemon**
- **1 tablespoon chopped fresh parsley**
- **salt and pepper**

Serves 4–6

Separate the mushroom caps and stalks. Slice the stalks and caps and put into a bowl. Pour in the oil and lemon juice, season with salt and pepper, and mix well. Sprinkle with the parsley and chill in the refrigerator for 2 hours before serving

Milk cap mushrooms

NÍSCALOS

- 1 pound 2 ounces milk cap mushrooms
- 1½ tablespoons olive oil
- 1 tablespoon chopped fresh parsley
- 1 clove garlic, very finely chopped
- salt

Serves 4

Separate the mushroom stalks and caps. Discard the stalks. Wash the caps under cold running water, rubbing each side carefully with your fingers to remove any earth or sand. Cut them into large pieces and put them into a skillet with no added oil. Cover and cook over medium heat, shaking the pan occasionally, for 10 minutes. Drain off the liquid released by the mushrooms. Season with salt, drizzle with the oil, and sprinkle with the parsley and garlic. Mix well and cook over low heat, stirring occasionally, for 3 minutes. Serve immediately.

Note: Milk cap mushrooms are usually used to garnish a meat dish, but if they are served as a first course allow 9 ounces per serving. If milk cap mushrooms are available, this recipe will work well with other wild mushroom varieties.

Wild mushrooms in sauce

SETAS EN SALSA

- 3 tablespoons olive oil
- 2 shallots, finely chopped
- generous finely chopped ½ cup Serrano ham or prosciutto
- 2¼ pounds wild mushrooms, such as porcinis, cut into large pieces
- 6 tablespoons sherry
- 3 tablespoons light cream
- salt and pepper

Serves 4

Heat the oil in a large skillet. Add the shallots and cook over low heat, stirring occasionally, for about 8 minutes, until beginning to brown. Add the ham and cook, stirring frequently, for 2–3 minutes, then add the mushrooms. Cook, stirring occasionally, for about 8 minutes, until lightly browned. Add the sherry and cook for 8 minutes more. Season to taste with salt and pepper. Pour the cream over the mushrooms and heat through, stirring constantly, but do not let the cream boil. Serve immediately.

479

Stuffed porcini
SETAS GRATINADAS

- 24 large porcini mushrooms
- ½ cup olive oil,
  plus extra for brushing
- 2 shallots, chopped
- 6 sprigs chopped fresh parsley
- 2 tablespoons bread crumbs
- 5 tablespoons white wine
- ¾ cup stock
  (homemade, canned or
  made with a bouillon cube)
- salt

Serves 6

Separate the mushroom caps and stalks. Chop the stalks. Heat 3 tablespoons of the oil in a skillet. Add the stalks and shallots and cook, stirring occasionally, for 4 minutes, then stir in the parsley. Preheat the oven to 375°F. Brush an ovenproof baking dish with oil. Put the mushroom caps in the prepared dish, gill sides up. Season with salt, divide the shallot mixture among the caps, and sprinkle with the bread crumbs. Combine the wine and stock in a pitcher and pour over the mushrooms. Bake for 10 minutes and serve straight from the dish.

480

Truffles
CRIADILLAS DE TIERRA

- 1 pound 10 ounces truffles,
  thinly sliced
- 4 tablespoons olive oil
- 1 onion, finely chopped
- 2 tablespoons all-purpose flour
- ¾ cup white wine
- salt

Serves 3

Put the truffles into a pan, pour in enough water to cover, and bring just to a boil. Lower the heat, cover, and simmer for 10 minutes. Meanwhile, make the sauce. Heat the oil in another pan. Add the onion and cook over low heat, stirring occasionally, for 8–10 minutes, until lightly browned. Stir in the flour and cook, stirring constantly, for 3–5 minutes, until lightly colored. Stir in the wine and 3 cups water, lightly season with salt, and cook for 2–3 minutes more. Drain the truffles and return them to the pan. Strain the sauce over them, cover, and cook over low heat for 30 minutes. Taste and adjust the seasoning, if necessary, and serve.

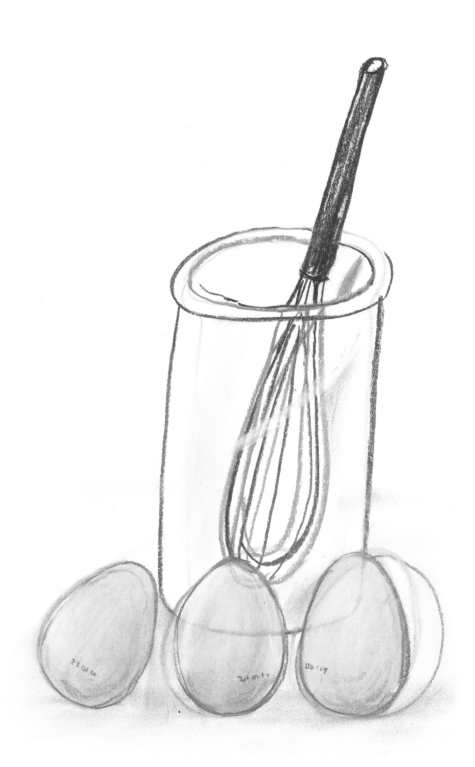

EGGS,
FLANS AND
SOUFFLÉS

Eggs

Buying eggs

Eggs may be farm-fresh, from intensively reared hens, or from birds that have limited access to the outside. If they are labeled organic, the producer will have observed regulations concerning the use of chemicals in the feed and pharmaceuticals. Although there are different grades of egg, most of those on sale in supermarkets and other retail outlets are the top grade, the lower grades mainly being used commercially. The grade is marked on the container, together with the size of the eggs, such as large or extra large, and the use-by date. It will also state whether the eggs are farm-fresh and organic. In Spain eggs are sold at different prices according to their category. There are extra, 1st and 2nd class eggs, etc., and on those sold in boxes there should be the date on which they were laid and the date by which they should be used. The most important thing about an egg is that it is fresh.

How to choose eggs

In the past, a customer could look at each egg to see the size of the air sac inside the shell, as the bigger the sac, the older the egg. This is not very practical nowadays and it is easier to rely on the use-by date. The color of the shell is no guide to the quality of the egg: a brown egg is as nutritious as a white one. The color simply varies according to the breed of hen. A large egg is not necessarily more nutritious than a smaller one because proportionately it contains less yolk.

Tricks

- A new-laid egg is indigestible—wait at least 24 hours before eating it
- Never wash eggs before storing them, as the shell becomes permeable in water
- When storing eggs in the refrigerator do not put them near strong-smelling foods such as melon, which can flavor the eggs as their shell is porous. Store them in the refrigerator in their container or put them in the egg rack, pointed end down
- Remember to wash your hands after handling eggs as the shells may carry harmful bacteria
- Whenever possible, remove the eggs from the refrigerator at least an hour before they are needed. This ensures that whites will whisk stiffly, mayonnaise will come out better, and so on
- Fresh eggs may be stored in the refrigerator for up to 2 weeks. An unshelled hard-cooked egg will keep for 4 days. A leftover egg yolk covered in a little cold water will keep for 2 days
- Don't let eggs come into contact with silver containers or cutlery as it turns them black
- When whisking egg whites do not let even a drop of egg yolk fall into them as it will prevent them frothing. Always use a clean, dry bowl, preferably copper or other metal, glass, or china. Plastic bowls are less suitable
- Eggs can be frozen as long as they are beaten first.

Soft-cooked eggs

How to cook

Pour enough water into a saucepan to cover all the eggs (never more than six at a time) and add salt (1 tablespoon for 4–6 eggs). Bring to a boil, plunge in the eggs, and cook for exactly 3 minutes.

Variation

Put the eggs into a saucepan, add water to cover and 1 tablespoon salt. Bring to a boil over high heat, remove the eggs immediately, and serve. Soft-cooked eggs may be served in egg cups or even in coffee cups and are often accompanied by strips of buttered toast.

481

Soft-cooked eggs with anchovy and smoked trout butter

HUEVOS PASADOS POR AGUA CON MANTEQUILLA DE ANCHOAS Y TRUCHA

- 1½ ounces canned anchovy fillets, drained
- 2 tablespoons (¼ stick) butter, softened
- 2 ounces smoked trout
- 4 slices bread
- 2 eggs

Serves 2

Pound the anchovies in a mortar, or process in a mini-food processor, then mix with half the butter to a smooth paste. Transfer the mixture to a small bowl. Put the trout and remaining butter into the food processor and process to a smooth paste. Toast the bread, then cut into lengthwise strips, about ¾ inch wide. Spread half the strips with the anchovy butter and half with the smoked trout butter. Boil the eggs as described on page 390 and serve in egg cups, accompanied by the strips of buttered toast.

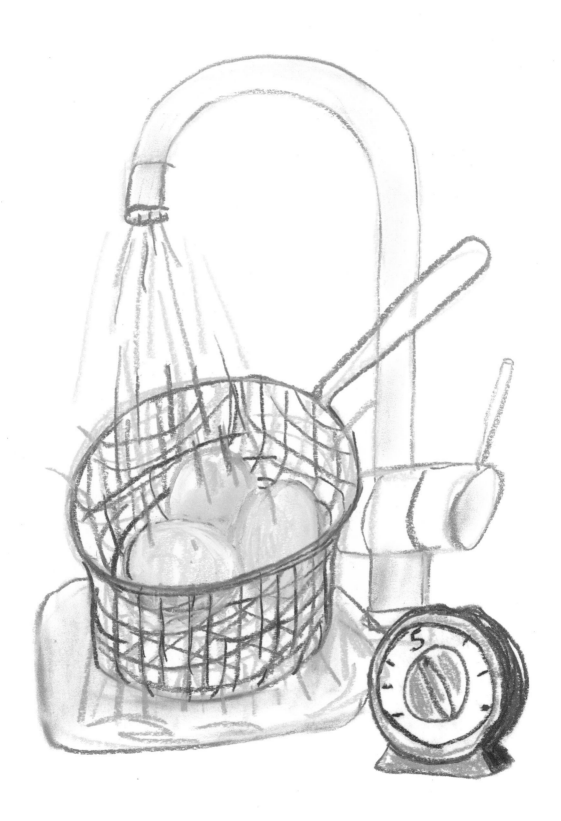

Hard-cooked eggs

How to cook

Pour enough water to cover the eggs into a saucepan, add 1 table-spoon salt, and bring to a boil. Add the eggs carefully and stir gently with a wooden spoon so that when they set the yolks will be in the middle. Cook large eggs for 12 minutes. (Add 1 minute for bigger eggs and subtract 1 minute for smaller eggs.) Drain off the hot water, fill the pan with cold water, and leave the eggs in the water until required.

482

Hard-cooked egg croquettes
CROQUETAS DE HUEVOS DUROS

- 8 eggs
- 2 tablespoons olive oil,
  plus extra for brushing
- 2 tablespoons (¼ stick) butter
- 4 tablespoons all-purpose flour
- 3 cups milk
- 1½–2 cups fine bread crumbs
- sunflower oil, for deep-frying
- 4 deep-fried parsley sprigs
  (see recipe 918)
- salt

Serves 6

Hard-cook six of the eggs as described on page 392. Shell and halve lengthwise, then cut each half into three pieces. Brush a baking sheet with olive oil. Melt the butter with the olive oil in a pan. Stir in the flour and cook, stirring constantly, for 2 minutes. Gradually stir in the milk, a little at a time. Season with salt and cook, stirring constantly, for 10 minutes. Remove the pan from the heat. Using two spoons, add the pieces of egg, one at a time, and coat in the béchamel sauce, then place on the prepared baking sheet. Let cool for 1 hour in the refrigerator. Beat the remaining eggs in a shallow dish and pour the bread crumbs into another shallow dish. Dip the eggs first in the beaten egg and then in the bread crumbs to coat. Heat the sunflower oil in a deep-fryer or deep skillet to 350–375°F or until a cube of day-old bread browns in 30 seconds. Add the egg pieces, in batches if necessary, and cook until golden brown. Remove and drain on paper towels. Serve the croquettes garnished with the parsley.

483

Eggs mimosa
HUEVOS DUROS MIMOSA

- 9 eggs
- 1 quantity Classic Mayonnaise
  (see recipe 105)
- 1½ ounces canned anchovy
  fillets, drained and chopped
- fresh parsley or watercress
  sprigs
- salt

Serves 6

Hard-cook the eggs as described on page 392. Shell and halve lengthwise, then scoop out the yolks with a teaspoon, without piercing the whites, and set the whites aside. Combine 1 cup of the mayonnaise, five of the egg yolks, and the anchovies in a bowl. Cut a thin slice off the base of each egg white half so that it stands straight. Using a teaspoon, fill the egg white halves with the mayonnaise mixture. Place on a serving dish, cover with the remaining mayonnaise, and sift the remaining egg yolks over them. (Use a nylon rather than a metal strainer.) Garnish with the parsley or watercress and chill in the refrigerator for 1–2 hours before serving.

484

Hard-cooked egg fritters
BUÑUELOS DE HUEVOS DUROS

- 11 eggs
- 2 tablespoons (¼ stick) butter
- sunflower oil, for deep-frying
- 3 tablespoons all-purpose flour
- 3 cups milk
- 2 cups bread crumbs
- salt
- 1 quantity Classic Tomato Sauce
  (see recipe 73)

Serves 6

Hard-cook nine of the eggs as described on page 392. Shell and halve widthwise, then scoop out the yolks with a teaspoon without piercing the whites. Melt the butter with 2 tablespoons of oil in a pan. Stir in the flour and cook, stirring constantly, for 2 minutes. Gradually stir in the milk, a little at a time. Season with salt and cook, stirring constantly, for 8–10 minutes. Add the cooked egg yolks and stir until they are fully incorporated into the sauce. Using a teaspoon, fill the egg white halves with this mixture, letting the outside of the egg halves be coated too. Let stand in the refrigerator for at least 30 minutes. Beat the remaining eggs in a shallow dish and pour the bread crumbs into another shallow dish. Dip the egg halves first in the beaten egg and then in the bread crumbs. Heat the oil in a deep-fryer or deep skillet to 350–375°F or until a cube of day-old bread browns in 30 seconds. Add the egg halves, in batches if necessary, and cook until golden brown. Remove with a slotted spoon and drain on paper towels. Serve immediately, offering the tomato sauce separately.

485

Hard-cooked eggs with shrimp
HUEVOS DUROS CON GAMBAS

- 12 ounces raw shrimp
- 9 eggs
- 3 tablespoons sunflower oil
- 1 onion, chopped
- 3 tablespoons all-purpose flour
- 5 tablespoons white wine
- salt

Serves 6

Bring a large saucepan of salted water to a boil. Add the shrimp and cook for 2–3 minutes. Drain well, reserving scant 2 cups of the cooking liquid. Peel the shrimp, then cut each into two or three pieces. Hard-cook the eggs as described on page 392. Shell and halve lengthwise, then scoop out the yolks with a teaspoon, without piercing the whites. Preheat the oven to 350°F. Heat the oil in a skillet. Add the onion and cook over low heat, stirring occasionally, for about 8 minutes, until beginning to brown. Stir in the flour and cook, stirring constantly, for 2 minutes. Gradually stir in the wine, a little at a time, then stir in the reserved cooking liquid. Cook, stirring constantly, for 5 minutes. Strain into a bowl, season to taste with salt and keep warm. Combine three-quarters of the egg yolks, the shrimp, and 2–3 tablespoons of the sauce in another bowl. Cut a thin slice off the base of each egg white half so it stands straight. Using a teaspoon, fill the egg whites with the shrimp mixture. Put them into an ovenproof baking dish, pour the remaining sauce over them, and bake for about 5 minutes. Sift the remaining egg yolks over the dish and serve immediately. (Use a nylon rather than a metal strainer.)

Hard-cooked eggs with salad

HUEVOS DUROS CON ENSALADILLA

- **9 eggs**
- **1 bunch watercress or arugula**

  Vegetable salad:
- **1 pound 2 ounces peas, shelled**
- **scant 1½ cups diced carrots**
- **2 potatoes, unpeeled**
- **1 quantity Classic Mayonnaise (see recipe 105)**
- **salt**

Serves 6

First cook the vegetables. Bring a pan of salted water to a boil. Add the peas and cook for 20–30 minutes, until tender. Put the carrot in another pan, pour in water to cover, and add a pinch of salt. Bring to a boil and cook for 20–30 minutes, until tender. Put the potatoes into a third pan, pour in water to cover, and add a pinch of salt. Bring to a boil and cook for 20–30 minutes, until tender but not falling apart. Drain all the vegetables well and let cool. Peel and dice the potatoes. Meanwhile, hard-cook the eggs as described on page 392. Shell and halve lengthwise, then scoop out the yolks with a teaspoon, without piercing the whites. Cut a thin slice off the base of each egg white half so it stands straight. Mix the mayonnaise with the vegetables. Using a teaspoon, fill the egg white halves with this mixture. Sift the egg yolks over the top. (Use a nylon rather than metal strainer.) Chill in the refrigerator for 1 hour. Serve garnished with the watercress or arugula leaves.

Note: The potatoes can be replaced with 1 pound 2 ounces Russian Salad (see recipe 21).

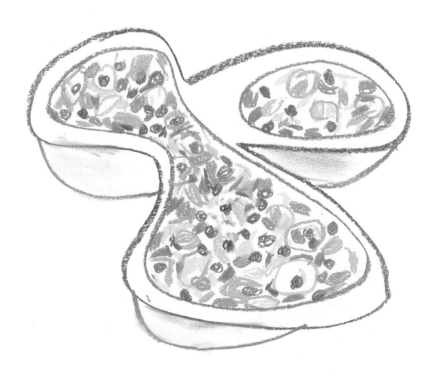

487 Hard-cooked eggs au gratin

HUEVOS DUROS GRATINADOS

- 9 eggs
- 5 tablespoons butter,
  plus extra for greasing
- 9 ounces mushrooms,
  thinly sliced
- juice of ½ lemon
- 4 tablespoons sunflower oil
- 2 onions, finely chopped
- 2 tablespoons all-purpose flour
- 2¼ cups milk
- pinch of freshly grated nutmeg
- 3 tablespoons bread crumbs
- salt

Serves 6

Hard-cook the eggs as described on page 392. Shell and halve lengthwise, then scoop out the yolks with a teaspoon, without piercing the whites. Cut a thin slice off the base of each egg white half so it stands straight. Preheat the oven 400°F. Grease an ovenproof baking dish with butter. Put the mushrooms, 1½ tablespoons of the butter, and the lemon juice into a pan, cover, and cook over low heat for 6 minutes. Heat half the oil in a skillet. Add the onion and cook over low heat, stirring occasionally, for about 8 minutes, until beginning to brown. Melt 2 tablespoons of the remaining butter with the remaining oil in a pan. Stir in the flour and cook, stirring constantly, for 2 minutes. Gradually stir in the milk, a little at a time. Season with salt and cook, stirring constantly, for 8–10 minutes. Combine 2 tablespoons of the sauce, the egg yolks, onion, mushrooms, and nutmeg in a bowl and mix well. Using a teaspoon, fill the egg white halves with this mixture, place them in an ovenproof baking dish, and pour the remaining sauce over them. Sprinkle with the bread crumbs, dot with the remaining butter, and bake for 10–15 minutes, until golden brown. Serve immediately straight from the dish.

488 Hard-cooked eggs with hunter's sauce

HUEVOS DUROS CON SALSA CAZADORA

- ½ clove garlic
- 9 eggs
- 4 tablespoons olive oil
- 7 ounces onions, thinly sliced
- 2¼ pounds ripe tomatoes,
  peeled, seeded, and chopped
- 9 ounces mushrooms, chopped
- 1 sprig fresh thyme
- 5 tablespoons white wine
- 1 teaspoon sugar
- salt and pepper

Serves 6

Crush the garlic with a pinch of salt in a mortar, or process in a mini-food processor. Mix in 5 tablespoons water. Hard-cook the eggs as described on page 392. Shell and halve lengthwise, then cut a thin slice off the base of each egg half so it stands straight and put on a serving dish. Heat the oil in a skillet. Add the onion and cook over low heat, stirring occasionally, for about 5 minutes, until softened and translucent. Add the tomato and cook, stirring occasionally and breaking it up with the side of the spoon, for 5 minutes. Add the mushrooms, garlic mixture, thyme, and wine, season with pepper, and cook for 10 minutes. Stir in the sugar and stir until it dissolves. Pour the sauce over the eggs and serve immediately.

Eggs in port gelatin

HUEVOS EN GELATINA AL OPORTO

- **8 leaves gelatin or 2 envelopes (½ ounce) unflavored gelatin**
- **4 cups chicken stock (homemade, canned or made from a bouillon cube)**
- **8 eggs**
- **2 tablespoons port or other sweet, fortified wine**
- **4 slices of ham, chopped**
- **3½ ounces cooked green beans**
- **1 pound 2 ounces Russian Salad (see recipe 21)**

Serves 4

Is you are using gelatin leaves, soak them in a small bowl of cold water for 10 minutes. Meanwhile, pour the stock into a pan and bring to a boil. Squeeze out the gelatin and stir it into the stock. Remove the pan from the heat and let cool, stirring occasionally. If you are using powdered gelatin, see the glossary for directions. Meanwhile, hard-cook the eggs as described on page 392, then let stand in cold water until required. Stir the port into the cooled stock. Spoon a little of the stock into the base of some four individual oval aspic molds or gratin dishes to make a layer about ½ inch deep. Chill in the refrigerator for 15 minutes, until set. Shell the eggs. Cut the beans into thin strips and arrange decoratively on the base of the molds once the stock has set. Cover with the ham, put the eggs on top, and surround with some of the Russian Salad. Pour in the remaining stock to fill the molds and chill in the refrigerator until set. To serve, dip the base of the molds in warm water and turn out onto individual plates. If using hard-cooked eggs, the dish can be kept in the refrigerator for up to 2 days.

Note: This dish is delicious with coddled eggs (see page 398) instead of hard-cooked eggs.

Coddled eggs

How to cook

Bring a pan of water with 2 tablespoons salt to a boil. Pass the eggs under cold running water, put them into a wire basket, and plunge into the boiling water. When the water comes back to a boil, cook for exactly 5 minutes, and remove the pan from the heat. Run cold water into the pan until it is completely cold. This must happen quickly to prevent any further cooking. Leave the eggs in cold water until needed. Shell the eggs very carefully and gently. The eggs can be reheated in warm water for a maximum of 2–3 minutes.

490

Coddled eggs with wine sauce

HUEVOS MOLLETS CON SALSA DE VINO

- 6 eggs
- 1 pounds 2 ounces ripe tomatoes
- 3 tablespoons olive oil
- 2 onions, chopped
- 2 tablespoons all-purpose flour
- ⅔ cup dry white wine
- ¼ teaspoon meat extract
  or Maggi Seasoning
- generous ½ cup chopped
  Serrano or other dry-cured ham
- salt and pepper

Serves 6

Coddle the eggs as described on page 398 and let stand in cold water. Peel, seed and chop the tomatoes. Heat the oil in a skillet. Add the onion and cook over low heat, stirring occasionally, for about 8 minutes, until lightly browned. Stir in the flour, add the tomato, and cook, stirring frequently, for 5 minutes. Pour in the wine and generous 1 cup water and season with salt and pepper. Increase the heat to medium and cook for 10 minutes more. Carefully shell the eggs and put them into a warm deep serving dish. Stir the meat extract into the skillet and strain the sauce over the eggs. Sprinkle with the ham, and serve immediately with triangles of fried bread (see recipe 130).

491

Little spinach tarts with coddled eggs

TARTALETAS DE ESPINACAS Y HUEVOS MOLLETS

- 6 eggs
- pinch of baking soda
  (optional)
- 2¼ pounds spinach,
  coarse stalks removed
- 3 tablespoons olive oil
- 1 pound 10 ounces tomatoes,
  seeded and coarsely chopped
- ½ teaspoon sugar
- 6 baked tartlet shells
  (see recipe 2)
- 1½ tablespoons butter
- 1 tablespoon all-purpose flour
- 1 cup milk
- salt

Serves 6

Coddle the eggs as described on page 398 and let stand in cold water. Bring a pan of salted water to a boil, add a pinch of baking soda, then add the spinach, pushing it down into the water with a spoon. Bring back to a boil and cook for 5 minutes, then drain well, pressing down with the back of a spoon to squeeze out as much liquid as possible. Chop very finely. Preheat the oven to 350°F. Heat 2 tablespoons of the oil in a skillet. Add the tomato and cook over medium-low heat, stirring occasionally and breaking it up with the side of the spoon, for 20 minutes. Transfer to a food processor or blender and process to a thick purée. Scrape into a bowl, season with salt, and stir in the sugar. Keep warm. Place the tartlet shells on a baking sheet and warm through in the oven. Melt the butter with the remaining oil in a pan. Stir in the flour and cook, stirring constantly, for 2 minutes. Gradually stir in the milk, a little at a time. Season with salt and cook, stirring constantly, for 10 minutes. Stir in the spinach and cook for a few minutes more, until heated through. Divide the spinach mixture among the tartlets and keep warm. Carefully shell the eggs and put one on top of each tartlet. Pour a spoonful of hot tomato sauce over each one and serve immediately.

Poached eggs

How to cook

The most important thing when poaching eggs is to make sure that the eggs are fresh. Pour some water into a pan or deep skillet, add 1 tablespoon lemon juice or a good dash of vinegar for every 4 cups water, and bring to a boil. Crack each egg into a cup and pour it into the water from just above the water level, to prevent the yolk breaking and the white spreading. (Poach up to three eggs at a time.) When the water comes back to a boil, turn the heat down to low and cook for 3 minutes in very hot but not boiling water. Remove with a slotted spoon, put into a cake pan, and let cool. When the eggs are needed, gradually pour in hot, but not boiling water, a little at a time, to warm them. Do not leave them for more than 3 minutes in this water. Remove very carefully. If they are still dripping water, drain well on a dishtowel.

492 Poached eggs with asparagus

HUEVOS ESCALFADOS CON ESPÁRRAGOS

- 18 fresh or canned
  asparagus spears
- ¼ cup (½ stick) butter
- 8 eggs
- 2 cups milk
- 6 slices of bread
- 2 tablespoons sunflower oil
- 2 tablespoons all-purpose flour
- pinch of freshly grated nutmeg
- 2 tablespoons white-wine
  vinegar
- salt

Serves 6

If using fresh asparagus, trim and cook in a pan of salted boiling water for 20 minutes, until tender. If using canned asparagus, drain and heat gently. Melt half the butter in a skillet. Lightly beat two of the eggs in a shallow dish and pour the milk into another shallow dish. Dip the slices of bread first in the milk and then in the beaten eggs. Reserve the remaining milk. Add the bread to the skillet, in batches, and cook until golden brown on both sides. Remove with a spatula and keep warm. Melt the remaining butter with the oil in a skillet. Stir in the flour and cook, stirring constantly, for 2 minutes. Gradually stir in the reserved milk, a little at a time. Cook, stirring constantly, for 6–8 minutes, until thickened. Season with salt, stir in the nutmeg, and keep warm. Poach the remaining eggs, three at a time, with the vinegar, as described on page 400. Transfer the bread to a warm serving dish and put an egg on each slice. Cover with the sauce and place the asparagus on top. Serve immediately.

Note: You can use chopped truffles or ham instead of asparagus.

493 Poached eggs with mushrooms

HUEVOS ESCALFADOS CON CHAMPIÑONES

- 11 ounces mushrooms
- 5 tablespoons butter
- juice of ½ lemon
- 6 slices of bread
- 8 eggs
- 2 cups milk
- 2 tablespoons white-wine
  vinegar
- 1 tablespoon sunflower oil
- 2 tablespoons all-purpose flour
- salt

Serves 6

Separate six of the mushroom caps from the stalks and keep the caps whole. Thinly slice the remainder. Put all the mushrooms into a pan with 1½ tablespoons of the butter and the lemon juice. Cover and cook over low heat for 6 minutes, then remove from the heat, and keep warm. Soak and fry the bread, using two of the eggs, the milk, and 1½ tablespoons of the remaining butter, as described in recipe 492. Meanwhile, poach the remaining eggs, three at a time, with the vinegar as described on page 400. Melt the remaining butter with the oil in a pan. Stir in the flour and cook, stirring constantly, for 2 minutes. Gradually stir in the reserved milk, a little at a time. Season with salt and cook, stirring constantly, for 6–8 minutes, until thickened. Transfer the slices of bread to a warm serving dish and divide the sliced mushrooms among them. Top each with an egg and cover with a tablespoonful of sauce. Finally, put a whole mushroom cap on top of each egg to garnish. Serve immediately.

494

Poached eggs in gelatin

HUEVOS ESCALFADOS EN GELATINA

- 1 envelope (¼ ounce) unflavored gelatin
- 1 tablespoon sherry or other sweet, fortified wine (optional)
- scant 1 cup drained canned peas
- 1 thick slice ham, about 3½ ounces, cut into 6 squares
- 6 eggs
- 2 tablespoons white-wine vinegar
- lettuce leaves

Serves 6

Make the gelatin according to the instructions on the package and, when cool, stir in the sherry, if using. Pour 3 tablespoons of gelatin into each of six individual molds or ramekins to cover the base. Chill in the refrigerator for about 15 minutes, until nearly set. Arrange a "necklace" of peas on the gelatin and put a square of ham in the middle. Poach the eggs, three at a time, with vinegar, as described on page 400, then drain, and let cool. Carefully put 1 egg into each mold or ramekin and pour in the remaining gelatin to cover (it should not be too hot or it will set the eggs). Chill in the refrigerator until set. Make a bed of lettuce on individual plates, turn out the molds, and serve. This dish can be made the night before it is needed.

Eggs en cocotte

How to cook

These eggs are somewhere between poached and shirred eggs. To cook them successfully you will need individual ovenproof ramekins or individual gratin dishes. Preheat the oven to 400°F. Put a small pat of butter, about the size of a hazelnut, into each ramekin or gratin and melt it in the oven or over a pan of barely simmering water for about 1 minute. Alternatively, grease the dishes with the butter. Break an egg into each dish, making sure that the yolk remains whole. Season with salt and put the dishes into a roasting pan. Pour in enough boiling water to come about halfway up the sides, and bake for 4–5 minutes, until the whites have set but the yolks are still runny. Serve the eggs straight from the dishes or remove them carefully, making sure that the yolks do not break. They can also be served cold.

495

Eggs en cocotte with kidneys in sherry
HUEVOS EN CAZUELITAS CON RIÑONES AL JEREZ

- 1 kidney, about 14 ounces, trimmed, cored, and diced
- 3 tablespoons olive oil
- 1½ tablespoons all-purpose flour
- ¾ cup sherry or other sweet, fortified wine
- 6 eggs
- salt

Serves 6

Put the pieces of kidney into a skillet, cover, and cook over medium heat, gently shaking the pan, for 2 minutes. Drain off and discard the cooking juices and transfer the pieces of kidney to a plate. Preheat the oven to 400°F. Heat the oil in a pan. Stir in the flour and cook, stirring constantly, for 10 minutes. Gradually stir in the sherry and scant 2 cups water, a little at a time. Season with salt and cook, stirring constantly, for 5 minutes. Add the pieces of kidney and cook for 3 minutes more. Divide the pieces of kidney among six ramekins or individual gratin dishes, adding about 1 tablespoon of the sauce to each one. Break an egg into each dish, season with salt, and cook as described on page 403. Top each egg with a little of the remaining sauce and serve immediately.

496

Eggs en cocotte with cheese and ham
HUEVOS EN CAZUELITAS CON QUESO EN PORCIONES Y JAMÓN

- 6 chunks of cheese
- 1½ tablespoons butter
- 6 eggs
- generous ½ cup chopped Smithfield or Black Forest Ham, Prosciutto, or other dry-cured ham
- 6 small pieces of truffle
- salt

Serves 6

Preheat the oven to 400°F. Put a cheese portion and a pat of the butter, about the size of a hazelnut, into each of six ovenproof ramekins or individual gratin dishes. Put the dishes into a roasting pan, pour in boiling water to come about halfway up the sides, and bake for about 15 minutes, until the cheese is very soft or almost melted. Break an egg into each dish, season lightly with salt, and cook as described on page 403. Sprinkle the ham around the edge of each dish and top each yolk with a piece of truffle. Serve immediately.

497

Eggs en cocotte with mushrooms

HUEVOS EN CAZUELITAS CON CHAMPIÑONES

- 9 ounces mushrooms,
  thinly sliced
- 3 tablespoons butter
- juice of ½ lemon
- 6 eggs
- salt

Serves 6

Preheat the oven to 400°F. Put the mushrooms, half the butter, and the lemon juice into a pan, season with salt, cover, and cook over low heat for 6 minutes. Meanwhile, divide the remaining butter among six ovenproof ramekins or individual gratin dishes. Break an egg into each, season lightly with salt, and cook as described on page 403. Remove from the oven and top the eggs with the mushrooms. Serve immediately.

498

Eggs en cocotte with ham, cream, and grated cheese

HUEVOS EN CAZUELITAS CON JAMÓN, NATA Y QUESO RALLADO

- 12 tablespoons light cream
- ½ cup chopped Smithfield
  or other dry-cured ham
- 6 eggs
- ½ cup grated gruyere cheese
- salt

Serves 6

Preheat the oven to 400°F. Put 2 tablespoons of the cream into each of six ovenproof ramekins or individual gratin dishes and divide the ham among them. Break an egg into each one, season lightly with salt, and sprinkle with the gruyere. Cook as described on page 403. Serve immediately.

499

Eggs en cocotte with tomato sauce and bacon

HUEVOS EN CAZUELITAS CON SALSA DE TOMATE Y BACON

- 5 tablespoons olive oil
- 1 pound 10 ounces very ripe
  tomatoes, peeled, seeded,
  and chopped
- 1 teaspoon sugar
- 6 thin slices bacon,
  halved lengthwise
- 6 eggs
- salt

Serves 6

Preheat the oven to 400°F. Make a tomato sauce with 3 tablespoons of the oil, the tomatoes, and sugar, as described in recipe 73. Meanwhile, heat the remaining oil in a skillet. Add the bacon and cook, stirring occasionally, for about 5 minutes, until lightly browned. Remove from the skillet and drain. Roll up and secure with wooden toothpicks. Keep warm. Put 1 heaping tablespoon of the tomato sauce into each of six ovenproof ramekins or individual gratin dishes. Break an egg into each one, season lightly with salt, and cook as described on page 403. Remove the toothpicks from the bacon rolls and top each egg with two rolls. Serve immediately.

Shirred eggs

How to cook

You will need individual ovenproof gratin dishes or ramekins to cook these eggs successfully. Put about ½ tablespoon butter into each dish and melt in a preheated oven, at 325°F, for 1–2 minutes. Remove from the oven and break an egg into each dish. Season the egg whites lightly with salt and cook for 3–4 minutes until the whites have set but the yolks are still runny. Serve immediately.

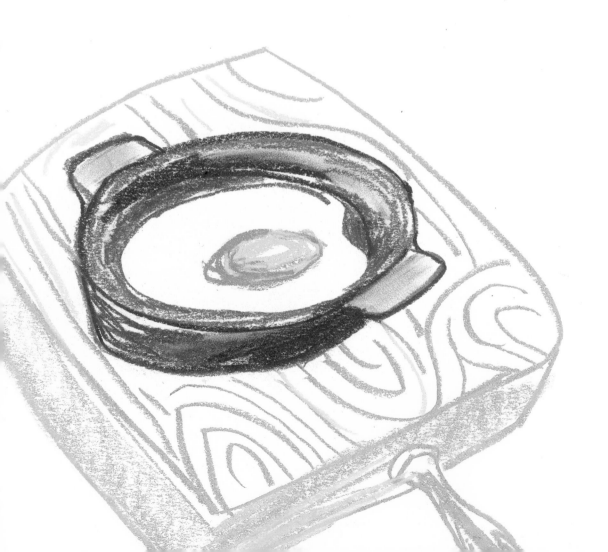

500 Shirred eggs with chicken livers

HUEVOS AL PLATO CON HIGADITOS DE POLLO

- 3 tablespoons olive oil
- 1 small onion, finely chopped
- 6 small chicken livers, trimmed and cut into 4 pieces
- 1 tablespoon potato starch
- 2 tablespoons sherry or other sweet, fortified wine
- ¼ cup (½ stick) butter
- 6 eggs
- 1 tablespoon chopped fresh parsley
- salt

Serves 6

Preheat the oven to 325 °F. Heat the oil in a small skillet. Add the onion and cook over low heat, stirring occasionally, for 5 minutes, until softened and translucent. Add the chicken livers and cook, stirring frequently, for 3 minutes. Remove from the skillet with a slotted spoon and set aside. Stir the potato starch into the skillet and cook, stirring constantly, for 2 minutes. Gradually stir in the sherry, a little at a time, then stir in generous 1 cup water. Cook, stirring constantly, for 2–3 minutes, then return the livers and onion to the skillet, and season with salt. Remove from the heat and keep warm. Divide the butter among six individual ovenproof gratin dishes or ramekins and melt in the oven. Break an egg into each dish and cook as described on page 406. Gently reheat the sauce and spoon it over the egg whites. Sprinkle with the parsley and serve immediately.

501 Shirred eggs with green asparagus

HUEVOS AL PLATO CON ESPÁRRAGOS VERDES

- 1 bunch of green asparagus, trimmed
- 6 tablespoons (¾ stick) butter
- 6 eggs
- salt

Serves 6

Bring a large pan of salted water to a boil. Add the asparagus and cook over medium heat for about 20 minutes, until tender. Meanwhile, preheat the oven to 325°F. Drain the asparagus well. Melt half the butter in a skillet. Add the asparagus and cook over low heat for 5–10 minutes. Meanwhile, divide the remaining butter among six individual ovenproof gratin dishes or ramekins. Melt in the oven, then break an egg into each dish and cook as described on page 406. Remove the asparagus from the pan and divide among six warm plates. Add the eggs and serve immediately.

502

Shirred eggs with mashed potato
HUEVOS AL PLATO CON PURÉ DE PATATAS

• 2¼ pounds potatoes
• 6 tablespoons (¾ stick) butter
• 1 cup warm milk
• scant 1 cup grated gruyere
  cheese
• 6 eggs
• salt

Serves 6

Boil and mash the potatoes with 4 tablespoons of the butter and the milk as described in recipe 230. Stir in all but 2 tablespoons of the gruyere. Preheat the oven to 325°F. Melt ½ tablespoon of the remaining butter in an ovenproof baking dish, then add the mashed potato. Using the back of a spoon, make six hollows in the potato, sprinkle with the remaining cheese, and bake for 5 minutes. Remove the dish from the oven and break an egg into each hollow. Lightly season the whites with salt and top the egg yolks with the remaining butter. Return to the oven and cook as described on page 406. Serve immediately straight from the dish.

503

Shirred eggs, soufflé style, with grated cheese and ham
HUEVOS AL PLATO, ESTILO SOUFFLÉ, CON QUESO RALLADO Y JAMÓN

• 1½ tablespoons butter
• 6 eggs, separated
• 3 egg whites
• 1 cup grated Parmesan cheese
• 1 slice of ham, chopped
• salt

Serves 6

Preheat the oven to 325°F. These eggs are best served in one large dish. Put the butter into an ovenproof baking dish and melt in the oven. Meanwhile, stiffly whisk all the egg whites in a clean, dry bowl, then fold in all but 3 tablespoons of the Parmesan. Spoon the egg whites into the prepared baking dish and with the butter smooth the surface, then, using the back of a spoon, make six hollows. Pour the egg yolks into the hollows, sprinkle the remaining cheese over the egg whites and lightly season the yolks with salt. Bake for about 10 minutes, until lightly browned. Sprinkle the ham over the yolks and serve immediately.

Fried eggs

How to cook

To fry eggs well it is best to cook them one at a time. If you need to cook them more quickly, use two small skillets simultaneously. Always use the freshest possible eggs and check that they are not cracked. Break the egg into a cup. Heat plenty of oil in a small skillet. Slide the egg into the pan and use a spatula or slotted spoon to baste the white with oil. When the white has set and the egg is loose in the pan, remove with a spatula and serve. Season the eggs after they have been removed from the skillet, otherwise the oil will spatter.

504

Fried eggs with straw potatoes and bacon

HUEVOS FRITOS CON PATATAS PAJA Y BACON

- 2 ¼ pounds potatoes,
  cut into julienne strips
- sunflower oil, for deep-frying
- 6 slices smoked bacon
- 6 eggs
- salt

Serves 6

Deep-fry the potato strips in the oil in a deep skillet as described in recipe 243. Drain well, season with salt, place in the center of a round serving dish, and keep warm. Drain off half the oil and reheat the pan. Add the bacon and cook for 4–5 minutes, until lightly browned. Remove from the pan, drain well, and place around the edge of the serving dish like the rays of the sun. Fry the eggs as described on page 411. Arrange the eggs between the slices of bacon and serve immediately.

505

Eggs in buns

HUEVOS EN BOLLOS

- 6 muffins or individual brioches
- 6 egg yolks
- 4 egg whites
- 1 teaspoon all-purpose flour,
  sifted
- sunflower oil, for deep-frying
- salt

Tomato sauce:
- 1 ½ tablespoons sunflower oil
- 1 pound 10 ounces ripe
  tomatoes, peeled, seeded,
  and chopped
- 1 teaspoon sugar
- salt

Serves 6

Make a thick tomato sauce as described in recipe 73. Cut a thin layer off the top of each muffin or brioche and scoop out a hollow in the center of each. Put a little tomato sauce in the hollows and add an egg yolk to each. Lightly season with salt and put some more tomato sauce around the yolks. Stiffly whisk the egg whites with a pinch of salt in a clean, dry bowl and gently fold in the flour. Divide the egg whites among the muffins or brioches, spooning some on top of each egg yolk, and making an attractive pyramid shape using the tines of a fork. Heat the oil in a deep-fryer or deep skillet to 350–375°F or until a cube of day-old bread browns in 30 seconds. Put a muffin or brioche onto a slotted spoon and lower it into the oil without taking it off the spoon. Use a tablespoon to baste the egg white quickly with oil so that it cooks without the yolk setting. Remove from the oil, transfer to a serving dish, and keep warm while cooking the remaining muffins or brioches in the same way. Serve immediately. Keep the cooked muffins or brioches in a preheated oven, now turned off to prevent the yolks setting.

Note: Some people like to stick pine nuts into the egg white. It is attractive but is optional.

506

Fried eggs with rice
HUEVOS FRITOS CON ARROZ

• 1¾ cups long-grain rice
• ¼ cup (½ stick) butter
• sunflower oil, for deep-frying
• 6 slices smoked bacon or
  3 bananas, peeled and
  halved lengthwise
• 1 quantity Classic Tomato Sauce
  (see recipe 73)
• 6 eggs
Serves 6

Boil and drain the rice, then cook in the butter as described in recipe 173. Heat the oil in a skillet. Add the bacon or bananas and cook for about 5 minutes, until lightly browned. Remove from the skillet, drain, and keep warm. Heat the tomato sauce. Fry the eggs as described on page 411. Make a ring of rice on a warm round serving dish. Spoon the tomato sauce into the middle and put the bacon or bananas on top of the rice. Place the fried eggs around the rice and serve immediately.

507

Fried eggs in bread crumbs
HUEVOS FRITOS ENCAPOTADOS

• 3 cups sunflower oil,
  plus extra for brushing
• 8 eggs
• 1½ tablespoons butter
• 2 tablespoons olive oil
• 3 tablespoons all-purpose flour
• 3 cups milk
• 1 cup bread crumbs
• deep-fried parsley sprigs
  (see recipe 918)
• 1 quantity Classic Tomato Sauce
  (see recipe 73)
• salt
Serves 6

Brush a marble slab or baking sheet with sunflower oil. Heat half the sunflower oil in a skillet. Fry six of the eggs as described on page 411. Transfer to the marble slab or baking sheet and trim the edges to give them a neat round shape. Melt the butter with the olive oil in a pan. Stir in the flour and cook, stirring constantly, for 2 minutes. Gradually stir in the milk, a little at a time. Cook, stirring constantly, for about 8 minutes, until thickened. Season with salt, remove the pan from the heat, and let cool slightly, stirring occasionally. Spoon enough sauce over each fried egg to cover it completely. Refrigerate the eggs until completely cold. Beat the remaining eggs in a shallow dish and pour the bread crumbs into another shallow dish. Dip the coated eggs first in the beaten eggs and then in the bread crumbs. Add the remaining sunflower oil to the skillet and heat to 350–375°F or until a cube of day-old bread browns in 30 seconds. Add the coated eggs and cook, in batches, until golden brown. Serve immediately, garnished with the fried parsley, and offer the tomato sauce separately.

Scrambled eggs

How to cook

Allow 2 eggs per serving. Break the eggs into a pan and beat for 30 seconds with a fork. Immediately add a pinch of salt, 2 tablespoons milk for every 4 eggs, and 1½ tablespoons butter (also for every 4 eggs). Put the pan in a roasting pan half filled with very hot water set over low heat. Whisk constantly, especially around the sides of the pan where the eggs will set first. When the mixture is thick and creamy, remove the pan from the heat as the eggs will continue to cook off the heat. Stir in a dash of light cream and serve immediately.

508 Scrambled eggs with rice and shrimp

HUEVOS REVUELTOS CON ARROZ Y GAMBAS

- pinch of saffron threads
- 2 cups long-grain rice
- 9 ounces raw shrimp, peeled
- generous ½ cup butter
- 12 eggs
- 6 tablespoons milk
- 4 tablespoons light cream
- salt

Serves 6

Bring 3¼ quarts unsalted water to a boil in a pan. Crush the saffron in a mortar, or small bowl, with a little water and add to the pan. Add the rice and cook over high heat for about 15–18 minutes, until tender. Drain well, refresh under cold running water, drain again, and set aside. Put the shrimp, 1½ tablespoons of the butter, and a pinch of salt into a small pan. Cover and cook for about 5 minutes. Melt 4 tablespoons of the remaining butter in a skillet. Add the rice, season with salt, and heat through. Meanwhile, beat the eggs with a fork in another pan. Add the shrimp, milk, remaining butter, and a pinch of salt. Put the pan into a roasting pan half filled with very hot water and cook as described above. Stir in the cream. If you like, spoon the rice into a ring mold and turn out onto a warm serving plate. Transfer the scrambled eggs and shrimp to the middle of the rice and serve immediately. Alternatively, serve the scrambled eggs and prawns with the rice on the side.

Note: You can add scant 1 cup cooked or canned peas to the rice while it is frying.

509

- **2 ounces truffles**
- **2¼ cups sunflower oil**
- **6 slices of bread**
- **6 tablespoons milk**
- **13 eggs**
- **7 tablespoons butter**
- **4 tablespoons light cream**
- **salt**

Serves 6

Scrambled eggs on toast with truffles

HUEVOS REVUELTOS EN TOSTADAS CON TRUFAS

Drain the truffles, reserving the liquid from the cans. Cut six thin slices of truffle for the garnish and set aside. Finely chop the remainder. Heat the oil in a skillet. Put the slices of bread in a shallow dish, add the milk, and let soak. Lightly beat one of the eggs in another shallow dish. Add the slices of bread, then transfer to the skillet, in batches, and cook until golden brown on both sides. Remove from the skillet, drain, and keep warm. Lightly beat the remaining eggs with the soaking milk, the butter, and the reserved truffle liquid in a saucepan with a fork. Put the pan into a roasting pan half filled with very hot water and cook as described on page 415. Stir in the cream and chopped truffles. Divide the scrambled eggs among the slices of fried bread, garnish each portion with a truffle slice if you like, and serve immediately.

510

- **13 eggs**
- **2¼ cups sunflower oil**
- **6 slices of bread**
- **6 tablespoons milk**
- **6 frankfurters**
- **3 tablespoons butter**
- **4 tablespoons light cream**
- **6 tablespoons Classic Tomato Sauce (see recipe 73)**
- **salt**

Serves 6

Scrambled eggs on toast with sausages

HUEVOS REVUELTOS EN TOSTADAS CON SALCHICHAS

Heat the oil in a skillet and lightly beat one egg in a shallow dish. Soak the slices of bread in the milk and then in the beaten egg, and fry as described in recipe 509. Remove from the pan, drain, and keep warm. Bring a pan of water just to the boiling point, add the frankfurters, then lower the heat, and warm through. Lightly beat the remaining eggs with the butter and the soaking milk in a saucepan. Put the pan into a roasting pan half filled with very hot water and cook as described on page 415. Stir in the cream and divide the scrambled egg among the slices of fried bread. Halve the frankfurters and put a half on either side of each slice of fried bread. Spoon the warmed tomato sauce on the other two sides. Serve immediately.

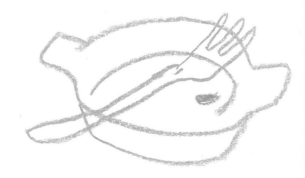

511

Artichoke hearts with scrambled eggs
FONDOS DE ALCACHOFAS CON HUEVOS REVUELTOS

- 4–6 large globe artichokes
- ½ lemon
- 8 eggs
- 4–5 tablespoons milk
  or light cream
- 3 tablespoons butter
- 1 truffle, cut into 6 slices
- salt

Serves 4–6

Break off the stems from the artichokes and cut off and discard the tough outer leaves. Trim the remaining leaves to about halfway and remove and discard the chokes. Trim the bases of the artichokes so they will not tip over when filled. Rub all over with the lemon half to prevent discoloration. Bring a pan of salted water to a boil, add the artichokes, and cook for about 30 minutes, until tender. Remove from the pan and drain upside down, covered with a dishtowel to keep warm. Lightly beat the eggs with half the milk or cream and 2 tablespoons of the butter in a saucepan. Put the pan into a roasting pan half filled with very hot water and cook as described on page 415. Stir in the remaining milk or cream and butter. Place the artichokes in a warm serving dish, fill with the scrambled eggs, and top each with a slice of truffle. Serve immediately.

512

Scrambled eggs with potatoes and peas or asparagus
HUEVOS REVUELTOS CON PATATAS Y GUISANTES O ESPÁRRAGOS

- 4½ cups shelled peas
- pinch of baking soda
- 3 cups sunflower oil
- 5¼ cups diced potatoes
- 8 eggs
- salt

Serves 4

Bring a pan of salted water to a boil. Add the peas and baking soda and cook for about 30 minutes, until tender. Drain well. Meanwhile, heat the oil in a skillet to 350–375°F or until a cube of day-old bread browns in 30 seconds. Add the potato and cook for about 15 minutes, until golden brown. Remove from the skillet with a slotted spoon, drain, and keep warm. Drain off most of the oil from the skillet, leaving just enough to prevent the eggs sticking, and heat. Meanwhile, lightly beat the eggs with a pinch of salt in a bowl. Add to the skillet and cook, whisking constantly, until creamy. Stir in the peas and potato and serve immediately.

Note: You can use drained canned peas instead of fresh or replace the peas with fresh or canned green or white asparagus. Instead of stirring the potato into the eggs, you could arrange it around the edge of a serving dish with the eggs in the center.

513

Portuguese scrambled eggs with straw potatoes and salt cod

HUEVOS REVUELTOS CON PATATAS PAJA Y BACALAO (A LA PORTUGUESA)

- 9 ounces salt cod fillet
  (not soaked)
- 2½ pounds potatoes,
  cut into fine julienne strips
- sunflower oil, for deep-frying
- 1 large onion, finely chopped
- 8 eggs

Serves 4

To serve the cod raw, Portuguese-style, remove and discard any skin and bones, then flake the flesh finely. If you prefer to cook it, put it into a pan, pour in water to cover, and bring to a boil. Lift out the fish with a slotted spatula, remove and discard any skin and bones, and flake the flesh. Cook the potato strips in the hot oil as described in recipe 243. Drain well and set aside. Transfer about 6 tablespoons of the oil to a large skillet and heat. Add the onion and cook over low heat, stirring occasionally, for about 10 minutes, until golden brown. Increase the heat to high, add the straw potatoes and fish, break the eggs into the pan, and cook, stirring constantly, until the eggs begin to set. Serve immediately.

514

Scrambled eggs with tomato

HUEVOS REVUELTOS CON TOMATES

- 9 eggs
- 3 tablespoons milk
- 2 tablespoons butter
- salt

Tomato sauce:
- 2 tablespoons sunflower oil
- 2 onions, finely chopped
- 2¼ pounds ripe tomatoes,
  peeled, seeded, and chopped
- ½ teaspoon sugar
- salt

Serves 6

Make a thick tomato sauce as described in recipe 73 and keep warm. Beat the eggs with a pinch of salt in a pan for 30 seconds, then add the milk and butter. Put the pan into a roasting pan half filled with very hot water and cook as described on page 415. Stir in the tomato sauce and serve immediately, with triangles of fried bread (see recipe 130).

Scrambled eggs with grated cheese

HUEVOS REVUELTOS CON QUESO RALLADO

- **12 eggs**
- **5 tablespoons milk**
- **3 tablespoons butter**
- **1 cup grated gruyere or Parmesan cheese**
- **salt**

Serves 6

Beat the eggs in a pan for 30 seconds, add the milk, half the butter, and the gruyere. Put the pan into a roasting pan half filled with very hot water and cook as described on page 415. Remove the pan from the heat and stir in the remaining butter. Season to taste with salt and serve immediately, with triangles of fried bread (see recipe 130).

Omelets

How to cook

Allow 1 ½ – 2 eggs per serving, but it is advisable not to use more than 6 eggs at a time, as the fatter the omelet, the more difficult it is to produce a good one. Over high heat, heat enough sunflower oil to cover the base of a skillet. Meanwhile, beat the eggs vigorously with a pinch of salt in a bowl for 1 minute. Pour the eggs into the skillet and pull them from the edge of the pan to the center with a fork or spatula. Cook until the underside is set and lightly browned. Fold the omelet, using a spatula.

Tricks

- To make a Spanish omelet succulent, add 1 teaspoon baking powder to the eggs and, if it is a potato omelet, add ⅔ cup milk to the eggs. Add a dash of milk to the beaten eggs when preparing a folded omelet
- To flip an omelet professionally, tilt the pan, holding the handle in your left hand so that the omelet slides toward the edge. Holding a spatula in your right hand, roll the omelet under from the edge opposite the handle. Then gently hit the handle of the pan with your right hand and the omelet will slide in the pan and roll over on itself. Adjust the shape slightly with a fork, slide the omelet onto a plate, and serve immediately. If you cannot flip the omelet this way the first time, do not despair. Even great chefs take time to learn the trick.

516

French omelet

TORTILLA A LA FRANCESA

- **2 tablespoons sunflower oil**
- **4 eggs**
- **½ tablespoon chopped fresh parsley**
- **salt**

Serves 2

Heat the oil in a skillet. Beat the eggs vigorously with a pinch of salt for 1 minute. Add the parsley and cook as described above. Serve immediately.

517

Soufflé omelet with parsley or cheese

TORTILLA SOUFFLÉ CON PEREJIL O QUESO

- **3 eggs**
- **3 tablespoons sunflower oil**
- **½ teaspoon chopped fresh parsley or 2 tablespoons grated gruyere cheese**
- **salt**

Serves 2

Separate two of the eggs. Whisk the whites in a clean, dry bowl until they form soft peaks. Heat the oil in a skillet. Beat the remaining egg and the egg yolks with a pinch of salt in a bowl. Fold in the egg whites and parsley, if using, and cook as described on page 422. Alternatively, beat the egg and egg yolks with the cheese, fold in the egg whites and cook as described on page 422. Serve immediately.

518

Omelet with grated cheese, ham, and croûtons

TORTILLA CON QUESO RALLADO, JAMÓN Y CUSCURROS DE PAN FRITO

- **1 cup sunflower oil**
- **2 slices of bread, crusts removed, cubed**
- **6 eggs**
- **½ cup grated gruyere cheese**
- **5 tablespoons milk**
- **scant 1 cup chopped Serrano ham, prosciutto or other dry-cured ham**
- **salt**

Serves 6

Heat the oil in a skillet. Add the bread cubes and cook, stirring occasionally, for a few minutes, until golden brown. Remove from the pan and drain well. Beat the eggs vigorously in a bowl for 1 minute. Add the gruyere, milk, and ham and season lightly with salt. (Bear in mind that the cheese and ham are salty.) Transfer enough oil to another skillet just to cover the base, and heat. Add the egg mixture and cook as described on page 422, until beginning to set. Sprinkle with the croûtons and cook until the omelet sets around the edges but is still liquid in the middle—about 6 minutes. Fold it in half, transfer to a warm dish, and serve immediately.

519

Ham omelet

TORTILLA DE JAMÓN

- 3 tablespoons sunflower oil
- 3 tablespoons diced
  Serrano ham, prosciutto or
  other dry-cured ham
- 4 eggs
- salt

Serves 2

If the ham is very salty, let soak in warm milk for 10 minutes, then drain, and pat dry. Heat 1 tablespoon of the oil in a skillet. Add the ham and cook, stirring occasionally, for a few minutes, until lightly browned. Remove with a slotted spoon. Add the remaining oil to the skillet and heat. Meanwhile, beat the eggs vigorously in a bowl for 1 minute. Add the ham and season lightly with salt. Pour into the skillet and cook as described on page 422. Serve immediately.

520

Omelet with mushrooms, asparagus, spinach, truffles, or shrimp

TORTILLA DE CHAMPIÑONES O ESPÁRRAGOS, O ESPINACAS, O TRUFAS, O GAMBAS

- 3½ ounces mushrooms,
  thinly sliced or 3½ ounces
  asparagus tips, trimmed or 2
  ounces leftover cooked spinach
  or 2 truffles, thinly sliced or 3½
  ounces raw shrimp, peeled
- 1–2 tablespoons butter
- dash of lemon juice (optional)
- 1 tablespoon Madeira wine
  (optional)
- 3 tablespoons sunflower oil
- 3 eggs
- salt

Serves 2

If using the mushrooms, cook them with 1 tablespoon butter and the lemon juice as described in recipe 470. If using the asparagus, bring a pan of salted water to a boil. Add the asparagus and cook for about 10 minutes, until tender. Drain well and gently pat dry. Melt 1½ tablespoons butter in a skillet. Add the asparagus and cook over low heat for a few minutes. If using leftover cooked spinach, melt 2 tablespoons butter in a skillet. Add the spinach and cook, stirring occasionally, for a few minutes. If using truffles, put them into skillet, and add 1½ tablespoons butter and the Madeira, and heat gently. If using shrimp, melt 2 tablespoons butter in a skillet. Add the shrimp and a pinch of salt and cook over medium-high heat, stirring frequently, for 3–5 minutes, until opaque. Remove from the pan. Heat the oil in a skillet. Meanwhile, beat the eggs vigorously with a pinch of salt in a bowl for 1 minute. If using mushrooms, asparagus, spinach, or truffles, pour the eggs into the pan and cook as described on page 422. Using a slotted spoon put the chosen filling in the middle, fold over the omelet, and serve. If using shrimp, put them into the skillet before adding the eggs. Serve immediately.

521

- 5 tablespoons sunflower oil
- 1 small onion, chopped
- 2 ounces canned tuna in brine
- 4 eggs
- salt

Serves 2

Omelet with tuna in brine

TORTILLA DE ATÚN ESCABECHADO

Heat 2 tablespoons of the oil in a skillet. Add the onion and cook over low heat, stirring occasionally, for about 5 minutes, until softened but not browned. Add the tuna and cook for a few minutes, breaking up the fish with a fork or slotted spoon. Heat the remaining oil in another skillet. Meanwhile, beat the eggs vigorously with a pinch of salt in a bowl for 1 minute. Pour into the skillet and cook as described on page 422. When the eggs begin to set, put the tuna mixture in the middle, fold over the omelet, and serve immediately.

Note: This dish can be served with Classic Tomato Sauce (see recipe 73) poured around the omelet.

522

- 1 pound 2 ounces eggplant, peeled
- 5 tablespoons sunflower oil
- 9 ounces onions, finely chopped
- 1 heaping tablespoon all-purpose flour
- 1¼ cups milk
- 8 eggs
- ½ cup grated gruyere cheese
- salt

Tomato sauce:
- 3 tablespoons sunflower oil
- 3½ ounces onion, chopped
- 3¼ pounds tomatoes, peeled, seeded, and chopped
- 1 teaspoon sugar
- salt

Serves 4

Little omelets filled with eggplant

TORTILLITAS RELLENAS DE BERENJENAS

Make the tomato sauce as described in recipe 73. Process the eggplant in a food processor or grind in a grinder. Heat 3 tablespoons of the oil in a skillet. Add the onion and eggplant and cook over low heat, stirring occasionally, for 8–10 minutes, until lightly browned. Stir in the flour and cook, stirring constantly, for 2 minutes. Gradually stir in the milk, a little at a time. Season with salt and cook, stirring constantly, for about 10 minutes, until thickened. Preheat the oven to 400°F. Using the remaining oil and the eggs, make little one-egg omelets in a small skillet as described on page 422. As each one sets, put a spoonful of the eggplant mixture in the middle, fold over, and slide onto an ovenproof baking dish. When all the omelets have been cooked, pour the tomato sauce over them, sprinkle with the gruyere, and bake for about 8 minutes, until golden brown. Serve immediately straight from the dish, allowing two omelets per serving.

Spanish potato omelet

TORTILLA DE PATATAS A LA ESPAÑOLA

- 2¼ cups sunflower oil
- 2¼ pounds potatoes, halved lengthwise and thinly sliced
- 8 eggs
- 2 tablespoons olive oil
- salt

Serves 6

Heat the sunflower oil in a skillet. Add the potato slices and cook, stirring occasionally, until softened and lightly browned. Season with salt, remove from the skillet, and drain well. Beat the eggs vigorously with a pinch of salt in a large bowl for 1 minute. Add the potato slices and stir with a fork. Heat the olive oil in a large skillet. Pour in the egg mixture and cook, gently shaking the skillet occasionally, until the underside is set and lightly browned. Invert the omelet onto the pan lid or a plate, then gently slide it back into the skillet, cooked side up. Cook, gently shaking the skillet occasionally, until the underside is set and golden brown. Serve immediately.

Note: The omelet can be made with French Fries (see recipe 242) and accompanied by Classic Mayonnaise (see recipe 105), either poured over it or offered separately.

524

Spanish potato omelet with sauce
TORTILLA DE PATATAS GUISADA

- 2¼ cups sunflower oil
- 3 pounds potatoes, halved
  lengthwise and thinly sliced
- 8 eggs
- 2 tablespoons olive oil
- salt

  Sauce:
- 4 tablespoons olive oil
- 1 onion, finely chopped
- 1½ tablespoons flour
- pinch of saffron threads
- 1 tablespoon chopped
  fresh parsley
- generous ½ cup chopped
  Serrano ham, prosciutto
  or other dry-cured ham
- scant 1 cup drained canned peas
- salt

  Serves 6

Make a thick Spanish Potato Omelet with the sunflower oil, potatoes, eggs, olive oil, and salt (see recipe 523). Keep it warm in the skillet. To make the sauce, heat the olive oil in another skillet. Add the onion and cook over low heat, stirring occasionally, for about 7 minutes, until beginning to brown. Stir in the flour and cook, stirring constantly, for 2 minutes. Gradually stir in 3 cups water, a little at a time. Crush the saffron and parsley in a mortar, or process in a mini-food processor, and mix in a little of the sauce, then stir into the skillet. Simmer for 5 minutes, then strain into a pan. Add the ham and simmer for 5 minutes more, then add the peas and season lightly with salt (bearing in mind that the ham is salty). Pour the sauce over the omelet and cook over low heat for 2 minutes. Slide the omelet onto a warm serving dish with the sauce-covered side up. Cut into squares and serve. Alternatively, slide the omelet onto a serving dish before adding the sauce. Cut the omelet into squares, and pour the sauce over them. This way, the omelet will be drier in the middle.

525

Green bell pepper omelet
TORTILLA DE PIMIENTOS VERDES

- 3 tablespoons olive oil
- 1 green bell pepper,
  seeded and cut into strips
- 4 eggs
- salt
- 1 quantity Classic Tomato Sauce
  (see recipe 73)

  Serves 2

Heat the oil in a skillet. Add the bell pepper, season with salt, cover, and cook over low heat for 15 minutes. Drain off the oil. Beat the eggs vigorously with a pinch of salt in a bowl for 1 minute. Add to the bell pepper, and mix well, then cook as described in recipe 523. Serve immediately, covered in tomato sauce if you like.

Three-layer omelet with tomato sauce

TRES PISOS DE TORTILLAS CON SALSA DE TOMATE

- 2 ¼ cups sunflower oil
- 4 large potatoes, halved lengthwise and thinly sliced
- 12 eggs
- 5 ounces canned tuna, drained and flaked
- 4 ½ cups drained canned peas
- generous ½ cup finely chopped Serrano ham, prosciutto or other dry-cured ham
- 1 quantity Classic Tomato Sauce (see recipe 73)
- salt

Serves 6

Make a Spanish potato omelet with half the sunflower oil, the potatoes, four of the eggs, and salt as described in recipe 523. Transfer to a serving dish and keep warm. Beat four of the remaining eggs vigorously with a pinch of salt in a bowl for 1 minute and add the tuna. If necessary, add more oil to the pan and reheat. Pour in the egg mixture and cook as described in recipe 523. Put the tuna omelet on top of the potato omelet and keep warm. Beat the remaining eggs vigorously with a pinch of salt in a bowl for 1 minute and add the peas and ham. If necessary, add more oil to the pan and reheat. Pour in the egg mixture and cook as described in recipe 523. Put the ham and pea omelet on top of the tuna omelet. Pour the warmed tomato sauce over the stack of omelets and serve immediately.

Note: The base of this dish should always be a potato omelet but you can vary the other two layers according to taste. For example, instead of tuna, use shrimp, and substitute asparagus for the peas or chorizo for the ham.

Savory custards and soufflés

527

Egg custard with tomato sauce
FLAN DE HUEVOS CON SALSA DE TOMATE

- 2 tablespoons (¼ stick) butter, plus extra for greasing
- 2 tablespoons sunflower oil
- 4 tablespoons all-purpose flour
- 2¼ cups milk
- 5 eggs, separated
- 2¼ cups cooked peeled shrimp or scant 1 cup finely chopped Serrano ham, prosciutto or other dry-cured ham (optional)
- 3 egg whites
- 1 quantity Classic Tomato Sauce (see recipe 73)
- pinch of freshly grated nutmeg or ground pepper
- salt

Serves 6–8

Make the tomato sauce as described in recipe 73. Preheat the oven to 350°F. Generously grease a 7-inch tart pan with butter. Melt the butter with the oil in a skillet. Stir in the flour and cook, stirring constantly, for 2–3 minutes, but do not let the flour brown. Gradually stir in the milk, a little at a time. Season with salt and the nutmeg or pepper and cook, stirring constantly, for about 10 minutes, until thickened. Remove the skillet from the heat and let cool. Stir in the egg yolks one at a time. Stir in the shrimp or ham, if using. Stiffly whisk all the egg whites with a pinch of salt in a clean, dry bowl until stiff. Gently fold them into the sauce in three or four batches, then pour the mixture into the prepared pan. Put the pan in a roasting pan and pour in boiling water to come about halfway up the sides. Bake for about 1 hour, until set. Just before serving, reheat the tomato sauce. Remove the pan from the oven, run a round-bladed knife around the edge, and turn the custard out onto a warm serving dish. Pour the hot tomato sauce over it and serve immediately.

Note: The custard may also be served with a Classic Béchamel Sauce (see recipe 77) mixed with 2–3 tablespoons tomato sauce or 1 table-spoon tomato paste. Alternatively, make a béchamel sauce with half milk and half stock.

Savory custard

FLAN SALADO

- butter, for greasing
- 8 eggs
- generous ½ cup finely chopped Serrano ham, prosciutto or other dry-cured ham
- 5 tablespoons sherry or other sweet fortified wine
- pinch of freshly grated nutmeg
- 3 cups warm milk
- salt

Béchamel sauce:
- 1½ tablespoons butter
- 2 tablespoons sunflower oil
- 1 tablespoon all-purpose flour
- generous 1 cup milk
- 1 tablespoon tomato paste or 2 tablespoons Classic Tomato Sauce (see recipe 73)
- salt

Serves 6

Preheat the oven to 325°F. Grease a ring mold with butter. Beat the eggs in a bowl, add the ham, sherry, and nutmeg and season with salt (bearing in mind that the ham is salty). Mix well, then gradually stir in the milk, a little at a time. Pour the mixture into the prepared mold and bake (not in a water bath) for 30–40 minutes, until set. Meanwhile, make the béchamel sauce as described in recipe 77 and stir in the tomato paste or tomato sauce. Keep the sauce warm. Remove the custard from the oven and turn out onto a serving dish. Fill the center with the béchamel sauce and serve immediately.

529

Savory custard with mushrooms

FLAN SALADO CON CHAMPIÑONES

- 1½ tablespoons butter, plus extra for greasing
- 8 eggs
- generous ½ cup finely chopped Serrano ham, prosciutto or other dry-cured ham
- 5 tablespoons sherry or other sweet fortified wine
- pinch of freshly grated nutmeg
- 3 cups warm milk
- 1 quantity Classic Béchamel Sauce (see recipe 77)
- 7 ounces mushrooms
- juice of ½ lemon
- salt

Serves 6

Preheat the oven to 325°F. Grease a ring mold with butter. Beat the eggs in a bowl, add the ham, sherry, and nutmeg and season with salt (bearing in mind that the ham is salty). Mix well, then gradually stir in the milk, a little at a time. Pour the mixture into the prepared mold and bake (not in a water bath) for 30–40 minutes, until set. Meanwhile, make the béchamel sauce as described in recipe 77. Keep the sauce warm. Cut the mushrooms into large pieces and put into a pan with the butter, lemon juice and a pinch of salt. Cook over medium heat for 6 minutes. Remove the custard from the oven and turn out onto a serving dish. Fill the center with the béchamel sauce and place the mushrooms around the custard. Serve immediately.

530

SOUFFLÉ DE QUESO

Cheese soufflé

- 6 tablespoons (¾ stick) butter, plus extra for greasing
- 4 tablespoons all-purpose flour
- 4 teaspoons potato starch
- 2¼ cups milk
- scant 1 cup grated gruyere cheese
- 5 eggs, separated
- 3–4 egg whites
- salt

Serves 6–8

Preheat the oven to 350°F. Generously grease an 8 ½ inch soufflé dish with butter. Melt the butter in a skillet. Stir in the flour and potato starch and cook, stirring constantly, for 2 minutes. Gradually stir in the milk, a little at a time. Bring to a boil, stirring constantly, then lower the heat, and simmer, still stirring, for 5 minutes. Remove the pan from the heat and stir in the gruyere. Let cool slightly. Stir in the egg yolks, one at a time, then season to taste with salt. Whisk half the egg whites in a clean, dry bowl until stiff. Gently fold into the mixture. Repeat with the remaining egg whites. Pour the mixture into the prepared soufflé dish and bake for 20 minutes. Increase the oven temperature to 425°F and bake for 10–15 minutes more, until risen and golden brown. Serve immediately. A soufflé cannot wait even a few minutes as it will collapse.

Note: The basic method for soufflés is always the same, only the flavoring ingredients change. For a shrimp soufflé, put 9 ounces peeled raw shrimp into a pan with 2 tablespoons butter and a pinch of salt. Cover and cook over medium heat for 6–8 minutes, then stir the mixture into the sauce. Continue as above.

Custards with tomato sauce

FLANECILLOS CON SALSA DE TOMATE

- **butter, for greasing**
- **7 eggs**
- **½ cup milk**
- **pinch of freshly grated nutmeg**
- **salt**

  Tomato sauce:
- **3 tablespoons sunflower oil**
- **1 pound 10 ounces ripe tomatoes, peeled, seeded, and chopped**
- **1 teaspoon sugar**
- **salt**

Serves 4

Make the tomato sauce as described in recipe 73. Preheat the oven to 325°F. Grease four individual tartlet pans with butter. Beat the eggs in a bowl, add the milk and nutmeg, season with salt, and mix well. Pour the egg mixture into the prepared pans. Put the tartlet pans into a roasting pan, pour in boiling water to come halfway up the sides, and bake for about 15 minutes, until set. Pour the tomato sauce into a warm serving platter and turn the custards out on top of the sauce. Serve immediately.

Note: This dish can also be served with Béchamel Sauce with Tomato (see recipe 78) instead of tomato sauce.

532

Potato soufflé

SOUFFLÉ DE PATATAS

- 2 ¼ pounds potatoes,
  cut into pieces
- ¼ cup (½ stick) butter,
  cut into small pieces,
  plus extra for greasing
- 1 cup hot milk
- 4 eggs, separated
- pinch of freshly grated nutmeg
- 3 egg whites
- salt

Serves 4–6

Put the potato into a pan, pour in water to cover, and add a pinch of salt. Bring to a boil and cook for 20–30 minutes, until tender but not falling apart. Meanwhile, preheat the oven to 400°F. Grease an 8 ½ inch soufflé dish with butter. Drain the potato well and push through a strainer or press through a ricer into a bowl. Immediately add the butter, then gradually stir in the milk, a little at a time. Stir the egg yolks into the potato and add the nutmeg. Whisk half the egg whites with a pinch of salt in a clean, dry bowl until soft. Gently fold into the mixture. Repeat with the remaining egg whites. Pour the mixture into the prepared soufflé dish and bake for 45 minutes, until golden brown. Serve immediately.

533

Rice soufflé

SOUFFLÉ DE ARROZ BLANCO

- 3 tablespoons butter,
  plus extra for greasing
- 2 tablespoons sunflower oil
- 1 ½ tablespoons all-purpose
  flour
- 3 cups milk
- 4 eggs, separated
- 1 ⅓ cups cooked long-grain rice
- scant 1 cup grated
  gruyere cheese
- 2 egg whites
- salt

Serves 4–6

Preheat the oven to 350°F. Grease an 8 ½ inch soufflé dish with butter. Melt 2 tablespoons of the butter with the oil in a pan. Stir in the flour and cook, stirring constantly, for 2 minutes. Gradually stir in the milk, a little at a time. Season with salt and cook, stirring constantly, for 8 minutes, until thickened. Remove the pan from the heat and let cool slightly. Stir in the egg yolks, one at a time, then add half the rice and all but 2 tablespoons of the gruyere. Dot with the remaining butter. Whisk the egg whites with a pinch of salt in a clean, dry bowl until stiff. Fold in the remaining rice, then fold the rice and egg whites into the rice and egg yolk mixture. Pour into the prepared dish, sprinkle with the remaining cheese, and bake for 20 minutes. Increase the oven temperature to 425°F and bake for 15 minutes more, until risen and golden brown. Serve immediately.

FISH AND SHELLFISH

Fish

Before preparing fish for any recipe, rinse all fish under cold running water and immediately pat dry.

Fish poached in quick white wine stock

CALDO CORTO CON VINO BLANCO

- 2 ¼ pounds fish, such as sole, whiting or hake

Quick white wine stock:
- 1 bay leaf
- 1 thick slice of onion
- 1 large carrot, sliced
- ¾ cup white wine
- juice of ½ lemon
- salt

Serves 4–6

Put all the stock ingredients into a large pan, pour in 8 ¾ cups water, and bring to a boil. Lower the heat and simmer for about 10 minutes, then remove the pan from the heat, and let cool. When ready to poach the fish, remove the rack from a fish poacher and pour in the stock. Put the fish on the rack and replace the rack so that it is positioned over the vegetables. If the stock does not cover the fish, add some water. Set the poacher over medium heat, cover, and bring just to a boil. If you are cooking flat fish, such as sole, turn off the heat immediately and leave the fish in the stock for 5–6 minutes. If you are cooking round fish, such as hake, lower the heat and simmer gently for a few minutes, until the flesh flakes easily. Lift up the rack and place it diagonally across the top of the fish poacher so that the fish drains well without getting cold. Wring out a clean dishtowel in very hot water and place it over the fish to keep it warm until you are ready to serve.

Notes: To cook fish in a red wine or red-wine vinegar stock, prepare the stock and cook as described above, substituting red wine or red-wine vinegar for the white wine. This stock can be used to give color and flavor to fish such as trout and pike. If you do not have a fish poacher, you can cook the fish in the stock in a skillet. Lift it out with a slotted spoon and drain in a colander set over the skillet.

535

Fish poached in quick stock with milk

CALDO CORTO CON LECHE

- 2¼ pounds fish, such as sole, whiting or hake

Quick stock with milk:
- 1 cup milk
- ½ lemon, peeled and sliced
- 1 bay leaf
- salt

Serves 4

Bring the milk just to a boil in a saucepan, then remove from the heat, and let cool. Remove the rack from a fish poacher, pour in the milk, add the lemon, bay leaf, and a pinch of salt, and pour in 6¼ cups water. Put the fish on the rack and replace the rack. There should always be plenty of stock to cover the fish. Increase the quantities as necessary. Poach the fish until the flesh flakes easily. This stock is mainly used for large flat fish.

Note: If you do not have a fish poacher, you can cook the fish in the stock in a skillet. Lift it out with a slotted spoon and drain in a colander set over the skillet.

Fish cooked in salt crust
PESCADO A LA SAL

• 1 whole fish, such as sole,
  red porgy, grouper, or sea bass,
  about 3¼ pounds, gutted but
  not skinned
• 6½–8¾ pounds coarse sea salt

Serves 4–6

Do not clean the fish. (Cleaning the fish allows the salt to enter through the cut flesh and spoils the flavor). Scale the fish with the back of a knife, then rinse, and pat dry. Preheat the oven to 400°F. Make a thick layer of salt in the base of a deep earthenware baking dish large enough to hold the fish. Place the fish on top and cover it completely with more salt, then sprinkle a little water over the top to form a crust. Bake for about 40 minutes, depending on the size of the fish. Remove the baking dish from the oven, cover the crust with a dishtowel or some thick paper, and break it with a hammer or a pestle. Carefully transfer the fish to a serving dish without breaking, and serve. Mayonnaise and its variations or hollandaise sauce make excellent accompaniments.

Note: This dish is easy to prepare but it is essential to use a thick, meaty, chunky fish.

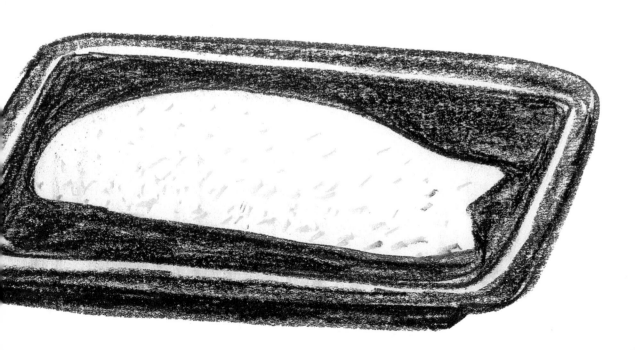

637

Gulas in garlic
GULAS AL AJILLO

- **2 tablespoons olive oil**
- **1 clove garlic, sliced**
- **1 chile, sliced**
- **4 ounces gulas**

Serves 2–4

Heat the oil in a stovetop-safe casserole. Add the garlic and cook, stirring frequently, for a few minutes, until browned. Add the chile and then the gulas, stirring them with a wooden fork. Serve piping hot.

Note: Usually made from ling, a member of the cod family, gulas are white "sausages" with a dark line down the back made from squid ink. They are healthy and nutritious, with no cholesterol, are low in calories, and have a high protein content. You may find them in Spanish specialty shops but they are not widely available outside Spain. If you can't find gulas, you can try other seafood sausages, but follow the cooking time and temperature specified by your fishmonger or on the package.

Eel

Baby eels, also known as glass-eels, are white or transparent and 2½–3½ inches long. They are highly valued in Spain and parts of France and fetch extremely high prices during their short season.

How to prepare

For perfect results, buy live eels. Take great care as they escape easily! To kill an eel, hold it firmly by the tail with a cloth and hit it hard on the head with something heavy. To remove the skin, cut around the head with a small sharp knife. Using a cloth, grasp the skin and pull it firmly toward the tail. It should come off in one piece. It is some-times easier to do this if you hang the eel from a meat hook or other firm support. You can also buy fish pliers that make keeping hold of the skin easier. Cut off the head and the tail. Slit open the belly and remove the intestines. Wash the eel thoroughly in cold water and cut into pieces.

538

Baby eels in individual dishes

ANGULAS EN CAZUELITAS

- **12 tablespoons olive oil**
- **12 cloves garlic**
- **1 pound 5 ounces baby eels**
- **2 chiles, sliced**

Serves 6

Put 2 tablespoons of the oil and 2 garlic cloves into each of six individual gratin dishes and set over high heat until the garlic browns. Remove and let the oil cool, then divide the eels among them, and add 2 slices of chile to each. Return to high heat and cook, stirring frequently with a wooden fork, until the mixture comes to a boil. Remove from the heat, place each dish on a plate, and cover with another plate. Serve immediately with wooden forks.

539

Broiled herring served with mustard sauce

ARENQUES ASADOS, SERVIDOS CON SALSA DE MOSTAZA

- **6 fresh herring,**
  scaled, cleaned, and boned
- **sunflower oil, for brushing**
- **salt**

  Mustard sauce:
- **6 tablespoons (¾ stick) butter**
- **1 tablespoon all-purpose flour**
- **1 cup hot water**
- **2 egg yolks**
- **1–2 teaspoons mustard**
- **salt**

Serves 6

Preheat the broiler. Lightly season the herring inside and out with salt. Brush oil all over the insides of the fish, then slash the outside twice with a sharp knife, and brush with oil. Gently reshape the fish and place on the broiler rack. Cook, turning once, for 15–20 minutes, until the flesh flakes easily. Meanwhile, make the mustard sauce. Melt the butter in a pan. Add the flour and cook, stirring constantly, for 2 minutes. Gradually stir in the water, a little at a time. Cook, stirring constantly for 10 minutes, until thickened. Remove the pan from the heat and stir in the egg yolks one at a time, then the mustard and season to taste with a little salt. When the fish are ready, transfer them to a warmed dish and serve immediately, offering the mustard sauce separately.

540

Broiled herring with anchovies

ARENQUES ASADOS CON ANCHOAS

- **4 ounces canned anchovy**
  fillets in oil
- **¼ cup (½ stick) butter**
- **8 sprigs fresh parsley**
- **6 fresh herring,**
  scaled, cleaned and boned
- **3 tablespoons olive oil**
- **1 teaspoon mustard**
- **salt**

Serves 6

Preheat the broiler. Cut six fillets in half lengthwise and set aside. Drain the remainder and process in a mini-food processor. Divide among the herring cavities, close the fish, and secure with wooden toothpicks. Place the fish on a broiler rack. Combine the oil and mustard and brush half over one side of each herring, then broil for about 10 minutes. Carefully turn the fish, brush with the remaining oil and mustard mixture and broil for 5–10 minutes more, until the flesh flakes easily. Transfer to a warm serving dish and garnish with the reserved anchovies in the shape of crosses and the remaining parsley sprigs. Serve immediately.

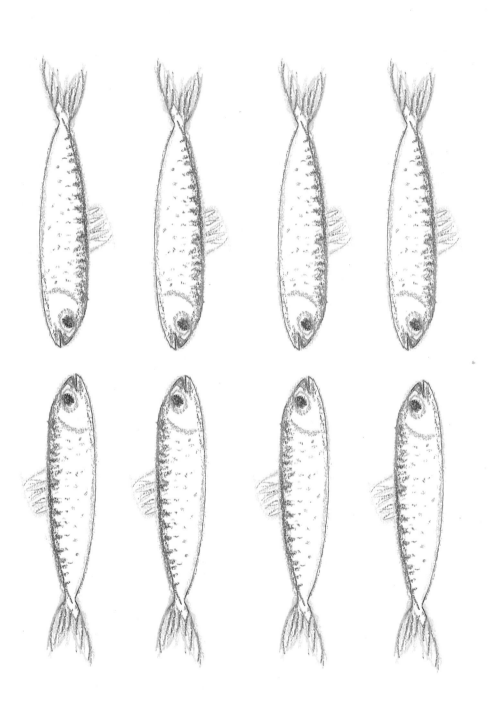

Tuna

As tuna is closely related to bonito (see recipes 557–565), the same recipes can be used for both fish.

541

Tuna au gratin
GRATINADO DE ATÚN DE LATA

- 2¼ pounds mussels
- 5 tablespoons white wine
- ¼ cup (½ stick) butter
- 2 tablespoons sunflower oil
- 3 tablespoons all-purpose flour
- 2¼ cups milk
- 1 pound 2 ounces canned tuna,
  drained and flaked
- 1 tablespoon chopped
  fresh parsley
- 2 scallions or large shallots,
  very finely chopped
- juice of 1 lemon
- 2 eggs, separated (optional)
- 3 tablespoons bread crumbs
- salt

Serves 6

If your mussels have not been pre-scrubbed, scrape their shells with the blade of a knife and remove the "beards," then scrub under cold running water. Discard any mussels with broken shells or any that do not shut immediately when sharply tapped. Put them into a pan with the wine, 5 tablespoons water, and a pinch of salt. Cover and cook over high heat, shaking the pan occasionally, for 4–5 minutes, until the shells have opened. Remove the mussels with a slotted spoon and reserve the cooking liquid. Discard any mussels that remain closed. Strain the cooking liquid through a cheesecloth-lined strainer into a bowl. Remove the mussels from their shells, cut in half with kitchen scissors if they are large, and put into the bowl of cooking liquid. Preheat the oven to 400°F. Heat half the butter with the oil in a pan. Stir in the flour and cook, stirring constantly, for 2 minutes. Gradually stir in the milk, a little at a time. Cook, stirring constantly, for about 10 minutes until thickened. Add the tuna, parsley, and scallions or shallots. Using a slotted spoon, add the mussels and stir in ¾ cup of the reserved cooking liquid. Season to taste with salt and add the lemon juice. Whisk the egg whites, if using, in a clean, dry bowl until stiff. Beat the egg yolks, if using, in another bowl, stir in a little of the sauce to prevent them from curdling, and add to the pan. Remove the pan from the heat and fold in the egg whites. Divide the mixture among individual gratin dishes, sprinkle with the bread crumbs, and dot with the butter. Bake for 5–10 minutes, until golden brown. Serve immediately straight from the dishes.

Salt cod

How to de-salt

Choose pieces of salt cod that are very white with dark skin and not too thick. Soak them in a bowl of cold water for 12 hours, changing the water four times. Each time the water is changed, remove the cod and thoroughly rinse the bowl before adding fresh water and replacing the fish, as salt tends to deposit on the bottom. If time is short, flake the salt cod and soak in warm water for 3 hours, changing the water three times, as described above. However, this method is only recommended for such dishes as croquettes and purées.

542

Salt cod with garlic

BACALAO AL AJO ARRIERO

- 1 pound 2 ounces salt cod fillet
- 3½ ounces canned red bell peppers, drained, or 2 dried red bell peppers, soaked in water
- generous 1 cup sunflower oil
- 1 large onion, finely chopped
- 3–4 cloves garlic, finely chopped
- 2 tablespoons olive oil

Serves 6

The night before you are going to cook the cod, remove and reserve the skin and flake the flesh. Soak the cod as described above. The next day, drain the cod and pat dry. Cut the skin into fine strips with kitchen scissors. Seed the bell peppers, if necessary, and cut into strips. Heat the sunflower oil in a stovetop-safe casserole. Add the onion and garlic and cook over very low heat, stirring occasionally, for about 10 minutes, until very soft and translucent. If using dried bell peppers, add them to the casserole, and cook for a few minutes more. If using canned bell peppers, heat the olive oil in a small skillet, add the bell peppers, and cook over low heat, stirring occasionally, for 5 minutes. Add the cod and strips of skin to the casserole and cook, shaking the casserole occasionally to release the gelatin, for 10 minutes. Add the canned bell peppers, if using. Mix well and simmer over low heat for about 1 hour, until cooked through.

Note: As a variation, prepare the dish as described above, but omit the bell peppers. Just at the end of the cooking time, beat 2–3 eggs in a bowl, then stir them into the casserole, and cook, stirring constantly, for a few minutes, until the eggs are scrambled with the salt cod. Serve immediately.

Salt cod bites

FRITOS DE BACALAO

- 2¼ pounds potatoes, unpeeled
- 1 pound 2 ounces salt cod fillet
- 1 clove garlic, chopped
- 1 tablespoon chopped
  fresh parsley
- 3 eggs, separated
- sunflower oil, for deep-frying
- salt

Serves 6

Put the potatoes and cod (not desalted) into a pan, pour in water to cover, and bring to a boil. Lower the heat and simmer for about 30 minutes, until tender. Lift the cod out of the pan and set aside to cool slightly. Drain the potatoes and when they are cool enough to handle, peel, and mash them in a bowl. Remove and discard any skin and bones from the cod and flake the flesh, then mix into the mashed potatoes. Stir in the garlic and parsley and add the egg yolks one at a time. Whisk the egg whites with a pinch of salt in a clean, dry bowl until stiff, then gently fold into the mixture. Heat the oil in a deep-fryer or deep saucepan to 350–375°F or until a cube of day-old bread browns in 30 seconds. Use two spoons to shape the fish and potato mixture into little balls, then carefully add them to the hot oil, and cook, in batches, until golden brown. Remove with a slotted spoon, drain well, and keep warm while you cook the remaining batches. Serve immediately.

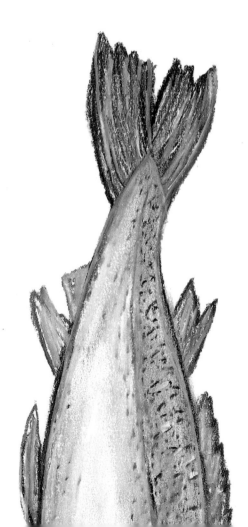

Salt cod fritters with tomato sauce

BUÑUELOS DE BACALAO CON SALSA DE TOMATE

- **1 pound 2 ounces salt cod fillet, soaked overnight as described on page 448**
- **sunflower oil, for deep-frying**
- **1 quantity Classic Tomato Sauce (see recipe 73)**

Batter:
- **2¼ cups all-purpose flour**
- **½ teaspoon rapid-rise active dry yeast**
- **1 egg, separated**
- **1 tablespoon sunflower oil**
- **1 tablespoon rum or brandy**
- **1 egg white**
- **salt**

Serves 6

Put the cod into a pan, pour in water to cover, and bring just to a boil. Remove the pan from the heat, cover, and let stand for 10 minutes. Lift out the fish, remove any skin and bones, and flake the flesh into large pieces. To make the batter, combine the flour, yeast, and a pinch of salt in a bowl. Make a well in the center and add the egg yolk, oil, and rum or brandy. Mix well and add just enough water to give the consistency of a thin purée. Cover and let stand for 2 hours. Just before frying the fritters, whisk both the egg whites with a pinch of salt in a clean, dry bowl until stiff, then gently fold them into the batter. Heat the oil in a deep-fryer or deep saucepan to 350–375°F or until a cube of day-old bread browns in 30 seconds. Dip the pieces of cod into the batter, three at a time, add to the hot oil, and cook until golden brown. Remove with a slotted spoon, drain well, and keep warm while you cook the remaining fritters. Reheat the tomato sauce. Serve the fritters immediately, offering the tomato sauce separately.

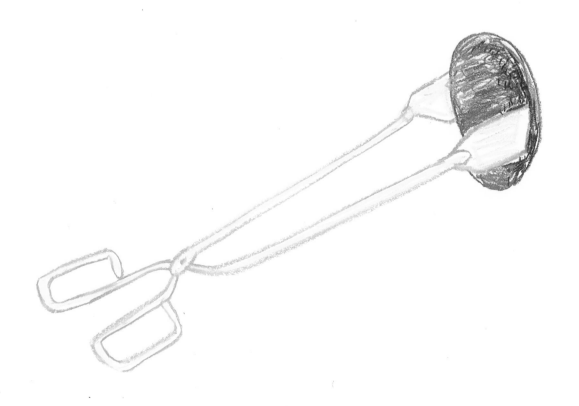

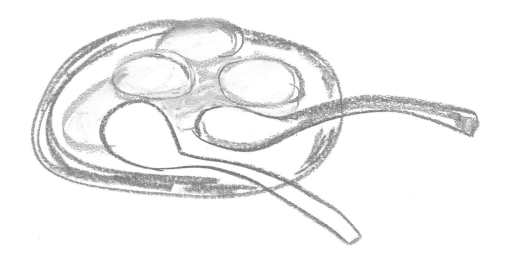

545

Potato and salt cod bouillabaisse
BOUILLABAISSE DE PATATAS Y BACALAO

- 5 tablespoons olive oil
- 2 onions, finely chopped
- 3 cloves garlic, lightly crushed
- 2 tomatoes,
  peeled, seeded, and chopped
- pinch of dried mixed herbs or
  1 bouquet garni (1 sprig fresh
  thyme, 1 bay leaf and 1 sprig
  fresh parsley tied together in
  cheesecloth)
- 2¼ pounds red-skinned
  potatoes, cut into ½-inch
  thick slices
- pinch of saffron threads
- 14 ounces salt cod fillet,
  soaked overnight as described
  on page 448
- fried bread (see recipe 130)
- salt

Serves 6

Heat the oil in a large, heavy pot. Add the onions and cook over low heat, stirring occasionally, for about 5 minutes, until soft and translucent. Add the garlic and cook, stirring frequently, for a few minutes, then add the tomatoes, and cook, stirring occasionally, for 5 minutes. Pour in 8 ¾ cups water, add the herbs or bouquet garni and potatoes, and bring to a boil. Crush the saffron in a mortar or small bowl and stir in 2–3 tablespoons of the cooking liquid, then add to the pot. Simmer for about 20 minutes. Meanwhile, drain the cod, remove any skin and bones and coarsely flake the flesh. Add to the pot and cook for 10 minutes more, until the potatoes are tender. Season to taste with salt. Serve immediately with slices of fried bread if you like.

Note: Bouillabaisse is a traditional Provençal fish soup which is more like a stew in its consistency. This Spanish version uses the salt cod fillet so prized in Spain.

546

Salt cod with spinach and béchamel sauce

BACALAO CON ESPINACAS Y BECHAMEL

- 1 pound 2 ounces salt cod fillet, soaked overnight as described on page 448
- 6½ pounds spinach, coarse stalks removed
- 1½ tablespoons butter, plus extra for greasing
- 5 tablespoons olive oil
- 1 onion, finely chopped
- ½ cup grated gruyere cheese
- salt

Béchamel sauce:
- 2 tablespoons (¼ stick) butter
- 2 tablespoons sunflower oil
- 1½ tablespoons all-purpose flour
- 2¼ cups milk
- salt

Serves 6

Drain the cod and put into a pan. Pour in water to cover, and bring just to a boil. Remove the pan from the heat, cover, and let stand for 10 minutes. Lift out the fish, remove any skin and bones, and finely flake the flesh. Cover and set aside. Bring a large pan of salted water to a boil. Add the spinach, push it down into the water with a spoon, and cook for about 10 minutes. Drain well, refresh under cold running water, and drain again, pressing out as much liquid as possible with the back of a spoon, then chop. Preheat the oven to 400°F. Grease an ovenproof baking dish with butter. Make the béchamel sauce as described in recipe 77. Heat the olive oil in a skillet. Add the onion and cook over low heat, stirring occasionally, for about 5 minutes, until softened and translucent. Add the spinach and cook, stirring frequently, for a few minutes more. Spoon the spinach mixture into the prepared baking dish, spreading it evenly over the base. Add the cod and pour in the béchamel sauce. Sprinkle with the gruyere, dot with the butter, and bake for 10–15 minutes, until golden brown. Serve immediately straight from the dish.

Salt cod in green sauce

BACALAO EN SALSA VERDE

- 2 ¼ pounds salt cod, cut into pieces, soaked overnight as described on page 448
- sunflower oil, for deep-frying
- 2 tablespoons all-purpose flour, plus extra for dusting
- 6 tablespoons olive oil
- 1 large onion, finely chopped
- 1 clove garlic
- 2–3 sprigs fresh parsley
- 1 cup white wine
- 1 bay leaf
- 1 tablespoon chopped fresh parsley
- salt

Serves 6–8

Drain the cod and put into a pan. Pour in water to cover, and bring just to a boil. Remove the pan from the heat, cover, and let stand for 10 minutes. Lift out the pieces of fish and pat dry. Reserve the cooking liquid. Heat the sunflower oil in a deep-fryer or deep skillet to 350–375°F or until a cube of day-old bread browns in 30 seconds. Dust each piece of fish in flour, add to the hot oil, and cook in batches until golden brown. Remove with a slotted spoon and drain. Heat the olive oil in a deep skillet. Add the onion and cook over low heat, stirring occasionally, for 7–8 minutes, until beginning to brown. Meanwhile, crush the garlic with a pinch of salt and the parsley sprigs in a mortar, or process in a mini-food processor. Mix in 3–4 tablespoons of the reserved cooking liquid. Stir the flour into the skillet and cook, stirring constantly, for 2 minutes. Stir in the garlic mixture, wine, and 2 ¼ cups of the reserved cooking liquid. Add the bay leaf and cook for 5–8 minutes. Place the cod in a stovetop-safe dish and strain the sauce over it. Cook over low heat, gently shaking the dish occasionally, for 10 minutes. Sprinkle with the chopped parsley and serve immediately straight from the dish.

548

- 1 pound 10 ounces–2¼ pounds salt cod fillet, cut into 12 pieces, soaked overnight as described on page 448
- 1 pound 2 ounces canned red bell peppers, drained, seeded, and cut into ¾-inch wide strips
- sunflower oil, for deep-frying
- ¾ cup all-purpose flour
- 1 quantity Classic Tomato Sauce (see recipe 73)

Serves 6

Salt cod with bell peppers and tomato sauce
BACALAO CON PIMIENTOS Y SALSA DE TOMATE

Drain the cod. Wrap each piece in a red bell pepper strip and secure with a wooden toothpick. Heat the oil in a deep-fryer or deep skillet to 350–375°F or until a cube of day-old bread browns in 30 seconds. Coat each piece of wrapped cod in some of the flour, add to the hot oil, four at a time, and cook until golden brown. Remove with a slotted spoon, drain, and put into a stovetop-safe casserole. Pour the tomato sauce over the pieces of cod and cook over low heat, shaking the dish occasionally, for about 10 minutes, until the sauce has thickened. Serve immediately, straight from the dish.

Note: You can substitute fresh roasted bell peppers for canned ones if you like.

549

- 1 pound 2 ounces salt cod fillet, soaked overnight as described on page 448
- 2¼ cups milk
- 1 pound 2 ounces potatoes, unpeeled
- sunflower oil, for deep-frying
- ¾ cup all-purpose flour
- 1 quantity Classic Mayonnaise (see recipe 105)
- salt

Serves 6

Salt cod with potatoes and mayonnaise
BACALAO CON PATATAS Y MAYONESA

Put the cod into a dish, pour in the milk, and let soak for 1 hour. Drain, remove the skin and any bones, and flake the flesh into large pieces. Put the potatoes into a pan, pour in water to cover, and add a pinch of salt. Bring to a boil and cook for about 30 minutes, until tender. Meanwhile, heat the oil in a deep-fryer or deep skillet to 350–375°F or until a cube of day-old bread browns in 30 seconds. Lightly dust the pieces of cod with some of the flour, add to the hot oil, in batches, and cook until golden brown. Remove with a slotted spoon, drain well and keep warm while you cook the remaining batches. Drain the potatoes, then peel, and cut them into large pieces. Put them around the edge of a warm serving dish and put the cod in the middle. Serve immediately with the mayonnaise either poured over the dish or served separately in a sauceboat.

550

Salt cod and mashed potato baked with mayonnaise
BACALAO CON PURÉ DE PATATAS Y MAYONESA, AL HORNO

• 1 pound 10 ounces salt cod, soaked overnight as described on page 448

Mashed potatoes:
• 2¼ pounds potatoes, unpeeled
• 3 tablespoons butter
• scant 2 cups hot milk
• salt

Mayonnaise:
• 2 eggs
• 3 cups sunflower oil
• juice of 1 lemon
• salt

Serves 6

Make the mayonnaise in a food processor or blender as described in recipe 105. Put the potatoes into a pan, pour in water to cover, and add a pinch of salt. Bring to a boil and cook for about 30 minutes, until tender. Drain well, then peel, and mash. Stir in the butter, then gradually stir in the milk, a little at a time. The mixture should be quite thick, so you may not need all the milk. Preheat the oven to 325°F. Drain the cod and put into a pan. Pour in water to cover, and bring just to a boil. Remove the pan from the heat, cover, and let stand for 10 minutes. Lift out the fish, remove any skin and bones, and flake the flesh into large pieces. Spoon the mashed potato around the edge of an ovenproof baking dish and put the cod in the middle. Cover with the mayonnaise. Roll a small piece of aluminum foil around your finger to make a funnel and insert it into the mashed potatoes one side of the dish. Bake for about 15 minutes, until the top is golden brown. Tip the dish a little so that excess liquid drains out of the aluminum foil funnel. You can also remove the liquid with a spoon. Serve immediately, straight from the dish.

551

Salt cod with straw potatoes and scrambled eggs
BACALAO CON PATATAS PAJA Y HUEVOS REVUELTOS

• 12 ounces salt cod fillet
• sunflower oil, for deep-frying
• 1 pound 2 ounces potatoes, cut into thin julienne strips
• 3 onions, thinly sliced and pushed out into rings
• 4 eggs
• salt

Serves 6

Flake the cod and rinse well under cold running water. Set aside. Heat the oil in a skillet to 350–375°F or until a cube of day-old bread browns in 30 seconds. Add the potatoes, in batches, and cook for a few minutes, until golden brown. Remove with a slotted spoon, drain, and set aside. Drain off all but about 4–5 tablespoons of the oil from the skillet and reheat. Add the onion and cook over low heat, stir-ring occasionally, for about 8 minutes, until lightly browned. Add the cod and cook for about 5 minutes, until lightly browned. Break the eggs straight into the skillet and quickly mix with a fork, as if making scrambled eggs. When they begin to set but are still creamy, add the straw potatoes. Lightly season with salt, stir rapidly, and then pour the mixture into a warm serving dish. Serve immediately.

552

Brandade
BRANDADA (PURÉ DE BACALAO)

- **11 ounces salt cod fillet, soaked overnight as described on page 448**
- **¾ cup heavy cream**
- **triangles of fried bread (see recipe 130)**

Béchamel sauce:
- **5 tablespoons olive oil**
- **4 tablespoons all-purpose flour**
- **1 cup milk**
- **salt**

Serves 4

Drain the cod and remove any skin and bones and flake the flesh. Put it into a pan, pour in water to cover, and bring just to a boil. Remove the pan from the heat, cover, and let stand for 10 minutes. Drain the cod and process to a purée in a food processor or blender. Make the béchamel sauce as described in recipe 77, using the olive oil instead of a mixture of butter and oil. Stir the cod into the béchamel sauce, then stir in the cream, and heat through gently. Serve the purée immediately, garnished with fried bread triangles.

Note: Brandade or brandada is a salt cod purée that is much loved throughout Spain.

Red porgy

Red porgy is a mediterranean variety of Sea Bream. It is bigger than porgy (also known here as scup). If you cannot find red porgy, use the same weight of porgy, or other firm-fleshed fish such as hake, whiting or sea bass.

553

Red porgy baked with lemon juice, parsley and butter

BESUGO AL HORNO CON ZUMO DE LIMÓN, PEREJIL Y MANTEQUILLA

- **4 tablespoons sunflower oil**
- **1 red porgy (sea bream), about 3¼ pounds, trimmed, scaled, and cleaned**
- **1 sprig fresh parsley**
- **2 lemon slices**
- **juice of 1 lemon**
- **6 tablespoons (¾ stick) butter**
- **salt**

Serves 6

Preheat the oven to 375°F. Pour the oil into an ovenproof baking dish. Season the fish inside and outside with salt. Using a sharp knife, slash the fish diagonally once on either side, place the parsley in the cavity, and insert the lemon slices into the slashes. Put the fish into the dish, pour in the lemon juice, dot with the butter, and bake for 20–25 minutes. Serve immediately, straight from the dish.

554 Red porgy baked with garlic, parsley, and vinegar

BESUGO AL HORNO CON AJO, PEREJIL Y VINAGRE

- 1 cup olive oil
- 1 large potato, sliced
- 1 red porgy (sea bream), about 3¼ pounds, trimmed, scaled and cleaned
- 2–3 large sprigs fennel
- 3 tablespoons white-wine vinegar
- 3 cloves garlic, finely chopped
- 1 tablespoon chopped fresh parsley
- salt

Serves 6

Preheat the oven to 350°F. Heat the oil in a small skillet. Add the potato slices and cook, turning occasionally, for about 10 minutes, until softened but not browned. Remove with a spatula, lightly season with salt, and put into a large ovenproof baking dish. Reserve the oil. Season the fish inside and out with salt and reshape. Put one of the fennel sprigs in the cavity and put the fish in the dish. Insert one of the remaining fennel sprigs underneath it and place the other on top. Pour 2 tablespoons of the reserved oil over the fish and bake for about 10 minutes. Remove the dish from the oven and increase the oven temperature to 425°F. Remove and discard the fennel. Carefully pour half the vinegar inside the cavity, then sprinkle in half the garlic and half the parsley. Close the fish, pour the remaining vinegar over it, and sprinkle with the remaining garlic and parsley. Return to the oven for about 8 minutes, until the flesh flakes easily, and serve immediately straight from the dish.

555 Red porgy baked with white wine and bread crumbs

BESUGO AL HORNO CON VINO BLANCO Y PAN RALLADO

- 4 tablespoons olive oil
- ½ small onion, thinly sliced
- 1 red porgy (sea bream), about 3¼ pounds, trimmed, scaled, and cleaned
- ¾ cup white wine
- juice of 1 lemon
- 4 tablespoons bread crumbs
- ¼ cup (½ stick) butter
- salt

Serves 6

Preheat the oven to 375°F. Heat the oil in a stovetop-safe casserole. Add the onion and cook over low heat, stirring occasionally, for about 5 minutes, until softened and translucent. Remove the casserole from the heat and scoop the onion into the center. Season the fish inside and out with salt and slash twice with a sharp knife. Place on top of the onion. Mix the wine with 5 tablespoons water in a bowl and pour it over the fish. Add the lemon juice, sprinkle with the bread crumbs, and dot with the butter, making sure that there is a large piece in each slash. Bake the fish, basting occasionally, for about 20 minutes, until the flesh flakes easily. Serve immediately straight from the dish.

Broiled red porgy with mayonnaise sauce

BESUGO A LA PARRILLA CON SALSA MAYONESA

- 1 red porgy (sea bream), about
  3¼ pounds, trimmed, scaled,
  and cleaned
- 2 thin slices bacon, halved
- olive oil, for brushing
- 2 sprigs fresh fennel or thyme
- salt

  Mayonnaise sauce:
- 1 egg
- 1 cup sunflower oil
- juice of ½ lemon
- 1 tablespoon capers,
  rinsed, drained and chopped
- 2 canned anchovy fillets,
  drained and chopped
- 1 teaspoon chopped
  fresh parsley
- salt

Serves 6

Preheat the broiler. To make the sauce, first make a mayonnaise with the egg, oil, lemon juice, and salt in a food processor or blender as described in recipe 107. Transfer to a bowl and stir in the capers, anchovies, and parsley. Cover and leave in the refrigerator. Slash the fish twice on each side with a sharp knife. Season with salt and put a piece of bacon into each of the slashes. Brush the fish all over with oil and brush the broiler rack with oil. Put the fennel or thyme sprigs into the cavity of the fish and broil, turning the fish and brushing it with more oil occasionally, for 15 minutes, until the flesh flakes easily. Serve immediately with the mayonnaise sauce offered separately.

Bonito

As bonito is closely related to tuna, the same recipes can be used for both fish (see recipe 541).

557

Bonito with onion and tomato

BONITO CON CEBOLLA Y TOMATE

- **6 tablespoons olive oil**
- **2 large onions, chopped**
- **1 teaspoon all-purpose flour**
- **1 pound 10 ounces ripe tomatoes, peeled, seeded, and chopped**
- **¾ cup white wine**
- **pinch of dried mixed herbs or 2 bay leaves or 1 sprig fresh thyme**
- **2½ pounds thick bonito fillets**
- **salt**

Serves 6

Heat the oil in a large skillet. Add the onion and cook over low heat, stirring occasionally, for about 5 minutes, until softened and translucent. Stir in the flour and cook, stirring constantly, for 2 minutes. Add the tomato and cook, stirring occasionally and breaking it up with the side of the spoon, for 5 minutes. Pour in the wine, add the herbs, season, and cook for about 15 minutes. Add the bonito, cover, and cook over low heat for 10 minutes more. Serve immediately.

558

- ½ cup olive oil
- 3 large onions, finely chopped
- 2 bonito fillets,
  about 2½ pounds total weight
- ¾ cup white wine
- 1 bay leaf
- salt

Serves 6

Bonito with onion and white wine

BONITO CON CEBOLLA Y VINO BLANCO

Heat the oil in a skillet. Add the onion and cook over low heat, stirring occasionally, for 5 minutes, until softened and translucent. Place the bonito fillets on top, season with salt, and pour in the wine. Add the bay leaf, cover, and cook over low heat, shaking the skillet occasionally, for 15 minutes. If necessary, add a little water during the cooking. Transfer the fish to a warm serving dish, top with the onion, and serve.

559

- 3¼-pound bonito tail
- 6 slices smoked bacon
- 5 tablespoons olive oil
- 1 onion, chopped
- 2 carrots, thinly sliced
- 1 cup white wine
- 1 sprig fresh thyme
- cooked potatoes (optional)
- salt

Serves 6

Bonito cooked with bacon

BONITO ASADO CON BACON

Ask your fishmonger to fillet the fish or do it yourself: remove and discard the skin from the bonito. Cut out the backbone and remove any other bones, then put the two fillets back together. Lightly season with salt and cover the fish with the bacon. Tie together in several places with kitchen string, rather like a rolled roast. Heat the oil in a large pan. Add the onion and carrot and cook over low heat, stirring occasionally, for 5 minutes. Add the fish and cook, turning once, for a few minutes, until lightly browned on both sides. Pour in the wine, add the thyme, cover, and cook, stirring occasionally, for 25 minutes. Lift out the fish and remove the string and bacon. Remove and discard the thyme and stir in a little water if the sauce seems too thick. Heat well, then pass the sauce through a food mill into a bowl. Cut the fish into slices like meat and serve it with the sauce on top. Garnish with a few cooked potatoes if you like.

Note: If there is any fish left over, flake it and mix with a thin béchamel sauce (see recipe 77). Put it into an ovenproof baking dish, sprinkle with grated cheese, and dot with butter. Bake in a preheated oven, 400°F, for 10–15 minutes, until golden and serve immediately straight from the dish.

560

Roasted bonito with green mayonnaise
BONITO ASADO CON MAYONESA VERDE

- 2½ pounds bonito
- 5 tablespoons olive oil
- 3 tablespoons white wine
- 3 sprigs fresh parsley
- salt

Green mayonnaise:
- 2 eggs
- juice of ½ lemon
- scant 2 cups sunflower oil
- 1 teaspoon chopped
  fresh parsley
- 2 tablespoons capers, rinsed,
  drained and coarsely chopped
- 2 small pickled gherkins,
  coarsely chopped
- salt

Serves 6

Preheat the oven to 400°F. Make the green mayonnaise as descibed in recipe 107, and set aside in a cool place or in the refrigerator. Season the bonito with salt and brush both sides with the oil. Put the fish into a roasting pan and pour the white wine over it. Roast, basting occasionally and turning once, for 20 minutes, until golden brown. Transfer to a warm serving dish, garnish with the parsley sprigs, and serve with the green mayonnaise.

561

Fried bonito with green mayonnaise
BONITO EMPANADO CON MAYONESA VERDE

- 2 eggs
- 2 cups bread crumbs
- sunflower oil, for deep-frying
- 2½ pounds thin bonito fillets
- salt
- sprigs fresh parsley

Green mayonnaise:
- 4 eggs
- juice of 1 lemon
- 3¾ cups sunflower oil
- 2 teaspoons chopped
  fresh parsley
- 4 tablespoons capers, rinsed,
  drained and coarsely chopped
- 4 small pickled gherkins,
  coarsely chopped
- salt
  Serves 6

Make the green mayonnaise as described in recipe 107, and set aside in a cool place or in the refrigerator. Beat the eggs in a shallow dish and pour the bread crumbs into another shallow dish. Heat the oil in a deep-fryer or deep skillet to 350–375°F or until a cube of day-old bread browns in 30 seconds. Lightly season the fish with salt and coat first in the beaten egg, and then in the bread crumbs, gently pressing them into place. Add the fish to the skillet, in batches, and cook until golden brown. Remove from the skillet, drain, and keep warm while you cook the remaining batches. Garnish with the parsley and serve immediately, offering the green mayonnaise separately.

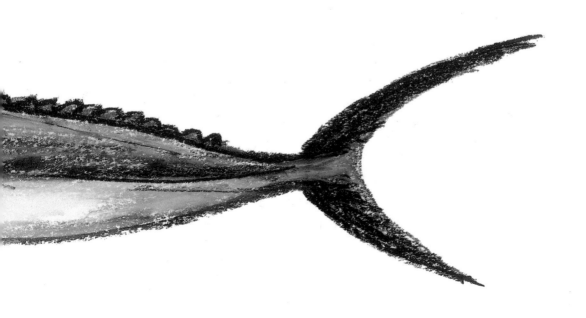

Bonito marmitako

MARMITAKO DE BONITO

- **4 tablespoons olive oil**
- **14 ounces bonito fillet,**
  cut into ¾-inch cubes
- **1 large onion, finely chopped**
- **2 tomatoes,**
  peeled, seeded, and chopped
- **2¼ pounds potatoes,**
  thickly sliced
- **2 cloves garlic**
- **2 sprigs fresh parsley**
- **1 bay leaf**
- **½ chile,**
  seeded and finely chopped
- **1 fish or vegetable bouillon cube**
- **scant 1 cup drained canned peas**
- **3½ ounces canned red bell**
  peppers, drained, and diced
- **salt**

Serves 6–8

Heat the oil in a stovetop-safe casserole. Add the bonito and cook, stirring frequently, for 2–3 minutes, until lightly browned. Remove from the casserole with a slotted spoon and set aside. Add the onion to the casserole and cook over low heat, stirring occasionally, for about 8 minutes, until lightly browned. Add the tomato and cook, stirring occasionally, for 5 minutes more, then add the potato slices, and pour in water to cover. Season with salt and bring to a boil, then lower the heat. Pound the garlic with the parsley and a pinch of salt in a mortar, or process in a mini-food processor. Mix in 2 tablespoons of the cooking liquid, then add to the casserole along with the bay leaf and chile. Mix well and cook over low heat for 30 minutes. Crumble in the bouillon cube, add the peas, bell peppers, and bonito, and cook for 10 minutes more. Remove and discard the bay leaf and serve the marmitako straight from the casserole.

Note: Marmitako is a Basque word meaning 'from the pot'.

563

Cold bonito loaf
PASTEL DE BONITO FRÍO

- 2¼ pounds bonito fillets
- 6 tablespoons bread crumbs
- 1 egg, lightly beaten
- ¾ cup sherry or other sweet
  fortified wine
- 1 thick slice Serrano ham
  or other dry-cured ham,
  cut lengthwise into ¼-inch
  wide strips
- 1 thick slice of bacon,
  cut lengthwise into
  ¼-inch wide strips
- salt and pepper

Quick stock:
- 2 bay leaves
- ½ small onion, halved
- 5 tablespoons white wine
- salt

Serves 6–8

Chop the bonito fillets and put into a bowl. Sprinkle with the bread crumbs, add the egg and sherry, and season with salt and pepper. Using your hands, mix together well, then spread out the mixture into a rectangle on a clean dishtowel. Top with alternating strips of ham and bacon. Using the dishtowel to help, roll up the mixture, then wrap the dishtowel around it, and tie at both ends. Put the roll into a pan. Pour in water to cover, add all the quick stock ingredients, and season with salt. Bring to a boil, then lower the heat, cover, and cook for 45 minutes. Drain off the stock and transfer the roll, still wrapped in the dishtowel, to a flat dish. Place a weight, such as a cutting board, on top and let stand in the refrigerator for at least 2 hours. Remove the dishtowel and cut the loaf into slices. Serve garnished with lettuce and tomato.

564

Cold bonito pie
BUDÍN DE BONITO FRÍO

- 1 pound 10 ounces potatoes,
  unpeeled
- 3 tablespoons olive oil,
  plus extra for brushing
- 1 onion, finely chopped
- 7 ounces canned chunk light
  tuna (bonito) in oil, drained
- 1 tablespoon tomato paste
- tomato slices and lettuce
  or shrimp (optional)
- 1 quantity Classic Mayonnaise
  (see recipe 105)
- salt

Serves 6

Put the potatoes into a pan, pour in water to cover, and add a pinch of salt. Bring to a boil, then lower the heat, and simmer for about 30 minutes, until tender. Meanwhile, heat the oil in a skillet. Add the on-ion and cook over low heat, stirring occasionally, for 5 minutes, until softened and translucent. Mash the tuna in a bowl and mix with the tomato paste. Drain the potatoes, then peel, and mash them. Stir in the tuna mixture and onion, together with the oil from the skillet, and mix well. Brush a loaf pan with oil and spoon in the mixture, pressing it down with the back of the spoon to eliminate any air pockets. Chill in the refrigerator for at least 4 hours. Run a round-bladed knife around the edge of the pan and turn the pie out onto a serving dish. Garnish with slices of tomato and lettuce or shrimp, if you like, and serve, offering the mayonnaise separately.

565

Bonito in aspic with mayonnaise
ASPIC DE BONITO CON MAYONESA

- 1 envelope fish aspic
  gelatin powder
- 5 ounces canned peas, drained
- 3½ ounces canned red bell
  peppers, drained
- 11 ounces canned chunk light
  tuna (bonito) in oil, drained
- 2 hard-cooked eggs, chopped
- 1 onion, finely chopped
- tomato slices and lettuce leaves

  Mayonnaise:
- 1 egg
- 1 cup sunflower oil
- juice of ½ lemon
- ½ teaspoon mustard
- salt

Serves 6–8

Make the mayonnaise in a food processor or blender as described in recipe 106, and set aside in a cool place or the refrigerator. Dissolve the aspic powder according to the instructions on the package but use only half the quantity of water. Pour a thin layer of aspic into a tart pan. Put some of the peas in a ring around the edge of the pan. Cut two strips of bell pepper and put them in an X in the middle of the pan. Chill in the refrigerator until set. Put the remaining aspic in a cool place but not the refrigerator. Dice the remaining bell peppers. Flake the tuna, and mix it with the hard-cooked eggs, onion, the remaining peas, and the diced bell peppers in a bowl. Stir in the mayonnaise and the cooled aspic. Mix well, then pour into the tart pan, and chill in the refrigerator for at least 2 hours. To serve, run a round-bladed knife around the edge of the pan and turn the aspic out onto a round serving dish. Garnish with slices of tomato and a few lettuce leaves.

566

Mackerel with garlic sauce and lemon juice
CABALLA CON SALSA DE AJO Y ZUMO DE LIMÓN

- 6 mackerel, about 14 ounces
  each, cleaned and boned
- 1 cup olive oil
- ¾ cup all-purpose flour
- 4 cloves garlic, lightly crushed
- 2 bay leaves
- ½ lemon, sliced
- juice of 1½ lemons
- salt

Serves 6

Season the mackerel inside and out with salt. Heat the oil in a skillet. Coat the mackerel, two at a time, in the flour, shaking off the excess, add to the skillet, and cook for about 5 minutes on each side until golden brown. Remove from the skillet and place in a single layer in an ovenproof baking dish. Preheat the oven to 350°F. Drain off all but 5–6 tablespoons of the oil from the skillet and reheat. Add the garlic and cook, stirring frequently, for a few minutes, until beginning to brown, then add the bay leaves, and cook for a few minutes more. Add the lemon slices and heat well, then remove the skillet from the heat, and stir in the lemon juice and ¾ cup water. Strain the sauce over the mackerel and warm through in the oven for about 5 minutes. Serve hot.

567

Mackerel fillets with mustard sauce

FILETES DE CABALLA CON SALSA DE MOSTAZA

- 12 mackerel fillets
- 5 tablespoons butter
- 1 tablespoon sunflower oil
- 1 tablespoon all-purpose flour
- 2¼ cups milk
- 3 tablespoons Bordeaux,
  Dijon or tarragon mustard
- juice of ½ lemon
- 1 tablespoon chopped
  fresh parsley
- salt

Serves 6

Preheat the oven to 350°F. Put the mackerel fillets in a single layer in a large ovenproof baking dish. Make the mustard sauce. Melt 1½ tablespoons of the butter with the oil in a pan. Stir in the flour and cook, stirring constantly, for 2 minutes. Gradually stir in the milk, a little at a time. Cook, stirring constantly, for about 10 minutes, until thickened. Remove the pan from the heat, stir in the mustard and lemon juice, and season to taste with salt. Pour the sauce over the mackerel fillets, sprinkle with the parsley, and dot with the remaining butter. Bake for 10–15 minutes, then serve straight from the dish.

Squid

How to clean

Pull the head away from the body—the intestines will come away at the same time. Cut away the ink sac, if required, from among the intestines and put it in a bowl of water. Cut off the tentacles from the head, if using, and squeeze out the beak. Discard the head and beak. Remove and discard the transparent quill from the body sac and remove any remaining membrane. Rinse well under cold running water and peel off the skin. Pat dry.

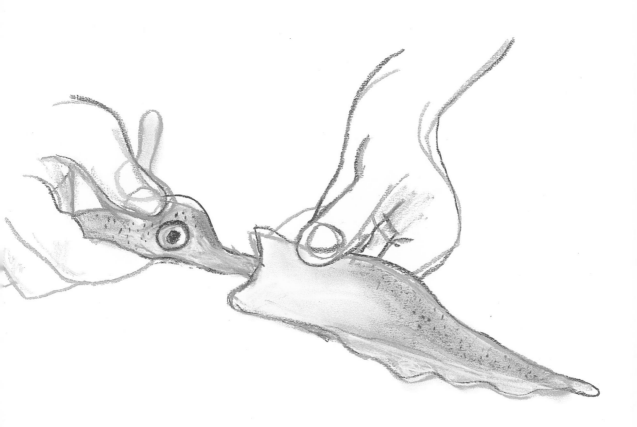

568

- 4 tablespoons all-purpose flour, plus extra for dusting
- 1 cup club soda
- sunflower oil, for deep-frying
- 2½ pounds squid, cleaned and cut into ½-inch wide rings
- 1 lemon, cut into wedges
- salt

Serves 6

Calamari

CALAMARES FRITOS ENVUELTOS

Sift the flour with a pinch of salt into a bowl. Gradually stir in the club soda, a little at a time, to make a thick batter. Heat the oil in a deep-fryer or saucepan to 350–375°F or until a cube of day-old bread browns in 30 seconds. Dust the squid rings with flour, shaking off the excess, then dip them into the batter to coat. Add them to the hot oil, in batches, and cook until golden brown. Remove with a slotted spoon, drain well, and keep warm while you cook the remaining batches. Serve with the lemon wedges.

Note: A pinch of saffron powder added to the batter of these squid rings gives it a nicer color.

569

- 2½ pounds squid, cleaned and cut into ½-inch wide rings
- ¾ cup all-purpose flour
- sunflower oil, for deep-frying
- lemon wedges
- salt

Serves 6

Simple fried squid

CALAMARES FRITOS SENCILLOS

Lightly season the squid rings with salt and coat them in the flour, shaking off the excess. Heat the oil in a deep-fryer or saucepan to 350–375°F or until a cube of day-old bread browns in 30 seconds. Add the squid rings, in batches, and cook until golden brown. Remove with a slotted spoon, drain well, and keep warm while you cook the remaining batches. Serve garnished with lemon wedges.

Note: This dish can be made with bread crumbs added to the flour.

Squid in its ink with rice (first version)

CALAMARES EN SU TINTA CON ARROZ BLANCO

- 2 ¼ pounds small squid, cleaned with their ink sacs reserved
- ¾ cup red wine
- 5 tablespoons olive oil
- 1 onion, chopped
- 1 tomato, peeled, seeded, and chopped
- 1 tablespoon all-purpose flour
- 1 cup sunflower oil
- 1 slice of bread, crusts removed
- 1 sprig fresh parsley
- 1 clove garlic
- 1 bag squid ink
- 2 cups long-grain rice
- 3 tablespoons butter
- salt

Serves 6

Put the ink sacs into a bowl with half the red wine. Leave the squid body sacs whole if they are very small or cut into pieces if larger. Heat the olive oil in a skillet. Add the onion and cook over low heat, stirring occasionally for about 10 minutes, until lightly browned. Add the tomato and cook, stirring occasionally, for 5 minutes more. Stir in the flour and cook, stirring constantly, for 2 minutes. Gradually stir in 2 ¼ cups water, a little at a time. Heat the sunflower oil in another skillet. Add the bread, parsley, and garlic and cook, stirring and turning the bread, for a few minutes, until golden brown. Transfer the fried bread, parsley, and garlic to a mortar and pound together, or process in a mini-food processor, then add to the onion and tomato mixture. Stir in the remaining red wine. Use the back of a spoon to mash the ink sacs into the wine, stir in the bag of ink, and pour the mixture into the skillet. Add the squid before the sauce comes to a boil and simmer over low heat for 1 ½ – 2 hours. Cook and refresh the rice as described in recipe 173, frying it in the butter afterward. Spoon it into a ring mold and turn out onto a warm serving dish. Season the squid to taste with salt and spoon it and its sauce into the middle of the rice. Serve immediately. Alternatively, serve the rice on the side.

Note: To prepare this recipe using small squid or cuttlefish, allow 4–6 squid/cuttlefish per serving, depending on size. Clean the squid, chop the tentacles, and use them to stuff the body sacs, then prepare and cook as in the recipe above.

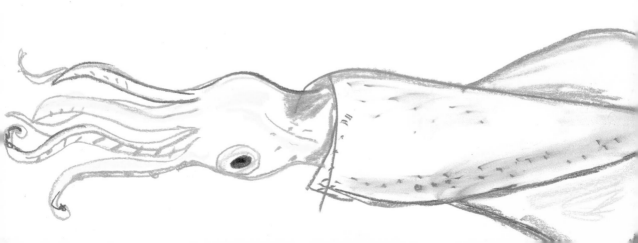

571

Squid in its ink with rice (second version)

CALAMARES EN SU TINTA CON ARROZ BLANCO

- 2 ¼ pounds small squid,
  cleaned with their ink
  sacs reserved in water
- ¾ cup olive oil
- 2 ¼ pounds onions,
  finely chopped
- 1 clove garlic, finely chopped
- 2 sprigs fresh parsley
- 1 bag squid ink
- 2 tablespoons Classic Tomato
  Sauce (see recipe 73)
- 5 tablespoons white wine
- 1 tablespoon bread crumbs
  (optional)
- salt

Serves 6

Leave the squid body sacs whole if they are very small or cut into pieces if larger. Put the oil, onion, and garlic into a stovetop-safe casserole and heat gently. Cook over very low heat, stirring occasionally, for about 10 minutes, until softened but not colored. Add the squid and cook, stirring occasionally, for 15 minutes. Meanwhile, crush the ink sacs with the parsley and stir in the bag of ink. Pour the mixture into the pan, and add the tomato sauce and wine. Simmer gently for about 10 minutes. If the sauce seems too thin, stir in the bread crumbs to thicken. Season to taste with salt and serve.

Note: To prepare this recipe using small squid or cuttlefish, allow 4–6 squid/cuttlefish per serving, depending on size. Clean the squid, chop the tentacles, and use them to stuff the body sacs, then prepare and cook as in the recipe above.

572

Stuffed squid

CALAMARES RELLENOS

- 6–8 squid, about 2 ½ ounces
  each, cleaned
- 11 ounces lean pork, ground
- 2 hard-cooked eggs, chopped
- 1 cup olive oil
- 1 tablespoon all-purpose flour,
  plus extra for dusting
- 1 onion, finely chopped
- 5 tablespoons white wine
- 1 sprig fresh parsley
- very small pinch of saffron
  powder
- salt

Serves 6

Finely chop the squid tentacles and leave the body sacs whole. Combine the chopped squid, pork, and hard-cooked eggs in a bowl. Divide the mixture among the body sacs, but do not overfill them or they will burst during cooking. Secure with trussing thread or wooden toothpicks. Heat ⅔ cup of the oil in a skillet. Dust the squid with flour and add them to the pan, two at a time, and cook, turning occasionally, for a few minutes, until lightly browned. Remove from the pan and set aside. Heat the remaining oil in a pan. Add the onion and cook over low heat, stirring occasionally, for about 8 minutes, until beginning to brown. Stir in the flour and cook, stirring constantly, for 5 minutes, until lightly colored. Gradually stir in the wine and 4 cups water and add the parsley and saffron. Add the squid to the pan, cover, and cook over low heat for 1 hour. Season to taste with salt. Remove and discard the trussing thread or toothpicks and serve the squid in a warm deep dish with the sauce.

Pomfrets

European (mediterranean) pomfret is not readily available in the US, but the similar pacific pomfret is available. You could also use butterfish, a tiny fish similar in flavor and texture to European pomfret, You will need 4–6 per person. Remove the head and tails and rub off the scales. Reduce the cooking time if using smaller fish.

573

Baked pomfret fillets

FILETES DE CASTAÑOLA AL HORNO

- 1 small pomfret, 1 pound
  10 ounces–2¼ pounds, cleaned,
  filleted, and skinned
- ¾ cup sunflower oil
- 5 tablespoons white wine
- 1 large onion, finely chopped
- 1 tablespoon chopped
  fresh parsley
- salt

Serves 6–8

Preheat the oven to 350°F. Put the fish fillets into an ovenproof baking dish in a single layer, season with salt, and pour the oil and wine over them. Combine the onion and parsley and sprinkle a little over each fillet. Bake for about 20 minutes, until the flesh flakes easily, and serve immediately straight from the dish.

574

Pomfret fillets with onions and tomatoes
FILETES DE CASTAÑOLA CON CEBOLLA Y TOMATE

- 6 tablespoons olive oil
- 2 onions, very finely chopped
- 1 clove garlic
- 3 large ripe tomatoes,
  peeled, seeded, and chopped
- ½ teaspoon sugar
- 1 pomfret, 1 pound 10 ounces–
  2¼ pounds, cleaned,
  filleted, and skinned
- ¾ cup white wine
- 1 sprig fresh thyme
  or 2 bay leaves
- salt

Serves 4

Heat the oil in a large skillet. Add the onion and cook over low heat, stirring occasionally, for 5–6 minutes, until softened and translucent. Add the garlic, tomato, and sugar and cook, stirring occasionally and breaking up the tomato with the side of the spoon, for 10 minutes. Add the pomfret fillets, wine, and thyme sprig or bay leaves and season with salt. Cover and simmer gently, adding a little water if necessary, for about 20 minutes, until the fish flakes easily. Remove and discard the thyme sprig or bay leaves and garlic and serve im-mediately.

Note: This dish can be made in advance and reheated before serving.

575

Dentex in sauce
DENTÓN EN SALSA

- 3 cups sunflower oil
- 6 x 5-ounce slices dentex, red
  porgy (sea bream), or snapper
- 1 tablespoon all-purpose flour,
  plus extra for dusting
- 1 onion, chopped
- 2 cloves garlic
- pinch of saffron threads
- 2¼ cups fish stock
  (home-made or canned)
- 1 tablespoon chopped
  fresh parsley
- scant 1 cup drained canned peas
- 1 bay leaf
- salt

Serves 6

Reserve 3 tablespoons of the oil and heat the remainder in a skillet. Season the fish with salt on both sides and dust with flour. Add the fish to the skillet and cook for 4–5 minutes, until golden brown. Transfer the fish to a stovetop-safe casserole. Heat the reserved oil in a small skillet. Add the onion and garlic and cook over low heat, stirring occasionally, for about 10 minutes, until lightly browned. Remove the skillet from the heat. Pound the onion and garlic with the saffron and a pinch of salt in a mortar, or process in a mini-food processor. Mix in 2 tablespoons of the stock, and pass the mixture through a vegetable mill into a bowl. Return the skillet to the heat and stir in the flour. Cook, stirring constantly, for 2 minutes. Gradually stir in the remaining fish stock, a little at a time, and strain in the mixture from the mortar. Cook, stirring constantly, for 2 minutes, season to taste with salt, and pour the sauce over the fish. Sprinkle with the parsley, add the peas and bay leaf, and cook over medium heat, gently shaking the casserole occasionally, for 10 minutes. Remove and discard the bay leaf and serve immediately, straight from the casserole.

Note: See also recipes for sea bream (553–556) for alternative ways to prepare dentex.

Sole

How to prepare

To prevent the fillets shrinking, once they have been removed from the fish, hold them by one end and gently bang both sides onto a work surface. A thin-bodied European fish, John Dory is similar to pomfret and butterfish. Although not a flat fish, it is often prepared in the same way as sole. It has a similar flavor and texture, but is not quite such good quality.

Sole fillets with spinach, béchamel sauce, and langoustines

FILETES DE LENGUADO CON ESPINACAS, BECHAMEL Y LANGOSTINOS

- 3–4 sole, about 11 ounces each, cleaned, filleted, and skinned, trimmings reserved
- 1 pound 10 ounces unpeeled langoustines or lobsterettes
- 4½ pounds spinach, coarse stalks removed
- ¼ cup (½ stick) butter, plus extra for greasing
- ½ cup grated gruyere or Parmesan cheese
- salt

Quick stock:
- 1 bay leaf
- 1 thick slice of onion
- 1 large carrot, sliced
- ¾ cup white wine
- juice of ½ lemon
- salt

Béchamel sauce:
- 2 tablespoons (¼ stick) butter
- 3 tablespoons sunflower oil
- 1 tablespoon all-purpose flour
- ½ cup milk
- small pinch of curry powder (optional)
- salt

Serves 6

Make the quick stock in advance as described in recipe 534. Remove the rack from a fish poacher, put the fish trimmings on the base, and pour in the stock. Fold the sole fillets in half and put them on the rack with the langoustines. Replace the rack and bring the stock just to a boil. Remove the fish poacher from the heat and lift the rack to rest diagonally across the top so that the fish and shellfish drain. Strain and reserve ½ cup of the stock. Meanwhile, put the spinach into a large pan with just the water clinging to its leaves after washing. Add a pinch of salt and cook for 8–10 minutes, until tender. Drain well, pressing out as much liquid as possible with the back of a spoon. Chop coarsely. Melt the butter in a pan. Add the spinach and cook, stirring frequently, for 5 minutes. Grease an ovenproof baking dish with butter and spoon the spinach over the base. Place the fish fillets on top. Peel the langoustines and put them in the dish. Preheat the oven to 400°F. Make the béchamel sauce. Melt the butter with the oil in a pan. Stir in the flour and cook, stirring constantly, for 2 minutes. Gradually stir in the milk and reserved stock. Cook, stirring constantly, for about 10 minutes, until thickened. Season to taste with salt and stir in the curry powder, if using. Pour the sauce over the fish, sprinkle with the gruyere, and bake for 15–20 minutes, until golden brown. Serve immediately, straight from the dish.

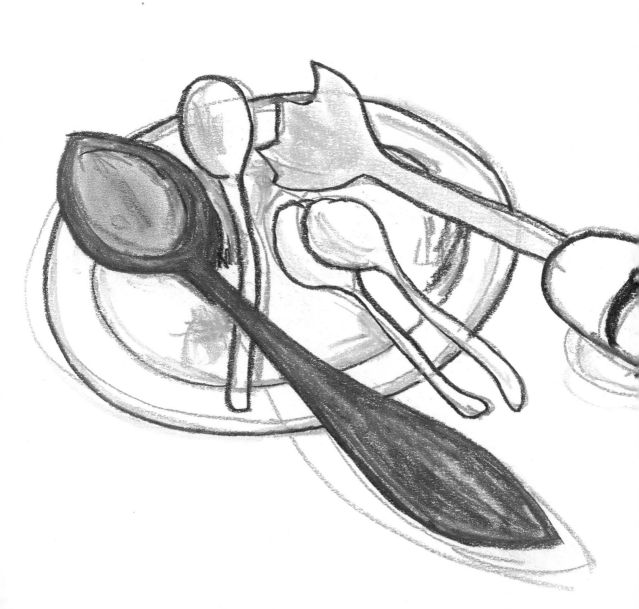

577

Sole fillets in whiskey
FILETES DE LENGUADO AL WHISKY

- 3 sole, about 12 ounces each, cleaned, filleted, and skinned, trimmings reserved
- ¼ cup (½ stick) butter, plus extra for greasing
- 2 cups sliced mushrooms
- juice of ½ lemon
- 2 tablespoons sunflower oil
- 1 tablespoon all-purpose flour
- 3 tablespoons whiskey
- 2 egg yolks
- scant 1 cup heavy cream
- pinch of curry powder
- ¼ grated cup gruyere cheese
- salt

Quick stock
- 1 bay leaf
- 1 thick slice onion
- 1 large carrot, sliced
- ¾ cup white wine
- juice of ½ lemon
- salt

Serves 6

Make the quick stock as described in recipe 534. Remove the rack from a fish poacher, pour in half the stock, and set aside to cool. Put the fish trimmings in a pan, add the remaining stock, and bring to a boil. Lower the heat and simmer for 35 minutes, then remove the pan from the heat, and strain into a bowl. Put the sole fillets on the rack of the fish poacher and replace the rack. Bring the stock to a boil, then remove the poacher from the heat. Lift the rack to rest diagonally across the top of the fish poacher so that the fish can drain. Grease an ovenproof baking dish with butter, put the sole fillets in it, and cover with a dishtowel wrung out in hot water, or with aluminum foil to keep them warm. Put the mushrooms, 1½ tablespoons of the butter, the lemon juice, and a pinch of salt into a pan. Cook over low heat for 6 minutes, then set aside. Preheat the oven to 400°F. Melt the remaining butter with the oil in a pan. Stir in the flour and cook, stirring constantly, for 2 minutes. Gradually stir in scant 2 cups of the strained concentrated stock, a little at a time. Cook, stirring constantly, for 5 minutes, add the whiskey, and cook, still stirring for 3–4 minutes more, until thickened. Add the mushrooms and their cooking juices. Remove the pan from the heat. Mix the egg yolks with the cream in a bowl and stir into the sauce, then add the curry powder, and season to taste with salt. Pour the sauce over the fish, sprinkle with the gruyere, and bake for about 15 minutes, until golden brown. Serve immediately.

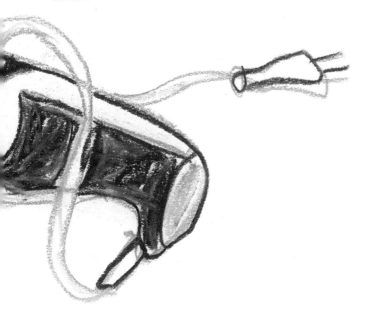

578

Sole fillets with béchamel sauce au gratin
FILETES DE LENGUADO CON BECHAMEL GRATINADA

- 9 ounces raw shrimp, shells on and heads attached, if available
- 3 large sole, 12–14 ounces each, cleaned, filleted, and skinned, trimmings reserved
- 2 tablespoons (¼ stick) butter
- 2 tablespoons sunflower oil
- 1 heaping tablespoon all-purpose flour
- generous 1 cup milk
- pinch of curry powder (optional)
- 2 egg yolks
- ⅔ cup grated gruyere cheese
- salt

Serves 6

Peel the shrimp, reserving the shells and heads, if attached. Set the shrimp tails aside. Put the shells and heads, if using, with the trimmings from the sole in a pan, pour in water to cover, and add a pinch of salt. Bring to a boil, then lower the heat, and simmer for 5 minutes. Strain the stock into a bowl, pressing down on the contents of the strainer to extract all the liquid. Lightly season the sole fillets with salt, fold them in half, and put into an ovenproof baking dish in a single layer. Preheat the oven to 350°F. Melt the butter with the oil in a pan. Stir in the flour and cook, stirring constantly, for 2 minutes. Gradually stir in the milk, a little at a time, then stir in generous 1 cup of the shrimp and fish stock. Cook, stirring constantly, for about 10 minutes, until thickened. Add the shrimp and cook, stirring constantly, for 5 minutes more. Season to taste with salt and stir in the curry powder, if using. Lightly beat the egg yolks in a bowl and stir in a little of the béchamel sauce to prevent them curdling, then stir them into the sauce. Pour the sauce over the fish fillets, sprinkle with the gruyere, and bake for 10 minutes. Increase the oven temperature to broil and broil for 10 minutes more, until golden brown. Serve immediately, straight from the dish.

579

Sole fillets baked with white wine and chopped onions
FILETES DE LENGUADO AL HORNO, CON VINO BLANCO Y PICADITO DE CEBOLLAS

- Sole fillets baked with white wine and chopped onions
- 2 large sole, 12–14 ounces each, cleaned, filleted, and skinned, trimmings reserved
- ¾ cup sunflower oil
- ¾ cup white wine
- 1 small onion, finely chopped
- 1 tablespoon finely chopped fresh parsley
- ½ teaspoon dried mixed herbs
- salt

Serves 4

Put the fish trimmings into a pan, pour in just enough water to cover, and add a pinch of salt. Bring to a boil, then lower the heat, and cook for 30 minutes. Strain the stock into a bowl. Preheat the oven to 350°F. Pour ¼ cup of the oil into an ovenproof baking dish. Lightly season the sole fillets with salt and put them in the dish in a single layer. Pour the wine over them, then pour in the remaining oil. Combine the onion, parsley, and dried herbs in a bowl and sprinkle over the fish. Pour in ¾ cup of the fish stock and gently shake the dish to make sure it penetrates. Bake for 15–20 minutes, until the fish flakes easily. Serve immediately, straight from the dish.

Note: Grouper fillets can be used in place of sole in this dish but the cooking time should be increased slightly.

580

Baked sole fillets with tomato sauce, mushrooms, mussels, and grated cheese

FILETES DE LENGUADO AL HORNO CON SALSA DE TOMATE, CHAMPIÑONES, MEJILLONES Y QUESO RALLADO

- 1 quantity Classic Tomato Sauce (see recipe 73)
- 1 pound 2 ounces mussels
- ¾ cup white wine
- 1 bay leaf
- generous 2¾ cup sliced mushrooms
- 1½ tablespoons butter
- juice of ½ lemon
- 3 large sole, 12–14 ounces each, cleaned, filleted, and skinned
- ½ cup grated gruyere or Parmesan cheese
- salt

Serves 6

Strain the tomato sauce, and set aside. Preheat the oven to 400°F. If your mussels have not been pre-scrubbed, scrape their shells with the blade of a knife and remove the "beards," then scrub under cold running water. Discard any mussels with broken shells or any that do not shut immediately when sharply tapped. Put the mussels into a pan and add ¼ cup of the wine, ½ cup water, the bay leaf, and a pinch of salt. Cover and cook over medium heat, shaking the pan occasionally, for 4–5 minutes, until the shells have opened. Remove the mussels from the pan with a slotted spoon and discard any that remain shut. Strain the cooking liquid through a cheesecloth-lined strainer into a bowl. Remove the mussels from their shells and put them into the bowl. Put the mushrooms, butter, lemon juice, and a pinch of salt into a pan. Cover and cook over low heat for 8 minutes. Stir the mushrooms into the tomato sauce and add the remaining wine. Spoon a little sauce on to the base of an ovenproof baking dish and add the sole fillets in a single layer. Drain the mussels and put them on top of the fish in an even layer. Pour the remaining tomato sauce mixture over them, and sprinkle with the gruyere or Parmesan. Bake for about 10 minutes, until golden brown. Serve immediately, straight from the dish.

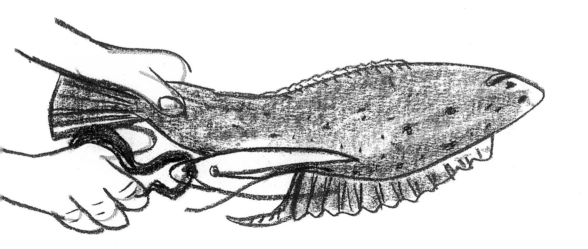

581

Sole fillets in tartlets with mushroom and béchamel sauce

CAZOLETAS DE FILETES DE LENGUADO CON CHAMPIÑONES Y BÉCHAMEL

- 2 large sole, 14 ounces–1 pound 2 ounces each, cleaned, filleted, and skinned, trimmings reserved
- 1 ⅔ cups sliced mushrooms
- 1½ tablespoons butter
- juice of ½ lemon
- 8 cooked tartlet shells (packaged or see recipe 1)
- 1 black truffle, sliced (optional)
- salt

Quick stock:
- 1 bay leaf
- 1 thick slice of onion
- 1 large carrot, sliced
- ¾ cup white wine
- juice of ½ lemon
- salt

Béchamel sauce:
- 2 tablespoons (¼ stick) butter
- 2 tablespoons sunflower oil
- 1 heaping tablespoon all-purpose flour
- 1 cup milk
- 2 egg yolks
- salt

Serves 8

Make the quick stock as described in recipe 534. Remove the rack from a fish poacher and pour in the cold stock. Loosely roll up the sole fillets and secure with wooden toothpicks. Place them on the rack and return it to the fish poacher. Bring to a boil, then lift out the fish, and transfer to a plate. Cover with a dishtowel wrung out in hot water or aluminum foil and keep warm. Add the fish trimmings to the stock and cook for 20 minutes. Strain and set aside. Put the mushrooms, butter, lemon juice, and a pinch of salt into a pan. Cover and cook over medium heat for 6 minutes. Remove from the heat and set aside. Preheat the oven to 350°F. Make the béchamel sauce. Melt the butter with the oil in a pan. Stir in the flour and cook, stirring constantly, for 2 minutes. Gradually stir in the milk, a little at a time, then stir in ⅔ cup of the strained concentrated stock. Cook, stirring constantly, for about 10 minutes, until thickened. Lightly beat the egg yolks in a bowl and gradually stir in some of the béchamel sauce to prevent them curdling, then add them to the pan. Drain the mushrooms and add to the sauce, then remove the pan from the heat. Season to taste with salt. Heat the tartlet shells in the oven for about 5 minutes or according to the instructions on the package. Remove and discard the toothpicks from the rolled fish fillets and place a roll in each tartlet shell. Pour in some of the béchamel sauce and place a slice of truffle on top of each one, if you like. Serve immediately.

Note: This dish can be served with or without the tartlet shells. If you are not using the tartlet shells, simply place the rolls of fish in an ovenproof baking dish, allowing at least two fillets per serving.

Sole fillets stuffed with ham in sauce

ROLLITOS DE FILETES DE LENGUADO RELLENOS CON JAMÓN EN SALSA

- **6 sole, 7 ounces each, cleaned, filleted, and skinned**
- **generous 1 cup chopped Serrano ham or prosciutto**
- **2 hard-cooked eggs, chopped**

Quick stock:
- **1 bay leaf**
- **1 thick slice of onion**
- **1 large carrot, sliced**
- **3 tablespoons white wine**
- **juice of ½ lemon**
- **salt**

Béchamel sauce:
- **2 tablespoons (¼ stick) butter**
- **2 tablespoons sunflower oil**
- **1 tablespoon all-purpose flour**
- **1 cup milk**
- **1 tablespoon chopped fresh parsley**
- **salt**

Serves 6

Make the quick stock as described in recipe 534, and let cool. Remove the rack from a fish poacher and pour in the cold stock. Loosely roll up the sole fillets and secure with wooden toothpicks. Place them on the rack and return it to the fish poacher. Bring to a boil over medium heat. Turn off the heat and lift the rack to rest diagonally across the fish poacher. Cover the sole fillets with a clean dishtowel wrung out in hot water to keep them warm. Make the béchamel sauce. Melt the butter with the oil in a pan. Stir in the flour and cook, stirring constantly, for 2 minutes. Gradually stir in the milk, a little at a time. Cook, stirring constantly, for 5 minutes, then stir in 1 cup of the quick stock, and cook, stirring constantly, for 5 minutes more. Season to taste with salt, remove the pan from the heat, and stir in the parsley. Remove and discard the toothpicks from the fish rolls and put the rolls on a warm dish. Fill the centers with the ham. Pour the béchamel sauce over the rolls and sprinkle with the hard-cooked eggs (this should be mostly yolk with just a little white). Serve immediately.

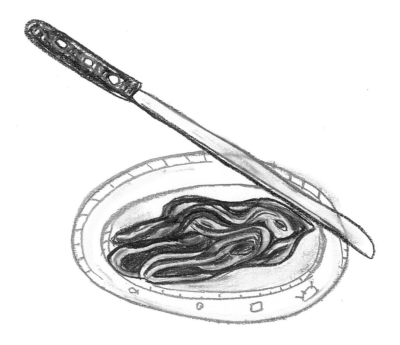

583

Sole fillets with rice

- 4 ounces mushrooms, finely chopped
- scant ½ cup (1 stick) butter
- a few drops of lemon juice
- ⅔ cup chopped Serrano or Smithfield ham, prosciutto, or other dry-cured ham
- 2½ cups long-grain rice
- pinch of saffron threads
- 3 large sole, 12–14 ounces each, cleaned, filleted, and skinned
- 2 tablespoons sunflower oil
- 1 heaping tablespoon all-purpose flour
- 1 cup milk
- salt

Quick stock:
- 1 bay leaf
- 1 thick slice onion
- 1 carrot, sliced
- 3 tablespoons white wine
- juice of ½ lemon
- salt

Serves 6

Make the quick stock as described in recipe 534, and let cool. Put the mushrooms, 1 tablespoon of the butter, the lemon juice, and a pinch of salt into a pan. Cover and cook over medium heat for 6 minutes. Add the ham, mix well, and set aside. Cook the rice and sauté in ¼ cup of the remaining butter as described in recipe 173, but do not add any peas. Put the rice into a tart pan, pressing down lightly, then turn out onto the center of a warm round serving dish, and keep warm. Remove the rack from a fish poacher and pour in the cold stock. Fold the sole fillets, put them on the rack, and return it to the fish poacher. Bring to a boil over medium heat. Turn off the heat, and lift the rack to rest diagonally across the fish poacher. Cover the sole fillets with a clean dishtowel wrung out in hot water, to keep them warm. Melt the remaining butter with the oil in a pan. Stir in the flour and cook, stirring constantly, for 2 minutes. Gradually stir in the milk, a little at a time. Cook, stirring constantly, for 5 minutes, then add about ⅔ cup of the quick stock and cook, stirring constantly, for a further 5 minutes. Season to taste with salt. Arrange the sole fillets around the edge of the rice on the serving dish. Use a spoon to fill the fillets with the mushroom mixture, then pour the béchamel sauce over them, and serve immediately.

584

Sole fritters

- sunflower oil, for deep-frying
- 3 large sole, 12–14 ounces each, cleaned, filleted, and skinned
- 1 quantity Fritter Batter (see recipe 58–60)
- 2 sprigs fresh parsley
- 1 quantity Classic Tomato Sauce (see recipe 73)
- salt

Serves 6

Heat the oil in a deep-fryer or deep skillet to 350–375°F or until a cube of day-old bread browns in 30 seconds. Lightly season the sole fillets with salt and dip them into the batter. Add them to the hot oil, in batches, and cook until golden brown. Remove with a slotted spoon, drain, and keep warm while you cook the remaining batches. Serve immediately, garnished with the parsley, and offer the tomato sauce, if using, separately.

585

Breaded sole fillets with rice and tomato sauce

FILETES DE LENGUADO EMPANADOS CON ARROZ BLANCO Y SALSA
DE TOMATE

- 2 eggs
- 1½ cups bread crumbs
- sunflower oil, for deep-frying
- 4 sole, about 7 ounces each,
  cleaned, filleted, and skinned
- 1 quantity Classic Tomato Sauce
  (see recipe 73)

Rice:
- 2½ cups long-grain rice
- ¼ cup (½ stick) butter
- salt

Serves 4–6

Cook the rice and refresh under cold running water as described in recipe 173. Beat the eggs in a shallow dish and pour the bread crumbs into another shallow dish. Heat the oil in a deep-fryer or deep skillet to 350–375°F or until a cube of day-old bread browns in 30 seconds. Dip the sole fillets first in the beaten egg and then in the bread crumbs, pressing them on well with your hands. Add to the hot oil, in batches, and cook until golden brown. Remove with a slotted spatula, drain, and keep warm while you cook the remaining batches. Heat the tomato sauce. Finish cooking the rice by sautéing in the butter as described in recipe 173, then put it into a tart pan, pressing down lightly. Turn out onto the center of a warm serving dish and place the breaded fish fillets around the edge. Pour 2 tablespoons of the tomato sauce over the rice and serve im-mediately, offering the rest of the tomato sauce separately.

586

Fried sole fillets with brandy and tomato mayonnaise

FILETES DE LENGUADO REBOZADOS Y FRITOS, SERVIDOS CON MAYONESA
DE COÑAC Y TOMATE

- 2 eggs
- ¾ cup all-purpose flour
- sunflower oil, for deep-frying
- 4 large sole, 11–14 ounces each,
  cleaned, filleted, and skinned
- salt
- 2 quantities Mayonnaise with
  Brandy and Tomato (see recipe
  108, but using ½ the mustard)

Serves 4–6

Beat the eggs in a shallow dish and pour the flour into another shallow dish. Heat the oil in a deep-fryer or deep skillet to 350–375°F or until a cube of day-old bread browns in 30 seconds. Lightly season the sole fillets with salt and coat them first in the flour, shaking off any excess, and then in the beaten eggs. Add to the hot oil, in batches, and cook until golden brown. Remove with a slotted spatula, drain, and keep warm while you cook the remaining batches. Serve immediately, offering the mayonnaise separately.

587

Sole with butter
LENGUADOS MOLINERA CON MANTEQUILLA

- sunflower oil, for deep-frying
- 6 sole, 5–7 ounces each, cleaned, filleted and skinned
- ½ cup all-purpose flour
- 2 tablespoons chopped fresh parsley
- lemon wedges
- ⅔ cup butter
- juice of 1 lemon, strained
- salt

Serves 6

Heat the oil in a deep-fryer or deep skillet to 350–375°F or until a cube of day-old bread browns in 30 seconds. Lightly season both sides of the sole with salt and coat them in flour, shaking off any excess. Add them to the hot oil, two at a time, and cook until golden brown. Remove with a fish slice and keep warm while you cook the remaining fish. Transfer the cooked fish to a warm serving dish, sprinkle with the parsley, and garnish with the lemon wedges. Melt the butter in a pan but do not let it brown. Remove the froth that rises to the surface with a spoon. Stir in the lemon juice and pour the hot butter over the fish. Serve immediately.

588

Baked sole with white wine
LENGUADO GRANDE ENTERO CON VINO BLANCO, AL HORNO

- 3 tablespoons sunflower oil
- 1 extra-large sole, about 3¼ pounds, or 2 large sole, about 1 pound 5 ounces each, cleaned and skinned
- juice of 1 lemon
- ¾ cup white wine
- ¼ teaspoon paprika (optional)
- 2 tablespoon bread crumbs
- 1 tablespoon chopped fresh parsley
- ¼ cup (½ stick) butter
- salt

Serves 6

Preheat the oven to 350°F. Pour the oil into a large ovenproof baking dish. Lightly season both sides of the sole with salt and place in the dish. Pour the lemon juice over the top, then the wine, and gently rub the paprika, if using, over the fish with your fingertips. Sprinkle with the bread crumbs and parsley and dot with the butter. Cover the dish with aluminum foil and bake for 15 minutes. Remove the aluminum foil and bake the fish for 5 minutes more. Serve immediately, straight from the dish.

Note: Grouper can be used in place of sole in this dish but the cooking time should be increased slightly.

589

Baked stuffed sea bass

LUBINA RELLENA AL HORNO

- 1 sea bass or grouper, about
  3 ¼ pounds, scaled, trimmed,
  cleaned, and boned
- 5 tablespoons sunflower oil
- juice of 1 lemon
- ¼ cup (½ stick) butter
- 1 small onion
- salt

Stuffing:
- 1 thick slice of bread,
  crusts removed
- ¾ cup hot milk
- 4 ounces mushrooms,
  finely chopped
- ½ tablespoon butter
- a few drops of lemon juice
- 2 tablespoons olive oil
- 1 small onion, finely chopped
- 1 teaspoon chopped
  fresh parsley
- 1 egg, lightly beaten
- salt

Serves 6

Season the fish inside and out with salt. Prepare the stuffing. Put the bread into a bowl, add the milk, and let soak. Meanwhile, put the mushrooms, butter, lemon juice, and a pinch of salt into a pan. Cover and cook over medium heat for about 6 minutes. Heat the olive oil in a skillet. Add the onion and cook over low heat, stirring occasionally, for about 8 minutes, until beginning to brown. Remove the pan from the heat. Preheat the oven to 350°F. Gently squeeze out the bread, if necessary, and put it into a bowl with the onion, mushrooms, parsley, egg, and a pinch of salt. Mix well and then use to fill the cavity of the fish. Sew up the opening with fine trussing thread, leaving a length hanging to help to pull out the stitches when the fish is ready to be served. Alternatively, secure the cavity with wooden toothpicks. Pour the sunflower oil into an ovenproof baking dish and add the fish. Slash the uppermost side twice without cutting into the flesh. Pour the lemon juice over the fish, sprinkle with salt, and place pats of butter under the fish. Bake, basting occasionally, for about 20 minutes, until the flesh flakes easily. Remove and discard the trussing thread or toothpicks and serve immediately.

590

Fried sea bass

LUBINAS DE RACIÓN FRITAS

- 6 sea bass or grouper,
  11–14 ounces each, scaled,
  trimmed, and cleaned
- sunflower oil, for deep-frying
- ½ cup all-purpose flour
- 2 tablespoons (¼ stick) butter
- juice of 1 lemon
- 1 tablespoon chopped
  fresh parsley
- salt

Serves 6

Slash the fish twice on both sides with a sharp knife. Season inside and out with salt. Heat the oil in a deep-fryer or deep skillet to 350–375°F or until a cube of day-old bread browns in 30 seconds. Coat the fish in the flour, shaking off the excess, add them, two at a time, to the hot oil and cook until golden brown. Transfer to a serving dish and keep warm while you cook the remaining fish. Drain off the oil from the skillet, add the butter, and melt over low heat. Remove the pan from the heat and stir in the lemon juice and parsley. Return the pan to the heat and warm through, stirring constantly. Pour the lemon butter over the fish and serve immediately.

Hake

Whiting can be used in place of hake in recipes 591, 592, 603, 604 and 605. If you can't find fillets of hake, ask your fishmonger to fillet the fish for you.

591

Cooked hake, served with mayonnaise, vinaigrette, or hollandaise sauce

MERLUZA COCIDA, SERVIDA CON SALSA MAYONESA, VINAGRETA U HOLANDESA

- 3¼–4½ pounds hake fillet, in a single piece
- sprigs fresh parsley and lemon slices

To serve:
- 1 quantity Classic Mayonnaise (see recipe 105) or Vinaigrette (see recipes 98–101) or Hollandaise Sauce (see recipe 84)

Quick stock:
- 1 large carrot, sliced
- 1 large onion, cut into 4 slices
- juice of ½ lemon
- 1 bay leaf
- ¾ cup white wine
- salt

Serves 6

Remove the rack from a fish poacher. Pour in 10 ⅔ cups water and add all the stock ingredients. Bring to a boil, then lower the heat, and simmer for 15 minutes. Remove the fish poacher from the heat and let the stock cool completely. Put the hake on the rack and replace the rack in the fish poacher so that the vegetables are underneath. Bring to a boil over medium heat, then lower the heat, and simmer very gently for 15–17 minutes, until the flesh flakes easily. Lift the rack to rest diagonally on top of the fish poacher and cover the hake with a clean dishtowel wrung out in hot water, to keep it warm. Let drain for 5–10 minutes. Place a folded napkin in the base of a serving dish, put the hake onto it, and garnish with parsley sprigs and lemon slices. Serve with your chosen sauce.

592

Hake baked with tomatoes and cheese
COLA DE MERLUZA AL HORNO, CON TOMATES Y QUESO RALLADO

- **1 hake tail,**
  about 3¼ pounds, boned
- **¼ cup (½ stick) butter**
- **1¼ cups grated gruyere cheese**
- **3 tablespoons sunflower oil**
- **4 ripe tomatoes,**
  peeled and halved
- **salt**

Serves 6

Preheat the oven to 350°F. Lightly season the hake inside and out with salt. Put half the butter and half the gruyere in the cavity and close the cavity to reshape the tail. Put the oil into an ovenprooof baking dish. Reserve two tomato halves and put the remainder into the center of the dish. Lightly season with salt. Place the hake on top of the tomatoes. Slash the fish twice and rub the tail with the remaining butter. Place a tomato half on each slash and sprinkle with the remaining cheese. Bake for about 20 minutes, until the fish is browned and the flesh flakes easily when pressed gently with a fork. Serve immediately, straight from the dish.

593

Hake steaks with tomato, onion, and grated cheese
RODAJAS DE MERLUZA CON TOMATE, CEBOLLA Y QUESO RALLADO

- **5 tablespoons olive oil**
- **6 hake steaks**
- **1 large onion**
- **3 large ripe tomatoes,**
  peeled, halved, and seeded
- **scant 1 cup grated**
  gruyere cheese
- **salt**

Serves 6

Preheat the oven to 325°F. Put 4 tablespoons of the oil into an ovenproof baking dish and add the hake steaks in a single layer. Lightly season with salt and drizzle ½ teaspoon of the remaining oil over each steak. Cut the onion into six thin slices, discarding the thick end pieces, and place a slice on each fish steak. Put a tomato half on top. Sprinkle each steak with the gruyere and bake for about 25 minutes, until the fish flakes easily. Serve immediately straight from the dish.

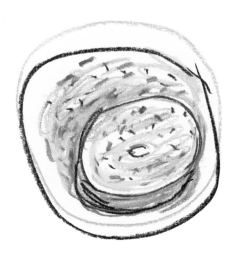

594 Breaded hake fillets with green mayonnaise

FILETES DE MERLUZA EMPANADOS, SERVIDOS CON SALSA MAYONESA VERDE

- 6 hake fillets,
  2½ pounds total weight
- 1 cup milk
- 2 eggs
- 1½ cups bread crumbs
- sunflower oil, for deep-frying
- 6 canned rolled anchovies,
  drained
- salt

  Green mayonnaise:
- 2 eggs
- juice of 1 lemon
- 2¼ cups sunflower oil
- 1 sprig fresh parsley
- 3 tablespoons rinsed capers,
  drained and coarsely chopped
- 2 pickled gherkins, chopped
- salt
Serves 6

Make the green mayonnaise as described in recipe 107. It should be quite thick. Put the hake fillets in a shallow dish, pour in the milk and let soak, turning occasionally, for 30 minutes. Meanwhile, beat the eggs in a shallow dish and pour the bread crumbs into another shallow dish. Drain the fish fillets, season with salt, and dip them first in the beaten egg and then in the bread crumbs. Heat the oil in a deep-fryer or deep skillet to 350–375°F or until a cube of day-old bread browns in 30 seconds. Add the hake fillets, in batches, and cook until golden brown. Remove with a slotted spatula, drain well, transfer to a serving dish, and keep warm while you cook the remaining batches. Place a rolled anchovy on each fillet to garnish and serve immediately, offering the green mayonnaise separately.

Note: If using frozen hake fillets, let thaw completely before soaking in the milk.

595 Fried hake

FILETES DE MERLUZA REBOZADOS Y FRITOS

- 2 eggs
- ¾ cup all-purpose flour
- sunflower oil, for deep-frying
- 6 hake or whiting fillets,
  2½ pounds total weight
- 1 lemon, cut lengthwise
  into 6 slices
- salt
Serves 6

Beat the eggs in a shallow dish and pour the flour into another shallow dish. Heat the oil in a deep-fryer or deep skillet to 350–375°F or until a cube of day-old bread browns in 30 seconds. Season the fillets with salt, then coat first in the flour, shaking off any excess, and then in the beaten egg. Add to the hot oil, in batches, and cook until golden brown. Remove with a slotted spatula, drain well, transfer to a serving dish, and keep warm while you cook the remaining batches. Garnish with the lemon slices, and serve immediately.

Note: To make the fillets more succulent, put them into a shallow dish, pour in milk to cover, and let soak for 10 minutes. Turn the fish over, leave for 10 minutes more, then drain, and pat dry. Proceed as described above.

596

Fillets of hake wrapped in ham
FILETES DE MERLUZA ENVUELTOS EN JAMÓN DE YORK

- 12 hake fillets, 1 pound 10 ounces–2¼ pounds total weight
- 1 cup milk
- 6 thin slices of Smithfield or other dry-cured ham, halved
- 2 eggs
- ½ cup all-purpose flour
- sunflower oil, for deep-frying
- 1 lemon, cut into wedges
- salt

Serves 6

Put the hake fillets into a deep dish, pour the milk over them, and let soak for 30 minutes, turning them twice. Drain and pat dry. Season with salt, wrap each fillet in half a slice of the ham, and secure with a wooden toothpick. Beat the eggs in a shallow dish and pour the flour into another shallow dish. Heat the oil in a deep-fryer or deep skillet to 350–375°F or until a cube of day-old bread browns in 30 seconds. Dip the wrapped fillets first in the flour and then in the beaten egg. Carefully add to the hot oil, in batches, and cook until golden brown. Remove with a slotted spatula, drain well, and keep warm while you cook the remaining batches. Serve immediately, garnished with the lemon wedges.

597

Hake in garlic sauce
MERLUZA EN ALLADA

- 2 large potatoes, thickly sliced
- 3 tablespoons olive oil
- 1 onion, chopped
- 8 cloves garlic, sliced
- 1 heaping teaspoon paprika
- 4 hake or other white fish steaks
- salt

Serves 4

Put the potato slices into a stovetop-safe casserole, pour in water to cover, and add a pinch of salt. Bring to a boil, lower the heat, and cook for 20 minutes. Meanwhile, heat the oil in a skillet. Add the onion and cook over low heat, stirring occasionally, for about 5 minutes, until softened and translucent. Add the garlic and cook, stirring occasionally for 5 minutes more. Remove the skillet from the heat and stir in the paprika. Season the hake steaks lightly with salt and add to the potato slices at the end of the cooking time. Bring back to a boil and cook for 5 minutes. Drain off nearly all the water from the casserole, add the onion mixture and cook for 5 minutes more. You can either serve the dish immediately or heat it through in a preheated oven at 350°F for a few more minutes.

Baked hake tail with béchamel sauce and mushrooms

COLA DE MERLUZA AL HORNO CON BECHAMEL Y CHAMPIÑONES

- 1 hake tail, 2¼–3¼ pounds
- ¼ cup (½ stick) butter
- 2 tablespoons sunflower oil
- 1 heaping tablespoon
  all-purpose flour
- 2¼ cups milk
- ¾ grated cup gruyere cheese
- 4 ounces mushrooms,
  stalks removed
- a few drops of lemon juice
- salt

Serves 6

Preheat the oven to 350°F. Lightly season the hake with salt and put it into a deep ovenproof baking dish. Melt half the butter with the oil in a pan. Stir in the flour and cook, stirring constantly, for 2 minutes. Gradually stir in the milk, a little at a time. Season with salt and cook, stirring constantly, for about 10 minutes, until thickened. Pour the sauce over the fish, sprinkle with the gruyere, and bake for about 25 minutes, until golden brown. Put the mushroom caps, remaining butter, the lemon juice, and a pinch of salt into a pan and cook for about 6 minutes, until tender. Remove from the heat and set aside. At the end of the cooking time, remove the baking dish from the oven and place the mushroom caps in a line along the fish, then return the dish to the oven, and cook for 5 minutes more. Serve immediately, straight from the dish.

599

Hake fried in flour
RODAJAS DE MERLUZA FRITA SÓLO CON HARINA

- **6 thick hake steaks**
- **sunflower oil, for deep-frying**
- **½ cup all-purpose flour**
- **1 lemon, cut into 6 thick slices**
- **salt**

Serves 6

Season the hake steaks on both sides with salt. Heat the oil in a deep-fryer or deep skillet to 350–375°F or until a cube of day-old bread browns in 30 seconds. Coat the fish steaks with the flour, shaking off any excess, add to the oil, in batches of two, and cook until golden brown. Remove with a slotted spatula, drain, and keep warm while you cook the remaining batches. Garnish each steak with a slice of lemon and serve immediately.

600

Fried hake steaks
RODAJAS DE MERLUZA FRITAS REBOZADAS

- 6 thick hake steaks
- sunflower oil, for deep-frying
- ½ cup all-purpose flour
- 2 eggs, beaten
- 1 lemon, cut into wedges
- salt

Serves 6

Season the hake steaks on both sides with salt. Heat the oil in a deep-fryer or deep saucepan to 350–375°F or until a cube of day-old bread browns in 30 seconds. Coat the fish steaks first in the flour, shaking off any excess, and then in the beaten egg. Add the steaks to the hot oil, in batches of two, and cook until golden brown. Remove with a slotted spatula, drain, and keep warm while you cook the remaining batches. Serve immediately, garnished with the lemon wedges.

601

Fried frozen hake
RODAJAS DE MERLUZA CONGELADA FRITAS

- 6 frozen hake steaks
- 1 cup milk
- ½ cup all-purpose flour
- 2 eggs, beaten
- sunflower oil, for deep-frying
- 1 lemon, cut into wedges
- salt

Serves 6

Put the hake steaks into a bowl of cold water with 3 tablespoons salt and let thaw. Drain well, put the steaks into a deep dish, and pour in the milk to cover. Let soak, turning several times, for 30 minutes. Drain well, then coat the steaks first in the flour, shaking off any excess, and then in the beaten egg. Cook the steaks in hot oil as described in recipe 600. Serve immediately, garnished with lemon.

602

Hake steaks garnished with croûtons and capers
RODAJAS DE MERLUZA FRITAS ADORNADAS CON CURRUSQUITOS DE PAN
FRITO Y ALCAPARRAS

- sunflower oil, for deep-frying
- 3 slices of bread, about ¾ inch thick, crusts removed, cut into small squares
- 6 thick hake steaks
- ½ cup all-purpose flour
- 1 tablespoon chopped fresh parsley
- 3 tablespoons butter
- 3 tablespoons capers, rinsed and drained
- salt

Serves 6

Heat the oil in a skillet. Add the bread squares and cook for a few minutes, until lightly golden. Remove with a slotted spoon, drain, and set aside. Reserve the oil in the skillet. Season the hake steaks on both sides with salt and coat them in the flour, shaking off any excess. Sprinkle some of the parsley over each steak and press down gently to make sure it adheres to the fish. Reheat the oil to 350–375°F or until a cube of day-old bread browns in 30 seconds. Add the steaks to the hot oil, in batches of two, and cook until golden brown all over. Remove with a slotted spatula, drain, and keep warm while you cook the remaining steaks. Drain off most of the oil from the skillet, leaving just enough to cover the base. Melt the butter in the pan and skim off the froth with a spoon. Add the capers and croûtons and stir for 1–2 minutes. Pour the sauce over the steaks and serve immediately.

603

Hake cooked with clams

RODAJAS DE MERLUZA GUISADA CON CHIRLAS

- sunflower oil, for deep-frying
- 6 thick hake steaks
- ½ cup all-purpose flour
- 9 ounces littleneck clams
- 4 tablespoons olive oil
- 1 small onion, chopped
- 1 clove garlic, chopped
- 5 tablespoons white wine
- ½ teaspoon meat extract
  or Maggi Seasoning
- 1 tablespoon chopped
  fresh parsley
- salt

Serves 6

Heat the sunflower oil in a deep-fryer or deep skillet to 350–375°F or until a cube of day-old bread browns in 30 seconds. Season the hake steaks on both sides with salt and coat in the flour, shaking off the excess. Reserve the remaining flour. Add the steaks to the hot oil, in batches, and cook until golden brown. Remove with a slotted spatula, drain, and keep warm in a stovetop-safe casserole, while you cook the remaining batches. Wash the clams under cold running water and discard any with broken shells or any that do not shut immediately when sharply tapped. Put them into a pan and pour in water to cover. Cover and cook over high heat, shaking the pan occasionally, for 3–5 minutes, until the shells have opened. Remove the pan from the heat and lift out the clams with a slotted spoon. Discard any that remain shut. Strain the cooking liquid through a cheesecloth-lined strainer into a bowl. Remove the clams from their shells, put into another bowl, and add a little of the reserved cooking liquid. Heat the olive oil in a skillet. Add the onion and garlic and cook over low heat, stirring occasionally, for 5 minutes, until softened and translucent. Stir in the reserved flour and cook, stirring constantly, for about 4 minutes, until lightly colored. Gradually stir in the wine, a little at a time, and the reserved cooking liquid. Cook, stirring constantly, for 10 minutes, then remove the pan from the heat and stir in the meat extract or Maggi Seasoning. Pass the sauce through a food mill and then pour it over the hake steaks. Scatter the clams and sprinkle the parsley on top. If there does not seem to be enough sauce, add a little warm water. Season to taste with salt and cook over medium heat, gently shaking the dish occasionally, for about 10 minutes, until the sauce has thickened. Serve immediately, straight from the dish.

📷

Hake steaks in green sauce

RODAJAS DE MERLUZA EN SALSA VERDE

- **4 tablespoons olive oil**
- **1 onion, chopped**
- **1 clove garlic**
- **2–3 sprigs fresh parsley**
- **1 tablespoon all-purpose flour**
- **6 thick hake or whiting steaks, about 7 ounces each**
- **1 tablespoon very finely chopped fresh parsley**
- **1 cup drained canned peas (optional)**
- **1–2 hard-cooked eggs, chopped (optional)**
- **salt and pepper**

Serves 6

Heat the oil in a skillet. Add the onion and cook over low heat, stirring occasionally, for 5 minutes, until softened and translucent. Meanwhile, crush the garlic with the parsley sprigs and a pinch of salt in a mortar, or process in a mini-food processor. Stir the flour into the skillet and cook, stirring constantly, for 2 minutes. Gradually stir in scant 2 cups water, a little at a time. Cook, stirring constantly, for 5 minutes. Stir 2 tablespoons of the sauce into the garlic mixture, mix well, and then stir into the skillet. Pass the sauce through a food mill or push through a coarse strainer into a stovetop-safe casserole. Lightly season the hake steaks with salt and add to the dish. The sauce should just cover them, but if not, add a little more water. Lightly season with pepper, sprinkle with the parsley, and add the peas, if using. Cook over medium heat, gently shaking the dish occasionally, for about 15 minutes. Taste and adjust the seasoning, if necessary. Sprinkle with the hard-cooked eggs, if using, and serve immediately straight from the dish.

Note: This dish can be made using 3¼ pounds grouper steaks in place of the hake but the cooking time will need to be increased.

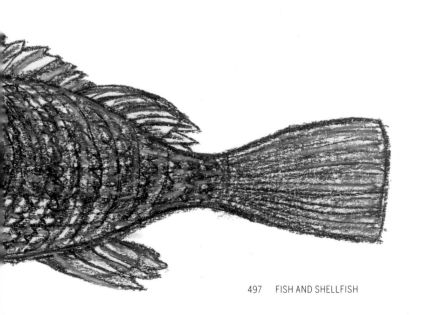

605

Basque hake
RODAJAS DE MERLUZA A LA VASCA

- 1 bunch thin asparagus, trimmed
- 1 pound 2 ounces peas, shelled
- 4 tablespoons olive oil
- 1 onion, chopped
- 1 clove garlic, chopped
- 1 tablespoon all-purpose flour
- 1 sprig fresh parsley
- 6 thick hake steaks,
  about 7 ounces each
- 1 tablespoon chopped
  fresh parsley
- 1 hard-cooked egg, chopped
- salt

Serves 6

Bring a large pan of salted water to a boil. Add the asparagus, submerging it completely, cover, bring back to a boil, and cook for about 10 minutes, until tender. Drain well and set aside. Bring another pan of salted water to a boil, add the peas, and cook for 20–30 minutes, until tender. Drain well and set aside. Heat the oil in a skillet. Add the onion and garlic and cook over low heat, stirring occasionally, for 5–7 minutes, until the onion is softened and translucent. Stir in the flour and cook, stirring constantly, for 2 minutes. Gradually stir in 1 cup water and add the parsley sprig. Cook, stirring constantly, for 8 minutes. Remove from the heat and pass through a food mill or push through a strainer into a bowl. Lightly season the hake steaks with salt, put them into a stovetop-safe casserole, and pour the sauce over them, adding scant 2 cups water, if necessary (the fish should be covered). Cook over medium heat, gently shaking the dish occasionally, for 12 minutes. Sprinkle the parsley over the steaks, add the peas, asparagus, and hard-cooked egg, and heat gently for about 5 minutes to warm through. Season to taste with salt and serve immediately, straight from the dish.

Notes: You can substitute drained canned asparagus and/or peas for the fresh vegetables. Grouper or whiting can be used in place of hake in this dish.

498   FISH AND SHELLFISH

606 Baked hake with wine and cream sauce

RODAJAS DE MERLUZA AL HORNO CON SALSA DE VINO Y NATA

- **5 tablespoons olive oil**
- **6 thick hake steaks**
- **3–4 tablespoons bread crumbs**
- **2 tablespoons (¼ stick) butter**
- **1 shallot, very finely chopped**
- **¾ cup white wine**
- **1 cup light cream**
- **salt**

Serves 6

Preheat the oven to 350°F. Pour 3 tablespoons of the oil into an oven-proof baking dish. Season the hake steaks on both sides with salt, put them into the dish, sprinkle with the bread crumbs, and dot with the butter. Bake for about 15 minutes. Meanwhile, heat the remaining oil in a skillet. Add the shallot and cook over low heat, stirring occasionally for about 5 minutes, until softened and translucent. Add the wine and cook for 8 minutes more. Remove the skillet from the heat and gradually stir in the cream. Pour the sauce over the fish and return the dish to the oven but turn off the heat. Leave for about 5 minutes to warm through, then serve immediately straight from the dish.

607

Baked hake with cream and mushroom sauce

RODAJAS DE MERLUZA AL HORNO CON SALSA DE NATA Y CHAMPIÑONES

- 3 tablespoons sunflower oil
- 6 thick hake steaks
- ½ cup white wine
- juice of 1½ lemons
- 4 sprigs fresh parsley
- 2 tablespoons bread crumbs
- 3 tablespoons butter
- scant 1½ cups sliced
  mushrooms
- 1 cup light cream
- salt

Serves 6

Preheat the oven to 350°F. Pour the oil into an ovenproof baking dish. Season the hake steaks on both sides with salt and arrange the steaks in the dish in a single layer. Pour in the wine and 5 tablespoons of the lemon juice and place the parsley sprigs between the steaks. Sprinkle 1 teaspoon of the bread crumbs over each steak and dot with 2 tablespoons of the butter. Bake for about 10 minutes, until golden brown on top. Meanwhile, put the mushrooms, the remaining butter, and the remaining lemon juice into a pan. Cover and cook over medium heat for 6 minutes until cooked. Stir in the cream and warm the sauce through but do not let boil. Remove the parsley sprigs from the dish and discard. Lower the oven temperature to 225°F. Pour the mushroom sauce over the hake steaks, return the dish to the oven, and continue to cook for a further 5 minutes. Serve immediately, straight from the dish.

Note: Grouper can be used in place of hake in this dish.

608

Quick hake

MERLUZA RÁPIDA

- fresh or frozen hake steaks
- 1 cup sunflower oil
- 2 potatoes, thinly sliced
- 2 cloves garlic, finely chopped
- 1 tablespoon chopped
  fresh parsley
- juice of 1 lemon
- salt

Serves 6

If using frozen hake, put the steaks into a bowl of cold water with 3 tablespoons salt and let thaw for about 1 hour. Drain, rinse under cold running water, and pat dry. Preheat the oven to 350°F. Heat the oil in a skillet. Add the potato slices and cook over low heat for 5–8 minutes, until softened but not browned. Remove with a slotted spoon and put into an ovenproof baking dish. Put the hake steaks on top. Drain off nearly all the oil from the skillet, leaving just enough to coat the base. Add the garlic and cook over low heat, stirring frequently, for a few minutes, until beginning to brown. Remove the skillet from the heat, stir in the parsley, and pour the mixture over the fish. Bake for about 15 minutes, until the steaks are opaque and the flesh flakes easily. Remove the dish from the oven, season with salt, and sprinkle with the lemon juice.

Notes: This dish can be cooked on the stovetop rather than in the oven, but it will be drier. The secret of this dish's flavor is that neither the salt nor the lemon juice are added until just before serving.

609

Frozen hake with onion

RODAJAS DE MERLUZA CONGELADA CON CEBOLLA

- 5 tablespoons sunflower oil
- 2 large onions, chopped
- 6 thick frozen hake steaks,
  thawed (see recipe 608)
- juice of 1 lemon
- salt

Serves 6

Pour the oil into a large pan and add about two-thirds of the onion. Season the hake steaks on both sides with salt, put them on top of the onion, and pour in the lemon juice. Sprinkle the remaining onion on top of the fish. Cover and cook over low heat for 15 minutes. Carefully transfer the steaks to a warm serving dish with a slotted spatula and serve immediately.

610

Hake with almond, garlic, and white wine sauce
COLA DE MERLUZA AL HORNO CON SALSA DE ALMENDRAS, AJOS
Y VINO BLANCO

- 2 ¼ cups sunflower oil
- 2 potatoes, thinly sliced
- 2 ½–3 ¼ pounds hake, cleaned and filleted
- ½ cup all-purpose flour
- salt

Sauce:
- 3 slices of bread, ½ inch thick, crusts removed
- 2 tablespoons olive oil
- 1 small onion, chopped
- 3 cloves garlic
- 2 sprigs fresh parsley
- 8 almonds
- generous 1 cup white wine
- salt

Serves 4

Heat the sunflower oil in a skillet. Add the slices of bread for the sauce and cook, turning occasionally, until golden brown on both sides. Remove from the skillet and set aside. Add the potato slices to the pan and cook for 5–10 minutes, until softened and just beginning to color. Transfer to an ovenproof baking dish with a slotted spoon. Lightly season the hake fillets with salt and coat with the flour, shaking off the excess. Add the hake fillets to the skillet, one at a time, and cook until golden brown. Remove with a slotted spatula and place on top of the potatoes. Preheat the oven to 350°F. To make the sauce, heat the oil in a skillet. Add the onion and cook over low heat, stirring occasionally, for about 8 minutes, until beginning to brown. Pound the fried bread with the garlic, parsley, and almonds in a mortar, or process in a mini-food processor, then add to the pan. Pour in the wine and 5 tablespoons water, lightly season with salt, and cook for 5 minutes. Pass the mixture through a food mill and pour it over the hake fillets. Bake for 10 minutes, then serve immediately straight from the dish.

611

Fried hake cheeks
COCOCHAS REBOZADAS FRITAS

- 1 pound 5 ounces hake cheeks
- sunflower oil, for deep-frying
- ½ cup all-purpose flour
- 2 eggs, beaten

Serves 6

Ask your fish supplier to skin and bone the hake cheeks. Heat the sunflower oil in a deep-fryer or deep skillet to 350–375°F or until a cube of day-old bread browns in 30 seconds. One at a time, lightly coat the cheeks first in the flour, then in the beaten egg. Add to the hot oil, in batches of two, and cook until golden brown. Remove with a slotted spoon, drain on paper towels, and keep warm while you cook the remaining batches. Serve immediately.

Note: This dish can be made with cod cheeks.

Fried whiting biting their tails

PESCADILLAS FRITAS QUE SE MUERDEN LA COLA

- **6 whiting, ling, or pout,**
  12–14 ounces each, scaled,
  trimmed, and cleaned,
  with heads and tails on
- **sunflower oil, for deep-frying**
- **⅓ cup all-purpose flour**
- **1 lemon, cut into wedges**
- **salt**

Serves 6

Season the whiting inside and out with salt. Place the tails in the mouths and press down gently so that the teeth get a good grip. Heat the oil in a deep-fryer or deep skillet to 350–375°F or until a cube of day-old bread browns in 30 seconds. Coat the fish in the flour, shaking off any excess, add to the hot oil, in batches of two, and cook until golden brown. Remove with a slotted spatula, drain, and keep warm while you cook the remaining batches. Serve immediately, garnished with the lemon wedges.

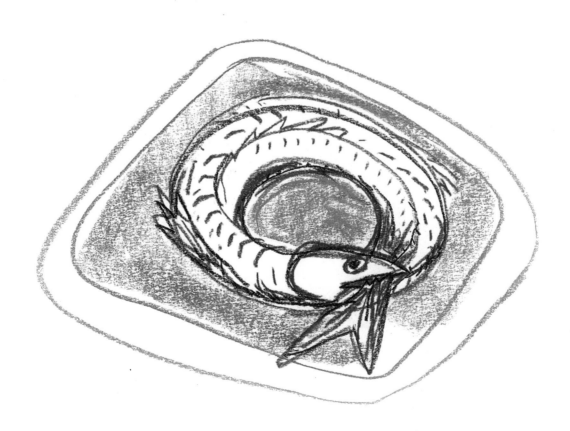

613   Fried breaded whiting

PESCADILLAS ABIERTAS, REBOZADAS Y FRITAS

- 6 whiting, ling, or pout,
  12–14 ounces each, scaled,
  trimmed, cleaned, and boned
- 2 eggs
- ⅓ cup all-purpose flour
- sunflower oil, for deep-frying
- salt
- 1½ lemons, cut into wedges

Serves 6

Season the whiting with salt. Beat the eggs in a shallow dish and pour the flour into another shallow dish. Heat the oil in a deep-fryer or deep skillet to 350–375°F or until a cube of day-old bread browns in 30 seconds. Dip the fish first in the flour, shaking off any excess, and then in the beaten egg. Add to the hot oil, in batches, and cook until golden brown. Remove with a slotted spatula, drain, and keep warm while you cook the remaining batches. Serve immediately, garnished with the lemon wedges.

614   Whiting baked with wine and currants

PESCADILLAS AL HORNO CON VINO Y PASAS

- 3 tablespoons olive oil
- 6 whiting, ling, or pout,
  12–14 ounces each, scaled,
  trimmed, cleaned, and boned
- 1 tablespoon bread crumbs
- ¼ cup (½ stick) butter
- ¾ cup muscatel wine
- juice of 1½ lemons
- ⅓ cup currants
- 2 egg yolks
- salt

Serves 6

Preheat the oven to 350°F. Pour the oil into an ovenproof baking dish. Season the whiting with salt, fold them in half, skin side outside, and put into the dish. Sprinkle with bread crumbs and dot with 1 ½ tablespoons of the butter. Pour in half the wine and half the lemon juice and bake for 15 minutes. Meanwhile put the currants and the remaining wine into a small pan and heat gently until warmed through. Remove the pan from the heat and set aside. Melt the remaining butter in a skillet. Stir in the remaining lemon juice and the wine and currants and cook for a few minutes, stirring constantly. Lightly beat the egg yolks in a bowl and gradually stir in a little of the sauce to prevent the yolks curdling, then stir into the skillet. Pour the sauce over the whiting, shaking the dish so it penetrates. Return the dish to the oven, switch off the heat, and leave for about 5 minutes. Serve straight from the dish.

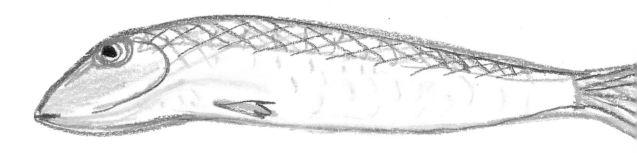

615

Baked whiting
PESCADILLA AL HORNO

- 4 tablespoons sunflower oil
- 3¼-pounds whiting, ling,
  or pout fillet
- 2 sprigs chopped fresh parsley
- 1½ tablespoons bread crumbs
- ¼ cup (½ stick) butter
- juice of 1 lemon
- salt

Serves 6   .

Preheat the oven to 350°F. Pour the oil into an ovenproof baking dish and add the fish, skin side down. Season with salt, sprinkle with the parsley and bread crumbs, and dot with the butter and drizzle with the lemon juice. Bake for about 15 minutes. Serve immediately, straight from the dish.

616

Swordfish with onions and white wine
PEZ ESPADA CON CEBOLLA Y VINO BLANCO

- scant 2 cups sunflower oil
- 2¼ pound thin swordfish steaks
- ½ cup all-purpose flour
- 2 large onions,
  cut into long thin strips
- ¾ cup white wine
- salt

Serves 6

Heat the oil in a skillet. Lightly season the swordfish steaks on both sides with salt and coat in the flour, shaking off any excess. Add to the skillet, in batches, and cook over medium heat until golden brown. Remove from the skillet and set aside. Transfer 3 tablespoons of the oil from the skillet to a pan and reheat. Add the onion and cook over low heat, stirring occasionally, for about 5 minutes. Pour in the wine and ¾ cup water and simmer, stir-ring occasionally, for 10 minutes. Add the steaks and simmer for 10 minutes more, until the flesh flakes easily. Serve immediately.

617

Swordfish with toasted sauce
PEZ ESPADA CON SALSA TOSTADA

- 1½ tablespoons flour
- 1 cup sunflower oil
- 4 swordfish steaks
- 2 small onions, thinly sliced
  and pushed out into rings
- ¾ cup fish stock
  (homemade or canned)
- 2 tablespoons sherry (optional)
- 1 tablespoon capers,
  rinsed and drained
- salt and pepper

Serves 4

Heat the flour in a non-stick skillet, stirring constantly, until browned, then set aside. Heat the oil in a large skillet. Add the swordfish steaks and cook for about 5 minutes on each side. Remove from the pan and set aside. Pour off nearly all the oil from the skillet, leaving just enough to cover the base. Add the onion and cook over low heat, stirring occasionally, for about 5 minutes, until softened and translucent. Stir in the flour, then gradually stir in the stock, a little at a time, followed by the sherry, if using. Season to taste with salt and pepper and cook, stirring constantly, for a few minutes more, until thickened a little. Add the steaks and simmer very gently for 5 minutes. Stir in the capers and warm through. Serve immediately.

Swordfish with shrimp and clam sauce

FILETES DE PEZ ESPADA CON SALSA DE GAMBAS Y ALMEJAS

- 9 ounces littleneck or cherrystone clams
- 9 ounces raw shrimp, shells on and heads attached, if available
- 2¼ pounds thin swordfish steaks
- ⅓ cup all-purpose flour
- 2¼ cups sunflower oil
- 1 large onion, chopped
- 3 tablespoons sherry or other sweet fortified wine
- pinch of saffron threads or powder
- 1 clove garlic
- salt

Serves 6

Scrub the clams under cold running water and discard any with damaged shells or any that do not shut when sharply tapped. Put them into a pan, pour in ¾ cup water, cover, and cook over high heat, shaking the pan occasionally, for 3–5 minutes, until the shells have opened. Remove the clams with a slotted spoon and discard any that remain shut. Strain the cooking liquid through a cheesecloth-lined strainer into a bowl. Remove the clams from their shells and put them in the bowl. Peel the shrimp and set them aside. Put the shells and heads, if using, in a pan, pour in water to cover, and add a pinch of salt. Bring to a boil, then lower the heat, and simmer for 10 minutes. Strain the stock into a bowl and set aside. Lightly season the swordfish steaks with salt. Reserve 1 tablespoon of the flour and pour the remainder into a shallow dish. Heat the oil in a skillet. Lightly coat the fish steaks in the flour, shaking off any excess, add to the hot oil, and cook for about 5 minutes on each side, until golden brown. Remove from the skillet with a slotted spatula, drain, and put into a stovetop-safe casserole. Measure the shrimp stock and add enough of the reserved cooking liquid from the clams to make it up to 2 cups. Transfer about 4 tablespoons of the oil from the skillet to a pan and reheat. Add the onion and cook over low heat, stirring occasionally, for about 8 minutes, until beginning to brown. Stir in the reserved flour and cook, stirring constantly, for 2 minutes. Gradually stir in the sherry, a little at a time, then the shrimp and clam stock. Crush the saffron with the garlic in a mortar, or process in a mini-food processor. Mix in 2 tablespoons water, and add to the sauce. Strain the sauce over the swordfish steaks and add the shrimp and clams. Season to taste with salt and cook over medium heat, shaking the dish occasionally, for about 8 minutes, until the sauce has thickened. Add a little more water if necessary. Serve immediately, straight from the dish.

619

Monkfish with milk

RAPE CON LECHE

- 2 tablespoons (¼ stick) butter
- 3 tablespoons sunflower oil
- 1 large onion, finely chopped
- 1½ tablespoons all-purpose flour
- 3 cups milk
- ½ tablespoon tomato paste
- 6 monkfish fillets, about 3¼ pounds total weight
- salt

Serves 6

Ask your fish supplier for the monkfish backbone. Melt the butter with the oil in a skillet. Add the onion and cook over very low heat, stirring occasionally, for about 10 minutes, until softened but not browned. Stir in the flour and cook, stirring constantly, for 2 minutes. Gradually stir in the milk, a little at a time, then stir in the tomato paste, add the monkfish bone, if available, and lightly season with salt. Lightly season the monkfish fillets with salt and add them to the sauce. Simmer gently for about 8 minutes, until the flesh flakes easily. Remove and discard the bone and serve immediately.

620

American-style monkfish with tomatoes, Cognac, and white wine

RAPE A LA AMERICANA CON TOMATE, COÑAC Y VINO BLANCO

- ½ cup olive oil
- 6 monkfish fillets,
  about 3 ¼ pounds total weight
- ⅓ cup all-purpose flour
- 5 tablespoons Cognac
  or other brandy
- 1 shallot,
  very finely chopped
- 1 large clove garlic,
  lightly crushed
- pinch of dried mixed herbs
- generous 1 cup dry white wine
- 6 very ripe tomatoes,
  seeded and chopped
- juice of 1 lemon
- 1 tablespoon finely chopped
  fresh parsley
- salt and pepper

Serves 6

Heat 6 tablespoons of the oil in a skillet. Season the monkfish fillets with salt and coat lightly in the flour, shaking off any excess. Add to the skillet and cook for about 5 minutes, until the flesh has become opaque. Drain off and discard the liquid released by the fish, add the remaining oil, and cook for 5 minutes more, until the fillets are light golden brown. Meanwhile, warm the Cognac or brandy in a small pan, ignite, and leave until the flames have died down. Set aside. Sprinkle the shallot over the fillets, add the garlic, sprinkle in the dried herbs, and pour in the brandy. Add the wine and tomato, lightly season with salt and pepper, cover, and cook over medium-high heat for 10 minutes. Lift out the fillets with a slotted spatula and put them into a warm deep serving dish. Pass the sauce through a food mill, stir in the lemon juice, and pour it over the monkfish. Sprinkle with the parsley and serve immediately.

621

Monkfish in sauce with tomatoes and peas

RAPE EN SALSA CON TOMATES Y GUISANTES

- 1 cup sunflower oil
- ⅓ cup all-purpose flour
- 6 monkfish fillets,
  about 3 ¼ pounds total weight
- 1 large onion, finely chopped
- 2 tomatoes,
  peeled, seeded, and chopped
- 2 cloves garlic
- pinch of saffron threads
- scant 1 cup drained canned peas
- 1 tablespoon chopped
  fresh parsley
- salt

Serves 6

Heat the oil in a skillet. Reserve 1 tablespoon of the flour and pour the remainder into a shallow dish. Lightly coat the monkfish fillets in the flour, shaking off any excess, add to the skillet, and cook for about 5 minutes. Remove from the skillet with a slotted spatula and set aside. Transfer 4 tablespoons of the oil from the skillet to a pan and reheat. Add the onion and cook over low heat, stirring occasionally, for about 8 minutes, until lightly browned. Add the tomato and cook, stirring frequently, for 10 minutes. Stir in the reserved flour and cook, stirring constantly, for 2 minutes. Gradually stir in scant 2 cups water, a little at a time. Crush the garlic with the saffron and a pinch of salt in a mortar, or process in a mini-food processor. Mix in 2 tablespoons of the sauce, then add to the pan. Season and simmer for 10 minutes. Add the fillets, and a little water if necessary. Cook for 10 minutes more, then add the peas, and heat through gently. Transfer to a warm serving dish, sprinkle with the parsley, and serve.

622

Monkfish and potato soup

BOUILLABAISSE DE RAPE Y PATATAS

- 2 ¼ pounds monkfish fillet,
  cut into chunks
- pinch of saffron threads
- 2 cloves garlic
- 5 tablespoons white wine
- 6 tablespoons olive oil
- juice of ½ lemon
- 1 onion, very finely chopped
- 1 pound 2 ounces potatoes,
  cut into fairly thick slices
- scant 2 cups fish stock
  (homemade or canned)
- 1 tablespoon chopped
  fresh parsley
- salt

Serves 6

Put the monkfish chunks into a nonmetallic bowl. Crush the saffron with one of the garlic cloves and a pinch of salt in a mortar, or process in a mini-food processor. Stir in the wine, then pour the mixture over the fish, and add 2 tablespoons of the oil, the lemon juice, and 5 tablespoons water. Mix well and let marinate in the refrigerator, stirring occasionally, for 3–4 hours. Heat the remaining oil in a pan. Add the onion and the remaining garlic clove and cook over low heat, stirring occasionally, for about 10 minutes, until lightly browned. Add the potato slices and cook, stirring frequently, for 5 minutes. Pour in the fish stock. If there is not enough liquid to cover the ingredients, add a little water. Season with salt and cook over high heat for 20 minutes. Add the monkfish chunks, together with their marinade, stir well, and cook for 10 minutes more. Taste and adjust the seasoning if necessary. Serve immediately, sprinkled with the parsley.

Monkfish and vegetable stew

ESTOFADO DE RAPE CON VERDURAS

- 1 ¾ pounds monkfish fillets
- ⅓ cup all-purpose flour
- 4 tablespoons olive oil
- 1 cup diced mixed vegetables,
  fresh, frozen and thawed,
  or canned and drained
- scant ½ cup white wine
- scant 1 cup fish stock
  (homemade or canned)
- ⅔ cup light cream
- 2 tablespoons Classic Tomato
  Sauce (see recipe 73)
- 1 sprig fresh parsley, chopped
- salt and pepper

Serves 4

Cut the monkfish fillets into medallions, coat them in the flour, and shake off any excess. Heat half the oil in a skillet, add the fish, and cook for 7 minutes, until the flesh flakes easily. Remove with a slotted spatula and keep warm. Heat the remaining oil in another skillet. Add the mixed vegetables and cook over medium-low heat, stirring occasionally, until tender. Remove the skillet from the heat, drain off the oil, and keep warm. Drain off most of the oil from the first skillet, add the wine, and cook over medium heat until reduced by half. Lower the heat, add the stock and cream, and cook until thickened, then stir in the tomato sauce, and heat through. Spoon the sauce over individual warm serving plates, add the fish and vegetables, and garnish with the parsley.

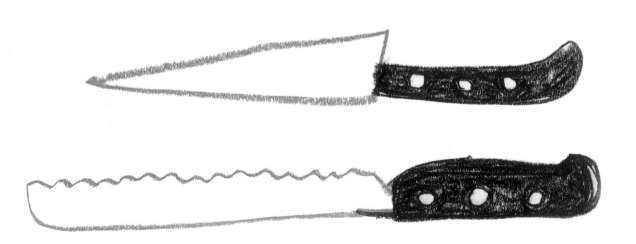

624

Skate in black butter and caper sauce

RAYA COCIDA CON SALSA DE MANTEQUILLA NEGRA Y ALCAPARRAS

- 3 ¼ pounds skate wings
- ⅔ cup butter
- 2 tablespoons pickled capers, drained, plus 2 tablespoons vinegar from the jar
- salt

Stock:
- 5 tablespoons white-wine vinegar
- 1 onion, cut into wedges
- 2 bay leaves
- 10 black peppercorns

Serves 6

Put the skate into a pan with all the stock ingredients, season with salt, and pour in water to cover. Bring to a boil, lower the heat, and simmer gently for 15 minutes. Lift out the skate wings with a slotted spatula and remove and discard the skin, if this has not already been done. Drain the fish well and transfer to a warm serving dish. Melt the butter in a skillet. As soon as it begins to turn brown and smell nutty, remove the skillet from the heat and carefully add the capers and vinegar. Return the skillet to the heat and warm through, then pour the sauce over the fish, and serve immediately.

Skate in gelatin with green mayonnaise

RAYA EN GELATINA CON MAYONESA DE ALCAPARRAS

- 2¼ pounds skate wings
- 2 envelopes (½ ounce) unflavored gelatin
- 2 tablespoons sherry or other sweet fortified wine
- lettuce leaves and 2 sliced tomatoes
- 1 quantity Green Mayonnaise (see recipe 107)
- salt

Stock:
- 5 tablespoons white-wine vinegar
- 1 onion, cut into wedges
- 2 bay leaves
- 10 black peppercorns

Serves 6

Cook the skate with the stock ingredients and add enough water to cover as described in recipe 624. Drain well and flake the fish. Pour 2¼ cups water into a heatproof bowl and sprinkle the gelatin over the surface. Let sponge for 5 minutes, then set the bowl over a pan of barely simmering water, and heat until the gelatin has dissolved and the mixture is clear. Remove from the heat and stir in the sherry. Put a little gelatin into a 2-inch deep round mold to cover the base, and chill in the refrigerator for 15 minutes, until set. Put the fish into the mold, pour in the remaining gelatin, and chill for about 3 hours, until set. Run a round-bladed knife around the edge of the mold and invert on to a serving dish. Garnish with the lettuce leaves and slices of tomato and serve with the mayonnaise.

Note: This dish can be made with any fish that has quite firm flesh, such as red porgy, hake, and sea bass.

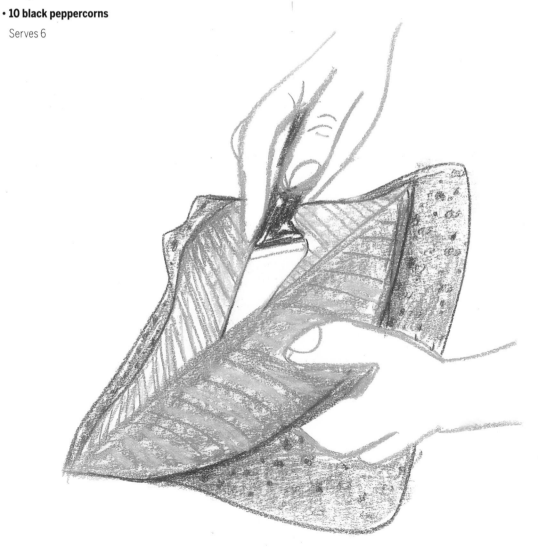

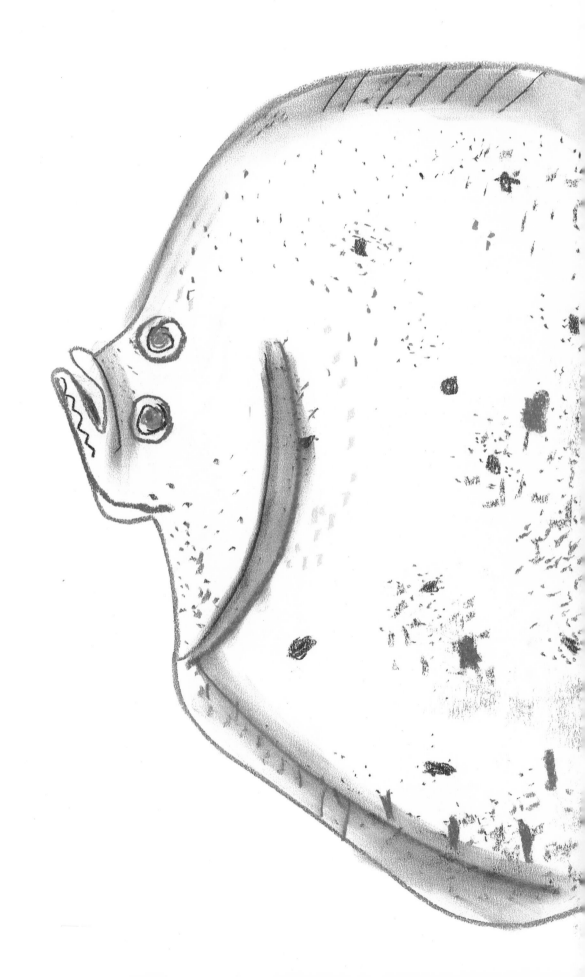

Turbot

A large European flatfish that is highly prized for its fine flavor, turbot is sold whole, and as fillets and steaks. It can be difficult to obtain outside Europe, in which case substitute the best-quality local flatfish available, such as halibut.

How to prepare
When buying a whole turbot, ask the fishmonger to prepare the fish for you (removing the head, tail, and frill and cleaning it). Rinse the fish thoroughly, sprinkle with salt, and put it on a slightly inclined rack in a diamond-shaped fish poacher to drain for about 2 hours. Rinse the fish again and rinse the fish poacher and rack. Put the turbot on the rack, dark side down. Using a sharp knife, make two very deep incisions, one on each side of the backbone. If you don't have a diamond-shaped fish poacher, you can cut the fish into large pieces and place them in an oblong fish poacher or a skillet.

626

Poached turbot
RODABALLO COCIDO

- 7 ounces turbot per person, trimmed and cleaned

Quick stock with milk:
- 1 cup milk
- ½ lemon, peeled and sliced
- 1 bay leaf
- salt

Makes enough for 1 serving

Make the stock as described in recipe 534 and allow to cool. Remove the rack from a diamond-shaped fish poacher and pour in the stock. Place the turbot in the rack and replace it. Bring the stock just to a boil over high heat, then lower the heat, and poach the fish very gently for 15–20 minutes. Do not take the fish out of the stock in advance of serving it, unlike other fish. It can be left in its concentrated stock for up to 30 minutes, but should not cook any further before being served. If it is to be served cold, let the fish cool in the stock before removing it. Put it onto a doubled-over napkin to drain. Remove the skin before serving.

Note: To serve turbot hot, it may be accompanied by Hollandaise Sauce (see recipe 84), Mousseline Sauce (see recipe 87), or Black Butter and Caper Sauce (see recipe 96). To serve it cold, it can be accompanied by all varieties of mayonnaise (see recipes 105–109).

627

Turbot with mussels
RODABALLO AL HORNO CON MEJILLONES

- 1 turbot, 2½–3¼ pounds,
  trimmed and cleaned
- 2¼ pounds mussels
- ¾ cup white wine
- 2 tablespoons (¼ stick) butter
- 2 tablespoons sunflower oil
- 1 heaping tablespoon
  all-purpose flour
- 1 cup fish stock
  (homemade or canned)
- 2 egg yolks
- 1 tablespoon chopped
  fresh parsley
- salt

Quick stock with milk:
- 1 cup milk
- ½ lemon, peeled and sliced
- 1 bay leaf
- salt and black peppercorns

Serves 6

Remove the rack from a diamond-shaped fish poacher. Prepare the stock as described in recipe 534 in the poacher. Put the turbot on the rack and return it to the fish poacher. Bring the stock just to a boil, then lower the heat, and poach the fish very gently for 20 minutes. Meanwhile, if your mussels have not been pre-scrubbed, scrape their shells with the blade of a knife and remove the "beards," then scrub under cold running water. Discard any mussels with broken shells or any that do not shut immediately when sharply tapped. Put them into a pan, pour in the wine, cover, and cook over high heat, shaking the pan occasionally, for 4–5 minutes, until they have opened. Remove the mussels with a slotted spoon and discard any that remain shut. Strain the cooking liquid through a cheesecloth-lined strainer into a bowl. Remove the mussels from their shells and set aside. Melt the butter with the oil in a pan. Stir in the flour and cook, stirring constantly, for 2 minutes. Gradually stir in the reserved cooking liquid, a little at a time, followed by the stock. Cook, stirring constantly, for about 10 minutes, until thickened. Season to taste with salt. Remove the turbot from the fish poacher and carefully remove the skin and bones. Cut the flesh into large pieces and put into a warm serving dish. Lightly beat the egg yolks in a bowl and stir in a little of the sauce to prevent them curdling, then add to the sauce, together with the mussels. Mix well and pour the sauce over the turbot. Sprinkle with the parsley and serve.

Poached salmon

SALMÓN COCIDO

- **7 ounces salmon per person**

Special quick stock:
- **1 bay leaf**
- **1 thick slice of onion**
- **1 large carrot, sliced**
- **¾ cup white wine**
- **juice of ½ lemon**
- **salt**

Serves 4–6

Make the stock as described in recipe 534. Let cool, then remove the rack from a fish poacher and pour in the stock. Place the salmon in the rack and return it to the poacher. Bring the stock just to a boil, then lower the heat so that the salmon cooks very gently. Allow about 20 minutes per 2 ¼ pounds fish. Salmon may be served hot or cold, with various sauces.

Notes: For this dish you can use fillets, steaks, a whole tail or even the whole fish if there are a lot of guests and a big enough fish poacher is available. To serve cooked salmon hot, it may be accompanied by Hollandaise Sauce (see recipe 84) or Mousseline Sauce (see recipe 87). To serve it cold, it can be accompanied by all varieties of mayonnaise (see recipes 105–109). It is usual to put a doubled-over napkin into the serving dish to absorb any water from the cooked fish. Garnish with cooked potatoes and sprigs of fresh parsley. For this dish, you can also cook the salmon in quick white wine stock (see recipe 534).

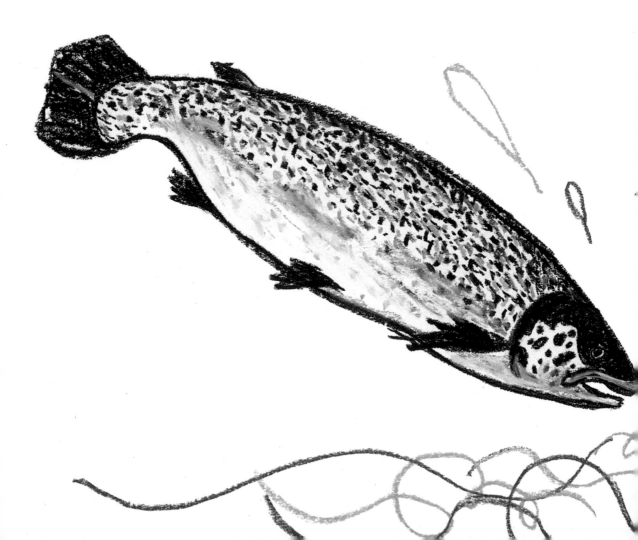

629

Broiled salmon
SALMÓN ASADO

- 1 cup sunflower oil
- 3 large salmon steaks or
  6 small salmon steaks
- salt

Serves 6

Pour the oil into a large dish and add the salmon steaks in a single layer, turning to coat. Let marinate in the refrigerator, turning occasionally, for 1 hour. Preheat the broiler. Remove the steaks from the marinade and drain slightly, then season with salt on both sides. Brush the broiler rack with oil (from marinating the salmon) and discard any remaining marinade. Cook the steaks under the broiler for about 4 minutes on each side. They are fully cooked when the central bones can be removed easily with a fork. Serve in a warm dish, offering a sauce separately.

Note: Serve mayonnaise with this dish (see recipes 105 –109).

630

Oven-roasted salmon with butter
RODAJAS DE SALMÓN AL HORNO CON MANTEQUILLA

- 1 cup sunflower oil
- 3 large salmon steaks or
  6 small salmon steaks
- 7 tablespoons butter
- 1 tablespoon chopped
  fresh parsley
- 1 lemon, cut into wedges
- salt

Serves 6

Put the oil into a large dish and add the salmon steaks in a single layer, turning to coat. Let marinate in the refrigerator, turning occasionally, for 1 hour. Preheat the oven to 350°F. Remove the steaks from the marinade and drain slightly, then season with salt on both sides. Discard any remaining marinade. Put the steaks into an ovenproof baking dish in a single layer, dot with the butter, and roast, basting oc-casionally, for about 20 minutes, until golden brown. Take the salmon out of the oven, sprinkle with the parsley, and garnish with the lemon wedges on the side of the dish. To do this, separate the rind from the flesh to just over halfway up each wedge, then hook the wedges over the edge of the dish. Serve immediately.

Salmon medallions cooked in egg and bread crumbs

MEDALLONES DE SALMÓN EMPANADOS

- 1 pound 2 ounces mushrooms
- 3 tablespoons butter
- juice of ½ lemon
- 2 eggs
- ⅓ cup all-purpose flour
- 1½ cups bread crumbs
- 4 cups sunflower oil
- 2¼ pounds salmon fillets, skinned
- 2¼ cups light cream
- salt

Serves 6

Put the mushrooms, butter, lemon juice, and a pinch of salt into a pan and cook over medium heat, shaking the pan occasionally, for 6 minutes. Remove from the heat and keep warm. Beat the eggs in a shallow dish, pour the flour into another shallow dish, and pour the bread crumbs into a third. Heat the oil in a deep-fryer or deep skillet to 350–375°F or until a cube of day-old bread browns in 30 seconds. Season the salmon fillets with salt and coat first in the flour, then in the beaten egg, and finally in the bread crumbs. Add the fish to the hot oil, in batches, and cook until golden brown. Remove with a slotted spatula, drain, and keep warm in a serving dish while you cook the remaining butter. Return the pan of mushrooms to low heat, gradually stir in the cream, and heat gently but do not let boil. Pour the mushroom sauce over the salmon and serve immediately.

Note: You can substitute a thin béchamel sauce for the cream. Make it with 1 tablespoon all-purpose flour, 1 ½ tablespoons butter, 2 tablespoons sunflower oil, and 2 ¼ cups milk, as described in recipe 77.

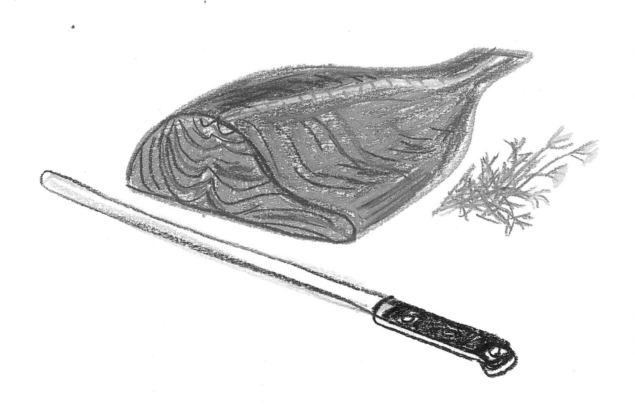

Fisherwoman's salmon, baked with shrimp and mussels

SALMÓN A LA PESCADORA (AL HORNO CON GAMBAS Y MEJILLONES)

- 2 large salmon fillets,
  1 pound 2 ounces each
- ⅓ cup all-purpose flour
- 6 tablespoons olive oil
- 1 small onion, finely chopped
- generous 1 cup white wine
- juice of 1 lemon
- 9 ounces large raw shrimp,
  peeled
- 5 tablespoons butter
- 1 pound 2 ounces mussels
- 2 egg yolks
- 1 tablespoon milk
- 1 tablespoon chopped
  fresh parsley
- salt

Serves 6

Preheat the oven to 180°C/350°F/Gas Mark 4. Season the salmon fillets with salt on both sides and coat with the flour, shaking off any excess. Pour the oil into a large ovenproof baking dish and add the onion, salmon fillets, wine, and lemon juice. Sprinkle in the shrimp and dot the fillets with half the butter. Cover the dish with foil and bake for about 15 minutes. Meanwhile, if your mussels have not been pre-scrubbed, scrape their shells with the blade of a knife and remove the "beards," then scrub under cold running water. Discard any mussels with broken shells or any that do not shut immediately when sharply tapped. Put them into a pan, pour in 1 cup water, and add a pinch of salt. Cook over high heat, shaking the pan occasionally, for 3–5 minutes, until the shells have opened. Remove the mussels with a slotted spoon and discard any that remain closed. Strain the cooking liquid through a cheesecloth-lined strainer into a bowl. Remove the mussels from their shells and add them to the bowl. Using a slotted spatula, carefully transfer the salmon fillets to a warm serving dish. Place the shrimp around them and cover the dish with aluminum foil. Keep warm. Strain the salmon cooking liquid into a pan. Lightly beat the egg yolks with the milk in a bowl. Place the pan of salmon cooking liquid over low heat, add the mussels with their cooking liquid, and warm through, stirring occasionally. Stir a little of this mixture into the egg yolks to prevent them curdling, then stir into the pan. Stir in the parsley, pour the sauce over the salmon, and serve immediately.

Note: For a slightly thicker sauce, mix 2 teaspoons potato flour with the milk, then add it to the salmon cooking liquid, and cook, stirring constantly, for 2–3 minutes. Then add this to the egg yolks.

633

Salmon fillets marinated in watermelon juice
LOMOS DE SALMON MARINADOS CON ZUMO DE SANDÍA

- 4 tablespoons soy sauce
- 4 tablespoons sake
- 4 tablespoons watermelon juice
- pinch of freshly grated ginger
- 1 pound 2 ounces salmon fillets, skinned
- 2 tablespoons sunflower oil
- 3 tablespoons sesame seeds
- ¼ watermelon, peeled, seeded, and cubed

Serves 4

Combine the soy sauce, sake, watermelon juice, and ginger in a large non-metal dish, add the salmon fillets, turning to coat, and let mari-nate for at least 2 hours in the refrigerator. Preheat the oven to 350°F. Pour the oil into an ovenproof baking dish. Drain the salmon fillets, discarding the marinade, add the fillets to the baking dish in a single layer, and sprinkle with the sesame seeds. Bake for about 7 minutes, until the flesh flakes easily. Transfer to a warm serving dish, garnish with the watermelon, and serve.

Note: To cook the salmon on a barbecue, brush both sides with oil. To make watermelon juice, process chunks of watermelon and strain.

634

Salmon with orange vinaigrette
SALMON CON VINAGRETA DE NARANJA

- 1 cup olive oil
- 4 salmon fillets
- salt

Vinaigrette:
- 10 strips of shallot
- ½ orange
- 2 tablespoons balsamic vinegar
- 2 tablespoons olive oil
- salt

Serves 4

Pour the oil into a large non-metal dish and add the salmon fillets, turning to coat. Let marinate, turning occasionally, for about 20 min-utes. Preheat the broiler. Brush the broiler rack with a little of the oil from the marinade and discard the remaining marinade. Season the salmon fillets on both sides and cook under the broiler for about 4 minutes on each side, until the flesh flakes easily. Meanwhile, prepare the vinaigrette. Cut the shallots into pieces. Squeeze the juice from the orange and cut three strips of zest from the rind, avoiding the pith. Chop the zest finely. Combine the juice, balsamic vinegar, oil, and a pinch of salt in a bowl. Stir in the shallots and orange zest. Serve the salmon in a warm serving dish and offer the vinaigrette separately.

635

Baked red mullet
SALMONETES AL HORNO

- 6 red mullet or snapper, 7 ounces each, scaled and cleaned
- 6 lemon slices, halved
- 4 tablespoons olive oil
- juice of 1 lemon
- 6 tablespoons (¾ stick) butter
- salt

Serves 6

Preheat the oven to 350°F. Season the cavities of the fish with salt. Slash the fish on either side of the backbones with a sharp knife and insert a half slice of lemon into each cut. Pour the oil into an ovenproof baking dish and add the fish in a single layer. Lightly season with salt, pour the lemon juice over, and dot with the butter. Bake for about 15 minutes, until the flesh flakes easily, and serve immediately straight from the dish.

Red mullet cooked in packages

SALMONETES AL HORNO ENVUELTOS EN PAPEL (PAPILLOTES)

- 6 red mullet or snapper, about 7 ounces each, scaled and cleaned
- 6 tablespoons olive oil
- ½ teaspoon dried mixed herbs or 6 sprigs fresh thyme or fennel
- 1 large onion, very finely chopped
- salt

Serves 6

Preheat the oven to 350°F. Cut out six squares of parchment paper or aluminum foil with sides 2 inches longer than the fish, then cut into heart shapes. Season the fish inside and out with salt. Brush the sheets with some of the oil, brush both sides of each fish with oil, and place each one on a parchment or foil sheet. Sprinkle the dried herbs over the fish or put a fresh herb sprig into each cavity. Divide the onion among them and wrap the parchment or foil around them. Put the packages onto a baking sheet and bake for about 15 minutes. Serve the fish in a dish with the packages half open.

Note: This dish has the advantage that the fish can wait quite some time before being served without drying out. Also, the smell of fish is not so strong. If you use parchment, it might require a shorter cooking time than foil.

637

Red mullet baked with bread crumbs and rancio wine

SALMONETES AL HORNO CON PAN RALLADO Y VINO RANCIO

- 6 red mullet or snapper, about 7 ounces each, scaled and cleaned
- 4 tablespoons olive oil
- 1 small onion, very finely chopped
- juice of ½ lemon
- ¾ cup rancio-style wine such as muscatel
- 2 tablespoons bread crumbs
- ¼ cup (½ stick) butter
- salt

Serves 6

Preheat the oven to 350°F. Season the fish with salt inside and out and slash on either side of the backbones with a sharp knife. Pour the oil into an ovenproof baking dish and sprinkle in the onion. Add the fish in a single layer and pour the lemon juice and wine over them. Sprinkle with the bread crumbs and dot with the butter. Bake for about 15 minutes, until the fish are browned. Serve immediately, straight from the dish.

Note: A tawny brown, rich uniquely flavored wine with a full aroma of overly ripe fruit, rancio wines are wood-aged and heated fortified wines, such as Madeira. Vino raucio, or raucio-style, is not rancid, as the name suggests, but is made by aging the wine in barrels left in the hot sun, which gives it a unique, fruity flavor.

638

Broiled red mullet with green mayonnaise

SALMONETES EMPANADOS A LA PARRILLA, CON SALSA MAYONESA VERDE

- 1 cup olive oil
- juice of 1 lemon
- 6 red mullet or snapper, about 7 ounces each, scaled and cleaned
- 1½ cups bread crumbs
- salt
- 1 quantity Green Mayonnaise (see recipe 107)

Serves 6

Combine the oil and lemon juice in a dish. Season the fish with salt inside and out and add to the dish, turning to coat. Let marinate in the refrigerator, turning occasionally, for 2 hours. Preheat the broiler. Drain the fish and coat them in the bread crumbs. Brush the broiler rack with a little of the marinade and discard the remaining marinade. Put the fish on the rack, and cook under the broiler for about 10 minutes on each side, until the flesh flakes easily. Serve immediately, offering the mayonnaise separately.

639

- 3¼ pounds fresh sardines or sprats, scaled, cleaned, and boned
- sunflower oil, for deep-frying
- ½ cup all-purpose flour
- 2 eggs, lightly beaten
- 1 lemon, cut into wedges
- salt

Serves 6

Sardines coated in egg and fried

SARDINAS REBOZADAS CON HUEVO Y FRITAS

Open out the fish and lightly season with salt on both sides. Heat the oil in a deep-fryer or deep skillet to 350–375°F or until a cube of day-old bread browns in 30 seconds. Coat each fish first in the flour, holding it by the tail and shaking to remove any excess, and then in the beaten egg. Add to the hot oil, in batches, and cook until golden brown. Remove with a slotted spoon, drain well, and keep warm while you cook the remaining batches. Garnish with the lemon wedges and serve immediately.

640

- 5 tablespoons olive oil
- 3¼ pounds large fresh sardines or sprats, scaled, cleaned, and boned
- ⅔ cup white wine
- juice of ½ lemon
- 1 tablespoon chopped fresh parsley
- 3 tablespoons bread crumbs
- 3 tablespoons butter
- salt

Serves 6

Baked sardines with white wine and bread crumbs

SARDINAS AL HORNO CON VINO BLANCO Y PAN RALLADO

Preheat the oven to 350°F. Pour the oil into an ovenproof baking dish. Lightly season the fish with salt on both sides and put them into the dish in a single layer. Pour in the wine and lemon juice, sprinkle with the parsley and bread crumbs, and dot with the butter. Bake, basting occasionally, for about 15 minutes, until the flesh flakes easily. Serve immediately, straight from the dish.

641 📷 Baked sardines stuffed with spinach

SARDINAS AL HORNO RELLENAS DE ESPINACAS

- 3¼ pounds spinach,
  coarse stalks removed
- 7 tablespoons butter
- 3¼ pounds large fresh sardines
  or sprats, scaled, cleaned,
  and boned
- 4 tablespoons olive oil
- 2 tablespoons bread crumbs
- salt

Serves 6

Preheat the oven to 350°F. Cook the spinach as described on page 315. Drain well, pressing out as much liquid as possible with the back of a spoon, then chop. Melt 6 tablespoons of the butter in a skillet, add the spinach, and cook, stirring occasionally, for 5 minutes. Season to taste with salt. Remove from the heat and keep warm. Put the fish on a work surface, skin side down. Lightly season with salt and divide the spinach among them, then roll up the fish. Pour the oil into an ovenproof baking dish, making sure that the base is covered. Put the rolled-up fish into the dish in a single layer, sprinkle with the bread crumbs, and dot with the remaining butter. Bake for 15 minutes, then serve immediately straight from the dish.

642 Sardines in pastry packages

SARDINAS EN HOJAS DE BRICK

- 12 canned sardines or
  18 canned sprats, drained
- 4 sheets of brik or puff pastry
  or 8 sheets of phyllo pastry,
  thawed if frozen
- ¼ cup (½ stick) butter, melted
- 4 small tomatoes,
  peeled, seeded, and chopped
- 6 fresh basil leaves, chopped
- 4 cloves garlic, finely chopped
- 4 fresh chives
- 1 lemon, cut into wedges
- mixed salad greens dressed with
  an oil and lemon vinaigrette

Serves 4

Preheat the oven to 400°F. Remove the backbones from the fish, flake the flesh, and set aside. Spread out the pastry sheets on a work surface and brush with some of the melted butter. If using phyllo, put the sheets together in pairs at an angle to each other. Divide the flaked fish, tomato, basil, and garlic among the pastry sheets. Gather up the edges like money pouches and tie each with a chive. Brush a baking sheet with some of the remaining melted butter and place the packages on it. Brush them all over with melted butter and bake for about 20 minutes, until golden brown. Serve the packages on a bed of dressed mixed salad greens, garnished with the lemon wedges.

Notes: Brik is the name of a North African dish made with a very flaky pastry. This pastry (also known as malsouqa, wasqa, and ouarka) is extremely difficult to make but is available from specialist stores. Phyllo pastry and puff pastry are good alternatives or you could even use wonton wrappers, which are available from Chinese supermarkets. When they are in season, use fresh sardines for this dish.

643

• 6 trout, about 5 ounces each
• 1 cup milk
• ½ cup all-purpose flour
• sunflower oil, for deep-frying
• salt

Serves 6

Fried trout

TRUCHAS FRITAS

Scale and clean the trout, then wash, and pat dry. Season inside and out with salt and let stand for about 10 minutes to allow the salt to soak in. Heat the oil in a deep-fryer or deep skillet. Dip the fish first in the milk, and then in the flour. Add the fish to the hot oil, in batches of two, for about 10 minutes. Drain and keep warm while you cook the remaining fish. Serve immediately, garnished with lemon wedges if you like.

Note: Choose trout that weigh about 5 ounces each (smaller ones do not have much flesh and larger ones do not fry well).

644

• 4 trout, cleaned
• 11 ounces canned red bell peppers, drained and cut into strips
• 1 chile, seeded and cut into pieces
• 4 thin slices of Serrano ham or prosciutto
• 3 tablespoons olive oil
• 1 clove garlic, finely chopped
• 1 tablespoon white-wine vinegar or lemon juice
• salt

Serves 4

Trout with ham and bell peppers

TRUCHAS CON JAMON Y PIMIENTOS

Preheat the oven to 400°F. Season the trout with salt and pepper. Divide the bell pepper and the chile among the slices of ham. Roll up each slice of ham and put one inside the cavity of each fish. Put the trout into an ovenproof casserole that can be used on the stove in a single layer. Pour the oil over them and sprinkle with the garlic. Season with salt and bake for about 12 minutes, until the flesh flakes easily. Transfer the trout to a warm serving dish. Add the vinegar or lemon juice to the casserole and bring the mixture to a boil, then pour it over the trout, and serve immediately.

645

Sea trout poached in special quick stock

TRUCHA ASALMONADA EN CALDO CORTO ESPECIAL

- 2 tablespoons (¼ stick) butter
- 2 tablespoons olive oil
- ¾ cup chopped carrots
- 1 onion, chopped
- 1 slice of smoked bacon, chopped
- pinch of dried mixed herbs
- 2 ¼ cups white wine
- 1 sea trout, or salmon or actic char fillet, about 1 pound 2 ounces, scaled and cleaned
- Hollandaise Sauce (see recipe 84)
- salt and pepper

Serves 3

Melt the butter with the oil in a deep skillet. Add the carrot, onion, and bacon and cook over low heat, stirring occasionally, for 10 minutes. Lightly season with salt and pepper and add the mixed herbs. Stir in the wine and 2 ¼ cups water, bring to a boil, lower the heat, and simmer gently for 30 minutes. Strain the stock into a bowl and let cool. Season the trout inside and out with salt and let stand for about 10 minutes. Remove the rack from a fish poacher. Pour in the stock, put the trout on the rack, and return the rack to the fish poacher. The fish should be completely covered in liquid. Cover the fish poacher and set over very low heat so that the stock is barely simmering. Cook for about 15 minutes, until the flesh flakes easily. Place a folded napkin in a serving dish, add the trout, and serve immediately, offering the hollandaise sauce separately.

Note: This stock is also suitable for salmon, sea bass or grouper.

646

Trout with ham, almonds, and garlic

TRUCHAS CON JAMÓN, ALMENDRAS Y AJO

- 6 trout, about 9 ounces each, cleaned
- 2 ¼ cups sunflower oil
- 6 small slices of Serrano ham or prosciutto
- ⅓ cup all-purpose flour
- generous ½ cup finely chopped cooked ham
- 8 blanched almonds, finely chopped
- 3 cloves garlic, finely chopped
- 2 sprigs fresh parsley, finely chopped
- 3 tablespoons sherry or other sweet fortified wine
- juice of 1 lemon
- salt and pepper

Serves 6

Season the trout with salt and pepper. Heat the oil in a skillet. Add the Serrano ham and cook, turning once, for 1–2 minutes, then remove and drain. Put a slice of Serrano ham into the cavity of each fish. Coat the trout in the flour, shaking off any excess, and then add to the skillet, in batches, and cook until golden brown all over. Transfer to an ovenproof baking dish in a single layer. Preheat the oven to 400°F. Transfer ½ cup of the oil to a small skillet and heat. Add the chopped ham, almonds, garlic, and parsley and cook for about 5 minutes, until the garlic and almonds are lightly browned. Stir in the sherry and lemon juice, then pour the sauce over the trout. Bake for 10 minutes and then serve immediately, straight from the dish.

647 Navarra trout with ham

TRUCHAS CON JAMÓN (A LA NAVARRA)

- 6 trout, about 9 ounces each,
  scaled and cleaned
- 6 thin slices of Serrano ham
  or prosciutto
- 3 cups sunflower oil
- 1 onion, finely chopped
  (optional)
- 2¼ pounds tomatoes,
  peeled, seeded, and chopped
- 1 teaspoon sugar
- 1 large red bell pepper, seeded
  and cut into strips
- ½ cup all-purpose flour
- salt

Serves 6

Season the trout inside and out with salt and let stand for about 10 minutes. Place a slice of ham inside the cavity of each fish and close the cavity with a wooden toothpick. Using 3 tablespoons of the oil, the onion, if using, the tomatoes, and sugar, make a thick tomato sauce as described in recipe 73. Stir in the bell pepper and cook, stirring occasionally, for 10 minutes, then transfer to a serving dish, and keep warm. Meanwhile, heat the remaining oil in a skillet. Coat the trout in the flour, shaking off any excess, add to the hot oil, in batches if necessary, and cook until golden brown. Transfer to the serving dish and serve immediately.

Note: Some people prefer to serve the trout without the tomato sauce. Also, some people prefer to wrap the ham around the trout, holding it in place with a wooden toothpick, and frying the fish without coating them in flour.

648 Trout au bleu

TRUCHAS AZULADAS

- 6 very fresh trout,
  about 9 ounces, cleaned,
  but not scaled or rinsed
- 1 cup red-wine vinegar

Quick stock with red wine:
- scant 2 cups red wine
- 2 carrots, sliced
- 1 onion, cut into wedges
- 1 bay leaf
- 1 sprig fresh parsley
- 2–3 black peppercorns
- 1 tablespoon salt
- 1 quantity Hollandaise Sauce
  (see recipe 84) or
  Special Vinaigrette
  (see recipe 99 or 100)

Serves 6

Make a quick stock with 10 ⅔ cups water and all the stock ingredients as described in recipe 534. Remove the rack from a fish poacher, pour in the stock, and bring to a boil. Meanwhile, put the trout into a deep dish. Bring the vinegar to a boil in a pan and pour it over the trout, turning to coat. Transfer the trout to the rack and return the rack to the fish poacher. Cover the poacher and cook the trout over a very low heat for 10 minutes. Place a folded napkin in a serving dish. Lift out the rack, drain the fish, and place them on the napkin. Serve immediately with the hollandaise sauce or special vinaigrette.

Note: The name of this dish, which translates as "bluish trout," refers to a method of cooking fish (especially trout) where a freshly killed fish is immersed in boiling stock, which turns its skin a bluish color.

649

Cold trout in gelatin
TRUCHAS FRÍAS EN GELATINA

- **6 trout, about 9 ounces, cleaned but not scaled**
- **¾ cup red-wine vinegar**
- **2 envelopes (½ ounce) unflavored gelatin**
- **1 quantity Classic Mayonnaise (see recipe 105)**
- **lettuce leaves or watercress or tomato slices or hard-cooked egg slices**

Quick stock:
- **1 bay leaf**
- **1 thick slice of onion**
- **2 carrots, sliced**
- **juice of ½ lemon**
- **4–5 black peppercorns**
- **1 tablespoon salt**
- **generous 1 cup white wine**

Serves 6

First prepare the quick stock, using all the ingredients and 13 cups water as described in recipe 534. Add the wine just as the stock comes to a boil and simmer for 20 minutes. Remove the rack from a fish poacher, pour in the stock, and bring to a boil. Meanwhile, put the trout into a deep dish. Pour the vinegar and 2 ¼ cups water into a small pan and bring to a boil. Remove the pan from the heat, let cool slightly, then pour the mixture over the trout, turning to coat. Transfer the trout to the rack and return the rack to the fish poacher, plunging the fish into the boiling stock. Immediately remove the poacher from the heat and let cool completely. Lift out the rack and drain the trout. Carefully remove the skin from the base of the head until just before the tail, then place the fish in a serving dish. Strain 2 ¼ cups of the stock into a heatproof bowl. Sprinkle the gelatin over the surface and let sponge for 5 minutes. Set the bowl over a pan of barely simmering water and leave until the gelatin has dissolved completely and the mixture is clear. Remove the bowl from the heat and let cool until beginning to set. Brush some of the gelatin over each trout and repeat three or four times. Chill in the refrigerator for at least 3–4 hours. Allow the remaining gelatin to set, then chop it, and place it around the trout. Garnish with lettuce leaves or watercress, tomatoes, and hard-cooked eggs. Serve the trout accompanied by the mayonnaise in a sauceboat.

Shellfish

650

Small crabs
CANGREJOS DE MAR PEQUEÑOS

- **36 small crabs,**
  such as blue crabs
- **4 tablespoons olive oil**
- **1 clove garlic**
- **pinch of dried mixed herbs**
  or 1 bouquet garni
  (1 sprig fresh thyme, 2 bay
  leaves, and 1 sprig fresh parsley
  tied together in cheesecloth)
- **3 black peppercorns**
- **salt**

Makes 36 appetizers

Wash the crabs in salted water, but do not leave them in the water. Remove the legs, if you like. Crush four or five crabs in a mortar or sturdy bowl. Heat the oil in a skillet. Add the garlic and cook, stirring occasionally, for a few minutes, until lightly browned. Add the crushed crabs, stir well, and add the whole crabs (with or without legs) and the dried herbs or bouquet garni. Pour in water to cover, add the peppercorns, and season with salt. Bring to a boil and cook over high heat for 5 minutes. Remove the pan from the heat, drain the crabs, and let cool. Serve as an appetizer or add to a paella just before serving.

Note: The crabs are served as appetizers and used to garnish paella when crayfish are not available.

651 **Fisherman's cold spider crab**

CENTOLLO FRÍO A LA PESCADORA

- ¾ cup white-wine vinegar
- 10 black peppercorns
- 3 bay leaves
- 2 spider crabs or Dungeness crabs, thawed if frozen
- 11 ounces hake fillet
- 1 tablespoon white wine
- 1 thick slice of onion
- 3 hard-cooked egg yolks
- ¼ teaspoon mustard
- juice of 1 lemon
- 4 tablespoons sunflower oil
- salt

Serves 2

Pour 5 ¼ quarts water into a pan, add the vinegar, peppercorns, two of the bay leaves, and a pinch of salt, and bring to a boil over high heat. Plunge in the crabs, cover, bring back to a boil, and cook over high heat for 8 minutes. Drain well and let cool. Meanwhile, put the hake fillet into a pan, pour in water to cover, and add the remaining bay leaf, and the wine, onion, and a pinch of salt. Bring to a boil, then remove the pan from the heat. Lift out the hake, remove and discard any skin and bones, and flake the flesh. Once the crabs are cold, open them carefully without breaking the back shells. Remove and discard the gills. Take out the white meat from the body and the legs and cut it into pieces. Scoop out any brown meat into a bowl and reserve any roe from a hen crab. Wash and dry the back shells and set aside. Pound the brown meat, roe, hard-cooked egg yolks, mustard and lemon juice in a mortar, or process in a food processor. Gradually mix in the oil, a little at a time, and season to taste with salt. Combine the hake, white crab meat, and the sauce in a bowl, then divide between the crab shells. Store in the refrigerator until ready to serve.

Crayfish

Crayfish are freshwater crustaceans that look like small lobsters. Also called crawfish in parts of the United States, crayfish can be purchased live or cooked, peeled or shell on, refrigerated or frozen.

How to clean

Wash in plenty of cold water just before cooking (if done in advance, they release all their water). Twist off the tail and peel, otherwise twist the central lamina at the end of the tail and pulling it so that the gut comes out whole. The crayfish are now ready to be cooked.

652

Crayfish

CANGREJOS DE RÍO

- **24 crayfish, thawed if frozen**
- **1 cup white wine**
- **2 carrots, chopped**
- **1 onion, chopped**
- **6 black peppercorns**
- **2 bay leaves**
- **1 sprig fresh parsley**
- **1 sprig fresh thyme**
- **1 tablespoon sunflower oil**
- **salt**

Serves 4

Prepare the crayfish as described above. Put all the remaining ingredients into a pan, pour in 8 ¾ cups water, and add a pinch of salt. Bring to a boil over high heat and plunge in the crayfish so that they are covered by the stock. Bring back to a boil and cook for 4–6 minutes, depending on the size of the crayfish. Drain well and serve warm or cold.

Crayfish tails in béchamel sauce with brandy

COLAS DE CANGREJOS CON SALSA BECHAMEL Y COÑAC

- **36–48 cooked crayfish, thawed if frozen**
- **6 tablespoons (¾ stick) butter**
- **2 tablespoons sunflower oil**
- **2 tablespoons all-purpose flour**
- **2¼ cups milk**
- **1 teaspoon tomato paste**
- **2 tablespoons brandy**
- **1 truffle**
- **salt and pepper**

Serves 6

Pull off and reserve the crayfish heads and peel the tails. Set the tails aside in a pan. Put the heads, if using, and 4 tablespoons of the butter into a pan and heat gently, stirring constantly. Pour the mixture into a mortar and pound or process in a mini-food processor. Strain through a cheesecloth-lined strainer into a bowl, then twist the cheesecloth with your hands to extract all the juices. Set aside. Melt the remaining butter with the oil in a pan. Stir in the flour and cook, stirring constantly, for 2 minutes. Gradually stir in the milk, a little at a time. Cook, stirring constantly, for about 10 minutes, until thickened. Season to taste with salt and pepper and stir in the tomato paste. Heat the brandy in a small pan for about 30 seconds, ignite it, and pour it over the crayfish tails, stirring until the flames die down. Stir into the béchamel sauce along with the truffle and the crayfish juices. Cook, stirring constantly, for 1 minute more. Taste and adjust the seasoning, if necessary, and serve immediately in individual dishes.

654

Bordeaux crayfish
CANGREJOS DE RÍO AL ESTILO BURDEOS

- 3 tablespoons olive oil
- 2 large carrots,
  very finely chopped
- 1 small onion, finely chopped
- 1 shallot, very finely chopped
- 36 large crayfish,
  thawed if frozen
- 1 cup dry white wine
- 3 tablespoons brandy
- 2 very ripe tomatoes,
  seeded and chopped
- pinch of dried mixed herbs or
  1 bouquet garni (1 clove garlic,
  1 sprig fresh parsley, 1 sprig
  fresh thyme, and 2 bay leaves
  tied together in cheesecloth)
- pinch of cayenne pepper
- 2 tablespoons (¼ stick) butter
- 1 tablespoon chopped
  fresh parsley
- salt and pepper
Serves 6

Heat the oil in a pan. Add the carrot, onion, and shallot, cover, and cook over low heat for 5 minutes. Add 1 cup water, re-cover, and cook for 10 minutes more. Meanwhile, prepare the crayfish as described on page 536. Put them into a skillet with the wine and a pinch of salt, cover, and cook over high heat until they change color. Warm the brandy in a small pan for a few seconds, ignite it, and pour it over the crayfish, stirring until the flames have died down. Remove the pan from the heat and set aside. Add the tomato to the pan of vegetables and cook, stirring occasionally and breaking it up with the side of the spoon, for 5 minutes. Add the crayfish mixture and dried herbs or bouquet garni, season with pepper, and cook for about 5 minutes, then remove the crayfish with a slotted spoon, and keep warm. Cook the sauce for 10 minutes more, then pass it through a strainer into a clean pan, pressing down hard and adding a little hot water if necessary. Add the cayenne pepper, season to taste with salt, and add the butter and crayfish. Sprinkle with the parsley and cook for a few minutes more. Serve immediately.

655

Crayfish omelet
TORTILLA DE COLAS DE CANGREJOS DE RÍO

- 6 crayfish, thawed if frozen
- 1½ tablespoons butter
- 2 eggs
- 3 tablespoons sunflower oil
Serves 1

Clean and cook the crayfish as described on page 536, then remove the heads and peel the tails. If the tails are large, cut them into two or three pieces. Melt the butter in a pan. Add the crayfish, season with salt and pepper, and cook, stirring occasionally, for 1–2 minutes. Lightly beat the eggs with a pinch of salt. Heat the oil in a skillet, pour in the eggs and cook as described on page 422. Drain the crayfish and sprinkle them over the omelet, then fold the omelet, and slide it out of the pan. Serve immediately.

Mediterranean shrimp

Also known as crevettes, these European shrimp are not quite so large or so fine as langoustines (lobsterettes). They are very good for soups and can be served as a less expensive substitute for langoustines. Remove their heads before cooking, as they have a very strong flavor, and cook in the same way as langoustines as described in page 552). Any jumbo shrimp would be a good substitute and royal red shrimp would be perfect.

656

Crevette and asparagus fan
ABANICO DE CARABINEROS Y ESPARRAGOS

- **24 asparagus spears, trimmed**
- **24 raw crevetttes, or other large shrimp, shells on and heads attached, if available**

Sauce:
- **2 tablespoons olive oil**
- **1 onion, chopped**
- **1 carrot, chopped**
- **¾ cup white wine**
- **4 cups heavy cream**
- **1 bouquet garni**
  (1 sprig fresh thyme, 2 bay leaves, and 1 sprig fresh parsley tied together in cheesecloth)
- **2 sprigs fresh tarragon**
- **3 tablespoons butter (optional)**
- **salt and pepper**

Serves 6

Bring a pan of salted water to a boil, add the asparagus with the tips pointing upward, cover, and bring back to a boil. Lower the heat and simmer for about 15 minutes, until the asparagus is tender. Remove the pan from the heat but leave the asparagus in the water. Meanwhile, bring another pan of salted water to a boil. Add the crevettes and cook for 3 minutes, then drain well. Remove the heads, if available, and peel the crevettes. Pound the shells and heads, if using, into a mortar or process in a mini-food processor. Heat the oil in a skillet. Add the crushed shells and heads, if using, and cook, stirring frequently, for 3–4 minutes. Add the onion and carrot and cook, stirring occasionally, for 3 minutes more. Pour in the wine and cook until reduced by half. Stir in the cream, add the bouquet garni and tarragon, and cook over low heat for 30 minutes. Pass the sauce through a food mill into a clean pan. If it seems too thin, cook until reduced to the desired consistency. (You could also stir in 3 tablespoons butter to thicken it). Season to taste with salt and pepper, add the crevettes, and heat through. Place the asparagus spears and crevettes alternately on a warm serving dish and serve immediately accompanied by the sauce.

Spiny lobsters

Varieties

There is confusion about the names of some crustaceans. The French word cigale refers to slipper or flat lobsters, while the Spanish cigalas is more usually applied to spiny lobsters in spite of the similar-sounding name. To add to the confusion, the spiny lobster is also known as the rock lobster, Florida lobster, thorn lobster, crawfish, and langouste. It is often mistakenly called a crayfish, which is a smaller freshwater crustacean, and crayfish are also often called crawfish, especially in the United States. In the end, it makes little difference whether you use slipper lobsters or spiny lobsters as they have a similar flavor, neither has claws, all the meat is in the tail, and both make good eating.

How to cook

Bring a large pan of salted water to a boil. Add the lobsters, making sure that they are fully immersed. When the water comes back to a boil, remove the pan from the heat, and let cool for 8 minutes. Lift out the lobsters, drain well, and serve cold.

Spiny lobster with mayonnaise and spiny lobster with vinaigrette

CIGALAS CON MAYONESA Y CIGALAS CON VINAGRETA

- 2 x 1⅓ pounds spiny lobsters
- 1 quantity Classic Mayonnaise (see recipe 105) or Vinaigrette (see recipe 98)
- 1 tablespoon finely chopped fresh parsley (optional)
- 1 tablespoon finely chopped scallion (optional)
- 1 tablespoon brandy (optional)
- salt and pepper

Serves 4

To serve with mayonnaise, cook the lobsters as described on page 540 and serve cold, offering the mayonnaise separately. To serve with vinaigrette, make a salpicón the night before it is required. To do this, take the vinaigrette and add the onion, parsley, hard-cooked egg, and brandy. Season to taste with salt and pepper. Cook the lobsters as described on page 540 and let cool, then remove the meat from the tails, and cut into slices about ¾ inch thick. Put the slices into a deep dish, pour the salpicón over them, and leave in the refrigerator for 3–5 hours. Serve cold.

Note: This dish can be made with shrimp rather than spiny lobster, leaving the peeled shrimp whole. It can also be made with lobster, for which allow 1 lobster, weighing about 1 pound 5 ounces for 2 servings.

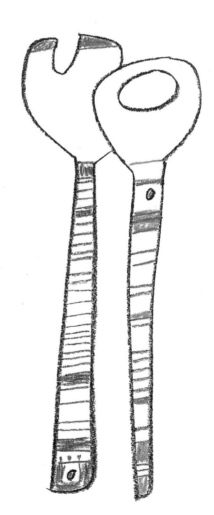

Shrimp

How to cook

Bring a large pan of salted water to a boil. Add the raw shrimp, lower the heat, and simmer for 2–4 minutes, depending on their size. Drain well and let cool.

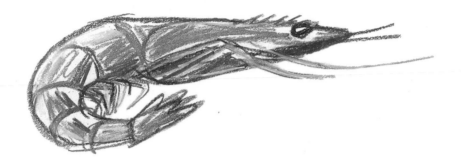

658

Shrimp cocktail

CÓCTEL DE GAMBAS

- 3¼ pounds raw shrimp
- 1 large lettuce
- 1 quantity Mayonnaise with Tomato and Brandy (see recipe 108)
- 1 hard-cooked egg, finely chopped
- salt

Serves 6

Cook the shrimp as described above. Drain well and let cool. Shred the lettuce and peel the shrimp. Make a bed of lettuce in the base of six champagne glasses or sundae dishes and top each with 1 tablespoon of the mayonnaise. Divide the shrimp among the glasses or dishes and cover them with the remaining mayonnaise. Sprinkle with the hard-cooked egg and chill in the refrigerator for 1–2 hours before serving.

Fish and shrimp salad

ENSALADA DE PESCADO Y GAMBAS

- **6 tablespoons olive oil**
- **12 large shrimp, peeled**
- **2 strips of chile**
- **5 ounces kingklip fillets**
- **5 ounces precooked crabmeat**
- **juice of 2 lemons**
- **1 tablespoon chopped fresh mint**
- **1 lettuce, shredded**
- **salt and pepper**

Serves 4

Heat half the oil in a skillet. Add the shrimp and chile and cook over medium heat, stirring occasionally, for a few minutes, until the shrimp are opaque. Remove from the pan, drain well, and set aside. Steam the kingklip fillets for 3 minutes . Cut the shrimp into pieces and flake the fish and crabmeat. Put into a bowl with the remaining oil, and the lemon juice, and mint, season with salt and pepper, and let marinate in the refrigerator. To serve, make a bed of lettuce on a round dish and put the fish mixture on top. Pour the marinade over the salad and serve.

Note: Kingklip, also called congrio, is an eel-like fish with pink, orange, brown or black markings. It can be found off the coasts of South America and South Africa. If you can't find it, use another firm-fleshed, mild fish such as monkfish.

Lobster

Spanish cooks distinguish between hen lobsters (langosta) and their male counterparts (bogavante). In fact, chefs and gourmets throughout the world generally agree that female lobsters are usually heavier, are better value, and have a better flavor. Cook and prepare bogavante the same way as langosta. It is not advisable to buy one that weighs more than 2 ¼ pounds as the meat will not be as good.

How to prepare

Allow 1 pound 2 ounces–1 pound 5 ounces lobster for 2 servings. Tie the lobster. Pour 3 ¼–4 ¾ quarts water into a pan, add 1 thickly sliced carrot, 1 wedge of onion, 1 bay leaf, 1 sprig fresh thyme, 1 sprig fresh parsley, 5 tablespoons dry white wine, 1 teaspoon salt, and 6 black peppercorns. Cook over high heat for 20 minutes, then plunge in the lobster so that it is completely submerged, cover the pan, lower the heat, and cook for 8 minutes per 2 ¼ pounds. Remove the pan from the heat and let cool for about 15 minutes. Then lift the lobster out of the water, untie it, and let it drain. Remove the head from the tail. Cut open the tail on the underside of the shell with a large pair of scissors. Remove the meat in one piece. Using the point of a knife, remove and discard the black intestinal tract that runs along its length. Remove and discard the stomach sac from the head. Remove and reserve the tomalley (liver) and any roe. To kill lobster painlessly, put it into the freezer for 2 hours before plunging it into boiling liquid.

Lobster served with mayonnaise

LANGOSTA COCIDA, SERVIDA CON SALSA MAYONESA

• **2 lobsters,**
  about 1 pound 2 ounces each
• **1 quantity Classic Mayonnaise**
  (see recipe 105)
• **lettuce leaves**
• **2 tomatoes, thickly sliced**
• **2 hard-cooked eggs, sliced**

Serves 4

Prepare the lobster as described on page 546 and remove the meat. Cut the tail meat into slices. Put the head and tail shell on an elongated dish. Place the slices of tail meat in the tail shell and put the legs around the edge of the dish with the edible parts of the head and claw meat. Garnish with the lettuce leaves, tomato, and hard-cooked egg. Offer the mayonnaise in a sauceboat.

661 Lobster and melon salad

ENSALADA DE LANGOSTA Y MELON

- 14 ounces green beans, trimmed
- 2 lobsters,
  about 1 pound 5 ounces each
- 1 cantaloupe melon,
  halved and seeded
- juice of 1 lemon
- ½ cup olive oil
- 7 ounces mixed salad greens
- 1 sprig fresh dill, chopped
- 6 fresh chives
- salt and ground pink
  peppercorns

Stock:
- 1 carrot, sliced
- 1 onion, sliced
- 1 leek, sliced and rinsed well
- 1 bouquet garni
  (1 sprig fresh thyme, 1 bay leaf,
  1 sprig fresh parsley tied
  together in cheesecloth)
- 5 tablespoons dry white wine
- 6 black peppercorns
- 1 teaspoon salt

Serves 4

Cook the beans in salted boiling water for 5–10 minutes, until crisp-tender. Drain, refresh under cold water, and drain again. Put into a bowl and set aside. Put all the ingredients for the stock into a pan, pour in 10 ⅔ cups water, and bring to a boil. Lower the heat and simmer for 30 minutes. Plunge in the lobsters so that they are completely submerged, cover, and cook for 8 minutes. Remove the lobsters with a slotted spoon and let drain and cool. Using a melon baller, scoop out balls of the melon flesh. Set aside. Separate the heads from the tails of the lobsters and cut open the tails on the underside of the shell with a large pair of scissors. Remove the flesh from the tails, then remove and discard the black intestinal tracts. Cut the flesh from the tails in half. Remove the edible meat from the head and crack the claws and remove the edible meat. Combine a pinch of salt, a pinch of pink pepper, and the lemon juice in a bowl, then whisk in the oil. Toss the salad greens with some of the dressing and toss the green beans separately with some of the dressing. Make a bed of the salad greens on a serving dish and pile a cone of green beans in the center. Put the halved lobster tails and other meat on top and brush with the remaining dressing. Sprinkle with the dill and chives, arrange the melon balls around the edge and serve.

Note: A few drops of port poured over the melon adds extra flavor.

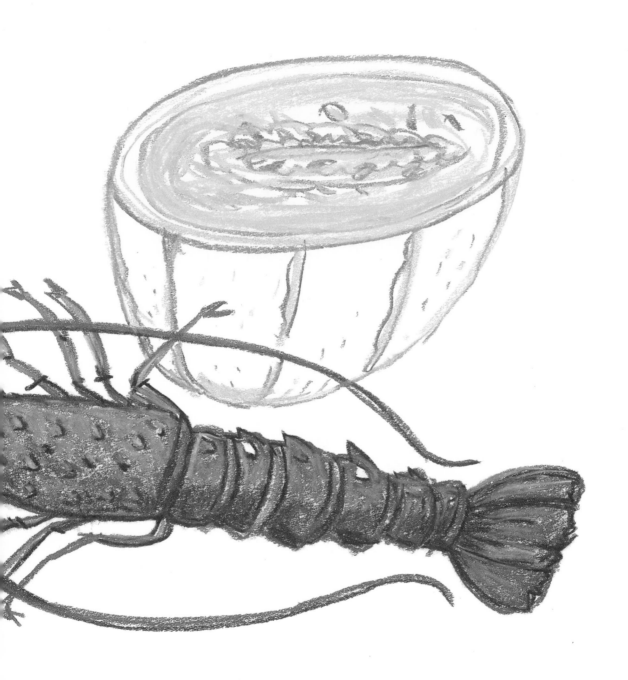

662 Lobster mousse with leek fondue
ESPUMA DE LANGOSTA EN MOLDE CON FONDUE DE PUERROS

- 1 gelatin leaf
- 1¼ cups canned lobster bisque
  or other creamy lobster soup
- 1 teaspoon Dijon mustard
- 1¼ cups heavy cream
- 2 tablespoons brandy
- 1½ tablespoons butter
- 3 leeks,
  cut into strips and rinsed well
- 1 tablespoon sliced almonds,
  toasted
- salt and pepper

Serves 4

Put the gelatin into a small bowl of cold water to soak for 5 minutes. Meanwhile, pour the soup into a bowl and stir in the mustard. Whisk the cream in another bowl until stiff. Heat the brandy in a small pan, then remove from the heat. Squeeze out the gelatin and stir it into the brandy until dissolved, then stir into the soup mixture. Fold in the cream and divide the mixture among four individual molds. Cover and chill in the refrigerator for 6 hours, until set. Melt the butter in a skillet. Add the leek and cook over low heat, stirring occasionally, for a few minutes, until crisp-tender. Turn the mousse out of the molds onto individual plates and surround each one with strips of leek. Sprinkle the almonds over the mousses and serve.

Note: If using plastic molds, brush them with a little oil to make it easier to turn out the mousses. If the molds are not plastic, put aluminum foil in the base of each one.

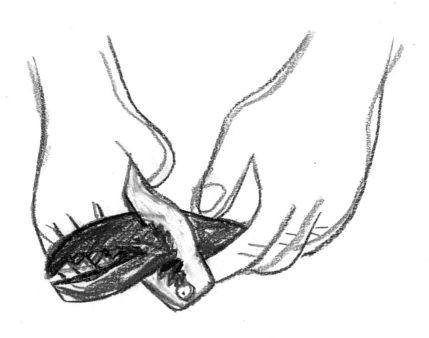

663

Lobster with béchamel sauce
LANGOSTA CON BECHAMEL AL HORNO

- 2 lobsters,
  about 1 pound 5 ounces each
- generous ½ cup butter
- 2¼ cups hot milk
- 1 heaping tablespoon
  all-purpose flour
- a pinch of curry powder
- 1 large truffle, thinly sliced
- 2 egg yolks
- juice of ½ lemon
- ⅔ cup grated Parmesan cheese
- salt

Quick stock:
- 1 carrot, thickly sliced
- 1 onion wedge
- 1 bouquet garni (1 sprig
  fresh thyme, 1 bay leaf,
  1 sprig fresh parsley tied
  together in cheesecloth)
- 5 tablespoons dry white wine
- 6 black peppercorns
- 1 teaspoon salt

Serves 4

Pour 4 ¾ quarts water into a pan, add all the stock ingredients, and cook the lobsters as described on page 546. When the lobsters have cooled, cut them in half lengthwise. Cut off the legs and break off the claws. Loosen the meat in the tail and remove the black intestinal tracts. Remove and reserve the tomalley and any roe from the heads, and remove and discard the stomach sac. Break the claws into pieces at the joints and crack them open. Place the lobster halves, cut sides uppermost, in a large stovetop-safe dish. Put the tomalley, roe, claws, and legs into a pan with 7 tablespoons of the butter. Heat gently, stirring and breaking up the lobster pieces as much as possible. When the butter begins to froth, add the milk and bring to a boil. Strain through a cheesecloth-lined strainer into a bowl and reserve. Twist the cheesecloth to extract any remaining liquid. Let stand for 15 minutes, then skim off any pink colored butter that has risen to the surface, and set the butter aside in a bowl. Melt the remaining butter in a pan. Stir in the flour and cook, stirring constantly, for 2 minutes. Gradually stir in the strained milk, a little at a time. Cook, stirring constantly, for about 10 minutes, then season to taste with salt, and add the curry powder and truffle. Gradually stir in the reserved pink butter. Remove the pan from the heat. Preheat the broiler. Lightly beat the egg yolks and lemon juice in a bowl and stir in a few spoonfuls of the béchamel sauce, then stir into the pan. Pour the sauce over the lobsters, sprinkle with the Parmesan, and cook under the broiler for 4–5 minutes, until golden. Serve immediately.

Langoustines

Langoustines are also known as lobsterettes, Dublin Bay prawns and, in some places, as scampi, especially when deep-fried.

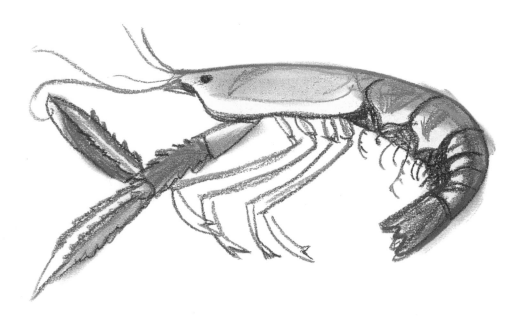

How to cook

Allow about 6 langoustines per serving. Do not cook them too far in advance or they will not be so juicy. If using frozen langoustines, let them thaw fully before using. To cook langoustines, bring a pan of salted water to a boil. Add the langoustines so that they are completely submerged and cook for 2 minutes, then remove them from the water with a slotted spoon. However, as langoustines can survive only a short time once they are out of the water, they are usually sold already cooked.

664 Breaded scampi

LANGOSTINOS EMPANADOS Y FRITOS

- 36 langoustines (lobsterettes), peeled
- 2 eggs
- ½ cup all-purpose flour
- 2 cups bread crumbs
- sunflower oil, for deep-frying
- 1 quantity Classic Mayonnaise (see recipe 105)
- salt and pepper

Serve 6

Bend the langoustines into nice shapes, season with salt and pepper, and let stand for about 10 minutes. Meanwhile, beat the eggs in a shallow dish. Pour the flour into another shallow dish and pour the bread crumbs into a third. Heat the oil in a deep-fryer or deep saucepan to 350–375°F or until a cube of day-old bread browns in 30 seconds. One at a time, coat the langoustines in the flour, then in the beaten egg, and, finally, in the bread crumbs. Thread them onto six metal skewers, submerge in the hot oil, and cook for 5–6 minutes, until golden brown. Remove from the oil and drain, then serve immediately, offering the mayonnaise separately.

665 Langoustines with American sauce and rice

LANGOSTINOS CON SALSA AMERICANA Y ARROZ BLANCO

- 36 langoustines (lobsterettes), unpeeled
- 2½ cups long-grain rice
- ½ cup (1 stick) butter
- ¾ cup sunflower oil
- 2 shallots, chopped
- 3 large ripe tomatoes, seeded and chopped
- pinch of dried mixed herbs
- pinch of cayenne pepper
- 1 sprig fresh parsley
- ¾ cup dry white wine
- 5 tablespoons brandy
- a few drops of red food coloring (optional)
- 4–5 tablespoons light cream
- salt and pepper

Serves 6

Pull off and reserve the heads of the langoustines and peel the tails. Put the tails in a bowl and cover with plastic wrap. Boil the rice and fry it in half the butter as described recipe 173. Spoon it into a cake pan. To make the American sauce, melt half the remaining butter with half the oil in a skillet. Add the langoustine heads, season with salt and pepper, and cook over high heat, stirring frequently, for about 5 minutes. Remove the heads from the pan and set aside. Add the shallots, tomato, dried herbs, cayenne pepper, and parsley to the pan and cook, stirring occasionally, for 5 minutes. Reduce the heat to medium, pour in the wine, and cook for 10–15 minutes. Melt the remaining butter with the remaining oil in another skillet. Add the langoustine tails and cook, stirring occasionally, for a few minutes, until golden. Heat the brandy in a small pan, ignite it, and pour it over the langoustines. When the sauce has finished cooking, add the langoustine heads and strain into a bowl, pressing down hard with the back of a spoon. Pour the sauce over the langoustine tails, adding food coloring, if using. Cook over low heat for 6 minutes, then remove the pan from the heat, and stir in the cream. Season to taste with salt and pepper. Put the langoustines and their sauce in a warm serving dish, turn out the rice, and serve immediately.

Notes: If the sauce is too thin, stir in a paste made from 1 teaspoon potato starch mixed with a little water before adding the cream. This dish can be made using crayfish in place of langoustines.

666

Langoustines in sauce

LANGOSTINOS EN SALSA

- 9 ounces langoustines
  (lobsterettes), unpeeled
- 1 bay leaf
- 1 tablespoon olive oil
- 1 clove garlic, chopped
- 1 onion, chopped
- 1 leek, sliced and rinsed well
- 1 sprig fresh tarragon
- 2 tablespoons fried tomato
- 2 tablespoons brandy
- boiled rice or pasta
- salt

Serves 4

Peel the langoustines, reserving the heads and shells, put the tails in a dish, and cover with plastic wrap. Put the heads and shells in a pan, pour in 1 cup water, add the bay leaf and a pinch of salt, and bring to a boil. Lower the heat and simmer for 20 minutes. Heat the oil in a skillet. Add the garlic, onion, and leek and cook over low heat, stirring occasionally, for 5 minutes, until softened. Add the tarragon and tomato and cook for a few minutes more, then add the langoustine tails, and cook for about 4 minutes, until opaque. Add the brandy and ignite. Transfer the heads and shells mixture to a food processor or blender, discarding the bay leaf. Process to a purée and strain the sauce over the langoustine tails. Heat through briefly, taste and adjust the seasoning, if necessary, and serve immediately with rice or pasta.

Notes: A little Tabasco sauce or other hot sauce can be added at the last minute for a spicy flavor. This dish can also be made with jumbo shrimp.

667

Seafood cocktail

COCTEL DE MARISCOS

- 4 tablespoons Classic
  Mayonnaise (see recipe 105)
- 1 tablespoon tomato paste
- 2 tablespoons lemon juice
- 2 tablespoons heavy cream
- 6 grapes, peeled and seeded
- 1 stalk celery, sliced
- 1 apple,
  peeled, cored, and chopped
- 1 red bell pepper,
  seeded and diced
- 1 head endive, cut into strips
- 1 pound 2 ounces cooked peeled
  langoustines (lobsterettes),
  shrimp, and spiny lobster
- pinch of paprika
- salt and pepper

Serves 4

Combine the mayonnaise, tomato paste, and lemon juice in a bowl and season with pepper. Whisk the cream in another bowl until stiff, and fold it into the mayonnaise mixture. Combine the grapes, celery, apple, bell pepper, endive, and shellfish in another bowl. Add half the sauce and mix well. Stir the paprika into the remaining sauce and pour it over the top.

Note: This dish looks lovely served in glasses or glass sundae dishes on a bed of crushed ice or in glasses that have been rinsed in cold water and put into the freezer.

Mussels

How to clean and cook

These days mussels often come precleaned, but if yours are not (you'll see the thread-like beard hanging from the shell and sandy water around them) you must clean them. Holding each mussel in your hand with the wide part of the shell near your fingers and the pointed end in the palm of your hand, scrape the shells with a knife and pull off the "beards." Scrub under cold running water and discard any mussels with broken shells or any that do not shut immediately when sharply tapped. Put the mussels into a pan with 1 cup water (for 4½–6½ pounds mussels) and a pinch of salt. Cover and cook over high heat, shaking the pan occasionally, for 4–5 minutes, until the shells have opened. Remove the pan from the heat and lift out the mussels with a slotted spoon. Discard any that remain closed. Depending on the dish you are preparing, either remove the mus-sels from their shells or leave them on the half shell and discard the empty half shells. Strain the cooking liquid through a cheesecloth-lined strainer into a bowl. The mussels are now ready to cook according to the recipe chosen.

668

Mussels in vinaigrette
MEJILLONES EN VINAGRETA

- 2¼ pounds mussels
- ½ onion, finely chopped
- 7 ounces canned red peppers, drained and chopped
- 7 ounces canned peas
- 1 quantity Vinaigrette (see recipe 98)

Serves 4

Prepare and cook the mussels as described above, pouring enough water into the pan to cover them completely. Drain and reserve the mussels on the half shell, discarding any that remain closed. Combine the onion, red bell pepper, and peas and spread this mixture over each mussel. Spoon the vinaigrette over the mussels.

Note: These are also ideal served as an appetizer.

669

- 2 ¼ pounds large mussels
- 1 egg
- 1 ½ cups bread crumbs
- sunflower oil, for deep-frying
- salt
- 1 quantity Classic Mayonnaise
  (see recipe 105)

Serves 4

Fried mussels

MEJILLONES REBOZADOS Y FRITOS

Prepare and cook the mussels as described on page 555. Drain and discard any mussels that remain closed. Remove the mussels from their shells, put them between two clean dishtowels, and place a weight, such as a heavy cutting board, on top. Beat the egg with a pinch of salt in a shallow dish and pour the bread crumbs into another shallow dish. Heat the oil in a deep-fryer or deep skillet to 350–375°F or until a cube of day-old bread browns in 30 seconds. Coat each mussel first in the beaten egg and then in the bread crumbs, add carefully add them to the hot oil, and cook until golden brown. Remove with a slotted spoon and drain. Stick a wooden toothpick into each mussel and serve immediately, offering the mayonnaise separately if you like.

Note: These are also ideal served as an appetizer.

670

- 6 ½ pounds mussels
- 5 tablespoons white wine
- 2 tablespoons (¼ stick) butter
- 2 tablespoons sunflower oil
- 1 heaping tablespoon
  all-purpose flour
- 2 egg yolks
- juice of 1 lemon
- 1 tablespoon chopped
  fresh parsley
- salt

Serves 6

Mussels with poulette sauce

MEJILLONES EN SALSA BECHAMEL CLARITA (POULETTE)

Prepare the mussels as described on page 555 and cook in the wine mixed with generous 1 cup water. Drain, and reserve the mussels on the half shell, discarding any that remain closed. Strain the cooking liquid through a cheesecloth-lined strainer into a bowl. Melt the butter with the oil in a pan. Stir in the flour and cook, stirring constantly, for 2 minutes. Gradually stir in the reserved cooking liquid, a little at a time, adding more water if necessary. Cook, stirring constantly, for 5 minutes. Lightly beat the egg yolks and lemon juice in a bowl and stir in a few spoonfuls of the sauce to prevent the yolks curdling, then stir into the pan. Season to taste with salt, stir in the parsley, and add the mussels. Cook for a few minutes to warm through. Serve in a warm deep serving dish.

Note: Poulette sauce is a variety of béchamel sauce that is thickened with egg and usually includes parsley.

671

Curried mussels
CONCHAS DE MEJILLONES AL CURRY

- 3¼–4½ pounds mussels
- ¾ cup white wine
- 1 shallot, finely chopped
- ¼ cup (½ stick) butter
- 2 tablespoons sunflower oil
- 2 tablespoons all-purpose flour
- 2¼ cups milk
- ½ teaspoon curry powder
- 1 tablespoon chopped
  fresh parsley
- 2 egg yolks
- juice of ½ lemon
- 3 tablespoons bread crumbs
- salt

Serves 6

Prepare the mussels as described on page 555. Put them into a pan, pour in ¾ cup water and the wine, and add the shallot and a pinch of salt. Cover and cook over high heat, shaking the pan occasionally, for 4–5 minutes, until the shells have opened. Remove the pan from the heat and lift out the mussels with a slotted spoon. Discard any that remain closed. Remove the mussels from their shells, cut them in half, put them into a bowl, and cover. Return the pan to the heat and cook for 10 minutes more to concentrate the cooking liquid. Strain through a cheesecloth-lined strainer into a bowl and set aside. Preheat the oven to 400°F. Melt 3 tablespoons of the butter with the oil in a pan. Stir in the flour and cook, stirring constantly, for 2 minutes. Gradually stir in the milk, a little at a time, then stir in 1 cup of the reserved cooking liquid. Cook, stirring constantly, for about 5 minutes, until thickened. Stir in the curry powder and parsley and season lightly to taste with salt. Lightly beat the egg yolks and lemon juice in a bowl and stir in a little of the sauce to prevent the yolks curdling, then stir into the pan. Add the mussels, then divide the mixture among six individual ovenproof baking dishes or scrubbed scallop shells. Sprinkle with the bread crumbs, dot with the remaining butter, and bake for about 10 minutes, until golden brown on the top. Serve immediately.

672

Mussels with garlic and parsley butter
MEJILLONES CON MANTEQUILLA, AJO Y PEREJIL, (AL ESTILO CARACOLES)

- 4½ pounds large mussels
- ¾ cup white wine
- 1 shallot, chopped
- pinch of dried mixed herbs
- salt

  Garlic and parsley butter:
- generous 1 cup butter, softened
- 2 cloves garlic,
  very finely chopped
- 3 tablespoons chopped
  fresh parsley

Serves 6

Preheat the oven to 400°F. Prepare the mussels as described on page 555. Put them into a pan, pour in the wine and ¾ cup water, and add the shallot, dried herbs, and a pinch of salt. Cover and cook over high heat, shaking the pan occasionally, for 4–5 minutes, until the shells have opened. Remove the pan from the heat and lift out the mussels with a slotted spoon. Discard any that remain closed. Divide the mussels on the half shells, open side up, among four individual ovenproof gratin dishes or ramekins. Beat the butter with the garlic and parsley until thoroughly combined. Using a round-bladed knife, place a little of the flavored butter on each mussel, covering it well. Put the gratin dishes or ramekins into the oven for just 3 minutes, until the garlic and parsley butter has melted. Serve immediately.

Mussel, bacon, and mushroom brochettes

PINCHOS DE MEJILLONES, BACON Y CHAMPIÑONES

- 6½ pounds large mussels
- 9 ounces mushrooms
- juice of ½ lemon
- 9 thin slices of bacon
- sunflower oil, for brushing
- salt

Serves 6

Preheat the oven 400°F. Prepare and cook the mussels as described on page 555. Drain, discarding any mussels that remain closed. Remove them from their shells. Separate the mushroom caps from the stalks. Cut the bacon into pieces twice the size of the mussels and fold them in half. Thread six skewers so that there is a mushroom cap at both ends and in the middle with pairs of mussels alternating with the folded pieces of bacon in between. Season the brochettes with salt and brush with the oil. Place the brochettes in a roasting pan or ovenproof baking dish so that the skewers are resting on the rim. Bake, turning the brochettes occasionally, for 8–10 minutes, until cooked through. Serve immediately.

Queen or king scallops

VIEIRAS O CONCHAS PEREGRINAS

- 9 scallops, thawed if frozen
- ⅔ cup butter
- 1 onion, very finely chopped
- pinch of dried mixed herbs
- pinch of cayenne pepper
- generous 1 cup white wine
- 2 ¾ cups sliced mushrooms
- juice of ½ lemon
- 4 tablespoons Classic Tomato Sauce (see recipe 73)
- 4 tablespoons bread crumbs
- salt

Serves 6

If your scallops have not been shelled, hold one of them flat side uppermost, in one hand and slide a thin-bladed knife between the two shells. Keeping the blade flat against the top shell, sever the ligament attaching the scallop to the shell and lift off the top shell. Remove and discard the "skirt" and the black stomach sac. Slide the knife under the scallop and sever the ligament attaching the scallop to the shell. Pull off and discard the ligament from the scallop. Separate the white muscle and orange coral and reserve. Repeat with the remaining scallops. Thoroughly scrub the rounded half shells and dry with paper towels. Melt 3 tablespoons of the butter in a pan. Add the onion and cook over low heat, stirring occasionally, for 5 minutes, until softened. Add the white scallop meat, sprinkle with the dried herbs and cayenne pepper, season with salt, and pour in the wine. Cook for 5 minutes. Put the mushrooms, 2 tablespoons of the remaining butter, the lemon juice, and a pinch of salt into a pan and cook over low heat for 6 minutes. Remove from the heat and set aside. Remove the scallops from the pan with a slotted spoon and cut them into slices about 5/8 inch thick. Slice the coral if you have it. Generously grease the inside of the reserved shells with some of the remaining butter and divide the scallop meat, mushrooms, and coral, if using, among them, placing the coral on top in the centre. Stir the tomato sauce into the onion and wine mixture and cook for a few minutes, then pour this sauce over the scallops. Sprinkle with the bread crumbs, dot with the remaining butter, and bake for about 5 minutes, until golden brown. Serve immediately.

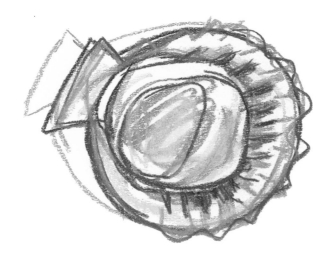

675

Scallop salad with Parmesan tuiles

ENSALADA DE VIEIRAS CON TEJAS DE PARMESANO

- **16 shelled scallops (see recipe 674) without coral, thawed if frozen**
- **6 tablespoons olive oil**
- **juice of ½ lemon**
- **1 tablespoon balsamic vinegar**
- **5 ounces watercress**
- **sea salt and pepper**

Tuiles:
- **butter, for greasing**
- **2 slices of bread, left out overnight to harden**
- **generous 1 cup grated Parmesan cheese**

Serves 4

Preheat the oven to 350°F. Grease a baking sheet with butter. To make the tuiles, put the bread in a food processor or blender and process to make bread crumbs, then mix with the Parmesan. Spoon small heaps of the mixture onto the prepared baking sheet and flatten gently into rounds with a teaspoon. Bake for 5 minutes, then lift the rounds off the baking sheet with a metal spatula, and drape them over a rolling pin or bottle to give them the shape of a curved roof tile. Let cool. Meanwhile, brush both sides of the scallops with some of the oil. Combine the remaining oil, the lemon juice, vinegar, and a little salt and pepper in a bowl. Make a bed of watercress on four individual plates and sprinkle with the dressing. Heat a nonstick skillet, add the scallops, and cook for 20 seconds on each side until cooked through. Divide them among the plates and pour the cooking juices over them. Serve immediately with the Parmesan tuiles.

Note: You can also sprinkle a little curry powder over the scallops at the last minute to add extra flavor.

Oysters au gratin

OSTRAS GRATINADAS

- **36 oysters**
- **1 clove garlic**
- **4 ½ pounds rock salt**
- **grated zest of 2 green lemons**
- **⅔ cup butter,**
  chilled and cut into pieces
- **1 sprig fresh parsley**
- **salt and pepper**

Serves 6

If your oysters have not been shucked, wrap one hand in a dishtowel and grasp one of the oysters, flat side uppermost. Insert an oyster knife into the hinge—the narrowest point of the shell. Work the knife backward and forward or twist to prize open the shells. Slide the blade of the knife along the inside of the top shell and sever the ligament that joins the oyster to the upper shell. Remove the upper shell. Keeping the bottom shell upright to avoid spilling the juices, slide the blade under the oyster, and sever the second ligament. Lift out the oyster and strain the juices through a cheesecloth-lined strainer into a pan. Repeat with the remaining oysters. Add the garlic to the pan and cook over medium-low heat until the liquid has reduced by two-thirds. Meanwhile, wash and dry the cup-shaped oyster shells, then stand them on a bed of rock salt on a baking sheet. Return the oysters to their shells and sprinkle with the lemon zest. Preheat the broiler. Remove the garlic from the pan and gradually whisk in the butter, one piece at a time. Cook over medium heat, whisking constantly, until creamy. Season to taste with salt and pepper. Pour a spoonful of this sauce over each of the oysters and cook under the broiler for 2–3 minutes, until beginning to brown. Garnish with the parsley and serve immediately.

Note: You can add 1 cup dry white wine to the oyster juices before reducing them. If you don't like the flavor of green lemons, substitute a pinch of saffron.

Assorted pies and fish dishes

677

- 1 pound 10 ounces hake or other white fish fillets
- 8 ounces day-old French bread, crusts removed
- scant 2 cups hot milk
- 2 tablespoons (¼ stick) butter, plus extra for greasing
- 4 eggs, separated
- pinch of freshly grated nutmeg
- 2 egg whites
- salt

Béchamel sauce:
- 2 tablespoons (¼ stick) butter
- 2 tablespoons sunflower oil
- 2 tablespoons all-purpose flour
- 2¼ cups milk
- 1 egg yolk

Serves 6

Fine hake pie
BUDÍN FINO DE MERLUZA

Put the fish into a pan, pour in water to cover, add a pinch of salt, and bring to a boil. Remove the pan from the heat and let cool. Meanwhile, put the bread into a bowl, pour in the milk, and let soak. Preheat the oven to 350°F. Grease an 8-inch cake pan with butter. Lift the fish out of the pan, reserving the cooking liquid, remove and discard any skin and bones, and flake the flesh. Add the soaked bread and any remaining hot milk, breaking it up with a fork, then add half the butter. Stir in the egg yolks, nutmeg, and a pinch of salt. Whisk all the egg whites in a clean, dry bowl until stiff, and fold into the fish mixture. Spoon the mixture into the prepared pan. Put the pan in a roasting pan and pour in boiling water to come about halfway up the sides. Bake for about 1 hour, until set. Meanwhile, make the béchamel sauce as described in recipe 77, adding 1 cup of the reserved cooking liquid. Lightly beat the egg yolk in a bowl, stir in a little of the sauce to prevent it curdling, then stir into the sauce. Run a round-bladed knife around the edge of the cake pan and turn the pie out onto a warm serving dish. Pour the sauce over it and serve immediately.

Note: You can also serve this pie with Classic Tomato Sauce (see recipe 73) or a slightly thicker béchamel with cooked, peeled shrimp.

678

Hot or cold fish pie with potatoes and tomatoes

BUDÍN DE PESCADO CON PATATAS Y TOMATE, FRÍO O CALIENTE

- 1 pound 10 ounces white fish fillets, such as hake or whiting
- 2 potatoes, unpeeled
- 2 tablespoons (¼ stick) butter, plus extra for greasing
- 2–3 tablespoons bread crumbs
- 2 eggs
- 1 egg white
- salt

Tomato sauce:
- 1 pound 2 ounces ripe tomatoes
- 2 tablespoons sunflower oil
- 1 teaspoon sugar
- salt

Quick stock:
- 2 tablespoons white wine
- 2 thick slices of onion
- 1 bay leaf
- salt

Serves 6

Make the quick stock as described in recipe 534 and set aside to cool. Make the tomato sauce as described in recipe 73. After processing it in a food processor or blender, simmer the tomato sauce for 25–35 min-utes more, until thickened, then remove from the heat, and set aside. Remove the rack from a fish poacher. Pour in the quick stock, put the fish on the rack, and return the rack to the fish poacher. Bring the stock to a boil, then remove the fish poacher from the heat, and let stand for 10 minutes. Lift out the fish and let cool, then remove and discard any skin and bones, and flake the flesh carefully. Meanwhile, put the potatoes into a pan, pour in water to cover, and add a pinch of salt. Bring to a boil and cook for about 30 minutes, until tender. Preheat the oven to 350°F. Grease a loaf pan with butter, sprinkle with the bread crumbs, and pour out any excess. Drain, peel, and mash the potatoes, then put them into a pan. Stir in the butter, flaked fish, and tomato sauce. Separate one of the eggs and beat the yolk with the whole egg in a bowl, then stir into the potato mixture. Whisk both egg whites in a clean, dry bowl until they form soft peaks, then fold them into the mixture. Spoon the mixture into the prepared pan. Put the pan in a roasting pan, pour in boiling water to come about halfway up the sides, and bake for 30–45 minutes, until a knife inserted into the pie comes out clean. Run a round-bladed knife around the edge of the pan and turn the pie out onto a serving dish.

Note: The pie may be served hot covered with Classic Tomato Sauce (see recipe 73) or Classic Béchamel Sauce (see recipe 77). It may also be served cold, garnished with slices of tomato and hard-cooked egg or with shrimp, and with a sauceboat of mayonnaise.

Glasses of fish and shellfish with vegetable sauce

COPAS DE PESCADO Y MARISCO CON SALSA DE HORTALIZAS (PIPIRRANA)

- **1 pound 2 ounces raw unpeeled shrimp**
- **3 bay leaves**
- **9 ounces monkfish fillet**
- **1 pound 2 ounces white fish fillet, such as hake or whiting**
- **1 quantity Vegetable Sauce (see recipe 113)**
- **salt**

Serves 6

Bring a large pan of salted water to a boil. Add the shrimp and one of the bay leaves, lower the heat, and simmer for 2–4 minutes, depending on the size of the prawns. Drain well, let cool, then peel the prawns. Put the monkfish and white fish in separate pans. Add 1 bay leaf and a pinch of salt to each and pour in water to cover. Bring to a boil, then remove the pans from the heat, and let stand for 10 minutes. Lift out the fish and remove and discard any skin and bones. Cut the flesh into bite-size pieces. Divide the shrimp and fish among individual glasses or glass sundae dishes and let stand in the refrigerator. About 10 minutes before serving, stir the vegetable sauce well and divide it among the glasses.

Note: You can vary the fish and shellfish according to taste.

Fish balls

ALBÓNDIGAS DE PESCADO

- 4 ½ ounces day-old bread,
  crusts removed
- 1 cup hot milk
- 1 pound 2 ounces hake fillet
- 1 egg
- 1 clove garlic, finely chopped
- 1 teaspoon chopped
  fresh parsley
- sunflower oil, for deep-frying
- ½ cup all-purpose flour
- triangles of fried bread
  (see recipe 130) or boiled rice
- salt

Sauce:
- 1 onion, chopped
- 1 tablespoon all-purpose flour
- 1 bay leaf
- pinch of saffron threads
- salt

Serves 6

Put the bread into a bowl, pour in the milk, and let soak. Put the hake into a pan, pour in water to cover, add a pinch of salt, and bring to a boil. Immediately remove the pan from the heat. Drain the fish well, reserving the cooking liquid, then remove any skin and bones, and flake the flesh with a fork. Strain the cooking liquid and let cool. Put the fish into a bowl and add the soaked bread, egg, garlic, parsley, and a pinch of salt. Mix well, then form the mixture into small balls like meatballs. Heat the oil in a deep-fryer or deep skillet to 350–375°F or until a cube of day-old bread browns in 30 seconds. Coat the fish balls in the flour, add to the hot oil, in batches of five at a time, and cook until golden brown. Remove with a slotted spoon and drain. Make the sauce. Transfer 6 tablespoons of the oil into another skillet and reheat. Add the onion and cook over low heat, stirring occasionally, for about 10 minutes, until golden brown. Stir in the flour and cook, stirring constantly, for about 5 minutes, until lightly browned. Gradually stir in 2 ¼ cups of the reserved cooking liquid and add the bay leaf. Crush the saffron in a mortar or small bowl and stir in 2 tablespoons of the sauce, then add to the pan, and cook for 10 minutes more. Strain the sauce, add the fish balls, and serve immediately with the triangles of fried bread or the boiled rice in molds.

Note: The fish balls can be served with Classic Tomato Sauce (see recipe 73) instead of the sauce in this recipe.

Provençal fish stew

BOUILLABAISSE

- 2 onions, coarsely chopped
- 3 cloves garlic, lightly crushed
- 2 tomatoes, peeled, seeded, and coarsely chopped
- 1 bay leaf
- 1 sprig fresh parsley
- 1 sprig fresh fennel
- thinly pared zest of 1 orange
- 1 pound 2 ounces monkfish fillet, sliced
- 1 pound 2 ounces blue or Jonah crabs
- 1 red porgy (sea bream) or 1 porgy (scup) or other firm-fleshed fish, about 1 pound 2 ounces, trimmed, scaled, and cleaned
- ½ cup olive oil
- pinch of saffron threads
- 1 pound 2 ounces hake steaks
- 2 red mullet or snapper, scaled and cleaned
- 1 sea bass, about 1 pound 2 ounces, trimmed, scaled, and cleaned
- 1 sprig fresh thyme
- 1 day-old French bread loaf, about 1 pound 2 ounces, cut into ½-inch thick slices
- salt and pepper

Serves 8

Put the onion, garlic, tomato, bay leaf, parsley, fennel, and orange zest into a pan and put the monkfish, crabs, and porgy on top. Add the oil, pour in boiling water to cover the fish, and season with salt and pepper. Crush the saffron in a mortar or small bowl, stir in 1 tablespoon water, and add to the pan. Bring to a boil over high heat and cook for 5 minutes. Add the remaining fish and more water if necessary. Bring back to a boil and cook for 8 minutes. Remove the pan from the heat and transfer the fish to a warm serving dish. Put the slices of bread in a soup tureen and strain the cooking liquid over them. Serve immediately with the fish.

Note: For a similar recipe using salt cod, see recipe 545.

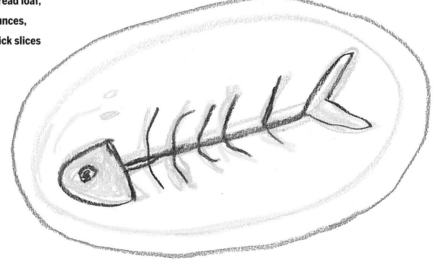

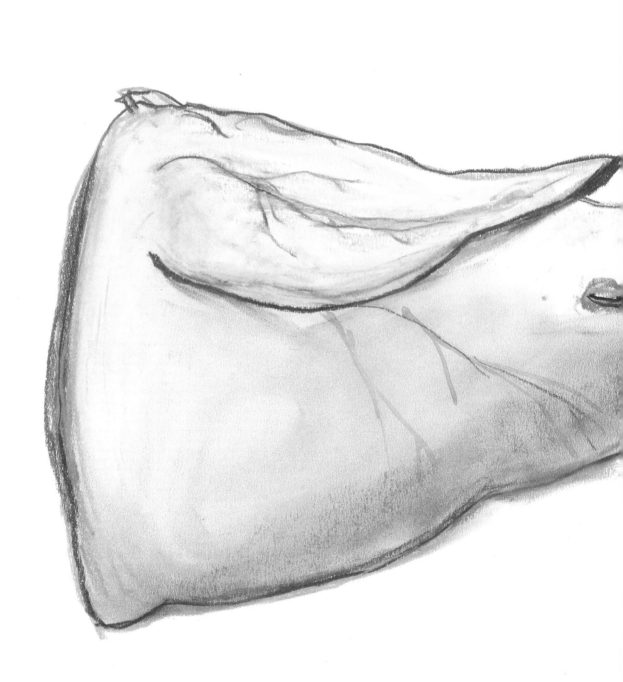

MEAT

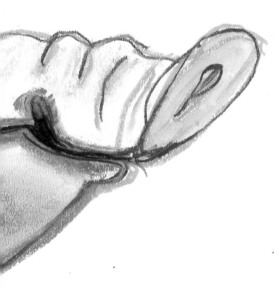

Meat has been an important part of the human diet since prehistoric times—ever since the invention of weapons to hunt animals and tools to turn them into food.

Frozen meat

Once frozen meat has thawed, it should never be refrozen. This is because freezing does not destroy microorganisms but leaves them "sleeping," stopping their reproduction. However, once the meat has thawed, the bacteria "wake up" again and start to multiply rapidly. If you buy frozen meat, do not leave it in the back of a parked auto-mobile for any length of time and, ideally, put it into the freezer within an hour of purchase, so that any bacteria do not have a chance to proliferate. Can meat be cooked without defrosting it first? It depends on the kind of meat and the way it is to be cooked. If it is to be cooked for a long time on low heat in a sauce, there is no problem if it hasn't thawed first; just make sure it is fully cooked, through and through. It is especially important for ground meat to be cooked through evenly. This is because most bacteria reside on the outside of the meat (due to contact with other contaminated surfaces) which, in the case of ground meat, then get mixed into the interior. Ground meat can also be used without defrosting it first, but roasts or large cuts for broiling must be defrosted to avoid the outside cooking while the inside remains raw. The best way to defrost frozen meat is slowly in the refrigerator. Remove all the packaging, put it on a plate, and cover with plastic wrap. If you're in a hurry, it can be defrosted more quickly in a microwave oven, following the manufacturer's instructions.

Selection

The color of meat is a guide to its quality and flavor. Beef, for example, should be a dull, dark red rather than a shiny coral. This shows that it has been aged long enough to become tender. Similarly, the fat should be firm and waxy and either cream or white in color, depending on the type of meat. It is important to choose the appropriate cut of meat for the method of cooking. The flank, for example, is ideal for pot-roasting or making meatballs, but is not so good for frying, as it releases a lot of juice and will dry out. The round is much better for this purpose, as it is succulent but does not release too much juice when cooked. Other good cuts for braising and pot roasts are rump roast, chuck roast or bottom round and brisket. Wonderful cutlets, perfect for broiling and frying, can be obtained from the top of the leg, while brisket, breast, and ribs are perfect for stews and casseroles. Other less commonly used parts, such as the tail and snout, have a delicious texture because of their gelatin content.

Beef

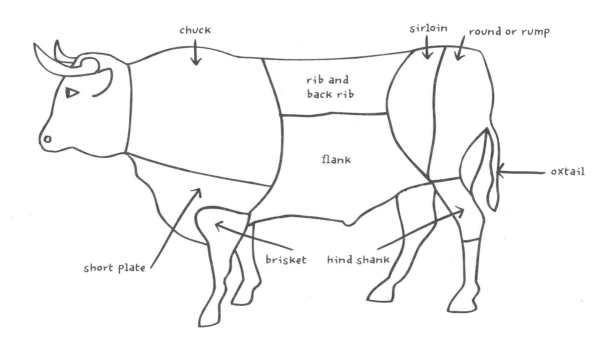

Allow about 4½ ounces boneless beef per serving for broiling and frying. Allow about 5 ounces boneless beef per serving for roasting, as it shrinks slightly. Allow 7 ounces boneless beef per serving for stewing, as it is the method which reduces most.

Buying beef	Suitable cuts	Weight per serving	Cooking time
Fried, broiled or grilled	Tenderloin steak, Hamburgers, Sirloin, Rib steak	4½–5 ounces	2 minutes each side for rare 3–4 minutes each side for medium 4–6 minutes each side for well done
Roasted *	Tenderloin, Rolled rib, Sirloin, Rolled rump, Silverside, Standing rib	5 ounces (boneless) 9 ounces (on the bone)	10–15 minutes per pound
Stewed or braised	Pot roast, Oxtail, Blade pot roast, Flank, Brisket	6½–7 ounces	2–2½ hours

*Make sure that the oven is preheated

Tips

Grilled or fried steak:

Tenderloin steak, sirloin, club steak, porterhouse, T-bone, and rib eye (Delmonico) steak are the best cuts. There are many suitable accompaniments for steak, including

- Fries: traditional, thin, or straw potatoes
- Mashed potatoes
- All kinds of vegetables: peas, green beans, fried green bell peppers
- onion fritters, fried tomatoes, roasted tomatoes, etc.
- Salad greens

Accompaniments are not suggested for each recipe as this is a matter of personal taste.

Stews, casseroles and pot roasts:

Use a good-quality, heavy pan or stovetop-safe casserole to insure even cooking.

Broiled or grilled steak

FILETES A LA PLANCHA

- 1 tenderloin steak,
  about 5 ounces
- olive oil, for brushing
- 1 thin slice of lemon
- ½ teaspoon mustard or
  1 tablespoon butter mixed
  with a little finely chopped
  fresh parsley, chilled

Serves 1

Brush both sides of the steak with the oil and let stand in the refrigerator for 30–60 minutes. Preheat the broiler or a ridged grill pan. Broil or grill the steak for 2–4 minutes on each side, until done to your liking. Season with salt after cooking. Serve garnished with the lemon and mustard or parsley butter.

Note: Tenderloin steak and tournedos may be served with Béarnaise Sauce (see recipe 84) or Butter and Anchovy sauce (see recipe 95), offered separately.

683

Fried steak

FILETES FRITOS

- 1 tenderloin steak,
  about 5 ounces
- 1 tablespoon olive oil

Serves 1

Season both sides of the steak with salt. Pour just enough of the oil into a skillet to cover the base and heat. Add the steak and cook over high heat for about 2–6 minutes on each side, until done to your liking. (4 minutes each will produce medium steaks.) Put the steak on a warm serving dish and pour the cooking juices over it.

Note: Seasoning the steak with salt before cooking helps release the juices, which then mix with the oil to make a delicious sauce.

684

Tenderloin steaks with port and mustard sauce

FILETES DE SOLOMILLO CON SALSA DE OPORTO Y MOSTAZA

- 6 tenderloin steaks,
  about 5 ounces each
- 4 tablespoons olive oil
- ½ teaspoon mustard
- 5 tablespoons port
- salt

Serves 6

Brush both sides of the steaks with a little of the oil and let stand in the refrigerator for 30 minutes. Heat the remaining oil in a skillet. Season the steaks with salt, add to the skillet, and cook over high heat for 2–4 minutes on each side, until done to your liking. Transfer to a serving dish and keep warm. Stir the mustard and port into the skillet and cook for 2–3 minutes. Pour the sauce over the steaks and serve immediately.

685

Tenderloin steaks in wine sauce

SOLOMILLO CON SALSA DE VINO

- 2 thick tenderloin steaks, about 5 ounces each
- 2 tablespoons sunflower oil
- 1 tablespoon chopped fresh parsley
- 4 raspberries
- salt and ground pink peppercorns

Wine sauce:
- 5 tablespoons olive oil
- 2 large shallots, chopped
- 2¼ cups red wine
- 1 tablespoon all-purpose flour
- 3 tablespoons butter

Serves 2

Make the sauce. Heat the oil in a skillet. Add the shallots and cook over low heat, stirring occasionally, for 6–8 minutes, until lightly browned. Pour in the wine, add ¾ cup water, and simmer gently for about 10 minutes. Mash the flour into the butter in a small bowl, then stir into the skillet. Heat a ridged grill pan. Brush both sides of the steaks with the oil, add to the pan, and cook over high heat for 2–4 minutes on each side, until done to your liking. Season with salt and pepper. Transfer the steaks to a warm serving dish. Stir the cooking juices into the sauce, then pour the sauce over the steaks. Garnish with the parsley and raspberries and serve immediately.

Note: To create a decorative effect, rotate the steaks on the griddle pan halfway through cooking so the ridges make a diamond pattern on the meat. Turn and repeat on other side.

686

Tenderloin or sirloin steaks with mushrooms, shallots, and ham

FILETES DE SOLOMILLO O LOMO, CON UN PICADITO DE CHAMPIÑON, CEBOLLA Y JAMÓN

- 6 tenderloin or sirloin steaks, about 5 ounces each
- 5 tablespoons olive oil
- 2¾ cups sliced mushrooms
- 1½ tablespoons butter
- juice of ½ lemon
- 5 ounces shallots, chopped
- generous ½ cup chopped Serrano ham or prosciutto
- salt

Serves 6

Brush both sides of the steaks with a little of the oil and let stand in the refrigerator for 30 minutes. Put the mushrooms, butter, and lemon juice into a pan, season with salt, and cook over medium heat for 6 minutes. Remove from the heat and set aside. Heat 3 tablespoons of the oil in a skillet. Add the shallots and cook over low heat, stirring occasionally, for about 5 minutes, until softened and translucent. Stir in the ham and cook for 2–3 minutes, then add the mushrooms and their cooking juices. Keep warm over very low heat. Heat the remaining oil in a skillet or ridged grill pan, add the steaks, and cook over high heat for 2–4 minutes on each side, until done to your liking. Season with salt, transfer to a warm serving dish, and spoon a little of the mushroom, onion, and ham mixture, together with the cooking juices, on top of each steak. Serve immediately.

Note: This dish can also be made using veal in place of beef.

687

Tenderloin steaks with butter and anchovies
FILETES DE SOLOMILLO CON MANTEQUILLA Y ANCHOAS

- **6 tenderloin steaks,**
  about 5 ounces each
- **3 tablespoons olive oil**
- **8 canned anchovy fillets, drained**
- **7 tablespoons butter**
- **juice of 1 lemon**
- **1 tablespoon chopped**
  fresh parsley
- **salt**

Serves 6

Brush both sides of the steaks with a little of the oil and let stand for 30 minutes in the refrigerator. Heat the remaining oil in a skillet or ridged grill pan. Add the steaks and cook over high heat for 2–4 minutes on each side, until done to your liking. Lightly season with salt, transfer to a serving dish, and keep warm. Pound the anchovies and 2 tablespoons of the butter to a paste in a mortar or small bowl. Stir in the remaining butter and heat gently in the skillet or grill pan. When the butter has melted, stir in the lemon juice and parsley. Mix well and pour the sauce over the steaks or serve separately in a sauceboat.

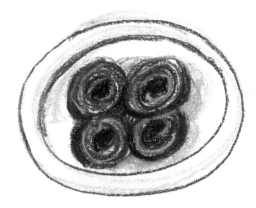

688

Flambéed pepper steaks
FILETES DE SOLOMILLO A LA PIMIENTA Y FLAMEADOS CON COÑAC

- **6 tenderloin steaks,**
  about 5 ounces each
- **3 tablespoons black**
  peppercorns, lightly crushed
- **3 tablespoons olive oil**
- **6 tablespoons brandy**
- **salt**

Serves 6

Season both sides of each steak with salt. Spread the peppercorns over both sides of each steak, pressing them down firmly. Heat the oil in a heavy skillet. Add the steaks, three at a time, and cook over high heat for 2–4 minutes on each side, until done to your liking. Return the first batch of steaks to the pan when the second batch has finished cooking. Pour the brandy into a small pan and heat gently, then ignite it, and carefully spoon it over the steaks while it is still burning. Transfer the steaks to a warm serving dish, pour the sauce over them, and serve immediately.

689

Tenderloin steaks with mushrooms, truffles, and cream
FILETES DE SOLOMILLO CON CHAMPIÑON, TRUFA Y NATA

- scant 1½ cups
  chopped mushrooms,
- juice of ½ lemon
- 3 tablespoons butter
- 1 canned or bottled truffle,
  drained and chopped,
  liquid reserved
- 6 slices of bread
- 6 tenderloin steaks,
  5 ounces each
- sunflower oil, for brushing
- 3 tablespoons brandy
- 4–5 tablespoons light cream
- salt and pepper

Serves 6

Put the mushrooms, lemon juice, half the butter, and a pinch of salt into a pan. Cook over medium heat, stirring occasionally, for 6 minutes. Add the truffle and its liquid and mix well. Remove the pan from the heat and keep warm. Toast the bread on both sides and spread with the remaining butter. Keep warm. Heat a heavy skillet. Brush both sides of the steaks with the oil, add to the skillet, and cook over high heat for 2–4 minutes. Season with salt, turn the steaks, and cook for 2–4 minutes more, until done to your liking. Transfer the steaks to a warm serving dish. Heat the brandy in a small pan, ignite it, and carefully pour it over the steaks while still burning. When the flames have died down, place a slice of toast under each steak. Stir the cream into the mushroom mixture and heat through gently but do not let it boil. Season to taste with salt, pour the sauce over the steaks, and serve immediately with Mashed Potato (see recipe 230) or Potato Balls (see recipe 231).

690

Steak with olives and white wine
FILETES CON ACEITUNAS Y VINO BLANCO

- generous 1 cup olives, pitted
- 4 tablespoons olive oil
- 6 sirloin or rib eye (Delmonico)
  steaks, 4½ ounces each
- 5 tablespoons white wine
- 1 teaspoon tomato paste or
  Classic Tomato Sauce
  (see recipe 73)
- ½ teaspoon meat extract
  or Maggi Seasoning
- salt

Serves 6

Put the olives into a pan, pour in water to cover, bring to a boil, and simmer for 2 minutes. Drain well, pat dry, and cut in half. Heat the oil in a skillet. Season both sides of the steaks with salt, add them to the skillet, in three batches, and cook over high heat for 2–4 minutes on each side, until done to your liking. Remove from the skillet and keep warm. Pour off half the cooking juices and return the skillet to the heat. Add the olives, stir in the wine, tomato paste or tomato sauce, and meat extract or Maggi Seasoning, and cook for 3–4 minutes. Transfer the steaks to a warm serving dish and pour the sauce over them. Serve immediately.

Note: This dish can also be made using veal in place of beef.

Breaded steak

FILETES EMPANADOS

- **6 club steaks,**
  about 4½ ounces each
- **1 clove garlic**
- **1 sprig fresh parsley**
- **2 eggs**
- **1½ cups bread crumbs**
- **sunflower oil, for deep-frying**
- **salt**

Serves 6

One at a time, place the steaks between two sheets of waxed paper and pound thinly and evenly with a meat bat, the bottom of a small saucepan or the side of a rolling pin. Pound the garlic with the parsley and a pinch of salt to a paste in a mortar or process in a mini-food processor. Spread the paste over both sides of each steak. Lightly beat the eggs in a shallow dish and pour the bread crumbs into another shallow dish. Dip the steaks first in the beaten egg and then in the bread crumbs, making sure they are evenly covered. Chill in the refrigerator for 15 minutes. Heat the oil in a deep-fryer or deep skillet to 350–375°F or until a cube of day-old bread browns in 30 seconds. Add the steaks, in batches, and cook until golden brown. Remove with a slotted spatula, drain well, and keep warm while you cook the remaining batches. Serve immediately.

Note: You can omit the garlic and parsley mixture if you like. Simply season the steaks with a little salt before coating them with egg and bread crumbs.

Beef roulades with ham, olives, and hard-cooked eggs

FILETES DE CEBÓN, RELLENOS DE JAMÓN, ACEITUNAS Y HUEVO DURO

- 6 round or flank steaks, about 4½ ounces each
- 12 olives, pitted and chopped
- generous ½ cup chopped Serrano ham or prosciutto
- 2 hard-cooked eggs, chopped
- ⅓ cup all-purpose flour
- 1 cup sunflower oil
- 1 small onion, very finely chopped
- 5 tablespoons white wine
- 1 clove garlic
- 1 sprig fresh parsley
- salt

Serves 6

One at a time, place the steaks between two sheets of waxed paper and pound thinly and evenly with a meat bat, the bottom of a small saucepan or the side of a rolling pin. Combine the olives, ham, and hard-cooked eggs. Reserve 2 tablespoons of the mixture and divide the remainder among the steaks. Roll up the steaks and secure with a wooden toothpick or tie with fine kitchen string. Reserve 1 tablespoon of the flour and pour the remainder into a shallow dish. Heat the oil in a skillet. Lightly coat the steaks in the flour, shaking off any excess, add to the skillet, in two batches, and cook over medium heat, turning frequently for 4–5 minutes until golden brown all over. Remove with a slotted spatula, drain, and keep warm. Transfer 6 tablespoons of the oil from the skillet into a pan and reheat. Add the onion and cook over low heat, stirring occasionally, for about 10 minutes, until golden brown. Stir in the reserved flour and cook, stirring constantly, for 2 minutes. Gradually stir in the wine and 4 cups water. Add the steaks to the pan. Pound the garlic with the parsley and a pinch of salt in a mortar or process in a mini-food processor, mix in 2–3 tablespoons of the sauce, and stir into the pan. Cook over medium-low heat for about 25 minutes, or until the roulades are tender and cooked through. Just before serving, lift out the roulades and remove and discard the toothpicks or string, then place on a warm serving dish. Stir the reserved stuffing into the sauce and bring to a boil, then pour the sauce over the meat. Serve immediately, with croûtons, boiled rice, or Mashed Potato (see recipe 230).

Note: This dish can also be made using veal in place of beef.

693

Beef roulades with ham and olives

FILETES RELLENOS DE JAMÓN YORK Y ACEITUNAS

- 6 round or flank steaks,
  about 4½ ounces each
- 3 large, thin slices of Smithfield,
  Black Forest or other dry-cured
  ham, halved
- scant 1 cup pimiento-stuffed
  green olives, chopped
- 1 cup sunflower oil
- 1 onion, chopped
- 1 clove garlic, chopped
- 2 tablespoons all-purpose flour
- 1¼ cups white wine
- 2 beef bouillon cubes
- pinch of mixed dried herbs
- juice of 1 lemon
- salt and pepper

Serves 6

One at a time, place the steaks between two sheets of waxed paper and pound thinly and evenly with a meat bat, the bottom of a small saucepan or the side of a rolling pin. Lightly season each steak with salt and pepper, top with a half-slice of ham, and divide the olives among them, putting them in the center of each steak. Roll up each steak and secure with a wooden toothpick or tie with fine kitchen string. Heat the oil in a pan. Add the roulades, two at a time, and cook over medium heat, turning frequently, for 4–5 minutes, until evenly browned. Remove with a slotted spoon, drain and set aside. Pour off most of the oil from the pan, leaving 2–3 tablespoons, and reheat. Add the onion and garlic and cook over low heat, stirring occasionally, for about 10 minutes, until golden brown. Stir in the flour and cook, stirring constantly, for 2 minutes. Gradually stir in the wine and scant 2 cups water, crumble in the bouillon cubes, add the herbs, and bring to a boil. Lower the heat, add the roulades, and simmer for 1 hour. Add the lemon juice and simmer for 15 minutes more, or until the roulades are tender and cooked through. Lift the roulades out of the pan, remove and discard the toothpicks or string, and put them on a warm serving dish. Pass the sauce through a food mill or process in a food processor and pour it over the meat. Serve with Mashed Potato (see recipe 230) or boiled rice.

Note: This dish can also be made using veal in place of beef.

694

Beef in beer with onions

FILETES DE CEBÓN GUISADOS CON CERVEZA Y CEBOLLA

- 5 tablespoons olive oil
- 6 thick slices of beef, such as
  flank steak, or rump roast
- 3 large onions, thinly sliced
  and pushed out into rings
- 2¼–3 cups beer
- salt

Serves 6

Heat the oil in a pan. Add the beef, in batches, and cook over medium heat for 1 minute on each side, then remove from the pan, and set aside. Put half the onion rings into the pan, place the beef on top, and season with salt, then put the remaining onion rings on top of the meat. Cover and cook over low heat for about 10 minutes, until the onion is softened and translucent. Pour in enough beer to cover the meat. Re-cover the pan and cook over medium-low heat for 1–1½ hours, or until tender and cooked through. (Move the meat occasionally with a wooden spoon or tongs during the cooking time to prevent it sticking to the pan.) Transfer the meat and sauce to a warm serving dish, top with the onion, and serve immediately with the boiled rice or Mashed Potato (see recipe 230).

695

Rib-eye with parsley, butter, and lemon

LOMO DE VACA CON PEREJIL, MANTEQUILLA Y LIMÓN

- 1–2 thick boneless rib-eye steaks, 1¾–2¼ pounds total weight
- 2 tablespoons olive oil
- ¼ cup (½ stick) butter
- juice of 1 lemon
- 1 tablespoon chopped fresh parsley
- salt and pepper

Serves 6

Preheat the broiler. Brush both sides of the beef with the oil and cook under the broiler for 4 minutes, then turn over, and cook over medium heat for 8 minutes more or until done to your liking. Remove the meat from the broiler, season both sides with salt and pepper, and place on a serving dish. Cut it into strips about 1½ inches wide and keep warm. Drain all the juices released into a pan, add the butter, and melt over low heat. Stir in the lemon juice and parsley, pour the sauce over the meat, and serve immediately.

Note: You can also make this dish with round steak.

696

Rib-eye with red wine sauce

LOMO DE VACA CON SALSA DE VINO TINTO

- 4 tablespoons sunflower oil
- 1–2 slices of thick boneless rib-eye steaks, 1¾–2¼ pounds total weight
- 2 shallots, chopped
- 1¼ cups red wine
- 3 tablespoons light cream
- salt and pepper

Serves 6

Heat the oil in a large skillet. Add the beef and cook over medium heat for 5 minutes on each side. (Cook for a little longer if you prefer your beef well done.) Season with salt and pepper on both sides, then transfer to a serving dish, cut into strips about 1½ inches wide, and keep warm. Add the shallots to the skillet and cook over low heat, stirring occasionally, for about 5 minutes, until softened and translucent. Add the wine and cook over low heat for 8–10 minutes, until reduced. Stir in the cream and heat gently but do not let it boil. Pour the sauce over the meat and serve immediately, with boiled or sautéed potatoes, or a side salad.

Note: You can substitute 6 tablespoons butter for the cream. Add one-third to the sauce and beat well until it has been incorporated, then add half the remaining butter, and beat well again. When that has been completely incorporated, beat in the rest.

697   Ground beef or hamburgers

FILETES PICADOS O HAMBURGUESAS

• 1 pound 10 ounces ground meat

Preheat the grill. Mix the meat with the onion in a bowl, then add the eggs and season. Shape into eight evenly sized balls and flatten into patties, before drizzling with oil. Cook under a medium grill for 4 minutes each side, depending on how rare you like your meat.

Note: Generally, hamburgers are tastier if made with a mixture of ground beef and sausage meat or lean minced pork. Good proportions for hamburger meat are about 1 pound 2 ounces ground beef to 9 ounces pork or sausage meat. For meatballs or meat loaf it is usual to combine about 14 ounces ground beef with 5 ounces pork or sausage meat.

698   Hamburgers in a light batter

FILETES PICADOS (HAMBURGUESAS) REBOZADOS

• 6 hamburgers (see recipe 697)
• 2 eggs
• ⅓ cup all-purpose flour
• 1 cup sunflower oil
• salt

Serves 6

Season the hamburgers on both sides with salt. Beat the eggs in a shallow dish and pour the flour into another shallow dish. Coat the hamburgers first in the flour, shaking off the excess, and then in the beaten egg. Heat the oil in a skillet. Add the hamburgers, in batches, and cook over medium heat for 4–5 minutes on each side, until cooked through. Serve immediately.

Note: These hamburgers are also delicious if simply seasoned with salt and coated in flour before frying.

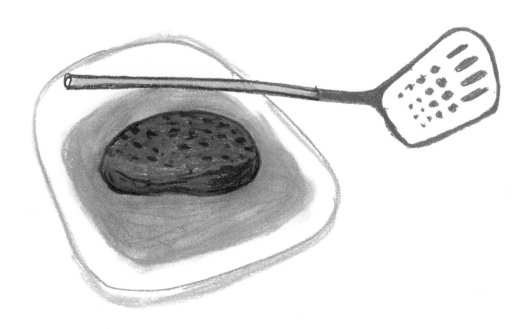

699

Hamburgers in onion sauce
FILETES PICADOS (HAMBURGUESAS) EN SALSA CON CEBOLLA

- ⅓ cup all-purpose flour
- 1 cup sunflower oil
- 6 hamburgers (see recipe 697)
- 1 large onion, thinly sliced
- ¾ cup white wine
- salt

Serves 6

Reserve 1 teaspoon of the flour and pour the remainder into a shallow dish. Heat the oil in a skillet. Season the hamburgers on both sides with salt and coat them in the flour, shaking off any excess. Add to the pan, in batches, and cook over medium heat for 4–5 minutes on each side until cooked through. Transfer the cooked hamburgers to a large pan, arranging them in a single layer. Drain off nearly all the oil from the skillet, leaving about 3 tablespoons to cover the base, and reheat. Add the onion and cook over low heat, stirring occasionally, for about 8 minutes, until beginning to brown. Stir in the reserved flour and cook, stirring constantly, for 1 minute. Gradually stir in the wine and 5 tablespoons water, a little at a time. Cook, stirring constantly, for about 5 minutes, until thickened, then pour the sauce into the pan with the hamburgers. Bring to a boil, then lower the heat, and simmer for 8 minutes. Place the hamburgers on a warm serving dish. Scoop up the onion with a slotted spoon and place it on top. Pour the sauce over the dish and serve immediately with Mashed Potato (see recipe 230) or fried potatoes.

700

Meatballs
ALBÓNDIGAS

- 1 pound 2 ounces ground beef
- 1 sprig fresh parsley, chopped
- 1 clove garlic,
  very finely chopped
- 1 egg, lightly beaten
- 4 tablespoons bread crumbs
- 3 tablespoons white wine
- ⅓ cup all-purpose flour
- 1¼ cups sunflower oil
- salt

  Sauce:
- 4 tablespoons olive oil
- ⅓ cup chopped onion
- 2 ripe tomatoes, chopped
- small pinch of saffron threads
- salt

Serves 6

Put the ground beef, parsley, garlic, egg, bread crumbs, wine, and a pinch of salt into a bowl and mix well. Shape the mixture into small balls, rolling them between the palms of your hands. Lightly coat the meatballs in the flour. Heat the oil in a skillet. Add the meatballs, in batches, and cook over medium heat, turning frequently, until golden brown all over. Using a slotted spoon, transfer the meatballs to a pan, arranging them in a single layer. Heat the oil in another skillet. Add the onion and cook over low heat, stirring occasionally, for about 5 minutes. Add the tomato and cook, stirring occasionally and breaking them up with the side of the spoon, for 6–8 minutes. Stir in 2¼ cups water and season with salt. Bring the sauce to a boil, let it cool slightly, then pass it through a food mill and pour it over the meatballs. Crush the saffron threads in a mortar or small bowl, then stir in ½ cup water, and pour into the pan. Simmer the meatballs in the sauce for 15–20 minutes, then serve.

Note: You can also make the meatballs with ground veal or a mixture of ground beef and pork. Simmer veal meatballs for 10 minutes only.

701

- 1 small onion or 1 shallot,
  finely chopped
- 1 clove garlic, finely chopped
- 1 heaping tablespoon
  finely chopped fresh parsley
- ½–1 teaspoon mustard
- 1 egg yolk
- 14 ounces ground lean steak,
  such as tenderloin
- salt and pepper

Serves 2

Steak tartar (first version)
STEAK TÁRTARO

Put the onion or shallot, garlic, parsley, mustard, and egg yolk into a bowl, season with salt and quite a lot of pepper, and mix well to form a paste. Add the meat and shape into patties.

Note: This dish and the one following are classics. Modern times have given rise to concern over foodborne illnesses caused by uncooked or undercooked meat or eggs. Many people continue to enjoy such dishes, but caution should be applied, especially when serving the very young or very old, or those with compromised immune systems.

702

- 1 small onion or 1 shallot,
  finely chopped
- 1 clove garlic, finely chopped
- 1 heaping tablespoon
  finely chopped fresh parsley
- ½–1 teaspoon mustard
- 2 egg yolks
- 14 ounces ground lean steak,
  such as tenderloin
- 7 ounces spinach,
  coarse stalks removed
- 1½ cups chopped mushrooms
- salt and pepper

Serves 2

Steak tartar (second version)
STEAK TÁRTARO

To give steak tartar an original touch, cook about 7 ounces spinach as described on page 315, then chop. Prepare the paste as described in recipe 701, then add the spinach and mushrooms. Add the meat and shape into patties.

703

Pepper steak
STEAK A LA PIMIENTA

- **6 rib steaks**
  or large pieces of tenderloin
- **4 tablespoons black or green**
  peppercorns, lightly crushed
- **salt**

  Serves 4–6

Press the peppercorns firmly onto both sides of each steak. Cook the steaks under the broiler or in a skillet over high heat for 2–4 minutes on each side, until done to your liking. Season both sides of the meat with salt after cooking. It is important to warm the plates on which the meat will be served. There are several recipes in this book for sauces to accompany these steaks, such as Red Wine Sauce (see recipe 88) and Shallot Sauce for Fried Meat (see recipe 93). See Chapter 4 for more ideas.

704

Carpaccio with lemon
CARPACCIO DE CARNE AL LIMÓN

- **8 very thin slices of sirloin steak**
  (see note below)
- **4 tablespoons olive oil**
- **juice of 1 lemon**
- **lettuce or watercress**
- **salt and pepper**

  Sauce:
- **1 egg**
- **juice and grated zest of 1 lemon**
- **scant 2 cups olive oil**
- **salt**

  Serves 4

Put the slices of sirloin in a nonmetallic dish. Beat the oil with the lemon juice in a bowl, then pour the mixture over the meat, and let marinate in the refrigerator for 30 minutes. Meanwhile, make the sauce. Put the egg, lemon juice, a pinch of salt, and a dash of the oil in a food processor or blender. Gently combine the ingredients with a spatula or the handle of a spoon, then process for 20 seconds. With the motor running, add the remaining oil through the feeder hole. Pour into a sauceboat, stir in the lemon zest, and chill in the refrigerator. Drain the steak, place on individual plates, and season with salt and pepper on both sides. Garnish with the lettuce or watercress and serve immediately, offering the sauce separately.

Notes: The secrets of a good carpaccio are to use high-quality meat and to slice it extremely thinly. Put a piece of sirloin weighing at least 1 pound 10 ounces into the freezer for 2–3 hours so that it firms up but does not freeze completely. It will then be easier to slice thinly. Foodborne illnesses can be caused by uncooked or undercooked meat or eggs. Many people continue to enjoy dishes with these ingredients, but caution should be applied, especially when serving the very young or very old, or those with compromised immune systems.

Ground beef and potato pie

CARNE PICADA CON PURÉ DE PATATAS Y HUEVOS DUROS, AL HORNO

- scant ½ cup raisins (optional)
- 2¼ pounds potatoes
- 3 tablespoons butter
- 1 cup hot milk
- 6 tablespoons olive oil
- 1 large onion, finely chopped
- 1 pound 2 ounces ground beef
- 2 hard-cooked eggs,
  cut into wedges or thickly sliced
- 1 egg, lightly beaten
- 1½ tablespoons sugar
- salt

Serves 6

Put the raisins, if using, into a bowl and pour in hot water to cover. Let soak. Cook and mash the potatoes, using the butter and hot milk as described in recipe 230. Keep warm. Preheat the oven to 400°F. Meanwhile, heat 4 tablespoons of the oil in a skillet. Add the onion and cook over low heat, stirring occasionally, for about 8 minutes, until beginning to brown. Add the ground beef and cook, stirring frequently, for about 4 minutes, until lightly browned. Season with salt. Drain the raisins, if using, and stir them into the skillet. Spoon the mixture into an ovenproof baking dish and put the hard-cooked eggs on top. Combine the mashed potato and the beaten egg and spread over the meat. Drizzle with the remaining oil and sprinkle with the sugar. Bake for 15–20 minutes and serve straight from the dish.

Oven roasts

ASADO AL HORNO

- **1 boneless beef joint for roasting, 3¼ pounds**
- **lard or sunflower oil**
- **meat extract or Maggi Seasoning**
- **salt**

Serves 4–6

Preheat the oven to 400°F. Tie the beef with fine kitchen string so it forms a neat shape. Melt the lard or heat the sunflower oil in a roasting pan over medium heat. Add the beef and cook, turning frequently, until evenly browned all over. Season with salt and spread with meat extract or Maggi Seasoning, then place them in the oven and cook until done to your liking. A boneless piece of beef weighing 3¼ pounds cooked for about 30 minutes will be rare and quite red in the middle. Beef is often served rare, but this is a matter of personal taste. (See the table below for approximate cooking times.)

Remove the beef from the roasting pan, cover with aluminum foil, and let rest for 10–15 minutes before carving. Add a little boiling water to the roasting pan and bring to a boil, scraping up any bits from the base of the pan, then strain into a sauceboat, and serve with the meat.

Boneless beef
Rare—10–15 minutes per pound
Medium—15–20 minutes per pound
Well done—20–25 minutes per pound

Beef on the bone
Rare—15–20 minutes per pound
Medium—20–25 minutes per pound
Well done—25–30 minutes per pound

Fillet of beef in pastry

SOLOMILLO EN HOJALDRE

- 2 tablespoons sunflower oil
- 1 beef tenderloin, 2¼ pounds
- 2 tablespoons lard
  or 2 tablespoons olive oil
- ½ onion, finely chopped
- 1 pound 2 ounces mushrooms,
  sliced
- 1 canned or bottled truffle,
  drained, thinly sliced
  and cut into slivers
- 1–1½ sheets frozen puff pastry
  dough, thawed if frozen
- all-purpose flour, for dusting
- 1 egg yolk, lightly beaten
- scant 1 cup beef stock
  (homemade, canned or
  made with a bouillon cube)
- salt and pepper

Serves 6

Heat the sunflower oil in a stovetop-safe roasting pan. Season the beef with salt and pepper, add to the pan, and cook over medium heat, turning frequently, until evenly browned all over. Remove the meat from the roasting pan and put it onto a dishtowel to absorb any juice it releases. Preheat the oven to 400°F. Melt the lard or heat the olive oil in a skillet. Add the onion and cook over low heat, stirring occasionally, for 5 minutes, until softened and translucent. Add the mushrooms, increase the heat to high, and cook, stirring frequently, for 10 minutes, or until the mushrooms have released their juice and most of it has evaporated. Remove the pan from the heat, stir in the truffle, and let cool. Roll 1 sheet of the dough on a lightly floured surface to form a sheet large enough to enclose the beef completely. Trim the edges neatly and reserve the trimmings. Spread the mushroom mixture over the beef, then place the meat on the dough. Brush the edges with the egg yolk and wrap the dough around the beef to make a package. Roll out the dough trimmings and the additional half-sheet of dough, if using, and cut out leaf or star shapes. Brush them with beaten egg yolk and place them on top of the package. Cut a slit in the middle of the top and insert a rolled-up cylinder of aluminum foil to make a funnel. Brush the remaining egg yolk over the parcel to glaze. Carefully transfer the parcel to a baking sheet and bake for 25 minutes, then turn off the oven, open the oven, and cover the package with aluminum foil. Leave the covered beef en croûte in the warm oven for 10 minutes for rare and 18 minutes for medium before cutting the parcel into slices and serving.

Note: For an accompanying sauce, heat some cream in the pan used to cook the onion and mushrooms, adding a few extra slices of mushroom, the juice from the can or jar of truffle, and a little pepper. Do not let the sauce boil.

Roast beef in a pan

ASADOS EN CACEROLA

- **1 boneless sirloin or center cut of tenderloin, 3 pounds**
- **lard or sunflower oil**
- **meat extract or Maggi Seasoning**
- **salt**

Serves 4–6

You can "roast" in a Dutch oven or flameproof casserole, but this is not the same as a pot roast, which is typically cooked in liquid with vegetables. Melt the lard or heat the oil over medium heat. Add the beef and cook, turning frequently, until browned all over. Season with salt and spread with meat extract. Lower the heat and cook for 1½ hours, uncovered, turning the meat every 10 minutes. When the beef is cooked to your liking, remove it from the Dutch oven or flameproof casserole, and make a gravy by adding a little water to the pan juices and cook over a low heat until slightly thickened.

Note: Allow about 10–15 minutes per pound meat for rare or longer until cooked to your liking.

709

Beef, carrot, onion, and pea stew

RAGOÛT CON ZANAHORIAS, CEBOLLITAS FRANCESAS Y GUISANTES

- cup olive oil
- 3¼ pounds stewing beef, such as chuck, flank, rump or brisket, cut into 1½-inch cubes
- 1 onion, finely chopped
- 1 tablespoon all-purpose flour
- 1 cup white wine
- pinch of mixed dried herbs
- 1 pound 2 ounces carrots, sliced lengthwise
- 2 tablespoons Classic Tomato Sauce (see recipe 73)
- 9 ounces shallots
- 1½ tablespoons butter
- scant 1 cup drained canned, frozen, or shelled fresh peas
- salt

Serves 6

Heat the oil in a pan. Add the beef, in batches, and cook over medium heat, stirring occasionally, for 5–8 minutes, until evenly browned. Remove with a slotted spoon and set aside. Pour off nearly all the oil from the pan, leaving 2–3 tablespoons, and reheat. Add the onion, lower the heat, and cook, stirring occasionally, for 10 minutes, until lightly browned. Stir in the flour and cook, stirring constantly, for 5 minutes. Return the beef to the pan, stir in the wine, and add water to cover. Season with salt and sprinkle in the herbs. Bring to a boil, cover, and simmer for 1½ hours. Add the carrot, re-cover the pan, and simmer for 45 minutes more. Stir in the tomato sauce, if using. Meanwhile, put the shallots and butter into a small pan, add water to cover, and simmer gently for about 20 minutes, until tender but not falling apart. About 10–15 minutes before serving, add the shallots and the peas to the stew. Serve hot.

710

Beef cooked in red wine

CARNE ADOBADA Y GUISADA EN VINO TINTO

- 3¼ pounds boneless rump roast
  or flank, cut into 1½-inch cubes
- 1 large onion, halved
- 1 large carrot, thickly sliced
- 2 bay leaves
- 1 bouquet garni
  (1 sprig fresh parsley, 1 clove
  garlic, and 3 sprigs fresh thyme
  tied together in cheesecloth)
- 2¼ cups red wine
- ¼ cup red-wine vinegar
- 2 tablespoons olive oil
- 5 ounces slab bacon,
  cut into thin strips
- 2¼ cups hot water
- salt and pepper

Serves 6

Put the beef into a deep, nonmetallic dish. Cut one of the onion halves into three wedges and add to the dish along with the carrot, bay leaves, and bouquet garni. Season with salt and pour in the wine and vinegar. Cover with plastic wrap and let marinate in a cool place, but not the refrigerator, stirring occasionally, for 6–10 hours. Drain the beef, reserving the marinade. Put the oil and bacon into a large pan and cook over medium heat for 3–4 minutes. Meanwhile, chop the remaining onion half, add it to the pan, and cook, stirring occasionally, for 8–10 minutes, until lightly browned. Add the beef and cook, stirring frequently, for about 10 minutes, until evenly browned. Pour in the reserved marinade, bring to a boil, and cook until the liquid has reduced by half. Lower the heat, add the hot water, cover, and simmer for 2–3 hours, until the beef is tender. Remove and discard the bay leaves and bouquet garni and serve the stew in a warm deep dish, garnished with triangles of fried bread (see recipe 130) or accompanied by Mashed Potato (see recipe 230).

Beef bourguignonne

CARNE GUISADA CON VINTO TINTO (BOURGUIGNON, ESTILO FRANCES)

- 3 tablespoons olive oil
- generous 1 cup diced bacon
- 1 onion, chopped
- 3¼ pounds stewing beef, such as chuck, flank, rump or brisket, cut into 1-inch cubes
- 2 heaping tablespoons all-purpose flour
- 4 cups red wine
- pinch of freshly grated nutmeg
- 9 ounces shallots
- 1½ tablespoons butter
- salt and pepper

Serves 6

Heat the oil in a large pan. Add the bacon and onion and cook over low heat, stirring occasionally, for about 10 minutes, until the onion is lightly browned. Remove with a slotted spoon and set aside. Add the beef to the pan and cook over medium heat, stirring frequently, for 8–10 minutes, until evenly browned. Stir in the flour and cook, stirring constantly, for 2 minutes. Gradually stir in the wine, a little at a time. Add the nutmeg, season with pepper, and bring to a boil. Lower the heat, return the bacon and onions to the pan, and mix well. If necessary, add a little hot water to make sure the beef is covered. Cover the pan and simmer, stirring occasionally, for about 2 ½ hours, until the beef is tender. Meanwhile, put the shallots in a single layer in a pan. Add water to cover, a pinch of salt, and the butter. Cook for about 20 minutes, until tender. Taste the stew and adjust the seasoning, if necessary, then add the shallots, and cook, stirring occasionally, for 10 minutes. Serve in a warm deep dish, with the boiled or fried potatoes around the edge. An alternative accompaniment would be macaroni tossed with a little butter and grated cheese.

Note: If you like, you can stir in 3 tablespoons thick fresh Tomato Sauce (see recipe 73) or 1 ½ tablespoons tomato paste after browning the meat and before adding the flour.

712

Pot roast beef with carrots and onions

- **5 ounces slab bacon, cut into strips**
- **1 eye round, bottom round, chuck roast, or brisket, 3¼ pounds**
- **4 tablespoons olive oil**
- **4 pieces of ham rind or pork rind**
- **1 small onion, chopped**
- **1 pound 2 ounces veal shank**
- **3 tablespoons brandy**
- **2 carrots, sliced**
- **½ teaspoon mixed dried herbs or 1 bouquet garni (1 sprig fresh parsley, 1 clove garlic, 1 bay leaf, and 1 sprig fresh thyme tied together in cheesecloth)**
- **1 chicken bouillon cube**
- **¾ cup white wine**
- **9 ounces baby carrots, halved lengthwise**
- **9 ounces shallots**
- **1½ tablespoons butter**
- **salt and pepper**

Serves 6

Using a larding needle, thread the strips of bacon through the beef, then tie it into a neat shape with fine kitchen string. Heat the oil in a large pan. Add the ham or pork rind and onion and cook over low heat, stirring occasionally, for 5 minutes, until the onion is softened and translucent. Add the beef and veal shank and cook, turning occasionally, for about 10 minutes, until evenly browned all over. Meanwhile, heat the brandy in a small pan, ignite it, and add it to the meat when the flames have died down. Add the sliced carrots and dried herbs or bouquet garni, pour in water to cover, and season with salt and pepper. Cover and cook on medium-low heat for 3 hours. Dissolve the bouillon cube in 2–3 tablespoons of the cooking liquid in a bowl and add to the pan with the wine and baby carrots. Cook for 30 minutes more, then taste, and adjust the seasoning if necessary. Meanwhile, put the shallots in a single layer in a pan, add the butter and a pinch of salt, and pour in water to cover. Simmer for about 20 minutes, until tender. Lift the beef out of the pan and remove and discard the string. Cut into slices and place them on a warm serving dish. Lift out the veal shank, carve the meat off the bone, and place on top of the beef. Arrange the baby carrots and shallots around the edge. Remove and discard the bouquet garni, if used, pass the sauce through a food mill or process in a food processor or blender, and pour it over the meat.

Note: To serve cold, prepare in the same way as described above but use smaller quantities.

713

Terrine
PASTEL-TERRINA

- 1 envelope unflavored gelatin
- 1 cup cooking liquid from
  a stew or beef or veal stock
  (homemade, canned or
  made with a bouillon cube)
- 1 carrot, thinly sliced
- 2 ounces canned or cooked peas
- 5 ounces diced leftover beef
- 3½ ounces Serrano ham
  or prosciutto, finely diced
- 1 pound 2 ounces veal shank,
  finely diced
- 1 tomato sliced
- 1 beet, cooked and sliced
- lettuce leaves
  Serves 6

Dissolve the gelatin in 2¼ cups water, following the instructions on the package. Mix some of the sauce from the stew or the stock with the gelatin and spoon a layer into the base of a loaf pan or terrine mold. Transfer to the refrigerator and let set. Arrange half of the slices of carrot and peas in a layer on top of the gelatin. Add a layer of the beef, then one of the ham, and finally one of the veal. Top the terrine with the remaining carrot slices and peas and pour in the remaining gelatin mixture. Chill in the refrigerator for several hours until the gelatin is set. Turn the terrine out of the pan and serve it cold, garnished with the sliced tomato and beet, and the lettuce leaves.

714

Old clothes
ROPA VIEJA

- 4 tablespoons olive oil
- 1 large onion, chopped
- 2¼ pounds ripe tomatoes,
  seeded and chopped
- 1 teaspoon sugar
- 1 large red bell pepper
- 2¼ pounds leftover cooked beef
  pot roast, cut into large pieces
- boiled rice
- salt
  Serves 6

Preheat the oven to 400°F. Heat the oil in a skillet. Add the onion and cook over low heat, stirring occasionally, for about 5 minutes, until softened and translucent. Add the tomato and cook, stirring occasionally and breaking it up with the side of the spoon, for 15 minutes. Pass the mixture through a food mill or process in a food processor. Transfer to a clean pan. Stir in the sugar, and season with salt. Meanwhile, put the bell pepper on a baking sheet and roast for about 30 minutes, until soft. Remove from the oven, cover with a plate or dishtowel, and let cool, then peel, and seed. Cut the flesh into ¾-inch strips. Add the bell pepper and pieces of meat to the sauce and bring to a boil. Serve immediately with little mounds of the boiled rice (see recipe 173).

Note: This is one of the many variations on ropa vieja, a dish whose name translates as 'old clothes'. Typically the meat is cooked for so long that it can be shredded – or will fall apart by itself – hence the name. This version, using left-over meat, is a quick alternative.

715

Stewed pot roast
REDONDO GUISADO

- **4 tablespoons olive oil**
- **1 eye round, bottom round,
  chuck roast, or brisket,
  4½–5½ pounds**
- **2 large onions, chopped**
- **2 tablespoons all-purpose flour**
- **generous 1 cup white wine**
- **1 bay leaf**
- **salt**

  Serves 8–10

Heat the oil in a large pan. Add the beef and cook over medium heat, turning frequently, for 8–10 minutes, until evenly browned all over. Remove from the pan and set aside. Add the onion to the pan and cook over low heat, stirring occasionally, for about 10 minutes, until lightly browned. Stir in the flour and cook, stirring constantly, for 2 minutes. Gradually stir in the wine, a little at a time. Cook, stirring constantly, for 5 minutes, then return the beef to the pan. Season with salt, add the bay leaf, and pour in water to cover. Cover the pan and simmer gently, turning the beef occasionally, for about 2½ hours, until tender. Lift out the beef and cut into slices about ⅝ inch thick. Remove and discard the bay leaf and pass the sauce through a food mill or process in a food processor or blender. Serve the meat accompanied by Mashed Potato (see recipe 230) and the sauce in a sauceboat.

Notes: A peeled and halved apple can be added to the dish and passed through the food mill or process in a food processor with the sauce. If you have time, lard the topside with a few pieces of bacon. It makes it more succulent.

716

Leftover pot roast (first version)
RESTOS DEL REDONDO

- **sunflower oil, for deep-frying,
  plus extra for brushing**
- **2 tablespoons (¼ stick) butter**
- **2 heaping tablespoons
  all-purpose flour**
- **2¼ cups milk**
- **6–12 slices of cooked beef
  pot roast**
- **2 eggs**
- **1½ cups bread crumbs**
- **salt**

  Serves 6

Brush the inside of a ceramic dish with oil. Melt the butter with 3 tablespoons of the oil in a skillet. Stir in the flour and cook, stirring constantly, for 2 minutes. Gradually stir in the milk, a little at a time. Cook the sauce, stirring constantly, for about 10 minutes, until thickened. Season with salt and remove the pan from the heat. One at a time, dip the slices of beef into the sauce to coat, then put them in the prepared dish. Let stand for 1 hour in the refrigerator. Beat the eggs in a shallow dish and pour the bread crumbs into another shallow dish. Heat the remaining oil in a deep-fryer or deep skillet to 350–375°F, or until a cube of day-old bread browns in 30 seconds. Coat each slice of beef first in the beaten egg and then in the bread crumbs. Add to the hot oil, in batches if necessary, and cook until golden brown. Remove with a slotted spoon, drain, and keep warm while you cook the remaining batches. Serve immediately.

717

Leftover pot roast (second version)
RESTOS DEL REDONDO

- 3 tablespoons olive oil
- 2 onions, very finely chopped
- 1 bay leaf
- 1 clove garlic, lightly crushed
- 6 tablespoons (¾ stick) butter
- 2 tablespoons all-purpose flour
- 1 tablespoon white-wine vinegar
- 1 cup milk
- 1 cup chicken stock
- 6–12 slices of cooked
  beef pot roast
- 2 tablespoons capers
- 2 tablespoons bread crumbs
- ¼ cup (½ stick) butter
- salt

Serves 6

Preheat the oven to 400°F. Heat the oil in a skillet. Add the onion and cook over low heat, stirring occasionally, for about 5 minutes, until softened and translucent. Add the bay leaf and garlic and cook for a few minutes more. Add 2 tablespoons of the butter, stir in the flour, and cook, stirring constantly, for 2 minutes. Gradually stir in the vinegar, then the milk, and, finally, the stock. Cook the sauce, stirring constantly, for about 10 minutes, until thickened. Season with salt and remove the pan from the heat. Remove and discard the bay leaf and garlic and put 3 tablespoons of the sauce into the base of an ovenproof baking dish. Place the slices of beef on top. Rinse and drain the capers, then stir them into the remaining sauce. Pour the sauce over the beef. Sprinkle with the bread crumbs and dot with the remaining butter. Bake for about 15 minutes, until the top is golden brown. Serve immediately, straight from the dish.

718

Beef with tomatoes and olives
CARNE GUISADA CON TOMATES Y ACEITUNAS

- 1 cup sunflower oil
- 3¼ pounds stewing beef,
  such as chuck, flank, rump,
  or brisket, cut into chunks
- 2 large onions, finely chopped
- 2 tablespoons all-purpose flour
- 1 pound 2 ounces very ripe
  tomatoes, peeled and chopped
- scant 1 cup chopped
  Serrano ham or prosciutto
- ¾ cup white wine
- pinch of mixed dried herbs
  or 1 bouquet garni (1 sprig fresh
  parsley, 1 clove garlic, and 1 bay
  leaf tied in cheesecloth)
- scant 1 cup pimiento-stuffed
  green olives
- salt

Serves 6

Heat the oil in a pan. Add the beef, in batches if necessary, and cook, stirring occasionally, for about 10 minutes, until evenly browned. Remove with a slotted spoon and set aside. Drain off most of the oil, leaving about 4 tablespoons to cover the base of the pan, and reheat. Add the onion and cook over low heat, stirring occasionally, for about 8 minutes, until beginning to brown. Stir in the flour and cook, stirring constantly, for 2 minutes. Add the tomato and cook, stirring occasionally and breaking it up with the side of the spoon, for 5 minutes more. Return the beef to the pan, add the ham, and pour in the wine. Season with salt, add the dried herbs or bouquet garni, mix well, and cook for about 5 minutes. Pour in water to cover, cover the pan, and simmer over medium heat for about 2 hours, until tender. Meanwhile, put the olives in a pan, add water to cover, and bring to a boil, then lower the heat, and simmer for 1 minute. Drain well and set aside. Uncover the stew, stir in the olives, and cook, uncovered, for 10 minutes more. Remove and discard the bouquet garni, if used. Serve in a warm deep dish garnished, with triangles of fried bread (see recipe 130).

719

Pot roasted brisket

CONTRA GUISADA

- 5 ounces slab bacon,
  cut into strips
- 1 cup sunflower oil
- 1 brisket, 2½ pounds
- 2 large onions, chopped
- 8 black peppercorns
- 1 cup white wine
- 1 pound 2 ounces carrots,
  cut into chunks
- 1 eating apple, peeled, cored,
  and chopped (optional)
- salt

Serves 6

Using a larding needle, thread the strips of bacon through the beef, then tie it into a neat shape with fine kitchen string. Heat the oil in a large pan. Add the beef and cook over medium heat, turning frequently, for about 10 minutes, until evenly browned all over. Remove from the pan and set aside. Add the onion to the pan and cook over low heat, stirring occasionally, for 8–10 minutes, until beginning to brown. Return the beef to the pan, pour in 1 cup water, add the peppercorns, and season with salt. Cover and simmer over very low heat, stirring occasionally, for 1½ hours. Pour in the wine, add the carrot and the apple, if using, re-cover the pan, and cook for 45 minutes more, until the beef is tender. Lift out the beef from the pan, remove and discard the string, and carve the meat into fairly thin slices. Transfer to a warm serving dish. Remove all but two of the chunks of carrot from the pan and place on the serving dish. Pass the sauce through a food mill into a pan or process in a food processor and transfer to a pan. Heat through gently, adding more water if necessary, then pour over the beef, and serve.

Note: This dish can be served with boiled potatoes or Mashed Potato (see recipe 230), or with little piles of vegetables placed all around the serving dish.

720

Salt beef

CARNE FIAMBRE

- 1 ounce saltpeter
- 1 beef round, 2¼ pounds
- 1½ cups salt
- 6 black peppercorns
- 1 bay leaf
- 1 sprig fresh thyme
- 2 leeks, thickly sliced
  and rinsed well
- 2 carrots, thickly sliced
- 2 beef shank bones
- ¾ cup white wine

Serves 6–8

Spread the saltpeter over the beef and let stand in a cool place, but not the refrigerator, for a few hours or even overnight. Put the beef into a large pan, pour in 4¼ quarts water, and add the salt, peppercorns, bay leaf, and thyme. Let soak, stirring the brine occasionally, for 24 hours. Remove the beef, rinse it in cold water, and put it into a clean pan. Add the leek, carrot, and beef shanks, pour in the wine, and add water to cover. Bring to a boil, then lower the heat to medium, and cook for 3 hours. Drain the beef, then put it on a plate, and place a weight, such as a cutting board, on top. Let cool completely, then slice, and serve with Russian Salad (see recipe 21) or salad greens.

Note: Saltpetre is a restricted substance in many countries.

721

Stewed oxtail

RABO DE BUEY GUISADO

- **2 oxtails, cut into pieces**
- **2 large onions**
- **2 cloves**
- **4 black peppercorns**
- **1 bay leaf**
- **9 ounces carrots,**
  halved lengthwise
- **1½ cups white wine**
- **salt**

Serves 6

Pour 13 cups water into a pan and add the pieces of oxtail. There should be enough water for the meat to float; if not, add some more. Bring to a boil and skim off the froth that rises to the surface with a slotted spoon. Stud each onion with a clove and add to the pan with the peppercorns, bay leaf, carrots, wine, and a pinch of salt. Simmer, uncovered, for 2–3 hours, until the meat is falling off the bones and the cooking liquid has reduced.Lift out the pieces of oxtail, cut off the meat, and place on a warm serving dish. Remove and discard the bay leaf and peppercorns, then pass the sauce through a food mill or process in a food processor. Pour the sauce over the meat and serve immediately with Mashed Potato (see recipe 230) or French Fries (see recipe 242).

Note: Oxtails were once made from the tails of oxen, but the term now refers to the tail of any beef cattle. This cut of meat is quite boney and requires long, slow cooking.

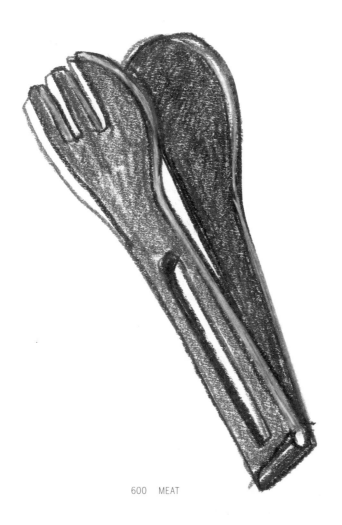

Veal

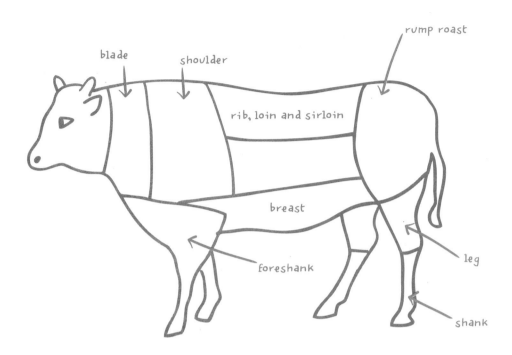

Allow 5 ounces boneless veal per serving
(4 ½ ounces for breaded cutlets).
Allow 7–8 ounces veal per serving for roasting,
as it will shrink considerably.
Allow 8–9 ounces stewing veal per serving.

Buying veal	Suitables cuts	Weight per serving	Cooking time
Fried, broiled or grillled	Chops, Rump roast, Cutlets**, Shoulder	6 ½ ounces 5 ounces (plain cutlets) 4 ½ ounces (breaded cutlets)	10 minutes for chops 1–1 ½ minutes per side for cutlets, first over a high heat and then over a lower one
Roasted *	Leg, Loin, Rib or Foreshank	9 ounces (boneless)	15–20 minutes per pound
Stewed or braised	Breast, Blade, Shoulder, Rump, Shank	7–9 ounces	2 hours for stews 1 ½–2 ½ hours for casseroles and pot roasts

*Make sure that the oven is preheated

**Cutlets are boneless slices of veal typically taken from the leg of sirloin of the calf. They are sold under a variety of names, including scallops, scallopini, schnitzel, medallions or slices. They come in different sized pieces, so you may need to adjust the cooking time slightly. For thin cutlets, 1–1 ½ minutes on each side should be sufficient.

722

Fried veal cutlets
FILETES FRITOS

- **6 veal cutlets,**
  about 5 ounces each
- **⅓ cup lard or 3 tablespoons**
  sunflower oil
- **salt**

Serves 6

Season the cutlets with salt on both sides. Melt the lard or heat the oil in a skillet. Add the veal, in batches, and cook over high heat for 3 minutes on each side. Turn the meat with tongs to avoid piercing it and so letting out the juices. Lower the heat, cover the pan, and cook for 2 minutes more, or until done to your liking. Serve immediately with vegetables, fried potatoes, or French Fries (see recipe 242).

723

Fried veal cutlets with lemon and butter
FILETES FRITOS CON LIMÓN Y MANTEQUILLA

- **6 veal cutlets**
- **4 tablespoons olive oil**
- **¼ cup (½ stick) butter**
- **juice of 1 lemon**
- **1 tablespoon chopped**
  fresh parsley
- **salt**

Serves 6

Season the cutlets with a little salt on both sides. Heat the oil in a skillet. Add the cutlets and cook over medium heat for 3–4 minutes on each side, or until done to your liking, turning them with tongs. Transfer to a serving dish and keep warm. Pour off most of the oil from the skillet, add the butter, and when it has melted, stir in the lemon juice. Add the parsley and pour the sauce over the cutlets. Serve immediately.

724

Veal cutlets filled with bacon and gruyere
FILETES DE TERNERA RELLENOS CON BACON Y GRUYÈRE

- **6 veal cutlets**
- **6 thin slices of bacon**
- **6 thin slices of gruyere cheese**
- **pinch of mixed dried herbs**
- **¼ cup (½ stick) butter**
- **2 tablespoons olive oil**
- **juice of ½ lemon**
- **2 tablespoons light cream**
  (optional)
- **1 teaspoon chopped**
  fresh parsley
- **salt**

Serves 6

Season the cutlets with salt on both sides. Place a slice of bacon in the center of each cutlet and top with a slice of gruyere. Sprinkle with some of the dried herbs, then fold the cutlet like a turnover, and pinch all around the edge with a toothpick. Melt half the butter with the oil in a skillet. Add the cutlets and cook over high heat for 2 minutes on each side. Lower the heat and cook for 5 minutes more on each side, or until done to your liking. Remove the cutlets from the skillet and keep warm. Drain off the oil from the skillet, then add the remaining butter and the lemon juice. If necessary, stir in 1–2 tablespoons hot water. Stir well, then remove the skillet from the heat, and stir in the cream, if using. Sprinkle the cutlets with the parsley and pour the sauce over them. Serve immediately, with straw potatoes (see recipe 243) or Mashed Potato (see recipe 230).

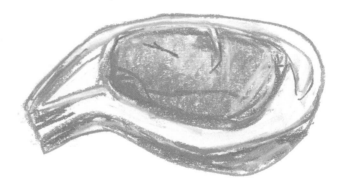

725

Veal cutlets with port, mustard, and parsley sauce
FILETES DE TERNERA CON SALSA DE OPORTO, MOSTAZA Y PEREJIL

- **6 veal cutlets**
- **5 tablespoons olive oil**
- **5 tablespoons port or**
  other fortified wine
- **2 teaspoons Dijon mustard**
- **1 tablespoon chopped**
  fresh parsley
- **salt**

Serves 6

Lightly season the cutlets with salt on both sides. Heat the oil in a skillet. Add the cutlets, in batches, and cook over medium heat for 3–4 minutes on each side, or until done to your liking, turning them with tongs. Set aside and keep warm. Pour off most of the oil from the skillet, leaving just enough to cover the base. Add the port and mustard and cook, stirring constantly, for 2–3 minutes. Add the parsley, pour the sauce over the cutlets, and serve immediately.

Veal tenderloin with mushrooms and béchamel sauce

FILETES MIGNON CON CHAMPIÑONES Y BECHAMEL

- 9 ounces cremini mushrooms
- ¼ cup (½ stick) butter
- juice of ½ lemon
- 1 cup sunflower oil
- 2 tablespoons all-purpose flour
- 3 cups milk
- 6 slices of bread, crusts removed and cut into rounds
- 6 slices of veal tenderloin
- salt

Serves 6

Separate the mushroom caps from the stalks and put the caps into a pan with 1½ tablespoons of the butter, the lemon juice, and a pinch of salt. Cook over low heat for about 6 minutes, then set aside and keep warm. Meanwhile, finely chop the stalks. Melt the remaining butter with 2 tablespoons of the oil in another pan. Stir in the flour and cook, stirring constantly, for 2 minutes. Gradually stir in the milk, a little at a time. Add the mushroom stalks and cook, stirring constantly, for about 10 minutes, until the sauce has thickened. Remove from the heat and keep warm. Preheat the broiler. Heat the remaining oil in a skillet. Add the bread and cook, turning occasionally, until golden brown on both sides. Remove with a slotted spatula, drain, and place on an ovenproof serving dish or casserole. Pour off most of the oil from the skillet. Season the veal slices with salt on both sides and add to the skillet, in batches, and cook over medium heat for 3–4 minutes on each side. Place a slice of veal on top of each fried bread round, pour the sauce over the top, and garnish with the mushroom caps. Put the dish under the broiler for about 5 minutes, or until lightly browned and cooked to your liking, then serve.

727

Veal cutlets with chopped mushrooms
ESCALOPINES DE TERNERA REBOZADOS Y CON PICADITO DE CHAMPIÑONES

- 1 pound 2 ounces mushrooms
- ¼ cup (½ stick) butter
- juice of ½ lemon
- sunflower oil, for deep-frying
- ⅓ cup all-purpose flour
- 3 tablespoons brandy
- 2 eggs
- 12 small veal cutlets
- salt and pepper

Serves 6

Separate the mushroom caps from the stalks. Put the caps into a pan with 2 tablespoons of the butter, the lemon juice, 2 tablespoons water, and a pinch of salt. Cook over low heat for about 8 minutes, until tender. Set aside and keep warm. Meanwhile, finely chop the stalks. Melt the remaining butter with 2 tablespoons of the oil in another pan. Stir in 1 tablespoon of the flour and cook, stirring constantly, for 5 minutes, until lightly browned. Gradually stir in the brandy and 1 cup water, a little at a time. Add the mushroom stalks, season with salt and pepper, and cook, stirring constantly, for about 8 minutes, until thickened. Remove from the heat and keep warm. Pour the remaining flour into a shallow dish and beat the eggs in another shallow dish. Heat the oil in a deep-fryer or deep skillet to 350–375°F or until a cube of day-old bread browns in 30 seconds. Season the cutlets with salt on both sides and coat them first in the flour, shaking off any excess, then in the beaten egg one at a time. Add them to the hot oil, in batches, and cook until golden brown. Remove the cutlets with a slotted spatula, drain, and keep warm while you cook the remaining batches. Put the cutlets on a warm serving dish, garnish with the mushroom caps, and serve immediately, offering the sauce separately.

728

Veal rolls with bacon and anchovies
ROLLITOS DE TERNERA CON BACON Y ANCHOAS

- 6 slices of veal breast
  or rump roast
- 12 thin slices of bacon
- 6 canned anchovy fillets, drained
- 4 tablespoons olive oil
- 1 onion, chopped
- 1 tablespoon all-purpose flour
- ¾ cup white wine
- 1 bay leaf
- salt and pepper

Serves 6

Season the veal slices with salt and pepper on both sides, place two slices of bacon on each slice of veal, and top with an anchovy fillet. Roll up each veal slice and tie with fine kitchen string. Heat the oil in a pan. Add the veal rolls and cook, turning frequently, until browned all over. Remove from the pan, drain, and set aside. Add the onion to the pan and cook over low heat, stirring occasionally, for about 8 minutes, until beginning to brown. Stir in the flour and cook, stirring constantly, for 2 minutes. Gradually stir in the wine, a little at a time, then stir in ¾ cup water. Add the bay leaf, return the veal rolls to the pan, and add ¾ cup water to cover them. Season with salt and bring to a boil. Lower the heat to medium, cover, and cook for 1–1¼ hours. Lift the veal rolls out of the pan, remove and discard the string, and place the rolls on a warm serving dish. Remove the bay leaf. Pass the sauce through a food mill or process in a food processor, then pour over the meat. Serve with Mashed Potato (see recipe 230).

729

Veal rolls with bacon and ground beef
ROLLITOS DE TERNERA CON BACON Y CARNE PICADA

- **6 slices of veal breast or rump roast**
- **9 ounces ground beef**
- **1 thick slice of bacon**
- **6 sprigs fresh parsley**
- **4 tablespoons olive oil**
- **1 onion**
- **1 tablespoon all-purpose flour**
- **¾ cup white wine**
- **1 bay leaf**
- **salt**

Serves 6

Season the veal slices with a little salt on both sides, then divide the ground beef among the slices, placing it on top and pressing it down gently. Cut the bacon into 6 strips. Put a strip of bacon and a parsley sprig in the middle of each slice. Roll up each slice of veal and tie it with fine kitchen string. From this point, proceed as described in recipe 728.

730

Veal chops with tomatoes and green bell peppers
CHULETAS DE TERNERA CON REVUELTO DE TOMATES Y PIMIENTOS VERDES

- **2¼ cups sunflower oil**
- **6 ripe tomatoes, peeled, seeded, and chopped**
- **1 teaspoon sugar**
- **4 green bell peppers, seeded and diced**
- **6 veal chops**
- **salt**

Serves 6

Heat 2 tablespoons of the oil in a skillet. Add the tomato and cook over high heat, stirring occasionally and breaking it up with the side of the spoon, for about 20 minutes, until pulpy. Stir in the sugar, season with salt, and set aside. Heat 1⅔ cups of the remaining oil with 2 tablespoons water in another skillet. Season the bell pepper with salt, add to the hot oil, cover, and cook over low heat for 10 minutes. Drain off the oil, add the bell pepper to the tomato, and mix well. Heat the remaining oil in a large skillet. Season the chops with salt on both sides, add them to the pan, in two batches, and cook over high heat for 1–2 minutes on each side, then lower the heat, and cook for 3–4 minutes more on each side. Put the chops on a warm serving dish and top each with some of the tomato and bell pepper mixture. Surround with fried potatoes and serve immediately.

731 Veal chops with almonds and Malaga wine

CHULETAS DE TERNERA CON ALMENDRAS Y VINO DE MÁLAGA

- 5–6 tablespoons olive oil
- 6 veal chops
- scant 1 cup sliced almonds
- ¾ cup Malaga wine
  or sweet sherry
- salt

Serves 6

Heat the oil in a skillet. Add the chops, in batches, and cook over high heat for 1–2 minutes on each side, then lower the heat, and cook for 3–4 minutes more on each side. Season with salt, transfer to a serving dish, and keep warm. Add the almonds to the skillet and cook, stirring frequently, for a few minutes, until golden brown. Stir in the wine or sherry, then spoon the almonds and sauce over the chops. Serve immediately.

Note: This dish can be made using pork chops in place of veal.

732 Veal chops in packages

CHULETAS DE TERNERA EN PAPILLOTE

- 2 tablespoons (¼ stick) butter
- 2 shallots, very finely chopped
- 1 ⅔ cups chopped mushrooms
- 1 teaspoon lemon juice
- 1 tablespoon chopped
  fresh parsley
- ½ cup olive oil,
  plus extra for brushing
- 6 veal chops
- 3 very thin slices of Serrano ham
  or prosciutto, halved
- salt and pepper

Serves 6

Preheat the oven to 325°F. Melt the butter in a skillet. Add the shallots and cook over low heat, stirring occasionally, for about 5 minutes, until softened. Add the mushrooms and lemon juice, season with salt, and cook, stirring occasionally, for 6 minutes or until the mushrooms have released their juice and some of it has been evaporated. Stir in the parsley and cook for 1 minute more. Set aside. Heat the oil in a skillet. Add the chops, in batches, and cook over high heat for 1 minute on each side. Remove from the skillet and set aside. Brush six sheets of parchment paper or aluminum foil with oil. Season both sides of each chop with salt and pepper and put a chop on each piece of parchment or foil. Put one-sixth of the mushroom mixture on top of each, and cover it with a half slice of ham. Fold over the parchment or foil and seal the edges. Put the packages on a baking sheet and bake, turning the parcels once, for 20 minutes. Serve the packages half open on a warm serving dish.

733

Veal chops and chicken livers in packages

CHULETAS DE TERNERA EN PAPILLOTE CON HIGADITOS DE POLLO

- **6 veal chops**
- **6 chicken livers, trimmed**
- **6 sprigs fresh parsley**
- **1 onion, thinly sliced**
- **6 tablespoons sunflower oil**
- **6 tablespoons white wine**
- **salt and pepper**

Serves 6

Preheat the oven 350°F. Season the chops on both sides with salt and pepper and place each one on a sheet of parchment paper or aluminum foil. Halve the chicken livers without cutting all the way through. Put a liver on each chop and season with salt. Place a parsley sprig on top and divide the onion slices among the chops. Pour 1 tablespoon oil and 1 tablespoon wine over each one. Fold over the parchment paper or foil and seal the edges. Place the packages on a baking sheet and bake for 20 minutes. Serve the packages half open on a warm serving dish.

Note: Foil provides more insulation than parchment, so the food inside a parchment package might need to be cooked for less time than food wrapped in foil.

734

Veal chops in sauce

CHULETAS EN SALSA

- **½ cup olive oil**
- **6 veal chops**
- **¾ cup dry or medium sherry or other fortified wine**
- **½ teaspoon potato starch**
- **2 tablespoons (¼ stick) butter**
- **½ teaspoon meat extract or Maggi Seasoning**
- **juice of ½ lemon**
- **1 teaspoon chopped fresh parsley**
- **salt**

Serves 6

Heat the oil in a skillet. Add the chops, in batches, and cook over high heat for 1–2 minutes on each side, then lower the heat, and cook for 3–4 minutes more on each side. Season the chops on both sides with salt, place on a serving dish, and keep warm. Drain off nearly all the oil from the skillet, then pour in the sherry and ¾ cup water, and cook over high heat, stirring frequently, until reduced by half. Mix the potato starch with a little water and stir into the skillet. Add the butter, meat extract or Maggi Seasoning, and lemon juice and mix well. Pour this sauce over the chops, sprinkle with the parsley, and serve with Mashed Potato (see recipe 230) or fried potatoes, French Fries (see recipe 242), or vegetables.

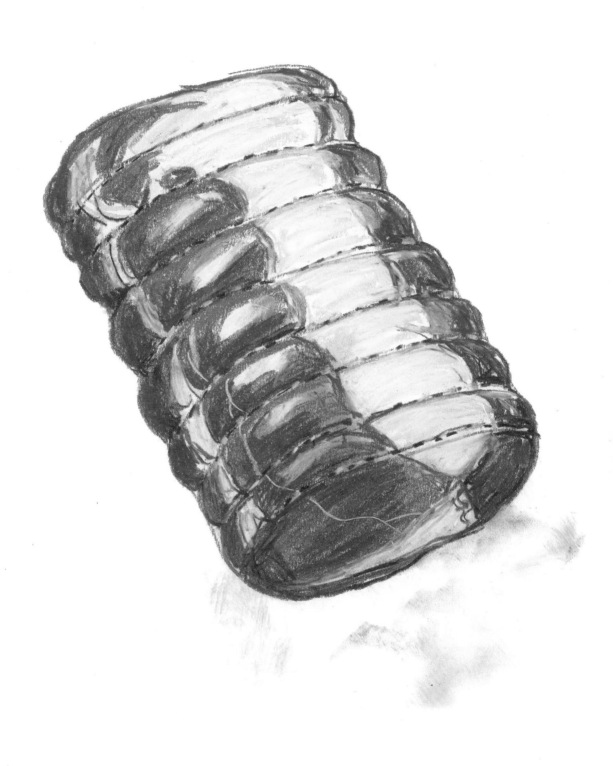

735

Roast veal

ASADO DE TERNERA AL HORNO

- 1 veal leg, loin, or rib roast,
  3¼ pounds
- generous ½ cup lard or
  5–6 tablespoons sunflower oil
- 1 small onion, cut into wedges
  (optional)
- ½ lemon
- salt

Serves 6

Preheat the oven to 325°F. Tie the veal into a neat shape with fine kitchen string. Rub the veal all over with the lard or brush with the oil and place it in a roasting pan. Roast, turning once or twice, for 30 minutes. Season with salt and pour 5 tablespoons hot water over the meat. Put the onion wedges, if using, around the veal and return the tin to the oven. Increase the oven temperature to 350°F and roast for 1 hour, turning the meat occasionally, adding more water if necessary and basting occasionally with the cooking juices. Turn off the oven, open the door for 2 minutes, close it again, and let the veal rest in the warm oven for about 5 minutes before carving it. Discard the onion wedges, if used, and serve the cooking juices separately in a sauceboat.

736

**Roast veal with mayonnaise
and hard-cooked eggs**

ASADO DE TERNERA, PRESENTADO CON MAYONESA Y HUEVO DURO

- 1 leg, loin or rib of veal,
  roasted, 3¼ pounds
- 2 eggs
- juice of ½ lemon
- 2¼ cups sunflower oil
- 2 hard-cooked eggs,
  finely chopped
- salt

Serves 6

Using the eggs, lemon juice, oil, and a pinch of salt, make the mayonnaise in a food processor or blender as described in recipe 105, second part. It should be quite thick. Carve the meat, place in a warm serving dish, and cover with the mayonnaise. Sprinkle with the hard-cooked eggs and garnish with vegetables. Serve immediately, offering the cooking juices separately. This dish is splendid and very tasty.

737

Veal pot roast
ASADO DE TERNERA HECHO EN CACEROLA

- 1 rump roast or leg of veal,
  3¼ pounds
- 5–6 tablespoons sunflower oil
  or generous ½ cup lard
- 1 onion, coarsely chopped
- pinch of mixed dried herbs
  or 1 bouquet garni
  (1 sprig fresh parsley, 2 bay
  leaves, and 1 clove garlic tied
  together in cheesecloth)
- 2 veal shank bones
- salt

Serves 6

Tie the veal into a neat shape with fine kitchen string. Heat the oil or melt the lard in a large, heavy pan. Add the veal and cook over medium heat, turning frequently, for about 10 minutes, until evenly browned all over. Add the onion, dried herbs or bouquet garni, shank bones, and a pinch of salt. Pour in ¾ cup water, cover, and cook over medium-low heat, turning the veal every 15 minutes, for 1 hour. Lift out the veal, remove and discard the string, and let rest for about 5 minutes before carving. Remove the bones and strain the cooking juices into a sauceboat. There is usually plenty, but if not, stir a little hot water into the pan before straining it.

Note: A cast-iron Dutch oven is ideal for cooking this dish.

738

Leg of veal with pineapple
BABILLA DE TERNERA CON PIÑA

- 1 leg of veal, about 3¼ pounds
- 8 cloves
- 5 tablespoons rum
- scant ¼ cup currants
- ¾-inch piece of chile pepper
- 20 ounce canned pineapple
  slices in juice
- 4 tablespoons olive oil
- 1 heaping tablespoon
  all-purpose flour
- generous 1 cup white wine
- 2 tablespoons (¼ stick)
  margarine or butter
- salt

Serves 6

Tie the veal into a neat shape with fine kitchen string and stud with the cloves. Put it into a Dutch oven or heavy pan and add the rum, currants, chile, and the juice from the pineapple slices. Chop two slices of the pineapple and add to the pan, then let the veal marinate in the refrigerator, turning it occasionally, for at least 1 hour. Reserve the remaining pineapple. Remove the veal from the pan, pour the marinade into a bowl, remove the currants with a slotted spoon, and reserve. Heat the oil in the Dutch oven or pan. Add the veal and cook, turning frequently, for about 10 minutes, until evenly browned all over. Sprinkle in the flour, pour in the marinade and wine, season with salt, and bring to a boil. Lower the heat and cook, turning the veal occasionally, for about 1½ hours, until tender. Toward the end of the cooking time, melt the margarine or butter in a skillet. Add the reserved pineapple slices and cook over high heat for 5 minutes until golden brown on both sides. Remove with a slotted spatula, drain, and keep warm. Lift the veal out of the pan, remove and discard the string, and carve the meat into thin slices. Pass the sauce through a food mill or process in a food processor. Put the veal on a serving dish and garnish with the pineapple slices and the reserved currants. Serve immediately, offering the sauce separately.

Note: The dish can be served with yellow rice (see recipe 191).

739

Roast veal with orange

CONTRA DE TERNERA ASADA CON NARANJA

- 1 veal boneless leg, sirloin, or rump roast, 3¼ pounds
- 5 tablespoons brandy
- generous ½ cup lard or 6 tablespoons sunflower oil
- 5 tablespoons hot water
- 2 tablespoons sugar
- 1½ tablespoons butter
- 1 large orange or 2 small oranges, sliced
- juice of 2 oranges
- 1 tablespoon grated orange zest
- Mashed Potato (see recipe 230)
- salt

Serves 6

Preheat the oven to 350°F. Tie the veal into a neat shape with fine kitchen string and put it into a roasting pan. Heat the brandy in a small pan, ignite it, and pour it over the veal. When the flames have died down, spread the lard over the veal or pour the oil over it. Roast for about 20 minutes, until beginning to brown, then season with salt, add the hot water, and baste the meat. Cook, turning the meat and basting occasionally, for 1 hour, until tender. Meanwhile, pour 1 cup water into a pan, add the sugar and butter, and bring to a boil, stirring until the sugar has dissolved. Cook for about 6 minutes, then add the orange slices, and bring back to a boil. Remove the pan from the heat and set aside. When the veal is tender, turn off the oven, open the door for 2 minutes, and then close it again, and let the meat rest for about 15 minutes before carving. Carve the veal and place the slices on a warm serving dish. Drain the orange slices. Garnish the meat with little mounds of the mashed potato and the orange slices. Stir the orange juice and grated zest into the cooking juices and heat through, then serve separately in a sauceboat.

740

Osso buco in mushroom sauce

OSSO BUCCO EN SALSA CON CHAMPIÑONES

- 5–6 tablespoons olive oil
- 6 slices of veal shank (osso buco)
- ⅓ cup all-purpose flour
- 3⅔ cups thickly sliced mushrooms
- 3 large, ripe tomatoes, peeled, seeded, and chopped
- 1 cup white wine
- 1 cup veal or chicken stock (homemade, canned or made with a bouillon cube)
- salt and pepper

Serves 6

Heat the oil in a large pan. Coat the pieces of veal in the flour, shaking off any excess, add to the pan, and cook over medium heat, turning occasionally, for 8–10 minutes, until lightly browned. Add the mushrooms and cook, stirring occasionally, for 5 minutes, then add the tomatoes. Pour in the wine and stock, season with salt and pepper, cover, and cook over low heat for about 1 hour, until tender. Serve in a warm deep dish.

741

Osso buco in sauce

OSSO BUCCO EN SALSA

- 2 cups sunflower oil
- 6 slices of veal shank
  (osso buco)
- ⅓ cup all-purpose flour
- 1 onion, finely chopped
- 1 clove garlic, finely chopped
- 3 tomatoes, seeded and chopped
- ½ teaspoon mixed dried herbs
  or 1 bouquet garni
  (1 sprig fresh parsley, 1 sprig
  fresh thyme, and 2 bay leaves
  tied together in cheesecloth)
- 1 tablespoon grated lemon zest
- 1 cup white wine
- 1 cup veal or chicken stock
  (homemade, canned or
  made with a bouillon cube)
- 9 ounces shallots
- 1½ tablespoons butter
- a dash of lemon juice
- 1 tablespoon chopped
  fresh parsley
- salt and pepper

Serves 6

Reserve 5 tablespoons of the oil and heat the remainder in a skillet. Coat the pieces of osso buco in the flour, shaking off any excess, add to the skillet, and cook over medium heat, turning occasionally, for 8–10 minutes, until golden brown on both sides. Remove from the skillet and keep warm. Heat 3 tablespoons of the reserved oil in another skillet. Add the onion and garlic and cook over low heat, stirring occasionally, for about 8 minutes, until beginning to brown. Add the tomato and cook, stirring occasionally and breaking it up with the side of the spoon, for about 10 minutes. Add the dried herbs or bouquet garni and stir in the lemon zest. Put the pieces of veal into a pan. Pour the wine and stock into the tomato and onion mixture, season with salt and pepper, and pour the sauce over the meat. Cover and simmer over low heat for 1 hour, until tender. Meanwhile, put the shallots, butter, lemon juice, and a pinch of salt into another pan, add water to cover, and cook for about 20 minutes, until tender. Drain well. Heat the remaining oil in a third pan. Add the shallots and cook, turning frequently, until browned all over. Remove from the pan and set aside. Transfer the pieces of veal to a warm serving dish. Remove and discard the bouquet garni, if used, pass the sauce through a food mill or process in a food processor or blender, and pour it over the meat. Garnish the dish with the shallots and sprinkle with the parsley. Serve immediately.

Note: Some people prefer not to pass the sauce through a food mill or process in a food processor or blender, which results in a sauce with more texture.

Veal stew with whiskey sauce and rice

GUISO DE TERNERA EN SALSA DE WHISKY CON ARROZ BLANCO

- **2 onions**
- **3¼ pounds veal, breast or shoulder, cut into cubes**
- **4 carrots, halved lengthwise**
- **1 bay leaf**
- **5 tablespoons white wine**
- **2½ cups long-grain rice**
- **6 tablespoons (¾ stick) butter**
- **2 tablespoons sunflower oil**
- **1 tablespoon all-purpose flour**
- **3 tablespoons whiskey**
- **1 tablespoon chopped fresh parsley**
- **salt**

Serves 6

Finely chop one of the onions and cut the other in half. Put the veal, carrots, onion halves, bay leaf, wine, and a pinch of salt into a pan, pour in water to cover, and bring to a boil. Skim off the froth that rises to the surface, then cover, and cook over medium heat for 1–1½ hours, until the veal is tender. Meanwhile, cook and rinse the rice as described in recipe 173. Remove the veal from the pan with a slotted spoon and set aside. Strain and reserve the cooking liquid. Melt 2 tablespoons of the butter with the oil in a pan. Add the chopped onion and cook over low heat, stirring occasionally, for about 10 minutes, until lightly browned. Stir in the flour and cook, stirring constantly, for 2 minutes. Stir in the whiskey, then gradually stir in 3 cups of the reserved cooking liquid, a little at a time. Cook, stirring constantly, for about 10 minutes, until thickened. Add the veal and heat through for about 5 minutes. Meanwhile, season the rice with salt and fry in the remaining butter (see recipe 173). Spoon the rice into a ring mold and turn it out onto a warm serving dish. Spoon the meat and sauce into the middle and sprinkle with the parsley. Alternatively, serve the rice in a mound on the side. Serve immediately.

743

Veal stew with lemon juice

GUISO DE TERNERA CON ZUMO DE LIMÓN

- 3¼ pounds veal, breast or shoulder, cut into cubes
- ⅓ cup all-purpose flour
- 6 tablespoons olive oil
- 1 onion, chopped
- juice of 3 lemons
- grated zest of 1 lemon
- 1 veal or chicken bouillon cube
- 9 ounces shallots
- 1 tablespoon butter
- 1 teaspoon sugar
- 1 teaspoon Dijon mustard
- ½ teaspoon meat concentrate
- ¾ cup muscatel wine
- salt and pepper

Serves 6

Coat the cubes of veal in the flour, shaking off any excess. Heat the oil in a pan. Add the onion and cook over low heat, stirring occasionally, for about 5 minutes, until softened and translucent. Add the veal and cook over medium heat, stirring frequently, for 8–10 minutes, until browned all over. Stir in 1 tablespoon of the flour and cook, stirring constantly, for 2 minutes. Gradually stir in 3 cups water and the lemon juice and add the lemon zest. Crumble in the bouillon cube and stir well. Cover and cook over medium heat for about 1½ hours, until the veal is tender. Meanwhile, put the shallots and butter into a pan, pour in water to cover, and cook for about 20 minutes, until tender. Shortly before serving, heat the sugar in another pan until it is the color of caramel. Stir in the mustard, meat concentrate, and wine, then stir the mixture into the stew. Season to taste with salt and pepper. Drain the shallots, add to the stew, and cook for 8 minutes more. Serve with triangles of fried bread (see recipe 130) or little mounds of boiled rice.

744

Veal stew with leeks
TERNERA GUISADA CON PUERROS

- 2 tablespoons (¼ stick) butter
- 2 tablespoons olive oil
- 2¼ pounds veal, breast
  or shoulder, cut into cubes
- 1¾ pounds leeks, thinly sliced
  and rinsed well
- ¾ cup dry white wine
- juice of ½ lemon
- 1 cup milk
- scant ¼ cup currants
- 1 bouquet garni (1 sprig fresh
  parsley, 1 bay leaf, and 1 clove
  garlic tied in cheesecloth)
- salt
Serves 6

Melt the butter with the oil in a pan. Add the veal and cook over medium heat, stirring frequently, for about 8 minutes, until golden brown all over. Remove with a slotted spoon and keep warm. Add the leek to the pan and cook over low heat, stirring occasionally, for 10 minutes, until softened. Return the veal to the pan, pour in the wine, lemon juice, and milk and add the currants and bouquet garni. Cover and simmer gently for 40 minutes, until the veal is tender. Remove and discard the bouquet garni and serve immediately with boiled rice or tagliatelle.

745

Veal stew
TERNERA GUISADA

- 1 pound 5 ounces veal, breast
  or shoulder, cut into cubes
- 2 tablespoons all-purpose flour
- 4 tablespoons olive oil
- 1 onion, chopped
- ½ cup dry white wine
- ½ cup veal or chicken stock
  (homemade, canned or
  made with a bouillon cube)
- 1 sprig fresh thyme, chopped
- 1 sprig fresh sage, chopped
- pinch of freshly grated nutmeg
- 2 eggs
- juice of ½ lemon
- 1 tablespoon chopped
  fresh parsley
- salt and pepper
Serves 4

Coat the veal in the flour, shaking off any excess. Heat the oil in a pan. Add the onion and cook over low heat, stirring occasionally, for about 8 minutes, until beginning to brown. Add the veal, in batches, and cook over medium heat, stirring frequently, for about 5–8 minutes, until evenly browned. Return all the veal to the pan. Pour in the wine and cook over high heat until reduced, then add the stock. Lower the heat and simmer gently for 45 minutes, adding more stock or water, if necessary, until the veal is tender. Season with salt and pepper halfway through the cooking time and add the thyme, sage, and nutmeg. Beat the eggs with the lemon juice and parsley and stir into the pan, then remove from the heat, and serve.

Stewed veal breast

FILETES DE FALDA DE TERNERA GUISADOS

- 5 tablespoons olive oil
- 3 pounds boneless veal breast,
  cut into 6 slices
- 1 onion, finely chopped
- 3 cloves garlic, lightly crushed
- 2 ripe tomatoes,
  peeled, seeded, and diced
- generous 1 cup white wine
- a pinch of mixed dried herbs
  or 1 bouquet garni
  (1 sprig fresh parsley, 1 sprig
  fresh thyme, and 2 bay leaves
  tied together in cheesecloth)
- 9 ounces shallots
- 3 tablespoons butter
- juice of ½ lemon
- generous 2 ¾ cups thickly sliced
  mushrooms
- ½ cup olives, pitted
  and halved lengthwise
- salt

Serves 6

Heat the oil in a heavy pan or a Dutch oven. Add the veal, in batches, and cook over medium heat, stirring frequently, for 5–8 minutes until evenly browned on both sides. Remove the veal from the pan and set aside. Add the onion and garlic to the pan and cook over low heat, stirring occasionally, for about 5 minutes, until softened and translucent. Return the veal to the pan, add the tomato, and pour in the wine and ¾ cup water. Season with salt, stir in the dried herbs or bouquet garni, and bring to a boil. Lower the heat, cover. and simmer for 1 hour, until the veal is tender. Meanwhile, put the shallots, half the butter, half the lemon juice, and a pinch of salt into a pan and cook for about 20 minutes, until tender. Drain and set aside. Put the mushrooms, the remaining lemon juice, the remaining butter, and a pinch of salt into a pan. Cover and cook for 6 minutes. When the veal is tender, add the shallots, the mushrooms and their cooking juices, and the olives to the stew, mix well, and cook over medium heat for 5 minutes more. Remove and discard the bouquet garni, if used, and serve immediately.

747

Blanquette of veal
BLANQUETA DE TERNERA

- 3 ¼ pounds boneless veal breast, cut into cubes
- 1 bay leaf
- 1 small onion, halved
- 2 carrots, sliced
- 5 tablespoons white wine
- 2 ½ cups long-grain rice
- 6 tablespoons (¾ stick) butter
- 2 tablespoons sunflower oil
- 1 ½ tablespoons flour
- 1 cup milk
- 2 egg yolks
- juice of ½ lemon
- 2 teaspoons chopped fresh parsley
- salt

Serves 6

Put the veal into a pan, pour in water to cover, and add the bay leaf, onion, carrot, wine, and a pinch of salt. Bring to a boil and skim off the froth that rises to the surface, then lower the heat, and simmer for 1–1 ½ hours, until the veal is tender. Meanwhile, cook and rinse the rice as described in recipe 173. Remove the veal from the pan with a slotted spoon and keep warm. Strain and reserve the cooking liquid. Melt 2 tablespoons of the butter with the oil in a pan. Stir in the flour and cook, stirring constantly, for 2 minutes. Gradually stir in the milk and 2 ¼ cups of the reserved cooking liquid. Beat the egg yolks with the lemon juice and stir in a little of the sauce, then pour into the pan. Sprinkle in the parsley and season to taste with salt. Remove the pan from the heat and keep warm. Season the rice with salt and fry in the remaining butter (see recipe 173). Fill half of a long serving dish with the rice and the other half with the veal and sauce. Serve immediately.

748

Classic stuffed breast of veal
ALETA DE TERNERA RELLENA CLÁSICA

- 3 carrots
- 1 boneless veal breast, 3 ¼ pounds
- 9 ounces ground veal
- 4-ounce piece of Serrano ham or prosciutto, cut into ¾-inch wide strips
- 1 hard-cooked egg, cut into wedges
- 4 tablespoons olive oil
- 1 large onion, chopped
- 1 apple, peeled, cored, and chopped
- ¾ cup dry white wine
- salt

Serves 8–9

Cut two of the carrots into lengthwise strips, discarding the centers. Slice the remaining carrot. Open out the breast of veal, spread the ground veal in the center, and place the strips of ham and strips of carrot on top and all along it. Add the hard-cooked egg and season with salt. Roll up the veal and tie securely with fine kitchen string. Heat the oil in a pan. Add the veal and cook over medium heat, turning frequently, for 8–10 minutes, until evenly browned all over. Remove from the pan and set aside. Add the onion to the pan and cook over low heat, stirring occasionally, for about 10 minutes, until golden brown. Return the veal to the pan, add the apple, sliced carrot, and a pinch of salt, and pour in the wine. Bring to a boil, pour in enough water almost to cover the meat, and bring back to a boil. Lower the heat, cover, and simmer for 1 ¼ hours, until the veal is tender and the sauce has reduced. Lift the veal out of the pan and remove and discard the string. Cut into slices about ½ inch thick and place on a warm serving dish. Pass the sauce through a food mill or process in a food processor. Transfer to a sauceboat. Serve immediately with little mounds of vegetables or Mashed Potato (see recipe 230).

Rolled veal breast filled with spinach and omelet

ALETA DE TERNERA RELLENA CON ESPINACAS Y TORTILLAS

- 2 ¼ pounds spinach, coarse stalks removed
- 1 boneless veal breast, 1 pound 10 ounces
- 7 ounces ground veal
- ½ cup finely chopped Serrano ham or prosciutto
- 2 eggs
- ½ cup sunflower oil
- 5 tablespoons white wine
- ¾ cup hot water
- salt

Serves 6

Cook the spinach as described on page 315, drain well, and chop. Preheat the oven to 350°F. Open out the breast of veal and season lightly with salt. Combine the ground veal and ham and spread the mixture on top of the breast of veal. Using 1 egg and 1 ½ tablespoons of the oil each, make two flat omelets in a small skillet. Place the omelets on top of the ground meat, next to each other. Put the spinach on top of the omelets in a strip about 2 ½ inches wide. Carefully roll up the veal so that none of the filling moves, then tie it with fine kitchen string. Heat the remaining oil in a roasting pan. Add the veal roll and cook over medium heat, turning frequently, for 8–10 minutes, until evenly browned all over. Lightly season with salt and roast in the oven for 30 minutes. Pour the wine over the veal, return the tin to the oven, and roast for 15 minutes more. Pour half the hot water over the veal, return it to the oven, and roast, basting occasionally, for another 30 minutes, adding the remaining hot water, if necessary. If serving hot, let the meat rest for about 10 minutes before removing the string and carving. This dish is also very tasty served cold.

Stewed veal shoulder

ESPALDILLA DE TERNERA GUISADA

- ⅓ cup lard or 5 tablespoons sunflower oil
- 1 boneless, rolled veal shoulder, 4½ pounds, bones reserved
- 2 onions, coarsely chopped
- 9 ounces carrots, thickly sliced
- 2 ripe tomatoes, peeled, seeded, and chopped
- pinch of mixed dried herbs or 1 bouquet garni (1 sprig fresh parsley, 2 bay leaves, and 1 sprig fresh thyme tied together in cheesecloth)
- 1 cup white wine
- ¾ cup warm water
- 1 tablespoon potato starch
- ¼ teaspoon meat extract or Maggi Seasoning
- 1 teaspoon paprika
- salt

Serves 6

Preheat the oven to 350°F. Melt the lard or heat the oil in an ovenproof casserole that can be used on the stove. Add the veal, veal bones, onion, and carrot and cook over medium heat, turning the meat frequently, for 8–10 minutes, until evenly browned all over. Add the tomato, dried herbs or bouquet garni, and a pinch of salt, pour in the wine and the water, and bring to a boil. Transfer the casserole to the oven and cook, turning the veal and basting occasionally, for 1½ hours, until tender. Remove the veal from the casserole, cut it into slices, and keep warm. Set the casserole over medium-low heat and skim off any fat from the surface of the cooking liquid. Mix the potato starch with a little water and the meat extract or Maggi Seasoning in a bowl, then stir into the casserole. Remove and discard the bones and the bouquet garni, if used, and pass the cooking liquid through a food mill or process in a food processor or blender. Mix in the paprika, season to taste with salt, and add a little hot water if the sauce is very thick. If it is too thin, cook for a little longer before adding the paprika. Pour the sauce over the veal, and serve immediately with Mashed Potato (see recipe 230) or fried potatoes.

751

Veal with onions and sherry
TERNERA CON CEBOLLA Y VINO DE JEREZ

- 1 veal leg or rump roast,
  3¼ pounds
- 1 pound 10 ounces onions
- 5 tablespoons sunflower oil
  or ½ cup lard
- 2 cloves garlic, lightly crushed
- ⅔ cup sherry or other
  sweet fortified wine
- 2 cloves
- salt and pepper

Serves 6

Tie the veal into a neat shape with fine kitchen string. Coarsley chop the onions. Heat the oil or melt the lard in a heavy-based pan, or a Dutch oven. Add the veal and cook over medium heat, turning frequently, for 8–10 minutes, until evenly browned all over. Add the onion, garlic, sherry, cloves, and 1½ cups water, season with salt and pepper, and bring to a boil. Lower the heat, cover, and simmer for about 1¾ hours, until the veal is tender. Lift the veal out of the pan, remove and discard the string, and cut the meat into slices. Pass the cooking juices through a food mill or process in a food processor or blender. Serve immediately with boiled potatoes or macaroni tossed in butter and grated cheese.

752

Braised veal
TERNERA ESTOFADA

- 3¼ pounds veal breast,
  leg, or rib, cut into cubes
- ¾ cup white-wine vinegar
- ¾ cup olive oil
- 1 head garlic, peeled
- 1 large onion, chopped
- pinch of mixed dried herbs
  or 1 bouquet garni (1 bay leaf,
  2 sprigs fresh parsley, and
  1 sprig fresh thyme tied
  together in cheesecloth)
- 1 teaspoon paprika
- salt

Serves 6

Put all the ingredients into a large, heavy pan and season with the salt. Cover with a tight-fitting the lid and cook over low heat, stirring occasionally, for about 2 hours, until the veal is tender. If necessary, stir in a little hot water to prevent the meat drying out. Remove and discard the garlic and the bouquet garni, if used. Serve in a warm deep dish with triangles of fried bread (see recipe 130).

Veal casserole with porcini

TERNERA A LA CAZUELA CON SETAS

- generous ½ cup lard or
  6 tablespoons sunflower oil
- 1 veal rump roast, 3¼ pounds
- ¾ cup Malaga wine
  or sweet sherry
- 1 pound 10 ounces porcini,
  cut into large pieces
- 1 teaspoon potato starch
- ½ teaspoon meat concentrate
- salt

Serves 6

Melt the lard or heat the oil in a heavy pan or a Dutch oven. Add the veal and cook over medium heat, turning frequently, for 8–10 minutes, until evenly browned all over. Pour in the wine or sherry and ¾ cup water, season lightly with salt, cover, and cook, stirring occasionally, for 30 minutes. Add the porcini to the pan, re-cover, and cook for another 30 minutes, until the veal is tender. Lift out the meat, cut it into slices, place on a serving dish, and keep warm. Mix the potato starch and meat concentrate with a little water in a small bowl, then stir into the sauce. Bring to a boil, stirring constantly. Taste and adjust the seasoning, if necessary, then spoon the sauce and mushrooms over the veal. Serve immediately.

Note: This dish can also be made with dried porcini. Rehydrate them according to the instructions on the package.

754

Veal with garlic and tomato
TERNERA AL AJILLO CON TOMATE

- 4 tablespoons olive oil
- 3 ¼ pounds veal breast,
  cut into 2 ½-inch long strips
- 1 tablespoon bread crumbs
- 1 head garlic, peeled
- 1 veal or chicken bouillon cube
  dissolved in generous 1 cup
  boiling water
- salt

  Tomato sauce:
- 3 tablespoons sunflower oil
- 2 ¼ pounds very ripe tomatoes,
  peeled, seeded, and chopped
- pinch of mixed dried herbs
  or 1 bouquet garni (1 bay leaf and
  1 sprig fresh thyme tied together
  in cheesecloth)
- 1 teaspoon sugar
- salt

Serves 6

Make a thick tomato sauce as described in recipe 73. Remove and discard the bouquet garni, if used, before processing in a food processor or blender. Heat the oil in a heavy pan or a Dutch oven. Add the veal and cook over medium heat, stirring occasionally, for 8–10 minutes, until evenly browned. Sprinkle in the bread crumbs, add the tomato sauce, garlic cloves, and stock, and season lightly with salt. Cover and simmer over low heat for 1 ½ hours, until the veal is tender. Remove and discard the garlic and serve immediately accompanied by fried potatoes, boiled rice, or triangles of fried bread (see recipe 130).

Pork

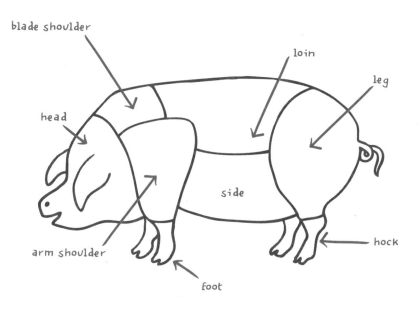

blade shoulder

loin

leg

head

arm shoulder

side

hock

foot

Selection

Pork should be pink or light red, depending on the cut. It shrinks considerably when roasted, fried, or stewed, losing almost one-third of its weight. A loin of pork weighing 3 ¼ pounds when raw will be just 1 2 ¼ pounds after roasting. Pork is very tasty but the meat from some of the traditional breeds can be quite fatty and indigestible. If you are worried about the fat content, look for specially bred lean pork (but be aware that meat is often drier, the more lean it is.)

Sausages

Method for poaching sausages

Some sausages, especially larger sausages popular in Spain, Italy and France are often poached rather than fried. Prick the skin in several places with a toothpick. Bring a large pan of water to a boil, add the sausages, and bring back to a boil. Lower the heat so that the water is barely simmering with just a few bubbles around the side of the pan. Poach for 10–12 minutes, depending on the type of sausage, then remove, and serve.

Method for frying sausages

Prick the skin in several places with a fork or a toothpick. Put them in a skillet, pour oil over them, and set the pan over low heat. Cook, turning occasionally, until they are cooked through and evenly browned.

Buying pork	Suitable cuts	Weight per serving	Cooking time
Fried, broiled or grilled	Chops, Ham, Tenderloin	7 ounces 5 ounces	6 minutes each side, first over a high heat and then over a low heat
Roasted *	Tenderloin Loin, Leg	7–8 ounces (boneless)	25–30 minutes per pound
Stewed or braised	Arm shoulder, Blade shoulder	7 ounces	1½–1¾ hours

*Make sure that the oven is preheated

755

Roast loin of pork

LOMO DE CERDO ASADO

- 1 boneless pork loin, 3¼ pounds
- 2–3 tablespoons lard
  or sunflower oil (optional)
- juice of ½ lemon
- salt and pepper

Serves 6

Tie the pork into a neat shape with fine kitchen string and season with salt and pepper at least 1 hour before cooking. Preheat the oven to 450°F. Put the pork into a roasting pan. If the meat has plenty of fat, put the pan into the oven without any additional fat. If most of the fat has been trimmed, spread the lard or brush the oil over the pork before putting it into the oven. Roast, turning frequently, for 10–15 minutes, until browned all over. Lower the oven temperature to 350°F, pour 3–4 tablespoons hot water over the pork, and return to the oven. Roast, occasionally basting the meat with the cooking juices, for 1¼ hours, until the juices run clear when the thickest part is pierced with the tip of a sharp knife. Remove the pork from the oven and let rest for 5 minutes before removing and discarding the string and carving the meat into thin slices. Mix a few drops of the lemon juice into the cooking juices and pour into a sauceboat. Serve the pork garnished with Mashed Potato (see recipe 230), fried parsley potatoes, Potato Balls (see recipe 231), watercress, noodles, or tagliatelle. Offer the sauce separately.

Notes: Some people like to rub the meat with a peeled garlic clove after it has been seasoned. As roast pork is delicious cold with a salad, remember to roast a larger quantity of meat and keep some to serve cold.

756

Pork loin with mustard

- 1 boneless pork loin, 3¼ pounds
- 2 tablespoons Dijon mustard
- ¾ cup white wine
- hot water
- salt

Serves 6

Tie the pork into a neat shape with fine kitchen string and season with salt 1 hour before cooking. Preheat the oven to 450°F. Spread the mustard all over the pork, then put the meat into a roasting pan.Put the pork into the oven and roast, turning frequently, for 10–15 minutes, until browned all over. Lower the oven temperature to 350°F. Pour the wine over the pork and baste well, then return to the oven, and roast, basting occasionally, for 1¼ hours, until the juices run clear when the thickest part is pierced with the tip of a sharp knife. Turn off the oven, open the door for 2–3 minutes, close it again, and let the pork rest for about 6 minutes. Take the pork out of the oven, remove and discard the string, and carve the pork into thin slices. Place them in a serving dish and keep warm. Put 2–3 tablespoons hot water into the roasting pan and bring to a boil over medium heat, stirring and scraping up any bits from the base of the pan. Strain into a sauceboat. Serve the pork with French Fries (see recipe 242), Mashed Potato (see recipe 230), or macaroni tossed in butter and grated cheese, offering the sauce separately.

Pork loin with milk

CINTA O LOMO DE CERDO CON LECHE

- 1 boneless pork loin, 4¼ pounds
- 2½ tablespoons lard,
  or 2 tablespoons sunflower oil
- 4 cups warm milk
- 4 cloves garlic
- 4 black peppercorns
- salt

Serves 6

Tie the pork into a neat shape with fine kitchen string and season with salt 1 hour before cooking. Melt the lard or heat the oil in a heavy pan or a Dutch oven. Add the pork and cook over medium heat, turning frequently, for about 10 minutes, until browned all over. Pour in the milk, add the garlic and the peppercorns, and bring to a boil over medium heat. Lower the heat, cover, and simmer gently, turning occasionally, for about 2½ hours, until the pork is tender. Remove the pork from the pan and keep warm. If the remaining cooking liquid is very thin, cook over high heat until reduced. Remove and discard the string from the pork, carve the meat into thin slices, and place on a warm serving dish. Garnish with Mashed Potato (see recipe 230) or applesauce. Strain the cooking liquid or put it through a food mill, or process in a food processor or blender. Beat well and serve separately in a sauceboat.

Pork loin in a salt crust

CINTA DE CERDO ASADA CON COSTRA DE SAL

- 9 ¾–13 ½ cups coarse salt
- 1 boneless pork loin, 3 ¼ pounds

Serves 6

Preheat the oven to 350°F. Make a ½-inch deep layer of salt in the base of a roasting pan. Put the pork on top and cover with the remaining salt in a thick layer. Press down firmly with wet hands so that the salt forms a crust. Put the roasting pan in the oven and cook for 1 ¾ hours, until the salt crust begins to crack. Remove the pan from the oven, break the salt crust, lift out the pork, and brush off any remaining salt. Carve into slices. Serve hot, with any accompaniment you like, or cold.

759

Braised pork loin with cabbage
LOMO DE CERDO BRASEADO CON REPOLLO

- 1 boneless pork loin, 3¼ pounds
- ⅓ cup lard or 3 tablespoons sunflower oil
- 1 thick slice of bacon, about 3½ ounces, diced
- 1 Savoy cabbage, shredded
- salt

Serves 6

Tie the pork into a neat shape with fine kitchen string and season with salt at least 1 hour before cooking. Melt the lard or heat the oil in a deep, heavy pan or a Dutch oven. Add the bacon and cook over medium heat, stirring frequently, for about 5 minutes, until browned. Add the pork and cook, turning frequently, for about 10 minutes, until browned all over. Lower the heat and cover the pan. Bring a large pan of salted water to a boil. Add the cabbage, pushing it under the surface with a slotted spoon, and cook for about 15 minutes, until tender. Drain well and add to the pan with the meat, placing it all around the pork. Re-cover the pan and cook, stirring occasionally, for 45 minutes more. Remove the pan from the heat and let stand for 5 minutes, then lift out the pork, remove and discard the string, and carve the meat into thin slices. Put them on a warm serving dish and arrange the cabbage all around the edge of the dish. Pour the cooking juices over the top of the pork or transfer to a sauceboat and serve separately.

760

Roast pork with pineapple
CERDO ASADO CON PIÑA

- 1 boneless pork loin, 3¼ pounds
- 2 tablespoons Dijon mustard
- 2½ tablespoons lard or 2 tablespoons sunflower oil
- 7 ounces canned pineapple slices in juice
- 1 teaspoon potato starch
- salt

Serves 6

Tie the pork into a neat shape with fine kitchen string and season with salt 1 hour before cooking. Preheat the oven to 450°F. Spread the mustard all over the pork. Melt the lard or heat the oil in a roasting pan over medium-low heat. Add the meat and cook, turning frequently, for about 10 minutes, until browned all over. Transfer to the oven, lower the temperature to 350°F, and roast, turning occasionally and basting with the cooking juices, for about 1¼ hours, until the juices run clear when the thickest part is pierced with the tip of a sharp knife. Add a little hot water, if necessary. Remove the pork from the oven. Remove and discard the string and carve the meat into thin slices. Place them on a serving dish and keep warm. Drain the slices of pineapple, reserving the juice. Coat the pineapple slices with the cooking juices in the roasting pan, then cut them in half. Put some of the half slices on top of the pork and the rest around the edge of the dish. Mix the potato starch with 3 tablespoons water in a bowl, pour into the roasting pan, and add the reserved pineapple juice. Cook over low heat, stirring frequently, until thickened and hot, then serve in a sauceboat.

Pork loin with apples

CINTA O LOMO DE CERDO CON MANZANAS

- **1 boneless pork loin roast, 3¼ pounds**
- **⅓ cup lard or 3 tablespoons sunflower oil**
- **6 small apples, peeled and cored**
- **3 teaspoons sugar**
- **¼ cup (½ stick) butter**
- **3 tablespoons sherry or other sweet fortified wine**
- **1 teaspoon potato starch**
- **salt**

Serves 6

Tie the pork into a neat shape with fine kitchen string and season with salt at least 1 hour before cooking. Preheat the oven to 450°F. Spread the lard or brush the oil all over the pork, place the meat in a roasting pan, and transfer to the oven. Roast, turning frequently, for about 10 minutes, until browned all over. Lower the temperature to 350°F, pour 1 tablespoon water over the pork, return it to the oven, and roast, adding 1–2 tablespoons water occasionally, for 45 minutes more. Remove the roasting pan from the oven and put the apples around the pork. Divide the sugar and butter among the cavities in the apples, pour the sherry over them, and return the pan to the oven. Lower the temperature to 325°F and roast for 30 minutes, until the pork juices run clear when the thickest part is pierced with the tip of a sharp knife and the apples are soft but not falling apart. Lift out the pork from the roasting pan, remove and discard the string, and carve the meat into thin slices. Put them on a warm serving dish and place the apples all around the edge. Mix the potato starch with a little cold water, stir into the cooking juices, and cook over low heat, stirring frequently, until thickened, then pour over the pork. Serve immediately.

Pork loin with apples and chestnuts

CINTA DE CERDO CON MANZANAS Y CASTAÑAS

- 2¼-pound pork tenderloin
- ⅓ cup lard or 3 tablespoons sunflower oil
- 5 apples, peeled and cored
- 3 teaspoons sugar
- ¼ cup (½ stick) butter
- 3 tablespoons sherry or other sweet fortified wine
- 7 ounces canned peeled and cooked chestnuts, drained
- ⅔ cup milk
- 1 teaspoon potato starch
- salt

Serves 6

Tie the pork into a neat shape with fine kitchen string and season with salt at least 1 hour before cooking. Preheat the oven to 450°F. Spread the lard or brush the oil all over the pork, place the meat in a roasting pan, and transfer to the oven. Roast, turning frequently, for about 10 minutes, until browned all over. Lower the temperature to 350°F and roast, turning occasionally and basting with 3 tablespoons water, for 45 minutes more. Meanwhile, put the apples into an ovenproof baking dish. Divide the sugar and butter among the cavities and pour the sherry over them. Thirty minutes before the end of the cooking time, arrange the apples alongside the pork and return it to the oven. If necessary, lower the oven temperature to 325°F. The apples should be soft but not falling apart. Shortly before the end of the cooking time, put the chestnuts in a small pan, add the milk, and heat through gently, then drain, and keep warm. Lift the pork out of the roasting pan, remove and discard the string, and slice the meat thinly. Put the slices on a warm serving dish with the apples and chestnuts around the edge. Mix the potato starch with 2–3 tablespoons water in a bowl. Stir into the cooking juices and cook over low heat, stirring frequently, for a few minutes, until thickened. Pour over the pork and serve immediately.

763

Braised marinated pork

CINTA DE CERDO ADOBADA Y GUISADA

- 1 pork loin, 3¼ pounds
- 2¼ cups white wine
- 3 tablespoons
  white-wine vinegar
- 1 onion, cut into 4 pieces
- 2 carrots, sliced
- 1 clove garlic
- 6 black peppercorns
- pinch of mixed dried herbs
  or 1 bouquet garni (1 bay leaf,
  1 clove garlic, 1 sprig fresh
  parsley, and 1 sprig fresh thyme
  tied together in cheesecloth)
- ⅓ cup lard or 3 tablespoons
  sunflower oil
- 1 teaspoon potato starch
- 1 tablespoon tomato paste
- salt

Serves 6

Tie the pork into a neat shape with fine kitchen string and put it into an earthenware, ceramic or glass bowl with the wine, vinegar, onion, carrot, garlic, peppercorns, and dried herbs or bouquet garni. Cover and let marinate in the refrigerator for 8–10 hours. Preheat the oven to 450°F. Drain the pork, reserving the marinade and vegetables. Season the meat generously with salt, spread the lard or brush the oil over it, and place in a roasting pan. Put the pieces of onion and carrot around it and transfer to the oven. Roast, turning frequently, for about 10 minutes, until the pork and onion pieces begin to brown. Reduce the oven temperature to 350°F, baste the pork with the reserved marinade, return it to the oven, and roast, turning the meat and basting occasionally with the cooking juices, for 1¼ hours, until the juices run clear when the thickest part is pierced with the tip of a sharp knife. Lift the pork out of the roasting pan, remove and discard the string, and carve the meat into thin slices. Put on a serving dish and keep warm. Mix the potato starch with 2–3 tablespoons water in a bowl, then stir into the cooking juices along with the tomato paste. Heat through, stirring, then pass the sauce through a food mill or process in a food processor or blender. Serve the pork with boiled potatoes or macaroni tossed in butter and grated cheese, with the sauce poured over the top.

764

Marinated pork confit

CINTA O LOMO DE CERDO EN ADOBO (PARA CONSERVAR)

- 1 tenderloin or loin of pork
- 2 cloves garlic
- pinch of paprika
- pinch of dried oregano
- ⅓ cup lard or 4 tablespoons
  sunflower oil
- salt

Serves 6

Cut the pork into slices and put into a bowl. Pound the garlic with the paprika and a pinch of salt in a mortar or process in a mini-food processor. Mix in a few spoonfuls of water, and pour over the pork. Add the oregano and pour in water to cover. Let stand in a cool place, but not the refrigerator, for 4–5 days. Drain the slices of pork. Melt the lard or the oil in a skillet, add the pork slices, and cook over medium heat for about 3 minutes on each side. As each slice is cooked, place it in an earthenware pot. Finally, pour in the oil or lard until the meat is completely covered. The meat will keep for a long time like this. To serve, heat the pork slices in the fat covering them.

765

Pork medallions with mustard, wine and orange juice

FILETES DE CINTA DE CERDO CON MOSTAZA, SALSA DE VINO Y ZUMO DE NARANJA

- 3 tablespoons Dijon mustard
- 12 thin pork tenderloin medallions
- scant 1 cup olive oil
- 1 onion, chopped
- 1 tablespoon all-purpose flour
- ¾ cup white wine
- juice of 1 large orange
- 1 tablespoon very finely chopped fresh parsley
- salt

Serves 6

Spread the mustard over both sides of each medallion and sprinkle with a little salt. Heat the oil in a heavy skillet. Add the medallions, in batches, and cook over medium heat for 3–5 minutes on each side, or until done to your liking. Remove with a slotted spatula and keep warm. Pour off most of the oil from the skillet, leaving just enough to cover the base, and reheat. Add the onion and cook over low heat, stirring occasionally, for 6–8 minutes, until beginning to brown. Stir in the flour and cook, stirring constantly, for 2 minutes. Gradually stir in the wine, orange juice, and scant 2 cups water, a little at a time. Cook, stirring constantly, for 5–10 minutes, until thickened, then pass through a food mill or process in a food processor or blender. Transfer to a clean pan. Add the parsley and pork medallions and heat for about 2 minutes. Using a slotted spoon, transfer the pork medallions to a warm serving dish, and spoon a little sauce over them. Serve immediately, with Mashed Potato (see recipe 230), offering the remaining sauce separately.

766

Pork medallions with mustard and cream sauce

FILETES DE CERDO CON SALSA DE MOSTAZA Y NATA LÍQUIDA

- 12 thin pork tenderloin medallions
- 1 tablespoon lard (optional)
- 4–5 tablespoons sunflower oil
- 1 tablespoon Dijon mustard
- 1 cup light cream

Serves 6

Season the pork medallions on both sides with salt about 1 hour before cooking. Heat the oil with the lard, if using, in a skillet. Add the medallions, in batches, and cook over medium heat for 3–5 minutes on each side, or until done to your liking. Using a slotted spatula, transfer the medallions to a serving dish and keep warm. Stir the mustard into the skillet, add the cream, and cook gently, stirring constantly, but do not let boil. Pour the sauce over the pork, and serve immediately with fried potatoes.

767

Pork medallions with béchamel
FILETES DE CINTA DE CERDO CON BECHAMEL

- 12 thin pork tenderloin
  medallions
- 1 tablespoon lard (optional)
- 4–5 tablespoons sunflower oil
- 1 tablespoon Dijon mustard
- 1 cup all-purpose flour
- 1 cup milk

Serves 6

Season the pork medallions on both sides with salt about 1 hour before cooking. Heat the oil with the lard, if using, in a skillet. Add the medallions, in batches, and cook over medium heat for 3–5 minutes on each side, or until done to your liking. Using a slotted spatula, transfer the medallions to a serving dish and keep warm. Stir the mustard into the skillet along with the flour and cook, stirring constantly, for 2 minutes. Gradually stir in the milk, a little at a time. Cook, stirring constantly, for about 6 minutes, until thickened, then pour the sauce over the pork medallions.

768

Pork chops with onion sauce
CHULETAS DE CERDO CON CEBOLLAS EN SALSA

- 6 pork chops
- 1 cup sunflower oil
- 3 large onions, thinly sliced
- 1½ tablespoons butter
- 1 tablespoon all-purpose flour
- scant 1 cup milk
- salt and pepper

Serves 6

Season the chops with salt and pepper 1 hour before cooking. Reserve 2 tablespoons of the oil and heat the remainder in a skillet. Add the chops, in batches, and cook over medium heat for 4–5 minutes on each side. Transfer to a plate and keep warm. Pour off nearly all the oil from the skillet, leaving 2–3 tablespoons to cover the base, and reheat. Add the onion and cook over low heat, stirring occasionally, for about 5 minutes, until softened and translucent. Pour in just enough hot water to cover the onion and simmer for about 15 minutes. Remove the skillet from the heat and keep warm. Melt the butter with the reserved oil in another skillet. Stir in the flour and cook, stirring constantly, for 2 minutes. Gradually stir in the milk, a little at a time. Cook, stirring constantly, for about 5 minutes, until thickened. Stir in the onions with their cooking juices and cook for 5 minutes more. Put the chops into a warm serving dish, pour the onion sauce over them, and serve immediately.

Note: This dish can be garnished with sautéd potatoes.

769 Pork chops with honey, lemon, and curry powder

CHULETAS DE CERDO CON MIEL, LIMÓN Y CURRY

- 6 tablespoons olive oil
- 6 tablespoons honey
- 3 tablespoons lemon juice
- 1½ teaspoons curry powder
- 6 pork chops
- 1 cup sunflower oil
- salt

Serves 6

Combine the olive oil, honey, lemon juice, curry powder, and a pinch of salt in a nonmetallic dish. Add the chops, turning to coat, and set aside to marinate in the refrigerator, turning occasionally, for 30 minutes. Heat the sunflower oil in a skillet. Drain the chops, reserving the marinade. Add the chops to the skillet, in batches, and cook over medium heat for 4–5 minutes on each side. Remove from the skillet and keep warm. Pour the reserved marinade into the skillet and bring to a boil, then pour over the chops and serve immediately.

Note: This dish may be accompanied by boiled rice or Mashed Potato (see recipe 230). It is also delicious with fried apple slices.

770 Pork chops with prunes

CHULETAS DE CERDO CON CIRUELAS PASAS

- 1 pound 2 ounces prunes, pitted
- scant 2 cups red wine
- 2 cinnamon sticks
- 2 tablespoons sugar
- 6 pork chops
- ⅓ cup lard or
  3 tablespoons olive oil
- 2¼ pounds small new potatoes
- 1 tablespoon chopped
  fresh parsley
- generous 1 cup sunflower oil
- 1 tablespoon potato starch
  or cornstarch
- salt and pepper

Serves 6

If using traditional prunes, put them in a bowl, pour in water to cover, and let soak for at least 6 hours, then drain. If using ready-to-eat prunes, soaking is not necessary. Put the prunes, wine, cinnamon, and sugar into a pan, pour in water to cover, stir well, and cook over low heat for about 20 minutes, until the prunes are tender. Set aside to cool. Meanwhile, season the chops with salt and pepper 1 hour before cooking. Melt the lard or heat the olive oil in a skillet. Add the potatoes and cook, occasionally shaking the pan, for 35–40 minutes, until tender and golden brown on all sides. Remove from the heat, season with salt, sprinkle with the parsley, and keep warm. Heat the sunflower oil in another skillet. Add the chops, in batches, and cook over medium heat for 4–5 minutes on each side. Drain the prunes, reserving the cooking liquid. Put the chops on a warm serving dish, and arrange the potatoes on one side of them and the prunes on the other. Gently heat the reserved cooking liquid in a pan. Mix the potato starch or cornstarch with a little water in a small bowl, stir it into the pan, and cook over low heat, stirring frequently, for a few minutes, until thickened. Pour into a sauceboat and serve with the chops.

771

Pork chops with tomato sauce
CHULETAS DE CERDO CON SALSA DE TOMATE

- 6 pork chops
- ½ cup olive oil
- 1 onion, chopped
- 6 tomatoes, seeded and chopped
- 1 clove garlic, chopped (optional)
- ½ cup white wine
- pinch of mixed dried herbs
  or 1 bouquet garni (1 bay leaf
  and 1 sprig fresh thyme, tied
  together in cheesecloth)
- salt

Serves 6

Heat 2 tablespoons of the oil in a skillet. Add the onion and cook over low heat, stirring occasionally, for about 5 minutes, until softened and translucent. Add the tomato, garlic, wine, dried herbs or bouquet garni, and a pinch of salt. Mix well, increase the heat to high, and cook, stirring occasionally and breaking up the tomato with the side of the spoon, for about 20 minutes. Remove and discard the bouquet garni, if used. Pass the sauce through a food mill or process in a food processor or blender and pour it back into the skillet. Cook over low heat, stirring occasionally, until thickened to your liking. Heat the remaining oil in another skillet. Working in batches, add the chops and cook over medium heat for 4–5 minutes on each side. Transfer to a warm serving dish, cover each chop with tomato sauce, and keep warm while you cook the remainig chops. Garnish with French Fries (see recipe 242).

772

Pork chops with onion and mustard sauce
CHULETAS DE CERDO CON SALSA DE CEBOLLAS Y MOSTAZA

- 3 tablespoons sunflower oil
- 1 onion, coarsely chopped
- 1 tablespoon all-purpose flour
- 1 cup chicken stock
  (homemade, canned or
  made with a bouillon cube)
- 2 tablespoons
  white-wine vinegar
- 2½ tablespoons lard
  or 2 tablespoons olive oil
- 4 pork chops
- 1 teaspoon Dijon mustard
- salt and pepper

Serves 4

Heat the sunflower oil in a skillet. Add the onion and cook over low heat, stirring occasionally, for about 8 minutes, until beginning to brown. Stir in the flour and cook, stirring constantly, for 2 minutes. Gradually stir in the stock, a little at a time. Stir in the vinegar, cover, and simmer very gently for 5–6 minutes. Meanwhile, melt the lard or heat the olive oil in another skillet. Season the chops with salt and pepper, add to the skillet, and cook over low heat for about 8 minutes on each side. Transfer the chops to the pan of sauce and simmer over low heat for 5 minutes. Transfer the chops to a warm serving dish. Stir the mustard into the sauce, then pour it over the chops, and serve.

Suckling pig

COCHINILLO ASADO

- **1 piglet**
- **generous pinch
  mixed dried herbs**
- **olive oil, for brushing**
- **1 cup white wine**
- **salt**

Serves 6

You will require a young piglet about a month and a half old. It should be thoroughly cleaned, with no hairs or stubble remaining, then halved lengthwise. Season generously with salt several hours before roasting. Preheat the oven to 325°F. Put the dried herbs inside the animal and brush inside and out with oil. Put the piglet in a large roasting pan and place in the oven. Roast, turning occasionally and basting with the cooking juices, for about 1½ hours. Pour the wine over the skin of the animal and continue to roast, basting frequently, until the wine has all been used up and a meat thermometer inserted into the thickest part of the rump reads 165–170°F. Serve the meat carved into large pieces.

Note: The classic method of cooking this dish is to roast a suckling pig in a baker's oven—it tastes much better than when roasted at home, but can be difficult to arrange!

Pork hock with sausages, cabbage, and potatoes

CODILLOS DE JAMÓN FRESCO CON SALCHICHAS, REPOLLO Y PATATAS

- **1 onion**
- **4 cloves**
- **2 pork hocks**
- **8 ounces slab bacon in a single piece**
- **2 carrots**
- **3¼ pounds Savoy cabbage, shredded**
- **6 small potatoes**
- **3 tablespoons olive oil**
- **6 frankfurters**
- **salt**

Serves 6

Stud the onion with the cloves. Put the studded onion, pork hocks, bacon, and carrots into a flameproof casserole. Pour in 13 cups water and bring to a boil, then lower the heat, and simmer gently for 30 minutes. Bring a large pan of salted water to a boil. Add the cabbage, pushing it down under the surface with a slotted spoon. Cover, bring back to a boil, and cook over high heat for 5 minutes. Remove with a slotted spoon, drain, and add to the meat. Simmer gently for 20 minutes more, then add the potatoes. Cook for another 30 minutes, until the potatoes are tender but not falling apart. Remove the cabbage with a slotted spoon and set aside. Heat the oil in a skillet. Prick the frankfurters with a toothpick, add to the skillet, and cook over low heat for a few minutes. Remove from the skillet and keep warm. Add the cabbage to the skillet and cook for a few minutes, then transfer to a warm serving dish. Put the potatoes around the edge. Add the pork hocks and frankfurters to the dish. Cut the bacon into ¾-inch strips and sprinkle it over the cabbage. Serve immediately.

Notes: Pork hocks are also called shanks, and sometimes knuckles, and come from the hog's lower leg. Use the cooking liquid fom this dish to make a delicious soup, with the carrots and any leftover potatoes, diced.

Sausages in cloaks

SALCHICHAS ENCAPOTADAS

- **12 frankfurters**
- **1 egg, lightly beaten**

Dough:
- **2 ¾ cups all-purpose flour, plus extra for dusting**
- **⅔ cup butter**
- **½ teaspoon salt**

Makes 12

First make the dough as described in recipe 1, and let rest for at least 1 hour. Preheat the oven to 400°F. Roll out the dough on a lightly floured surface and cut out 12 rectangles measuring about 7 x 6 ¼ inches each. Put a frankfurter on each dough rectangle at an angle. Roll over the dough diagonally, pressing down a little with your fingers to seal. Brush the beaten egg over the frankfurter rolls, place them on a baking sheet, and bake for about 30 minutes, turning them over once the tops have browned and brushing the undersides with the egg. Serve hot.

Note: This dish can be made with frozen dough that has been thawed. Bake according to the directions on the package.

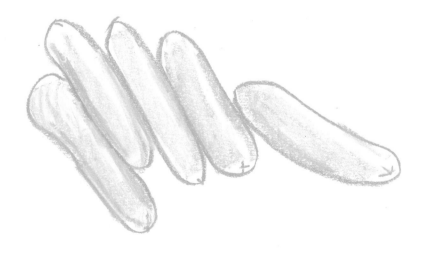

776

Frankfurters with mustard sauce
SALCHICHAS DE FRANKFURT CON SALSA DE MOSTAZA

- 3 tablespoons butter
- 1 tablespoon sunflower oil
- 1 tablespoon all-purpose flour
- 1 cup milk
- 1 tablespoon Dijon mustard
- 12 frankfurters
- 6 slices of bread
- 3 tablespoons bread crumbs
- salt

Serves 6

Melt half the butter with the oil in a skillet. Stir in the flour and cook, stirring constantly, for 2 minutes. Gradually stir in the milk, a little at a time. Cook, stirring constantly, for 5 minutes, then remove the skillet from the heat, and stir in the mustard. Season to taste with salt and keep warm. Preheat the broiler. Bring a pan of water to a boil, add the frankfurters, and bring back to a boil. Lower the heat so that the water is barely simmering and poach for 6 minutes. Meanwhile, toast the slices of bread on both sides, then place them on an ovenproof serving dish. Remove the frankfurters from the water, drain well, and halve widthwise. Place them on top of the toast. Spoon a little of the sauce over each frankfurter, leaving their ends uncovered. Sprinkle with the bread crumbs and dot with the remaining butter. Cook under the broiler for a few minutes, until the topping is golden brown. Serve immediately.

Ham with spinach and Madeira sauce

JAMÓN DE YORK CON ESPINACAS Y SALSA DE VINO MADEIRA

- **6 thick slices of Smithfield, Black Forest or other dry-cured ham**
- **1 quantity Madeira Sauce (see recipe 89)**

Spinach with béchamel sauce:
- **5½ pounds spinach, coarse stalks removed**
- **2 tablespoons (¼ stick) butter**
- **2 tablespoons sunflower oil**
- **1 tablespoon all-purpose flour**
- **generous 1 cup milk**
- **salt**

Serves 6

First, prepare the spinach with béchamel sauce as described in recipe 393. Put the slices of ham and the Madeira sauce into a pan and warm through. To serve, put the creamed spinach on one side, or at each end, of a warm serving dish. Remove the slices of ham from the sauce, using a fork to separate them, fold them in half and place them on the other side of the dish. Reheat the sauce, pour it over the ham and serve.

Note: This dish is best made with small slices of ham that are a little thicker than usual. You can substitute 2¼ pounds frozen spinach for fresh spinach if you like.

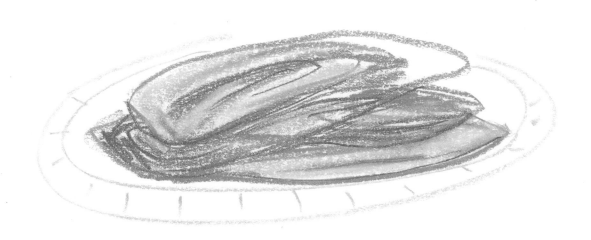

778

Ham with béchamel sauce and mushrooms
JAMÓN DE YORK CON BECHAMEL Y CHAMPIÑONES

- 1⅔ cups sliced mushrooms
- 1½ tablespoons butter
- juice of ½ lemon juice
- 6 thick slices of Smithfield, or other dry-cured ham
- salt

Béchamel sauce:
- 2 tablespoons (¼ stick) butter
- 2 tablespoons sunflower oil
- 2 tablespoons all-purpose flour
- scant 2 cups milk
- scant 2 cups chicken stock (homemade or made with a bouillon cube)
- small pinch of curry powder
- salt

Serves 6

Put the mushrooms, butter, lemon juice, and a pinch of salt into a pan. Cover and cook over low heat for 6 minutes. Meanwhile, make the béchamel sauce. Melt the butter with the oil in a skillet. Stir in the flour and cook, stirring constantly, for 2 minutes. Gradually stir in the milk, a little at a time. Cook, stirring constantly, for 2 minutes, then gradually stir in the stock, a little at a time. Sprinkle in the curry powder and season to taste with salt. Cook, stirring constantly, for 5 minutes, then add the mushrooms and cooking juices. Remove the pan from the heat. Pile the slices of ham together and add to the sauce. Let stand until they have warmed through. Just before serving, use a fork to separate the slices of ham and place them, one at a time, on a warm serving dish, folding them in half. Reheat the béchamel sauce and pour it over the ham. Serve immediately.

779

California ham with pineapple
JAMÓN CALIFORNIANO CON PIÑA

- 1 canned ham, 6½ pounds
- 1⅓ cups brown sugar
- 10–14 cloves
- 2¼ cups grapefruit juice
- 3–4 canned pineapple slices, drained and halved
- 6 canned or bottled morello, montmercy or other sour cherries in syrup, drained and halved

Serves 10–14

Preheat the oven to 350°F. Trim the edges of the ham, leaving a piece about the size of a large beef roast. (The trimmings can be used for another recipe.) Using a sharp knife, score a diamond pattern in the top. Coat the ham all over with the sugar, pressing it into the meat to prevent it falling off. Insert a clove into each corner of the diamonds. Put the ham into a roasting pan, pour the grapefruit juice over it, and bake for 1 hour or according to the instructions on the can. Arrange the pineapple slices and cherries on top of the ham and return to the oven for about 5 minutes to let the pineapple warm through. Cut the ham into slices, place on a warm serving dish, and serve with boiled rice or Potato Balls (see recipe 231).

780

Californian ham in beer
JAMÓN CALIFORNIANO EN CERVEZA

- **1 canned ham, 6½ pounds**
- **1⅓ cups brown sugar**
- **10–14 cloves**
- **2¼ cups beer**
- **3–4 canned pineapple slices, drained and halved**
- **6 canned or bottled morello, montmercy or other sour cherries in syrup, drained and halved**

Serves 10–14

Preheat the oven to 350°F. Trim the edges of the ham, leaving a piece about the size of a large beef roast. Using a sharp knife, score a diamond pattern in the top. Coat the ham all over with the sugar, pressing it into the meat to prevent it falling off. Insert a clove into each corner of the diamonds. Put the ham into a roasting pan, pour the beer over it, and bake for 1 hour or according to the instructions on the can. Arrange the pineapple slices and cherries on top of the ham and return to the oven for about 5 minutes to let the pineapple warm through. Cut the ham into slices, place on a warm serving dish, and serve with boiled rice or Potato Balls (see recipe 231).

Ham sandwiches

EMPAREDADOS DE JAMÓN DE YORK

- **3 large slices or 6 small slices of Smithfield, Black Forest or other dry-cured ham**
- **12 slices of bread**
- **1¼ cups milk**
- **2 eggs**
- **sunflower oil, for deep-frying**

Makes 6

If using the large slices of ham, cut in half. Using the bread, make six ham sandwiches and soak them briefly in the milk. Put the sandwiches on a surface, lightly weigh them down with a lid or a plate, and let stand for 30 minutes. Remove the weight and cut each sandwich diagonally in half. Lightly beat the eggs in a shallow dish. Heat the oil in a deep-fryer or deep skillet to 350–375°F or until a cube of day-old bread browns in 30 seconds. One at a time, coat the sandwiches in the beaten egg. Add to the hot oil, in batches, and cook, turning once, until golden brown on both sides. Remove with a slotted spatula, drain, and keep warm while you cook the remaining batches.

782

Ham croquettes
CROQUETAS DE JAMÓN DE YORK

- 2 tablespoons sunflower oil
- 3 tablespoons butter
- 4 tablespoons all-purpose flour
- 3 cups milk
- 2 eggs
- 3 cups bread crumbs
- vegetable oil, for deep-frying
- salt
- fresh or deep-fried parsley
  sprigs (see recipe 918), optional

Filling:
- 1 cup very finely chopped
  Smithfield or Black Forest
  ham, prosciutto or other dry
  cured ham

Serves 6

Make a béchamel sauce by heating the sunflower oil in a pan. Add the butter, and when it has melted, stir in the flour with a wooden spoon. Gradually stir in the milk, a little at a time, and cook, stirring constantly, until the béchamel sauce thickens. Season with salt and stir in your chosen filling, then spread the mixture out in a large dish to cool for at least 2 hours. Using two tablespoons, shape scoops of the mixture into croquettes. Finish forming the croquettes with your hands. Beat the eggs in a shallow dish. Pour the bread crumbs into another shallow dish. Roll each croquette lightly in the bread crumbs, then in the beaten egg, and finally in the bread crumbs again, making sure that each one is evenly covered. Heat the vegetable oil in a deep-fryer or deep pan to 350–375°F or until a cube of day-old bread browns in 30 seconds. Working in batches of about 6 at a time, add the croquettes, and cook until crisp and golden brown. Using a slotted spoon, transfer them to a large colander set over a baking dish and place in a warm oven until all the croquettes have been cooked. Serve immediately on a dish garnished with sprigs of fresh or deep-fried parsley.

783

Fried fillets of York ham with béchamel sauce
FILETES DE JAMÓN DE YORK CON BECHAMEL Y EMPANADOS

- 3 thick slices of Smithfield,
  Black Forest or other dry-cured
  ham, about 4 ounces each
- sunflower oil, for deep-frying,
  plus extra for brushing

Béchamel sauce:
- 2 tablespoons (¼ stick) butter
- 2 tablespoons sunflower oil
- 2 tablespoons all-purpose flour
- 2¼ cups milk
- salt

Breading:
- 2 eggs
- 1½ cups bread crumbs

Serves 3

Preheat the oven to 400°F. Cut the slices of ham into strips about ¾ inch wide. Make the béchamel sauce as described in recipe 77. Coat and cook the ham as described in recipe 716. Serve garnished with fried parsley sprigs as described in recipe 918.

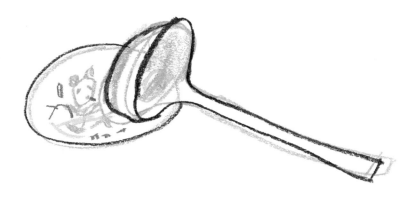

Lamb

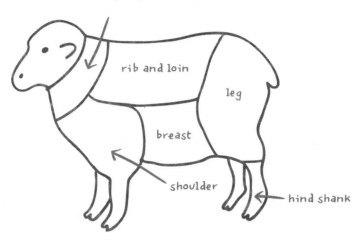

Spring lamb

This is the name given to lamb that is less than one year old—usually between five and seven months—but has been weaned. It is the most commonly available type of lamb. The meat of spring lamb should be a clear red color with firm, creamy white fat. Allow about 7 ounces per serving.

Milk lamb

The meat from milk lamb—an animal 30–40 days old—is a pale rosy pink. Also called milk-fed lamb in some places, it has less nutrtional value than spring lamb but is delicious. Although very popular in Spain and other southern European countries, milk lamb is less widely available elsewhere. Allow about 9 ounces per serving.

Spring lamb

Buying lamb	Suitable cuts	Weight per serving	Cooking time
Fried, broiled or grilled	Rib chops, Loin chops	7–8 ounces (with bone)	5 minutes on each side (medium)
Roasted *	Leg, Shoulder	7–8 ounces (with bone)	15–20 minutes per pound
Stewed or braised	Shoulder, Neck slice, Breast	7–8 ounces	1¼ hours for stews 1½ hours for casseroles

*Make sure that the oven is preheated

Milk lamb

Buying lamb	Suitable cuts	Weight per serving	Cooking time
Fried, broiled or grilled	Rib chops, Loin chops	9 ounces	3 minutes on each side
Roasted *	Half a milk lamb	9 ounces	25–30 minutes per pound
Stewed or braised	Chops, Shoulder, Neck slice	9 ounces	1½ hours

*Make sure that the oven is preheated

784

Roast milk lamb
CORDERO LECHAL ASADO

- ½ milk lamb
- 1 clove garlic
- ¼ cup lard or 3–4 tablespoons sunflower oil
- 1 teaspoon white-wine vinegar
- salt

Serves 6

Preheat the oven to 350°F. Rub the lamb with the garlic, spread the lard or oil all over it, and sprinkle with salt. Put it into a roasting pan and roast until cooked to your liking, basting occasionally with the cooking juices, allowing 25–30 minutes per pound. About 15 minutes before the end of the cooking time, brush the vinegar all over the lamb. Serve hot.

785

Roast leg of spring lamb
PIERNA DE CORDERO PASCUAL ASADA

- 1 leg of lamb, 3¼–4½ pounds
- 2 cloves garlic
- ¼ cup lard or 3–4 tablespoons sunflower oil
- 1 teaspoon white-wine vinegar
- navy bean garnish (see recipe 221)
- salt

Serves 6–8

Rub the lamb all over with the garlic, spread the lard or brush the oil all over it, and sprinkle with salt. Let stand in the refrigerator for 1 hour. Preheat the oven to 450°F. Put the lamb into a roasting pan and roast for 15 minutes, then lower the oven temperature to 350°F. Roast, basting occasionally, until the lamb is cooked to your liking, allowing about 15–20 minutes per pound. About 15 minutes before the end of the cooking time, brush the vinegar all over the lamb. When the meat is cooked, turn off the oven but leave the lamb to rest in it for about 5 minutes. Remove the leg from the roasting pan and carve, collecting all the juices released. Put a little hot water into the roasting pan, add the juices from the carving, and cook over medium heat, stirring and scraping up any bits from the base of the pan. Garnish the lamb with the navy bean garnish and serve immediately, offering the sauce separately. The meat can be accompanied by fried or Mashed Potato (see recipe 230), if you like.

Sepulvedana roast lamb

CORDERO ASADO A LA SEPULVEDANA

- ¼ cups lard or
  3–4 tablespoons sunflower oil
- 1 milk lamb
- salt

  Basting sauce:
- 2 sprigs fresh parsley
- 2 cloves garlic, unpeeled
- 1 bay leaf
- ½ large onion
- 2 tablespoons
  white-wine vinegar
- juice of 1 lemon
- salt, to taste

  Serves 6–8

Preheat the oven to 350°F. Spread the lard or brush the oil all over the lamb, season with salt, and put the meat into a roasting pan. Roast for about 15 minutes, until the lamb is beginning to brown. Meanwhile, put all the ingredients for the basting sauce in a pan, pour in generous 1 cup water, and bring to a boil. Lower the heat and simmer for 5 minutes. Remove from the heat and strain into a pitcher. When the lamb is beginning to brown, pour the basting sauce over it. (You could put some potatoes in the roasting pan around the lamb if you like.) Roast, basting occasionally, until the lamb is cooked to your liking, allowing about 25–30 minutes per pound. When the lamb is cooked, turn off the oven but leave to rest in it for about 5 minutes before carving it.

Note: This style of cooking roast lamb is popular in the Sepulvedana region of Spain.

787

Roast lamb with egg and tomato sauce

CORDERO ASADO SERVIDO CON SALSA DE YEMAS Y PURÉ DE TOMATE

- ¼ cup lard or 3–4 tablespoons sunflower oil
- 1 leg of lamb, 3¼–4½ pounds
- 1 small onion, halved
- 1 bouquet garni
  (2 sprigs fresh parsley, ½ bay leaf, and 1 clove garlic tied together in cheesecloth)
- ¾ cup white wine
- 4 tablespoons tomato paste
- 2 egg yolks
- juice of 1 lemon
- 1½ tablespoons chopped fresh parsley
- 2 tablespoons (¼ stick) butter
- salt and pepper

Serves 6–8

Preheat the oven to 450°F. Spread the lamb with the lard or brush with the oil, season with salt and pepper, and put the meat into a roasting pan. Put an onion half on either side, add the bouquet garni, and roast for 10 minutes. Lower the oven temperature to 350°F and roast for 15 minutes more, then pour the wine over the lamb. Return to the oven and roast, basting occasionally with the cooking juices, for 15 minutes more. Add the tomato paste to the cooking juices and return the lamb to the oven for another 5–10 minutes, until cooked to your liking. Carve the lamb, place it on a serving dish, cover it with aluminum foil, and keep warm. Pour the cooking juices into a heatproof bowl and use a tablespoon to skim off the fat from the surface. Set the bowl over a pan of barely simmering water. Beat the egg yolks with the lemon juice and parsley in another bowl. Stir in a little of the cooking juices to prevent the egg yolks curdling, then add to the cooking juices, together with the butter, beating constantly with a whisk. Continue to beat until the sauce is shiny, then remove from the heat, and pour into a warm sauceboat. Serve the lamb with the sauce immediately.

788

Stuffed leg of lamb

PIERNA DE CORDERO PASCUAL RELLENA

- scant 1½ cups finely chopped mushrooms
- 1½ tablespoons butter
- juice of ½ lemon
- 6 sausages, skinned
- 5 tablespoons sherry or other sweet fortified wine
- pinch of mixed dried herbs
- 1 boneless leg of lamb, 2½–3¼ pounds
- ⅓ cup all-purpose flour
- 3 tablespoons olive oil
- salt

Serves 6–8

Preheat the oven to 350°F. Put the mushrooms, butter, lemon juice, and a pinch of salt in a pan, cover, and cook over low heat for 6 minutes. Remove the pan from the heat. Combine the meat from the sausages, half the sherry, the dried herbs, and the mushrooms in a bowl, spoon the mixture into the center of the leg of lamb, and sew or tie up the leg with fine kitchen string, forming a neat shape. Season the lamb with salt and lightly coat it in the flour, shaking off any excess. Put the lamb into a roasting pan with the oil and remaining sherry and roast, turning it several times and basting occasionally with the cooking juices, for 1–1¼ hours, until browned all over and cooked to your liking. Lift the lamb out of the roasting pan, remove and discard the string, and carve the meat into slices. Make a sauce with the cooking juices as described in recipe 785. Serve the lamb with French Fries (see recipe 242) or Mashed Potato (see recipe 230), offering the sauce separately.

Roast lamb in a salt and rosemary crust

ASADO DE CORDERO EN COSTRA DE SAL Y ROMERO

- ¾ cup coarse salt
- 1 egg white
- 2 sprigs fresh rosemary
- 2¼ cups all-purpose flour
- 1 tablespoon olive oil
- 1 boned rack of lamb,
  bones and fat reserved
- 1 carrot, sliced
- 1 leek, sliced and rinsed well
- 1 clove garlic, lightly crushed
- 1 cup bread crumbs
- 1 tablespoon chopped
  fresh parsley
- 2 egg yolks
- salt and pepper

Serves 4

Prepare the salt crust the night before. Combine the coarse salt and egg white in a bowl, then add the rosemary needles, flour, and 5–6 tablespoons water. Work the mixture with your fingers until it is even, then let stand in the refrigerator overnight (or at least 2 hours). Heat the oil in a pan. Add the lamb bones and any scraps of meat and cook over medium heat, stirring occasionally, for about 10 minutes, until browned. Add the carrot, leek, and garlic and cook, stirring occasionally, for about 10 minutes, until browned. Drain off as much fat as possible, and reserve, then pour in just enough water to cover, and cook over medium heat until the liquid has reduced by a third. Strain through a fine-mesh strainer into a clean pan.Preheat the oven to 425°F. Combine the bread crumbs and parsley. Season the lamb with salt and pepper and sprinkle the bread crumb and parsley mixture over it, then roll it in its fat. Spread out the salt crust on a clean surface, wrap the lamb in it, put it in a roasting pan, and bake for 20 minutes. Remove from the oven and let stand for 25 minutes (the salt crust will keep it warm).Lightly beat the egg yolks with 1 tablespoon water and a pinch of salt in a bowl. Heat the strained liquid and stir 2 tablespoons into the egg yolks, then stir them into the liquid and heat through. Pour into a sauceboat. Break the salt crust and remove the lamb, brushing off all traces of salt. Carve into slices and serve immediately with the sauce.

Note: For a luxurious touch, stir a little light cream and a finely chopped truffle into the sauce.

790

- 1 small head of celery
- 3 carrots
- 1 onion
- 1 teaspoon mixed dried herbs
  or 1 bouquet garni (1 sprig fresh
  parsley, 2 bay leaves, 1 sprig
  fresh thyme, and 1 clove garlic
  tied in cheesecloth)
- 4 black peppercorns
- 1 boneless leg of lamb,
  3¼–4½ pounds
- salt

Serves 6–8

English-style leg of lamb
PIERNA DE CORDERO COCIDA A LA INGLESA

Put the celery, carrots, onion, dried herbs or bouquet garni, pepper-corns, and a pinch of salt into a large heavy pot full of water, leaving enough room to add the lamb, and bring to a boil. Add the lamb and bring back to a boil, then lower the heat, and simmer gently until cooked to your liking, allowing 10–15 minutes per pound. Lift the lamb out of the pan, drain, and carve. Serve hot with mint jelly.

791

- 4 tablespoons olive oil
- 1 boneless leg of lamb,
  2½ pounds, boned and the
  bone reserved
- 1 onion
- 3 cloves
- 2 carrots, chopped
- 1 bay leaf
- pinch of mixed dried herbs
- 1 ham hock
- 1¾ cups fresh or frozen peas
- ¾ cup white wine
- 8 spinach leaves
- salt and pepper

Serves 4

Leg of lamb with pea sauce
PIERNA DE CORDERO CON SALSA DE GUISANTES

Ask your butcher for the bone when he has removed it from the leg. Heat the oil in a heavy pan or a Dutch oven. Add the lamb and cook over medium heat, turning frequently, for about 10 minutes, until browned all over. Stud the onion with the cloves and add to the pan with the carrot, bay leaf, dried herbs, ham hock, and lamb bone. Season with salt and pepper, pour in 2¼ cups water, and bring to a boil. Add the peas, lower the heat, and simmer gently for 45 minutes. Add the wine and simmer for 45 minutes more. Meanwhile, put the spinach in a pan with just the water clinging to its leaves after washing. Add a pinch of salt, cover, and cook for 8 minutes. Remove from the heat and drain well, squeezing out as much liquid as possible. Remove the lamb from the pan, wrap in aluminum foil, and keep warm. Remove and discard the hem hock, lamb bones, carrot, bay leaf, and onion (if it has not disintegrated) from the pan. Transfer the cooking liquid to a food processor or blender, add the spinach, and process until smooth. Carve the lamb, put it on a warm serving dish, and spoon a little of the sauce over it. Serve immediately, offering the remaining sauce separately.

Note: This dish may be accompanied by fried potato balls or steamed potatoes, placed around the edge of the serving dish.

792

Boned shoulder of lamb

PALETILLA DE CORDERO DESHUESADA

- 1 boneless lamb shoulder,
  2¼–2½ pounds
- 2 cloves garlic
- ¼ cup lard or 3–4 tablespoons
  sunflower oil
- 1 teaspoon white vinegar
- salt

Serves 4–6

Tie the lamb into a neat shape with fine kitchen string. Rub the lamb all over with the garlic, spread the lard or brush the oil all over it, and sprinkle with salt. Let stand in the refrigerator for 1 hour. Preheat the oven to 450°F. Put the lamb into a roasting pan and roast for 15 minutes, then lower the oven temperature to 350°F. Roast, basting occasionally, until the lamb is cooked to your liking, allowing about 15–20 minutes per pound. About 15 minutes before the end of the cooking time, brush the vinegar all over the lamb. When the meat is cooked, turn off the oven but leave the lamb to rest in it for about 5 minutes. Remove the leg from the roasting pan and carve, collecting all the juices released. Put a little hot water into the roasting pan, add the juices from the carving, and cook over medium heat, stirring and scraping up any bits from the base of the pan. Transfer the sauce to a sauceboat and serve immediately, alongside the meat This roast lamb can be accompanied by fried or Mashed Potato (see recipe 230), if you like.

793

Shoulder of lamb with potato and onion

PALETILLA DE CORDERO CON PATATAS Y CEBOLLA (PANADERA)

- 1 clove garlic
- 1 boneless, rolled lamb shoulder,
  2½–3¼ pounds
- ½ cup lard or 5 tablespoons
  sunflower oil
- 2 large onions, thinly sliced
- 1 pound 5 ounces potatoes,
  preferably new potatoes,
  cut into ⅝-inch thick slices
- generous 1 cup chicken stock
  (homemade, canned or
  made with a bouillon cube)
- salt

Serves 4–6

Preheat the oven to 450°F. Rub the garlic all over the lamb, then spread some of the lard or oil over it, reserving the remaining lard or oil. Put the lamb into a roasting pan and roast for 10 minutes. Lower the oven temperature to 350°F and roast, turning the lamb occasionally, for 20 minutes more. Meanwhile, melt the remaining lard or heat the remaining oil in a skillet. Add the onions and cook over low heat, stirring occasionally, for 6–8 minutes, until beginning to brown. Add the potatoes, increase the heat to medium, season with salt, and cook for 5–10 minutes more. Put the potato slices and onion in the roasting pan around the lamb. Pour the stock over the lamb and return the tin to the oven. Roast, basting three or four times, for another 20 minutes until the potatoes are tender and the meat is cooked to your liking. Lift the lamb out of the roasting pan, remove and discard the string, carve the meat into slices, and put them in the center of a warm serving dish. Arrange the potatoes and onions around the lamb. Pour the cooking juices into a sauceboat and serve with the roast.

Braised lamb shoulder

PALETILLA DE CORDERO DESHUESADA BRASEADA

- **4 tablespoons olive oil**
- **2 large onions, chopped**
- **1 boneless, rolled lamb shoulder, 3¼–4 pounds**
- **⅓ cup all-purpose flour**
- **5 tablespoons white wine**
- **scant 2 cups chicken stock (homemade, canned or made with a bouillon cube)**
- **½ teaspoon mixed dried herbs or 1 bouquet garni (1 sprig fresh parsley, 2 bay leaves, 1 sprig fresh thyme, and 1 clove garlic tied together in cheesecloth)**
- **salt**

Serves 6

Heat the oil in a heavy pan or a Dutch oven. Add the onion and cook over low heat, stirring occasionally, for 10–12 minutes, until golden brown. Remove with a slotted spoon and set aside. Lightly coat the lamb in the flour, tapping off any excess, add to the pan, and cook over medium heat, turning frequently, for 8–10 minutes, until evenly browned all over. Return the onion to the pan, pour in the wine and stock, and add the dried herbs or bouquet garni and a pinch of salt. Mix well, cover the pan with a tight-fitting lid, increase the heat to medium, and bring to a boil. Lower the heat and simmer gently for 45–60 minutes, until the lamb is tender. Lift the lamb out of the pan, remove and discard the string, carve the meat into slices, and place on a warm serving dish. Remove and discard the bouquet garni, if used, and pass the cooking liquid through a food mill or process in a food processor or blender. Pour the sauce over the meat and serve immediately with fried potatoes or fried whole green bell peppers.

Note: Some people like to add sliced pitted olives to this dish. Simmer the olives in a little water for 2 minutes, then drain, and add to the meat about 5 minutes before the end of the cooking time.

795

Lamb with quinces
CORDERO CON MEMBRILLOS

- juice of 1 lemon
- 12 black peppercorns
- 1 teaspoon Dijon mustard
- ⅔ cup plain yogurt
- 1 boneless leg of lamb or
  lamb shoulder, 4½ pounds
- 6 tablespoons olive oil
- 1 onion, chopped
- 1 carrot, chopped
- 1 leek, chopped and rinsed well
- 1 head garlic, unpeeled
- 6 quinces, cut into small pieces
- 1¼ cups beef or veal stock
  (homemade, canned or
  made with a bouillon cube)
- 1 bay leaf
- 1 tablespoon sugar
- salt

Serves 4

The night before you are planning to serve, combine the lemon juice, peppercorns, mustard, and yogurt in a bowl. Rub this mixture all over the lamb, put the meat on a plate, and let marinate overnight in the refrigerator. Remove the lamb from the refrigerator and scrape off the marinade. Heat 4 tablespoons of the oil in a large pan. Add the lamb and cook over medium heat, turning frequently, for 8–10 minutes, until evenly browned all over. Remove from the pan and set aside. Add the onion, carrot, leek, garlic head, and one of the quinces to the pan and cook over low heat, stirring occasionally, for 8–10 minutes, until golden brown. Pour in 1 cup of the stock, add the bay leaf, season with salt, and return the lamb to the pan. Cover and simmer gently for 3 hours, until the lamb is tender. Meanwhile, heat the remaining oil in a skillet. Add the remaining quinces and cook over low heat, stirring occasionally, for 5 minutes. Add the remaining stock and the sugar and cook, turning the quinces once, for about 10 minutes, until softened. Remove the lamb from the pan, carve into slices, and put on a warm serving dish. Place the quinces all around it. Remove and discard the bay leaf from the sauce and pass the sauce through a food mill or process in a food processor or blender. Season with salt if necessary. Serve immediately.

Note: This dish can be made with other fruit, such as pears, peaches, dried peaches, or dried apricots.

796

Braised lamb
CORDERO ESTOFADO

- 3¼ pounds stewing lamb, such
  as boneless shoulder, breast,
  or neck slices, cut into pieces
- ¾ cup white-wine vinegar
- ¾ cup olive oil
- 1 head garlic, unpeeled
- 1 large onion, halved
- 1 bay leaf
- 1 teaspoon paprika
- salt

Serves 6

Put all the ingredients into a pan, mix well, and cover the pan. Cook over low heat, stirring occasionally, for about 2 hours, until the meat is tender. If necessary, add a little hot water during cooking.

Lamb stew with peas, artichokes, and potatoes

GUISO DE CORDERO CON GUISANTES, ALCACHOFAS Y PATATAS

- **2 lamb shoulders, each 3¼–4 pounds, cut into pieces**
- **1 lemon, halved**
- **2¼ pounds globe artichokes**
- **5–6 tablespoons olive oil**
- **1 large onion, finely chopped**
- **2¼ pounds peas, shelled**
- **1 tablespoon all-purpose flour**
- **5 tablespoons white wine**
- **2¼ cups sunflower oil**
- **1 pound 2 ounces potatoes, diced**
- **salt**

Serves 6

Ask your butcher to cut the lamb shoulders into pieces. Squeeze the juice from one of the lemon halves and add it to a large bowl of water. Break off the artichoke stalks and remove the coarse outer leaves. Cut off the tips of the remaining leaves, open them out, and remove the chokes. Cut the artichokes lengthwise into halves or fourths, depending on their size. Rub them with the remaining lemon half and put them into the acidulated water. Heat the olive oil in a large, heavy pot. Add the onion and cook over low heat, stirring occasionally, for about 5 minutes, until softened and translucent. Add the lamb and cook, turning frequently, for about 8 minutes, until evenly browned. Drain the artichokes and add to the pan along with the peas. Stir in the flour and cook, stirring constantly, for 2 minutes. Gradually stir in the wine and add water to cover. Season with salt, cover, and cook over medium-low heat, stirring occasionally, for about 45 minutes. Meanwhile, heat the sunflower oil in a skillet. Add the potatoes and cook over low heat for 5–6 minutes without browning. Remove with a slotted spoon, drain well, and add to the stew. Mix well, re-cover the pan, and cook, stirring occasionally, for 20 minutes more, until the lamb is tender. Serve in a warm deep dish.

Lamb stew with zucchini
RAGÚ DE CORDERO CON CALABACINES

- **2 tablespoons olive oil**
- **⅓ cup finely chopped onion**
- **1 cup diced zucchini**
- **1 small eggplant,**
  peeled and diced
- **5 ounces green bell peppers,**
  seeded and cut into thin strips
- **5 ounces tomatoes,**
  peeled, seeded, and diced
- **2¼ pounds boneless stewing**
  lamb, cut into cubes
- **1 sprig fresh thyme**
- **pinch of paprika**
- **6 fresh mint leaves, chopped**
- **salt and pepper**

Serves 4

Heat the oil in a pan. Add the onion and cook over low heat, stirring occasionally, for 5 minutes, until softened and translucent. Add the zucchini, eggplant, bell pepper, and tomato and cook, stirring frequently, for 10 minutes. Add the lamb and cook, stirring, for 5 minutes more. Season with salt and pepper, then add the thyme and paprika. Cover the pan and cook over low heat for 30 minutes, until the lamb is tender. Sprinkle with the mint and serve immediately.

Note: You could add sliced green beans to the stew.

Lamb stew with carrots and turnips

GUISO DE CORDERO CON ZANAHORIAS Y NABOS

- 5 tablespoons olive oil
- 1 onion, chopped
- 3¼–4½ pounds stewing lamb, such as shoulder, breast, neck slices, cut into pieces
- 9 ounces young carrots, thinly sliced
- 1 whole clove
- 1 sprig fresh thyme
- 1 clove garlic
- 2 very ripe tomatoes, peeled, seeded, and cut into fourths, or 1 tablespoon tomato paste
- 5 tablespoons white wine
- 1 ⅔ cups diced turnips
- 1 ½ cups diced potatoes
- 1 cup chicken stock (homemade, canned or made with a bouillon cube)
- salt

Serves 6

Heat the oil in a pan. Add the onion and cook over low heat, stirring occasionally, for about 5 minutes, until softened and translucent. Add the lamb and cook over medium heat, stirring frequently, for about 8 minutes, until evenly browned. Add the carrot, clove, thyme, garlic, tomatoes or tomato paste, and a pinch of salt and pour in the wine. Cover the pan and cook for 45 minutes. Add the turnip and potato, pour in the stock, re-cover the pan, and cook for about 1 hour more, until the lamb is tender. Serve in a warm deep dish, garnished with fried bread (see recipe 130), if you like.

800

Lamb with garlic and tomato
CORDERO AL AJILLO Y TOMATE

- **4 tablespoons olive oil**
- **3¼–4½ pounds stewing lamb, such as breast or neck slices, cut into pieces**
- **1 tablespoon bread crumbs**
- **1 head garlic, peeled**
- **1 veal or chicken bouillon cube dissolved in generous 1 cup boiling water**
- **salt**

Tomato sauce:
- **3 tablespoons sunflower oil**
- **2¼ pounds very ripe tomatoes, peeled, seeded, and chopped**
- **pinch of mixed dried herbs or 1 bouquet garni (1 bay leaf and 1 sprig fresh thyme tied together in cheesecloth)**
- **1 teaspoon sugar**
- **salt**

Serves 6

Make a thick tomato sauce as described in recipe 73. Remove and discard the bouquet garni, if used, before processing in a food processor or blender. Heat the oil in a heavy pan or a Dutch oven. Add the lamb and cook over medium heat, stirring occasionally, for 8–10 minutes, until evenly browned. Sprinkle in the bread crumbs, add the tomato sauce, garlic cloves, and stock, and season lightly with salt. Cover and simmer over low heat for 1½ hours, until the lamb is tender. Remove and discard the garlic and serve immediately accompanied by fried potatoes, boiled rice, or triangles of fried bread (see recipe 130).

801

Rib chops with béchamel sauce

CHULETITAS DE CORDERO CON BECHAMEL

- **18 lamb rib chops**
- **sunflower oil, for deep-frying,**
  plus extra for brushing
- **2 eggs**
- **1½ cups bread crumbs**
- **salt**

  Béchamel sauce:
- **2 tablespoons (¼ stick) butter**
- **2 tablespoons sunflower oil**
- **2 tablespoons all-purpose flour**
- **2¼ cups milk**
- **salt**

  Serves 6

Scrape away the meat and connective tissue from the top 2 inches of the chop bones. Season the cutlets with salt. Heat 6 tablespoons of oil in a skillet. Add the chops, in batches, and cook over medium heat for about 3 minutes on each side, or until cooked to your liking. Remove from the skillet and set aside. Reserve the oil in the skillet. Brush a surface or cutting board with oil. Make the béchamel sauce. Melt the butter with the oil in another skillet. Stir in the flour and cook, stirring constantly, for 2 minutes. Gradually stir in the milk, a little at a time. Season with salt and cook, stirring constantly, for about 10 minutes, until thickened. Remove the skillet from the heat. Holding the chops by the bone, dip them, one at a time, into the béchamel sauce to coat. Put them onto the oiled surface or cutting board and let cool. Beat the eggs in a shallow dish and pour the bread crumbs into another shallow dish. Add the remaining oil to the reserved oil in the skillet or transfer both lots of oil to a deep-fryer and heat until a cube of day-old bread browns in 30 seconds. Coat each lamb chop, first in the beaten egg and then in the bread crumbs. Add to the hot oil, in batches, and cook until golden brown all over. Remove with a slotted spatula, drain, and keep warm while you cook the remaining batches. Serve immediately.

802

Lamb chops with kidneys
CHULETAS DE CORDERO CON RIÑONES

- **5 tablespoons butter, softened**
- **1 tablespoon chopped fresh parsley**
- **1 tablespoon chopped fresh tarragon**
- **8 lamb chops**
- **6 tablespoons olive oil**
- **4 slices of bacon**
- **4 lambs' kidneys, cored**
- **16 cherry tomatoes**
- **salt**

Serves 4

Beat the butter with the herbs in a bowl until thoroughly combined. Cover and chill in the refrigerator until required. Season the chops with salt. Heat the oil in a skillet. Add the chops and cook over medium heat for about 3 minutes on each side, until evenly browned and cooked to your liking. Remove from the pan and keep warm. Add the bacon and kidneys to the pan and cook for a few minutes on each side, until the bacon is golden brown and the kidneys are just firm. Remove and keep warm. Melt 1 tablespoon of the herb butter in a small pan. Add the tomatoes and cook, stirring occasionally, for 3–5 minutes, until softened but not falling apart. Remove the pan from the heat. Divide the chops, bacon, kidneys, and tomatoes among four warm individual plates. Top each chop with ½ tablespoon of the remaining herb butter and serve immediately.

PouLTRY

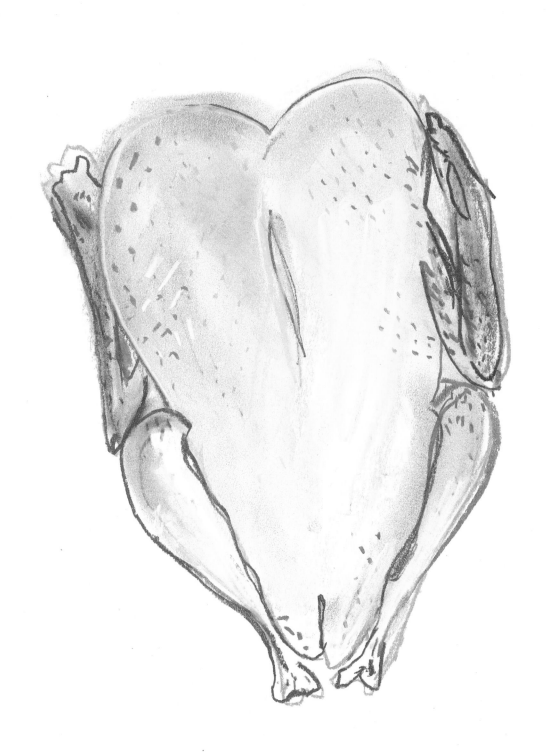

Chicken

History and curious facts

Chickens are domestic birds that originated in Asia more than six thousand years ago. They are mem-bers of the Gallinacean family. Their heads are adorned with a red crest and they have abundant plumage and strong ankles armed with spurs. These days their size and weight can vary greatly, depending on the breed and place of origin. There are noticeable differences between male and female birds as a result of many years of careful cross-breeding designed to improve either meat or egg production. Today chicken is a very popular foodstuff and a favorite with all consumers, although not long ago it was seen only on the tables of the better-off. This development is the result of research by the agricultural and farming industries into improving the birds' diet and using procedures in their rearing that cut the costs of production and, consequently, the price to the consumer. There are many different breeds of chicken, coming from a variety of geographical locations. The most widespread and inten-sively reared chickens are the American and Mediterranean breeds, which, in turn, subdivide into different groups with similar sizes and characteristics.

Value for money

The quality of chicken meat is assessed on the age, weight, and sex of the bird. Much can be judged from the bird's appearance–the texture of the leg and breast meat and the cleanness and smooth-ness of the skin. The colour of their skin, however, is not an indicator of quality; some chickens have yellow skin, while others, white. This is the result of variations in feed and processing. Intensively reared chickens cost considerably less than organic and barnyard birds and supermarkets, in particular, sell whole chickens and chicken portions at very low prices. In fact, chicken is currently one of the cheapest animal proteins available.

Nutrition

Chicken is a rich source of high-quality protein and provides all the essential amino acids that the human body requires for growth and maintenance. It is relatively low in calories and the white meat, in particular, is low in fat.

Chicken meat (per 3 ½ ounces)	Calories (kcal)	Protein (grams)	Carbohydrates (grams)	Fats (grams)
Raw chicken	173	20	0.5	10
Roast chicken	192	28	0	10
Braised chicken	233	20	0	17
Fried chicken	305	20	0	25

Chicken is easily digestible. Traditionally, it has been considered suitable for people suffering from a wide variety of digestive disorders and in the diet of the elderly. It is a good source of iron, phosphorus, and B group vitamins, espe-cially niacin. Younger birds have less fat and are good for roasting and frying, while older birds are better for stewing and braising. The amount of fat varies according to the age, type, and quality of the bird. Contrary to popular belief, there is no difference in the nutritional value of white and dark meat, except that the former contains more nicotinic acid, a B group vitamin, than the latter. The white meat contains less connective tissue and fat than the dark meat, making it slightly more digestible. The fat content is higher in the skin than in the rest of the meat, so people with dietary concerns may be advised to eat skinless chicken.

How to prepare

These days, most chickens are sold as oven-ready. However, if this is not the case, here is what you do. To make plucking easier, submerge the chicken in boiling water for 1 minute, holding it by the legs. This process does have the disadvantage that the meat may lose some flavor. After doing this it is advisable to singe the bird over a candle or other flame. First, check carefully that no wrapping or identification tag is left on the bird, then begin the process of opening the wings and extending them. Stretch out the bird, holding it by the neck and legs. Pass the whole surface of the chicken over a flame so that all the remaining feathers are scorched, but take care not to burn the skin. The next step is to clean the chicken. Put it on a work surface, breast side up, and then pull hard on the skin of the neck so that it is smooth. Make a small cut near the parson's nose (the protuberance from the rear end of the bird) and under it. Insert two fingers into this hole and pull gently. All the innards should come out together: liver, lungs, heart, etc. Check that nothing remains. To clean the feet, which are delicious when used in stock, submerge them in boiling water for 30 seconds, then use a cloth to pull the skin off as if it were a glove. Another way is to burn the skin and remove it in pieces.

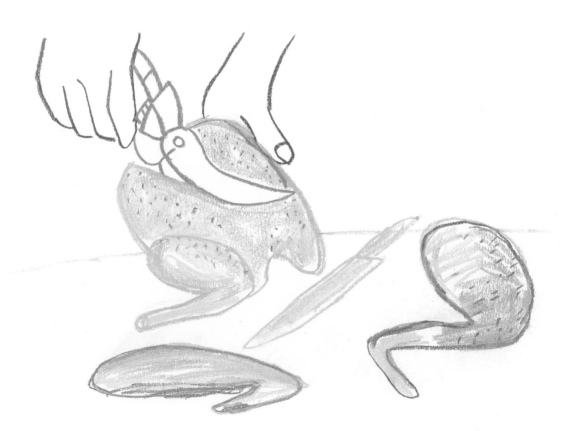

How to truss a chicken

Cover the opening at the neck with the overhanging skin. Take quite a long piece of fine kitchen string with both hands. Pass the string under the wings, also catching the neck, then cross it over the central breastbone, and fold the wings. Cross it again underneath, bring it back to the top, and tie it where the legs join.

How to cut up a raw chicken

The most important thing is to find the joints. Put the chicken breast side up, put the knife between the thigh and body, then hold the thigh, and dislocate the joint, finally cutting the skin. Repeat on the other side of the bird. Cut the legs in two. Also cut the wings in two, putting the knife in at the joint. Now separate the breast from the back, cutting along the base of the ribs. Pull the chest cavity with your hand. Cut the back section in half by cutting out the backbone. Finally, cut the breasts in half lengthwise along the breastbone.

How to carve a roast chicken

This requires a carving board or tray, a carving knife and fork, and a warm serving dish. If you're not going to serve the chicken immediately, have some aluminum foil ready to cover the dish to prevent it becoming cold. To separate the legs from the body, put the chicken in the center of the carving board or tray and hold it steady with the carving fork. Then cut through the thigh joints. Next cut off the wings, putting the knife into the joint with the back. Next, separate the breast from the carcass, cutting along the breastbone to separate the breast into two parts. Slip the knife under the breast to separate it from the carcass. Cut the legs in two at the joint. Never cut the cooked chicken on the same board, or with the same utensils, that you used to prepare it when raw. Doing so could infect the bird with harmful bacteria that were present in the bird when it was raw. These bacteria are destroyed in cooking, but can be reintroduced if the meat comes into contact with tools used to prepare the raw bird.

803

Chicken cooked in a Dutch oven, or casserole

POLLO ASADO EN «COCOTTE» O CACEROLA

- 1 chicken, 3¼–4½ pounds
- 3 thin slices of bacon
- 2½ tablespoons lard or butter
- 2 tablespoons sunflower oil
- juice of ½ lemon
- salt

Serves 4–6

Season the chicken with salt and put one bacon slice over the breast, one over the back, and the third inside the chicken. Truss with fine string as described on page 676. Melt the lard or butter with the oil in a Dutch oven or heavy pan. Add the chicken and cook over medium heat, turning frequently, for 8–10 minutes, until lightly browned on all sides. Cover the pan and continue to cook over medium heat, allowing 15–20 minutes per pound. Check that the chicken is done by piercing the thickest part of the thigh with the tip of a sharp knife; if the juices run clear and the meat is no longer pink, the chicken is cooked. Remove the lid from the pan, turn up the heat, and brown the chicken, turning frequently. Lift the chicken out of the pan, remove and discard the string and bacon, carve the meat, and put it on a warm serving dish. Stir 4–5 tablespoons hot water and the lemon juice into the cooking juices and bring to a boil, then pour into a sauceboat, and serve with the chicken.

804

Chicken with lemons

POLLO CON LIMONES

- ⅔ cup olive oil
- 1 chicken, 3¼–4½ pounds
- 1 large onion, finely chopped
- 3 lemons, cut into fourths
- ¾ cup white wine
- 1 cup chicken stock
  (homemade, canned or
  made with a bouillon cube)
- 1 bay leaf
- 1 tablespoon sugar
- salt

Serves 4

Heat the oil in a Dutch oven or heavy based pan. Add the chicken and cook over medium heat, turning frequently, for 8–10 minutes, until browned all over. Remove from the pan and keep warm. Add the onion to the pan and cook over low heat, stirring occasionally, for 6–7 minutes, until lightly browned. Put three of the lemon quarters into the cavity of the chicken and return the chicken to the pan. Put the remaining lemon quarter around it. Pour the wine and then the stock into the pan, add the bay leaf, sprinkle in the sugar, and season with salt. Cover and simmer for about 45 minutes, until the chicken is cooked through and tender. Check that the chicken is done by piercing the thickest part of the thigh with the tip of a sharp knife; if the juices run clear and the meat is no longer pink, the chicken is cooked. Lift the chicken out of the pan, carve the meat, and put it on a warm serving dish. Strain the sauce through a coarse strainer into a sauceboat. Serve the chicken with the sauce, accompanied by yellow rice (see recipe 191) or croûtons.

805 📷 Roast chicken with grapefruit or oranges

POLLO ASADO CON POMELOS O NARANJAS

- 1 chicken, 3¼–4 pounds
- 2 tablespoons brandy
- 2 grapefruit or 4 oranges
- 2 slices of bacon
- ⅓ cup lard or
  3 tablespoons sunflower oil
- 4–5 watercress sprigs
  or mesclun
- salt and pepper

Serves 6

Preheat the oven to 400°F. Season the chicken inside and out with salt and pepper and place in a roasting pan. Peel one of the grapefruit or two of the oranges and cut out the segments, discarding the bitter white pith. Heat the brandy in a small pan for a few seconds and ignite. When it has burned for a moment, pour it into the chicken and add the citrus segments. Put one of the slices of bacon over the breast of the chicken and the other over the back and spread with the lard. Truss with fine kitchen string as described on page 676. Roast, turning occasionally and basting with the cooking juices, for 30 minutes. Meanwhile, squeeze the juice from the remaining citrus fruit. Add to the cooking juices and continue to roast the chicken, turning occasionally and basting, for 30 minutes more, until the chicken is cooked through and tender. Check that the chicken is done by piercing the thickest part of the thigh. Lift the chicken out of the roasting pan , discard the string and bacon, and carve. Serve with the fruit segments and watercress.

806 Fried Rock Cornish hens

POLLITOS FRITOS

- 2 Rock Cornish hens,
  1 pound 10 ounces each
- 4 tablespoons olive oil
- 1 lemon, sliced
- 1 onion, sliced
- 7 sprigs fresh parsley
- sunflower oil for deep frying
- ½ cup flour mixed with 3
  tablespoons bread crumbs
- salt and pepper

Tomato sauce:
- 2 tablespoons sunflower oil
- 1 onion, finely chopped
- 1 pound 10 ounces tomatoes,
  peeled, seeded, and chopped
- 1 teaspoon sugar
- salt

Serves 4

Using poultry shears or strong kitchen scissors, cut each Rock Cornish hen in half. Season with salt and pepper, put the halves into a deep dish, and pour the olive oil over them. Add the lemon, onion, and three of the parsley sprigs. Let marinate in the refrigerator, turning occasionally, for 2 hours. Meanwhile, make the tomato sauce as described in recipe 73. Heat the sunflower oil in a deep-fryer or deep skillet to 325–340°F or until a cube of day-old bread browns in 45 seconds. Drain the hen halves, coat them in the flour and bread crumb mixture, and add to the hot oil. Cook for 10 minutes, then increase the temperature to 350–375°F, and cook for 5 minutes more, until the birds are cooked through and golden brown. Check by piercing the thickest part of the thigh with the tip of a sharp knife; if the juices run clear and the meat is no longer pink, the birds are cooked. Place the Rock Cornish hens on a serving dish and keep warm. Tie the remaining sprigs of parsley together with fine thread, add to the hot oil, and fry for 1–2 minutes. Reheat the tomato sauce and pour into a sauceboat. Garnish the birds with the fried parsley and serve immediately, offering the sauce separately.

807

Stuffed Andalusian chicken
POLLO RELLENO A LA ANDALUZA

- **6 tablespoons olive oil**
- **1 pound 2 ounces tart apples,**
  peeled, cored, and chopped
- **scant 1 cup diced Serrano ham**
  or prosciutto
- **⅓ cup pine nuts**
- **1 tablespoon chopped**
  fresh parsley
- **¼ teaspoon ground cloves**
- **1½ cup amontillado**
  or other sherry
- **¼ cup anisette**
- **1 chicken, 3¼ pounds**
- **⅓ cup lard or 3 tablespoons**
  sunflower oil
- **1 large onion, cut into 2–3 pieces**
- **salt and pepper**

Serves 6

Heat the oil in a pan. Add the apple and cook over low heat for 2 minutes. Add the ham, pine nuts, parsley, and cloves, season with salt and pepper, and cook, stirring occasionally, for 3–4 minutes. Pour in half the sherry and the anisette, stir well, cover, and simmer, stirring occasionally, for 30 minutes. Remove from the heat and let cool slighty. Preheat the oven to 400°F. Stuff the chicken with the mixture, reserving any extra cooking liquid. Sew up the opening or secure with skewers. Spread the lard or brush the oil all over the bird and place it in a roasting pan. Pour the reserved apple cooking liquid around the chicken. Season with salt and put the pieces of onion on either side of the chicken. Roast, turning occasionally, for 20 minutes, then pour the remaining sherry over the chicken. (If the tips of the legs start to brown during cooking, cover them in foil). Return to the oven and roast, basting occasionally, for about 40 minutes more, until the chicken is tender and cooked through. Check that it is done by piercing the thickest part of the thigh with the tip of a sharp knife; if the juices run clear and the meat is no longer pink, the chicken is cooked. Carve the chicken and spoon out the stuffing onto a warm serving dish. Serve immediately with the sauce.

Chicken with mushroom sauce

POLLO CON SALSA DE CHAMPIÑON

- 5 tablespoons olive oil
- 5½ pounds chicken parts
- 1 small onion,
  very finely chopped
- 1 (4-cup) package of dehydrated
  mushroom soup
- ¾ cup white wine
- 3 cups hot water
- 1 bouquet garni (1 clove garlic,
  1 bay leaf, 1 sprig fresh thyme,
  and 1 sprig fresh parsley tied
  together in cheesecloth)
- scant 4½ cups sliced
  mushrooms
- 2 tablespoons (¼ stick) butter
- juice of ½ lemon
- ¾ cup light cream (optional)
- salt

Serves 8

Heat the oil in a pan. Add the pieces of chicken, in batches, and cook over medium heat, turning frequently, for 8–10 minutes, until evenly browned. Remove from the pan and set aside. Add the onion and cook over low heat, stirring occasionally, for 7–8 minutes, until beginning to brown. Return the chicken parts to the pan. Combine the soup, wine, and hot water in a bowl and pour the mixture over the chicken. Add the bouquet garni and lightly season with salt. Cover and cook over medium heat for 35–60 minutes, until the chicken is tender. Check that it is done by piercing the thickest part of the thigh with the tip of a sharp knife; if the juices run clear and the meat is no longer pink, the chicken is cooked. Meanwhile, put the mushrooms, butter, lemon juice, and a pinch of salt into a pan and cook over low heat for 6 minutes. Just before serving, remove and discard the bouquet garni, add the mushrooms and their cooking juices to the chicken, and stir in the cream if using. Mix well and serve in a warm deep dish. The dish may be garnished with triangles of fried bread (see recipe 130) or served with boiled rice (see recipe 173).

809

Chicken with leeks and cream

POLLO CON PUERROS Y NATA

- **8 leeks, trimmed and halved lengthwise and rinsed well**
- **¾ cup olive oil**
- **1 chicken, quartered**
- **1 tablespoon all-purpose flour**
- **5 tablespoons white wine**
- **10 black peppercorns**
- **¾ cup light cream**
- **salt**

Serves 4

Cut off the white parts of the leeks, cut them into ¾-inch pieces, and set aside. Cook the green parts in salted boiling water for about 15 minutes, until tender. Drain well and set aside, covered to prevent them drying out. Heat the oil in a heavy based pan or Dutch oven. Add the chicken pieces and cook over medium heat, turning frequently, for 8–10 minutes, until evenly browned. Remove from the pan and set aside. Drain off nearly all the oil from the pan, leaving about 4 table-spoons, and reheat. Add the white parts of the leeks and cook over low heat, stirring occasionally, for 8 minutes. Stir in the flour, return the chicken to the pan, and pour in the wine and ¾ cup water. Add the peppercorns, cover the pan, and cook for about 30–40 minutes, until the chicken is cooked through and tender. Check that it is done by piercing the thickest part with the tip of a sharp knife; if the juices run clear and the meat is no longer pink, the chicken is cooked. Add the reserved leeks and the cream and heat through, shaking the pan gently. Serve immediately.

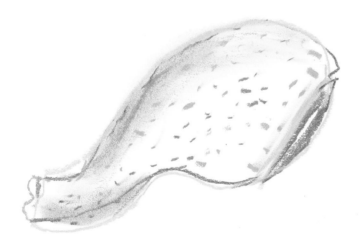

810

Chicken with dried porcini, shallots, cream, and egg

POLLO EN SALSA CON SETAS SECAS, CEBOLLITAS, NATA Y YEMAS

- 1 cup dried porcini
- ⅔ cup sunflower oil
- 3 ½ pounds chicken parts
- 18 shallots
- 1 cup white wine
- 1 teaspoon sugar
- 1½ tablespoons butter
- ¾ cup light cream
- 2 egg yolks
- juice of ½ lemon
- 1 tablespoon cornstarch
- 6 triangles of fried bread
  (see recipe 130)
- salt and pepper

Serves 6

Put the dried porcini into a bowl, add warm water to cover, and let soak for 15 minutes. Drain well. Heat 7 tablespoons of the oil in a pan. Add the chicken, in batches, and cook over medium heat, turning frequently, for 8–10 minutes, until evenly browned all over. Return all the chicken parts to the pan, then add half of the shallots and cook, occasionally shaking the pan, for 8–10 minutes, until golden brown. Pour in the wine and ⅔ cup water, add the porcini, and season with salt and pepper. Cover and cook over low heat for 20–30 minutes. Check that it is done by piercing the thickest part of the thigh with the tip of a sharp knife; if the juices run clear and the meat is no longer pink, the chicken is cooked. Put the remaining shallots into a pan, pour in water to cover, and add the sugar, butter, and a pinch of salt. Cook over low heat for about 20 minutes, until tender, then drain. Heat the remaining oil in a skillet, add the drained shallots and cook over low heat, stirring occasionally, for 5–8 minutes, until golden brown. Remove the pan of chicken from the heat. Lift out the pieces of chicken, set aside in a serving dish, and keep warm. Strain the cooking liquid into a bowl. Beat the cream with the egg yolks and lemon juice in a bowl. Mix the cornstarch with 1 tablespoon water in another bowl, then stir in the strained cooking liquid. Pour into a pan and bring to a boil, stirring constantly, then gradually stir into the cream and egg yolk mixture, a little at a time. Put the triangles of fried bread and the browned shallots around the edge of the serving dish, pour the sauce over the chicken, and serve immediately.

Note: You can use 11 ounces fresh porcini instead of using dried mushrooms, if you like. They do not need to be soaked.

811

📷

Braised chicken with pine nuts, green bell peppers, and tomatoes

GUISO DE POLLO CON PIÑONES, PIMIENTOS VERDES Y TOMATES

- 2 onions, chopped
- 3¼–4 pounds chicken parts
- 4 tomatoes, peeled, seeded, and chopped
- 3 green bell peppers, seeded and thinly sliced into rings
- 1 tablespoon bread crumbs
- ½ cup pine nuts
- ¼ teaspoon mixed dried herbs or 1 bouquet garni (1 sprig fresh thyme, 2 bay leaves, and 1 sprig fresh parsley tied together in cheesecloth)
- 2 cloves garlic
- ¾ cup olive oil
- 2 chicken bouillon cubes
- ¾ cup white wine
- salt and pepper

Serves 6

Preheat the oven to 350°F. Put the onion into an ovenproof casserole, place the pieces of chicken on top, and add the tomatoes and bell pepper. Sprinkle with the bread crumbs, pine nuts, and dried herbs or bouquet garni, and season with salt and pepper. Put the garlic cloves among the pieces of chicken, pour the oil over the top, and mix well. Put the casserole into the oven and cook for 15 minutes. Dissolve the bouillon cubes in 3 tablespoons hot water. Remove the casserole from the oven, stir well, and add the wine and stock. Return to the oven and cook, stirring occasionally, for 20–30 minutes more. Remove and discard the bouquet garni, if used, and try to put the rings of bell pepper back on top of the chicken. Check that it is done by piercing the thickest part of the thigh with the tip of a sharp knife; if the juices run clear and the meat is no longer pink, the chicken is cooked. Serve immediately, straight from the casserole.

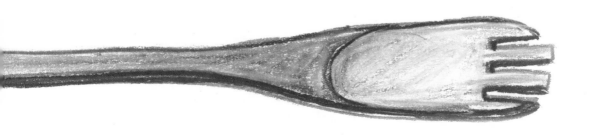

812

Chicken in sauce
POLLO EN SALSA

- 1 cup sunflower oil
- 3¼–4½ pounds chicken parts
- 2–3 slices of bread,
  crusts removed
- 1 onion
- 1 small clove garlic
- 2 sprigs fresh parsley
- pinch of saffron powder
- ¾ cup white wine
- 1 teaspoon mixed dried herbs
  or 1 bouquet garni (1 sprig fresh
  thyme, 2 bay leaves, and 1 sprig
  fresh parsley tied together in
  cheesecloth)
- 1 teaspoon very finely chopped
  parsley
- salt

Serves 6

Heat the oil in a skillet. Add the pieces of chicken, in batches, and cook over medium heat, turning frequently, for 8–10 minutes, until evenly browned. Remove from the skillet and set aside. Add the bread to the skillet and cook until golden brown on both sides. Remove from the skillet and set aside. Drain off and reserve most of the oil from the skillet, leaving just enough to cover the base, and reheat. Add the onion and cook for 4–6 minutes, until beginning to brown. Remove with a slotted spoon and transfer to a mortar or mini-food processor. Add the garlic to the skillet and cook for a few minutes, until beginning to brown. Add to the onion, along with the parsley, saffron, and fried bread and pound with a pestle or pulse in the processor. Put 3 tablespoons of the reserved oil into a large, deep pot and heat. Add the chicken pieces and pour the wine over them. Gradually mix 3 cups water into the onion mixture, then pass it through a food mill or process in the food processor or blender. Add the mixture to the chicken. Mix well and add the dried herbs or bouquet garni. If necessary, add some water so that the chicken is covered. Season with salt, stir well, and bring to a gentle simmer, then cook, partially covered, for 20 minutes. Sprinkle with the chopped parsley and cook for 10 minutes more, until the chicken is tender but not falling apart. Check that it is done by piercing the thickest part with the tip of a sharp knife; if the juices run clear and the meat is no longer pink, the chicken is cooked. Remove the bouquet garni, if used. Serve in a warm deep dish with boiled rice, served separately.

813

- ⅓ cup all-purpose flour
- 4 pounds chicken parts
- 1 cup sunflower oil
- 2½ tablespoons lard or butter
- 1 small onion,
  very finely chopped
- 1 clove garlic, peeled
- 2 sprigs fresh parsley
- pinch of saffron threads
- ¾ cup white wine
- salt

Serves 6

Chicken casserole

POLLO EN SALSA AL HORNO

Reserve 1 tablespoon of the flour. Season the chicken pieces with salt and coat them in the remaining flour, shaking off any excess. Heat the oil with the lard or butter in a skillet. Add the pieces of chicken and cook over medium heat, turning frequently, for 8–10 minutes, until evenly browned. Transfer to an ovenproof casserole. Preheat the oven to 350°F. Add the onion to the skillet and cook over low heat, stirring occasionally, for about 10 minutes, until golden brown. Stir in the reserved flour and cook, stirring constantly, for 2 minutes, then remove the skillet from the heat. Crush the garlic with the parsley and saffron in a mortar, or process in a food processor and mix in the wine. Return the skillet to the heat and gradually stir in the wine mixture. Bring to a boil, stirring constantly, then pour the mixture over the pieces of chicken. Put the casserole into the oven and cook for 30–45 minutes, until the chicken is cooked through and tender. Check that it is done by piercing the thickest part with the tip of a sharp knife; if the juices run clear and the meat is no longer pink, the chicken is cooked. Serve immediately straight from the casserole.

Note: This dish can be made in advance and refrigerated up to the stage where the chicken goes into the oven.

Roast chicken with orange juice

POLLO ASADO CON SALSA DE ZUMO DE NARANJAS

- **1 chicken,**
  about 3½ pounds
- **2½ tablespoons lard**
  or sunflower oil
- **3 thin slices of bacon**
- **1 orange, sliced**
- **salt**

  Sauce:
- **1½ tablespoons confectioners'**
  sugar
- **1 tablespoon white-wine vinegar**
- **juice of 2 large oranges**
- **½ teaspoon meat extract**
  or Maggi Seasoning
- **1 teaspoon potato starch**

  Serves 6

Preheat the oven 400°F. Season the chicken with salt and spread the lard or brush the oil all over it. Put one of the bacon slices over the breast, one over the back, and the third inside the chicken. Truss the chicken with fine kitchen string as described on page 676, and put into a roasting pan. Roast, turning and basting occasionally with the cooking juices, for about 1 hour, until cooked through and tender. Check that the chicken is done by piercing the thickest part of the thigh with the tip of a sharp knife; if the juices run clear and the meat is no longer pink, the chicken is cooked. (If the tips of the legs start to brown during cooking, cover them in foil). Remove the chicken from the roasting pan, cover with aluminum foil, and keep warm. Skim off the fat from the cooking juices. Stir 3–4 tablespoons hot water into the roasting pan, scraping up any bits from the base. Heat the confectioners' sugar in a skillet and when it begins to brown, remove the pan from the heat and stir in the vinegar. Immediately add the orange juice, scant ½ cup water, and the meat extract or Maggi Season-ing. Mix well, return the pan to the heat, cover, and simmer gently for 5 minutes. Halve the orange slices. Carve the chicken, place on a warm serving dish, and garnish with the half slices of orange and little mounds of mashed potato. Cover and keep warm. Mix the potato starch with a little water in a bowl, then stir into the sauce. Cook over low heat, stirring constantly, for 2 minutes, then stir in the cooking juices from the roasting pan. Serve the chicken, offering the sauce separately.

Note: When cooking several chickens, it is not necessary to multiply the sauce ingredients by the same amount. Among other things, the cooking juices will not double for each extra chicken. For 3 chickens, use 2 tablespoons sugar, the juice of 3 oranges, 2 tablespoons white-wine vinegar, 1 teaspoon meat extract or Maggi Seasoning, and 2 teaspoons potato starch.

Chicken cooked with shallots and tomatoes
POLLO GUISADO CON CEBOLLITAS Y TOMATE

- **4 tablespoons olive oil**
- **5½ pounds chicken parts**
- **generous ½ cup diced bacon**
- **6 small tomatoes, peeled**
- **pinch of mixed dried herbs**
- **½ cup white wine**
- **8 shallots**
- **1 tablespoon butter**
- **3½ ounces canned red bell pepper, drained, and cut into thin strips**
- **1 tablespoon chopped fresh parsley**
- **salt**

Serves 6–8

Heat the oil in a pan. Add the pieces of chicken, in batches, and cook over medium heat, turning frequently, for 8–10 minutes, until golden brown all over. Return all the chicken pieces to the pan, add the bacon and cook for a few minutes, then add the tomatoes. Season with salt, add the dried herbs, stir well, and pour in the wine and ½ cup water. Cover the pan and cook over medium heat for about 45 minutes, until the chicken is tender but not falling apart. Check that it is done by piercing the thickest part of the thigh with the tip of a sharp knife; if the juices run clear and the meat is no longer pink, the chicken is cooked. Meanwhile, put the shallots, butter, and a pinch of salt into a pan and pour in water to cover. Bring to a boil, lower the heat, and simmer for about 20 minutes, then drain. When the chicken is done, add the shallots, bell pepper, and parsley. Stir and heat through briefly, then serve.

816

Chicken with curry sauce
POLLO CON SALSA AL CURRY

- **1 chicken, 4 pounds**
- **3 slices of bacon**
- **2½ tablespoons lard**
  or sunflower oil
- **salt**

  Sauce:
- **2 tablespoons (¼ stick) butter**
- **2 tablespoons sunflower oil**
- **1 tablespoon all-purpose flour**
- **½ cup milk**
- **1 cup chicken stock**
  (preferably homemade)
- **¼ teaspoon curry powder**
- **1 egg yolk**
- **salt**

  Rice:
- **2½ cups long-grain rice**
- **¼ cup (½ stick) butter**
- **scant 1 cup drained canned peas**
- **salt**

  Serves 6

Season the chicken with salt and put one of the bacon slices over the breast, one over the back, and the third inside the chicken. Truss with fine kitchen string as described on page 676. Melt the lard or heat the oil in a Dutch oven or heavy pan and cook the chicken as described in recipe 803 for about 45 minutes. Check that it is done by piercing the thickest part of the thigh with the tip of a sharp knife; if the juices run clear and the meat is no longer pink, the chicken is cooked. Meanwhile, cook the rice as described in recipe 173. To make the sauce, melt the butter with the oil in a skillet. Stir in the flour and cook, stirring constantly, for 2 minutes. Gradually stir in the milk and then the stock, a little at a time. Cook, stirring constantly, for about 10 minutes, until thickened. Season to taste with salt and stir in the curry powder. Lightly beat the egg yolk in a bowl, stir in a little of the sauce, then add to the pan. Remove from the heat. Lift out the chicken from the pan, remove and discard the string and bacon, and carve the meat. Transfer the meat to a serving dish and keep warm. Skim off the fat from the cooking liquid, then stir the cooking liquid into the curry sauce, and pour it over the chicken. Serve immediately with the rice.

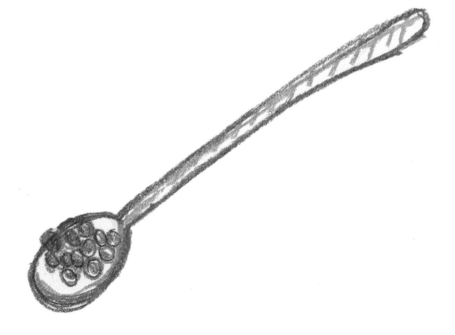

817

Chicken cooked in beer with onions

POLLO GUISADO CON CERVEZA Y CEBOLLAS

- 1 chicken, 4 pounds
- 1 cup sunflower oil
- 1 pound 2 ounces onions, thinly sliced and pushed out into rings
- 1½ cups beer
- 1 teaspoon potato starch
- ½ teaspoon meat extract or Maggi Seasoning
- salt

Serves 6

Season the cavity of the chicken with salt and truss with fine kitchen string as described on page 676. Heat the oil in a heavy pan or a Dutch oven. Add the chicken and cook over medium heat, turning frequently, for 8–10 minutes, until evenly browned all over. Remove from the pan and set aside. Drain off most of the oil from the pan, leaving just enough to cover the base, and reheat. Add the onion and cook over low heat, stirring occasionally, for about 5 minutes, until softened and translucent. Return the chicken to the pan and pour in the beer. Lightly season with salt, add the meat extract, cover, and bring to a boil, then lower the heat, and simmer, turning and basting the chicken occasionally, for about 45 minutes, until tender. Check that it is done by piercing the thickest part of the thigh with the tip of a sharp knife; if the juices run clear and the meat is no longer pink, the chicken is cooked. Lift out the chicken, remove and discard the string, carve the meat, and put it on a warm serving dish. Strain the cooking liquid into a clean pan and spoon the onion around the chicken. Mix the potato starch with 1 tablespoon water in a bowl and stir into the cooking liquid. Bring to a boil, stirring constantly, and cook for 2 minutes. Stir in any juices released when the chicken was carved, then pour into a sauceboat, and serve with the chicken.

818

Chicken supremes with grapefruit sauce

SUPREMAS DE AVE CON SALSA DE POMELOS

- 2 tablespoons olive oil
- 4 chicken breast quarters
- 2 grapefruit
- 4 tablespoons light cream
- pinch of ground turmeric
- pinch of saffron threads
- salt and pepper

Serves 4

Heat the oil in a skillet. Add the chicken breasts and cook over a medium heat for 6 minutes, then turn them over, season with salt, and cook the other sides for 6–10 minutes more. Remove from the pan and set aside. Check that it is done by piercing the thickest part of the thigh with the tip of a sharp knife; if the juices run clear and the meat is no longer pink, the chicken is cooked. Squeeze the juice from one of the grapefruit. Peel the other grapefruit and cut out the segments from between the membranes, discarding the bitter white pith. Drain off nearly all the oil from the skillet and reheat. Stir in the grapefruit juice and cream and cook until reduced and thickened, but do not let it boil. Season with salt and pepper and stir in the turmeric and saffron. Return the chicken to the pan and heat through for a few minutes. Add the grapefruit segments and serve immediately.

819

Chicken breasts with liver and bacon

PECHUGAS DE POLLO ASADAS CON HIGADITOS Y BACON

- 6 boneless chicken breast halves
- ½ teaspoon mixed dried herbs
- 6 chicken livers, trimmed
- 6 thin slices of bacon
- scant ½ cup lard or
  5 tablespoons sunflower oil
- salt

Serves 6

Preheat the oven to 400°F. Season the chicken breast halves with salt and sprinkle with the dried herbs. Place a chicken liver in the center of each breast half, then roll the chicken up. Wrap a slice of bacon around the roll and tie securely with fine kitchen string. Spread each roll with a little lard or oil and put into a roasting pan. Roast, turning the rolls occasionally and basting them with the cooking juices, for 30 minutes. Lift out the chicken rolls from the roasting pan, remove and discard the string, place on a serving dish, and keep warm. Skim off the fat from the cooking juices in the roasting pan, add 4–5 tablespoons hot water, and bring to a boil, stirring constantly. Pour over the chicken rolls and serve immediately with straw potatoes (see recipe 243) or Baked Tomatoes with Parsley and Garlic (see recipe 453).

820

Chicken quesadillas

QUESADILLAS DE POLLO

- 1 tablespoon corn oil
- 2 skinless boneless chicken
  breast halves, diced
- 1½ cups drained canned corn
- 4 flour tortillas
- 1¾ cups grated gruyere cheese

Salsa:
- 3–4 large ripe tomatoes,
  peeled and chopped
- 10 fresh green chiles,
  seeded and chopped
- ¼ onion, chopped
- 1 bunch of fresh cilantro,
  chopped
- salt

Serves 4

First make the salsa. Combine the tomato, chiles, onion, and cilantro in a bowl. Season to taste with salt, stir in ⅔ cup water, and set aside. Heat the oil in a nonstick skillet. Add the chicken and cook over low heat, stirring occasionally, for about 5 minutes, until beginning to brown and cooked through. Add the corn and salsa, mix well, and heat through. Warm the tortillas in the microwave or in a heavy skillet, following the instructions on the package, then place each one on a plate. Spoon the chicken mixture into the middle of each tortilla, sprinkle with some of the gruyere, then roll up the tortilla or fold it into a triangle, and serve immediately.

Note: This dish, of Mexican origin, uses tortillas, which are thin, flat, round breads made from flour or cornmeal.

821

Chicken with cucumber
POLLO CON PEPINO

- 1 cucumber, peeled and seeded
- 3 tablespoons olive oil
- 4 skinless boneless chicken breast halves, cut into strips
- 2 shallots, chopped
- juice of 3 lemons
- 2¼ cups chicken stock (homemade, canned or made with a bouillon cube)
- 6 fresh mint leaves, chopped
- salt and pepper

Serves 4

Dice the cucumber and cook in salted boiling water for 3 minutes, then drain, and set aside. Heat the oil in a deep skillet. Add the strips of chicken and cook over medium heat, stirring frequently, for 5 minutes, until golden brown and cooked through. Remove from the skillet and set aside. Add the shallots to the pan and cook over low heat, stirring occasionally, for about 5 minutes, until softened and translucent. Add the lemon juice and stock, return the chicken to the pan, season with salt and pepper, and cook over low heat for 10 minutes. Add the cucumber and cook for 5 minutes more. Sprinkle with the mint and serve.

822

Chicken supreme
SUPREMA DE POLLO

- 4 chicken breast halves
- 2 large carrots, cut into large pieces
- 1 large onion, cut into 4 wedges
- 1 chicken bouillon cube
- 1 truffle, sliced (optional)
- salt

Supreme sauce:
- 2 tablespoons (¼ stick) butter
- 1½ tablespoons all-purpose flour
- 2 egg yolks
- salt

Serves 4

Put the chicken into a pan, pour in water to cover, and add the carrot, onion, bouillon cube, and a small pinch of salt. Bring to a boil, then lower the heat, and simmer for about 30 minutes, until the chicken is tender and no longer pink when the tip of a sharp knife is inserted into the thickest part. Lift out the chicken breast halves, remove the skin, place them on a serving dish, and let cool. Strain and reserve the cooking liquid For the supreme sauce, melt the butter in a pan. Stir in the flour and cook, stirring constantly, for 2 minutes. Gradually stir in 6¼ cups of the reserved cooking liquid, a little at a time. Cook, stirring constantly, for about 5 minutes, until thickened, then remove the pan from the heat, and let cool slightly. Lightly beat the egg yolks in a bowl, stir in a little of the sauce, then stir into the pan. Pour the sauce over the chicken and let cool, then chill in the refrigerator. Serve cold, garnished with the slices of truffle, if using.

Chicken terrine with ham and pepper sauce

TERRINA DE POLLO CON JAMON Y SALSA DE PIMIENTO

- 12 ounces skinless boneless chicken breast halves, chopped
- 4 tablespoons dry vermouth
- 2 egg whites
- ⅔ cup heavy cream
- ⅓ cup chopped ham
- 3–4 pickled gherkins, diced
- sunflower oil, for brushing
- salt and pepper

Sauce:
- 1 large red bell pepper
- ½ chicken bouillon cube, dissolved in ⅔ cup warm water
- 3–4 tablespoons light cream
- salt and pepper

Serves 4

Season the chicken with salt and pepper, put it into a food processor or blender, add the vermouth, and process. Transfer to a bowl. Whisk the egg whites in a clean, dry bowl until they form soft peaks, then gently fold them into the chicken mixture. Lightly beat the cream with a fork, then fold into the mixture. Chill in the refrigerator. Meanwhile, preheat the broiler. To make the sauce, put the bell pepper on a baking sheet and cook under the broiler, turning occasionally, for 10–15 minutes, until blistered and charred. Remove with tongs, place in a plastic bag, and seal the top. When the bell pepper is cool enough to handle, peel and seed it and cut the flesh into pieces. Put the pieces of bell pepper and the stock into a food processor or blender and process until smooth, then pour into a pan. Combine the ham and pickled gherkins. Remove the chicken mixture from the refrigerator and divide it into fourths. Mix one fourth with the ham and gherkin mixture. Brush a heatproof mold with oil, cover the base with alumi-num foil, and brush the foil with oil. Spoon in the mixture, cover and set the mold over a pan of barely simmering water for about 15–20 minutes, until thoroughly cooked. Remove the mold from the heat, let cool slightly, then run a knife around the edge of the mold, and turn it out. Just before serving, bring the bell pepper sauce to a boil, stir in the cream, and heat gently, but do not let it come back to a boil. Season to taste with salt and pepper. Serve the terrine, offering the sauce separately. For the others we suggest a mixture of beef and Serrano ham or proscuitto, carrots and shrimp, or any other ingredients which go well with chicken, using the same proportions.

Note: The remaining chicken cream can be mixed with chopped mushrooms that have been sautéed with onion.

Blanquette of chicken

BLANQUETA DE GALLINA

- 1 boiling fowl, 3¼ pounds
- 1 bay leaf
- 1 small onion,
  studded with 3 cloves
- 2 carrots, sliced
- 5 tablespoons white wine
- 2½ cups long-grain rice
- 6 tablespoons (¾ stick) butter
- 2 tablespoons sunflower oil
- 1½ tablespoons all-purpose
  flour
- 1 cup milk
- 2 egg yolks
- juice of ½ lemon
- 1 tablespoon chopped
  fresh parsley
- salt

Serves 6

Put the boiling fowl into a pan, pour in water to cover, and add the bay leaf, onion, carrot, wine, and a pinch of salt. Bring to a boil and skim off the froth that rises to the surface, then lower the heat, and simmer for 1½–2 hours, until the boiling fowl is tender. Check that it is done by piercing the thickest part of the thigh with the tip of a sharp knife; if the juices run clear and the meat is no longer pink, the chicken is cooked. Meanwhile, cook and rinse the rice as described in recipe 173. Remove the boiling fowl from the pan with a slotted spoon and keep warm. Strain and reserve the cooking liquid. Melt 2 tablespoons of the butter with the oil in a pan. Stir in the flour and cook, stirring constantly, for 2 minutes. Gradually stir in the milk and 2¼ cups of the reserved cooking liquid. Beat the egg yolks with the lemon juice and stir in a little of the sauce, then pour into the pan. Sprinkle in the parsley and season to taste with salt. Remove the pan from the heat and keep warm. Season the rice with salt and fry in the remaining butter (see recipe 173). Fill half of a long serving dish with the rice and the other half with the boiling fowl and sauce. Serve immediately.

Note: A regular chicken can be used in this dish in place of a boiling fowl.

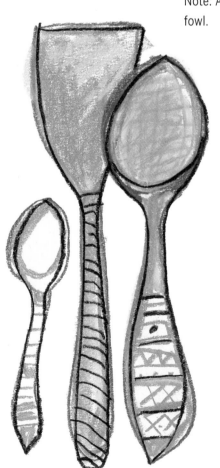

825

Chicken roll
PECHUGA DE GALLINA RELLENA

- 1 boneless breast portion of boiling fowl, 1 pound 2 ounces
- 9 ounces ground beef
- 9 ounces ground pork
- 1 thick slice of Serrano ham or prosciutto, cut widthwise into thin strips
- 1 truffle, thinly sliced (optional)
- ¾ cup white wine
- 2 leeks, white parts only, cut into short lengths and rinsed well
- 1 stalk celery, cut into short lengths (optional)
- 2 carrots, cut into short lengths
- pinch of mixed dried herbs or 1 bouquet garni (1 sprig fresh thyme, 2 bay leaves, and 1 sprig fresh parsley tied together in cheesecloth)
- 4 black peppercorns
- 1 envelope gelatin (see Notes)
- salt

Serves 6

Lay the breast of boiling fowl out on a dishtowel, skin side down. Combine the ground beef and pork in a bowl and spread over the breast. Arrange parallel strips of ham on top and add the truffle slices, if using. Roll up the breast portions, wrap in the dishtowel, and tie the dishtowel at both ends. Put the roll into a pan, pour in water to cover, and add the wine, leek, celery, if using, carrot, dried herbs or bouquet garni, peppercorns, and a pinch of salt. Cover and bring to a boil, then lower the heat, and cook for 1½–2 hours, until the breast portion is tender and no longer pink when the tip of a sharp knife is inserted. Remove the roll from the pan, weigh it down with a cutting board, and let cool. Strain and reserve the stock. Once it is cold, unwrap, slice, and serve the roll with gelatin (see Notes) and salad.

Notes: Make the gelatin with the strained stock from cooking the boiling fowl and the powdered gelatin, following the instructions on the package. When it has set, chop it and place it around the meat. Alternatively, use the stock to make a delicious soup. You can use 2 large boneless chicken breast halves in place of the boiling fowl.

826

Chicken in red wine

GALLO AL VINO TINTO

- Scant 1 cup brandy
- ½ cup chicken's or pig's blood (optional)
- 1 chicken, 5½ pounds
- generous 1 cup chopped bacon
- ⅔ cup butter
- 12 shallots
- 1 bottle (3 cups) red wine
- 1 teaspoon sugar
- 1 clove garlic, lightly crushed
- 1 bouquet garni
  (1 sprig fresh thyme, 2 bay leaves, and 1 sprig fresh parsley tied together in cheesecloth)
- 9 ounces mushrooms
- 2 tablespoons all-purpose flour
- salt and pepper

Serves 6

Combine 2 tablespoons of the brandy and the blood, if using, in a bowl and set aside. Cut the chicken into parts and season with salt and pepper. Blanch the bacon in boiling water for 2 minutes, then drain. Melt ¼ cup of the butter in a large skillet. Add the bacon and shallots and cook over low heat, stirring occasionally, until lightly browned. Add the chicken and cook, turning frequently, until evenly browned all over. Drain off the fat released. Heat the remaining brandy in a small pan, pour it into the pan with the chicken, and ignite. When the flames have died down, add the wine, season with salt and pepper, and add the sugar, garlic, and bouquet garni. Cover and simmer for 2½ hours. Add the mushrooms and stir well. Reserve 1½ tablespoons of the remaining butter and mix the rest to a paste with the flour. Add to the pan, in small pieces at a time, and cook, gently shaking the pan until fully incorporated. Cook for 15–30 minutes more, until the chicken is tender. Check that it is done by piercing the thickest part of the thigh with the tip of a sharp knife; if the juices run clear and the meat is no longer pink, the chicken is cooked. Just before serving, remove and discard the bouquet garni, and add the brandy and blood mixture, if using, and remaining butter to the sauce. Serve in a warm deep dish, covered with the sauce and garnished with triangles of fried bread (see recipe 130).

Turkey

History and curious facts

Like chicken, turkey is a member of the Gallinacean family. It lives wild in its native North America. Farmed turkeys may grow up to 39 inches high and weigh up to 25 pounds. There are many breeds. The most common is the white-feathered or broad-breasted white, specifically bred to have smooth, clean-looking skin after plucking. Traditional turkey has thick, dark—almost black—plumage and a speckled skin. Bronze turkeys also have dark plumage with metallic highlights. Turkeys have bald heads and a red wattle. The female of all breeds is smaller than the male. The turkey has long been used for food and remains very popular today. It is highly valued in the United States and is the nearly universal main course for Thanks-giving. It is the traditional Christmas dish in many European countries, including Spain and Britain, but has also increasingly become an every-day option. It has a high nutritional value, being a good source of proteins, B vitamins, and some minerals, including phosphorus and iron. It is easily digested and is suitable for people with some digestive disorders and for growing children. Younger birds have less fat and are good roasted or fried, while older birds are better stewed or braised. Roasting and stewing are the traditional ways to prepare this bird, but nowadays turkey is more often eaten as fillets. In the United States, it can be purchased in ground form, as sausages, and in deli-style meats.

Nutrition

Turkey is a source of high-quality proteins, vitamins, especially niacin, iron, zinc, phosphorus, potassium, and magnesium. There is no difference in the nutritional value of white and dark meat. Turkey contains 21.5 g protein, 19 g fat, and 58 g water per 3 ½ pounds meat. There are no carbohydrates in its composition and it has about 280 calories per 100 g / 3 ½ ounces.

Value for money

Turkey meat is not a seasonal product and frozen turkey, especially, can be found in stores and supermarkets all year around. Oven-ready fresh birds are more widely available at specific times of the year. Whole birds, fillets, drumsticks, crowns, diced, and ground meat are all on sale. Check the quality by looking at the cleanness of the skin and legs and the texture of the meat.

Selection

Avoid buying a very heavy turkey. If it weighs more than 8¾ pounds, its meat will be less tender. If possible, choose a turkey hen which will be both more tender and tastier.

How to clean and prepare

Clean and prepare the turkey in the same way as chicken. When roasting it, put some slices of bacon over the breast, if you like. To prevent it browning too quickly, cover it with aluminum foil.

Roasting times

3¼–4½-pound turkey—1¼ hours at 360—400°F
4½–6½-pound turkey –1½ hours at 360—400°F
6½–11-pound turkey—2–2½ hours at 360—400°F

Fried slices of turkey are delicious with a salad. When preparing stuffed turkey, it is advisable to cook the stuffing separately to make sure that it is cooked through. If you have cooked it inside the bird, the stuffing should reach at least 160°F before you serve it.

Turkey with chestnuts

PAVO CON CASTAÑAS

- 1 small turkey, 6 ½ pounds
- 6 slices of bacon
- dash of lemon juice
- generous ½ cup lard or
  5 tablespoons sunflower oil
- salt and pepper

Stuffing:
- ¼ cup (½ stick) butter
- 7 ounces porcini
- 7 ounces white mushrooms
- 3 skinless boneless chicken
  breast halves, coarsely chopped
- 2 eggs
- scant 1 cup light cream
- 9 ounces duck foie gras, diced
- 9 ounces canned peeled and
  cooked chestnuts, drained
- 1 ¾ cups bread crumbs
- dash of lemon juice
- salt and pepper

Serves 6

Preheat the oven to 350°F. Season the inside of the turkey with salt and pepper. Make the stuffing. Melt the butter in a skillet. Add the porcini and mushrooms and cook over a low heat, stirring occasionally, for 5 minutes or until much of the liquid has been released and evaporated. Remove the pan from the heat. Put the chicken in a food processor or blender and process until finely chopped. Add the eggs and cream and process again. Then add the porcini and mushrooms, foie gras, chestnuts, and bread crumbs and process again to combine. Season with salt and pepper. Stuff the turkey with the chicken mixture, adding one of the slices of bacon. Rub the outside of the bird with the lard or oil and cover with the remaining slices of bacon. Place in a roasting pan and cover with aluminum foil. Roast for 1 hour, then remove and discard the foil, and increase the temperature to 425°F. Roast, turning and basting occasionally, for 1–1½ hours more, until the turkey is cooked through and golden brown. Test by piercing the thickest part with the tip of a sharp knife; if the juices run clear and the meat is no longer pink, the turkey is cooked. Lift the turkey out of the roasting pan, discard the bacon, carve the meat, and put the slices on a warm serving dish. Skim off the fat from the cooking juices, add 4 tablespoons hot water and the lemon juice, and cook, stirring and scraping up any bits from the base of the roasting pan, then pour into a sauceboat. Serve immediately.

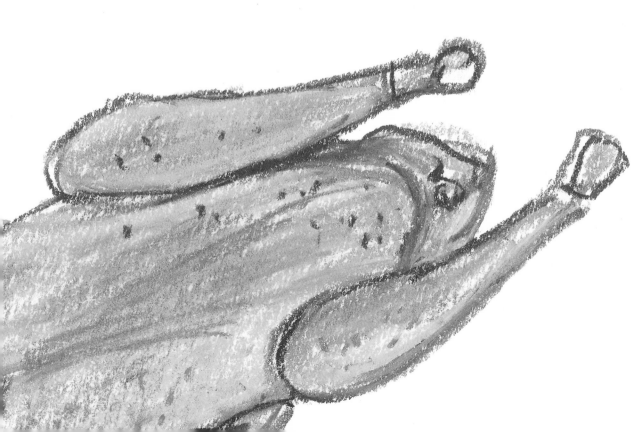

Capon

A capon is a young rooster that has been castrated and then fattened on a special diet that makes it especially flavorsome, with a high proportion of white meat. The production of capons is banned in a number of countries including the UK, and Australia (where it is illegal to castrate the birds using chemicals). A large chicken or small turkey may be substituted in traditional recipes for capon.

828 Capon stuffed with pears

CAPON RELLENO DE PERAS

- 2 slices of bread, crusts removed
- scant ½ cup milk
- 1 capon, chicken, or turkey, with giblets, 7–8 pounds
- 10 pears
- 11 ounces bulk sausage
- generous ½ cup diced bacon
- pinch of freshly grated nutmeg
- 1 egg
- 1 egg yolk
- scant 1 cup chopped pistachio nuts
- 3 tablespoons pine nuts
- 1 stalk celery, chopped
- 1 onion, chopped
- 2 tablespoons green peppercorns
- generous ½ cup lard or goose fat or 5 tablespoons sunflower oil
- 1 bottle (3 cups) red wine
- 1½ tablespoons honey
- salt and pepper

Serves 6

Put the bread in a bowl, pour in the milk, and let soak for 10 minutes, then drain. Preheat the oven to 475°F. Season the inside of the bird with salt and pepper. Chop the liver and heart. Slit the gizzard, remove and discard the gravel sac, then chop. Put the chopped giblets in a bowl. Peel, core, and chop two of the pears and add to the bowl along with the bulk sausage, bacon, nutmeg, egg, egg yolk, pistachio nuts, pine nuts, celery, onion, half the peppercorns, and the soaked bread. Mix well, then stuff the bird with this mixture. Close the cavities with trussing thread. Spread the lard or fat over the bird or brush it with the oil and put into a roasting pan. Roast for 15 minutes, then lower the temperature to 350°F, and roast, basting frequently, for 2 hours more. Check that it is done by piercing the thickest part of the thigh with the tip of a sharp knife; if the juices run clear and the meat is no longer pink, the chicken is cooked. Meanwhile, peel and core the remaining pears, put them into a pan, and add the wine, the remaining peppercorns, and the honey. Cook over medium heat for 20 minutes, then remove the pan from the heat, and let cool. Remove the bird from the roasting pan and cover with aluminum foil. Skim off the fat from the cooking juices and add scant 1 cup of the cooking liquid from the pears. Cook over medium heat until reduced by half. Season to taste with salt and pepper. Carve the bird and scoop out the stuffing and place on a warm serving dish. Halve the pears, place a little stuffing in the cavities, and put on the dish. Serve immediately, offering the sauce separately.

Duck

Strictly speaking, duckling less than four months old is the bird most commonly found in stores and supermarkets, as the meat will be tender. It is usually sold oven-ready, but if you need to prepare it yourself follow the method for preparing a chicken. In addition, remove the glands from either side of the tail bone. Duck is sold whole or in parts, as breasts or legs. A whole duck is cut up slightly differently from a chicken. Cut the skin between the legs and body. Carve the breast into fillets. Carve the legs and wings in the same way as for a chicken.

To roast a duck, allow 15–20 minutes per pound. Bear in mind that the duck is a bird with a lot of fat, so only use a little lard or oil when preparing it and do not add bacon.

829

Duckling à l'orange (first version)
PATO A LA NARANJA

- 3 oranges
- 1 duckling, 3¼ pounds
- ⅓ cup lard or 3 tablespoons
  sunflower oil
- 1 large carrot, sliced
- 2–3 shallots, sliced
- ¾ cup white wine
- 1 cup duck or chicken stock
  (homemade, canned or
  made with a bouillon cube)
- juice of 2 oranges
- 1 tablespoon potato starch
- strip of thinly pared orange zest
- 2 tablespoons Curaçao
- salt

Serves 4–5

Peel one of the oranges and cut out the segments from between the membranes. Slice the remaining oranges and set aside. Put the orange segments inside the duckling and season with salt. Melt the lard or heat the oil in a large skillet. Add the duckling, carrot, and shallots and cook over medium heat, turning the duckling frequently, for about 8 minutes, until evenly browned all over. Pour in the wine, stock, and 3 tablespoons of the orange juice. Cover and cook over medium heat for 45 minutes. Lift out the duckling from the pan. Remove and discard the orange segments. Strain the cooking liquid into a clean pan. Mix the potato starch with 2 tablespoons water and the remaining orange juice in a bowl and add the orange zest. Skim off the fat from the cooking liquid, stir in the potato starch and juice, and cook over low heat, stirring constantly, for 2–3 minutes, until thickened. Stir in the Curaçao. Remove and discard the orange zest and pour the sauce into a sauceboat. Carve the duckling and serve, garnished with the orange slices, offering the sauce separately.

830

Duckling à l'orange (second version)
PATO A LA NARANJA

- 3 oranges
- 1 duckling (such as Muscovy),
  3¼ pounds
- ⅓ cup lard or sunflower oil
- 1 large carrot, sliced
- 2–3 shallots, sliced
- ¾ cup white wine
- 1 cup duck or chicken stock
  (homemade, canned or
  made with a bouillon cube)
- juice of 2 large oranges
- 1 duck liver
- 1½ tablespoons butter
- 1 tablespoon sunflower oil
- 1 tablespoon all-purpose flour
- 2 tablespoons Curaçao
- skimmed duck cooking juices
- salt

Serves 4–5

Peel one of the oranges and cut out the segments from between the membranes. Slice the remaining oranges and set aside. Put the orange segments inside the duckling and season with salt. Melt the lard or heat the oil in a large skillet. Add the duckling, carrot, and shallots and cook over a medium heat, turning the duckling frequently, for about 8 minutes, until evenly browned all over. Pour in the wine, stock, and 3 tablespoons of the orange juice. Cover and cook over medium heat for 45 minutes. Lift out the duckling from the pan. Remove and discard the orange segments. Strain the cooking liquid into a clean pan. Lightly fry the duck liver, then pound it well in a mortar or process in a food processor. Melt the butter with the oil in a skillet. Stir in the flour and the liver and cook over low heat, stirring constantly, for 2 minutes. Stir in the orange juice, Curaçao, and cooking liquid and cook over low heat, stirring constantly, for a few minutes. If the sauce is too thick, stir in 1 tablespoon hot water. Season to taste with salt and strain into a sauceboat.

831 Braised duckling with olives

PATO BRASEADO CON ACEITUNAS

- 3–4 tablespoons olive oil
- 1 duckling (such as Muscovy),
  3 ¼ pounds
- 1 large onion, chopped
- 2 large carrots, sliced
- 2 large, ripe tomatoes,
  peeled, seeded, and chopped
- ¾ cup white wine
- 2 ¼ cups duck or chicken stock
  (homemade, canned or
  made with a bouillon cube)
- scant 1 cup olives, pitted
- 1 heaping teaspoon
  potato starch
- salt and pepper

Serves 6

Heat the oil in a large, heavy pan or a Dutch oven. Add the duckling and cook over low heat, turning frequently, for 5 minutes. Add the onion and carrot and cook, turning the duckling frequently, for about 15 minutes, until the vegetables have softened and the duckling is evenly browned all over. Add the tomato and cook for 10 minutes, then pour in the wine and stock, and season with salt and pepper. Cover and simmer over low heat for 1 hour. Meanwhile, put the olives in a small pan, pour in cold water to cover, and bring to a boil, then lower the heat, and simmer for 1 minute. Drain well and cut each into two or three slices. Remove the duckling from the pan and keep warm. Pass the sauce through a food mill or press through a strainer into a clean pan. Mix the potato starch with 2–3 tablespoons of the sauce in a bowl, then stir into the pan with the olives. Place the duckling into the pan and cook for 8–10 minutes. Lift out the duckling from the pan and carve. Arrange the meat on a warm serving dish. Spoon the sauce over the top and serve with triangles of fried bread (see recipe 130).

832 Duck breast

MAGRET DE PATO

- ⅓ cup lard or goose fat or
  3 tablespoons sunflower oil
- 1 large duck breast fillet,
  1 pound 2 ounces

Serves 1–2

Grease a flat griddle pan with lard, goose fat or oil and set over high heat for 10 minutes to preheat. Add the duck fillet, skin side down, and cook for 8 minutes. Turn the fillet, season with salt and pepper, turn again, and cook for 2–3 minutes more, or until done to your liking. Using a very sharp carving knife, cut the fillet diagonally into slices. Collect the cooking juices and serve with any one of several sauces, such as Béarnaise (see recipe 84).

833

Duck salad with pears and raspberries
ENSALADA DE PATO CON PERAS Y FRAMBUESAS

- 1 lettuce
- 3 tablespoons butter
- 2 tablespoons olive oil
- 1 duck breast fillet, thinly sliced
- 2 pears
- ½ cup raspberries
- scant ½ cup pine nuts (optional)

Vinaigrette:
- 3 tablespoons olive oil
- 1 tablespoon raspberry vinegar
- salt and pepper

Serves 4

Put the lettuce leaves into a salad bowl. Melt the butter with the oil in a skillet. Add the slices of duck and cook over medium heat, turning once, for 2–5 minutes, until done to your liking. Remove with a slotted spatula and add to the salad bowl. Make the vinaigrette. Whisk together the oil and vinegar, season to taste with salt and pepper. Peel, core, and thinly slice the pears and place them on the salad. Add the raspberries and the pine nuts, if using, and pour over the salad. Serve immediately.

834

Stuffed squab with apple compote
PICHONES RELLENOS Y SERVIDOS CON COMPOTA DE MANZANA

- 3 squab, 1 pound 2 ounces each
- 12 sausages, skinned
- 5 tablespoons olive oil
- ¾ cup full-bodied red wine
- salt

Apple compote:
- 1 pound 2 ounces apples
- 2 tablespoons sugar
- 1 tablespoon brandy

Serves 6

Lightly season the squab with salt and fill the cavities with the meat from the sausages. Secure the openings with wooden toothpicks. Heat the oil in a large, heavy pan or a Dutch oven. Add the squab and cook over low heat, turning frequently, for about 8 minutes, until evenly browned all over. Pour in the wine and 1 cup water, season with salt, and cook over medium heat for about 40 minutes, until tender and cooked through. Meanwhile, make the apple compote. Peel, core, and dice the apples, put into a pan, and pour 3 tablespoons water over them. Mix well, cover, and cook over low heat for about 20 minutes, until most of the liquid has evaporated. If necessary, remove the lid and cook for a little longer. Stir in the sugar. Heat the brandy in a small pan, ignite it, and carefully pour it into the compote. Mix well, then remove from the heat, and keep warm. When the squab are ready, put the compote into the base of a warm serving dish. Remove and discard the toothpicks and cut the squab in half lengthwise. Put them on top of the compote and arrange the stuffing around the edge of the dish. This dish can be garnished with triangles of fried bread (see recipe 130) if you like. Serve immediately.

Note: Some people like to pass the compote through a food mill before adding the flaming brandy.

835

Squab in sauce

- ½ cup olive oil
- 2 squab, 1 pound 2 ounces each
- 1 onion, very finely chopped
- 1 tablespoon all-purpose flour
- 2 tomatoes,
  peeled, seeded, and diced
- 1 clove garlic
- 1 chicken bouillon cube
- 1 large sprig fresh parsley
- ½ cup white wine
- salt and pepper

Serves 4

Heat the oil in a pan. Add the squab and cook over a low heat, turning frequently, for about 8 minutes, until evenly browned all over. Remove from the pan and set aside. Add the onion to the pan and cook, stirring occasionally, for about 8 minutes, until beginning to brown. Stir in the flour and cook, stirring constantly, for about 5 minutes, until lightly browned, then add the tomato. Crush the garlic, bouillon cube, and parsley in a mortar, or process in a food processor and mix in ⅔ cup water, then add to the pan. Stir well, return the squab to the pan, and season with salt and pepper. Pour in the wine and 2 ¼ cups water, cover, and cook over very low heat for about 2 hours, until the birds are tender and cooked through. Remove the squab from the pan, halve them lengthwise, and place on a warm serving dish. Pass the sauce through a food mill or process in a blender or food processor and spoon it over the squab. Serve immediately, garnished with triangles of fried bread (see recipe 130) if you like.

836

Ostrich

- 2 ¼ pounds ostrich fillet
- 1 quantity Red Wine Sauce
  (see recipe 88) or Shallot Sauce
  for Fried Meat (see recipe 93)

Serves 6–8

Now that it is quite widely farmed, this bird is becoming increasingly popular. It has a good flavor and is very nutritious. Having very little fat, it is a great ally in the fight against cholesterol and weight gain. It can be cooked in the same ways as steak and can also be roasted, but as the steaks are thinner than beef steaks, they will need less time in the oven. A piece of ostrich weighing 2 ¼ pounds will be ready to serve in 17 minutes. It is worth pointing out that ostrich cannot be reheated as it becomes tough. Otherwise it is a delicious meat and compares well with beef.

GAME

Hunting is as old as the human race itself and depictions of hunting appear in even the most primitive art. So far as cooking game is concerned, the first written records of how to prepare it come from the ancient Romans. They developed the technique of hanging the game for a few days before eating it, a method of preparation that continues today in many places.

Furred Game

Traditionally, furred game meant any fur-bearing animal killed for sport, but it has always been an important source of food. Big game includes wild boar, deer, reindeer, elk, moose, and antelope, while small game covers animals such as rabbit and hare. It is becoming increasingly difficult to obtain game directly from hunters. In some places, such as the United States, the sale of hunted game is restricted by law. However, meats that were once found only in the wild are now being raised commercially, and they are available from specialist butchers or Internet purveyors. Game bought this way has the advantage of being bred for tenderness and flavour, and having been hung for the appropriate length of time. In addition, the butcher will prepare it for you. Rabbit can be found in some supermarkets, while meats such as wild boar and vension are avaliable from speciality purveyors or via the internet although the meat is more likely to be from farmed.

Selection and Storage

When buying game, check that there are no blue or greenish discolorations. If you're not planning to eat it immediately, it can be frozen. Otherwise it can be stored for several days in foil in the refrigerator.

How to prepare

Marinades were once used to mask unpleasant flavors, but nowadays they are used to tenderize meat. They also help to keep meat succulent during cooking. This is especially important with furred game, which is often very lean and can dry out easily. In general, game should be cooked until it is well done, but it has become fashionable to serve it almost raw, in a carpaccio for example. If such cases, it is important that the meat came from a reputable supplier, but even so, there is still the risk of infection from foodborne bacteria.

Suggestions

Game is delicious accompanied by both wild and cultivated mushrooms, Brussels sprouts, chestnuts, or even a mixture of the latter two. In this case, cook the sprouts and chestnuts separately, and then sauté them together and season. Marinades should always be made with a base of herbs, onion, carrot, celery, wine, and vinegar. Preparations called "a la cazadora" (hunter-style) are usually based on wild mushrooms, onion, thyme, wine, and bay leaves. From a nutritional viewpoint, game is typically low in fat and high in protein. The meat also contains minerals such as calcium, phosphorus, and iron, as well as B vitamins.

Tricks

• Traditionally, to tenderize game that you or someone you know had shot, you would hang it in a cool place for no more than five or six days, and draw, but not skin it until just before using. Today, many hunters don't hang game at all, both out of concern for foodborne illnesses that come with unrefrigerated meat and because they prefer the flavor.

Rabbit

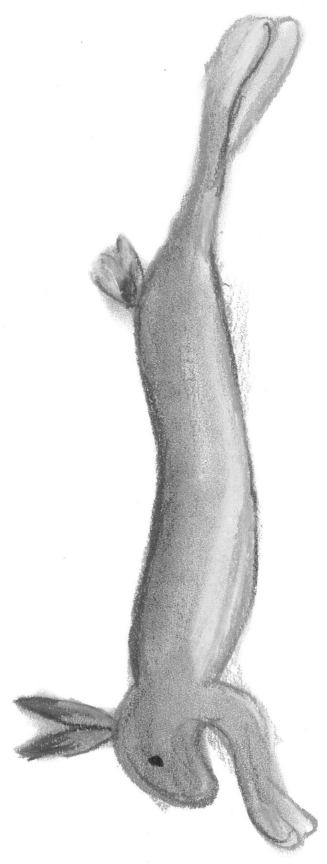

837

Rabbit with liver, pine nut, and bell pepper sauce
CONEJO CON SALSA DE HIGADITOS, PIÑONES Y PIMIENTOS

- 4 tablespoons olive oil
- generous ½ cup
  diced bacon
- 1 small onion, chopped
- 1 large rabbit or 2 small ones,
  cut into parts
- 4 tomatoes,
  peeled, seeded, and chopped
- pinch of mixed dried herbs
- ¼ cup pine nuts
- ½ cup white wine
- 2 rabbit or chicken livers,
  thawed if frozen, trimmed
- 3½ ounces canned red peppers,
  drained and cut into strips
- 1 tablespoon chopped
  fresh parsley
- salt

Serves 4

Heat the oil in a pan. Add the bacon and onion and cook over low heat, stirring occasionally, for 5 minutes, until the onion is soft and translucent. Add the pieces of rabbit and cook over medium heat, turning frequently, for about 10 minutes, until evenly browned all over. Add the tomato, season with salt, and stir in the dried herbs and nearly all the pine nuts. Mix the wine with ½ cup water and pour it over the rabbit. Cover and cook over medium heat for about 45 minutes, until the meat is tender but not falling apart. Put the livers, the remaining pine nuts, and a strip of red bell pepper into a mortar and pound with a pestle, or process in a mini-food processor, then stir into the pan. Add the remaining bell pepper and sprinkle in the parsley. Stir, heat through briefly, and serve.

838

Rabbit stewed with onions, tomatoes, and carrots
CONEJO GUISADO CON CEBOLLITAS, TOMATES Y ZANAHORIAS

- 6 tablespoons olive oil
- 2 small rabbits, 2½ pounds each, cut into parts
- generous ½ cup diced bacon
- 3–4 large, ripe tomatoes, peeled, seeded, and cut into quarters
- 3 carrots, thinly sliced
- ½ teaspoon mixed dried herbs or 1 bouquet garni (1 sprig fresh parsley, 2 bay leaves, 1 sprig fresh thyme, and 1 clove garlic tied together in cheesecloth)
- ½ cup white wine
- 8 shallots
- 1 tablespoon butter
- 3½ ounces canned red peppers, drained and cut into thin strips
- salt

Serves 6–8

Heat the oil in a pan. Add the pieces of rabbit and cook over medium heat, turning frequently, for about 10 minutes, until evenly browned all over. Add the bacon, tomato, and carrot, season with salt, and sprinkle in the dried herbs or add the bouquet garni. Mix well, pour in the wine and ½ cup water, cover the pan, and bring to a boil. Lower the heat and simmer for about 45 minutes, until the rabbit pieces are tender but not falling apart. Meanwhile, put the shallots, butter, and a pinch of salt into a pan. Pour in water to cover and cook for 10–15 minutes. Drain the shallots and add to the pan along with the bell pepper. Stir well, and transfer the rabbit and vegetables to a serving dish, removing the bouquet garni, if used. Serve immediately, garnished with triangles of fried bread (see recipe 130), if you like.

839

Rabbit cooked with white wine
CONEJO GUISADO CON VINO BLANCO

- ½ cup olive oil
- 1 onion, chopped
- 2 small rabbits, 2½ pounds each, cut into parts
- 1 tablespoon all-purpose flour
- ¾ cup dry white wine
- ½ teaspoon mixed dried herbs
- 1 tablespoon chopped fresh parsley
- salt

Serves 6–8

Heat the oil in a pan. Add the onion and cook over low heat, stirring occasionally, for about 5 minutes, until softened and translucent. Add the pieces of rabbit and cook over medium heat, turning frequently, for about 10 minutes, until evenly browned all over. Stir in the flour and cook, stirring constantly, for 2 minutes. Gradually stir in the wine and ½ cup water. Season with salt and add the dried herbs. Cover and cook over medium-low heat for about 45 minutes, until the rabbit pieces are tender and cooked through. Serve immediately, sprinkled with the parsley.

Note: This dish can be served with Mashed Potato (see recipe 230) or macaroni tossed in butter and grated cheese.

840 Rabbit cooked with olives and almonds
CONEJO GUISADO CON ACEITUNAS Y ALMENDRAS

- 1 small rabbit, 2½ pounds,
  cut into pieces
- ⅓ cup all-purpose flour
- 5 tablespoons olive oil
- 3 cloves garlic
- 1 large onion, finely chopped
- ¾ cup white wine
- scant 1 cup olives, pitted
- ½ cup toasted almonds
- salt and pepper

Serves 4

Season the pieces of rabbit with salt, then coat them in the flour, shaking off any excess. Heat the oil in a pan. Add the pieces of rabbit, in batches if necessary, and cook over medium heat, turning frequently, for about 10 minutes, until evenly browned all over. Remove from the pan and set aside. Lightly crush two of the garlic cloves and add to the pan. Cook, stirring occasionally, for a few minutes, until browned, then remove with a slotted spoon. Add the onion to the pan and cook, stirring occasionally, for about 8 minutes, until beginning to brown. Return the rabbit pieces to the pan, pour in the wine, and cook for about 10 minutes, until slightly reduced. Season with pepper and add just enough warm water to cover the rabbit. Cover the pan and cook over medium-low heat for about 30 minutes. Put the olives into another pan, cover with water, and bring to a boil. Lower the heat and cook for 2 minutes, then drain, pat dry, and cut each olive widthwise into two or three slices. Stir the olives into the pan. Pound the almonds with the remaining garlic clove in a mortar, or process in a mini-food processor, then add to the pan. Mix well, re-cover, and cook for 15 minutes more, until the rabbit is tender but not falling apart. Transfer to a warm dish, and pour the sauce over. Garnish with Potato Balls (see recipe 231).

841 Saddle of rabbit roasted with mustard
TRASERO DE CONEJO ASADO CON MOSTAZA

- saddle (loin) of 1 large
  or 2 small rabbits
- 2 tablespoons
  Dijon-style mustard
- 4 tablespoons olive oil
- 2 onions, coarsely chopped
- generous ½ cup diced
  slab bacon
- ½ teaspoon mixed dried herbs
  or 2–3 sprigs fresh thyme
- 4–5 tablespoons boiling water
- 1 cup heavy cream
- 1 tablespoon all-purpose flour
- salt

Serves 4

Preheat the oven to 400°F. Season the rabbit with salt and spread the mustard all over it. Pour the oil into a roasting pan or a deep, ovenproof baking dish and add the rabbit. Put the onion and bacon around it. Sprinkle with the dried herbs or put the thyme on top of the meat and roast, basting with the cooking juices and gradually adding the boiling water, for 30 minutes. Stir in 7 tablespoons of the cream, lower the temperature to 350°F, and cook for 10 minutes more. Combine the flour and remaining cream in a bowl. Remove the rabbit from the roasting pan, carve the meat, and put it onto a warm serving dish. Strain the cooking juices into the flour and cream mixture and mix well. Pour into a pan and heat gently, stirring constantly, for a few minutes. Pour the sauce over the rabbit and serve immediately.

Jugged rabbit
GUISO DE CONEJO CON SALSA DE SANGRE (CIVET)

- 1 small rabbit, about 2½ pounds, cut into pieces
- 2 tablespoons white-wine vinegar
- scant 1 cup diced lean bacon, Canadian bacon or turkey bacon
- 1 onion, chopped
- 2 tablespoons all-purpose flour
- 1 cup beef or veal stock (homemade, canned or made with a bouillon cube)
- salt and pepper

Marinade:
- 1 onion, cut into large pieces
- 2 small carrots, cut into 4 pieces
- 2 cloves garlic
- 1 sprig fresh thyme
- 1 bay leaf
- 2 cloves
- 6 black peppercorns
- 4 cups red wine

Serves 4–6

Place the rabbit pieces in a non-metallic dish and season with salt and pepper. To make the marinade, add the onion, carrot, garlic, thyme, bay leaf, cloves, and peppercorns and pour the wine over all the ingredients. Cover and let marinate overnight in a cool place but not in the refrigerator, stirring three or four times. Drain the pieces of rabbit, reserving the marinade. Heat the bacon in a large pan or a Dutch oven until the fat runs, then remove with a slotted spoon. Add the pieces of rabbit and cook over medium heat, turning frequently, for about 10 minutes, until evenly browned all over. Remove and set aside. Add the onion to the pan and cook over low heat, stirring occasionally, for about 8 minutes, until beginning to brown. Stir in the flour and cook, stirring constantly, for 2 minutes. Return the pieces of rabbit to the pan and strain the reserved marinade over them, reserving the solids. Tie the reserved thyme sprig, bay leaf, and garlic together in a piece of cheesecloth and add to the pan. Cover and bring to a boil, then lower the heat to medium, and cook, stirring occasionally and gradually adding the stock, for 1½ hours. If the sauce is too thin, remove the lid and cook until slightly reduced. Remove and discard the bouquet garni and serve the rabbit in a warm deep dish with the sauce poured over the top.

Rabbit in spiced sauce
CONEJO ESCABECHADO

- 1 cup olive oil
- 1 rabbit, 2½ pounds, cut into parts
- 3 cloves garlic
- 2 bay leaves
- 6 black peppercorns
- ¾ cup white-wine vinegar
- salt

Serves 4–5

Heat the oil in a skillet. Add the pieces of rabbit, in batches, and cook over medium heat, turning frequently, for about 10 minutes, until evenly browned all over. As each batch is cooked, transfer the meat to a large pan. Drain off most of the oil from the skillet, leaving 5–6 tablespoons to cover the base, and reheat. Add the garlic, bay leaves, and peppercorns, remove the skillet from the heat, and stir in the vinegar and ¾ cup water. Pour the sauce over the rabbit in the pan and, if there is not enough to cover it, add more water. Season with salt, cover the pan, and cook over low heat for about 45 minutes, until the rabbit is tender and cooked through. Serve hot or cold.

Hare

The hare is a relative of the rabbit, but is larger, weighing up to 13 or 14 pounds. If hare is not available, substitute rabbit or jack rabbit in the following recipes. Handle hare with caution. It can carry a harmful bacterial infection, so it is best to wear gloves when you prepare it and wash all utensils used with it separately.

844

Jugged hare

GUISO DE LIEBRE CON SALSA DE SANGRE (CIVET)

- 1 young hare,
  3¼–4½ pounds, skinned
- 2 tablespoons
  white-wine vinegar
- scant 1 cup diced lean bacon,
  Canadian bacon or turkey bacon
- 1 onion, chopped
- 2 tablespoons all-purpose flour
- 1 cup beef or veal stock
  (homemade, canned or
  made with a bouillon cube)
- salt and pepper

Marinade:
- 1 onion, cut into large pieces
- 2 small carrots, cut into 4 pieces
- 2 cloves garlic
- 1 sprig fresh thyme
- 1 bay leaf
- 2 cloves
- 6 black peppercorns
- 4 cups red wine

Serves 4–6

Start the preparation the day before you intend to cook the hare. In order for the civet—also known as jugged hare—to turn out well, the hare must be young and it must have blood. It is necessary to reserve the liver, having carefully removed the gall bladder. To collect the blood, pour the vinegar into the belly of the hare and collect the washed-out blood, including any clots, in a bowl. Set aside in the refrigerator. Cut the hare into medium-size pieces, put them into a non-metallic dish, and season with salt and pepper. To make the marinade, add the onion, carrot, garlic, thyme, bay leaf, cloves, and peppercorns and pour the wine over all the ingredients. Cover and let marinate overnight in a cool place but not in the refrigerator, stirring three or four times. Drain the pieces of hare, reserving the marinade. Heat the bacon in a large pan or a Dutch oven until the fat runs, then remove with a slotted spoon. Add the pieces of hare and cook over medium heat, turning frequently, for about 10 minutes, until evenly browned all over. Remove and set aside. Add the onion to the pan and cook over low heat, stirring occasionally, for about 8 minutes, until beginning to brown. Stir in the flour and cook, stirring constantly, for 2 minutes. Return the pieces of hare to the pan and strain the reserved marinade over them, reserving the solids. Tie the reserved thyme sprig, bay leaf, and garlic together in a piece of cheesecloth and add to the pan. Cover and bring to a boil, then lower the heat to medium, and cook, stirring occasionally and gradually adding the stock, for 1½ hours. If the sauce is too thin, remove the lid and cook until slightly reduced. Shortly before serving, pound the liver to a purée in a mortar, or process in a mini-food processor, add the blood and vinegar mixture, and mix in 2 tablespoons of the sauce and heat through. Stir the mixture into the sauce. Remove and discard the bouquet garni and serve the hare in a warm deep dish with the sauce poured over the top.

Note: This stew, which in French is also called a civet, is best when reheated, so save some of the stock in case the sauce is too thick. The liver and the blood should be added only just before serving.

Marinated hare stew

GUISO DE LIEBRE ADOBADA

- 1 hare, about 3¼ pounds,
  cut into parts
- 2 onions
- 1 bouquet garni (1 bay leaf,
  2 sprigs fresh parsley, 1 sprig
  fresh thyme, and 1 clove garlic
  tied together in cheesecloth)
- 2 tablespoons
  white-wine vinegar
- 2¼ cups white wine
- 5 tablespoons olive oil
- generous 1 cup diced bacon
- ⅓ cup all-purpose flour
- 2¼ cups beef or veal stock
  (homemade, canned or
  made with a bouillon cube)
- 1 tablespoon chopped
  fresh parsley
- salt and pepper

Serves 4

The night before you intend to cook the stew, put the pieces of hare into a nonmetallic dish and season with salt and pepper. Cut one of the onions into four pieces and add to the dish along with the bouquet garni, vinegar, and wine. Mix well and turn the pieces of hare to coat, then let marinate in the refrigerator for about 12 hours. The next day, finely chop the remaining onion. Drain the pieces of hare and reserve the marinade. Heat the oil in a large pan, add the bacon and chopped onion, and cook over low heat, stirring occasionally, for about 7 minutes, until just beginning to brown. Coat the pieces of hare lightly in the flour, shaking off any excess, and add to the pan. Cook, stirring constantly, for 2 minutes, then gradually stir in the reserved marinade, a little at a time. Cook, stirring constantly, for 5 minutes, then stir in the stock. Cover the pan with parchment paper that has been cut in a circle to fit snugly inside the pan or a clean dishtowel, then seal tightly with the lid. Cook over low heat, shaking the pan occasionally, for 1½–2 hours, until the hare is tender. Remove and discard the bouquet garni. Put the hare into a warm deep serving dish and pour the sauce over it. Sprinkle with the parsley and serve immediately garnished with triangles of fried bread (see recipe 130) and with macaroni tossed in butter and grated cheese if you like.

846

Saddle of hare roasted with mustard
TRASERO DE LIEBRE ASADO CON MOSTAZA

- 1 saddle of hare
- 2 tablespoons
  Dijon-style mustard
- 4 tablespoons olive oil
- 2 onions, coarsely chopped
- ½ cup diced slab bacon
- ½ teaspoon mixed dried herbs
  or 2–3 sprigs fresh thyme
- 4–5 tablespoons boiling water
- 1 cup heavy cream
- 1 tablespoon all-purpose flour
- salt

Serves 4–6

Preheat the oven to 400°F. Season the hare with salt and spread the mustard all over it. Pour the oil into a roasting pan or a deep, ovenproof baking dish and add the hare. Put the onion and bacon around it. Sprinkle with the dried herbs or put the thyme on top of the meat and roast, basting with the cooking juices and gradually adding the boiling water, for 30 minutes. Stir in 7 tablespoons of the cream, lower the temperature to 350°F, and cook for 10 minutes more. Combine the flour and remaining cream in a bowl. Remove the hare from the roasting pan, carve the meat, and put it onto a warm serving dish. Strain the cooking juices into the flour and cream mixture and mix well. Pour into a pan and heat gently, stirring constantly, for a few minutes. Pour the sauce over the hare and serve immediately.

847

Hare with chestnuts
LIEBRE CON CASTAÑAS

- 1 large hare, 4½ pounds
- 2 tablespoons red-wine vinegar
- generous ½ cup lard
  or 5 tablespoons sunflower oil
- 1 pound 2 ounces onions,
  chopped
- 1 sprig fresh thyme
- ¾ teaspoon black peppercorns
- 5 ounces bulk sausage
- ¾ cup dry sherry
  or other fortified wine
- 1 pound 5 ounces chestnuts
- salt

Serves 4

In order for this stew to turn out well, the hare needs to be young and must have blood. Reserve the liver, having carefully removed and discarded the gall bladder. Pound the liver to a purée in a mortar or process in a mini-food processor. To collect the blood, pour the vinegar into the belly of the hare and collect the washed-out blood, including any clots, in a bowl. Set aside in the refrigerator. Cut the hare into pieces and season with salt. Melt the lard or heat the oil in a stovetop-safe casserole. Add the onion and pieces of hare and cook over medium heat, stirring and turning frequently, for about 10 minutes, until evenly browned all over. Add the thyme and peppercorns and stir well. Cook the bulk sausage in a skillet until lightly browned, then add to the casserole. Pour in the sherry and add just enough water to cover the hare. Cover and cook over medium heat for 45 minutes. Add the chestnuts, re-cover the casserole, and cook for 40 minutes more. Stir 2 tablespoons of the sauce into the blood and vinegar mixture, then stir into the casserole, and cook for another 5 minutes. Taste and adjust the seasoning, if necessary, and serve immediately.

Venison

Tradition says that older deer should be hung for several days or even several weeks. Unlike most other game, deer are skinned and drawn before they are hung. Farmed venison is widely available, sold in oven-ready form, and surprisingly inexpensive. "A la cazadora" (hunter style) is prepared with mushrooms, Brussels sprouts, turnips, and potatoes. Red currant jelly can be served with the sauce. If you want to lard the venison before roasting, thread the strips of fat along the grain of the meat. Venison is suitable for most beef recipes, but it is a good idea to marinate it first. If you buy frozen venison, thaw it in a marinade. Discard this marinade afterward and then put the thawed meat in a fresh marinade.

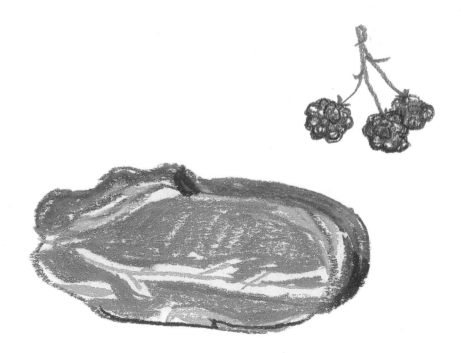

Leg of venison with red currant sauce

PIERNA DE CORZO CON SALSA DE GROSELLA

- 2 bay leaves
- 1 sprig fresh thyme
- 5 tablespoons olive oil
- 6 black peppercorns
- pinch of freshly grated nutmeg
- 1 leg of venison, 5½ pounds
- ⅔ cup hot water
- salt

  Red currant sauce:
- 4 tablespoons olive oil
- 2 shallots, chopped
- 1 small stalk celery, chopped
- 7 ounces boneless
  venison, chopped
- 3 cups full-bodied red wine
- 5 tablespoons brandy
- scant 1 cup red currant jelly
- 1 tablespoon potato starch
- salt and pepper

Serves 8–10

Pound the bay leaves and thyme in a mortar with a pestle or process in a mini-food processor. Add the oil, peppercorns, and nutmeg and pound again. Spread this mixture over the leg of venison, put it into a roasting pan, and let stand in the refrigerator for 3–4 hours. Preheat the oven to 375°F. Roast the venison for 1 hour, then season with salt, and gradually add the hot water. Return to the oven and roast for 30 minutes more, but do not baste the meat. Meanwhile, make the red currant sauce as described in recipe 97. Lift out the leg of venison and carve it like a leg of lamb. Serve immediately, offering the sauce on the side.

Pan-cooked venison

CIERVO O CORZO EN CAZUELA

- 1 venison loin, haunch,
  or tenderloin, 4½ pound
- 6¼ cups milk
- 4 tablespoons brandy
- ¾ cup olive oil
- 1 pound 10 ounces onions,
  chopped
- 1 sprig fresh thyme
- 10 black peppercorns
- 5 cloves
- generous 1 cup game or beef
  stock (homemade, canned
  or made with a bouillon cube)
- ⅔ cup raisins
- 8 prunes, pitted
- 9 ounces shallots
- 1½ tablespoons butter
- 1 teaspoon sugar
- salt and pepper

Serves 8–10

The night before you intend to serve, put the venison into a dish and pour in the milk. Let soak in the refrigerator, turning occasionally, for 12 hours. Drain the venison and put into a pan. Cook over high heat, turning twice, for 5 minutes. Meanwhile, heat the brandy in a small pan. Pour it over the venison and ignite. When the flames have died down, pour in the oil, add the onion, thyme, peppercorns, and cloves, and season with salt. Cook over medium heat, gradually adding the stock, a little at a time. Cover the pan and simmer, turning the meat occasionally, for 1 hour. Add the raisins and prunes, re-cover the pan, and cook for 45 minutes more. Put the shallots, butter, sugar, and a pinch of salt into a pan, add water to cover, and cook for 20 minutes. Remove the pan from the heat and set aside. Lift out the venison, carve it into slices, put it on a serving dish, and keep warm. Pass the sauce through a food mill or process in a blender or food processor. Drain the shallots and place them around the meat. Serve immediately, offering the sauce separately.

Note: Boiled potatoes or Apple Compote (see recipe 973) can also be served with this dish.

Feathered game

Game birds have always featured among the most common dishes in the Spanish kitchen and many different birds are popular throughout the world. They may be prepared in many different ways. As some species that were once hunted have become, or are becoming, endangered, wild birds are now protected and many countries have "closed" seasons when game cannot be shot. "Open" seasons may vary depending on the type of bird, and differ from state to state. The principle, however, is to give breeding birds an opportunity to recoup their numbers. Fresh game may be sold only during the open season, but in some countries frozen game is available throughout the year.

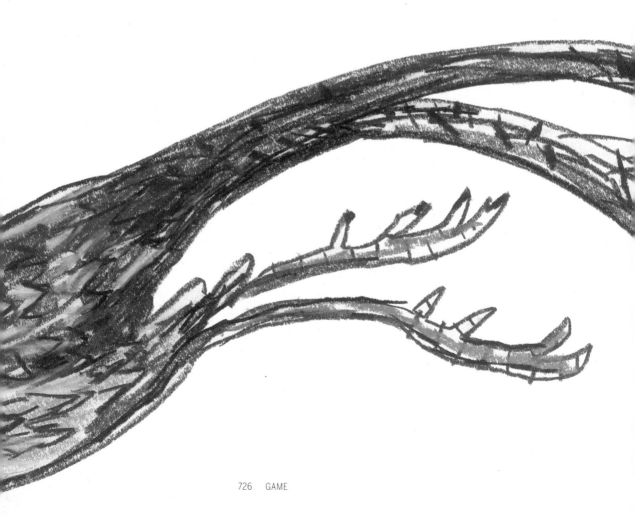

Selection and storage

Shiny feathers are a clear indicator of freshness. Avoid birds with severe injuries, such as broken limbs or badly damaged skin. Although game birds have quite a strong aroma, they should not smell unpleasant. It is best to buy from a specialist butcher or reputable Internet supplier, although in Europe supermarkets now stock increasing quantities of oven-ready game birds in season. Keep game in a cool, dry place rather than in the refrigerator. Nowadays, most feathered game is eaten fresh. Quail and other small birds should be drawn as soon as they are killed. Keep them in a cool place and eat within a couple of days. If you choose to hang your game, partridge, pheasant, and other large birds are better briefly hung. Hang them by the head in a dry, cool place without plucking or drawing them. Allow about 3 days for partridges and 4–5 for pheasants. Wild duck should be plucked and drawn, then let stand for a couple of days before being cooked. Always pluck and draw game birds before freezing them and never keep them in the freezer for more than 6 months.

How to prepare

As game is quite expensive, it is usually served as a main course, but it can also be used to make pâté. This is easy to prepare and the meat is usually mixed with pork or other lean meat and with bacon. A slightly more complicated but absolutely delicious way to prepare game birds is to bone them and stuff them with mushrooms, pistachios, etc. Wrap in cheesecloth and poach in flavored liquid, then put a weight on top to press out all the fat. Remove the cheesecloth and serve in slices. Delicious stuffings can be made by mixing the meat with bread crumbs soaked in milk, egg yolks, mushrooms, and spices.

Partridge

Characteristics and curious facts

The American partridge, valued as a game bird in its native land, has now been introduced to Europe and is highly prized, especially in France. Hunters in the United States tend to use the word partridge fairly casually and often apply it to the related bobwhite quail and ruffed grouse. Both of these can also be used in the following recipes. The ruffed grouse is particularly fine but remember that it is larger than the partridge. These are birds that live in open spaces on moors and arable land. They live in flocks or coveys and have a tendency to burst into flight when flushed. Breeding adults form monogamous pairs in the winter and the hens lay 8–16 eggs in the spring in a rudimentary nest made on the ground. Both parents incubate the eggs and rear the chicks.

How to prepare and cook

Like most game meat, partridge can be hung to make it more tender and tastier. Three to four days are all that is required. Younger birds and hens are usually more tender and can be hung for a shorter time. Partridge has a fine, delicate flavor and a texture similar to that of chicken. It may be roasted, braised, or made into pies and pâtés but however it is cooked, it is always tasty. As it has a high calorie content, is packed with protein, and contains a lot of mineral salts, partridge was not traditionally recommended for people who are overweight, hypertensive, or rheumatic or who have high levels of uric acid. On the other hand, because it contains high-quality protein it is believed to be excellent for children and adolescents, especially during periods of growth and intense physical exercise.

How to pluck and draw

Simply pull the feathers, which will usually come out easily. Hold the bird by the legs and pull out the feathers, starting with the back. Then cut the skin close to the tail end at the back and remove the intestines. Remove the gall bladder from the liver. Singe the remaining feathers over a flame or use cotton wool soaked in alcohol. Cut the legs and the neck toward the middle of their length. Pull the skin toward the wings and then cut the neck down by the wings. Join the skin and sew, or hold, it in place with a wooden toothpick. Rinsing the bird is not recommended, but if you do rinse it, dry it carefully afterward with a clean dishtowel.

Nutrition

Partridge contains all the essential amino acids that form the protein "building blocks" of the body. Partridge has about 22 g protein, 4 g fat and 0.5 g carbohydrate per 100 g meat. Its calorie content is about 130 calories per 100 g / 3 ½ ounces and it is 72 percent water. It has high quantities of B vitamins and is a good source of potassium, calcium, magnesium, and iron.

Partridge meat per 3 ½ oz	Calories (Kcal)	Carbohydrates (g)	Fats (g)	Protein (g)
Raw	130	0.5	4	22
Braised	220	0.5	10	36
Roasted	212	0	7	36

Value for money

Fresh partridge is available during the "open season" in the fall and winter. In some countries, frozen partridge is available all year round. You can buy it from specialist butchers, online or from some supermarkets. It is widely available oven-ready. The best way to guarantee the quality of a partridge is to know its origin and when and where it was shot. Otherwise, you must judge by its appearance—the shininess and cleanness of its plumage, the brightness of its eyes, and the texture of its muscles. Do not buy birds with severe wounds or obvious deterioration resulting from being stored badly.

Selection

The hen is tastier and more tender than the cock. It can be recognized because it does not have a spur shaped like a button on its foot. To tell if it is tender look at the beak—the lower part a young bird's beak is soft.

850

Partridge with sausages and carrots

PERDICES CON SALCHICHAS Y ZANAHORIAS

- **3 partridges**
- **9 sausages**
- **¾ cup olive oil**
- **1 large onion, chopped**
- **1 pound 2 ounces carrots, thickly sliced**
- **1 cup white wine**
- **1 bay leaf**
- **salt**

Serves 6

Season the partridges with salt and put one sausage in the cavity of each bird. Cut lengthwise along the center of each remaining sausage, open it out like a book, and place one sausage on the breast and one on the back of each partridge. Tie the partridges and the sausages with fine kitchen string. Heat the oil in a large pan or a Dutch oven. Add the birds and cook over medium heat, turning frequently, for 8–10 minutes, until evenly browned all over. Remove from the pan and set aside. Add the onion to the pan and cook over low heat, stirring occasionally, for about 8 minutes, until beginning to brown. Add the carrot and cook, stirring occasionally, for 5 minutes. Return the partridges to the pan, pour in the wine and 2 ¼ cups water, and add the bay leaf. Bring to a boil, lower the heat, cover, and simmer for about 1 ¼ hours, until the partridges are tender and cooked through. Check by piercing the thickest part with the tip of a sharp knife; if the juices run clear, the partridge is done. Lift out the partridges from the pan, and remove and discard the string. Remove the sausages from the outside of the birds and put them in a food processor or blender with the sauce and process until smooth. Return the sauce to the pan and set aside. Cut each bird in half lengthwise and place on a warm serving dish. Halve the sausages from the cavities and put them around the dish. Spoon a little of the sauce over the partridges and serve immediately, offering the rest of the sauce in a sauceboat.

Note: Always use good quality butcher's sausages in this recipe. For a particularly attractive presentation, garnish the serving dish with little mounds of Brussels sprouts (1 pound 2 ounces), cooked and then fried in butter, alternated with shallots (1 pound 2 ounces), cooked and then fried in oil until golden brown. The dish could also be garnished with straw potatoes (see recipe 243).

851

Partridge stuffed with raisins and cooked in milk
PERDICES RELLENAS DE PASAS Y GUISADAS CON LECHE

- ¾ cup raisins
- 2 partridges
- 5 tablespoons olive oil
- 1 onion, chopped
- 1½ tablespoons
  all-purpose flour
- 3 tablespoons brandy
- 2¼ cups warm milk
- salt and pepper

Serves 4

Put the raisins in a bowl, pour in warm water to cover, and let soak for 20 minutes, then drain. Season the cavities of the partridges with salt and fill them with the raisins. Secure the openings with wooden toothpicks. Heat the oil in a large pan or a Dutch oven. Add the partridges and cook over medium heat, turning frequently, for 8–10 minutes, until evenly browned all over. Remove the birds from the pan and set aside in a heatproof dish. Add the onion to the pan and cook over low heat, stirring occasionally, for about 5 minutes, until softened and translucent. Stir in the flour and cook, stirring constantly, for about 5 minutes, until light golden brown. Remove the pan from the heat. Heat the brandy in a small pan, ignite it, and carefully pour it over the partridges. When the flames have died down, place the birds into the large pan, together with any cooking juices. Pour in the milk, season, and bring to a boil. Lower the heat, cover, and simmer for 1 hour, until the partridges are tender. Lift out the birds from the pan, cut them in half lengthwise, and put them on a warm serving dish. Pass the sauce through a food mill or process in a food processor and pour it over the birds. Serve with Potato Balls (see recipe 231), if you like.

852

Partridges in cream sauce
PERDICES CON SALSA DE NATA

- 2 partridges
- 4 tablespoons olive oil
- 1 onion, coarsely chopped
- 5 tablespoons white wine
- pinch of mixed dried herbs
  or 1 bouquet garni (2 bay leaves,
  1 sprig fresh thyme, and 1 sprig
  fresh parsley tied together
  in cheesecloth)
- ¼ teaspoon meat extract
  or Maggi Seasoning
- 1 teaspoon potato starch
- juice of ½ lemon
- 1 cup light cream
- salt and pepper

Serves 4

Season the cavities of the partridges with salt. Heat the oil in a large pan or a Dutch oven. Add the birds and the onion and cook over medium heat, turning and stirring frequently, for 8–10 minutes, until the partridges are evenly browned all over. Pour in ¾ cup water and the wine, season with salt and pepper, and add the dried herbs or bouquet garni. Cover and cook over low heat for about 1 hour, until the partridges are tender. Lift out the birds from the pan, cut them in half lengthwise, and put them on a serving dish. Keep warm. Remove and discard the bouquet garni, if used. Pass the sauce through a food mill or process in a blender or food processor. Transfer to a clean pan and stir in the meat extract or Maggi Seasoning. Mix the potato starch with 1 tablespoon water and the lemon juice in a bowl, stir in a little of the sauce, and add to the pan. Heat gently, stirring constantly, then stir in the cream. Heat the sauce for a few minutes more but do not let it boil. Pour the sauce over the partridges and serve.

853

Partridges with grapes

PERDICES CON UVAS

- **3 partridges**
- **⅓ cup lard or 3 tablespoons sunflower oil**
- **3½ cups seedless white grapes, peeled**
- **3 tablespoons olive oil**
- **¾ cup white wine**
- **3 tablespoons brandy**
- **salt and pepper**

Serves 6

Season the cavities of the partridges with salt, spread a little of the lard or sunflower oil over the outsides, then season the outsides with salt. Put a handful of grapes into the cavity of each bird. Heat the olive oil in a large pan or a Dutch oven. Add the birds and cook over medium heat, turning frequently, for 8–10 minutes, until evenly browned all over. Pour in the wine and ¾ cup water, season with pepper, and bring to a boil. Lower the heat, cover, and simmer, turning the birds occasionally, for about 1 hour, until the partridges are tender. Add the remaining grapes. Heat the brandy in a small pan, ignite it, and carefully pour it over the partridges. When the flames have died down, put the lid back on the pan, and cook over medium heat for 5 minutes more. Lift out the partridges from the pan, cut them in half lengthwise, and place on a warm serving dish. Spoon the grapes around them and pour the sauce over them. If there is not very much sauce, stir in a few tablespoons of very hot water.

Note: You can use ¾-inch cubes of sweet ripe melon in place of the grapes, if you like.

854

Stuffed partridge wrapped in cabbage
PERDICES ESTOFADAS Y ENVUELTAS EN REPOLLO

- **2 partridges**
- **1 cup white wine**
- **1 cup olive oil**
- **1 bouquet garni (1 clove garlic, 1 bay leaf, 2 sprigs fresh parsley, and 1 sprig fresh thyme tied together in cheesecloth)**
- **1 onion, cut into 4 wedges**
- **2 ripe tomatoes, seeded and cut into fourths**
- **6–12 Savoy cabbage leaves**
- **1½ tablespoons butter**
- **2 tablespoons sunflower oil**
- **1½ tablespoons all-purpose flour**
- **1 cup milk**
- **scant 1 cup grated gruyere cheese**
- **salt**

Serves 6

Season the cavities of the partridges with salt and put them into a large pan or a Dutch oven with the wine, olive oil, bouquet garni, onion, tomatoes, and a pinch of salt. Pour in 1 cup water, cover, and cook over low heat for about 1¼ hours, until the partridges are tender. Meanwhile, bring a large pan of salted water to a boil. Add the cabbage leaves, pushing them down into the water with a slotted spoon, cover, and cook for about 20 minutes. Drain well and set aside. Lift out the partridges from the pan, reserving the cooking liquid, and carve the meat, like chicken. Divide the meat among the cabbage leaves, then fold over the leaves to form packages. Transfer to an ovenproof baking dish. Discard the bouquet garni from the reserved cooking liquid and pass the liquid through a food mill or process in a blender or food processor, then set aside. Preheat the oven to 400°F. Melt the butter with the sunflower oil in a skillet. Stir in the flour and cook, stirring constantly, for 2 minutes. Gradually stir in the milk, a little at a time. Cook, stirring constantly, for about 6 minutes, until thickened, then add ½ cup of the cooking liquid. Mix well, cook for 5 minutes more, season with salt, and pour the sauce over the cabbage packages. Sprinkle with the gruyere and bake for about 15 minutes, until the topping is golden brown. Serve immediately, straight from the dish.

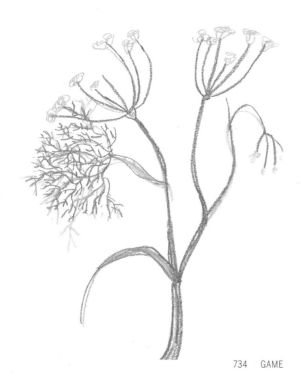

Partridges with orange
PERDICES EN SALSA CON CÁSCARA DE NARANJA

- 5 tablespoons olive oil
- 2 partridges
- 2 large onions, chopped
- 1 heaping tablespoon
  all-purpose flour
- ¾ cup white wine
- 1 chicken bouillon cube
- finely grated zest of 2 oranges
- juice of 1 orange
- salt

Serves 4

Heat the oil in a large pan or a Dutch oven. Add the birds and cook over medium heat, turning frequently, for 8–10 minutes, until evenly browned all over. Remove from the pan and set aside. Add the onion to the pan and cook over low heat, stirring occasionally, for 8 minutes, until beginning to brown. Stir in the flour and cook, stirring constantly, for 5 minutes. Return the partridges to the pan, pour the wine over them, and add warm water to cover. Crumble the bouillon cube, mix with a little hot water, and add to the pan along with the orange zest. Season to taste with salt, cover, and bring to a boil, then lower the heat, and simmer gently for 1¼–1½ hours, until the partridges are tender. Remove the birds from the pan, cut them in half lengthwise, and put on a warm serving dish. Pass the sauce through a food mill or process in a blender or food processor, stir in the orange juice, and season to taste with salt. Spoon a little of the sauce over the meat and serve immediately, offering the rest of the sauce separately. The dish can be served with macaroni tossed in butter and grated cheese, Mashed Potato (see recipe 230), or Brussels sprouts sautéed in butter.

Note: If the sauce becomes too thin when the orange juice is added, mix in 1 teaspoon potato starch dissolved in 1 tablespoon water. Cook the sauce over low heat, stirring constantly, for 2–3 minutes, then serve as above.

856

Partridges with cabbage

PERDICES CON REPOLLO

- **2 partridges**
- **4 slices of lean bacon,**
  Canadian bacon or turkey bacon
- **3 tablespoons olive oil**
- **1 tablespoon all-purpose flour**
- **pinch of mixed dried herbs**
  or 1 bouquet garni (1 clove garlic,
  2 sprigs fresh parsley, 1 sprig
  fresh thyme, and 1 bay leaf tied
  together in cheesecloth)
- **5 ounces slab bacon,**
  cut into strips
- **1 Savoy cabbage, shredded**
- **½ teaspoon meat extract**
  or Maggi Seasoning
- **salt**

Serves 4

Season the cavities of the partridges with salt, put a slice of lean bacon over the breast and back of each one, and tie in place with fine kitchen string. Heat the oil in a large pan or a Dutch oven. Add the birds and cook over medium heat, turning frequently, for 8–10 minutes, until evenly browned all over. Sprinkle the flour into the pan and pour in warm water to come halfway up the partridges. Add the dried herbs or bouquet garni and season with salt. Bring to a boil, lower the heat to medium, cover, and cook for about 1¼ hours. Bring a pan of salted water to a boil and add the slab bacon. When it comes back to a boil, add the cabbage, pushing it down into the water with a slotted spoon, and cook for 20 minutes. Drain well and place the cabbage and bacon around the partridges. Cook for 10 minutes more, until the partridges are tender. Lift the birds out of the pan, and remove and discard the bacon and string. Cut the partridges in half lengthwise, and put on a warm serving dish. Remove and discard the bouquet garni, if used. Drain the cabbage and bacon, reserving the cooking liquid, and place around the partridges. If the cooking liquid is too thin, cook, uncovered, over high heat, until slightly reduced. Strain, stir in the meat extract or Maggi Seasoning, and serve in a sauceboat with the partridges.

Partridges cooked with hot vinegar

PERDICES GUISADAS CON VINAGRE CALIENTE

- 3 small partridges
- generous ½ cup lard
  or ¾ cup olive oil
- 1 large onion, chopped
- 3 carrots, sliced
- ¾ cup white wine
- 5 tablespoons
  white-wine vinegar
- 1 chicken bouillon cube
- pinch of mixed dried herbs
  or 1 bouquet garni (1 sprig fresh
  thyme, 2 bay leaves, 1 sprig fresh
  parsley, and 1 clove garlic tied
  together in cheesecloth)
- salt

Serves 6

Season the cavities of the partridges with salt. Melt the lard or heat the oil in a large pan or a Dutch oven. Add the partridges and cook over medium heat, turning frequently, for 8–10 minutes, until evenly browned all over. Remove from the pan and set aside. Add the onion to the pan and cook over low heat, stirring occasionally, for about 5 minutes, until softened and translucent. Add the carrot and cook, stirring occasionally, for 10 minutes more. Return the partridges to the pan and pour in the wine and vinegar. Dissolve the bouillon cube in a little water in a bowl, add to the pan, and pour in just enough hot water to cover the birds completely. Add the dried herbs or bouquet garni, season with salt, cover, and cook over low heat for about 1 ¼ hours, until the partridges are tender. Lift out the birds from the pan, cut them in half lengthwise, and put on a warm serving dish. Remove and discard the bouquet garni, if used. Pass the sauce through a food mill or process in a blender or food processor and pour over the partridges. Serve immediately, garnished with triangles of fried bread (see recipe 130), if you like.

Pickled partridges

PERDICES ESCABECHADAS

- **3 small partridges**
- **¾ cup olive oil**
- **1 onion, coarsely chopped**
- **3 carrots, sliced**
- **1 bouquet garni**
  (1 sprig fresh thyme, 2 bay
  leaves, 1 sprig fresh parsley,
  1 stalk celery, and 2 cloves garlic
  tied together in cheesecloth)
- **6 black peppercorns**
- **¾ cup white wine**
- **¾ cup white-wine vinegar**
- **salt**

Serves 6

Season the cavities of the partridges with salt. Heat the oil in a large pan or a Dutch oven. Add the birds and cook over medium heat, turning frequently, for 8–10 minutes, until evenly browned all over. Remove them from the pan and set aside. Drain off nearly all the oil from the pan, leaving just enough to cover the base. Return the birds to the pan, add the onion, carrot, bouquet garni, and peppercorns, and cook for 5 minutes. Pour in the wine and vinegar, cover, and cook over medium heat for 10 minutes. Pour in just enough water to cover the partridges, season with salt, re-cover the pan, lower the heat, and cook for about 1 ½ hours, until the partridges are tender. Remove the pan from the heat and let the birds cool in their sauce. If they are to be eaten immediately, lift them out when cold, cut in half lengthwise, and put on a serving dish. Remove and discard the bouquet garni and pass the sauce through a food mill or process in a blender or food processor. Spoon it over the partridges and serve. If you do not plan to eat them right away, transfer the whole partridges to an earthenware or glass container. Remove and discard the bouquet garni. Ladle in the sauce to cover the partridges completely. Add a few tablespoons of olive oil and seal the container. Store in a cool place. When serving, cut the partridges in half lengthwise, garnish with the slices of carrot, and strain the sauce before pouring it over the birds. In both cases, serve cold.

Woodcock

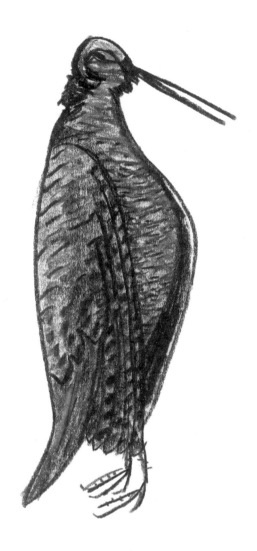

How to prepare

Allow 1 woodcock per 2–3 servings. If you hang them, woodcock
should be hung by their feet, without plucking, for 4–5 days in the
open air in a cool, but not damp place. When ready to cook, pluck
them, remove the eyes and gizzards, but do not draw them. The
innards, called the "trail", may be spread on toast and eaten. Singe
the woodcock over a flame to remove any remaining feathers and
season inside and out with salt and pepper. They are then ready to be
cooked as preferred. Like most game birds, woodcock are available
oven-ready. However, they are rarely sold in any form by commercial
butchers. You are more likely to obtain them from friends or acquaint-
ances who shoot or sometimes, from online sources.

859

Pan-cooked woodcock
BECADAS EN CACEROLA

- 3 woodcock
- ⅓ cup lard or 4–5 tablespoons olive oil
- 6 slices of bacon, diced
- 1 cup sherry or other sweet fortified wine
- 3–4 tablespoons boiling water
- salt and pepper

Serves 6

Season the woodcock inside and out with salt and pepper. Melt the lard or heat the oil in a large pan or a Dutch oven. Add the woodcock and bacon and cook over medium-high heat, stirring and turning frequently, for about 8 minutes, until evenly browned all over. Cover and cook, turning occasionally, over medium heat for 10 minutes. Pour in the sherry, re-cover, and cook for 10–15 minutes more, until the birds are tender. Lift out the birds from the pan and cut them in half lengthwise. Remove and reserve the intestines. Place the birds on a serving dish and keep warm. Stir the boiling water into the sauce and cook, stirring and scraping up any bits on the base of the pan. Chop the intestines, if using, and stir into the sauce. Pass the sauce through a food mill, pressing down well, or process in a blender or food processor. Pour it over the woodcock and serve with triangles of fried bread (see recipe 130) or Potato Balls (see recipe 231).

860

Woodcock with cognac
BECADAS CON COÑAC

- 3 woodcock
- generous ½ cup lard or 5 tablespoons sunflower oil
- ¾ cup cognac or other brandy
- juice of ½ lemon
- 1 tablespoon chopped fresh parsley
- salt and pepper

Serves 6

Preheat the oven to 475°F. Season the woodcock inside and out with salt and spread some of the lard or brush some of the oil over them. Divide the remaining lard or oil among the cavities and put the birds into a roasting pan. Roast for 12–15 minutes, until tender. Remove the birds from the roasting pan, cut off the breasts and legs, and put on a serving dish. Keep warm. Carefully collect the carving juices. Chop the carcass and intestines with a heavy knife or a cleaver. Heat the brandy in a small pan and ignite it. When the flames have died down, add the chopped carcass and the carving juices and season with salt and pepper. Cook over high heat, stirring constantly, for 10 minutes, then pass the sauce through a food mill, pressing down well, or process in a blender or food processor. Taste and adjust the seasoning if necessary, stir in the lemon juice and parsley, and pour the sauce over the woodcock. Serve with triangles of fried bread (see recipe 130) or Potato Balls (see recipe 231).

Quail

There are many species of New World quails so, unlike their European equivalent, they are popular game birds and not endangered. Nevertheless, some types of quail are also farmed and are therefore available all year round. Quails are small birds, 5–7 ounces, and their meat has a delicious flavor. Quails' eggs are also used in cooking. Fresh and frozen oven-ready quail are widely available. Depending on their size, allow 1–2 per serving.

861

Stewed quail
CODORNICES ESTOFADAS

- **4 quail**
- **1 large onion, finely chopped**
- **2 carrots, sliced**
- **1 tomato,
  peeled, seeded, and chopped**
- **3 cloves garlic**
- **1 bouquet garni
  (1 fresh sprig marjoram, 1 bay
  leaf, and 1 sprig fresh parsley
  tied together in cheesecloth)**
- **1 cup white wine**
- **½ chicken or game bouillon cube
  dissolved in 1 cup water**
- **1 cup olive oil**
- **salt and pepper**
  Serves 4

Season the cavities of the quail with salt. Put them into a pan with the onion, carrot, tomato, garlic, and bouquet garni, pour in the wine, bouillon cube mixture, and olive oil, and bring to a boil. Lower the heat and simmer for 1 hour, until the birds are tender. Transfer the quail to a warm serving dish. Remove and discard the bouquet garni and garlic and process the sauce in a food processor or blender or food processor. Pour the sauce over the quail and serve.

862

Roast quail
CODORNICES ASADAS

- **6 grape leaves**
- **6 quail**
- **⅓ cup lard**
- **6 thin slices of bacon**
- **6 slices of fried bread
  (see recipe 130)**
- **dressed watercress or augula**
- **salt**
  Serves 6

If using brined grape leaves, soak them in hot water for 20 minutes, then drain, rinse well, and pat dry. You do not need to soak fresh grape leaves. Preheat the oven to 425°F. Season the cavities of the quail with salt. Spread a little of the lard on the grape leaves and stick them onto the birds' breasts. Put the bacon over the birds' backs and spread with the remaining lard. Truss with fine kitchen string, put into a roasting pan, and roast for 15–20 minutes, until tender. Lift out the quail from the roasting pan, remove and discard the string and grape leaves, and reserve the bacon. Place each quail on a slice of fried bread and top with a bacon slice. Stir 3–4 tablespoons hot water into the cooking juices and cook over medium heat, scraping up any bits from the base of the roasting pan, for a few minutes. Pour the sauce over the quail and serve immediately, garnished with the watercress or arugula.

Quail in potato nests
CODORNICES EN NIDO DE PATATAS PAJA

- **6 quail**
- **⅓ cup lard**
- **6 thin slices of bacon**
- **6 slices of fried bread
  (see recipe 130)**
- **1 pound 2 ounces potatoes,
  thinly sliced then cut into
  fine straws**
- **sunflower oil, for deep frying**
- **salt**

  Serves 6

Preheat the oven to 425°F. Season the cavities of the quail with salt. Put the bacon over the birds' backs and spread with a little of the lard. Truss with fine kitchen string, put into a roasting pan and roast for 15–20 minutes, until tender. Meanwhile, heat the sunflower oil in a deep-fryer or pan to 350–375°F or until a cube of day-old bread browns in 30 seconds. Divide the potato straws into 6 equal amounts. Spread one amount over the base and slightly up the sides of a wire basket and lower into the hot oil. Cook for about 2 minutes, until golden brown, then remove from the oil and drain. Repeat with the remaining potato straws. Put a roasted quail, breast uppermost, in each potato nest, top with the bacon. Stir 3–4 tablespoons hot water into the roasting pan and cook over medium heat, scraping up any bits from the base of the roasting pan, for a few minutes. Pour into a sauceboat and serve immediately with the quail in potato nests.

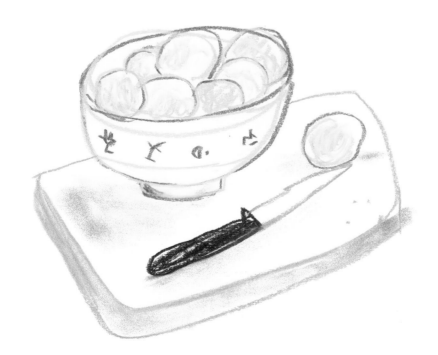

864

Pan-cooked quail

CODORNICES EN CACEROLA

- 6 grape leaves
- 6 quail
- ⅓ cup pork lard
- 6 thin slices of bacon
- 3 tablespoons olive oil
- 6 slices of fried bread
  (see recipe 130)
- salt

Serves 6

If using brined grape leaves, soak them in hot water for 20 minutes, then drain, rinse well, and pat dry. You do not need to soak fresh grape leaves. Season the cavities of the quail with salt. Spread a little of the lard on the grape leaves and stick them onto the birds' breasts. Put .the bacon over the birds' backs and spread with the remaining lard. Truss with fine kitchen string. Heat the oil in a heavy pan or a Dutch oven. Add the quail and cook over medium heat, turning frequently, for about 8 minutes, until evenly browned all over. Lower the heat and cook, uncovered, over medium heat for 15–20 minutes, until tender. Lift out the quail, remove and discard the string, bacon, and grape leaves, and put each bird on a slice of the fried bread. Put on a serving dish and keep warm. Stir in 4–5 tablespoons hot water into the pan and cook over medium heat, stirring and scraping up any bits from the base, for a few minutes, then serve the sauce in a sauceboat or poured over the quail.

865

Quail in white-wine sauce

CODORNICES EN SALSA

- 5 tablespoons olive oil
- 12 quail
- 3 large onions, finely chopped
- ¾ cup game or chicken stock
  (homemade, canned or
  made with a bouillon cube)
- 1 teaspoon mustard powder
- ¾ cup white wine
- pinch of freshly grated nutmeg
- pinch of ground cinnamon
- salt and pepper

Serves 6

Heat the oil in a pan. Add the quail and cook over medium heat, turning frequently, for about 5 minutes but do not let them brown. Remove from the pan and set aside. Add the onion to the pan and cook over low heat, stirring occasionally, for about 5 minutes, until softened and translucent. Put the quail on top of the onion, pressing them down well, and pour in the stock. Stir the mustard into the wine and pour into the pan, then season with salt and pepper, and sprinkle in the nutmeg and cinnamon. Cover and bring to a boil, then lower the heat, and simmer gently for 1–2 hours, until the birds are tender. Put the quail on a warm serving dish and spoon the sauce over them. Serve immediately with triangles of fried bread (see recipe 130).

Braised quail

CODORNICES GUISADAS

- **5 tablespoons olive oil**
- **1 large onion, chopped**
- **6 fat quail or 12 small quail**
- **⅓ cup all-purpose flour**
- **pinch of freshly grated nutmeg**
- **pinch of ground cinnamon**
- **1½–2¼ cups white wine**
- **1 bay leaf**
- **1 sprig fresh thyme**
- **salt and pepper**

Serves 6

Heat the oil in a pan. Add the onion and cook over low heat, stirring occasionally, for about 8 minutes, until beginning to brown. Coat the quail in the flour, shaking off any excess, put them into the pan, and cook over medium heat, turning frequently, for about 8 minutes, until evenly browned all over. Season with salt and pepper, sprinkle in the nutmeg and cinnamon, and pour in enough wine to half cover the birds. Add the bay leaf and thyme, cover the pan with parchment paper that has been cut in a circle to fit snugly inside the pan, and put the lid on top. Cook over medium heat, shaking the pan occasionally, for about 25 minutes, until the quail are tender. Lift out the birds and put them on a warm serving dish. Remove and discard the bay leaf and thyme sprig, pass the sauce through a food mill or process in a food processor or blender, and spoon it over the quail. Serve immediately, garnished with triangles of fried bread (see recipe 130).

Pheasant

Selection

Nowadays pheasants are widely available and relatively inexpensive. The best ones are about 12 months old and the hen pheasant has a finer flavor and texture than the cock pheasant, although he has the more colorful plumage. A hen and cock are often sold in pairs, called a brace. For tender, tasty meat the pheasant should be hung for at least 3 days and up to 2 weeks in cold weather. Farm-raised birds do not need to be hung. From a dietary point of view, the meat has some similarities to chicken and has about 200 calories per 3 ½ ounces. Young birds, weighing between 1 ¾ pounds and 2 ¼ pounds, can be roasted and will need to cook for 45–60 minutes. Older birds are better braised and most chicken recipes work well with pheasant.

How to clean

Like most other game birds, pheasants are widely available oven-ready. If you do have to pluck and draw a bird, chill it in the refrigerator for several hours as this will make it easier. First, remove the biggest feathers on the wings, twisting them, then pluck the body, neck, and wings in that order. Remove the entrails as you would a chicken and season the cavity with salt. Truss securely with fine kitchen string, especially if the bird is to be roasted.

867

Pheasant with apples

FAISAN CON MANZANAS

- 1 pheasant
- generous ½ cup goose fat or scant ½ cup butter
- 6 apples
- ¾ cup light cream
- ½ cup apple liqueur or applejack
- salt and pepper

Serves 4

Preheat the oven to 450°F. Season the pheasant inside and out with salt and truss with fine kitchen string. Melt half the goose fat or butter in a skillet. Add the pheasant and cook over medium heat, turning frequently, for about 10 minutes, until evenly browned all over. Meanwhile, peel, core, and slice the apples, season with salt and pepper, and make a thick layer of about half of them in the base of an ovenproof casserole. Dot with the remaining goose fat or butter and put the pheasant on top. Put the remaining apples around the bird, season with salt and pepper, cover, and roast for about 25 minutes, or until the pheasant is tender. Just before serving, gently heat the cream and apple liqueur or applejack in a pan and pour over the pheasant.

868

Roast pheasant
FAISANES O POULARDAS ASADOS

- 1 pheasant, 4 ½ pounds
- 4 thin slices of fatty bacon
- generous ½ cup lard
  or 5 tablespoons sunflower oil
- scant 2 cups game or chicken
  stock (homemade, canned
  or made with bouillon cubes)
- generous ½ cup diced
  Serrano ham or prosciutto
- 2 carrots, sliced
- 1 tablespoon bread crumbs
- scant 1 cup drained canned peas
- salt

Serves 4

Preheat the oven to 350°F. Season the pheasant inside and out with salt, cover the back and breast with the bacon, and truss with fine kitchen string. Spread the lard or brush the oil over the bird and put it into a roasting pan. Roast, turning occasionally, for 45 minutes. Lift out the pheasant, remove and discard the string and bacon, and carve the bird, collecting the carving juices. Put the meat into a pan with the carving juices, pour in the stock, and add the ham, carrot, and bread crumbs. Cook over medium-low heat for about 30 minutes, until the carrot is tender. Add the peas and cook for 5–6 minutes more, until heated through. Serve immediately.

Note: This dish can be garnished with raw mushroom salad (see recipe 476) or with artichoke hearts fried in a little oil and sprinkled with chopped fresh parsley.

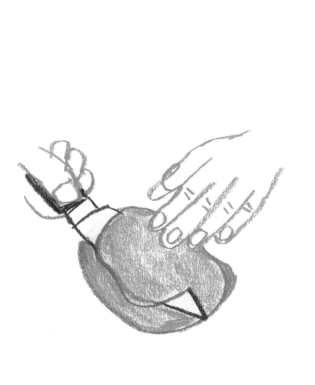

869

Meat and chicken liver terrine
PASTEL-TERRINA DE CARNES VARIADAS E HIGADITOS DE POLLO

- 9 ounces chicken livers, thawed if frozen, trimmed
- 14 ounces skinless boneless chicken breast halves
- 5 ounces bacon
- 12 ounces boneless pork
- 3 eggs, lightly beaten
- 4 tablespoons brandy
- ½ cup heavy cream
- 11 ounces lean bacon, such as Canadian bacon or turkey bacon, thinly sliced
- 6 cloves
- 1 sprig fresh thyme
- 2 bay leaves
- salt and pepper

Serves 8

Preheat the oven to 350°F. Chop the chicken livers, chicken breasts, bacon, and pork and combine in a bowl. Stir in the eggs and brandy. Whisk the cream in another bowl with an electric mixer, then add to the meat mixture. Season with salt and pepper and mix well. Cover the base and sides of a terrine mold with two-thirds of the slices of bacon. Fill the terrine mold with the meat mixture, pressing it down with a wooden spoon. Cover with the remaining slices of bacon and push the cloves into them, then put the thyme and the bay leaves on top. Put the lid on the terrine mold, place it in a roasting pan, and pour in hot water to come about halfway up the sides. Bake for 1½ hours, then turn off the oven, and leave the terrine inside until it has cooled. Remove the terrine mold from the oven, take off the lid, cover with aluminum foil, and put something heavy on top, such as an iron. Leave in the refrigerator for 3–4 hours. To serve, discard the thyme, bay leaves, cloves, and the top layer of bacon. Invert the terrine onto a serving dish and remove the remaining slices of bacon. Cut into slices and serve cold, garnished with watercress or lettuce.

Hare terrine

PASTEL-TERRINA DE LIEBRE

- 1 large boneless saddle of hare or rabbit
- 14 ounces lean boneless pork blade shoulder
- 14 ounces boneless breast or leg of veal
- 5 ounces bacon
- 12 ounces lean bacon, such as Canadian bacon or turkey bacon, thinly sliced
- pinch of freshly grated nutmeg
- pinch of dried tarragon
- 5 tablespoons brandy
- 1 sprig fresh thyme
- salt and pepper

Serves 8–10

Preheat the oven to 350°F. Cut the saddle of hare, pork, veal, and bacon into strips about ⅝ inch wide, keeping each type of meat separate. Line the base and the sides of a terrine mold with two-thirds of the slices of lean bacon. Make layers of veal, hare, and pork in the terrine, seasoning each layer with salt, pepper, nutmeg, and tarragon and separating the layers with strips of fatty bacon. When all the meat has been used up, pour the brandy over the top, cover with the remaining slices of bacon, and put the thyme on top. If you have any bones from the saddle of hare, you can add some of them for extra flavor. Cover the terrine mold, place it into a roasting pan, and pour in hot water to come about halfway up the sides. Bake for 3 hours. Remove the terrine from the roasting pan and let cool. Take off the lid, remove and discard the bones, if used, and the thyme, and cover the terrine with aluminum foil. Place something heavy on top, such as an iron, and leave in the refrigerator for 6–8 hours. This dish is served in the terrine mold after removing the covering of bacon.

871

Liver terrine
PASTEL-TERRINA DE HÍGADO DE CERDO

- 12 ounces lean bacon, such as Canadian bacon, thinly sliced
- 1 pound 2 ounces pork liver, trimmed and finely chopped
- 1 pound 2 ounces ground pork
- pinch of mixed dried herbs
- 2 eggs, lightly beaten
- 4 tablespoons brandy
- salt and pepper

Serves 8–10

Preheat the oven to 325°F. Line the base and sides of a terrine mold with two-thirds of the bacon. Combine the liver, ground pork, and dried herbs in a bowl and season with salt. Stir in the eggs and brandy and spoon the mixture into the terrine mold, pressing down well with a wooden spoon. Cover the top with the remaining slices of bacon and put the lid on the terrine. Put the terrine mold into a roasting pan and pour in hot water to come about halfway up the sides. Bake for 3 hours, then remove from the roasting pan, and let stand in the refrigerator for 48 hours before serving. This dish is usually served in the terrine mold, after removing the top covering of bacon.

872

Veal loaf
PASTEL DE TERNERA

- 2 cups bread crumbs
- scant 1 cup boiling milk
- 1 pound 2 ounces boneless veal shoulder
- 5 ounces boneless ham hock
- 1²⁄₃ cups finely chopped mushrooms
- 1 boneless veal breast, 1 pound 10 oz
- 5 ounces Serrano ham or prosciutto, in a single piece
- 3 tablespoons olive oil
- 1 onion, chopped
- ½ calf's foot, cut into pieces
- 1 teaspoon mixed dried herbs or 1 bouquet garni (2 bay leaves, 1 sprig fresh thyme, 1 sprig fresh parsley, and 1 clove garlic tied together in cheesecloth)
- 1 cup white wine
- salt and pepper

Serves 8–10

Put the bread crumbs into a bowl, pour in the boiling milk, and let soak. Meanwhile, grind the veal shoulder and ham hock together with a meat grinder or in a food processor or blender. Combine the ground meat, bread crumbs (if they are too liquid, squeeze gently), and mushrooms in a bowl and season with salt and pepper. Spread this mixture evenly over the veal breast. Cut the Serrano ham or proscuitto into strips about ¼ inch wide and arrange them over the meat. Roll up the veal breast and wrap it carefully in cheesecloth. Tie the ends with kitchen string and secure the center of the cheesecloth with a wooden toothpick. Heat the oil in a large pan. Add the onion and cook over low heat, stirring occasionally, for 7–8 minutes, until beginning to brown. Add the calf's foot and cook, turning occasionally, for about 8 minutes, until lightly browned. Add the dried herbs or bouquet garni and pour in the wine. Add the rolled veal breast, pour in water to cover, and season with salt. Cover and bring to a boil, then lower the heat, and simmer for 3 hours. Remove the rolled veal breast from the pan and drain it. Reserve the cooking liquid. Put the rolled meat on a surface, still wrapped in cheesecloth, and place something heavy on top until it has cooled completely. Remove the cheesecloth, wrap the meat in aluminum foil, and chill in the refrigerator. Meanwhile, bring the cooking liquid back to a boil, then simmer, uncovered, for 1 hour. Strain into a deep dish and chill in the refrigerator until set, then chop. To serve, cut the meat into slices, place on a serving dish, and garnish with lettuce, if you like.

Chicken, ham, and veal loaf

PASTEL DE POLLO, JAMÓN Y TERNERA

- ½ cup lard,
  plus extra for greasing
- 14 ounces ground veal
- 1 large skinless boneless chicken
  breast halves, coarsely chopped
- 1 tablespoon bread crumbs
- 2 eggs, lightly beaten
- 5 tablespoons sherry or
  other sweet fortified wine
- 5 ounces Serrano ham or
  prosciutto, cut into thin strips
- salt and pepper

Serves 4–6

Preheat the oven to 350°F. Grease a loaf pan with lard. Combine the lard, veal, chicken, bread crumbs, eggs, and sherry in a bowl and season with salt and pepper. Make alternate layers of the meat mixture and strips of ham in the prepared pan. Cover the pan with aluminum foil, put it into a roasting pan, and pour in boiling water to come about halfway up the sides. Bake for 2 hours. Remove the loaf pan from the roasting pan and let cool slightly, then place something heavy on top, such as an iron, until the loaf has cooled completely. To serve, run a knife around the edge of the loaf pan and turn out onto a serving dish. Garnish with watercress or lettuce, if you like, and serve.

874 Chicken and ham terrine

TERRINA DE POLLO Y JAMÓN

- 1 chicken, 2½ pounds,
  giblets reserved
- 4 tablespoons olive oil
- 1 small onion, cut into 4 wedges
- scant 1 cup finely chopped
  Serrano ham or prosciutto
- 3½ ounces thinly sliced bacon
- 2 tablespoons brandy
- 1 bay leaf
- 1 sprig fresh thyme
- salt and pepper

  Gelatin stock:
- 1 calf's foot, cut into pieces
- 2 carrots, chopped
- 1 leek, trimmed and rinsed well
- 2 stalks celery
- 1 bay leaf
- 5 tablespoons white wine
- salt

  Serves 8–10

First, make the stock. Pour 13 cups water into a pan and add the calf's foot, carrot, leek, celery, bay leaf, and the chicken giblets. Pour in the wine, season with salt, and bring to a boil. Lower the heat to medium and cook for 1½ hours. Remove the pan from the heat and strain the liquid into a bowl. Discard the contents of the strainer. Let the liquid cool completely and if a layer of fat forms on top, remove it with a spoon. Cut the chicken in half lengthwise. Heat the oil in a pan. Add the chicken and onion, season with salt, and cook, turning the chicken occasionally, for 20 minutes. Remove the pan from the heat and let cool. Remove the skin from the chicken, cut the meat into very small pieces, and mix it with the ham in a bowl. Preheat the oven to 350°F. Line the base of a terrine mold with the bacon, then make a layer of the chicken and ham mixture, and pour in a little of the stock. Continue making layers of chicken and ham, followed by more stock, until the terrine mold is full. Pour in the brandy and put the bay leaf and thyme sprig on top. Put the lid on the terrine, place it in a roasting pan, and pour in boiling water to come about halfway up the sides. Bake for 1 hour. Remove the terrine from the roasting pan, take off the lid, and let cool. If necessary, add a little more stock. Leave the terrine in the refrigerator for at least 6 hours, until completely set. Remove and discard the bay leaf and thyme. Turn the terrine out onto a serving dish, and remove and discard the bacon. The terrine can be served with a salad.

Pork loaf

PASTEL DE CABEZA DE CERDO

- **1 onion**
- **6 cloves**
- **olive oil, for drizzling**
- **2 carrots, halved lengthwise**
- **1 bay leaf**
- **1 sprig fresh thyme**
- **1 small nutmeg, halved**
- **9 ounces lean pork**
- **pig's feet, ears, and snout,**
  2¼ pounds total weight
- **5 tablespoons white wine**
- **salt and pepper**

Serves 8–10

Preheat the oven to 350°F. Stud the onion with the cloves and put into a small, ovenproof baking dish. Drizzle with oil and roast for 30 minutes. Remove from the oven and set aside. Cut the carrots in half widthwise and tie the bay leaf and thyme sprig together with fine kitchen string, then put them into a pan with the onion, nutmeg and pork. Singe the pig's feet, ear, and snout, if necessary, wash thoroughly, and add to the pan. Season with salt and pepper and pour in the wine and just enough water to cover the ingredients completely. Bring to a boil over high heat, then lower the heat, cover, and simmer gently for 4 hours. Remove the pan from the heat and let cool. Lift out the pork and dice finely. Lift out the feet, cut the meat off the bones, and dice finely. Dice the snout and cut the ears into very thin strips with kitchen scissors. Mix all the meats together. Strain the stock into a bowl and pour a little into a loaf pan, then add the meat mixture, and cover it with more stock. Stir well with a fork so that the stock penetrates and is evenly distributed. Leave in the refrigerator until set. To serve, run the blade of a knife around the edge of the pan, turn the loaf out onto a serving dish, and garnish with watercress or escarole if you like.

Note: Pig's feet are widely available, but the snout and ears are less commonly seen and may have to be ordered if you want to make the authentic dish. However, as pig's feet are very gelatinous, you could simply use 2¼ pounds feet.

876

Chicken liver mold
GELATINA DE HIGADITOS DE POLLO

- 1 small onion
- 2 cloves
- olive oil, for drizzling
- 1 calf's foot
- 2 veal knuckles
- 1 small leek,
  trimmed and rinsed well
- 1 celery stalk
- 2 carrots, cut into short lengths
- ¾ cup sherry or
  other sweet fortified wine
- 1 pound 2 ounces chicken livers,
  thawed if frozen, trimmed and
  coarsely chopped
- pepper

Serves 4–6

Preheat the oven to 350°F. Stud the onion with the cloves and put it into a small, ovenproof baking dish. Drizzle with oil and roast for 30 minutes. Remove from the oven and set aside. Put the calf's foot, veal knuckles, onion, leek, celery, and carrot into a large pan and pour in water to cover. Bring to a boil and skim off any froth that rises to the surface, then lower the heat, and simmer gently for 2 ½ – 3 hours. Strain the stock into a clean pan, discarding the contents of the strainer. Add the sherry and chicken livers to the stock in the pan, season to taste with pepper, and cook for 10 minutes more. Strain a layer of stock about ¾ inch deep into a mold or loaf pan. Chill in the refrigerator or freezer until set. Garnish with thin slices of carrot, making an attractive pattern all around the edge of the mold or tin. Using a slotted spoon, transfer the chicken livers to the mold or tin, spreading them out evenly. Pour in stock to cover and fill the mold. (Some stock will be left over and can be used for another recipe as it is delicious.) Chill in the refrigerator for 24 hours, until set. Serve with a salad.

877

'Foie gras'
FOIE-GRAS

- 1 pound 2 ounces pork livers,
  thawed if frozen, trimmed
- 1 pound 2 ounces lard
- 4 tablespoons brandy
- 1 egg, beaten

Serves 4–6

Put the livers and lard through a grinder together in batches. Stir in the brandy and egg. Spoon the mixture into a tart pan with a solid bottom or quiche pan and smooth the surface. Put the pan into a casserole and pour in hot water to come about halfway up the sides. Bring to a boil over medium-low heat and cook for about 1 hour, until the fat comes to the surface. Remove the pan from the water and leave the foie gras to cool in it, then turn it out, and cover with the lard that has oozed out.

Note: Foie gras is normally made from goose or duck livers and this recipe is not a direct substitute when foie gras is required within another dish.

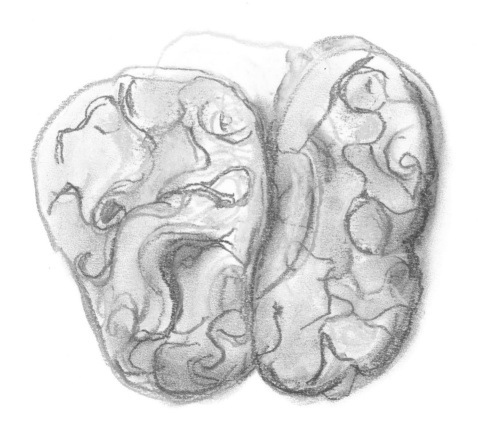

VARIETY MEATS

The nobility of variety meats

Sweetbreads, liver, kidneys, and more—variety meats are fine food. After all, they often appear on the menus of our best restaurants. It is all a matter of knowing how to get the best out of them. The most im-portant thing when preparing variety meats is freshness. Always buy your offal from a reliable source. The best criteria for quality is color—the clearer the better.

Liver

How to cook

Whatever sort of liver you are cooking, from calf's to chicken liver, the oil should not be too hot, especially at the beginning of the process. Liver can be cooked in slices, as kebabs, or roasted whole in the case of calf's liver and then cut into slices and served with a sauce.

Tricks

- To tenderize liver, soak it in milk for 1 hour before cooking. (Discard the milk and dry the livers before cooking.) This is particularly worthwhile with coarse-textured liver such as ox liver
- You might have to cut away visible ducts, veins or membranes from the liver before cooking
- If liver is lightly dusted with flour before frying, it will brown better and the oil will splatter less.

878

Simple fried calf's liver
HÍGADO DE TERNERA FRITO SENCILLO

- 6 (x 4-ounce) slices of calf's liver, trimmed
- ¾ cup olive oil
- 1 tablespoon white-wine vinegar or lemon juice (optional)
- 1 tablespoon chopped fresh parsley
- salt

Serves 6

Season the liver with salt. Heat the oil in a skillet. Add the slices of liver, in batches, and cook over medium-high heat for about 2 minutes on each side, until just firm. Transfer to a serving dish and keep warm while cooking the remaining batches. Remove the skillet from the heat and stir in the vinegar or lemon juice, if using. Return the skillet to the heat and cook, stirring constantly, for a few minutes, then pour the sauce over the liver. Sprinkle the parsley over the top and serve.

Note: Some people like to add a very finely chopped garlic clove. Put this into the skillet with the parsley and cook for a couple of minutes. Alternatively, substitute 2 tablespoons rinsed and drained capers for the garlic, parsley, and vinegar and sauté briefly in the skillet.

879

Calf's liver marinated in Malaga wine
FILETES DE HÍGADO DE TERNERA MACERADOS CON VINO DE MÁLAGA

- 6 (x 4-ounce) slices of calf's liver, trimmed
- ¾ cup Malaga wine or dry sherry
- ½ teaspoon mixed dried herbs
- generous 1 cup olive oil
- 1 tablespoon chopped fresh parsley
- salt

Serves 6

Put the liver into a fairly deep dish, pour the wine or sherry over it, sprinkle with the dried herbs, and let marinate in the refrigerator, turning occasionally, for 1 hour. Drain the liver, pat dry, and season with salt. Heat the oil in a skillet. Add the liver and cook over medium-high heat for about 2 minutes on each side, until just firm. Transfer the liver to a warm serving dish. Sprinkle the parsley over the liver and pour the cooking juices over the top. Serve immediately with Mashed Potato (see recipe 230), French Fries (see recipe 242), or seasonal vegetables.

880

- 1½ cups fine bread crumbs
- 2 eggs
- 1 garlic clove
- 1 sprig fresh parsley
- 6 thin slices of calf's liver,
  3½–4 ounces each, trimmed
- sunflower oil, for deep frying
- salt

Serves 6

Calf's liver in bread crumbs

FILETES DE HÍGADO DE TERNERA EMPANADOS

Pour the bread crumbs into a shallow dish. Lightly beat the eggs in another shallow dish. Pound the garlic with the parsley and a pinch of salt in a mortar, or process in a mini-food processor. Season the liver with salt and rub in the garlic mixture with your fingertips. Immediately coat the liver first in the bread crumbs, then in the beaten egg, and, finally, in bread crumbs again, making sure that the bread crumbs form an even coating. Heat the oil in a deep-fryer or deep skillet to 350–375°F or until a cube of day-old bread browns in 30 seconds. Add the liver and cook for few minutes, until golden brown. Remove with a slotted spatula, drain well, and serve immediately.

881

Liver with mustard and bacon
FILETES DE HÍGADO CON MOSTAZA Y BACON

- 6 (x 4-ounce) slices of calf's
  liver, trimmed
- 1–2 tablespoons Dijon mustard
- 1 cup olive oil
- 6 thin slices of bacon
- salt

Serves 6

Season one side of each slice of liver with salt and spread the mustard generously on the other side. Heat the oil in a skillet. Add the bacon and cook over medium-high heat for 2–4 minutes on each side, until browned. Remove from the skillet and keep warm. Drain off nearly all the oil from the pan, leaving just enough to cover the base. Working in batches, add the liver, and cook over medium-high heat for about 2 minutes on each side, until just firm. Put the slices of liver into a warm serving dish, mustard side up, and top with the bacon. Serve immediately.

882

Liver with onions and bell peppers
FILETES DE HÍGADO CON CEBOLLAS Y PIMIENTOS

- 6 tablespoons olive oil
- 2 large onions,
  cut into wedges ¾ inch wide
- 2 large green bell peppers,
  seeded and cut into
  ¾-inch wide strips
- 4 (x 4-ounce) slices of calf's
  liver, trimmed
- salt

Serves 4

Heat the oil in a skillet. Add the onion and cook over low heat, stirring occasionally, for about 8 minutes, until beginning to brown. Remove from the skillet and keep warm. Add the bell pepper to the skillet, cover, and cook over low heat for 12–15 minutes, until softened. Remove the bell peppers from the pan and keep warm. Season the liver with salt. Add to the skillet and cook over medium-high heat for about 2 minutes on each side, until just firm. Transfer to a warm serving dish. Return the onion and the bell pepper back to the skillet and heat through. Season them to taste with salt, arrange them around the liver, and serve.

883

Liver with onions and white wine
ESCALOPINES DE HÍGADO CON CEBOLLA Y VINO BLANCO

- 1 cup olive oil
- 1 pound 10 ounces calf's liver,
  very thinly sliced, trimmed
- ⅓ cup all-purpose flour
- 8 ounces onions,
  very finely chopped
- ¾ cup white wine
- pinch of dried tarragon
- salt

Serves 6

Reserve 4 tablespoons of the oil and heat the remainder in a skillet. Season the liver with salt and dust with the flour, shaking off the excess. Add to the pan, in batches, and cook over medium-high heat for about 2 minutes on each side, until just firm. Remove from the skillet and set aside. Heat the reserved oil in another skillet. Add the onion and cook over low heat, stirring occasionally, for 6 minutes, until softened and translucent, then add the wine, and cook for 5 minutes more. Add the liver and the tarragon to the skillet, cover, and simmer gently for 5 minutes. Serve immediately.

884

Braised calf's liver
HÍGADO DE TERNERA (EN UN TROZO) GUISADO

- **4 ounces bacon,**
  cut into thin strips
- **2 pounds calf's liver in**
  a single piece, trimmed
- **4 tablespoons olive oil**
- **1 onion, chopped**
- **pinch of mixed dried herbs**
  or 1 bouquet garni (1 bay leaf,
  1 sprig fresh thyme, and 1 sprig
  fresh tarragon tied together in
  cheesecloth)
- **generous 1 cup white wine**
- **salt**

Serves 6

Using a larding needle, thread some of the bacon through the liver and put the remainder on top, then tie with fine kitchen string like a roast. Heat the oil in a pan. Add the onion and cook over low heat, stirring occasionally, for about 5 minutes, until softened and translucent. Add the liver and cook, turning frequently, until evenly browned all over. Season with salt and sprinkle with the dried herbs or add the bouquet garni. Pour in the wine and ¾ cup water, cover the pan, and cook over medium heat, turning the liver occasionally, for 25–35 minutes, until the liver is firm. Lift out the liver from the pan, remove and discard the string and the bacon from the top, slice the meat, and put the slices on a warm serving dish. Remove and discard the bouquet garni, if used, pour the sauce into a food processor or blender, and process, or pass through a food mill. Pour the sauce over the liver or serve separately in a sauceboat.

Note: The liver can be served with macaroni tossed in butter and grated cheese, Mashed Potato (see recipe 230), or any kind of green vegetable such as Brussels sprouts, peas, or green beans.

885

Liver with onion, tomato, and cream
FILETES DE HÍGADO CON CEBOLLA, TOMATE Y NATA

- generous 1 cup olive oil
- 6 (x 4-ounce) slices of calf's liver, trimmed
- ⅓ cup all-purpose flour
- 1 large onion, sliced, in rings
- 4 tomatoes, peeled, seeded, and chopped
- ½ teaspoon meat extract or Maggi Seasoning
- 1 tablespoon chopped fresh parsley
- 3 tablespoons light cream
- salt

Serves 6

Heat the oil in a large skillet. Season the liver with salt and dust with the flour, shaking off any excess. Add to the skillet, in batches if necessary, and cook for about 2 minutes on each side, until just firm. Remove from the skillet and keep warm. Add the onion to the pan and cook over low heat, stirring occasionally, for about 5 minutes, until softened and translucent. Add the tomato and cook, stirring occasionally and breaking it up with the side of the spoon, for 15 minutes. Stir in the meat extract or Maggi Seasoning, return the liver to the skillet, cover, and cook for 3 minutes. Turn the liver and cook for 3 minutes more. Transfer the liver to a warm serving dish. Sprinkle the parsley into the skillet, remove it from the heat, and stir in the cream. Season to taste with salt and pour the sauce over the liver. Serve with Mashed Potato (see recipe 230), macaroni tossed with butter and grated cheese, or triangles of fried bread (see recipe 130).

886

Calf's liver and bacon brochettes (first version)
PINCHOS DE HÍGADO DE TERNERA CON BACON

- 1 pound 10 ounces calf's liver, trimmed and cut into cubes
- 6 medium-thick slices of bacon, cut into squares
- olive oil, for brushing
- 6 thin slices of bread
- salt

Serves 6

Preheat the oven to 425°F. Season the liver with salt, then thread the cubes, alternating with the squares of bacon, onto skewers. Brush the brochettes with oil. Put the slices of bread in a roasting pan and balance the ends of the skewers on the rim. Cook in the oven, turning occasionally, for about 20 minutes, until the liver is just firm and the bacon is brown. Transfer the slices of bread (soaked in the cooking juices) to a warm serving dish and put the brochettes on top.

887

Calf's liver and bacon brochettes (second version)
PINCHOS DE HÍGADO DE TERNERA CON BACON

- 1 pound 10 ounces calf's liver
- 6 medium-thick slices of bacon, cut into squares
- 2 eggs, beaten
- 1 cup bread crumbs
- sunflower oil, for deep frying

Serves 6

Season the cubed liver with salt, then thread the cubes, alternating with the squares of bacon, on to skewers. Coat the skewers first in the beaten egg, then in the bread crumbs, pressing the crumbs on firmly with your hands. Heat the oil in a frying pan to 350-375°F or until a cube of day-old bread browns in 30 seconds. Add the skewers and cook, turning occasionally, until golden brown. Serve immediately.

Chicken livers with tomatoes
HIGADITOS CON TOMATE

- **2 tablespoons olive oil**
- **1 onion, chopped**
- **1 pound 2 ounces chicken livers,**
  thawed if frozen, trimmed
- **3 tomatoes,**
  peeled, seeded, and chopped
- **1 sprig fresh basil, chopped**
- **3 tablespoons white wine**
- **½ chicken bouillon cube**
- **salt and pepper**

Serves 4–6

Heat the oil in a nonstick skillet. Add the onion and cook over low heat, stirring occasionally, for about 5 minutes, until softened and translucent. Add the chicken livers and cook, turning occasionally, for 3 minutes, then add the tomato and basil, and cook, stirring occasionally, for a few minutes more. Pour in the wine, crumble in the bouillon cube, and season with salt and pepper. Simmer gently over low heat for 15 minutes, then serve.

Kidneys

The most delicately flavored are veal kidneys, although pork and lamb kidneys are also delicious. Pig's kidneys have a robust flavor, while ox kidneys are very strongly flavored and may be quite tough. Lamb kidneys are smaller and quite tender. They are ideal for kebabs and for broiling or griddling. Whether veal or lamb kidneys, try to buy the smaller ones—their flavor is more exquisite and their consistency nicer, but they are harder to find. If possible, buy them with their fat intact, as they will keep better because they are protected from the air. In some places not all varieties are available; in the United States, lamb and sometimes calf's kidneys are most commonly sold.

How to clean and prepare

Kidneys must be properly prepared, otherwise they will taste bad. Veal and ox kidneys are multi-lobed. Remove the surrounding fat, if necessary, and peel off the membrane. Cut the kidney into small pieces, removing and discarding the core and any ducts or veins. Put the pieces of meat into a coarse strainer, add a handful of salt, and turn to coat. Let stand for about 2 hours, then rinse under cold running water, shaking the strainer occasionally, for 10 minutes. Drain well. They will now be ready to cook. Lamb's and pig's kidneys are shaped like a navy bean. Remove the surrounding fat, if necessary, and peel off the membrane. Cut the kidney in half lengthwise with a knife. Use kitchen scissors to cut out the core and any ducts or veins.

How to cook

Veal kidneys are delicious cooked in their own fat and are also excellent sautéed. They can be sautéed whole and then sliced or cut into ½-inch slices first. Whichever way they are pre-pared, cook them on all sides over high heat. If the fat or oil is not hot enough, they will boil, become hard, and taste frightful. In fact, you can simply heat kidneys in the sauce that is to accompany them. Prepare the sauce separately and add the kidneys just before serving.

889

Kidneys with white wine and rice

RIÑONES CON VINO BLANCO Y ARROZ

- 12 ounces onions, finely chopped
- 2 ¼ pounds veal or lamb kidneys, trimmed and cleaned
- 4 tablespoons olive oil
- 1 clove garlic, coarsely chopped
- 2 sprigs fresh parsley
- ¾ cup white wine
- 1 tablespoon bread crumbs

Rice:
- 2 cups long-grain rice
- ¼ cup (½ stick) butter
- salt

Serves 4

Cook and rinse the rice as described in recipe 173, then set aside. Put the onion into a pan, put the kidneys on top, pour in the oil, and cook over very low heat for 10 minutes. Pound the garlic with the parsley in a mortar, or process in a food processor, mix in the wine, and pour the mixture over the kidneys. Cook, stirring occasionally, for 5 minutes more. If the sauce seems thin, stir in the bread crumbs. Season with salt and cook for 5 minutes more. Season the rice and fry it in the butter as described in recipe 173, then spoon into a ring mold. Turn out onto a warm serving dish and spoon the kidneys and the sauce into the center. Serve immediately.

Veal kidneys in sherry sauce with rice

RIÑONES DE TERNERA CON SALSA DE JEREZ Y ARROZ BLANCO

- 2 tablespoons all-purpose flour
- 4 tablespoons olive oil
- generous 1 cup sherry or
  other sweet fortified wine
- 2¼ pounds veal or lamb kidneys,
  trimmed and cleaned
- salt

Rice:
- 2 cups long-grain rice
- ¼ cup (½ stick) butter
- salt

Serves 4

Cook and rinse the rice as described in recipe 173, then set aside. Put the flour into a skillet and cook over medium heat, stirring constantly, for about 10 minutes, until beginning to brown. Stir in the oil, then add the sherry, scant 2 cups water, and a pinch of salt. Cook for about 5 minutes. Add the kidneys, lower the heat, and cook for about 10 minutes, until firm. Meanwhile, season the rice with salt and fry in the butter as described in recipe 173. Spoon into a ring mold and turn out onto a warm serving dish. Spoon the kidneys and sauce into the center and serve immediately.

Kidneys in tomato sauce, served in rolls

RIÑONES CON SALSA DE TOMATE, PRESENTADOS EN PANECILLOS

- 1 tablespoon pine nuts
- 1 hard-cooked egg yolk
- 3 tablespoons sherry or other sweet fortified wine
- ½ teaspoon paprika
- 1 tablepsoon confectioner's sugar
- 6 round rolls
- sunflower oil, for deep frying
- 1 veal or 2 lamb kidneys, about 1 pound 10 ounces, trimmed, cleaned, and diced
- salt

Tomato sauce:
- 2 tablespoons sunflower oil
- 1 onion, chopped
- 1 pound 2 ounces ripe tomatoes, seeded and chopped
- 1 teaspoon sugar
- salt

Serves 4

Make the tomato sauce, as described in recipe 73, but do not transfer it to a food processor or blender. Pound half the pine nuts with the egg yolk in a mortar, or process in a mini-food processor, stir in the sherry, then pour the mixture into the skillet of tomato sauce. Stir in the paprika, sugar, and a pinch of salt. Mix well, then transfer to a food processor or blender, and process to a purée. Keep warm. Cut a thin layer off the tops of the rolls and scoop out the centers. Heat the oil in a deep skillet. Add the rolls upside down, in batches, and cook until golden brown. Remove with a slotted spoon, drain well, and keep warm. Transfer about ⅔ cup of the oil to another skillet. Add the diced kidney and cook, stirring occasionally, for 5–6 minutes, then drain off the fat. Lightly season the kidney with salt, then stir it into the tomato sauce. Add the remaining pine nuts and divide the mixture among the rolls. Serve immediately.

Note: This recipe can be made with pork or lamb's kidneys. The individual rolls can be replaced with a large loaf of bread.

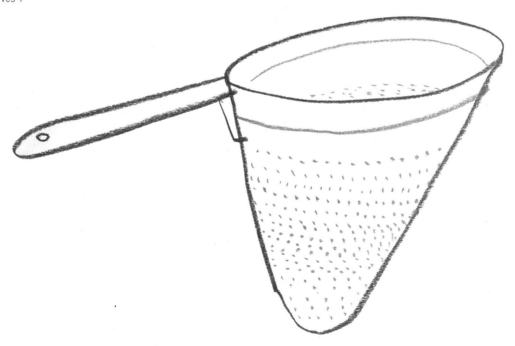

892

Kidney, bacon, and mushroom brochettes
PINCHOS DE RIÑONES DE CERDO O CORDERO, CON TOCINO Y CHAMPIÑONES

- **2 pork kidneys or 6 lamb kidneys, halved and trimmed**
- **juice of ½ lemon**
- **1 thick slice of bacon, cut into squares**
- **1½ cups small white mushrooms**
- **2 tablespoons olive oil**
- **salt and pepper**

Serves 2

Preheat the oven to 450°F. Put the kidneys into a bowl, pour in water to cover, and add the lemon juice. Stir the kidneys around with your hand, then drain, and pat dry. Cut the kidneys into large pieces and thread them onto skewers, alternating with the bacon squares and mushrooms. Season with salt and pepper and brush with the oil. Rest the ends of the skewers on the rim of a roasting pan or ovenproof baking dish. Cook in the oven, turning occasionally, for 15 minutes. Put the skewers on a warm dish and serve with watercress or straw potatoes (see recipe 243).

893

Simple kidney brochettes
PINCHOS SIMPLES DE RIÑONES DE CERDO O DE CORDERO

- **3 pork kidneys or 8 lamb kidneys, halved and trimmed**
- **juice of ½ lemon**
- **2 tablespoons olive oil**
- **3 slices of bread**
- **1 clove garlic, finely chopped**
- **1 teaspoon chopped fresh parsley**
- **salt**

Serves 2

Preheat the oven to 450°F. Put the kidneys into a bowl, pour in water to cover, and add the lemon juice. Stir the kidneys around with your hand, then drain, and pat dry. Thread the kidneys lengthwise onto skewers. Season with salt and brush with some of the oil. Put the slices of bread in a roasting pan or ovenproof baking dish and rest the ends of the skewers on the rim with the rounded sides of the kidneys uppermost. Cook in the oven for 5 minutes, turn the skewers, and sprinkle with the garlic, parsley, and a little more oil. Cook for 6 minutes more and serve on the slices of bread with straw potatoes (see recipe 243).

Brains

How to clean and prepare

Both lamb brains and calf brains are cleaned and prepared in the same way, regardless of how they will be cooked later. Put the brains in a colander that just holds them comfortably and place under a gentle flow of cold running water. Continue rinsing until there are no longer any traces of blood. Transfer them to a bowl, pour in water to cover, and add ¼ cup vinegar for each calf brain or each pair of lamb brains. Let soak for 15–20 minutes, then drain, and carefully remove the covering membrane, the veins, and any remaining blood. Put the brains in a pan, pour in water to cover, and bring to a boil. Skim off any froth that rises to the surface and simmer gently for a few minutes. Drain and rinse well. The brains are now ready for cooking.

894

Frittered brains
SESOS HUECOS (O EN BUÑUELOS)

- **1½ calf brains or 3 lamb brains**
- **sunflower oil, for deep frying**
- **deep-fried parsley sprigs (see recipe 918)**
- **1 quantity Classic Tomato Sauce (see recipe 73)**
- **1 quantity batter (see recipe 58)**

Serves 4

Prepare and blanch the brains as described on page 772. Drain and let cool, then cut them into pieces ¾–1¼ inches long. Make the batter as described in recipe 58. Heat the oil in a deep-fryer or deep skillet to 350–375°F or until a cube of day-old bread browns in 30 seconds. Coat the pieces of brain in the batter, add to the hot oil, and cook until golden brown all over. Drain well and transfer to a warm serving dish. Garnish with the fried parsley sprigs and serve immediately, offering the tomato sauce separately.

895

Breaded brains
SESOS EMPANADOS

- **1½ calf brains or 3 lamb brains**
- **2 eggs**
- **sunflower oil, for deep frying**
- **1½ cups bread crumbs**
- **salt**
- **1 quantity Classic Tomato Sauce (see recipe 73)**

Serves 4

Prepare and blanch the brains as described on page 772. Let cool, then cut them in half lengthwise, separating the two lobes, and slice thinly. Beat the eggs with 1 tablespoon of oil and a pinch of salt in a shallow dish. Pour the bread crumbs into another shallow dish. Coat the slices of brain first in the beaten egg and then in the bread crumbs, pressing the crumbs on firmly with your hands. Let the brains stand on a work surface or a cutting board. Heat the oil in a deep-fryer or deep skillet to 350–375°F or until a cube of day-old bread browns in 30 seconds. Add the brains, in batches, and cook until golden brown. Drain well, put them onto a serving dish, and keep warm. Serve with boiled rice, offering the tomato sauce separately.

896

Brains with black butter
SESOS CON MANTEQUILLA NEGRA

- 6 lamb brains
- ⅓ cup all-purpose flour
- 2¼ cups (4½ sticks) butter
- 2 tablespoons chopped fresh parsley (optional)
- 3 tablespoons white-wine vinegar
- salt

Serves 4

Prepare and blanch the brains as described on page 772. Let cool, then cut them in half lengthwise, separating the two lobes, and dust them with the flour. Melt 1 cup of the butter in a skillet. Add the brains, in batches, and cook, turning occasionally, until evenly golden brown all over. Transfer to a warm serving dish and sprinkle with the parsley, if using. Add the remaining butter to the skillet and heat until it turns dark brown, then remove the pan from the heat. Stir in the vinegar and return the skillet to the heat for a few minutes. Pour the sauce over the brains and serve immediately.

Note: The vinegar can be replaced with rinsed and drained capers.

897

Brains in béchamel sauce
SESOS EN SALSA BECHAMEL CLARITA

- 4 lamb brains
- 2 tablespoons (¼ stick) butter
- 2 tablespoons sunflower oil
- 1 small onion, finely chopped
- 2 tablespoons all-purpose flour
- ¾ cup milk
- generous 1 cup chicken stock (homemade, canned or made with a bouillon cube)
- 2 egg yolks
- juice of 1 lemon
- 1 tablespoon chopped fresh parsley
- salt

Serves 4

Prepare and blanch the brains as described on page 772. Let cool, then cut them in half lengthwise, separating the two lobes. Cut each lobe in half lengthwise and set aside. Melt the butter with the oil in a pan. Add the onion and cook over low heat, stirring occasionally, for 6–8 minutes, until beginning to brown. Stir in the flour and cook, stirring constantly, for 3–4 minutes, until lightly colored. Gradually stir in the milk, a little at a time, then stir in the stock. Cook, stirring constantly, for 2–3 minutes, until slightly thickened. Remove the pan from the heat and lightly season with salt. Lightly beat the egg yolks with the lemon juice in a bowl, then stir in 2 tablespoons of the sauce, 1 tablespoon at a time. Stir the mixture into the pan of sauce, add the pieces of brain, sprinkle in the parsley, and return the pan to low heat. Heat gently, spooning the sauce over the brains to warm them through. Transfer to a warm serving dish and serve immediately.

898

- **2 calf brains**
- **1½ cups small white mushrooms**
- **¼ cup (½ stick) butter**
- **juice of ½ lemon**
- **2 tablespoons sunflower oil**
- **2 tablespoons all-purpose flour**
- **1½ cups milk**
- **½ cup grated gruyere cheese**
- **salt**

Serves 4

Gratin of brains, béchamel sauce and mushrooms

SESOS AL GRATÉN, CON BECHAMEL Y CHAMPIÑONES

Prepare and blanch the brains as described on page 772. Let cool, then cut them in half lengthwise, separating the two lobes. Slice each lobe into ½-inch thick slices and put into a flameproof dish. Preheat the broiler. Put the mushrooms, 1½ tablespoons of the butter, the lemon juice, and a pinch of salt into a pan. Cover and cook over medium heat, shaking the pan occasionally, for about 6 minutes. Melt the remaining butter with the oil in a pan. Stir in the flour and cook, stirring constantly, for 2 minutes. Gradually stir in the milk, a little at a time. Cook over medium heat, stirring constantly, for about 6 minutes, until thickened. Drain the mushrooms and add them to the sauce, then season to taste with salt. Pour the béchamel sauce over the brains, sprinkle with the gruyere, and cook under the broiler for 5–10 minutes, until the topping is golden brown. Serve immediately.

899

- **2 calf brains or 4–5 lamb brains**
- **3 tablespoons sunflower oil**
- **1 onion (optional)**
- **2¼ pounds tomatoes, seeded and chopped**
- **1 teaspoon sugar**
- **3 tablespoons bread crumbs**
- **2 tablespoons (¼ stick) butter**
- **salt**

Serves 4

Broiled brains with tomato sauce

SESOS CON SALSA DE TOMATE GRATINADOS

Prepare and blanch the brains as described on page 772. Let cool, then cut into ¾-inch thick slices, and arrange in a ring in an ovenproof baking dish. Preheat the oven 400°F. Make a very thick tomato sauce with the sunflower oil, onion, if using, tomatoes, and sugar as described in recipe 73. Pour the tomato sauce over the brains, sprinkle with the bread crumbs, dot with the butter, and bake for 10–15 minutes, until the top is golden brown. Serve immediately, straight from the dish.

Tongue

How to cook

Allow 2½ pounds tongue for 6–8 servings. Tongue is usually sold cleaned and ready to cook. If not, carefully remove any gristle and fat. Put it in cold water to soak in the refrigerator for about 12 hours or overnight, then drain, and brush well. Bring a large pan of water to a boil, add the tongue, and cook at a rolling boil for 10 minutes. Remove the pan from the heat and put it under cold running water. When the tongue has cooled, remove it from the pan, and peel off the thick skin with a sharp knife. Some people prefer to remove the skin after the tongue has been braised in stock. It's simply a matter of personal preference. Put 5 ounces pork rind on the base of a large pan and put the tongue on top. Add 1 large halved onion, 2 sliced carrots, 2 veal shin bones, and 1 bouquet garni with 1 sprig fresh parsley, 1 sprig fresh thyme, 1 bay leaf, and 1 garlic clove. Season with salt, add some black peppercorns, pour in ¾ cup white wine, and add water to cover. Bring to a boil over high heat, then lower the heat, cover, and cook for 2½–3 hours, until the tongue is tender. The tongue is now ready to eat and can be accompanied by a variety of sauces or used in a number of different stews. Tongue can also be cooked in a pressure cooker, reducing the cooking time by 1 hour.

900

Tongue with special vinaigrette
LENGUA CON SALSA DE VINAGRETA HISTORIADA

• 1 ox tongue, 2 ¼ pounds, braised
• 1 quantity vinaigrette
  (see recipes 99 and 100)

Serves 4–6

Braise the tongue as described above. Cut it into diagonal slices and place them on a serving dish. Garnish with shredded lettuce and finely chopped hard-cooked egg, offering the vinaigrette separately. This dish can be served hot or cold.

901

Tongue in béchamel sauce with capers
LENGUA CON BECHAMEL Y ALCAPARRAS

- 1 ox tongue, 2 ¼ pounds, braised
- 1 quantity Béchamel Sauce with capers (see recipe 80)

Serves 4–6

Braise the tongue as described on page 776. Cut it into diagonal slices, and then cook as described in recipe 717.

.

902

Tongue with onion, tomato, and white wine sauce
LENGUA CON SALSA DE CEBOLLA, TOMATE Y VINO BLANCO

- 1 beef or ox tongue, 2 ¼ pounds
- 6 tablespoons olive oil
- 2 large onions, chopped
- 1 teaspoon all-purpose flour
- 1 pound 10 ounces ripe tomatoes, peeled, seeded, and chopped
- ¾ cup white wine
- pinch of mixed dried herbs or 1 bay leaf and 1 sprig fresh thyme
- salt

Serves 4–6

Braise the tongue as described on page 776, and cut it into diagonal slices. Substituting the tongue for the fish fillets, prepare in the same way as bonito with onion and tomato (see recipe 557). As the tongue is already cooked, it will not release any water, so it may be a good idea to add a few tablespoons of water. This dish can be served with molded rice.

903

Stewed tongue
LENGUA ESTOFADA

- 1 beef or ox tongue,
  2¼–2½ pounds
- ½ cup lard or ½ cup butter
- 2 onions, chopped
- 4 carrots, thickly sliced
- ¾ cups white wine
- ¾ cup, plus 2 tablespoons
  cooking liquid from braising
  the tongue
- pinch of mixed dried herbs or
  1 bouquet garni (1 bay leaf and 1
  sprig fresh thyme tied together)
- 1 slice of fried bread
  (see recipe 130)
- 1 clove garlic
- 2–3 black peppercorns
- 1 teaspoon potato starch
- salt

Serves 6

Braise the tongue as described on page 776, but only for 2 hours, and drain well, reserving the cooking liquid. Melt the lard or butter in a large pan. Add the onion and cook over low heat, stirring occasionally, for about 5 minutes, until softened and translucent. Put the tongue on top of the onion and place the carrot around it. Pour in the wine and ¾ cup of the reserved cooking liquid and add the dried herbs or bouquet garni. Pound the fried bread with the garlic in a mortar, or process in a mini-food processor, and mix in the remaining cooking liquid. Pour into the pan, add the peppercorns, and lightly season with salt. Bring to a boil over high heat, then lower the heat, cover the pan with parchment paper that has been cut into a circle to fit snugly inside the pan, put the lid on, and cook for 1½ hours. Remove the tongue from the pan and slice it. Put the slices on a warm serving dish and garnish with the carrot. Remove and discard the bouquet garni, if used, and process the sauce in a food processor or blender or pass through a food mill, then pour it over the tongue, and serve. If the sauce is too thin, mix 1 teaspoon potato starch with a little of the sauce in a bowl. Return the sauce to the pan, stir in the potato starch mixture, and cook, stirring, for 2–3 minutes, until thickened.

904

Breaded tongue
LENGUA REBOZADA

- 1 ox tongue
- 2 eggs, beaten
- 1½ cups bread crumbs
- sunflower oil, for deep frying
- 1 quantity Classic Tomato Sauce
  (see recipe 73), optional

Serves 4

Braise the tongue as described on page 776, and cut it into thin slices. Coat the slices first in the beaten egg and then in the bread crumbs, pressing the crumbs on with your fingertips. Heat the oil in a deep-fryer or deep skillet to 350–375°F or until a cube of day-old bread turns brown in 30 seconds. Fry the slices in the hot oil, in batches until golden brown. Remove with a slotted spatula, drain well, and keep warm while you cook the remaining slices. Serve them as they are or with the tomato sauce served separately in a sauceboat.

Sweetbreads

Two kinds of glands are used for Sweetbreads. The thymus gland, from the neck, shrinks as the young animal matures. The pancreas gland, also called belly Sweetbreads, does not shrink with age, but it becomes tougher and not so pleasant to eat. The most commonly eaten sweetbreads are veal and beef, and in Europe, lamb.

How to prepare

Allow 2 ¼ – 2 ½ pounds sweetbreads for 6 servings. No matter how they are to be cooked, the sweetbreads should be prepared as follows. Let soak in cold water in the refrigerator for about 4 hours, changing the water three or four times. Drain and blanch as described in the steps below. The quantities given are sufficient for 2 ¼ – 2 ½ pounds sweetbreads.

- 2 carrots, sliced
- 1 leek, halved and rinsed well or 1 small onion, halved
- 1 stalk celery (optional)
- 1 bay leaf
- juice of ½ lemon
- salt

Put the sweetbreads in a pan and pour in water to cover. Add the carrot, leek or onion, celery, if using, bay leaf, lemon juice, and a pinch of salt. Bring to a boil, lower the heat, and simmer gently for 5 minutes. Remove the pan from the heat, drain off the hot water, and refresh the sweetbreads in cold water, then drain well. Peel off the membrane, and remove any gristle, fat, ducts, membrane, or traces of blood. Place the sweetbreads on a dishtowel and fold it back over them so that they are covered, then put something heavy on top, such as a light cutting board. Let stand for 1 hour, then slice thickly, and cook according to taste.

905

Sweetbreads with mushrooms and shallots

MOLLEJAS GUISADAS CON CHAMPIÑONES FRESCOS Y CEBOLLITAS

- 2 ¼ pounds sweetbreads
- 3 ½ cups small white
  mushrooms
- 1 ½ tablespoons butter
- juice of ½ lemon
- 4 tablespoons olive oil
- 9 ounces grelots or shallots
- ⅓ cup all-purpose flour
- 1 ½ cups white wine
- ½ cup light cream or
  2 egg yolks, lightly beaten
- salt

Serves 6

Prepare and blanch the sweetbreads as described on page 779. Put the mushrooms, butter, lemon juice, and a pinch of salt into a pan. Cover and cook over low heat for 6 minutes. Set aside and keep warm. Heat the oil in another pan. Add the shallots and cook over low heat, stirring occasionally, for about 10 minutes, until beginning to brown. Slice the sweetbreads and coat in the flour, but do not shake off any excess, as it will serve to thicken the sauce. Add to the pan and cook, turning occasionally, until evenly browned. Pour in the wine and simmer over low heat, shaking the pan occasionally, for about 15 minutes. Stir in the mushrooms and their cooking juices and season to taste with salt. Remove the pan from the heat. Put the cream or egg yolks into a bowl and stir in a little of the sauce, then pour this mixture into the pan. Stir well and pour the contents of the pan into a warm serving dish. Serve with little mounds of boiled rice.

906

Sweetbreads cooked in sherry

MOLLEJAS GUISADAS AL JEREZ

- 2 ½ pounds sweetbreads
- 4 tablespoons olive oil
- 1 onion, chopped
- 2 carrots, sliced
- 1 large ripe tomato,
  seeded and cut into 4 wedges
- 1 heaping tablespoon
  all-purpose flour
- pinch of mixed dried herbs
  or 1 bouquet garni
  (2 bay leaves, 1 sprig fresh
  thyme, and 1 sprig fresh parsley
  tied together in cheesecloth)
- 5 tablespoons sherry
- 1 cup chicken stock
  (homemade, canned or
  made with a bouillon cube)
- salt and pepper

Serves 6

Prepare and blanch the sweetbreads as described on page 779, and slice. Heat the oil in a pan. Add the onion and cook over low heat, stirring occasionally, for about 5 minutes, until softened and translucent. Add the carrot and cook, stirring occasionally, for a few minutes more, then add the tomato and flour. Add the sweetbreads and cook, turning carefully, until evenly browned all over. Season with salt and pepper, add the dried herbs or bouquet garni, and pour in the sherry, followed by the stock. Bring to a boil, then lower the heat, cover, and simmer, stirring occasionally, for 30 minutes. Using a slotted spoon or spatula, transfer the sweetbreads to a warm serving dish. Remove and discard the bouquet garni, if used, and pass the sauce through a food mill or process in a food processor or blender. Pour the sauce over the sweetbreads and serve immediately with the fried bread (see recipe 130) around the dish, if you like.

907

Sweetbreads flamed in brandy and served with peas

MOLLEJAS FLAMEADAS CON COÑAC Y SERVIDAS CON GUISANTES

- 2¼ pounds sweetbreads
- generous ½ cup lard
  or sunflower oil
- 5 tablespoons brandy
- 1 tablespoon chopped
  fresh parsley
- 15 ounces canned peas or
  4½ pounds fresh peas, shelled
- ¼ cup (½ cup) butter
- salt and pepper

Serves 6

Prepare and blanch the sweetbreads as described on page 779, and slice. Melt the lard or heat the oil in a skillet. Add the sweetbreads and cook, turning occasionally, until lightly browned all over. Season with salt and pepper. Heat the brandy in a small pan, ignite it, and carefully pour it into the skillet, spooning it over the sweetbreads. When the flames have died down, sprinkle in the parsley and cook over medium heat for 15 minutes. Meanwhile, open the can of peas, if using, and stand it in a pan of hot water set over medium heat. Cook the fresh peas, if using, in a pan of salted boiling water for about 20 minutes, until tender. Drain the peas, put them into a pan, add the butter, and cook over low heat, stirring occasionally, for 5 minutes. Season to taste with salt. Put the sweetbreads on a warm serving dish, pour the sauce over them, and put the peas around the edge. Serve immediately.

908

Sweetbreads with spinach

MOLLEJAS CON ESPINACAS

- 2¼ pounds sweetbreads
- 6½ pounds spinach,
  coarse stalks removed
- 2 tablespoons (¼ stick) butter
- ½ cup all-purpose flour
- 1 cup milk
- 1½ cups sunflower oil
- salt

Serves 6

Prepare and blanch the sweetbreads as described on page 779, and slice. Cook the spinach as described on page 315. Drain well and chop finely or put it through a grinder or food processor. Heat the butter in a pan. Stir in 1 tablespoon of the flour and cook, stirring constantly, for 2 minutes. Gradually stir in the milk, a little at a time. Cook, stirring constantly, for about 5 minutes, until thickened, then stir in the spinach, and season to taste with salt. Remove the pan from the heat and keep warm. Heat the oil in a skillet. Coat the sweetbreads in the remaining flour, shaking off any excess. Add them to the pan and cook, turning occasionally, until golden brown. Remove with a slotted spatula and drain well. Spoon the spinach sauce onto a warm serving dish, place the sweetbreads on top, and serve immediately.

909

Breaded sweetbreads with tomato sauce

MOLLEJAS EMPANADAS CON SALSA DE TOMATE

• 2½ pounds sweetbreads

• 2 eggs

• 1 tablespoon olive oil

• 1½ cups bread crumbs

• 1 cup sunflower oil

• 2 sprigs fresh parsley

• 1 quantity Classic Tomato Sauce
  (see recipe 73)

• salt

Serves 6

Prepare and blanch the sweetbreads as described on page 779, and slice. Beat the eggs with the olive oil and a pinch of salt in a shallow dish. Pour the bread crumbs into another shallow dish. Coat the sweetbreads first in the egg mixture and then in the bread crumbs, pressing the crumbs on with your fingertips. Heat the sunflower oil in a skillet over low heat. Add the parsley sprigs and cook for a few minutes, then remove with a slotted spoon, and set aside. Increase the heat until the oil is hot enough to brown a cube of day-old bread in 30 seconds. Add the sweetbreads and cook until golden brown. Remove with a slotted spatula and drain well. Put the sweetbreads on a warm serving dish and garnish with the parsley. Serve immediately, offering the tomato sauce separately.

910

Vol-au-vent with sweetbreads, mushrooms, and truffles

VOL-AU-VENT DE MOLLEJAS, CHAMPIÑONES Y TRUFAS

• 1 pound 2 ounces sweetbreads

• 6 individual vol-au-vent cases
  or one large case, cooked

• 1 pound 2 ounces mushrooms

• 5 tablespoons butter

• juice of ½ lemon

• 2 tablespoons sunflower oil

• 2 tablespoons all-purpose flour

• 2¼ cups milk

• ½ teaspoon meat extract
  or Maggi Seasoning

• pinch of freshly grated nutmeg

• 1 small can or jar of truffles,
  drained and thinly sliced

• salt

Serves 6

Prepare and blanch the sweetbreads as described on page 779. Cut the sweetbreads into ¾-inch cubes. If the mushrooms are large, chop them coarsely. Put the mushrooms, 3 tablespoons of the butter, the lemon juice, and a pinch of salt into a pan. Cover and cook over medium heat, shaking the pan occasionally, for about 6 minutes. Preheat the oven to 350°F. Melt the remaining butter with the oil in a pan. Stir in the flour and cook, stirring constantly, for 2 minutes. Gradually stir in the milk, a little at a time. Cook, stirring constantly, for about 5 minutes, until thickened, then stir in the meat extract or Maggi Seasoning and nutmeg, and season to taste with salt. Add the sweetbreads to the sauce. Drain the mushrooms and add them to the sauce along with the truffles and stir well. Divide the mixture among the individual vol-au-vent cases or spoon it into the large case. Place on a cookie sheet and heat through in the oven. Serve hot.

Sweetbread croquettes

CROQUETAS DE MOLLEJAS

- 1 pound 2 ounces sweetbreads
- 2 tablespoons sunflower oil
- 1½ tablespoons butter
- 3–4 tablespoons all-purpose flour
- 3 cups milk
- 2 eggs
- 2–3 cups bread crumbs
- vegetable oil, for deep-frying
- salt

Serves 4

Prepare and blanch the sweetbreads as described on page 779. Cut the sweetbreads into small cubes. Then follow the method for making croquettes (see recipe 62).

Tripe

How to prepare

Tripe is the edible lining of the stomachs of cows, pigs or sheep. It is usually sold partly or fully cooked, so cooking times may vary. If you are in doubt, ask your butcher for advice. Uncooked tripe requires repeated and very careful cleaning and will need prolonged simmering—up to 5 hours.

912

Tripe in French sauce

- 3½ ounces bacon,
  cut into strips
- 2 onions
- 6 cloves
- 3 carrots, sliced
- 1 bouquet garni (2 bay leaves,
  1 sprig fresh thyme, 1 clove
  garlic, and 1 sprig fresh parsley
  tied together in cheesecloth)
- 3 tablespoons brandy
- 2¼ pounds prepared tripe,
  cut into large pieces
- 1 pound 2 ounces snout
- 1 calf's or ox foot, 1 pound
  10 ounces, cut into pieces
- 1 tablespoon chopped
  fresh parsley
- salt and pepper

French sauce:
- 4 tablespoons sunflower oil
- 2 tablespoons all-purpose flour
- 2¼ cups beef stock
  (homemade, canned or
  made with bouillon cubes)
- 3 egg yolks
- juice of 1 lemon
- salt

Serves 6–8

Put the bacon into a large pan. Stud the onions with the cloves and add them to the pan with the carrot, bouquet garni, brandy, tripe, snout, and calf's or ox foot. Season with salt and pepper and pour in water to cover. Bring to a boil, then lower the heat, and simmer for about 1½ hours, until the tripe is tender. Drain off the cooking liquid. Cut the tripe and snout into small pieces and set aside. Remove the meat from the foot and set aside with the tripe. To make the sauce, heat the oil in a pan. Stir in the flour and cook, stirring constantly, for 2 minutes. Gradually stir in the stock and season to taste with salt. Add all the meat to the sauce and simmer gently for 30 minutes. Just before serving, beat the egg yolks with the lemon juice in a bowl and stir in a few tablespoons of the sauce, then pour this mixture into the pan. Stir well and pour into a warm deep serving dish. Sprinkle with the parsley and serve immediately.

Madrid-style tripe
CALLOS A LA MADRILEÑA

- 2 small onions
- 3¼ pounds prepared tripe,
  cut into bite-size pieces
- 5 ounces andouille sausage
  (tripe sausage)
- 1 pound 2 ounces snout
- 1 calf's or ox foot,
  1 pound 10 ounces
- 1 bay leaf
- ½ chile, seeded
- 10 black peppercorns
- 4 cloves
- pinch of freshly grated nutmeg
- 2 cloves garlic, chopped
- 2 tomatoes,
  peeled, seeded and chopped
- 4 tablespoons olive oil
- 1 teaspoon paprika
- 2 chorizo sausages, 5 ounces
- 1 tablespoon all-purpose flour
- salt

Serves 6–8

Cut one of the onions into four pieces and chop the other. Put the tripe into a pan, pour in water to cover, and bring to a boil. When it reaches a rolling boil, drain off the water and add fresh water to cover. Add the andouille, snout, calf's or ox foot, bay leaf, chile, peppercorns, cloves, nutmeg, the pieces of onion, garlic, and tomato. Cook for about 1½ hours, until the tripe is tender. Heat the oil in a skillet. Add the chopped onion, paprika, chorizo, and flour. Cook, stirring occasionally, for 10 minutes, then add to the tripe, and cook for 1 hour more. Remove the pan from the heat and let cool. Cut the andouille into slices and cut the meat off the calf's or ox foot and return both to the pan. Reheat before serving.

Note: This dish should be prepared a day in advance and refrigerated, as it is much better when reheated. This quantity of tripe listed is the minimum that should be prepared in order for the dish to be tasty.

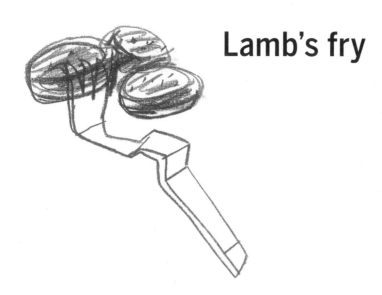

Lamb's fry

Lamb's fry, also known as animelles, or, in the United States, as Rocky Mountain oysters, are testicles and are not widely available. However, if you are lucky enough to obtain them, here's how they are prepared. If they are not sold ready skinned and sliced, you must blanch them in boiling water for 2 minutes, then drain, and refresh them under cold running water. Skin them immediately and then let soak in cold water for 10 hours. Drain and press between two plates before slicing and cooking.

914

Breaded lamb's fry with rice

CRIADILLAS EMPANADAS CON ARROZ BLANCO

- 1 egg
- 1½ cups bread crumbs
- sunflower oil, for deep frying
- 1 pound 2 ounces–1 pound 10 ounces prepared and sliced lamb's fry
- salt

Rice:
- 2 cups long-grain rice
- ¼ cup (½ stick) butter
- salt

Serves 6

Cook and refresh the rice as described in recipe 173, then set aside. Beat the egg with a pinch of salt in a shallow dish. Pour the bread crumbs into another shallow dish. Heat the oil in a deep-fryer or saucepan to 350–375°F or until a cube of day-old bread browns in 30 seconds. Cut the slices of lamb's fry into strips and coat first in the beaten egg and then in the bread crumbs. Add the strips, in batches, to the hot oil and cook until golden brown. Remove with a slotted spoon and drain well. Put them along one side of a serving dish and keep warm. Cook the rice with the butter as described in recipe 173 and season with salt. Spoon it onto the other side of the serving dish or shape it in little mounds. Serve immediately.

Note: This dish can be served with a sauce boat of Classic Tomato Sauce (see recipe 73).

Calf's heart in sauce
CORAZÓN DE TERNERA EN SALSA

- ½ cup olive oil
- 2½ pounds veal heart,
  thickly sliced
- 1 large onion, finely chopped
- 1 clove garlic, lightly crushed
- 4 carrots, sliced
- 1 tablespoon all-purpose flour
- 2 ripe tomatoes,
  peeled, seeded, and chopped
- pinch of mixed dried herbs
  or 1 bouquet garni
  (1 sprig fresh thyme, 2 bay
  leaves, and 1 sprig fresh parsley
  tied together in cheesecloth)
- ½ cup white wine
- 1 chicken bouillon cube
- salt

Serves 6

Heat the oil in a large pan or Dutch oven. Add the slices of heart, in batches, and cook, turning occasionally, until evenly browned all over. Remove from the pan and set aside. Add the onion to the pan and cook over low heat, stirring occasionally, for about 5 minutes, until softened and translucent. Add the garlic and cook, stirring occasionally, for 5 minutes more. Add the carrot and cook for 2–3 minutes, then stir in the flour, and cook, stirring constantly, for 2 minutes. Return the meat to the pan and add the tomato and dried herbs or bouquet garni. Pour in the wine and ½ cup water, season with salt, cover the pan, and bring to a boil. Lower the heat and simmer gently for 45 minutes. Crumble the bouillon cube into a bowl, stir in a little of the cooking liquid, and add to the pan. Stir well and cook for 30 minutes more, until the heart is tender. Taste and adjust the seasoning, if necessary. Serve immediately, with Mashed Potato (see recipe 230) or boiled potatoes cut into large pieces.

916

Breaded calf's heart
CORAZÓN DE TERNERA EMPANADO

- **1 quantity Classic Tomato Sauce (see recipe 73)**
- **2 eggs**
- **1½ cups bread crumbs**
- **sunflower oil, for deep frying**
- **2¼ pounds calf's heart, sliced**
- **salt**

Serves 6

Warm the Tomato Sauce. Beat the eggs in a shallow dish and pour the bread crumbs into another shallow dish. Heat the oil in a deep-fryer or saucepan to 350–375°F or until a cube of day-old bread browns in 30 seconds. Season the slices of heart with salt, and coat them first in the beaten egg and then in the bread crumbs, pressing the crumbs on with your fingers. Add the slices, in batches, to the hot oil and cook until golden brown. Remove with a slotted spatula, drain well, and put into a warm serving dish. Serve immediately with boiled rice or French Fries (see recipe 242). Offer the tomato sauce separately.

Feet and trotters

How to cook
If the feet are not already blanched and cleaned, remove any remaining skin and even singe them, over a flame or using cotton wool soaked in alcohol and lit with a match. Put the feet into a pan, pour in water to cover, and cook over high heat for 10 minutes. Drain, refresh under cold water, and drain again. Fill a large pan with water. Stir 2 tablespoons all-purpose flour into a bowl of cold water, then add it to the water in the pan with 1 large onion studded with 3 cloves, 2 bay leaves, 1 sprig fresh parsley, 1 clove garlic, the juice of ½ lemon, 1 sprig fresh thyme, and a pinch of salt. Bring to a boil and add the lamb's feet so that they are completely submerged. Bring back to a boil, cover, and cook, occasionally skimming off the froth that rises to the surface, for about 3 hours, until the lamb's feet are tender. Drain the lambs' feet, which are now ready to cook.

Lambs' feet stuffed with sausages, coated in bread crumbs and fried

MANOS DE CORDERO RELLENAS CON SALCHICHAS, EMPANADAS Y FRITAS

- **12 lamb's feet**
- **12 sausages**
- **3 eggs**
- **1½ cups bread crumbs**
- **sunflower oil, for deep frying**
- **salt**
- **1 quantity Classic Tomato Sauce (see recipe 73)**

Serves 6

Clean and precook the lamb's feet as described on page 788. When they are cool enough to handle, remove and discard the central bone. (It will come out very easily.) Prick the sausages in several places. Fill the cavities in the lamb's feet with the sausages and secure the opening with a wooden toothpick, if necessary. Beat the eggs with a pinch of salt in a shallow dish and pour the bread crumbs into another shallow dish. Heat the oil in a deep-fryer or skillet 350–375°F or until a cube of day-old bread browns in 30 seconds. Coat each foot first in the beaten egg and then in the bread crumbs, pressing the crumbs on with your fingertips. Add the feet, in batches, to the hot oil and cook until golden brown all over. Remove and drain, then put on a serving dish, and keep warm while you cook the remaining batches. Serve immediately, offering the tomato sauce separately, if using.

Note: You can omit the sausages if you like, but the dish will have less flavor.

918

Lambs' feet fritters
BUÑUELOS DE MANOS DE CORDERO

- **8 lamb's feet**
- **sunflower oil, for deep frying**
- **deep-fried parsley sprigs
  (see Note)**
- **salt**

  Fritter batter:
- **2 ¾ cups all-purpose flour**
- **3 tablespoons white wine**
- **3 tablespoons sunflower oil**
- **2 ¾ cups milk**
- **½ teaspoon baking powder**
- **salt**

  Serves 6

Clean and precook the lamb's feet as described on page 788. When they are cool enough to handle, remove the bones. Make the batter for the fritters as described in recipe 58. Heat the oil in a deep-fryer or saucepan to 350–375°F or until a cube of day-old bread browns in 30 seconds. One at a time, coat the lamb's feet in the batter. Add to the hot oil, in batches, and cook until golden brown. Remove from the pan and drain well, then put on a serving dish, and keep warm while cooking the remaining batches. Serve immediately garnished with the fried parsley.

Note: Tie parsley sprigs together with thread and fry in moderately hot oil for an attractive garnish.

Lambs' feet with tomato

MANOS DE CORDERO CON TOMATE

• 12 lamb's feet

Tomato sauce:
• 3 tablespoons sunflower oil
• 1 onion, chopped
• 2¼ pounds ripe tomatoes,
  peeled, seeded, and chopped
• 1 teaspoon sugar
• salt

Serves 6

Ask the butcher to remove the central bones from the feet. Clean them and precook as described on page 788. Meanwhile, make the tomato sauce as described in recipe 73. When the lamb's feet are tender, transfer them to the pan of tomato sauce and simmer gently for 25 minutes. Serve in a warm deep serving dish.

Lambs' feet in savory lemon sauce

MANOS DE CORDERO CON SALSA DE LIMÓN

- **12 lamb's feet**
- **salt**

Savory lemon sauce:
- **4½ tablespoons butter**
- **1 heaping tablespoon all-purpose flour**
- **1 chicken bouillon cube**
- **2 egg yolks**
- **juice of 1 lemon**
- **pinch of freshly grated nutmeg**
- **1 tablespoon chopped fresh parsley**
- **salt**

Serves 4

Clean and precook the lamb's feet as described on page 788. Meanwhile, make the savory lemon sauce as described in recipe 86. Drain the lamb's feet, put them into a warm serving dish, and pour the sauce over them. Serve immediately.

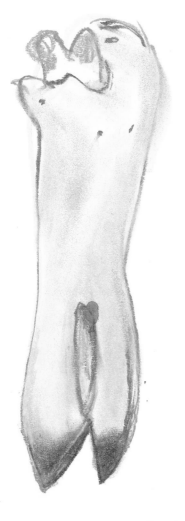

Pig's feet

Cooking method for 4 feet

Pig's feet are usually sold with the skin cleaned and the hair singed. If not, follow the method for lamb's feet (see page 788). Wash the feet in several changes of water. Make a cut in them from the hoof upward. Put them into a pan and pour in water to cover, then add ¾ cup white wine, 2 halved onions, 3 carrots, cut into four pieces, 2 cloves garlic, 1 bay leaf, 1 sprig fresh thyme, 1 sprig fresh parsley, 2 cloves, and a pinch of salt. Bring to a boil over high heat, then lower the heat, cover the pan, and simmer gently for about 4 hours, until the feet are tender. Drain well, then prepare them as preferred.

921

Pig's feet in bread crumbs

MANOS DE CERDO EMPANADAS

- **8 pig's feet**
- **2 eggs, beaten**
- **1½ cups bread crumbs**
- **sunflower oil, for deep frying**

Serves 4

Prepare and precook the feet as described on page 792, but before precooking wrap each one in cheesecloth and tie with fine kitchen string so that it does not lose its shape. When the feet are tender, drain well, and remove the cheesecloth. Remove as many bones as possible, then put the feet on a surface, and place a cutting board on top. Leave for 30 minutes. Coat the feet first in the beaten egg and then in the bread crumbs. Heat the oil in a skillet, add the trotters, two at a time, and cook until golden brown. Drain well and serve immediately.

Note: The trotters can be served with Classic Tomato Sauce (see recipe 73), Mayonnaise with Tomato and Brandy (see recipe 108), or Green Mayonnaise (see recipe 107). Offer the sauce separately.

922

Pig's feet with tomato

MANOS DE CERDO CON TOMATE

- **12 pig's feet**
- **salt**

Tomato sauce:
- **3 tablespoons sunflower oil**
- **1 onion, chopped**
- **2¼ pounds ripe tomatoes, peeled, seeded, and chopped**
- **1 teaspoon sugar**
- **salt**

Serves 6

Ask the butcher to remove the central bones from the feet. Clean them and precook as described on page 792. Meanwhile, make the tomato sauce as described in recipe 73. When the pig's feet are tender, transfer them to the pan of tomato sauce and simmer gently for 25 minutes. Serve in a warm deep serving dish.

923

Pig's feet fritters

BUÑUELOS DE MANOS DE CERDO

- **10 pig's feet**
- **sunflower oil, for deep frying**
- **deep-fried parsley sprigs**
  (see Note)
- **salt**

  Fritter batter:
- **2¾ cups all-purpose flour**
- **3 tablespoons white wine**
- **3 tablespoons sunflower oil**
- **2¾ cups milk**
- **½ teaspoon baking powder**
- **salt**

  Serves 5

Clean and precook the pig's feet as described on page 792. When they are cool enough to handle, remove the bones. Make the batter for the fritters as described in recipe 58. Heat the oil in a deep-fryer or saucepan to 350–375°F or until a cube of day-old bread browns in 30 seconds. One at a time, coat the pig's feet in the batter. Add to the hot oil, in batches, and cook until golden brown. Remove from the pan and drain well, then put on a serving dish, and keep warm while cooking the remaining batches. Serve immediately garnished with the fried parsley.

Note: Tie parsley sprigs together with thread and fry in moderately hot oil.

924

Pig's feet with Spanish sauce

MANOS DE CERDO CON SALSA ESPAÑOLA

- **8 pig's trotters**
- **1 quantity Spanish Sauce**
  (see recipe 82)

  Serves 4

Cook the pig's feet as described on page 792. When the feet are cool enough to handle, cut them in half, remove the bones, put the meat into the Spanish sauce, and bring to a boil.

Note: This dish is very good with the addition of 2 tablespoons pine nuts. Add them to the sauce at the same time as the pig's feet.

Pluck

925

Lamb's pluck
ASADURA DE CORDERO

- 4 tablespoons olive oil
- 2 large onions, finely chopped
- 1 pound 2 ounces lamb's pluck,
  cut into 1½-inch cubes
- 1 teaspoon paprika
- 2 tomatoes,
  peeled, seeded, and chopped
- ¾ cup white wine
- pinch of mixed dried herbs or
  1 bouquet garni (2 bay leaves,
  1 sprig fresh thyme, and 1 clove
  garlic tied in cheesecloth)
- 1 tablespoon chopped
  fresh parsley
- salt

Serves 4

Heat the oil in a pan. Add the onion and cook over low heat, stirring occasionally, for about 8 minutes, until beginning to brown. Add the lamb's pluck and cook, stirring frequently, until evenly browned. Stir in the paprika and add the tomato, wine, dried herbs or bouquet garni, and a pinch of salt. Cover and cook over a very low heat for 45 minutes. Remove and discard the bouquet garni, if used. Sprinkle with the parsley and serve with triangles of fried bread (see recipe 130) or Mashed Potato (see recipe 230).

Note: Pluck is a collective term that refers to the lungs, heart, liver and other offal of lamb. It is often hard to obtain outside the Mediterranean.

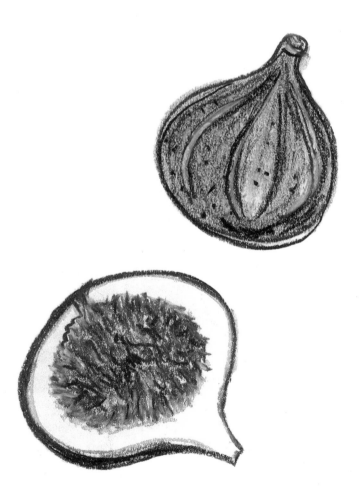

DESSERTS

926

Sponge cake made with milk and oil
BIZCOCHO CON LECHE Y ACEITE

- scant 1 cup sunflower oil,
  plus extra for brushing
- 2¼ cups all-purpose flour,
  plus extra for dusting
- 2 eggs
- scant 1 cup milk
- 1 cup superfine sugar
- grated zest of 1 lemon, or a pinch
  of vanilla powder or a few drops
  of vanilla extract
- ½ teaspoon baking powder
- pinch of salt

Serves 8

Preheat the oven to 300°F. Brush a long cake pan with oil and dust with flour, tapping out any excess. Beat the eggs in a bowl and stir in the milk, oil, sugar, and lemon zest or vanilla. Combine the flour, baking powder, and salt in another bowl, then sift them into the egg mixture in three batches, mixing well. Pour the sponge cake mixture into the prepared pan and bake until it starts to rise, then increase the oven temperature to 325°F. Bake for about 1 hour, until golden brown. Insert a wooden toothpick into the center of the sponge cake and if it comes out clean, the cake is cooked. Remove the cake from the oven, let cool until the pan is cold, then turn out onto a wire rack to cool completely.

Note: All sponge cakes can be kept for a couple of days, wrapped in aluminum foil once they are cooled.

927

Genoese sponge cake
BIZCOCHO GENOVESA

- scant ½ cup (1 stick) butter,
  melted, plus extra for greasing
- ¼ cup self-rising flour,
  plus extra for dusting
- 3 eggs, separated
- scant ½ cup superfine sugar
- grated zest of 1 lemon
- pinch of salt

Serves 8

Preheat the oven to 325°F. Grease a long cake pan with butter and dust with flour, tapping out any excess. Whisk the egg whites with a pinch of salt in a clean, dry bowl until stiff peaks form. Add the egg yolks and sugar and stir constantly with a wooden spoon and always in the same direction for 10 minutes. Add the flour, 1 tablespoon at a time, the lemon zest, and, finally, the melted butter. Pour the mixture into the prepared pan and bake for 45–60 minutes. Insert a wooden toothpick into the center of the cake and if it comes out clean, the cake is cooked. Remove the cake from the oven and let cool until the pan is cold, then turn onto a wire rack to cool completely.

928 Light orange sponge cake

BIZCOCHO LIGERO DE NARANJA

- **1 piece of candied orange zest, chopped**
- **2 tablespoons white rum**
- **margarine, for greasing**
- **¼ cup self-rising flour, plus extra for dusting**
- **generous ½ cup superfine sugar**
- **grated zest of 1 orange**
- **4 egg yolks**
- **¼ cup potato starch**
- **3 egg whites**
- **salt**

Serve 6–8

Put the candied orange zest in a bowl, pour in the rum, and let macerate for as long as possible. Grease a 10-inch long cake pan with margarine and dust with flour, tapping out any excess. Put the sugar and grated orange zest into another bowl, add the egg yolks, and whisk until pale and fluffy. Add the flour and potato starch sifted together and stir in. Whisk the egg whites with a pinch of salt in a clean, dry bowl until stiff peaks form. Gently fold them into the creamed mixture with a rubber spatula or metal spoon. Put half the sponge cake mixture into the prepared pan. Drain the candied orange zest, pat dry, and sprinkle it evenly in the pan. Cover with the remaining sponge cake mixture. Put the pan into the oven, turn it onto 325°F, and bake for 45 minutes. Insert a wooden toothpick into the center of the sponge cake and if it comes out clean, the cake is cooked. Remove the cake from the oven, let cool until the pan has cooled, then turn out onto a wire rack to cool completely.

929 Sponge cake made with egg whites

BIZCOCHO DE CLARAS DE HUEVO

- **scant ½ cup (1 stick) butter, melted, plus extra for greasing**
- **all-purpose flour, for dusting**
- **6 egg whites**
- **1 cup superfine sugar**
- **1¼ cups cornstarch**
- **pinch of vanilla powder or a few drops of vanilla extract**
- **salt**

Serves 6–8

Preheat the oven to 350°F. Grease a deep 8-inch cake pan with butter and dust with flour, tapping out any excess. Whisk the egg whites, three at a time, with a pinch of salt in a clean, dry bowl until stiff peaks form, then put them together in another bowl. Add alternate tablespoonfuls of sugar and cornstarch until they are used up. Finally, fold in the melted butter. Pour the mixture into the prepared pan and bake for about 50 minutes. Insert a wooden toothpick into the center of the sponge cake and if it comes out clean, the cake is cooked. Remove the cake from the oven, let cool until the pan is cold, then turn out onto a wire rack to cool completely.

930

Chocolate sponge cake

BIZCOCHO DE CHOCOLATE

- 6 tablespoons (¾ stick) butter,
  plus extra for greasing
- ¾ cup all-purpose flour,
  plus extra for dusting
- 3 ounces plain chocolate,
  broken into pieces
- scant ½ cup superfine sugar
- 3 eggs, separated
- ¾ teaspoon baking powder
- salt

Serves 6–8

Preheat the oven to 325°F. Grease a long cake pan with butter and dust with flour, tapping out any excess. Melt the butter in a pan over low heat, add the chocolate, and stir until melted. Remove the pan from the heat and stir in the sugar. Stir in the egg yolks, one at a time. Combine the flour and baking powder, sift into a bowl, and mix well, then add the chocolate mixture. Whisk the egg whites with a pinch of salt in a clean, dry bowl until stiff peaks form, then fold into the chocolate mixture. Pour the mixture into the prepared pan and bake for about 50 minutes. Insert a wooden toothpick into the center of the sponge cake and if it comes out clean, the cake is cooked. Remove the cake from the oven, let cool until the pan is cold, then turn out onto a wire rack to cool completely.

931

Rum baba

BIZCOCHO BORRACHO (BABA)

- butter, for greasing
- 3 egg whites
- 3 tablespoons superfine sugar
- 2 egg yolks
- 6 tablespoons all-purpose flour
- 1 tablespoon baking powder
- salt
- whipped cream and candied
  fruit, to decorate

Syrup:
- generous ½ cup superfine sugar
- scant 1 cup rum

Serves 6–8

Preheat the oven to 350°F. Grease a ring mold with butter. Whisk the egg whites with a pinch of salt in a clean, dry bowl until stiff peaks form. Fold in the sugar and then the egg yolks. Fold in half the flour, 1 tablespoon at a time, fold in the baking powder, and then fold in the remaining flour, 1 tablespoon at a time. Pour the mixture into the prepared mold and bake for about 45 minutes. Insert a wooden toothpick into the cake and if it comes out clean, the cake is cooked. Meanwhile, make the syrup. Pour 1 cup water into a pan, add the sugar and rum, and heat gently, stirring until the sugar has dissolved, then cook for 5 minutes more. Remove the pan from the heat but do not let the syrup cool. Remove the cake from the oven and while it is still in the pan, pour the hot syrup over it, a little at a time. When it is completely soaked, turn out onto a serving dish. Serve the baba with whipped cream in the middle and decorate it with candied fruit.

932

Rum baba made with bread crumbs
BIZCOCHO BORRACHO HECHO CON PAN RALLADO (BABA)

- butter, for greasing
- 4 eggs, separated
- 4 tablespoons superfine sugar
- 4–5 tablespoons bread crumbs
- 1 teaspoon baking powder
- salt
- whipped cream and candied
  fruit, to decorate

Syrup:
- ½ cup superfine sugar
- generous 1 cup rum

Serves 8

Preheat the oven to 350°F. Grease a ring mold with butter. Beat the egg yolks with the sugar until pale and fluffy, then stir in the bread crumbs and baking powder. Whisk the egg whites with a pinch of salt in a clean, dry bowl until stiff peaks form, then fold into the egg yolk mixture. Pour into the prepared mold and bake for about 45 minutes. Insert a wooden toothpick into the cake and if it comes out clean, the cake is cooked. Meanwhile, make the syrup. Put the sugar, rum and generous 1 cup water into a pan and heat, stirring until the sugar has dissolved, then cook for 5 minutes more. Remove the pan from the heat but do not let the syrup cool. Remove the cake from the oven and while it is still in the pan, pour the hot syrup over it, a little at a time. When it is completely soaked, turn out onto a serving dish. Serve it with whipped cream in the middle and decorate it with candied fruit.

Note: You could decorate the rum baba with Confectioner's Cream (see recipe 1010).

933

Sponge cake made with yogurt and lemon
BIZCOCHO CON YOGUR Y LIMÓN

- ¼ cup margarine, softened, plus extra for greasing
- 1 cup all-purpose flour, sifted, plus extra for dusting
- scant ⅔ cup superfine sugar
- ⅔ cup lemon yogurt
- 2 eggs
- 1 tablespoon baking powder
- grated zest of 1 lemon

Serves 6

Preheat the oven to 300°F. Grease a long cake pan with margarine and dust with flour, tapping out any excess. Using an electric mixer, beat the margarine with the sugar, yogurt, and eggs. Sift together the flour and baking powder and add to the mixture a spoonful at a time along with the lemon zest. Pour the mixture into the prepared pan and bake until the sponge cake is beginning to rise, then increase the oven temperature to 325°F, and bake for 45–60 minutes. Insert a wooden toothpick into the center of the sponge cake and if it comes out clean, the cake is cooked. Remove the sponge cake from the oven and turn out onto a wire rack to cool.

934

Fruitcake
PLUM-CAKE

- scant 1 cup softened margarine, plus extra for greasing
- 1¼ cups superfine sugar
- 5 eggs
- scant 1 cup candied fruit, chopped
- ½ cup raisins, soaked in hot water for 15 minutes, drained, and dried
- 2¾ cups all-purpose flour
- 2 teaspoons baking powder
- 6–7 tablespoons rum

Serves 6–8

Preheat the oven to 300°F. Grease a 12-inch long cake pan with margarine. Put the margarine and the sugar into a warmed bowl and beat until pale and fluffy. Add the eggs, one at a time and beat to incorporate. Coat the candied fruit and raisins in flour, shake them in a colander with large holes, and collect and reserve the excess flour. Set the fruit aside. Sift together all the flour and the baking powder and add to the margarine mixture, a little at a time. Stir in the rum and the coated fruit. Pour the mixture into the prepared pan and bake for 10 minutes, then increase the oven temperature to 325°F, and bake for about 50 minutes. Insert a wooden toothpick into the center of the cake and if it comes out clean, the cake is cooked. Remove the cake from the oven and let cool in the pan for about 10 minutes, then turn out onto a wire rack to cool completely. The cake will keep very well for several weeks if wrapped in aluminum foil.

935

Orange tart
BIZCOCHO-TARTA DE NARANJA

- butter, for greasing
- grated zest of 2 oranges
- generous ½ cup superfine sugar
- 4 eggs, separated
- ¼ cup self-rising flour
- ¼ cup potato starch
- ½ cup orange marmalade
- ¼ cup Cointreau, Curaçao or
  other orange-flavored liqueur

Syrup:
- 1 cup superfine sugar
- pinch of vanilla powder or
  a few drops of vanilla extract
- ¼ teaspoon orange extract

Serves 6

Preheat the oven to 325°F. Grease a 8- or 9-inch round cake pan with butter. Put half the orange zest into a bowl, add the sugar, and beat in the egg yolks, one at time. Stir with a wooden spoon for 15 minutes, then sift in the flour and potato starch. Finally, stir in the egg whites (not whisked). The mixture will be thick, smooth and pale yellow in color. Pour the mixture into the prepared pan and bake for about 30 minutes. Insert a wooden toothpick into the center of the sponge cake and if it comes out clean, the cake is cooked. Remove the cake from the oven, let cool until the pan is cold, then turn out onto a wire rack to cool completely. Using a sharp serrated knife, halve the cake horizontally. Combine the orange marmalade, the remaining grated orange zest, and the liqueur in a bowl and use to sandwich the two halves together. To make the syrup, put the sugar and vanilla into a pan, pour in 7 tablespoons water, and heat gently, stirring until the sugar has dissolved. Increase the heat to medium and cook for 10 minutes, then stir in 1 tablespoon cold water. Stir until thickened, add the orange essence, and pour the syrup over the cake. Let cool.

Note: The tart can be decorated with candied cherries or piped whipped cream.

Sweet walnut bread

PAN DE NUECES

- 1½ tablespoons butter, softened, plus extra for greasing
- 1 egg
- 1 cup superfine sugar
- 2¼ cups all-purpose flour, plus extra for dusting
- 1 cup milk
- ½ cup currants, soaked in warm water for 20 minutes and drained
- 1 cup walnuts, coarsely chopped
- ½ teaspoon active dry yeast

Makes 1 loaf

Cream the butter with the egg and sugar. Stir in half the flour, in batches alternating with the milk. Add the currants and walnuts. Mix the remaining flour with the yeast and stir in. Turn out the mixture onto a floured surface and mix with your fingertips. Generously grease a long loaf pan with butter and lightly dust with flour, tapping out the excess. Put the mixture into the pan and let stand in a warm place for 30 minutes, until risen. Meanwhile, preheat the oven to 350°F. Bake for about 1 hour. If necessary, cover the top of the loaf with aluminum foil during the cooking time to prevent it from burning. Insert a wooden toothpick into the center of the loaf and if it comes out clean, it is cooked. Remove the loaf from the oven and let cool in the pan for about 10 minutes, then turn out onto a wire rack to cool completely. Keep it wrapped in a damp dishtowel or aluminum foil for 24 hours before slicing and eating, as this will improve the flavor.

937

Madeleines
MAGDALENAS

- 3 eggs, separated
- 1¼ cups superfine sugar
- 1 cup sunflower oil
- ½ cup milk
- grated zest of 1 lemon
- 2¾ cups self-rising flour
- pinch of salt

Makes about 50

Preheat the oven to 350°F. Whisk the egg whites with a pinch of salt in a clean, dry bowl until stiff peaks form. Gradually stir in the yolks, then the sugar, oil, milk, lemon zest, and, finally, the sifted flour. Add these ingredients a little at a time, stirring them in well with a wooden spoon. Half fill about 50 foil baking cups for cupcakes with the mixture and place them on baking sheets. Bake for 18–25 minutes, until golden brown. Remove from the oven and transfer the cakes, in their baking cups, to wire racks to cool. They can be stored for 3–4 days in an airtight container.

938

Madeleines made with egg whites
MAGDALENAS DE CLARA DE HUEVO

- generous ⅔ cup butter, softened, plus extra for greasing
- 1¼ cups superfine sugar
- 6 egg whites
- 1 cup self-rising flour

Makes about 28

Preheat the oven to 350°F. Grease dariole or other cake molds with butter. (You will have to bake the mixture in batches). Beat the butter with the sugar until pale and fluffy, then beat in the egg whites (not whisked). Gradually sift in the flour, a little at a time, and mix well. Spoon the mixture into the prepared molds, leaving plenty of space for the cakes to rise during cooking. Bake for 20–25 minutes, until golden brown. Remove the cakes from the oven and turn them out onto wire racks to cool. Repeat with the remaining batter. They can be stored in an airtight container for 3–4 days.

Note: Dariole molds are small cylindrical baking molds. If not available you can use a muffin pan.

939

Coconut cakes
PASTAS DE COCO

- butter, for greasing
- 5 egg whites
- generous 1½ cups superfine sugar
- 3 cups shredded unsweetened dried coconut
- pinch of vanilla powder or a few drops of vanilla extract

Makes about 50

Preheat the oven to 300°F. Grease two baking sheets with butter. Put the egg whites and sugar into a pan and whisk together over medium-low heat until stiff. Whisk in the coconut and vanilla, then remove the pan from the heat. Using a teaspoon, put mounds of the mixture onto the prepared baking sheets. Bake for about 30 minutes, until lightly browned. Remove from the oven and let cool for 10–15 minutes, then lift the cakes off the baking sheets with a metal spatula, and place on a wire rack to cool completely.

940

Coconut rock cakes

ROCAS DE COCO

- butter, for greasing
- 5 egg whites
- 1½ cups superfine sugar
- 4 cups dry shredded coconut
- pinch of vanilla powder or
  a few drops of vanilla extract

Makes about 50

Make in the same way as coconut cakes (see recipe 939), but spoon larger mounds of the mixture on the baking sheets and use a fork, dipped in cold water, to give them an attractive shape before putting them into the oven.

941

Simple cakes

PASTAS SENCILLAS

- butter, for greasing
- 3 eggs
- 1 cup superfine sugar
- 2¼ cups self-rising flour, sifted
- pinch of vanilla powder or
  a few drops of vanilla extract

Makes about 50

Preheat the oven to 350°F. Grease two or three baking sheets with butter. Beat the eggs with the sugar, then stir in the flour, 2 table-spoons at a time, followed by the vanilla. Using a teaspoon, put small mounds of the mixture on the prepared baking sheets, spacing them well apart and working in batches if necessary. Bake for about 15 minutes, until lightly golden brown. Remove the baking sheets from the oven and lift off the cakes with a metal spatula. Transfer to wire racks to cool. These cakes will keep for up to 2–3 days in an airtight container.

942

Almond sablé biscuits

SABLÉS DE ALMENDRAS

- scant 1 cup (2 sticks) butter,
  softened
- scant ¾ cup superfine sugar
- 1 egg
- 2¾ cups all-purpose flour
- ⅔ cup blanched almonds,
  chopped

Makes about 35

Preheat the oven to 400°F. Cream the butter with the sugar until pale and fluffy. Gently stir in the egg, then the flour and almonds. Put the mixture into a churro machine, in batches, then spread it out on a surface, cutting the strips formed into 1½-inch lengths. Carefully transfer the cookies to a baking sheet with a metal spatula. Bake for about 15 minutes, until golden brown. Remove from the oven and let cool. They can be stored for 2–3 days in an airtight container.

Note: A machine for making churros (strips of fried dough) has a flat plate on one side and a ridged one on top. However, you can simply roll out the dough to ¼ inch thick and cut out the cookies with a round or oval cutter. Make a ridged pattern on the tops with a fork and bake as described.

943

Langues de chat
LENGUAS DE GATO

- ½ cup (1 stick) butter, softened
- generous ½ cup superfine sugar
- 4 egg whites
- pinch of vanilla powder or
  a few drops of vanilla extract
- 1 cup all-purpose flour, sifted

Makes about 55

Preheat the oven to 350°F. Beat the butter with the sugar in a bowl. Stir in the egg whites (not whisked), one at a time, and the vanilla, then stir with a wooden spoon for 8–10 minutes. Gradually stir in the flour, 1 tablespoon at a time. Use a spoon or a pastry bag to put ¾-inch wide strips of the mixture onto a baking sheet, spacing them well apart and working in batches if necessary. Bake for about 10 minutes, until golden brown around the edges but a lighter color in the center. Remove the baking sheet from the oven and loosen all the cookies with a metal spatula, then carefully transfer them to a flat surface to cool. The cookies can be stored for 2–3 days in an airtight container.

Note: These biscuits are called Langues de chat, or cats' tongues, because of their narrow shape.

944

Almond pastries
PASTAS DE TÉ CON ALMENDRAS RALLADAS

- 6 tablespoons (¾ stick) butter,
  softened
- scant ½ cup ground almonds
- ½ cup superfine sugar
- scant 1 cup all-purpose flour
- grated zest of 1 lemon
- 1 egg, lightly beaten

Decoration:
- 15 candied cherries, halved,
  or 30 blanched almonds

Makes about 30

Preheat the oven to 350°F. Beat the butter with the ground almonds and sugar in a bowl. Gently stir in the flour, lemon zest, and half the egg. Form teaspoonfuls of the mixture into balls, place on a baking sheet, and flatten them gently, working in batches if necessary. Brush the pastries with the remaining egg. Place a cherry half or an almond on top of each one, then bake for 15–20 minutes, until golden brown. Remove from the oven, lift the pastries off the baking sheet with a metal spatula, and let cool, preferably on a marble slab. The pastries can be stored for 2–3 days in an airtight container.

945

Teatime pastries
PASTAS DE TÉ

- 2 eggs
- 7 tablespoons butter, softened
- generous ½ cup superfine sugar
- 2¼ cups all-purpose flour,
  plus extra for dusting
- 1 tablespoon baking powder
- 1 tablespoon milk
- 50 blanched almonds,
  to decorate

Makes about 50

Preheat the oven to 350°F. Separate one of the eggs. Beat together the butter, sugar, whole egg, and the egg yolk in a bowl. Gradually sift in the flour and baking powder together, stirring to mix, and add the milk. Lightly flour your hands. Working in batches, form teaspoonfuls of the mixture into balls, place on a baking sheet and flatten them gently to make ⅝-inch rounds. Decorate each one with an almond. Beat the egg white in a bowl with a fork, then brush it over the pastries to glaze. Bake for 15–20 minutes, until golden brown. Remove from the oven, lift the pastries off the baking sheet with a metal spatula, and let cool, preferably on a marble slab. Repeat with the remaining batches. The pastries can be stored for 2–3 days in an airtight container.

946

Lemon doughnuts
ROSQUILLAS DE LIMÓN

- 3 eggs
- scant 1 cup lard, melted
- 1 cup milk
- grated zest of 1 lemon
- 3 tablespoons sweet anisette
- scant 1¾ cups superfine sugar
- 9 cups all-purpose flour,
  plus extra for dusting
- ½ teaspoon baking powder
  or baking soda
- 4 cups sunflower oil
- confectioner's sugar, for dusting

Makes about 35

Put the eggs, lard, milk, lemon zest, anisette, and sugar into a bowl and stir for 15 minutes. Gradually stir in the flour, a little at a time, and the baking powder or baking soda, until the mixture comes away from the sides of the bowl. (You may not need all of the flour). With floured hands, form the dough into little rolls about ⅝ inch thick. Heat the oil in a deep-fryer or deep skillet to 300–325°F or until a cube of day-old bread browns in 45 seconds. Add the doughnuts, in batches, and cook until puffed up, then turn up the heat and cook until golden brown. Remove the doughnuts from the oil with a slotted spoon, drain well, and dust with confectioner's sugar. Repeat with the remaining batter.

947

Almond doughnuts
ROSQUILLAS ALARGADAS DE ALMENDRAS

- 3 eggs
- 1 cup superfine sugar
- scant 1 cup blanched almonds, chopped
- 1 tablespoon kirsch
- 2 tablespoons (¼ stick) butter
- 2¾ cups all-purpose flour, plus extra for dusting
- 4 cups sunflower oil

Makes about 50

Put the eggs, sugar, almonds, and kirsch into a bowl and stir with a wooden spoon for 15 minutes. Melt the butter and stir it into the mixture. Finally, gently stir in the flour, stirring as little as possible. With floured hands, shape the mixture into little rolls, 1¼–1½ inches long and about ⅝ inch wide. Heat the oil in a deep skillet to 300–325°F or until a cube of day-old bread browns in 45 seconds. Remove the pan from the heat and add the first batch of doughnuts. When they have puffed up, return the pan to the heat, and cook until lightly browned. Remove with a slotted spoon and drain well. Repeat with the remaining batter. Once cooled, these doughnuts can be stored for 2–3 days in an airtight container.

948

Little almond cakes
POLVORONES DE ALMENDRA (MANTECADOS)

- 2¾ cups all-purpose flour
- generous 1¾ cups lard
- 1½ cups superfine sugar
- scant 1 cup ground toasted almonds
- pinch of ground cinnamon
- 1 egg, lightly beaten
- confectioner's sugar, for dusting
- salt

Makes about 50

Preheat the oven to 300°F. Heat the flour in a skillet, stirring constantly, for 7 minutes but do not let it brown. Pour the flour onto a work surface, preferably a marble slab, and spread it out into a round. Put the lard, sugar, almonds, cinnamon, a pinch of salt, and the egg in the middle and mix the ingredients with your hands until thoroughly combined. Shape pieces of the dough into balls about the size of a walnut, then flatten them. Working in batches if necessary, place the little cakes on a baking sheet and bake for about 30 minutes. Remove from the oven and leave on the baking sheet to cool completely, then dust with confectioner's sugar. Store them in an airtight container or wrap individually in tissue paper.

949

Fried bows
LAZOS FRITOS

- 2 ¼ cups self-rising flour,
  plus extra for dusting
- 2 eggs, lightly beaten
- 2 tablespoons (¼ stick) butter
- 2 tablespoons superfine sugar
- 1 tablespoon eau-de-vie or
  other fruit brandy
- 4 cups sunflower oil
- confectioner's sugar, for dusting
- salt

Makes about 25

Sift the flour with a pinch of salt into a bowl and add the eggs, butter, sugar, and eau-de-vie. Mix well with your hands, then turn out onto a lightly floured work surface, preferably a marble slab, and knead the mixture until smooth. Roll out the dough on a lightly floured surface and cut it into strips about ¾ inch wide and 10 inches long. Carefully tie the dough strips into bows. Heat the oil in a deep-fryer or skillet to 350–375°F or until a cube of day-old bread browns in 30 seconds. Add the bows, four at a time, and cook until golden brown. Remove with a slotted spoon and drain well. Repeat with the remaining batter. Serve sprinkled with plenty of confectioner's sugar.

950

Fried Marie cookies
GALLETAS «MARÍA» FRITAS

- 4 Marie cookies or tea biscuits
  per serving
- raspberry or red currant jam,
  about ½ teaspoon per biscuit
  sandwich
- sunflower oil, for deep frying
- confectioner's sugar, for coating

Serves 1

Sandwich the cookies together in pairs with the jam. Heat the oil in a large skillet to 300–325°F or until a cube of day-old bread browns in 45 seconds. When it is hot (but not too hot, as these cookies will burn easily), fry them quickly, about 10–12 seconds. Remove from the pan with a slotted spatula, drain, coat them in sugar, and serve immediately.

951

Choux puffs

PETITS-CHOUX

Choux pastry:
- 2 cups all-purpose flour
- 1 cup milk
- ¼ cup (½ stick) butter
- ⅓ cup lard
- ½ teaspoon sugar
  or 1 sugar lump
- sunflower oil, for brushing
- 2 egg whites
- salt

Custard filling:
- 3 egg yolks
- 2 tablespoons all-purpose flour
- 3 cups milk
- ¾ cup superfine sugar
- thinly pared zest of 1 lemon
- 1 egg white

Caramel topping:
- 3 tablespoons sugar

Makes about 30 large choux puffs
or 70 small choux puffs

Sift the flour onto a sheet of waxed paper. Put the milk, butter, lard, sugar, and a pinch of salt into a pan and heat gently, stirring with a wooden spoon. When the mixture comes to a boil, pour in the flour all at once, and stir rapidly for about 3 minutes. Remove the pan from the heat and let cool. Meanwhile, make the custard filling. Beat the egg yolks with the flour and 2 tablespoons of the milk in a bowl, then set aside. Put the remaining milk, the sugar, and lemon zest in a pan over medium heat and bring to a boil. Stir a ladleful of the hot milk into the egg yolk mixture, then pour the mixture into the pan, and cook, stirring constantly, for 3–5 minutes more, until thickened. Remove the pan from the heat, strain the custard through a coarse strainer into a bowl, and let cool, then chill in the refrigerator. Preheat the oven to 400°F. Brush 2 baking sheets with oil. Add the eggs, one at a time, to the cooled choux paste, making sure each is fully incorporated before adding the next. Finally, stir in the egg whites (not whisked). Using a teaspoon, put small mounds of the mixture, spaced well apart, onto the prepared baking sheets, working in batches if necessary. Alternatively, spoon the mixture into a pastry bag fitted with a plain tip and pipe small balls onto the baking sheets, spacing them well apart. Bake for 10 minutes, then lower the oven temperature to 350°F, and bake for 10 minutes more for small choux puffs or 20–25 minutes more for larger choux puffs, until they are golden brown. Remove from the oven. Using kitchen scissors, make a slit about 1¼ inches long in the side of each puff, then press gently to open it slightly and let the steam escape. (Make the slit about halfway up the puff so that the custard does not leak out when it is filled). Set aside to cool. To finish the custard filling, whisk the egg white in a grease-free bowl until soft peaks form, then gently fold it into the custard. Use a teaspoon to fill the puffs with the custard filling. To make the caramel topping, put the sugar into a pan with 1 tablespoon water and heat gently, stirring until the sugar has dissolved. Continue to heat without stirring until the caramel is golden. Remove the pan from the heat and quickly dip the top of each choux puff into the mixture, then remove immediately. Hold the choux puffs carefully to avoid burns.

Roulade

BRAZO DE GITANO

- **butter, for greasing**
- **4 tablespoons all-purpose flour**
- **2 tablespoons potato starch**
- **1 teaspoon baking powder**
- **pinch of vanilla powder or**
  a few drops of vanilla extract
- **3 eggs, separated**
- **1 egg white**
- **5 tablespoons superfine sugar**
- **salt**
- **confectioner's sugar,**
  to decorate

Serves 8

Preheat the oven to 325°F. Grease a jellyroll pan, about 15 x 10 inches, with butter. Line the base with waxed paper and grease with butter. Sift together the all-purpose flour, potato starch, baking powder, and vanilla powder, if using, into a bowl. Whisk all the egg whites with a pinch of salt in a clean, dry bowl until stiff peaks form. Add the egg yolks, and the vanilla extract, if using, then the sugar, and, finally, the flour mixture, a spoonful at a time. Spoon the mixture into the prepared pan. Bake for about 35 minutes, until firm but only lightly browned. Insert a wooden toothpick into the center of the sponge and if it comes out clean, the sponge is cooked. Wring out a clean dishtowel in warm water, spread it out on a work surface, and immediately turn the sponge out onto it. Remove and discard the waxed paper, spread your chosen filling over the sponge (see below), and use the dishtowel to help roll it up. Transfer to a dish, cover, and let cool. Before serving, trim off the ends of the roll and sprinkle confectioner's sugar on the top. Once the sponge is on the dishtowel, spread a thin layer of jam over it with a knife. Spread the whipped cream on top and quickly roll up the sponge. You will need about 2 ¼ cups heavy cream.

Note: The roulade can be filled with Confectioner's Cream (see recipe 1010) in place of the jam and cream.

Orange roulade

BRAZO DE GITANO DE NARANJA

- **butter, for greasing**
- **12 eggs, separated**
- **1¼ cups superfine sugar**
- **1 tablespoon cornstarch**
- **juice of 2 oranges**
- **grated zest of 1 orange**
- **salt**
- **confectioner's sugar,
  to decorate**

Serves 4–6

Preheat the oven to 300°F. Line a jellyroll pan with aluminum foil and grease with butter. Beat the egg yolks with the sugar and the cornstarch in a bowl. Add the orange juice and zest. Whisk the egg whites with a pinch of salt in a clean, dry bowl until stiff peaks form. Gently fold them into the egg yolk mixture. Pour the mixture into the prepared pan and bake for 30–45 minutes, until firm but only lightly browned. Remove from the oven and turn out onto a clean dishtowel. Roll up, using the dishtowel to help you, sprinkle confectioner's sugar on top, and let cool.

954

Walnut log
TRONCO DE NUECES

- butter, for greasing
- 4 tablespoons all-purpose flour
- 2 tablespoons potato starch
- 1 teaspoon baking powder
- pinch of vanilla powder or
  a few drops of vanilla extract
- 3 eggs, separated
- 1 egg white
- 5 tablespoons superfine sugar
- scant ½ cup freshly brewed
  strong coffee
- salt
- 2 ounces chocolate curls

  Filling:
- ⅓ cup superfine sugar
- 1¼ cups walnuts,
  peeled and chopped
- scant 1 cup milk
- 2 egg yolks
- 1½ teaspoons cornstarch
- ⅔ cup butter, softened
- dash of walnut liqueur

Serves 6

First make the filling. Put the sugar into a pan with 2 tablespoons water and heat gently, stirring until the sugar has dissolved. Continue to heat without stirring until the caramel is golden. Stir in the walnuts, remove the pan from the heat, and let cool. When the caramel has cooled, bring the milk to a boil, then stir it into the mixture. Beat the egg yolks with the cornstarch in a bowl and stir into the caramelized milk mixture. Return the pan to low heat and cook, stirring constantly, for a few minutes. Remove the pan from the heat and let cool. Pour the cooled mixture into a bowl, add the butter, and beat with an electric mixer on high speed. Stir in the liqueur and set aside. Preheat the oven to 325°F. Grease a large jellyroll pan, about 15 x 10 inches, with butter. Line the base with waxed paper and grease with butter. To make the sponge, sift together the all-purpose flour, potato starch, baking powder, and vanilla powder, if using, into a bowl and set aside. Whisk all the egg whites with a pinch of salt in a clean, dry bowl until stiff peaks form. Stir in the yolks and the vanilla extract, if using, then the sugar, and, finally, the flour mixture, a spoonful at a time. Pour the mixture into the prepared pan and bake for 35 minutes, until just firm but only lightly browned. Wring out a clean dishtowel in warm water and spread it out on a work surface. Remove the sponge from the oven and immediately turn it out onto the dishtowel. Remove and discard the waxed paper and sprinkle the coffee over the sponge. Spread the filling over the sponge, then roll it up using the dishtowel to help. Carefully transfer to a dish, cover, and let cool. Just before serving, trim off the ends diagonally and decorate the cake with the chocolate curls.

Note: You can make chocolate curls by shaving a bar of chocolate with a swivel-blade vegetable peeler. The cake can be filled with mango cream, creme anglaise with raspberries or chocolate cream.

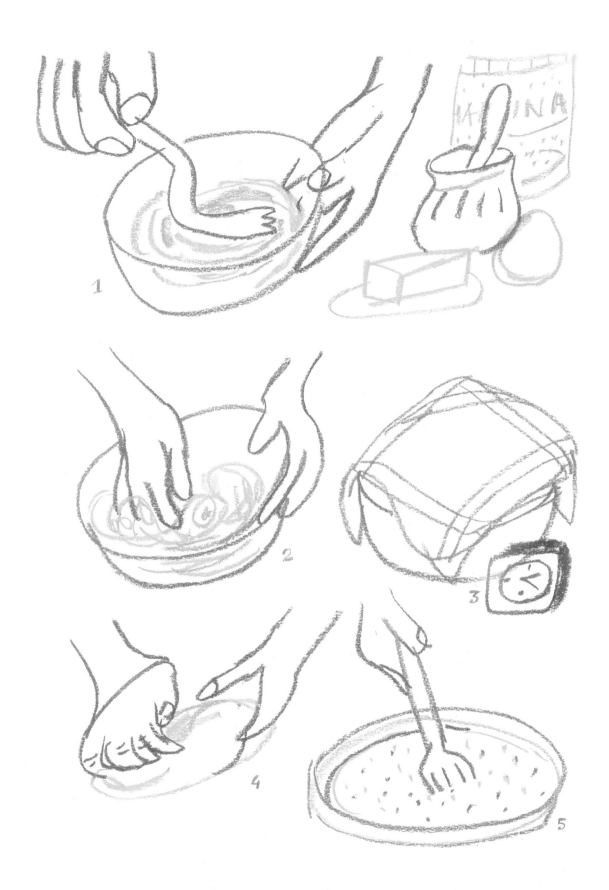

955

Pastry for tarts

MASAS PARA TARTAS

- 1¾ cups all-purpose flour,
  plus extra for dusting
- 1 tablespoon superfine sugar
- 6 tablespoons (¾ stick) butter,
  cut into pieces,
  plus extra for greasing
- 1 egg yolk
- 1 tablespoon peanut oil
- salt

Makes pastry for 1 tart, 10-inch
diameter

Sift the flour with a pinch of salt into a bowl. Sprinkle in the sugar and add the butter, egg yolk, and oil. Rub in the butter with your fingertips until the mixture resembles fine bread crumbs. Gradually stir in about ¾ cup water, a little at a time, until the dough forms. Turn out onto a lightly floured surface and knead lightly. Shape the dough into a ball, wrap in aluminum foil, and let rest in the refrigerator for at least 3 hours. Preheat the oven to 400°F. Grease a 10-inch tart pan with butter. Roll out the dough on a lightly floured surface, transfer to the prepared pan, trim the edge, and prick the base with a fork. Line the pie crust with waxed paper and half fill with pie weights. Bake blind for 10–15 minutes. Remove the pie crust from the oven. Remove the pie weights and paper and fill the crust according to your chosen recipe.

Note: If the tart is to be filled with fruit that will release juice, brush the base and sides of the pie crust with lightly beaten egg white before baking blind.

956

Sweet pie dough

MASA DULCE PARA TARTAS

- 1 cup all-purpose flour,
  plus extra for dusting
- 5 tablespoons butter, softened,
  plus extra for greasing
- 2 tablespoons superfine sugar
- 1 egg white

Makes pastry for 1 tart, 8-inch
diameter

Sift the flour onto a work surface, preferably a marble slab, and add the butter, sugar, and 2 tablespoons water. Work the ingredients together with your fingertips until combined. Shape the dough into a ball, wrap in aluminum foil, and let rest for about 30 minutes. Preheat the oven to 325°F. Grease a tart pan with butter. Roll out the dough on a lightly floured surface, transfer to the prepared pan, trim the edge, and prick the base with a fork. Lightly beat the egg white with a fork, then brush it over the base and sides of the pie crust. Bake blind for about 15 minutes. Remove the pie crust from the oven, add your chosen filling, and bake according to the recipe.

957

Sweet French pastry for tarts
MASA DULCE PARA TARTAS (3)

- 3 tablespoons lukewarm milk
- ¾ ounce dried active dry yeast
- scant ½ cup (1 stick) butter, softened, plus extra for greasing
- 2 egg yolks
- 2¼ cups all-purpose flour, plus extra for dusting
- 3 tablespoons superfine sugar
- salt

Makes 1 tart, 10 inches

Put the milk in a bowl, sprinkle the yeast over the surface, and let stand for about 10 minutes, until frothy. Stir well. Grease a baking sheet with butter. Pour the yeast mixture into a mixing bowl, add the egg yolks and butter, and sift in the flour with a pinch of salt. Bring the mixture together with your hands, then roll it out with a rolling pin or pat it out with your hand. Put the dough onto the prepared baking sheet, cover with a clean dishtowel, and let rise for 30 minutes. Prick the dough base all over with a fork, sprinkle with the sugar, and fill according to taste.

958

Sablé pastry for tarts
MASA SABLÉ PARA TARTAS

- ½ cup (1 stick) butter, softened, plus extra for greasing
- 1 egg
- 3 tablespoons superfine sugar
- 2¼ cups all-purpose flour, plus extra for dusting
- grated zest of ½ lemon
- salt

Makes 1 tart, 10 inches

Preheat the oven to 350°F. Grease an 8-inch tart pan with butter. Beat the egg with the sugar and a pinch of salt in a bowl until the sugar and salt have dissolved completely. Sift the flour into a mound on a work surface and make a well in the center. Pour the egg mixture into the well and dot the flour with the butter. Work the ingredients with your fingertips until combined but still grainy. Roll out the dough on a lightly floured surface, then transfer to the prepared pan, and trim the edge. Prick the base with a fork and bake until just dry or golden brown, depending on the recipe.

959

Almond pastry
MASA DE ALMENDRAS PARA TARTAS

- 1¾ cups all-purpose flour, plus extra for dusting
- scant ½ cup butter, cut into pieces, plus extra for greasing
- 3 tablespoons superfine sugar
- 1 medium egg, lightly beaten
- 2 tablespoons milk
- ½ cup ground almonds
- 3–4 tablespoons fine bread crumbs

Makes 1 tart 10 inches

Sift the flour with a pinch of salt into a bowl. Add the butter and rub in with your fingertips. Lightly work in the sugar, egg, milk, and almonds until combined. Shape the dough into a ball, cover with a clean dishtowel, and let rest for 1 hour. Preheat the oven to 350°F. Grease a 10-inch tart pan with butter and sprinkle with the bread crumbs, shaking out the excess. Roll out the dough on a lightly floured surface, transfer to the prepared pan, trim the edge, and prick the base with a fork. Bake blind for 25–30 minutes.

Note: This pie crust can be filled with cream and fresh berries. Brush the pie crust with lightly beaten egg white before baking.

250ml

Fruit for filling tarts

How to cook

Make a syrup with 2 ¼ cups water and ½ cup superfine sugar and heat for 10 minutes until the sugar has dissolved. Add the fruit—apple wedges, halved and pitted plums, cherries, apricots, etc. Simmer until softened but not falling apart. Drain well, reserving the syrup, and spoon into the prepared pie crust. Mix 2 teaspoons potato starch with a little water, add to the syrup, and cook for a few minutes, then pour it over the tart.

960

- 9 ounces strawberries, hulled
- ⅛ tablespoon powdered gelatin
- 2 tablespoons red currant or apricot jam
- 3 tablespoons superfine sugar

Serves 4–6

Strawberry tart
TARTA DE FRESA

Arrange the strawberries in a cooked pie crust (see recipe 956). Pour 3 tablespoons water into a small heatproof bowl, add the gelatin, and place the bowl over a pan of barely simmering water, stirring constantly until the gelatin has completely dissolved, then remove from the heat. Put the jam into a pan, add the sugar, dissolved gelatin, and 3 tablespoons water, and heat gently over low heat. Strain over the strawberries.

961

- 1 sweet pie dough pie crust (see recipe 956)

Filling:
- 1 tablespoon superfine sugar
- ⅓ cup currants
- 3 apples
- 2 tablespoons apricot jam
- whipped cream, to decorate (optional)

Serves 4–6

Apple tart
TARTA DE MANZANA

Preheat the oven to 325°F. Put the sugar and currants into a pan, pour in ½ cup water, and cook over medium heat for about 10 minutes. Remove the pan from the heat and set aside. Cut the apples into quarters, peel, core, and slice thinly. Arrange the slices around the edge of the cooked pie crust, overlapping slightly, then continue making similar concentric circles, until the pie crust is full. Put the tart onto a baking sheet and bake for about 20 minutes. Remove the tart from the oven. Drain the currants, reserving the syrup, and sprinkle them over the tart. Stir the jam into the syrup and cook over high heat for about 5 minutes. Remove the pan from the heat and let cool slightly, then strain the syrup over the tart. Let cool. Serve the tart plain or decorated with a little whipped cream.

962

Fruit tart

TARTA DE FRUTAS

- butter, for greasing
- 1 quantity pastry for tarts
  (see recipe 955)
- all-purpose flour, for dusting
- 1 egg white, lightly beaten

Fruit filling:
- generous ½ cup superfine sugar
- 3 large oranges,
  peeled and sliced, or
- 1 pound 10 ounces apricots,
  halved and pitted, or
- 1 pound 10 ounces pears,
  peeled, cored, and sliced, or
- 1 pound 10 ounces apples,
  peeled, cored, and sliced
- 2 tablespoons cornstarch
- 1½ cups milk
- 1 egg, lightly beaten
- 2 tablespoons apricot jam

Serves 6–8

Preheat the oven to 400°F. Grease a 10-inch tart pan with a removeable base with butter. Roll out the pastry for tarts on a lightly floured surface, transfer to the prepared pan, trim the edge, and brush the base and sides with the egg white. Bake blind for about 25 minutes. Meanwhile, prepare the filling. Put 5 tablespoons of the sugar into a pan, pour in scant ½ cup water, and cook over medium heat for 5 minutes. Add the fruit and cook in the syrup for about 8 minutes, until softened but not falling apart. Remove the pan from the heat and lift out the fruit with a slotted spoon and reserve. Reserve the syrup. Mix the cornstarch to a paste with 4 tablespoons of the milk in a bowl. Pour the remaining milk into a pan, add the remaining sugar, and bring to a boil. Stir in the cornstarch and cook, stirring constantly, for 3 minutes. Remove the pan from the heat. Remove the pie crust from the oven but do not switch off the oven. Gradually stir the egg into the cornstarch mixture, a little at a time. Pour the mixture into the pie crust and arrange the fruit on top. Return the tart to the oven for 5 minutes. Remove the tart from the oven and let cool. Remove the tart from the pan and place on a serving dish. Stir the jam into the reserved syrup and cook for about 10 minutes. Just before serving, strain the glaze over the tart in a thin layer.

Note: Do not fill the tart more than 30 minutes before serving or the pastry will become very soggy. You can omit the custard if you like, but more fruit will be needed. Sprinkle the base of the pie crust with a little sugar before adding the fruit, then continue as above.

963

Linzertorte
TARTA VIENESA CON MERMELADA DE FRAMBUESAS (LINZERTARTE)

- ⅔ cup butter, softened, plus extra for greasing
- 1¾ cups all-purpose flour
- ½ teaspoon baking powder
- 1 tablespoon unsweetened cocoa powder
- ¾ cup superfine sugar
- 1¼ cups ground almonds
- 1 teaspoon ground cinnamon
- 2 eggs, lightly beaten
- scant ½ cup raspberry or red currant jam

Serves 6

Preheat the oven to 325°F. Grease a 9-inch tart pan with a removeable base with butter. Sift together the flour, baking powder, and cocoa into a bowl and stir in the sugar, almonds, and cinnamon. Add the eggs and mix well, then mix in the butter. Reserve a little of the dough for decoration and put the remainder into the prepared pan, gently pressing it out with your hand to spread it all over the base and sides. Spread the jam over the base. Roll the reserved dough into thin strips between the palms of your hands and lay them over the jam in a diamond-shaped lattice. Put the tart on a baking sheet and bake for 10 minutes, then increase the oven temperature to 350°F, and bake for 10 minutes more. Increase the oven temperature to 375°F and bake for another 10 minutes, then increase the oven temperature to 400°F, and bake for 15–30 minutes more, until the pastry is lightly browned. Remove the tart from the oven and let cool in the pan, then remove it from the pan, and place on a serving plate.

Note: This Austrian pastry, usually made with raspberry jam, originates in Linz, hence its name. It can also be made with cranberries or apricots in the filling.

964

Lemon tart

TARTA DE LIMÓN

Dough:
- 1¾ cups all-purpose flour,
  plus extra for dusting
- 1 tablespoon superfine sugar
- 6 tablespoons (¾ stick) butter,
  cut into pieces,
  plus extra for greasing
- 1 egg
- 1 tablespoon sunflower oil
- 1 egg white, lightly beaten
- salt

Filling:
- 3 egg yolks
- grated zest of 1 lemon
- 1 can sweetened condensed milk
  (14 ounces)
- juice of 2–3 lemons

Meringue topping:
- 3 egg whites
- 2 tablespoons confectioner's
  sugar, sifted
- 1 teaspoon all-purpose flour,
  sifted
- salt

Serves 6

Make the dough with the flour, sugar, butter, egg, oil and salt as described in recipe 955. Shape it into a ball, wrap in aluminum foil, and let rest in the refrigerator for a few hours. Preheat the oven to 375°F. Grease a 10-inch tart pan with butter. Roll out the dough on a lightly floured surface, transfer to the prepared pan, trim the edge, and prick the base all over with a fork. Line the pie crust with waxed paper and half-fill with pie weights. Put the pan on a baking sheet and bake for about 30 minutes, until beginning to brown. Remove the pie crust from the oven but do not switch off the oven. Remove the pie weights and paper. Brush the base and sides of the crust with the egg white, return it to the oven, and bake for 5 minutes more. Meanwhile, make the filling. Beat the egg yolks with the lemon zest in a bowl, then gradually beat in the condensed milk, a little at a time, followed by the lemon juice. Remove the pie crust from the oven but do not switch off the oven. Pour the filling into the pie crust. To make the meringue topping, whisk the egg whites with a pinch of salt in a clean, dry bowl until stiff peaks form, then fold in the sugar and flour. Spread the meringue over the tart and return it to the oven. Bake for 10–15 minutes, until the meringue is beginning to brown. Remove the tart from the oven and let cool before serving.

Note: The tart can be filled with Lemon Curd (see recipe 1037).

Tipsy kiwi tart

TARTA BORRACHA DE KIWIS

- ⅔ cup butter, softened, plus extra for greasing
- generous ½ cup superfine sugar
- 4 eggs
- ⅔ cup all-purpose flour, sifted
- 1 tablespoon baking powder
- 4–5 kiwi fruits, peeled and sliced
- salt
- whipped cream, to decorate (optional)

Glaze:
- generous ½ cup superfine sugar
- ¾ cup rum

Serves 6–8

Preheat the oven to 325°F. Line the base of a 9-inch tart pan with a removeable base with aluminum foil and lightly grease the foil with butter. Pour hot water into a pan or metal bowl to warm it, pour it out, and immediately add the butter, sugar, and a pinch of salt. Mix well, then stir in the eggs, one at a time. Finally, sift in the flour and baking powder and mix well. Press the dough into the prepared pan with your fingers and place two sliced kiwis on top. Put the tart on a baking sheet and bake for 15 minutes, then increase the oven temperature to 350°F, and bake for 45 minutes more, until the pastry is golden. Meanwhile, prepare the glaze. Pour ¾ cup water into a pan, stir in the sugar, and cook over medium heat for 10 minutes. Stir in the rum and cook for 5 minutes more, then remove the pan from the heat, and let cool. Remove the tart from the oven and let cool in the pan. Remove the tart from the pan and place on a serving plate. Gradually spoon half the glaze over the tart, a little at a time. Put the remaining slices of kiwi on top and pour the rest of the glaze over them. Serve plain or decorated with whipped cream.

966

Grape tart

TARTA DE UVAS

- 1 cup all-purpose flour,
  plus extra for dusting
- 2 tablespoons superfine sugar
- 5 tablespoons butter,
  plus extra for greasing
- 1 egg white

Filling:
- 1 teaspoon cornstarch
- 1 cup milk
- 3 egg yolks
- ¾ cup confectioner's sugar
- ¼ cup Muscatel wine or
  other sweet white wine
- 2 tablespoons peach jam
- 1 bunch of seedless grapes
  (this can be a mixture of
  green and black grapes)

Serves 6

Sift the flour onto a work surface, add the sugar, butter, and 2 tablespoons water, and mix with your fingertips until combined. Shape the dough into a ball, wrap in aluminum foil, and let rest in the refrigerator for 30 minutes. Grease a 9-inch tart pan with butter and lightly dust with flour. Roll out the dough on a lightly floured surface, transfer to the prepared pan, trim the edge, and prick the base all over with a fork then brush with beaten egg white. Chill in the refrigerator. Make the filling. Mix the cornstarch to a paste with 1 tablespoon of the milk. Pour the remaining milk into a pan and bring to a boil. Beat the egg yolks with the sugar in another pan and stir in the cornstarch and boiling milk. Cook over low heat, stirring constantly, until thickened. Remove the pan from the heat and let cool, then stir in the wine. Preheat the oven to 400°F. Line the chilled pie crust with waxed paper and half-fill with pie weights. Place on a baking sheet and bake for 15 minutes. Remove the pie weights and paper, return the crust to the oven, and bake for 5 minutes more, until lightly browned. Remove the pie crust from the oven and lower the oven temperature to 300°F. Spread a thin layer of the custard on the base of the pie crust and return the crust to the oven for 15 minutes more. Remove the tart from the oven and let cool. Heat the jam in a pan over low heat. Pour the remaining custard into the pie crust and top with the grapes. Finally, pour the jam over them.

967

Egg custard tart

TARTA DE YEMA

- 1 quantity Sweet French pastry
  pie dough (see recipe 957)

Custard:
- 3 eggs
- scant ½ cup superfine sugar,
  plus extra for sprinkling
- 2 tablespoons ground almonds
  (optional)
- 3 tablespoons butter,
  plus extra for greasing

Serves 4–6

Leave the dough to rise for 30 minutes then prick with a fork. Grease a tart pan with a removeable base with butter. Preheat the oven to 350°F. Roll out the dough and press it into the prepared pan. Prick the bottom surface lightly with a fork. Make the custard. Beat the eggs in a bowl, then stir in the sugar and almonds, if using. Sprinkle the pie crust with sugar and pour in the custard. Dot with the butter, place on a baking sheet, and bake for about 20 minutes. Increase the oven temperature to 400°F and bake until the top is golden brown. Remove the tart from the oven and let cool. Turn it out of the pan and place on a plate so the custard is uppermost. This is easiest if you use a tart pan with a removeable base.

968

Puff pastry turnovers

HOJALDRE

- 1¾ cups all-purpose flour, plus extra for dusting
- ⅔ cup lard, softened
- ½ cup margarine, softened
- juice of 1 lemon
- 1 egg, lightly beaten
- salt

Makes 6

Try to prepare the puff pastry in a cool place, particularly in the summer time. Sift together the flour and a pinch of salt into a mound on a work surface, preferably a marble slab. Dot with the lard and margarine and mix lightly with a knife, then add the lemon juice and a little water (the amount depends on the type of flour, but never very much), and bring together with your fingers. Briefly knead the dough on a lightly floured surface, then roll out into a rectangle. Fold each of the short sides of the dough into the middle (see drawing). Let rest for 15 minutes. Give the dough a quarter turn and roll out again to a rectangle. Fold each of the short sides of the dough into the middle and let rest for 15 minutes. Repeat this procedure of turning the dough a quarter turn, rolling out, and folding three times, letting it rest for 15 minutes each time. Wrap the dough in aluminum foil and let rest in a cool place for at least 2 hours or overnight. Preheat the oven to 425°F. Roll out the dough on a lightly floured surface and make a turnover with your chosen filling, spooning the filling in the center of the dough, and folding one side of the dough over the filing to meet the other side. Leave a ½-inch border of pastry around the whole turnover and press to seal it with the tines of a fork or your fingertips. Place on a dampened baking sheet. Prick the turnover in several places with a skewer to allow steam to escape during cooking. You can also make a decorative pattern with a knife blade, if you like. Brush with the beaten egg to glaze, and bake for about 30 minutes, until puffed up and golden brown.

Note: To fill the turnovers, you can use a variety of fillings including: custard made with a lot of flour or cornstarch to make it very thick (see recipe 1008); Confectioner's Cream (see recipe 1010), without the addition of whisked egg white, and jam; Apple Compote (see recipe 972) which should be mixed with currants and walnuts (drain the purée well to prevent it spoiling the puff pastry); or fruit in syrup, such as pineapple, pears, etc., well drained.

Baked apples

MANZANAS ASADAS

- **1 apple per serving**
- **1 teaspoon sugar per serving**
- **1 pat of butter per serving**
- **apricot or other jam or custard (see recipe 1008)**

Serves 1

Preheat the oven to 350°F. Core the apples with an apple corer or sharp knife, but do not cut right through them. Score a line all the way around each apple, about halfway up, then place them in an ovenproof baking dish. Put the sugar into the cavities and put the butter on top. Put 3 tablespoons water (for 6 apples) into the base of the dish and bake for about 30 minutes, until the apples are tender. Test by piercing with a wooden toothpick. Serve warm or cold, filling the cavity in each apple with any variety of jam, or serve the apples covered with custard.

970

Baked apples with cream and caramel

MANZANAS ASADAS CON NATA Y CARAMELO

- 1 apple per serving
- 1 teaspoon sugar per serving
- 1 pat of butter per serving
- 1 tablespoon sweetened
  whipped cream
- 1 quantity Caramel Sauce
  (see recipe 117)

Serves 1

Bake the apples as described in recipe 969 and let cool. Fill them with the sweetened whipped cream and pour the caramel sauce over the top.

971

Baked apples with almonds

MANZANAS ASADAS CON ALMENDRAS

- 2 tablespoons rum
- ¼ cup currants
- 6 large apples
- ½ lemon
- 2 egg yolks
- 5 tablespoons superfine sugar
- 2 tablespoons (¼ stick) butter,
  softened
- ¼ cup blanched almonds,
  toasted and chopped
- 6 candied cherries

Serves 6

Preheat the oven to 350°F. Warm the rum in a pan for a few seconds, then remove from the heat. Add 1 tablespoon water and the currants and let soak. Meanwhile, core the apples with an apple corer or a sharp knife, then peel them, and rub them all over with the lemon to prevent discoloration. Place them in an ovenproof baking dish. Beat the egg yolks with the sugar in a small bowl and add the butter and almonds. Drain the currants, reserving the rum, and add to the mixture. Divide the mixture among the cavities in the apples. Stir 2 tablespoons water into the reserved rum and pour it into the dish. Bake for about 30 minutes, until the apples are tender. Remove from the oven and serve warm or cold, decorated with a candied cherry on top of each baked apple.

972

- **4 ½ pounds apples,
  peeled, cored, and sliced**
- **6 tablespoons superfine sugar**
- **1 cinnamon stick**
- **1 tablespoon rum (optional)**

Serves 6

Apple compote

COMPOTA DE MANZANAS

Put the apples into a pan, sprinkle the sugar over them, and add the cinnamon stick. Cook over medium heat, stirring occasionally, for about 20 minutes, until tender. Remove the cinnamon stick, pour the compote into a bowl, and let cool. Stir in the rum, if using. Pass the apples through a food mill or process in a food processor if you prefer a smoother texture.

973

- **4 ½ pounds apples,
  peeled, cored, and sliced**

Serves 4–6

Apple compote to accompany meat.

COMPOTA DE MANZANAS PARA ACOMPAÑAR LA CARNE

Prepare and cook the apples as described in recipe 972, omitting the cinnamon and sugar. Let cool, then pass through a food mill or pulse in a food processor.

974

- **4 ½ pounds apples,
  peeled, cored, and thickly sliced**
- **thinly pared strip of orange zest**
- **6 tablespoons orange juice**
- **6 tablespoons superfine sugar**
- **2 tablespoons rum (optional)**

Serves 6

Apple purée with orange juice

PURÉ DE MANZANAS CON ZUMO DE NARANJA

Put the apples into a pan with 3 tablespoons water and the orange zest. Cover and cook over low heat for about 20 minutes, until soft, then add the orange juice, and remove and discard the orange zest. Increase the heat to medium and cook for about 8 minutes, until the juice has been absorbed. Remove the pan from the heat and stir in the sugar, mixing well with a wooden spoon. Put the apple purée into a glass bowl and let cool. Stir in the rum, if using, and serve with Langues de Chat (see recipe 943) or other cookies.

975

Apple mousse with custard

MOUSSE DE MANZANAS CON NATILLAS

- 8 apples, about 2½ pounds,
  peeled, cored and chopped
- 6 tablespoons superfine sugar
- 2 tablespoons rum
- 4 egg whites
- salt

  Caramel:
- 3 tablespoons superfine
  sugar

  Custard:
- 3 cups milk
- 6 tablespoons superfine sugar
- 3 egg yolks
- 1 tablespoon cornstarch
- pinch of vanilla powder or
  a few drops of vanilla extract

Serves 6

Put the apples into a pan, sprinkle with the sugar, and cook over low heat for about 20 minutes, until softened. Drain well, then put the apples on a clean dishtowel or square of cheesecloth, gather up the corners, and hang over a bowl for about 10 minutes to drain completely. Make the caramel. Put the sugar into a pan, add 2 tablespoons water, and stir to dissolve, then cook over low heat until golden. Pour the caramel into a cake pan and pour it back and forth until the tin is completely coated. Make the custard as described in recipe 1008, let cool, then chill in the refrigerator. Preheat the oven to 350°F. Transfer the strained apples to a bowl and stir in the rum. Whisk the egg whites with a pinch of salt in a clean, dry bowl until stiff peaks form, then gently fold into the apple mixture. Pour the mixture into the prepared pan. Place in a roasting pan, pour in boiling water to reach about halfway up the sides of the pan, and bake for 1 hour. Remove the mousse from the oven and let cool in the pan. Just before serving, turn out onto a serving dish and pour some of the custard over it. Serve, offering the remaining custard separately.

976

Apple fritters

BUÑUELOS DE MANZANA

- 4 apples
- juice of ½ lemon
- 3 tablespoons superfine sugar,
  plus extra for coating
- 4 tablespoons rum
- 4 cups sunflower oil

  Batter:
- 2¾ cups all-purpose flour
- 3 tablespoons white wine
- 3 tablespoons sunflower oil
- 1 tablespoon superfine sugar
- 1¼ cups milk
- ½ teaspoon baking powder
- salt

Serves 4

Peel the apples, core with an apple corer or sharp knife, and cut into slices about ¼ inch thick. Toss them in the lemon juice to prevent discoloration. Combine the sugar, rum, and 1½ tablespoons water in a shallow dish, add the slices of apple, and let macerate, stirring occasionally, for 30 minutes. Meanwhile, make the batter. Sift the flour with a pinch of salt into a bowl, make a well in the center, pour in the wine and oil, and add the sugar. Mix well, then stir in the milk. Cover and let rest for 30 minutes. Heat the oil in a deep-fryer or deep skillet to 350–375°F or until a cube of day-old bread browns in 30 seconds. Drain the slices of apple and pat dry. Stir the baking powder into the batter. Dip the slices of apple into the batter, one at a time, add to the hot oil, in batches, and cook until golden brown. Remove with a slotted spoon and drain well, then coat the fritters in sugar while they are still hot. Put the fritters on a serving dish and keep warm as you cook the remaining fritters. Serve immediately.

Quick-and-economical fried apple purée

FRITOS DE PURÉ DE MANZANA, BARATOS Y RÁPIDOS

- **5 tablespoons all-purpose flour**
- **6 large apples, about**
  2½ pounds, peeled and grated
- **6 tablespoons superfine sugar,**
  plus extra for coating
- **4 cups sunflower oil**

Serves 6

Sift the flour into a bowl, add the apples and sugar, and mix well. Heat the oil in a deep-fryer or deep skillet to 350–375°F or until a cube of day-old bread browns in 30 seconds. Drop spoonfuls of the apple mixture into the hot oil and cook until golden. Remove with a slotted spoon, one at a time, coat in sugar, and place on a warm serving dish. Keep warm until all the purée has been fried. Serve immediately.

Flamed apple omelet

TORTILLA DE MANZANAS FLAMEADA

- **2 tablespoons (¼ stick) butter**
- **5–6 tablespoons sunflower oil**
- **3 apples,**
  peeled, cored, and sliced
- **6 eggs**
- **5 tablespoons superfine sugar**
- **5 tablespoons brandy or rum**
- **salt**

Serves 5–6

Melt the butter with 3 tablespoons of the oil in a skillet. Add the apples and cook, stirring occasionally, until golden brown. Put enough of the remaining oil into another skillet to cover the base, and heat it. Beat the eggs with a pinch of salt in a bowl, then pour them into the pan. Cook until the omelet is beginning to set, then spoon the apples in a semicircle on one half, and sprinkle 2 tablespoons of the sugar on top. Fold the uncovered half of the omelet over the apples. Slide the omelet onto a warm serving dish and sprinkle with the remaining sugar. Heat the brandy or rum in a small pan, ignite it, and carefully pour it over the omelet. Serve while it is still burning, spooning the rum or brandy over the omelet so that it is well flamed.

Tarte tatin

TARTA DE MANZANA CALIENTE Y HECHA AL REVÉS (TATIN)

- 1¾ cups all-purpose flour,
  plus extra for dusting
- ½ teaspoon salt
- 7 tablespoons butter,
  softened and cut into pieces
- 1 tablespoon sunflower oil
- 2 teaspoons superfine sugar
- whipped or pouring cream,
  to serve

Caramel:
- ½ cup superfine sugar
- 1 teaspoon lemon juice

Apples:
- 1 pound 2 ounces apples
- 2 tablespoons superfine sugar
- 1½ tablespoons butter

Serves 6

First, make the pastry dough. Sift together the flour and salt onto a work surface and put the pieces of butter on top. Pour on the oil and sprinkle with the sugar. Gently combine with your fingertips, gradually adding about 5 tablespoons warm water, a little at a time, until a smooth dough forms. Shape the dough into a ball, cover with aluminum foil, and let rest in the refrigerator. Make the caramel. Put the sugar into a pan, add 3 tablespoons water, and stir to dissolve, then cook over low heat until golden. Stir in the lemon juice, then pour the caramel into a tarte tatin pan or tart pan with a removeable base, and tip it back and forth until the tin is completely coated. Let cool. Peel, core, and slice the apples thickly. Arrange them in the prepared pan, bearing in mind that the first layer of apples will be on top when the tart is turned out so they should be placed attractively. Sprinkle the apples with the sugar and dot with the butter. Preheat the oven to 425°F. Knead the dough, pressing it out with your hands on a lightly floured surface. Fold it into four, then roll it into a round with a rolling pin. Lift the dough on the rolling pin and place it over the apples. Tuck it in around the edge. Bake the tart for about 45 minutes, until golden brown. Remove it from the oven and immediately turn out onto a warm serving dish. (If the caramel is allowed to cool, it is difficult to turn out the tart properly). This upside-down apple tart is served hot with whipped or pouring cream.

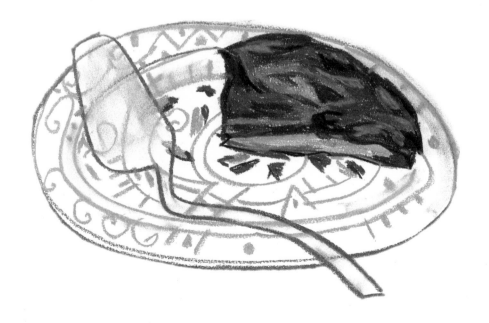

980

Apple tart with baked custard topping

FLAN-TARTA DE MANZANAS

- 1 pound 10 ounces apples,
  peeled, cored, and chopped
- ¾ cup superfine sugar
- 6 eggs
- scant 2 cups milk
- 2 tablespoons brandy
- pinch of vanilla powder or
  a few drops of vanilla extract
- grated zest of ½ lemon
- 3 day-old sugared doughnuts
  or sweet buns, thinly sliced
- 3 cups whipped cream and
  candied fruit, to decorate
  (optional)

Serves 6–8

Put the apples into a pan, add 2 tablespoons water and 2 tablepoons of the sugar, and cook, stirring occasionally, for about 20 minutes, until softened. Drain well, then put the apples on a clean dishtowel or square of cheesecloth, gather up the corners, and hang over a bowl for about 10 minutes to drain completely. Meanwhile, put 2 tablespoons of the remaining sugar into a pan, add 2 tablespoons water, and stir to dissolve, then cook over low heat until golden. Pour the caramel into a tart pan and pour it back and forth until the tin is completely coated. Preheat the oven to 325°F. Beat the eggs with the remaining sugar in a bowl, then mix in the milk, brandy, vanilla, and lemon zest. Arrange a layer of sliced doughnut or bun over the base of the coated tart pan and cover with a layer of apple purée. Continue making alternate layers until both ingredients are used up. Pour the egg mixture on top, but do not fill the pan completely so that there is room for the filling to rise. Put the pan into a roasting pan and pour in hot water to come about halfway up the sides. Bake for about 45 minutes, until set. Remove from the oven and let cool before turning out onto a serving dish. The tart can be covered with whipped cream and decorated with candied fruit if you like.

Note: This tart is delicious made with 14 ounces cherries. Pit them before cooking them in the same way as the apples.

Apple charlotte

POSTRE DE COMPOTA DE MANZANAS CON SOLETILLAS Y NATA

- **15–16 ladyfingers**
- **6 tablespoons superfine sugar**
- **3¼ pounds apples**
- **1 cup heavy cream,**
  stiffly whipped

Serves 6

Trim one end of the ladyfingers so that they will stand upright. Put half the sugar into a pan, add 2 tablespoons water, and stir to dissolve, then cook over low heat until golden brown. One at a time, dip the cut ends of the ladyfingers into the caramel to a depth of about ¾ inch. Place the ladyfingers upright, side by side, around a charlotte mold or round dish. Let cool. Peel, core, and dice the apples. Put the apples into a pan with the remaining sugar and ¾ cup water. Cook over low heat for about 20 minutes, until softened. Drain well, then put the apples on a clean dishtowel or square of cheesecloth, gather up the corners, and hang over a bowl for about 10 minutes to drain completely. Put the purée into a bowl and chill in the refrigerator. To serve, pour the purée into the center of the ring of ladyfingers, cover with the cream, and serve,

Note: Do not put the purée into the dish too far in advance of serving, as it will soften the ladyfingers and they will fall over. If you like, you can sweeten the cream with sugar before adding it to the charlotte. You could even fold in a whisked egg white. The cream can be decorated with chopped, caramel-coated almonds or with spun caramel, made from caramel beaten with a fork just as it is beginning to brown.

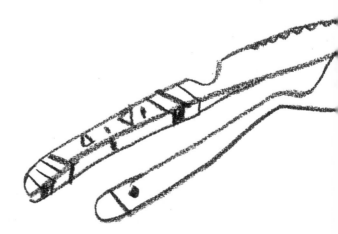

Pears with cream and chocolate
PERAS CON NATA Y CHOCOLATE

- **6 large pears**
- **scant ¾ cup superfine sugar**
- **1 small cinnamon stick**
- **1 cup heavy cream,**
  stiffly whipped
- **6 ounces semisweet chocolate,**
  broken into pieces
- **2 tablespoons (¼ stick) butter**

Serves 6

Peel and halve the pears and cut out the cores with a sharp knife. Put them in a pan in a single layer and sprinkle with 6 tablespoons of the sugar. Add the cinnamon and pour in just enough water to cover the fruit. Cook over medium heat for about 20 minutes, until softened and translucent but not falling apart. Lift out the pears with a slotted spoon, drain well, and let cool in a dish. Divide the cream among six glasses or sundae dishes and put two pear halves, cut sides down, on top. Chill in the refrigerator until ready to serve. Pour 1 ½ cups water into a pan, add the remaining sugar and the chocolate, and heat gently until the chocolate has melted and the sauce has thickened slightly. Add the butter and stir until it is fully incorporated, then remove the pan from the heat, and let the sauce cool slightly. Pour the sauce over the pears and serve immediately.

983

Tipsy cherries
BORRACHOS CON CEREZAS

Dough:
- ⅓ ounce fresh yeast
- ¼ cup lukewarm milk
- 1½ cups all-purpose flour,
  plus extra for dusting
- 6 tablespoons (¾ stick) butter,
  plus extra for greasing
- 3 tablespoons confectioner's
  sugar
- 2 eggs
- salt

Decoration:
- 3 tablespoons peach jam
- 1¾ pounds black cherries,
  pitted
- 2 tablespoons confectioner's
  sugar
- 1 tablespoon potato starch
- scant ½ cup kirsch

Syrup:
- 1½ cups superfine sugar
- scant ½ cup kirsch

Serves 4–6

Cream the yeast in a bowl with the lukewarm milk, mashing it well with a fork. Sift the flour into a bowl, make a well in the center, and pour in the yeast mixture. Mix well, cover with a clean dishtowel, and let rise in a warm place until cracks begin to appear on the surface. Melt the butter in a pan and beat in the sugar, a pinch of salt, and the eggs. Add the mixture to the dough and knead vigorously. Let rise for 15 minutes more. Grease individual ring molds with butter and dust them with flour. Divide the dough among the prepared molds, only half filling them. Let stand for about 15 minutes, until the dough has risen to the top of the molds. Meanwhile, preheat the oven to 425°F. Put the molds in the oven and bake for 15–20 minutes, until golden brown. Remove from the oven and turn out onto a wire rack to cool. Meanwhile, make the syrup. Pour 2¼ cups water into a pan, add the sugar, and stir to dissolve, then cook over low heat for about 6 minutes. Remove from the heat and let cool, then stir in the kirsch, and pour over the cake rings. Make the decoration. Heat the jam in a pan and pour it over the cake rings. Put the cherries and confectioner's sugar into a pan and pour in scant 1 cup water. Cover and cook for 4 minutes. Meanwhile, mix the potato starch with 2 tablespoons water in a bowl, add to the cherries, and cook, stirring constantly, for a few minutes, until the juice has thickened. Put the cake rings onto individual plates and divide the cherries among them, putting some in the middle and some around the edge. Spoon a little juice over them. Heat the kirsch in a pan, ignite it, and carefully pour it over the cherries. Serve immediately.

Melon and strawberry brochettes with raspberry sauce

BROCHETASDE MELON Y FRESON CON SALSA DE FRAMBUESAS

- ½ melon, preferably cantaloupe
- 12 strawberries, hulled
- 2 tablespoons (¼ stick) butter
- ¼ cup superfine sugar

For the sauce:
- Scant 1 cup raspberries
- juice of ½ lemon
- 1 tablespoon confectioner's sugar

Serves 2

Soak wooden skewers in water for 15–20 minutes and pat dry. Meanwhile, remove the seeds from the melon and scoop out the flesh with a melon baller or teaspoon. Halve the strawberries lengthwise. Thread the melon balls and strawberry halves alternately onto the skewers. Preheat the broiler. Put the raspberries, lemon juice, and sugar in a food processor or blender and process to a purée. Pass the purée through a strainer into a bowl and chill in the refrigerator. Melt the butter in a nonstick skillet over medium heat. Add the brochettes and cook quickly, turning frequently, until the fruit is lightly browned but remains firm. Sprinkle the sugar on the brochettes, place them on a baking sheet, and caramelize them under the broiler for a few minutes until they start to brown. Spread a little of the raspberry sauce on a plate and place the brochettes on top. Serve immediately, offering the remaining raspberry sauce separately.

Note: You can use metal skewers if you like. Other fruit, such as slices of banana or pieces of kiwi, can also be included.

985

Crunchy fruit in lemon sauce
CRUJIENTE DE FRUTAS CON SALSA AL LIMON

- juice of 2 limes
- ⅓ cup brown sugar
- 1 tablespoon chopped fresh mint
- 2 bananas
- 2 mangos
- 2 kiwi fruit
- 1 tablespoon butter,
  plus extra for greasing
- 8 sheets of phyllo pastry
- 8 fresh mint leaves

Sauce:
- juice of 5 lemons
- grated zest of 1 lemon
- 2 egg yolks
- ½ cup confectioner's sugar
- 1 tablespoon potato starch

Serves 4

Combine the lime juice, sugar, and chopped mint in a shallow dish. Peel and slice the bananas and put them in the dish. Peel, pit, and dice the mangos and add to the dish. Peel and dice the kiwis and put them in the dish. Let the fruit macerate. Make the sauce. Put the lemon juice and zest in a pan and bring to a boil. Beat the egg yolks with the sugar and potato starch in a bowl until light and fluffy. Pour in the boiling lemon juice, stirring constantly. Pour the mixture back into the pan and cook, stirring constantly, for a few minutes, until thickened, but do not let it boil. Remove the pan from the heat, let cool, then chill in the refrigerator. Preheat the oven to 425°F. Grease a baking sheet with butter. Melt the butter in a pan, then brush it over both sides of the phyllo pastry sheets. Cut the sheets in half and place two halves on top of each other to form a star shape. Place a mint leaf on each sheet of phyllo. Drain the fruit, reserving the liquid, and divide it among the phyllo sheets. Fold the pastry over the fruit and press the edges firmly to seal. Put the packets on the prepared baking sheet and bake for about 10 minutes, until the pasty is lightly browned. Meanwhile, stir the reserved liquid into the lemon sauce. Remove the packets from the oven and serve immediately, offering the sauce separately.

986

Grilled melon with sesame and honey
MELONES A LA BARBACOA CON SESAMO Y MIEL

- sunflower oil, for brushing
- 2 tablespoons orange blossom
  or other single flower honey
- 4 small melons, such as piel
  de sapo or cantaloupe, halved,
  seeded and cut into wedges
- 2 tablespoons grandulated
  (coarse) vanilla sugar
- juice of 1 lemon
- 2 tablespoons toasted sesame
  seeds
- 1 cup caramelized almonds,
  chopped

Serves 4

Brush the barbecue grill with oil. Pour the honey into a pan and place the pan on the side of the grill to warm through. Slice the melons and put them on the grill. Cook for 3–4 minutes on each side, until lightly marked with the bars of the grill. Transfer to a plate and sprinkle with the vanilla sugar and pour the lemon juice over them. Put the melon slices on individual plates or a serving dish and pour the warm honey over them. Sprinkle with the sesame seeds and almonds and serve.

Note: The melon is good served with raspberry sauce or melon or raspberry sherbet. Vanilla sugar is simply vanilla-flavored sugar. It is available in some markets and over the Internet. To make it yourself, bury a whole vanilla bean in 1 to 2 cups sugar, cover and let sit for several days.

987

Ricotta cheese with peaches in syrup
QUESO FRESCO CON MELOCOTONES EN ALMIBAR

- 14 ounces canned peach halves in syrup
- ½ cup superfine sugar
- ¼ cup peach liqueur or rum
- 16 ladyfingers
- generous 1 cup ricotta cheese
- 4 tablespoons red currant jam

Serves 4

Drain the peaches, reserving the syrup. Put the syrup into a pan and stir in 4 tablespoons of the sugar. Heat gently until the syrup thickens, then stir in the peach liqueur or rum. Remove the pan from the heat. Lightly coat the ladyfingers in the syrup and divide them among individual dessert plates. Beat the cheese with the remaining sugar. Spread the red currant jam on the ladyfingers and cover with the sweetened cheese. Decorate with the peach halves.

Note: The red currant jam can be replaced in the recipe with raspberry or blackberry jam.

988

Fresh fruit soup with cava
SOPA DE FRUTA FRESCA AL CAVA

- 1 small pineapple
- 20 lychees or 1 can lychees, drained
- scant 2 cups raspberries
- ⅓ cup brown sugar
- 1¼ cups cava or other sparkling white wine, chilled
- 5 fresh mint leaves

To serve:
- juice of ½ lemon
- superfine sugar
- marzipan petits fours

Serves 4

Lay the pineapple in a shallow dish to catch the juice and cut off the crown. Cut the pineapple into ½-inch slices. Cut off and discard the skin, then stand each slice on its side, and cut out the "eyes" with the tip of a sharp knife. Lay each slice flat again and stamp out or cut out the core. Chop the slices and put them into a bowl. Reserve the juice. If you are using fresh lychees, peel, halve, and pit them. Add the lychees to the pineapple with the raspberries. Stir in the sugar and chill in the refrigerator for 35 minutes. Prepare the glasses for serving the fruit soup. Brush the rims of four large goblets or water glasses with the lemon juice, then dip them into a saucer of superfine sugar to frost the rims. Set aside. Just before serving, pour the reserved juice and the wine over the fruit. Decorate with the mint leaves and serve in the prepared glasses. Offer the petits fours separately.

Note: The fruit may be varied. Oranges could be substituted for pineapple. Cut off the orange zests, removing all traces of pith, then cut the segments from between the membranes, and chop. Do this over a dish to collect the juice. Squeeze any juice out of the membranes. Pour the reserved juice over the fruit with the wine, just before serving.

989

Chestnut purée with layered ladyfingers
TARTA DE PURÉ DE CASTAÑAS Y SOLETILLAS

- sunflower oil, for brushing
- 2–3 tablespoons rum
- 3 tablespoons superfine sugar
- 35 ladyfingers
- 2 egg whites
- 1 pound 2 ounces canned sweet
  chestnut purée
- salt

Custard:
- 2¼ cups milk
- 3 tablespoons superfine sugar
- 2 eggs or 2 egg yolks
- 1 teaspoon cornstarch

Serves 6

Brush a 7-inch cake pan with oil. Put half the rum, half the sugar, and ⅔ cups water into a shallow dish and mix well. Dip about half the ladyfingers into the mixture. Place a layer of dipped ladyfingers in the base of the prepared pan. Line the sides of the pan with dipped ladyfingers, first cutting off one of the rounded ends, placing them upright side by side, cut ends down. Whisk the egg whites with a pinch of salt in a clean, dry bowl until stiff peaks form, then fold into the chestnut purée. Pour half the mixture into the pan. Dip some more ladyfingers into the rum mixture and place them on top of the purée. Combine the remaining rum and sugar, stir in ⅔ cup water, and dip the remaining ladyfingers into this. Add the remaining chestnut mixture to the pan and finish with a final layer of lightly dampened ladyfingers. Brush aluminum foil or waxed paper with oil and cover the tin. Put a lid or plate that is slightly smaller than the diameter of the cake pan on top so that it rests inside the pan. Put a light weight on top of the lid or plate and chill in the refrigerator for 6–8 hours. Make the custard as described in recipe 1008. To serve, remove the lid or plate and carefully take off and discard the foil or waxed paper. Carefully run a round-bladed knife around the edge of the pan, and turn the chestnut puree out on to a serving dish. Serve with the custard poured over the top or separately in a sauceboat.

990

Chestnut dessert
POSTRE DE CASTAÑAS

- 1½ envelopes
  (1½ tablespoons)
  unflavored powdered gelatin
- ¼ cup superfine sugar
- 4 ounces canned sweet
  chestnut purée
- scant ½ cup heavy cream
- 12 ladyfingers
- 3 marrons glacés and ⅔ cup
  chopped marrons glacés,
  to decorate

Serves 6

Pour ¼ cup water into a pan, add the sugar, and stir until it has dissolved. Bring to a boil and boil for 1 minute, then remove the pan from the heat. Add the gelatin, stir well to dissolve completely. Stir this mixture into the chestnut purée. Stiffly whisk the cream and fold it into the chestnut mixture, then pour into a fluted mold. Chill in the refrigerator for 2 hours, until set. Turn the chestnut mold out onto a serving dish and place the ladyfingers around it. Decorate with the whole marrons on top and the chopped marrons around the edge.

Note: To make it easier to turn out the dessert, first dip the mold into hot water for 30 seconds. Marron glacés are chestnuts that have been canned in syrup.

Ladyfinger, cream, and orange dessert

POSTRE DE SOLETILLAS, CREMA Y NARANJAS

- 5 navel oranges
- ¼ cup Cointreau, Curaçao or other orange-flavored liqueur
- 11 ounces ladyfingers
- 2¼ cups milk
- scant ¾ cup superfine sugar
- 4 egg yolks
- 1 tablespoon all-purpose flour
- 1 heaping tablespoon cornstarch
- sunflower oil, for brushing
- 6 candied cherries, halved

Serves 6–8

Prepare this dish the night before you intend to serve it. Peel the oranges, reserving the zest of one of them, then thinly slice on a plate in order to catch the juice. Rinse out a 7-inch cake pan with water and drain, then arrange the orange slices on the base and around the sides. Pour the juice into a shallow dish and add half the liqueur and 2 tablespoons water. Make a layer of ladyfingers on top of the oranges in the base of the pan, dipping them first in the juice mixture. Line the sides of the pan with ladyfingers, again dipping them first in the juice mixture. Pour the milk into a pan and add the reserved orange zest and half the sugar. Heat gently, stirring until the sugar has dissolved, and bring to a boil. Beat the egg yolks with the remaining sugar, the flour, cornstarch, and the remaining liqueur in a bowl, then stir in a few spoonfuls of the hot milk. Pour the egg yolk mixture into the pan and simmer, stirring constantly, for about 4 minutes, until thickened. Remove the pan from the heat, remove and discard the orange zest, and stir until cold. Pour half the custard into the cake pan, make a layer of ladyfingers (not soaked), add the remaining custard, and make a final layer of ladyfingers (not soaked). Brush aluminum foil or waxed paper with oil and cover the pan. Put a lid or plate that is slightly smaller than the diameter of the pan on top so that it rests inside the tin and add a light weight. Chill in the refrigerator for at least 6 hours before serving. To serve, remove the lid or plate and carefully take off the aluminum foil or waxed paper. Run a round-bladed knife around the edge of the pan and turn out onto a serving dish. Decorate with the cherries.

Note: You can serve this dessert with a thin custard (see recipe 1008) made with orange extract.

Ladyfingers with custard filling

SOLETILLAS RELLENAS DE CREMA

- **24 ladyfingers**
- **4 cups sunflower oil**
- **2 eggs**

  Custard filling:
- **2¼ cups milk**
- **3 tablespoons superfine sugar, plus extra for dredging**
- **thinly pared zest of 1 lemon**
- **3 egg yolks**
- **2 heaping tablespoons cornstarch**
- **1 tablespoon all-purpose flour**

Serves 6

First make the custard filling. Reserve 2 tablespoons of the milk and pour the remainder into a pan. Stir in 2 tablespoons of the sugar, add the lemon zest, and bring to a boil. Beat the egg yolks with the remaining sugar, the cornstarch, and flour in a bowl and stir in the reserved milk. Gradually stir in the boiling milk, a little at a time, then pour the custard back into the pan, and simmer gently, stirring constantly, for 3–4 minutes, until thickened. Remove the pan from the heat and let cool slightly. Cover the flat sides of half the ladyfingers with a generous layer of the warm custard filling. Put the remaining ladyfingers on top, but do not press down or the custard will squirt out. Heat the oil in a deep-fryer or skillet to 350–375°F or until a cube of day-old bread browns in 30 seconds. Beat the eggs in a shallow dish and coat the filled ladyfingers in them. Add to the hot oil and cook until golden brown. Remove with a slotted spatula, drain, and dredge with sugar while they are hot. Place them in a serving dish and let cool before serving.

993

Layered coffee and ladyfinger dessert

TARTA DE MOKA Y SOLETILLAS

- sunflower oil, for brushing
- 3 teaspoons instant coffee powder
- scant 1 cup superfine sugar
- 2 tablespoons rum
- 35 ladyfingers
- 2 egg yolks
- ⅔ cup butter, softened
- scant 1 cup toasted almonds, coarsely chopped

Serves 6–8

Prepare this dish the night before you intend to serve it. Brush a 7-inch cake pan with oil. Combine 1½ teaspoons instant of the coffee powder, 1½ tablespoons of the sugar, 1 tablespoon of the rum, and 3 tablespoons water in a shallow dish. Quickly dip about half the ladyfingers into the liquid, so that they absorb some flavor but are not sodden. Place a layer of dipped ladyfingers in the base of the prepared pan. Line the sides of the pan with dipped ladyfingers, first cutting off one of the rounded ends, and placing them upright side by side, cut ends down. Combine the remaining instant coffee, 1½ tablespoons of the remaining sugar, the remaining rum, and 3 tablespoons water. Beat the egg yolks with all the remaining sugar in a bowl until pale and fluffy. Gradually beat in the butter, small pieces at a time. Reserve one-third of this creamed mixture and store in the refrigerator until required. Pour half the remaining creamed mixture into the cake pan, cover with a layer of the remaining ladyfingers, first dipping them in the coffee mixture, pour in the other half of the remaining creamed mixture, and finish with another layer of lightly dampened ladyfingers. Brush aluminum foil or waxed paper with oil and cover the tin. Put a lid or plate that is slightly smaller than the diameter of the pan on top and add a light weight. Chill in the refrigerator for at least 6 hours. Remove the reserved creamed mixture from the refrigerator about 2 hours before serving to soften. About 1–1½ hours before serving, remove the lid or plate and carefully take off the aluminum foil or waxed paper. Run a round-bladed knife around the edge of the pan and turn out onto a serving dish. Cover the dessert with the reserved creamed mixture, spreading it evenly with a metal spatula. Sprinkle the almonds on top and chill in the refrigerator for 1 hour.

994

- sunflower oil, for brushing
- 5 tablespoons kirsch
- 2 tablespoons superfine sugar
- 36 ladyfingers
- 2¼ cups heavy cream
- 5¼ cups ripe strawberries, hulled

Sauce:
- 4 tablespoons superfine sugar
- 3⅔ cups strawberries, hulled

Serves 6–8

Layered strawberry dessert

BUDÍN DE SOLETILLAS Y FRESAS

Prepare this dish the night before it is needed. Brush a 7-inch cake pan with oil. Combine the kirsch, sugar, and ¾ cup water in a shallow dish. Dip about half the ladyfingers in the liquid. Line the sides of the prepared pan with dipped ladyfingers, first cutting off one of the rounded ends, placing them upright side by side, cut ends down. Make a layer of dipped ladyfingers over the base. Stiffly whisk the cream and spread half of it over the layer of ladyfingers in the base of the pan. Set six strawberries aside for decoration and halve the remainder. Put half of them on top of the cream, then cover with a layer of the remaining ladyfingers, after first dipping them in the kirsch mixture. Add the remaining cream, the remaining strawberries, and a final layer of lightly dampened ladyfingers. Brush aluminum foil or waxed paper with oil and cover the pan. Put a lid or plate that is slightly smaller than the diameter of the pan on top, so that it rests inside the pan and add a light weight. Chill in the refrigerator for at least 8 hours. To make the sauce, pour ¾ cup water into a pan, stir in the sugar, and bring to a boil. Cook for about 10 minutes, then remove the pan from the heat. and let cool. Put the strawberries in a fod processor or blender and process to a purée, then pass through a strainer into a bowl. Stir in the cooled syrup. Store in the refrigerator until required. To serve, remove the lid or plate and carefully take off the foil or waxed paper. Run a round-bladed knife around the edge of the pan and turn out onto a serving dish. Pour the sauce over the top and decorate with the reserved strawberries. Serve chilled.

Note: The filling can be made by crushing the strawberries with a fork and mixing them with the cream. Alpine strawberries can be used, if available, to make a more delicate pudding.

995

Ladyfingers with jam and chocolate
SOLETILLAS CON MERMELADA Y CHOCOLATE

- **6 tablespoons apricot or raspberry jam**
- **36 sponge fingers**
- **4 tablespoons cold milk**
- **7 ounces chocolate, coarsley grated**

Makes 18

Spread a little of the apricot or raspberry jam on the flat side of a ladyfinger and place another one on top, pressing them together. Dip them in the milk and then roll them in the chocolate. Repeat with the remaining ladyfingers. Place each prepared ladyfinger "sandwich" in a cupcake wrapper.

Tiramisu

TIRAMISÚ

- 3 tablespoons rum
- 1 cup very strong coffee
- 5 tablespoons superfine sugar
- 20 ladyfingers
- 4 egg yolks
- sunflower oil, for brushing
- 1⅓ cups mascarpone cheese
- 3 tablespoons unsweetened cocoa powder
- 3 cups thick custard (see recipe 1008)

Serves 4–5

Line an 8-inch cake pan with a removeable base with aluminum foil. Combine the rum, coffee, and 3 tablespoons of the sugar in a shallow dish. Dip the ladyfingers into the mixture and make a layer of them in the base of the pan. Beat the eggs yolks with the mascarpone in a bowl. Cover the layer of ladyfingers with a layer of the mascarpone mixture, sprinkle with a little of the remaining sugar, and make another layer of dipped ladyfingers on top. Continue making layers in this way until the pan is full, finishing with a layer of ladyfingers. Brush aluminum foil or waxed paper with oil and cover the pan. Put a lid or plate that is slightly smaller than the diameter of the pan on top so that it rests inside the pan, and add a light weight. Chill in the refrigerator for 24 hours. To serve, remove the lid or plate and carefully take off the foil or waxed paper. Turn the tiramisu out onto a serving dish, remove the aluminum foil, and sprinkle unsweetened cocoa powder over it. Serve the custard separately in a sauceboat.

Note: The name of this popular dessert of Italian origin means 'pick me up'.

997

Churros
CHURROS

- 1½ cups all-purpose flour
- 4–4¼ cups sunflower oil
- confectioner's sugar,
  for dredging
- salt

Makes about 25

Pour 1½ cups water into a pan, add a pinch of salt, and bring to a boil. Pour in the flour all at once and cook, stirring constantly, until the mixture comes away from the sides of the pan. Remove the pan from the heat and let cool. Heat the oil in a deep-fryer or deep skillet to 350–375°F or until a cube of day-old bread browns in 30 seconds. Put the cooled mixture into a churrera and make the churros, cutting them to the required length with a sharp knife as the dough is pushed out, and adding them immediately to the hot oil. Alternatively, spoon the cooled mixture into a pastry bag fitted with a star tip and pipe directly into the hot oil, cutting the churros to the required length with a sharp knife and working in batches if necessary. When the strips of fried dough are golden brown all over, carefully remove them with a slotted spoon, drain well, dredge with confectioner's sugar, and serve immediately while hot.

Note: These sweet, fried pastry strips are extremely popular in Spain, Latin America and the US.

998

Honey coated pastries
PESTIÑOS

- 2¾ cups all-purpose flour,
  plus extra for dusting
- 5 tablespoons white wine
- 2 tablespoons (¼ stick) butter
- 2½ tablespoons lard
- 4 cups sunflower oil
- generous 1 cup honey
- salt

Makes about 50

Sift the flour with a pinch of salt onto a sheet of waxed paper. Pour the wine and ¾ cup water into a pan, add the butter and lard and heat until the fat has melted. Pour in the flour all at once, remove the pan from the heat, and stir well with a wooden spoon. Turn out the dough onto a work surface and knead well. Shape the dough into a ball, wrap in aluminum foil, and let rest for 1–2 hours. Roll out the dough to a very thin sheet on a lightly floured surface. With a sharp knife, cut it into rectangles, about 6 x 3¼ inches. Starting at one corner, roll the rectangles up. Curl each one round like a miniature croissant, dampen one corner, and stick it to the other so that the roll does not open when frying. Heat the oil in a deep-fryer or deep skillet to 350–375°F or until a cube of day-old bread browns in 30 seconds. Add the pastries, in batches, and cook until golden brown. Remove with a slotted spoon, drain well, and let cool. Put the pastries on wire racks set over shallow dishes or trays. Spoon the honey over them (if it's not sufficiently runny, stir in a little warm water). Let stand until the honey is no longer running off the pastries, then transfer them to a serving dish.

999

Fritters
BUÑUELOS

- 2 ¾ cups all-purpose flour
- 3 tablespoons white wine
- 5 cups sunflower oil
- 1 ½ cups milk
- 5 eggs
- ½ teaspoon baking powde
- fresh fruit such as bananas or apples chunks, pineapple slices, figs or cooled rice or semolina pudding
- salt

Serves 4

Sift the flour with a pinch of salt into a bowl, make a well in the center, and pour in the wine and 3 tablespoons of the oil. Mix well with a wooden spoon, then gradually stir in the milk, and add the eggs, one at a time. Cover the bowl and let stand for at least 30 minutes. Stir in the baking powder when you are ready to start cooking. Use the batter to coat pieces of fresh fruit, such as banana, apple, pineapple, and figs, or cooled and set rice or semolina pudding, before deep-frying in hot oil. Heat the remaining oil in a deep-fryer or deep skillet to 350–375°F or until a cube of day-old bread browns in 30 seconds. Carefully add the fritters in batches, and cook until golden brown. Remove with a slotted spoon, drain well, and let cool. Repeat with the remaining fritters.

1000

Apricot fritters with raspberry and cinnamon sauce
BUÑUELOS DE ALBARICOQUE CON SALSA DE FRAMBUESA Y CANELA

- 12 apricots, halved and pitted
- 1 ¼ cups confectioner's sugar
- pinch of ground cinnamon
- 1 tablespoon raspberry liqueur
- 3 cups sunflower oil

Batter:
- 2 ¾ cups all-purpose flour
- 3 tablespoons beer
- 3 tablespoons sunflower oil
- 1 tablespoon superfine sugar
- 1 ¼ cups milk
- ½ teaspoon baking powder
- salt

Sauce:
- generous ½ cup raspberries
- juice of ½ lemon
- 1 ½ tablespoons superfine sugar
- pinch of ground cinnamon

Serves 4

First make the batter. Sift the flour with a pinch of salt into a bowl, make a well in the center, and pour in the beer and oil. Stir in the sugar and mix well with a wooden spoon. Gradually stir in the milk, then cover, and let rest for at least 30 minutes. Reserve half the apricots, put the rest into a food processor or blender with a little water, and process to a purée. Scrape into a pan, stir in ½ cup of the confectioner's sugar, and cook over low heat, stirring occasionally, for 10 minutes. Remove the pan from the heat and let cool. Stir in the cinnamon and the raspberry liqueur. Make the sauce. Put the raspberries, lemon juice, and sugar into a food processor or blender. Add the apricot purée and process until smooth. Strain into a bowl and stir in the cinnamon. Heat the oil in a deep-fryer or deep skillet to 350–375°F or until a cube of day-old bread browns in 30 seconds. Stir the baking powder into the batter. Dip the remaining apricots into the batter to coat, then add to the hot oil, and cook for about 2 minutes, until puffed up and golden brown. Remove with a slotted spoon and drain on paper towels, then dredge in the remaining confectioner's sugar. Serve the fritters with the sauce offered separately in a sauceboat.

1001

- 2 ¼ cups all-purpose flour
- 1 heaping teaspoon superfine sugar
- 2 eggs
- 1 tablespoon sunflower oil, plus extra for brushing
- 1 tablespoon rum or brandy
- ½ cup milk
- salt

Makes 15–20

Crepes
CRÊPES

Sift the flour with a pinch of salt into a bowl, stir in the sugar, and make a well in the center. Break the eggs into the well and pour in the oil and rum or brandy. Stir well, until the mixture is smooth. Combine the milk with ½ cup water and gradually stir it into the batter, a little at a time. The batter should have the consistency of thick custard and it may be necessary to add a little more liquid, depending on the type of flour. Cover the bowl with a clean dishtowel and let rest for at least 1 hour, longer if possible. When you are ready to cook, stir the batter. If it has become too thick, stir in a little more mixed milk and water. Brush oil over the bases of two small heavy skillets, about 5 ½ inches in diameter. Heat well. Pour a ladleful of the batter into a skillet and tilt the pan so that it covers the whole base evenly. Cook, gently shaking the pan to prevent the crepe from sticking or burning, until the underside is golden brown. Toss the crepe to turn, or flip it over with a metal spatula, and cook until the second side is lightly browned. Meanwhile, pour a ladleful of batter into the second skillet and cook in the same way. It is usual to make crepes in two pans simultaneously, as it is quicker. Put a pan full of very hot water over low heat, put a flat plate on top like a lid, and put a large sheet of aluminum foil on the plate. As the crepes are cooked, transfer them to the aluminum foil, then fold it over them to keep them warm while you cook the remaining crepes.

1002

- 2 tablespoons (¼ stick) butter
- 2 tablespoons Curaçao, or other orange-flavored liqueur
- 2 tablespoons superfine sugar
- ⅔ cup orange juice
- ½ quantity Crepes (see recipe 1001)
- 2 tablespoons rum or brandy

For 6–7 crepes

Sauce for crêpes suzette
SALSA DE CRÊPES SUZETTE

Melt the butter in a skillet. Add the Curaçao, sugar, and orange juice and cook for a few minutes. Add six or seven crepes, folded into four, to heat through in the sauce. Briefly warm the rum or brandy, ignite it, and carefully pour it over the crepes. Gently shake the pan until the flames die down, then serve the crepes immediately with the hot sauce on top.

1003

Crepes with custard filling
CRÊPES RELLENAS DE CREMA

- **1 quantity Crepes
  (see recipe 1001)**
- **5 tablespoons superfine sugar**
- **2 tablespoons rum or brandy**

  Custard:
- **2¼ cups milk**
- **5 tablespoons superfine sugar**
- **pinch of vanilla powder or
  a few drops of vanilla extract,
  or grated zest of 1 lemon**
- **3 egg yolks**
- **1½ teaspoons all-purpose flour**
- **1½ tablespoons cornstarch**

  Serves 2–4

Make the custard filling, as described in recipe 1008, in advance and let cool. Fill each crepe with custard and roll it up. Place the crepes next to each other, and sprinkle them with the sugar or flambé them with the rum or brandy as described in recipe 1005.

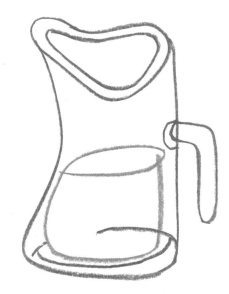

1004

Crepes filled with cream
CRÊPES RELLENAS DE NATA

- **1 quantity Crepes
  (see recipe 1001)**
- **1¼ cups whipped cream**
- **1 quantity Caramel Sauce
  (see recipe 117)**

  Makes 15–20

Make the crepes and, while they are fresh, fill them with whipped cream and pour the caramel sauce over the top.

Note: Crepes are delicious filled simply with apricot or other jam.

1005

Flambéed crepes
CRÊPES FLAMEADAS

- **1 quantity Crepes
  (see recipe 1001)**
- **5 tablespoons superfine sugar**
- **2 tablespoons rum or brandy**

  Makes 15–20

Fold the crepes in four and place them in a dish, then sprinkle the sugar over them. Heat the rum or brandy in a small pan, ignite it, and carefully pour it over the crepes. Scoop up the spirit from the dish with a tablespoon and pour it back over the crepes so that the flames do not die down too rapidly.

1006

Silver dollar pancakes

TORTITAS AMERICANAS

- 1¾ cups all-purpose flour
- ¾ teaspoon salt
- 1½ teaspoons baking powder
- 1 tablespoon superfine sugar
- 2 eggs
- 1 tablespoon sunflower oil
- 1 cup milk

Makes about 14

Sift the flour with the salt and baking powder onto a plate and add the sugar. Lightly beat the eggs in a bowl and stir in the oil and milk. Add the dry ingredients and beat briefly (it does not matter if there are lumps as these will dissolve on their own when the pancakes are cooked). Pour the batter into a pitcher. Heat a flat griddle or stove-top grill pan. Pour about 1 tablespoon of the batter onto it and cook for 2–3 minutes, until bubbles start to rise. Turn the pancake with a spatula and cook until golden brown on the underside. Try to serve these immediately. If they have to wait a while, keep them warm in little piles of no more than four.

Note: Serve these pancakes with cream and Caramel Sauce (see recipe 117), chocolate sauce, or jam. They can also be eaten spread with butter and jam.

1007

Bartolillos

BARTOLILLOS

- 1 quantity dough
  (see recipe 968)
- 1 quantity Confectioner's cream
  (see recipe 1010)
- 6¼ cups sunflower oil
- confectioner's sugar,
  for dredging

Makes about 20

Make the pastry dough as described in recipe 968 and let rest. Make the confectioners' cream as described in recipe 1010 and let cool. Roll out the dough to a thin sheet on a lightly floured surface. Cut out 4-inch rounds with a cookie cutter. Put 1 tablespoon of the confectioner's cream on each round and fold the bartolillo, pressing down firmly around the edges to seal. (You could use the metal wheel designed for cutting empanadillas, if you have one). Heat the oil in a deep-fryer or deep skillet to 350–375°F or until a cube of day-old bread browns in 30 seconds. Add the bartolillos, in batches, and cook until golden brown. Remove with a slotted spoon and drain well, then transfer to a serving dish, and dredge with confectioner's sugar. Serve warm or cold.

Note: Bartolillos are small cream-filled pastries popular in Madrid and throughout Spain.

Custards
and creams

Homemade custards and creams are delicious, but there is a trick to making them. From custard to confectioner's cream, many of them are used in the preparation of numerous desserts and also constitute desserts in themselves. They have a common denominator—their extreme fragility. Therefore you should use top-quality ingredients for them and eat them within hours of their being made.

Custards:
Making a traditional egg custard requires a little patience and care. It acquires its characteristic consistency because heat causes the egg yolks to coagulate. Therefore, the more egg yolks added, the thicker the custard will be.

- The usual proportion is 8 egg yolks for every 4 cups milk and 1 ¼ cups sugar, but add more yolks for a thicker custard
- Rinse out the pan with cold water before pouring in the milk. This prevents the milk sticking to the base and sides of the pan
- It is critical to be thorough when beating the egg yolks with sugar. Put the sugar in a bowl and make a well in the center. Add the eggs and beat quickly with a whisk until the mixture is smooth
- Remember to wash your hands after breaking the eggs to avoid bacterial contamination
- Be careful when heating the custard. It should thicken but not cook too much and should never boil, as it would spoil and lumps would form. However, if it doesn't cook enough, it will be too liquid. To find the ideal point, remove a little of the custard with a spatula and draw a line in it with your finger. The mark should be clear—if the sides rejoin, the custard is not yet cooked enough
- If the custard spoils, it may be possible to rescue it. Put a little cold water in a bowl and gradually pour in the custard, a little at a time, stirring vigorously.

Confectioner's cream:
- The base is the same as for custard, but it is usual to add flour or cornstarch to thicken it
- Add the cornstarch very carefully, beating with a whisk, but do not mix too much or the cream will harden
- To prevent a skin forming as the confectioner's cream cools, sprinkle confectioner's sugar over the top or cover it with plastic wrap.

1008

- 6 ¼ cups milk
- 6 heaping tablespoons superfine sugar
- thinly pared zest of 1 lemon or 2 vanilla beans
- 6 egg yolks
- 1 tablespoon cornstarch
- pinch of ground cinnamon (optional)

Serves 6–8

Custard
NATILLAS

Pour the milk into a pan, add 4 tablespoons of the sugar and the lemon zest, and bring just to a boil. Meanwhile, beat the egg yolks with the remaining sugar and the cornstarch in a bowl. Gradually stir in the hot milk, a little at a time, then pour the custard back into the pan, lower the heat, and cook, stirring constantly, for about 5 minutes until thickened and smooth. Do not let the mixture boil. Strain the custard and pour it into a deep dish or individual dishes or bowls. Chill in the refrigerator until required. Sprinkle a little ground cinnamon on the top before serving if you like.

1009

- 4 cups milk
- ⅔ cup superfine sugar
- thinly pared zest of 1 lemon
- 8 egg yolks
- 1½–2 tablespoons potato starch or cornstarch

Serves 6

Catalan cream
CREMA CATALANA

Pour the milk into a pan, add 4 tablespoons of the sugar and the lemon zest, and bring just to a boil. Meanwhile, beat the egg yolks with 2 tablespoons of the remaining sugar and the potato starch. Gradually stir in the hot milk, then pour the custard into the pan. Lower the heat and cook, stirring con-stantly, for about 5 minutes, until thickened. Strain into a serving dish or individual dishes and let cool, then chill in the refrigerator for at least 1 hour. Just before serving, sprinkle the remaining sugar on top and use a kitchen blow torch to caramelize it.

Note: Crema catalana is the best-known Spanish dessert and is said by some to be the predecessor of France's crème brûlée.

Confectioner's cream for fillings

CREMA PASTELERA (PARA RELLENOS)

- 2¼ cups milk
- 5 tablespoons superfine sugar
- thinly pared zest of 1 lemon,
  or pinch of vanilla powder or
  a few drops of vanilla extract
- 3 egg yolks
- 2 tablespoons cornstarch
- 1 tablespoon all-purpose flour
- 1 egg white (optional)
- salt (optional)

Serves 4–6

Reserve 3 tablespoons of the milk. Pour the remaining milk into a pan, add 3 tablespoons of the sugar and the lemon zest or vanilla, and bring just to a boil. Meanwhile beat the egg yolks with the remaining sugar, the cornstarch, flour, and reserved milk in a bowl. Gradually stir in the hot milk, a little at a time, then pour the custard back into the pan, and simmer over low heat, stirring constantly, for about 5 minutes, until thickened and smooth. Remove the pan from the heat, pour the custard into a dish or a bowl and let cool. Remove and discard the lemon zest, if using. If you like, whisk the egg white with a pinch of salt in a clean, dry bowl until stiff peaks form, then fold it into the custard.

1011

- 4 egg yolks
- 9 tablespoons superfine sugar
- 1 teaspoon all-purpose flour
- 2 heaping tablespoons
  cornstarch
- 4 cups milk
- 1 vanilla bean, pinch of vanilla
  powder or a few drops of vanilla
  extract

Serves 6–8

Confectioner's cream

CREMA PASTELERA

Combine the egg yolks, 3 tablespoons of the sugar, the flour, and cornstarch in a bowl. Pour the milk into a pan, add 3 tablespoons of the remaining sugar and the vanilla, and heat, stirring until the sugar has dissolved, then bring to a boil. Stir about 4 tablespoons of the milk into the egg yolk mixture, then pour the mixture into the pan. Cook, stirring constantly, for about 3 minutes, until thickened. Remove the pan from the heat and remove the vanilla bean, if used. Let cool, stirring occasionally. When the rum baba is cold and has been turned out onto a serving dish, pour the cooled confectioner's cream into the center and sprinkle with the remaining sugar. Caramelize the sugar with a kitchen blow torch. Serve immediately.

1012

Custard:
- 3 cups milk
- 6 tablespoons sugar
- pinch of vanilla powder or
  a few drops of vanilla extract
- 4 egg yolks
- 1 tablespoon cornstarch

Rock:
- 8 egg whites
- ½ cup superfine sugar

Caramel:
- 2 tablespoons superfine sugar

Serves 6

Custard with a floating island

NATILLAS CON ROCA FLOTANTE

First make the caramel. Put the sugar in a pan, add 1 tablespoon water, and stir to dissolve, then cook over low heat until golden. Pour the caramel into a cake pan and pour it back and forth until the base is completely coated. Let cool. Make the custard. Pour the milk into a pan, add half the sugar and the vanilla, and bring just to a boil. Meanwhile, beat the egg yolks with the remaining sugar and the cornstarch in a bowl. Gradually stir in the hot milk, a little at a time, then pour the custard back into the pan, and cook over medium heat, stirring constantly, for a few minutes, until thickened, but do not let it boil. Strain into a deep serving dish, let cool, and then chill in the refrigerator. Preheat the oven to 300°F. To make the island, whisk the egg whites in a clean, dry bowl until stiff peaks form, then whisk in half the sugar. Put the remaining sugar into a pan, add 2 tablespoons water, and stir to dissolve, then cook over low heat until a dark golden color, but do not let the caramel burn or it will taste bitter. Gradually pour the caramel onto the egg whites, a little at a time, stirring quickly so that it mixes well and no lumps of caramel form. Pour the mixture into the caramel-lined pan. Place it in a roasting pan, pour in hot water to come about halfway up the sides, and bake for about 25 minutes. Remove from the oven and let cool. To serve, pour the island out on top of the custard.

Chocolate custard

CREMA DE CHOCOLATE

- **8 ounces bittersweet chocolate**
- **3–4 tablespoons hot water**
- **4 cups milk**
- **6 tablespoons superfine sugar**
- **3 egg yolks**
- **1½ tablespoons cornstarch**

Serves 6

Put the chocolate and hot water into a pan and melt over low heat, stirring occasionally. Remove the pan from the heat. Pour the milk into another pan, add 4 tablespoons of the sugar, and stir to dissolve, then bring just to a boil. Meanwhile, beat the egg yolks with the remaining sugar and the cornstarch in a bowl. Gradually stir in the hot milk, a little at a time, then pour the custard back into the pan, and cook, stirring constantly, for a few minutes, until thickened. Stir in the melted chocolate mixture and cook, stirring constantly, for 3 minutes more, but do not let the mixture boil. Remove the pan from the heat and let the custard cool, then strain into a bowl, and chill in the refrigerator until required.

Note: To decorate the custard, stiffly whisk 2 egg whites in a grease-free bowl and fold in 2 tablespoons superfine sugar. Put spoonfuls of the mixture on top of the custard and sprinkle with 10 chopped toasted almonds.

1014

Sugared bun pudding
BUDÍN CON SUIZOS

- ¼ cup currants
- 3 tablespoons sherry or other sweet forified wine
- 5 tablespoons superfine sugar
- 2 cups milk
- 3–4 day-old sugared doughnuts or sweet buns, cut into ½-inch slices
- 3 eggs
- 1 quantity Jam Sauce (using red currant or apricot jam, see recipe 119)

Caramel:
- 3 tablespoons superfine sugar

Serves 6

Put the currants into a pan, add 5 tablespoons hot water and the sherry, and let soak. Make the caramel. Put the sugar into a pan, add 2 tablespoons water, and stir to dissolve, then cook over low heat until golden. Pour the caramel into a cake pan and pour it back and forth until the pan is completely coated. Let cool. Gently heat the pan of currants and simmer for a few minutes, then remove the pan from the heat. Strain the currants, reserving the liquid if you like (see note). Preheat the oven to 300°F. Stir 2 tablespoons of the sugar into half the milk in a shallow dish and add the slices of bun. Let soak for a few minutes, then turn over, and let soak for a few minutes more. Remove the slices from the milk, squeeze them out, and layer them in the cake pan alternating with the currants. Beat the eggs in a bowl with the remaining sugar, then beat in the remaining milk. Pour the mixture into the cake pan, shaking the pan gently so that the liquid penetrates. Put the pan into a roasting pan, pour in hot water to come about halfway up the sides, and bake for about 45 minutes. Check by inserting a wooden toothpick into the center of the pudding; if it comes out clean, the pudding is cooked. Remove the pan from the roasting pan and let cool. Run a round-bladed knife around the edge of the cake pan and turn the pudding out onto a long serving dish. Serve the sauce separately in a sauceboat.

Note: If you like, cook the reserved soaking liquid for 3 minutes more and pour it over the pudding when you remove it from the oven. This makes the pudding softer and some people prefer it. The pudding can also be served flamed with rum, instead of with jam sauce.

1015

• 4 pears
• 5 tablespoons superfine sugar
• 4 eggs
• 1 cup milk

Caramel:
• 3 tablespoons superfine sugar

Serves 6

Crème caramel with pears

FLAN CON PERAS

Make the caramel. Put the sugar into a pan, add 2 tablespoons water, and stir to dissolve, then cook over low heat until golden. Pour the caramel into a cake pan, 10 inches in diameter and 2 inches deep. Pour it back and forth until the base is completely coated. Let cool. Peel, core, and dice the pears, put them into a pan, pour in 1 cup water, and add 2 tablespoons of the sugar. Cover the pan and cook over medium heat until the pears are soft but not falling apart. Drain the pears and spoon them into the cake pan in an even layer. Preheat the oven to 300°F. Beat the eggs with the remaining sugar in a bowl, then beat in the milk. Pour the mixture over the pears. Put the pan into a roasting pan, pour in hot water to come about halfway up the sides, and bake for about 40 minutes, until set. Remove from the oven but leave the pan standing in the water. When the water has cooled to warm, remove the cake pan from the roasting pan and turn the crème caramel out onto a round serving dish. Serve this dessert slightly warm.

Note: The dish can also be made with apples.

1016

• 3 cups milk
• pinch of vanilla powder,
  a few drops of vanilla extract
  or 1 vanilla bean
• 2 eggs
• 6 yolks
• 1 cup superfine sugar

Caramel:
• 3 tablespoons superfine sugar

Serves 6

Classic crème caramel

FLAN CLÁSICO

Make the caramel. Put the sugar into a pan, add 2 tablespoons water, and stir to dissolve, then cook over low heat until golden. Pour the caramel into a cake pan and pour it back and forth until the pan is completely coated. Let cool. Preheat the oven to 300°F. Pour the milk into a pan, add the vanilla, and bring just to a boil. Meanwhile, beat the eggs and egg yolks with the sugar in a bowl. Gradually stir in the hot milk, a little at a time. Strain into the cake pan. Put the pan into a roasting pan, pour in hot water to come about halfway up the sides, and bake for about 50 minutes, until set. Remove the pan from the oven and let cool, then chill in the refrigerator. Turn out onto a round dish and serve.

1017

Crème caramel surprise

FLAN SORPRESA

- **3 cups milk**
- **pinch of vanilla powder,
  a few drops of vanilla extract
  or 1 vanilla bean**
- **2 eggs**
- **6 yolks**
- **1 cup superfine sugar**
- **1 cup heavy cream**
- **1 quantity Jam Sauce
  (using red currant or
  apricot jam, see recipe 119)**

Caramel:
- **3 tablespoons superfine sugar**

Serves 6

For crème caramel surprise, make the creme caramel as described in recipe 117. Stiffly whisk the cream. Whisk the egg white in a clean, dry bowl until stiff peaks form, then fold it into the cream. Turn out the chilled crème caramel and cover it with the cream mixture, then pour the jam sauce over it.

1018

- 3 eggs
- 1 can sweetened condensed milk
  (14 ounces)
- 3 cups milk
- pinch of vanilla powder or
  a few drops of vanilla extract

Caramel:
- 3 tablespoons superfine sugar

Serves 4

Crème caramel made with condensed milk

FLAN CON LECHE CONDENSADA

Make the caramel. Put the sugar into a pan, add 2 tablespoons water, and stir to dissolve, then cook over low heat until golden. Pour the caramel into a cake pan and pour it back and forth until the pan is completely coated. Preheat the oven to 300°F. Beat the eggs in a bowl, stir in the condensed milk, then stir in the milk and vanilla. Pour the mixture into the cake pan. Put the pan into a roasting pan, pour in hot water to come about halfway up the sides, and bake for 30–45 minutes, until set. Remove the pan from the oven and from the roasting pan and let cool. Do not chill this crème caramel in the refrigerator. Turn out and serve.

1019

- ½ cup superfine sugar
- 2 tablespoons cornstarch
- 1 tablespoon all-purpose flour
- 3 cups milk
- generous 1 cup shredded
  unsweetened dried coconut
- 5 egg

Serves 6–8

Coconut crème caramel

FLAN DE COCO

Put 2 tablespoons of the sugar into a pan, add 1 ½ tablespoons water, and stir to dissolve, then cook over low heat until golden. Pour the caramel into a ring mold and tip it back and forth until the mold is completely coated. Let cool. Preheat the oven to 300°F. Combine the cornstarch, flour, and 3 tablespoons of the milk in a bowl. Pour the remaining milk into a pan, stir in the remaining sugar, and heat gently. Add the flour mixture and cook, stirring constantly, for 3 minutes. Remove the pan from the heat and stir in the coconut. Beat the eggs in a bowl, then gradually stir in the milk and coconut mixture, a little at a time. Pour the custard into the mold. Put the mold into a roasting pan, pour in hot water to come about halfway up the sides, and bake for 35–45 minutes, until set. Remove the mold from the roasting pan and let cool, but do not chill in the refrigerator. Turn out and serve.

1020

Crème caramel with orange juice

FLAN CON ZUMO DE NARANJA

- 6 sugar lumps
- 5–6 oranges
- scant 1½ cups superfine sugar
- 2 tablespoons cornstarch
- 6 eggs

Caramel:
- 3 tablespoons superfine sugar

Serves 4

Make the caramel. Put the sugar into a pan, add 1½ tablespoons water, and stir to dissolve, then cook over low heat until golden. Pour the caramel into a cake pan and pour it back and forth until the pan is completely coated. Let cool. Preheat the oven to 300°F. Rub the sugar lumps all over the outside of a couple of the oranges, then put them in a pan. Squeeze the oranges, measure 2 ¼ cups juice, reserve 2 tablespoons, and pour the remainder into the pan. Stir in the superfine sugar. Combine the cornstarch and reserved orange juice in a bowl and add to the pan. Bring the mixture to a boil, stirring constantly. Cook, stirring constantly, for 1–2 minutes, until thickened. Remove the pan from the heat and let cool slightly. Beat the eggs in a bowl, then gradually stir in the orange juice mixture, a little at a time. Pour the mixture into the cake pan. Put the pan into a roasting pan, pour in hot water to come about halfway up the sides, and bake for about 40 minutes. Remove the pan from the roasting pan and let cool. Turn out onto a serving dish and serve.

1021

Argentinean caramel spread

DULCE DE LECHE CONDENSADA ESTILO ARGENTINO

- 1 can sweetened condensed milk (14 ounces)
- 2 eggs, separated
- salt

Serves 6

Put the unopened can of condensed milk into a pan, pour in water to come about halfway up the sides of the can, and bring to a boil. Lower the heat, and simmer gently for 3 hours, topping up with hot water as necessary. Remove the can from the water, open it, and let cool. Spoon the condensed milk into a small bowl or dish. Stir in the egg yolks. Whisk the egg whites with a pinch of salt in a grease-free bowl until soft peaks form, then fold into the mixture. Chill in the refrigerator for 1 hour, then serve, decorated with whipped cream and accompanied by Langues de Chat (see recipe 943) or other cookies.

Note: This popular caramel spread (most commonly called dulce de leche) is also widely available for purchase ready-made.

1022

Chinese-style crème caramel
FLAN CHINO

- **1 cup milk**
- **1¼ cups superfine sugar**
- **5 egg yolks**
- **3 egg whites**
- **salt**

Caramel:
- **3 tablespoons superfine sugar**

Serves 6

Make the caramel. Put the sugar and 2 tablespoons water into a 7-inch cake pan and cook over low heat until golden brown. Remove from the heat and tip the pan so that the caramel coats the base and sides evenly. Let cool. Pour the milk into a pan, stir in the sugar, and cook over low heat, stirring frequently, for about 15 minutes, until thickened. Beat the egg yolks in a bowl and gradually stir in the hot milk, a little at a time. Let cool, stirring occasionally with a wooden spoon. Preheat the oven to 300°F. Whisk the egg whites with a pinch of salt in a clean, dry bowl until stiff peaks form, then fold into the custard. Pour the mixture into the cake pan, place it in a roasting pan, and pour in water to come about halfway up the sides. Cover with a lid and bake for 20 minutes, then remove the lid, and cook for 15 minutes more, until set. Remove from the oven but leave the pan in the roasting pan to cool. Once it has cooled, transfer the pan to the refrigerator and chill for 30 minutes. Run a round-bladed knife around the edge of the pan, turn the dessert out onto a serving dish and serve.

1023 Custard and syrup dessert

TOCINO DE CIELO

- 1½ cups superfine sugar
- 2 strips of thinly pared lemon zest
- 7 egg yolks
- 1 egg

Caramel:
- 2 tablespoons superfine sugar

Serves 6

Make the caramel. Put the sugar into a pan, add 1 tablespoon water, and stir to dissolve, then cook over low heat until golden. Pour the caramel into a 5½-inch cake pan and tip it back and forth until the pan is completely coated. Let cool. Pour 1½ cups water into a pan, stir in the sugar, and add the lemon zest. Bring to a boil, then cook over low heat for 20 minutes. Remove the pan from the heat and let cool. Preheat the oven to 300°F. Beat the egg yolks and egg with 2 tablespoons water in a bowl, then gradually beat in the cooled syrup, a little at a time. Pour into the cake pan, cover with aluminum foil, and place a well-fitting lid on top. Put the cake pan into a roasting pan, pour in hot water to come about halfway up the sides, and bring to a boil. Lower the heat and simmer for 9 minutes, then transfer the cake pan in the roasting pan to the oven. Bake for 10 minutes. Remove the pan from the oven and let cool. Run a round-bladed knife around the edge and turn the dessert out onto a serving dish.

Note: This dessert can be made in individual dishes. In that case they will not need to bake for quite so long.

Quick custard and syrup dessert

TOCINO DE CIELO RAPIDO

- **2½ cups superfine sugar**
- **strip of thinly pared lemon zest**
- **18 egg yolks**

Serves 6

Pour scant ¼ cup water into a pan, stir in the sugar, add the lemon zest, and bring to a boil. Cook for about 5 minutes, until the syrup reaches thread stage and registers 225°F on a candy thermometer. Remove the pan from the heat and let cool, then use some of the syrup to coat the inside of a mold. Beat the egg yolks in a bowl and stir in the remaining syrup with a wooden spoon until the mixture acquires the consistency of mayonnaise. Strain this mixture into the mold and cover with aluminum foil. Fit the trivet into the base of a pressure cooker and pour in enough water to reach the edge. Place the mold on the trivet and put a plate on top of it. Close the pressure cooker, bring to high pressure, and cook for 10 minutes. Remove the pressure cooker from the heat and let cool with the lid on. When cooled, remove the mold from the pressure cooker, turn out the dessert, and serve.

Note: This is delicious accompanied by meringue, cream, or a raspberry sauce. If you prefer, make the dessert in individual molds.

1025

Capuchina

- butter, for greasing
- 10 egg yolks
- 1 egg white
- 2 tablespoons cornstarch

Syrup:
- ¾ cup superfine sugar
- thinly pared zest of 1 lemon

Topping:
- generous ½ cup superfine sugar
- 3 egg yolks

To decorate:
- 2 egg whites
- 3 tablespoons superfine sugar

Serves 8

Preheat the oven to 300°F. Generously grease a 9-inch cake pan with butter, then chill in the refrigerator. Beat the egg yolks and egg white with an electric mixer or by hand for about 20 minutes. Sift the cornstarch over the mixture and gently fold it in, then pour into the prepared cake pan. Put the pan in a roasting pan, pour in hot water to come about halfway up the sides, and simmer for 8–10 minutes, until bubbles begin to form on the surface of the mixture. Transfer the cake pan in the roasting pan to the oven and bake for 25–30 minutes, until set. Meanwhile, make a thin syrup. Pour ⅔ cup water into a pan, stir in the sugar, add the lemon zest, and bring to a boil. Lower the heat and simmer for 7 minutes. Remove the pan from the heat. Next, make the topping. Pour scant ½ cup water into a pan, stir in the sugar, and bring to a boil, then lower the heat, and simmer for 10 minutes, until a thick syrup forms. Remove the pan from the heat. Beat the egg yolks with 1 teaspoon water in a stovetop safe casserole. Gradually stir in the thick syrup, a little at a time. Cook over low heat, stirring constantly in a figure-eight movement with a whisk, for 3 minutes, until thickened. Remove from the heat and let cool. Remove the capuchina from the oven and prick it all over with a wooden toothpick without penetrating all the way through to the pan. Pour the thin syrup into these little holes. Run a round-bladed knife around the edge of the pan and turn the capuchina out onto a serving dish. Carefully pour the topping over it and spread it out to the edges with a metal spatula. Chill in the refrigerator for at least 6 hours or overnight. Just before serving, whisk the egg whites in a clean, dry bowl until stiff peaks form, then fold in the sugar. Spoon into a pastry bag and pipe decorations over the dessert.

Note: Capuchina is a light, pudding-like cake bathed in syrup.

1026

Sweet soufflé

SOUFFLÉ DÜLCE

- 6 tablespoons (¾ stick) butter,
  plus extra for greasing
- 1 tablespoon sunflower oil
- 4 tablespoons all-purpose flour
- 4 teaspoons potato starch
- 2¼ cups milk
- ½–⅔ cup superfine sugar
- pinch of vanilla powder or
  a few drops of vanilla extract
- 5 eggs, separated
- 5 egg whites
- salt

Serves 6–8

Melt the butter with the oil in a pan. Stir in the flour and potato starch and cook, stirring constantly, for 2 minutes. Gradually stir in the milk, a little at a time. Cook, stirring constantly, for about 5 minutes, until thickened, then remove the pan from the heat. Stir in the sugar and vanilla and let cool. When the sauce is just warm, beat in the egg yolks. Preheat the oven to 325°F. Grease a soufflé dish with butter. Stiffly whisk all the egg whites with a pinch of salt, in three batches, in a grease-free bowl and gently fold into the egg yolk mixture. Pour into the prepared dish and bake for 15 minutes, then increase the oven temperature to 350°F, and bake for 10 minutes more. Increase the oven temperature to 375°F and bake for another 10 minutes, until risen and golden brown. Serve immediately straight from the dish.

Note: The flavor of the soufflé can easily be altered in a variety of ways: substitute 3 tablespoons Grand Marnier or other orange-flavored liqueur for the same quantity of milk; steep thinly pared lemon zest in the milk and substitute the grated zest of a lemon for the vanilla powder or extract; stir 2–3 teaspoons instant coffee powder into the milk; or stir 3 tablespoons unsweetened cocoa powder into the milk.

1027 Orange soufflés

NARANJAS SUFLÉS

- **4 large oranges**
- **½–¾ cup superfine sugar**
- **2 heaping tablespoons cornstarch**
- **3 tablespoons Cointreau, Curaçao or other orange-flavored liqueur**
- **2 egg yolks**
- **3 egg whites**
- **salt**

Serves 4

Cut a thin slice off the base of each orange so that it stands flat. Cut a slice off the top and carefully squeeze out the juice without damaging the "shells." Scoop out the pulp and reserve the shells. Pour 1½ cups of the orange juice into a pan and stir in the sugar to taste. Mix the cornstarch to a paste with 5 tablespoons water in a bowl. Heat the orange juice and when bubbles begin to appear around the edge of the pan, stir in the cornstarch, and cook, stirring constantly, for 3 minutes. Remove the pan from the heat and let cool, stirring to prevent a skin forming. Preheat the broiler. Stir in the liqueur, then beat in the egg yolks. Whisk the egg whites with a pinch of salt in a clean, dry bowl until stiff peaks form, then gently fold into the egg yolk mixture. Divide the mixture among the orange shells and broil for 1 minute. Serve immediately.

1028 Floating strawberry and raspberry island with sugar-coated brochettes

ISLA FLOTANTE DE FRESONES Y FRAMBUESA
CON BROCHETAS REBOZADAS EN AZUCAR

- **4½ cups strawberries, hulled**
- **scant 1 cup confectioner's sugar**
- **juice of ½ lemon**
- **scant ½ cup raspberries**
- **1 cup milk**
- **10 egg whites**
- **1 teaspoon superfine sugar**
- **salt**

  Brochettes:
- **pineapple cubes**
- **mango cubes**
- **apple cubes**
- **strawberry halves**
- **2 egg whites, lightly beaten**
- **brown sugar**

Serves 4–6

Prepare the brochettes, alternating the fruit. Brush the fruit with the egg whites and coat in brown sugar. Let the brochettes dry or caramelize them in a skillet. Set aside 12 whole strawberries for decoration. Put the remainder in a bowl, sprinkle with the confectioner's sugar, and let macerate for 30 minutes. Put the strawberry mixture into a food processor or blender, add the lemon juice and raspberries, and process to a purée. Scrape into a bowl and chill in the refrigerator. Pour the milk into a pan and bring to a simmering. Whisk the egg whites with a pinch of salt in a clean, dry bowl until stiff peaks form. Fold in the superfine sugar. Drop large spoonfuls of the meringue into the milk and poach for 3 minutes. Remove with a slotted spoon and drain well. Divide the strawberry and raspberry sauce among individual dishes and place the meringues on top. Thinly slice the reserved strawberries and place them on the meringues. Serve immediately with the brochettes.

1029

Rice pudding with cream and almonds
ARROZ CON LECHE, CON NATA Y ALMENDRAS

- ¾ cup long or medium-grain rice
- 2 cups milk
- 6 tablespoons superfine sugar
- ½ cup toasted almonds
- 1 egg white
- 1 cup heavy cream
- salt
- canned or bottled morello, Montmercy or other cherries in syrup, to decorate

Serves 6–8

Bring a large pan of water to a rolling boil. Add the rice and cook for 8 minutes, then drain well. Meanwhile, heat the milk in another pan. Add the drained rice, bring to a boil, and cook over medium heat for about 20 minutes, until tender. Stir in the sugar, then remove the pan from the heat and let cool slightly. Coarsley chop the almonds, then stir into the pan and let cool completely. Whisk the egg white with a pinch of salt in a clean, dry bowl until stiff peaks form. Stiffly whisk the cream in another bowl. Fold the egg white into the cream, then fold into the rice. Serve cold decorated with the cherries in syrup.

1030

Rice dessert
BUDÍN DE ARROZ

- scant 1 cup long or medium-grain rice
- 5 cups milk
- 2 packets of crème caramel powder
- ⅔ cup superfine sugar
- 1 pound 2 ounces canned peaches in syrup, drained and diced
- 1 cup heavy cream, whipped
- candied cherries, to decorate

Serves 8–10

Bring a large pan of water to a boil. Add the rice and cook for 8 minutes, then drain well. Meanwhile, heat 4 cups of the milk in another pan. Add the drained rice, bring to a boil and cook over medium heat for about 20 minutes, until tender. Mix the crème caramel powder with the sugar, then stir in the remaining milk. Stir the mixture into the pan of rice and cook over medium heat, stirring constantly, according to the instructions on the packet. Remove the pan from the heat, add the peaches, and mix well. Pour the mixture into a mold and chill in the refrigerator for 3–4 hours. To serve, run a run a round-bladed knife around the edge of the mold and turn out the dessert. Decorate it with the cream and candied cherries.

1031

Rice pudding cones

CORNETES DE ARROZ CON LECHE

- 8 ¾ cups milk
- 1 small vanilla bean,
  halved lengthwise
- scant 1 cup long-
  or medium-grain rice
- ½ cup superfine sugar
- 4 ice cream cones
- ground cinnamon, grated lemon
  zest, or grated orange zest

Serves 4

Put the milk and vanilla bean into a pan and bring to a boil. Add the rice, cover the pan, and cook over low heat for about 40 minutes. Stir in the sugar and cook for 5 minutes more, until the rice is tender. Remove the pan from the heat, take out the vanilla bean, and let the rice cool. Put the rice in a food processor or blender and process to a creamy texture. Fill the ice cream cones with the rice, sprinkle with cinnamon or grated citrus zest, and serve.

1032

Chocolate mousse

MOUSSE DE CHOCOLATE

- 4 ounces semisweet chocolate,
  broken into pieces
- 3 tablespoons milk
- 6 tablespoons (¾ stick) butter,
  cut into pieces
- 3 egg yolks
- 3 tablespoons superfine sugar
- 4 egg whites
- salt
- whipped cream or morello or
  Montmercy cherries, to decorate

Serves 6

Put the chocolate into a pan, pour in the milk, and heat gently until the chocolate melts. Remove the pan from the heat and stir in the butter, one piece at a time. Beat the egg yolks with the sugar in a bowl, then add the chocolate mixture. Stir well to mix the ingredients and to cool the mixture. Whisk the egg whites with a pinch of salt in a clean, dry bowl until stiff peaks form, then gently fold them into the cooled chocolate mixture. Spoon the mousse into a serving bowl, individual little pots, or champagne glasses and chill in the refrigerator for at least 1 hour. Decorate the mousse with a little cream or cherries and serve with Langues de Chat (see recipe 943) or other cookies if you like.

Note: Whipped cream can be mixed into the mousse, but in this case whisk only 3 egg whites.

Chocolate mousse with ladyfingers

MOUSSE DE CHOCOLATE CON SOLETILLAS

- ¾ cup (1½ sticks) butter, softened,
  plus extra for greasing
- 3–4 tablespoons rum
- 6 tablespoons superfine sugar
- 35 ladyfingers
- 3½ ounces semisweet chocolate, broken into pieces
- 3 tablespoons milk
- 3 egg yolks
- 4 egg whites
- salt
- whipped cream, to decorate (optional)

Custard (optional):
- 2½ cups milk
- 5 tablespoons superfine sugar
- 3 egg yolks
- 1 tablespoon cornstarch

Serves 6–8

Grease an 8-inch cake pan with butter. Combine ¾ cup water, 1½ tablespoons of the rum, and 1 tablespoon of the sugar in a shallow dish. Dip about half the ladyfingers in the mixture and make a layer of them in the base of the prepared pan. Line the sides of the pan with dipped ladyfingers, first cutting off one of the rounded ends, placing them upright side by side, cut ends down. Make the mousse as described in recipe 1032, but using more butter so that when it is turned out of the pan it can stand up. Mix another batch of the liquid for dipping the ladyfingers. Spoon half the mousse into the pan and cover it with a layer of dipped ladyfingers. Spoon in the remaining mouse and add a final layer of lightly dampened ladyfingers. Put a greased lid or plate that is slightly smaller than the diameter of the pan on top so that it rests inside the tin, and add a light weight. Chill in the refrigerator for at least 5 hours. Make the custard, if using, as described in recipe 1008. To serve, remove the lid or plate, then run a round-bladed knife around the edge of the pan and turn the mousse out onto a round serving dish. Decorate with cream or serve with custard poured over the top.

1034

- ¼ cup (½ stick) butter,
  plus extra for greasing
- 5 ounces semisweet chocolate
- ¾ cup superfine sugar
- 2 egg yolks
- ½ cup ground almonds
- 4 egg whites
- salt
- whipped cream, to decorate
  (optional)

Custard (optional):
- 2¼ cups milk
- 2 egg yolks
- 5 tablespoons superfine sugar
- 1 tablespoon cornstarch
- pinch of vanilla powder or
  a few drops of vanilla extract

Serves 6

Light chocolate crown with custard

CORONA DE CHOCOLATE LIGERA CON NATILLAS

Preheat the oven to 300°F. Generously grease a ring mold with butter. Break the chocolate into pieces. Pour 5 tablespoons water into a pan, add the chocolate, and heat gently until the chocolate has melted. Remove the pan from the heat and let cool slightly. Stir in the butter, sugar, egg yolks, and ground almonds. Whisk the egg whites with a pinch of salt in a clean, dry bowl until stiff peaks form, then gently fold them into the mixture. Pour the mixture into the prepared mold, put it in a roasting pan, pour in boiling water to come halfway up the sides, and bake for 45–60 minutes, until set. Remove the mold from the roasting pan and let cool. Make the custard, if using, as described in recipe 1008. Turn the dessert out onto a serving dish and decorate with cream or serve with custard.

1035

- 7 ounces bittersweet chocolate,
  broken into pieces
- ⅔ cup butter, melted,
  plus extra for greasing
- scant 1 cup heavy cream
- generous 1 cup confectioner's
  sugar
- 3 eggs, separated
- 1 tablespoon vanilla sugar
- salt
- sliced kumquats, to decorate

Serves 6

Chocolate marquise

MARQUESA DE CHOCOLATE

Melt the chocolate in a heatproof bowl set over a pan of barely simmering water. Remove from the heat, stir in the butter, and let cool. Beat the cream into the chocolate mixture. Reserve 2 tablespoons of the confectioner's sugar and beat the egg yolks with the remainder and with the vanilla sugar in a bowl, until pale and fluffy. Stir in the chocolate mixture. Whisk the egg whites with a pinch of salt in a clean, dry bowl until stiff peaks form, then whisk in the reserved sugar. Gently fold the egg whites into the chocolate mixture. Grease a long or round mold with butter and pour the mixture into it. Chill in the refrigerator for 12 hours, until set. Turn the dessert out of the mold, decorate with slices of kumquat, and serve.

Note: Run the blade of the knife under cold water before attempting to slice the marquise. Vanilla sugar is simply vanilla-fla-vored sugar. It is available to buy, but to make it yourself, bury a whole vanilla bean in 1 to 2 cups sugar, cover and let sit for several days.

1036

- 1 tablespoon cornstarch
- 4 eggs
- grated zest of 2 lemons
- juice of 3 lemons
- 1 cup superfine sugar

Serves 5–6

Lemon cream

CREMA CUAJADA DE LIMÓN

Put the cornstarch into a bowl and gradually stir in 1 cup water to make a smooth paste. Beat the eggs in a stovetop safe casserole and add the lemon zest and juice, sugar, and the cornstarch mixture. Mix well, bring to a boil over low heat, stirring constantly, and cook, still stirring constantly, for 3 minutes. Remove from the heat and let cool, then chill in the refrigerator if you like. Serve with Langues de Chat (see recipe 943) or other cookies.

1037

- ¼ cup (½ stick) butter
- juice of 3 lemons
- grated zest of 1 lemon
- 1¼ cups superfine sugar
- 3 eggs, lightly beaten

Serves 4–6

Lemon curd

CREMA DE LIMÓN

Melt the butter in a pan and remove the pan from the heat. Add the lemon juice and zest, stir in the sugar, and beat in the eggs. Put the pan in a roasting pan, pour in hot water to come about halfway up the sides, and set over low heat. Cook, stirring constantly, for 15 minutes, until thickened. Remove the pan from the heat and pour the mixture into a sterilized screw-top jar. Seal the lid and store in a cool place, but not the refrigerator. Use to make lemon meringue pie or spread on bread like jam.

1038

- 4 egg yolks
- ¾ cup superfine sugar
- juice of 1 lemon
- grated zest of ½ lemon
- 4 egg whites
- salt
- 6 candied cherries, to decorate

Serves 5–6

Lemon mousse

MOUSSE DE LIMÓN

Beat the egg yolks with the sugar and lemon juice in a pan. Put the pan in a roasting pan, pour in hot water to come about halfway up the sides, and cook over low heat, stirring constantly, for 15–20 minutes, until almost doubled in volume. Remove the pan from the heat and let cool. Stir the lemon zest into the mixture. Whisk the egg whites with a pinch of salt in a clean, dry bowl until stiff peaks form, then gently fold them into the egg yolk mixture. Pour the mixture into little bowls or champagne glasses and chill in the refrigerator for about 2 hours. Serve the mousse decorated with candied cherries and accompanied by Langues de Chat (see recipe 943) or other cookies.

1039

Date mousse
MOUSSE DE DÁTILES

- 2¼ cups milk
- 5 tablespoons superfine sugar
- 1 cinnamon stick
- 3 egg yolks
- 2 tablespoons cornstarch
- 1 tablespoon all-purpose flour
- 30 dates
- 1 egg white

Serves 6

Reserve 3 tablespoons of the milk, pour the remainder into a pan, and add 3 tablespoons of the sugar and the cinnamon. Bring to a boil. Beat the egg yolks with the remaining sugar, the cornstarch, flour, and reserved milk in a bowl. Gradually stir in the hot milk, a little at a time, then pour the custard back into the pan, and simmer over low heat, stirring constantly, for 7 minutes. Pour the custard into a bowl, remove the cinnamon stick, and let cool. Set three of the dates aside. If your dates are ready-to-eat, peel and pit the remaining ones, put them into a food processor or blender, add the cooled custard, and process for 5 minutes, until thoroughly combined, then transfer to a bowl. Whisk the egg white in a clean, dry bowl until stiff peaks form, then gently fold into the mousse. Spoon the mousse into individual serving dishes. Cut the reserved dates in half and remove the pits, if necessary. Top each mousse with a date half and chill in the refrigerator until set.

Note: Ground cinnamon may be sprinkled on top of the mousse. This dessert is also delicious if a vanilla bean is substituted for the cinnamon stick.

1040

Coffee mousse with farmer cheese
MOUSSE DE CAFÉ CON REQUESÓN

- generous 1 cup farmer cheese, cut into pieces
- 4 tablespoons superfine sugar
- 3–4 tablespoons rum
- 2 tablespoons instant coffee powder
- ½ cup hot milk
- 2 egg whites
- salt

Serves 4

Put the farmer cheese into a bowl, sprinkle with the sugar, and add the rum. Dissolve the coffee powder in the hot milk, let cool slightly, then pour into the bowl. Mix well using a hand-held blender. Whisk the egg whites with a pinch of salt in a clean, dry bowl until stiff peaks form, then carefully fold them into the cheese mixture. Put the mousse into glasses and chill in the refrigerator for several hours. Serve with Langues de Chat (see recipe 943), if you like.

1041 Orange mousse

MOUSSE DE NARANJA

- juice of 3 large oranges
- ½–¾ cup superfine sugar
- 2 tablespoons cornstarch
- 3 tablespoons Cointreau, Curaçao or other orange-flavored liqueur
- 2 egg yolks
- 3 egg whites
- salt
- 1 orange, peeled and sliced, to decorate

Serves 6

Put the orange juice into a pan and stir in the sugar to taste. Mix the cornstarch with 4 tablespoons water in a bowl. Heat the juice and when bubbles begin to appear around the edge of the pan, stir in the cornstarch mixture and cook, stirring constantly, for 3 minutes. Remove the pan from the heat and let cool, stirring to prevent a skin forming. Stir in the liqueur and beat in the egg yolks. Whisk the egg whites with a pinch of salt in a clean, dry bowl until stiff peaks form, then gently fold them into the mousse. Divide the mixture among individual serving dishes or champagne glasses and chill in the refrigerator for about 3 hours until the mousse is set. Just before serving decorate the mousse with orange slices. Serve with Langues de Chat (see recipe 943).

1042 Fruit gelatin

GELATINA DE FRUTAS

- 1 pound 2 ounces mixed fruit, such as bananas, apples, peaches, plums, grapes, strawberries or raspberries
- 3 tablespoons rum or brandy
- generous ½ cup superfine sugar
- 1 cup orange juice
- 1 envelope (1 tablespoon) unflavored powdered gelatin

Serves 6

Make this dessert the night before you intend to serve it. Prepare the fruit in the appropriate way and cut it into pieces. Put them into a bowl, pour the rum or brandy over them, and let macerate, stirring occasionally. Pour ⅔ cup water into a pan, stir in the sugar, and cook for about 4 minutes to make a syrup. Pour the orange juice into a bowl, add the gelatin, and stir the warm syrup into the orange juice, mixing until the gelatin has dissolved completely. Line a round or ring mold with aluminum foil. Pour in the liquid to a depth of about ¾ inch and chill in the refrigerator or freezer until set. Arrange the fruit on top and pour in the remaining liquid. Chill in the refrigerator for several hours until set. Turn the dessert out of the mold to serve.

1043

Grape gelatin
GELATINA DE UVAS

- 9 ounces green grapes
- 9 ounces black grapes
- 1 cup grape juice
- 2 tablespoons lemon juice
- ½ cup white wine
- 1 cup superfine sugar
- 1½ envelopes (1½ tablespoons) unflavored powdered gelatin
- fresh mint leaves, to decorate

Serves 6–8

Reserve some of the grapes for decoration and halve and seed the remainder. Pour the grape juice, lemon juice, and wine into a pan, stir in the sugar, and cook, stirring until the sugar has dissolved. Add the gelatin, stir constantly until it has dissolved completely. Pour a little of the liquid into a bowl and chill in the refrigerator until set. Add a layer of grapes, pour in a little more liquid, and chill in the refrigerator until set. Continue making layers in this way until all the ingredients are used up, then chill in the refrigerator for at least 3 hours. Decorate with the reserved grapes and the mint leaves before serving.

1044

Coffee mousse
MOUSSE DE CAFÉ

- 2¼ cups milk
- ½ cup superfine sugar
- 2 egg yolks
- 1 tablespoon instant coffee powder
- 1½ tablespoons cornstarch
- 3 egg whites
- ½ cup toasted or caramel-coated almonds, chopped (optional)
- salt

Serves 6

Pour nearly all the milk into a pan, stir in ¼ cup of the sugar and bring to a boil. Beat the egg yolks with the remaining sugar and the coffee powder in a bowl. Mix the cornstarch with the remaining milk in another bowl. Stir the cornstarch mixture into the egg yolk mixture. Gradually stir the hot milk into the egg yolk mixture. Pour the custard back into the pan and cook, stirring constantly, for 3–4 minutes, until thickened. Remove the pan from the heat and let cool, stirring to prevent a skin forming. Whisk the egg whites with a pinch of salt in a clean, dry bowl until stiff peaks form, then gently fold them into the mixture. Divide the mousse among individual bowls or champagne glasses or pour into a large serving bowl. Chill in the refrigerator for 2–3 hours but no longer. Just before serving, sprinkle with the almonds, if using.

1045 📷 Small raspberry or strawberry Bavarians

BAVAROISES PEQUEÑAS DE FRESAS O FRAMBUESAS

- 2 ¾ cups strawberries, hulled,
  or 1 ½ cups raspberries, or
  4 tablespoons red currant jam
- 3 cups milk
- 4–8 tablespoons superfine
  sugar
- 6 tablespoons cornstarch
- ¾ envelope (¾ tablespoon)
  unflavored powdered gelatin
- 2 egg whites
- salt
- ½ cup whipped cream,
  or strawberries, or candied
  cherries, to decorate

Serves 6–8

Process the fresh fruit, if using, in a blender or food processor. Pour nearly all the milk into a pan, stir in 8 tablespoons sugar if using fresh fruit or 4 tablespoons if using jam, and bring to a boil. Mix the cornstarch with the remaining milk in a bowl. When the milk in the pan is about to boil, stir in the cornstarch mixture and cook, stirring constantly, for 3 minutes. Remove the pan from the heat and stir in the strawberries or raspberries or jam. Put the gelatin in a small pan of water and heat gently, stirring constantly until it has dissolved completely. Gradually stir it into the milk mixture, a little at a time. Whisk the egg whites with a pinch of salt in a clean, dry bowl until stiff peaks form, then gently fold them into the milk mixture. Rinse out individual molds with cold water, divide the Bavarian among them, and chill in the refrigerator for 2 hours. Run a knife around the edge of each mold and turn the Bavarian out onto a serving dish. If they do not come out easily, use the tip of a knife to separate them from the edge a little so that air enters, as this type of dessert sometimes forms a suction seal. Decorate with whipped cream or top each Bavarian with a strawberry or candied cherry.

1046 Praline Bavarians

BAVAROISE DE PRALINÉ

- 1 envelope (1 tablespoon)
  unflavored powdered gelatin
- 2 ¼ cups milk
- 6 tablespoons superfine sugar
- pinch of vanilla powder or
  a few drops of vanilla extract
- 5 egg yolks
- 1 tablespoon cornstarch
- 1 ¼ cups caramel-coated
  almonds, coarsely crushed
  or scant 2 cups coarsely
  chopped amaretti
- 2 egg whites
- 1 cup heavy cream
- salt

Serves 6

Pour ½ cup water into a small pan, add the gelatin, and heat gently, stirring constantly until the gelatin has dissolved completely. Pour the milk into another pan, stir in half the sugar and the vanilla, and bring to a boil over medium heat. Beat the egg yolks with the cornstarch and remaining sugar in a bowl. Gradually stir in the hot milk, a little at a time. Pour the custard back into the pan and cook, stirring constantly, for a few minutes, until thickened. Remove the pan from the heat, let cool for about 5 minutes, then stir in the gelatin. Add the almonds or amaretti and mix well. Stand the pan a bowl of cold water and stir the mixture until cold. Whisk the egg whites with a pinch of salt in a clean, dry bowl until stiff peaks form. Stiffly whisk the cream in another bowl, then fold in the egg whites. Gently stir the cream mixture into the custard. Rinse a mold with cold water and spoon the Bavarian into it. Chill in the refrigerator for at least 4 hours, until set. Turn the Bavarian out of the mold onto a serving dish to serve. If it does not come out easily, use the tip of a knife to separate it from the edge a little.

1047

Bavarian with peaches
BAVAROISE DE MELOCOTONES (DE LATA)

- 2¼ cups milk
- ¾ cup superfine sugar
- 4 egg yolks
- 1 teaspoon cornstarch
- 1 pound 2 ounces canned peaches in syrup
- 1¼ envelopes (1¼ tablespoon) unflavored powdered gelatin
- 4 egg whites
- sunflower oil, for brushing
- salt

Serves 6

Pour the milk into a pan, stir in half the sugar, and bring to a boil. Beat the egg yolks with the remaining sugar and the cornstarch in a bowl. Gradually stir in the hot milk, a little at a time, then pour the custard back into the pan, and cook over low heat, stirring constantly, for a few minutes, until thickened. Remove the pan from the heat and let cool, stirring occasionally. Drain the peaches, reserving the syrup. Set a peach aside for decoration. Put the remaining peaches in a food processor or blender and process to a purée. Stir the purée into the custard. Put the gelatin into a pan, add the reserved syrup, heat gently, stirring constantly until the gelatin has dissolved completely. Gradually stir it into the custard, a little at a time. Stir the custard until it is almost cooled. Whisk the egg whites with a pinch of salt in a clean, dry bowl until stiff peaks form, then gently fold them into the custard. Brush a mold with oil and spoon in the Bavarian. Chill in the refrigerator for at least 3 hours. (It can be made a day in advance). Run a round-bladed knife around the edge of the mold and turn the Bavarian out. If it does not come out easily, use the tip of a knife to separate it from the edge a little so that air enters, as this type of dessert sometimes forms a suction seal. Decorate with the reserved peach cut into wedges.

1048

Bavarian with pineapple
BAVAROISE DE PIÑA (DE LATA)

- 2¼ cups milk
- 1 cup superfine sugar
- 4 egg yolks
- 1 heaping teaspoon cornstarch
- 1 pound 2 ounces canned pineapple in juice
- 1 envelope (1 tablespoon) unflavored powdered gelatin
- 1 egg white
- 1 cup heavy cream
- sunflower oil, for brushing
- salt

Serves 6–8

Pour the milk into a pan, stir in half the sugar, and bring to a boil. Beat the egg yolks with the remaining sugar and the cornstarch in a bowl. Gradually stir in the hot milk, a little at a time, then pour the custard back into the pan. Cook over low heat, stirring constantly, for a few minutes, until thickened. Remove the pan from the heat. Drain the pineapple, reserving the juice in a pan. Add the gelatin to the juice, and heat gently, stirring constantly until it has dissolved completely. Gradually stir the gelatin into the custard, a little at a time, then stand the pan in a bowl of cold water, and stir until the cus-tard is almost cold. Chop half the pineapple slices into pieces and add to the custard. Halve the remaining slices and set aside. Whisk the egg white with a pinch of salt in a clean, dry bowl until stiff peaks form. Stiffly whisk the cream in another bowl, then fold in the egg white. Reserve a little of the mixture for decoration and gently fold the remainder into the custard. Brush a Bavarian mold or a cake pan with oil. Spoon the Bavarian into the mold and chill in the refrigerator for about 10 hours or overnight. To serve, dip the base of the mold or pan into hot water for a few seconds and then turn out the Bavarian. If it does not come out easily, use the tip of a knife to separate it from the edge a little so that air enters, as this type of dessert sometimes forms a suction seal. Decorate with the reserved cream mixture and the half slices of pineapple.

1049

- 3 eggs, separated
- 1 cup superfine sugar
- 1 envelope (1 tablespoon) unflavored powdered gelatin
- scant 1 cup orange juice, strained
- ¼ cup Cointreau or other orange-flavored liqueur
- 1 egg white
- sunflower oil, for brushing

Serves 6–8

Orange Bavarian
BAVAROISE DE NARANJA

Beat the egg yolks with the sugar for about 5 minutes, until the mixture is creamy. Put the gelatin into a small pan, add 4 tablespoons water and leave to soften for 5 minutes, then heat gently, stirring constantly until the gelatin has dissolved completely. Combine the orange juice and liqueur and add to the egg yolk mixture, then stir in the gelatin. Whisk all the egg whites in a clean, dry bowl until stiff peaks form, then gently fold them into the egg yolk mixture. Brush a cake pan with oil and pour in the Bavarian. Chill in the refrigerator for at least 6 hours, until set. (The Bavarian will need to be stirred a couple of times to prevent the gelatin sinking to the bottom). To serve, turn the Bavarian onto a serving dish. If it does not come out easily, use the tip of a knife to separate it from the edge a little so that air enters, as this type of dessert sometimes forms a suction seal.

Note: The Bavarian can be decorated with a little whipped cream or some thin slices of orange.

1050

- 5 ounces bittersweet chocolate, broken into pieces
- 1 cup milk
- 1 envelope (1 tablespoon) unflavored powdered gelatin
- 4 egg yolks
- ¾ cup superfine sugar
- 6 egg whites
- salt
- whipped cream or candied cherries, to decorate (optional)

Serves 6–8

Chocolate Bavarian
BAVAROISE DE CHOCOLATE

Put the chocolate in a pan, pour in the milk, and melt the chocolate over medium heat. Remove the pan from the heat and let cool. Pour 4 tablespoons water into a small pan, add the gelatin and leave to soften for 5 minutes, then heat gently, stirring constantly, until the gelatin has dissolved completely. Gradually stir the gelatin into the chocolate mixture, a little at a time. Let cool, stir-ring occasionally. Beat the egg yolks with the sugar in a bowl, then stir into the chocolate mixture. Whisk the egg whites with a pinch of salt in a clean, dry bowl until stiff peaks form, then gently fold into the chocolate mixture. Pour the Bavarian into a large mold or individual molds and chill in the refrigerator for at least 5 hours, until set. To serve, turn the Bavarian out onto a serving dish. If it does not come out easily, use the tip of a knife to separate it from the edge a little so that air enters, as this type of dessert sometimes forms a suction seal. Decorate with whipped cream or candied cherries if you like.

1051

- 4 ½ cups strawberries, hulled
- 2 tablespoons kirsch
- 3 eggs, separated
- 1 cup superfine sugar
- 1 envelope (1 tablespoon) unflavored powdered gelatin
- 3 drops of red food coloring (optional)
- 1 cup heavy cream
- sunflower oil, for brushing
- salt

Serves 6–8

Strawberry Bavarian

BAVAROISE DE FRESAS

Reserve a few strawberries for decoration and process the remainder in a blender or food processor. Mix the strawberry purée with the kirsch. Beat the egg yolks with the sugar in a bowl until pale and fluffy. Put the gelatin into a small pan, add 4 tablespoons water, and heat gently, stirring constantly, until it has dissolved completely. Stir the strawberry purée into the egg yolk mixture, then gradually stir in the gelatin, a little at a time. Stir in red food coloring, if using. Whisk the egg whites with a pinch of salt in a clean, dry bowl until stiff peaks form. Stiffly whisk the cream in another bowl. Fold half the cream into the strawberry mixture and then fold in the egg whites. Brush a cake pan with oil, spoon in the Bavarian, and chill in the refrigerator for at least 4 hours, until set. To serve, turn the Bavarian out onto a serving dish. If it does not come out easily, use the tip of a knife to separate it from the edge a little so that air enters, as this type of dessert sometimes forms a suction seal. Pipe the remaining cream over the top and sides of the Bavarian and decorate with the reserved strawberries.

1052

- 1 envelope (1 tablespoon) unflavored powdered gelatin
- 9 ounces nougat (see recipe 1080), cut into pieces
- 4 eggs, separated
- 2–3 tablespoons rum
- salt

Serves 6

Bavarian with nougat

BAVAROISE DE TURRÓN DE JIJONA

Put the gelatin into a small pan, add 4 tablespoons water and leave to soften for 5 minutes, then heat gently, stirring constantly, until the gelatin has dissolved completely. Remove the pan from the heat. Mash the nougat with a fork, then mix with the egg yolks and rum to make a smooth cream. Gradually stir in the gelatin, a little at a time. Whisk the egg whites with a pinch of salt in a clean, dry bowl until stiff peaks form, then fold them into the nougat cream. Pour the Bavarian into a ring mold and chill in the refrigerator for at least 4 hours, until set. (The dish can be made a day in advance). To serve, turn out the Bavarian. If it does not come out easily, use the tip of a knife to separate it from the edge a little so that air enters, as this type of dessert sometimes forms a suction seal. Serve with tuiles, or Langues de Chat (see recipe 943) or other cookies.

Raspberry Bavarian

BAVAROIS DE FRAMBUESA

- 3 cups raspberries
- 2 tablespoons raspberry liqueur
- 3 eggs, separated
- 1 cup superfine sugar
- 1 envelope (1 tablespoon) unflavored powdered gelatin
- 3 drops of red food coloring (optional)
- 1 cup heavy cream
- sunflower oil, for brushing
- salt
- whipped cream, to decorate

Serves 4–6

Set aside a few raspberries for decoration and beat the remainder to a purée with a wooden spoon in a bowl. Stir in the liqueur. Beat the egg yolks with the sugar in a bowl until pale and fluffy, then stir into the raspberry purée. Put the gelatin into a small pan, add 4 tablespoons water and leave to soften for 5 minutes, then heat gently, stirring constantly, until the gelatin has dissolved completely. Remove from the heat and stir into the raspberry mixture, then stir in the food coloring, if using. Whisk the egg whites with a pinch of salt in a clean, dry bowl until stiff peaks form. Stiffly whisk the cream in another bowl. Fold the cream into the raspberry mixture, then fold in the egg whites. Brush a mold with oil and spoon in the Bavarian. Chill in the refrigerator for at least 4 hours, until set. To serve, turn the Bavarian out. If it does not come out easily, use the tip of a knife to separate it from the edge a little so that air enters, as this type of dessert sometimes forms a suction seal. Pipe cream over the Bavarian and decorate it with the reserved raspberries.

1054

Vanilla ice cream
BISCUIT GLACÉ

- butter, for greasing
- 1 tablespoon cornstarch
- scant 1 cup milk
- scant 1 cup superfine sugar
- pinch of vanilla powder or
  a few drops of vanilla extract
- 6 eggs, separated
- few drops of yellow food coloring
  (optional)
- salt

Serves 6–8

Grease a metal mold with butter, then chill it in the freezer. Mix the cornstarch with 2–3 tablespoons of the milk in a bowl. Pour the remaining milk into a pan with 5 tablespoons of the sugar and the vanilla and bring to a boil. Stir in the cornstarch and cook, stirring constantly, for 3 minutes. Remove the pan from the heat and let cool slightly. Beat the egg yolks with 5 tablespoons of the remaining sugar in a bowl. Gradually stir in the milk mixture, a little at a time, then stir in the food coloring, if using. Whisk the egg whites with a pinch of salt in a clean, dry bowl until stiff peaks form, then fold in the remaining sugar. Gently fold the egg whites into the custard, then pour into the prepared mold, and put in the freezer for about 3 hours. Remove the mold from the freezer about 5 minutes before serving. Carefully run a round-bladed knife around the mold and turn the ice cream out onto a serving dish.

Note: The ice cream can be put into individual glass or foil molds.

1023

1068

1055

Lemon sherbet

SORBETE DE LIMÓN

- **1 cup superfine sugar**
- **grated zest and juice**
  of 4 large lemons
- **2 egg whites**
- **salt**

Serves 4

Pour 2 ¼ cups water into a pan, stir in the sugar, and bring to a rolling boil, then cook for 10–12 minutes, until syrupy. Remove the pan from the heat and let cool. Stir the lemon zest and juice into the cold syrup, pour into a freezerproof container, and put into the freezer. When the mixture begins to freeze, whisk the egg whites with a pinch of salt in a clean, dry bowl until stiff peaks form, then fold them into the mixture. Return to the freezer and freeze until firm. Serve in sundae glasses, accompanied by Langues de Chat (see recipe 943) or other cookies, if you like.

1056

- **4 oranges,**
  about 2¼ pounds, halved
- **2 lemons, halved**
- **2¼ pounds superfine sugar**

Makes 3 large jars

Orange marmalade

MERMELADA DE NARANJA (ESTILO INGLÉS)

Squeeze the oranges and lemons, reserving the seeds. Tie the seeds in a square of cheesecloth. Cut the zests into julienne strips, preferably with a mandoline. Mix the zests with the juice and add the bag of seeds. Let stand for 24 hours. Pour the mixture into a preserving pan or large pan, pour in 4 cups water, and bring to a boil. Lower the heat and simmer gently, stirring occasionally, for 1 hour. Remove the pan from the heat and let stand for 24 hours. Stir the sugar into the juice mixture and heat, stirring until the sugar has dissolved. Skim off the foam that rises to the surface and simmer for 1¼–1½ hours, until the temperature measures 220°F on a candy thermometer and the marmalade has reached setting point. To test for setting point, put a teaspoon of the marmalade on a cold saucer and cool quickly. When the surface has set, push it with your finger; if it wrinkles, the marmalade is at setting point. Remove the pan from the heat and let cool slightly, then remove and discard the bag of seeds, and ladle the marmalade into sterilized glass jars and seal.

1057

- **2¼ pounds very ripe fleshy**
  tomatoes, seeded and cut
  into pieces
- **1 pound 2 ounces**
  superfine sugar
- **juice of 1 lemon**

Makes 3 large jars

Tomato jam

MERMELADA DE TOMATES

This is an unusual recipe that is ideal for people who have a vegetable garden. Once the jam is made it does not taste like tomato. Put the pieces of tomato into a skillet and cook over medium heat, stirring occasionally and breaking them up with the side of the spoon, for 15 minutes. Pass the tomatoes through a food mill or food processor and pour the purée into a pan. Stir in the sugar and lemon juice and cook over low heat for about 30 minutes, depending on how thick you like your jam. Bear in mind it will thicken a little more as it cools.

1058

Quince jelly

MEMBRILLO

- **3 ¼ pounds ripe quinces, cored and cut into pieces**
- **2 ½ pounds superfine sugar**

Makes 3–4 jars

Put the quinces into a pan and add just enough cold water to cover. Cook over medium heat for about 1 hour, until the quinces have softened. Pass them through a food mill or food processor into a clean pan and stir in the sugar. Cook, stirring occasionally, for 30 minutes more. Pour the quince mixture into a square of cheesecloth. Bring the corners of the square together and suspend over a bowl to drain. Let drain for about 20 minutes, then pour the liquid into glass jars or bowls, and let cool and set. Run a round-bladed knife around the edge of the container and turn out the jelly once it is cold and set.

1059

Flamed quinces with red currant jam

MEMBRILLOS CON JALEA DE GROSELLA Y FLAMEADOS

- **4 quinces, peeled, cored, and thickly sliced**
- **3 tablespoons superfine sugar**
- **3 tablespoons red currant jam**
- **½ cup rum or brandy**

Serves 6

Put the quinces into a pan, add water to cover, cover the pan with a lid, and cook over medium heat for about 35 minutes, until softened. Drain off some of the water and sprinkle the sugar into the pan. Return it to the heat and cook for 10–15 minutes more. Remove the fruit from the syrup that will have formed and set aside. Just before serving, put the slices of quince onto a serving dish and put the jam in the center. Pour the rum or brandy into a pan and heat for a few seconds, then ignite it, and carefully pour it over the quinces. Spoon the spirit over the fruit while the alcohol is still burning. Serve before the flames die down.

1060

- 2¼ pounds sweet potatoes, peeled
- 1¾ cups superfine sugar
- 1 cinnamon stick
- 1 cup light cream (optional)

Serves 6

Sweetened sweet potatoes

BATATAS EN DULCE

If the sweet potatoes are fat, halve them lengthwise. Put them into a pan, pour in just enough water to cover, and add the sugar and cinna-mon. Cover the pan with parchment paper that has been cut in a cir-cle to fit snugly inside the pan, seal with a lid and bring to a boil, then lower the heat, and cook until a thick syrup forms. Pour the mixture into a bowl and let cool. Serve immediately with cream, if you like, or keep in the refrigerator for 3–4 days.

1061

- 1 cup wine
- generous ½ cup superfine sugar
- 1 cinnamon stick
- 1 pound 2 ounces pitted prunes, soaked in warm water for 3–6 hours and drained

Serves 6

Prunes with red wine

CIRUELAS PASAS CON VINO TINTO

Pour 1 cup water and the wine into a pan, stir in the sugar, and add the cinnamon and prunes. There should be enough liquid in the pan to cover the prunes but if not, add a little more wine or a mixture of water and wine. Cook over medium heat for about 30 minutes. Remove the pan from the heat, remove and discard the cinnamon, put the mixture into a bowl, and let cool. Serve cold, but do not chill in the refrigerator.

1062

- 9 large pears
- 4 tablespoons superfine sugar
- 2 cinnamon sticks
- 3 cups red wine
- 1 cup sweetened whipped cream (optional)

Serves 6

Pear compote with red wine

PERAS EN COMPOTA CON VINO TINTO

Peel the pears, then cut into four, and core them. Put them into a pan, sprinkle with the sugar, add the cinnamon, and pour in enough wine to cover. Cover and cook over medium heat for about 20 minutes, until the pears are tender. Spoon the pears into a bowl and let cool. Serve with whipped cream, if you like, offered separately.

Note: If the pears are fairly small, leave them whole. Peel them but leave the stalks intact. Allow 2 small pears per serving. The cream can be replaced with custard (see recipe 1008).

1063

Flamed peaches

MELOCOTONES FLAMEADOS

- **2 cylindrical bread rolls**
- **6 canned or bottled peach halves in syrup, drained**
- **6 teaspoons redcurrant or raspberry jam**
- **icing sugar, for sprinkling**
- **175 ml / 6 fl oz rum**

Serves 6

Preheat the grill. Cut the rolls into three and place a peach half on each piece with the cavity uppermost. Press down lightly on the fruit so it is firmly positioned. Fill the cavities in the peaches with redcurrant or raspberry jam and then put them into a flameproof dish. Sprinkle with icing sugar and cook briefly under the grill. Meanwhile, heat the rum in a saucepan for a few seconds. Remove the dish from the grill, ignite the rum and carefully pour it over the peaches. Keep spooning it back over the peaches until the flames die down. If possible, serve while the rum is still burning.

1064

- **6 canned or bottled peach halves in syrup, drained**
- **1½ cups rum**
- **3 cylindrical bread rolls, crusts removed**
- **2¼ cups vanilla ice cream**

Serves 6

Flamed peaches with vanilla ice cream

MELOCOTONES FLAMEADOS CON HELADO DE VAINILLA

Put the peach halves into a skillet. Heat the rum in a pan for a few seconds, ignite it, and carefully pour it over the peaches. Keep spooning the rum over the fruit. Halve the rolls and scoop out a little of the center from each half to make a cavity. When the flames have died down, place a peach half in each piece of roll with the cavity up. Press down gently so the peach is firmly positioned in the roll. Fill the cavities with the ice cream and spoon a little of the sauce from the skillet over the top. Serve immediately.

1065

- **6 large peaches, peeled, pitted, and cut into fourths**
- **1 cup superfine sugar**
- **3 cups white wine**
- **3 heaping tablespoons orange gelatin**

Serves 4–5

Peaches with white wine and orange gelatin

MELOCOTONES CON VINO BLANCO Y GELATINA DE NARANJA

It is better to prepare this dish a day in advance. Put the peaches into a pan in a single layer. Sprinkle them with the sugar and pour the wine over them. Bring to a boil, lower the heat, and simmer gently for about 30 minutes, until softened. Remove the pan from the heat, lift out the peaches with a slotted spoon, and put them into a serving bowl. Return the pan to the heat and cook the liquid for about 15 minutes, until syrupy. Transfer ¾ cup of the syrup to a pan and add the orange gelatin, stirring constantly until it has dissolved, then cook it for 1 minute. Stir in another generous 1 cup of the syrup and mix well. Pour the mixture over the peaches, let cool, and then chill in the refrigerator before serving.

1066

Peaches cooked with zabaglione
MELOCOTONES COCIDOS CON SABAYON

- **8 ripe peaches, peeled**

Syrup:
- **1¼ cups superfine sugar**
- **1 vanilla bean, halved lengthwise**

Zabaglione:
- **4 egg yolks**
- **¼ cup confectioner's sugar**
- **scant 1 cup Madeira wine
  or other fortified wine**
- **raspberries**
- **sliced almonds**

Serves 4

Make the syrup. Pour 2¼ cups water into a pan, stir in the sugar, add the vanilla, and bring to a boil. Add the peaches, cover, and cook for 5 minutes. Remove the pan from the heat and leave the peaches to cool in the syrup. Make the zabaglione. Beat the egg yolks with the sugar and Madeira in a heatproof bowl set over a pan of barely simmering water until thick and creamy. Remove the bowl from the heat and continue to beat until the mixture cools. Drain the peaches and divide them among individual plates. Spoon the zabaglione over them, decorate with raspberries and almonds, and serve.

Note: To make the peaches easier to peel, submerge them in boiling water for 8 seconds and then put them into cold water. The skin will then peel off more easily.

1067

Flamed bananas with vanilla ice cream
PLÁTANOS FLAMEADOS CON HELADO DE VAINILLA

- **6 bananas**
- **juice of 1 lemon**
- **2¼ cups sunflower oil**
- **¾ cup rum**
- **2¼ cups vanilla ice cream**
- **confectioner's sugar,
  for sprinkling**

Serves 6

Peel the bananas and cut them in half lengthwise. Sprinkle with the lemon juice to prevent discoloration. Heat the oil in a deep-fryer or deep skillet to 350–375°F or until a cube of day-old bread browns in 30 seconds. Add the bananas and cook until golden brown, working in batches if necessary. Remove with a slotted spoon, drain well, and set aside on a plate. Heat the rum in a small pan for a few seconds, ignite it, and carefully pour it over the bananas. Spoon the rum back over them until the flames have died down. Working quickly so that neither the rum nor the bananas have time to cool, divide the ice cream among individual plates, top with the banana halves crossed over each other, and spoon the rum over them. Sprinkle with confectioner's sugar and serve.

1068 Fig compote with red wine and spices

COMPOTA DE HIGOS CON VINO TINTO Y ESPECIAS

- 3 tablespoons red wine
- 2 large pieces of thinly pared orange rind
- 3 tablespoons caster sugar
- 1 cinnamon stick
- 6 cloves
- 1 sprig fresh mint
- 24 small figs or 12 large figs, peeled

Serves 4–6

Pour 135 ml / 4 ½ fl oz water and the wine into a saucepan, add the orange rind, sugar, cinnamon, cloves and mint and simmer for 10 minutes. Add the figs and cook over a low heat for 6 minutes. Lift out the figs with a slotted spoon and put them into a serving bowl. Simmer the cooking liquid for a further 15 minutes, then strain it into a dish, reserving the orange rind, and leave to cool. Cut the orange rind into very thin strips and add to the compote. Pour the sauce over the figs and chill in the refrigerator.

1069

Cointreau foam
ESPUMOSO DE COINTREAU

- 4 eggs, separated
- ⅔ cup superfine sugar
- 2 tablespoons Cointreau
- scant ½ cup heavy cream

Serves 4

Put the egg yolks and sugar into a pan and beat over low heat until the mixture is smooth and even, but do not let it boil. Remove the pan from the heat and add the liqueur; the mixture will thicken immediately. Let cool. Whisk the egg whites in a clean, dry bowl until stiff peaks form. Stiffly whisk the cream in another bowl. Fold the egg whites and cream into the egg yolk mixture. Divide the foam among glasses or sundae dishes and chill in the refrigerator.

1070

Caramelized pear compote
COMPOTA DE PERAS CARAMELIZADA

- ¼ cup slivered almonds
- juice of ½ lemon
- 1¾ cups confectioner's sugar
- 4 pears
- 2 tablespoons (¼ stick) butter, cut into small pieces

Serves 4

Toast the almonds in a small skillet, stirring frequently, for a few minutes until golden and fragrant, but be careful not to let them burn, then remove from the heat, and set aside. Pour 5 tablespoons water and the lemon juice into a pan, stir in the sugar, and cook over low heat until golden. Meanwhile, peel, core, and dice the pears. Add the pears and butter to the caramel, cover, and cook for 15 minutes. Divide the compote among individual pots or dishes and sprinkle with the almonds. Let cool slightly before serving.

1071

Green tea custard
NATILLAS AL TÉ VERDE

- 4 cups milk
- 2¼ cups confectioner's sugar
- 4 teaspoons green tea leaves
- 8 egg yolks
- ladyfingers, to serve

Serves 4

Reserve 1 tablespoon of the milk. Pour the remainder into a pan, stir in the sugar, and bring to a boil. Remove the pan from the heat, stir in the tea, and let steep for 30 minutes. Strain through a cheesecloth-lined strainer into a bowl and let cool completely. Beat the egg yolks with the reserved milk in a heatproof bowl. Add the steeped milk and set over a pan of barely simmering water. Cook, whisking constantly, until thickened. Remove the pan from the heat and pour the custard into a mold. Let cool, then chill in the refrigerator until ready to serve. Serve with ladyfingers.

1072

Grape and orange compote

COMPOTA DE UVAS Y NARANJAS

- **200 g / 7 oz muscatel grapes,
  seeded**
- **2 oranges, thinly sliced**
- **100 g / 3½ oz caster sugar**
- **100 g / 3½ oz raisins**
- **4 individual portions of fromage
  frais or other fresh cheese,
  to serve**

Serves 4

Put the grapes and oranges into a heavy-based saucepan, mix well and add the sugar and raisins. Cook over a low heat for about 1 hour, until the compote thickens. Remove the pan from the heat and leave to cool, then serve accompanied by the cheese.

1073

Grilled oranges with zabaglione
GRATINADO DE NARANJAS CON SABAYON

- **4 oranges**
- **4 egg yolks**
- **3 tablespoons confectioner's sugar**
- **¼ bottle of cava or other sparkling wine**

Serves 4

Peel the oranges and cut out the segments from the membranes. Put half of them in a decorative shape on ovenproof individual serving plates or individual souffle dishes. Beat the egg yolks with the sugar in a heatproof bowl until pale and fluffy. Add the cava and cook over a pan of barely simmering water, beating constantly, until thickened. Meanwhile, preheat the broiler. Pour the zabaglione over the oranges and top with the remaining orange segments. Cook under the broiler for about 3 minutes, until golden brown. Serve immediately.

Note: Prepare the orange segments a day in advance and leave them on a wire rack in the refrigerator so that they will not release too much juice when they are cooked. This dessert is delicious prepared with pink grapefruit.

1074

Melon and fig aspic
ASPIC DE MELÓN E HIGOS

- **1 envelope (1 tablespoon) unflavored gelatin powder**
- **½ cup port**
- **4 figs**
- **1 cantaloupe or other melon, halved and seeded**
- **4 sprigs fresh parsley, plus extra to decorate**
- **5 ounces Emmenthaler cheese, sliced**
- **12 thin slices of Serrano ham or prosciutto**

Serves 4

Prepare 2 ¼ cups gelatin following the instructions on the packet and stir in the port. Pour a ½-inch layer of warm gelatin into individual tart pans or dishes and chill in the refrigerator until set. Meanwhile, peel the figs and cut them into pieces. Scoop out balls of the melon flesh with a melon baller or teaspoon. Put pieces of fig, melon balls, and a parsley sprig on the set gelatin in each pan or dish. Pour in the remaining gelatin and return to the refrigerator until set. To serve, dip the bases of the pans or dishes into hot water for a few seconds and run a round-bladed knife around the edge of each one, then turn the molds out onto plates. Place alternating slices of cheese and ham around each mold and decorate with parsley.

1075

Marzipan cake
PONCHE AL ESTILO SEGOVIANO

Sponge cake:
- 3 eggs
- 2 tablespoons superfine sugar
- ¾ cup self-rising flour
- confectioner's sugar,
  to decorate

Filling:
- 2¼ cups milk
- 3 egg yolks
- 2 tablespoons superfine sugar
- ½ cup all-purpose flour
- pinch of vanilla powder or
  a few drops of vanilla extract
- pinch of ground cinnamon

Marzipan:
- 3 tablespoons superfine sugar
- 4 egg whites
- ½ cup ground almonds

Serves 4–6

Preheat the oven to 350°F. Grease a jelly-roll pan with butter. Line the base with waxed paper and grease with butter. First, make the sponge. Beat together the eggs, sugar, and flour in a bowl. Spoon the mixture into the prepared pan and bake for 10 minutes. Remove from the oven, remove and discard the waxed paper, and transfer to a wire rack to cool. Meanwhile, prepare the filling. Heat the milk in a pan. Beat the egg yolks with the sugar, flour, vanilla, and cinnamon in a bowl. Gradually stir in the hot milk, a little at a time, then return the custard to the pan, and cook, stirring constantly for a few minutes, until thickened. Remove the pan from the heat and set aside. Prepare the marzipan. Combine the sugar and 1 tablespoon water in a pan and heat gently for a few minutes to make a syrup, then remove the pan from the heat. Whisk the egg whites in a clean, dry bowl until stiff peaks form, then the almonds, then add the syrup. Mix well until firm, then heat gently in a pan, working the mixture until it acquires the desired consistency. To serve, cut the sponge cake into three long rectangles and pour the syrup over them. Spread half the filling on one sponge rectangle, put another sponge rectangle on top. Spread the remaining filling on top and add the remaining sponge rectangle. Cover with a layer of marzipan and sprinkle with confectioner's sugar. Caramelize the marzipan with a kitchen blow torch or on an ovenproof baking dish under a preheated broiler, just until caramelized.

1076

Santiago torte
TARTA DE SANTIAGO

- generous 1 cup butter, softened,
  plus extra for greasing
- 8 eggs
- 2½ cups superfine sugar
- 3½ cups all-purpose flour
- 4½ cups ground almonds
- grated zest of 1 lemon
- confectioner's sugar,
  to decorate

Serves 4–6

Preheat the oven to 350°F. Grease a cake pan with butter. Beat the eggs with the sugar in a bowl until pale and fluffy, then add the flour, butter, and 1 cup water. Mix well, then stir in the ground almonds and lemon zest. Pour the mixture into the prepared pan and bake for about 30 minutes, until cooked through. Insert a wooden toothpick into the center of the torte and if it comes out clean, the pie is cooked. Remove from the oven and let the torte cool in the pan, then turn it out. Sprinkle with confectioner's sugar. For an attractive effect, cut out a simple cardboard stencil, such as a star, and hold this over the pie when you sprinkle it with the sugar.

Note: The torte can be sprinkled with unsweetened cocoa powder.

1077 📷 Traditional Christmas cookies

MANTECADAS

- **butter, for greasing**
- **6½ cups all-purpose flour,
  plus extra for dusting**
- **3 tablespoons superfine sugar**
- **2⅓ cups lard**
- **juice of ½ lemon**
- **confectioner's sugar and
  ground cinnamon, to decorate**

Makes 8–9 dozen

Preheat the oven to 350°F. Grease a baking sheet with butter. Sift the flour onto a work surface, preferably a marble slab, make a well in the center, and add the sugar, lard, and lemon juice. Knead together until the dough is smooth, then let rest for 10 minutes. Using a floured rolling pin, roll out the dough on a lightly floured surface to about ⅜ inch thick. Cut out small rounds or ovals with a 2-inch round cookie cutter. Put the little cookies onto the prepared baking sheet (some people prefer to make a hole in the middle of each one). Bake for about 15 minutes, but do not let brown. Remove the cookies from the oven and sprinkle with confectioner's sugar and ground cinnamon.

1078 French toasts in wine

TORRIJAS AL VINO

- **1 day-old white bread loaf,
  cut into ¾-inch thick slices**
- **2¼ cups milk**
- **3 tablespoons superfine sugar**
- **2¼ cups red wine**
- **3 eggs**
- **2¼ cups sunflower oil**
- **sugar and ground cinnamon,
  for sprinkling**

Makes 20 slices

Put the slices of bread into a deep dish. Pour the milk into a pan, stir in the sugar, and bring just to a boil. Remove the pan from the heat and pour the sweetened milk over the bread together with the wine. Let soak. Beat the eggs in a shallow dish. Heat the oil in a skillet. One at a time, lift a slice of bread with a slotted spoon or tongs, coat it in the beaten eggs, and add to the hot oil. Cook until golden brown on both sides, then remove from the skillet, and drain. Sprinkle the with sugar and ground cinnamon and let cool. Serve warm or cold.

1079 Filled walnuts

NUECES RELLENAS

- **1¼ cups ground almonds**
- **1 egg white**
- **scant 1 cup confectioner's sugar**
- **2½ ounces semisweet
  chocolate, grated**
- **12 walnuts, halved and peeled**

Makes 24 petits fours

Combine the ground almonds, egg white, sugar, and chocolate in a bowl until well mixed. Shape the mixture into small balls. Place a walnut half on top of each ball and let harden in the refrigerator. Serve in petit four wrappers.

Note: Vary the flavor of these sweet treats by adding a spoonful of strong coffee or a favorite liqueur.

1080

Nougat

TURRON DE JIJONA

- 2¼ cups toasted almonds, chopped
- 2 egg whites
- scant ½ cup set honey
- 2½ cups superfine sugar
- 4–8 sheets of rice paper

Serves 8–10

Pound the almonds to a paste in a mortar or process in a food processor. Mix in the egg whites. Put the honey and sugar into a pan and bring to a boil, then remove the pan from the heat, and stir them into the almond paste. Continue to stir without stopping for 10 minutes. Line two baking sheets with rice paper. Shape the mixture into bars and place them on the prepared baking sheets. Cover with rice paper and place a weight on top. Let dry out for at least 8 days.

Note: Instead of only almonds, you could use 1¼ cups almonds and scant ½ cup hazelnuts.

MENUS FROM CELEBRATED SPANISH CHEFS

The following pages contain menus from some of the world's favorite chefs cooking Spanish or Spanish-influenced food. From Spain to the United States, these chefs celebrate the best of Spanish cuisine—its simplicity and emphasis on the finest of ingredients—but offer that little extra genius in the kitchen that has made these chefs acknowledged across the world.

1080 guest chefs

José Andrés	Washington, DC, USA
Pepe Balaguer	Valencia, Spain
Sam & Sam Clark	London, UK
Ramón Freixa	Barcelona, Spain
Andy Nusser	New York, USA
José Manuel Pizarro	London, UK
Alexandra Raij	New York, USA
Joan, Jordi & Joseph Roca	Gerona, Spain
Carme Ruscalleda	Sant Pol de Mar, Barcelona, Spain
Santi Santamaría	Sant Celoni, Barcelona, Spain

José Andrés

Restaurants: Zaytinya, Washington, DC; Jaleo, Maryland; Jaleo, Washington, DC; Minibar at Café Atlantico, Washington, DC

José Andrés is a multi-award winning Spanish chef. Early in his career he trained under Ferran Adrià at the famous restaurant El Bulli in Spain, and now he and his partners own several successful restaurants in Washington, DC. He has written a cookbook and produces and hosts a popular food programme on Spanish television.

Chilled tomato soup with garlic shrimp
GAZPACHO CONGAMAS AL AJILLO

- 2 pounds ripe red tomatoes
- 1 medium cucumber
- ½ green bell pepper
- 1 clove garlic, peeled
- 1 tablespoon sherry vinegar
- ¾ cup Spanish extra-virgin olive oil
- sea salt
- finely chopped chives, to garnish

Garnish:
- 1 medium cucumber
- 4 plum tomatoes
- 1 red bell pepper
- 1 green bell pepper
- 2 shallots
- 4 slices of rustic bread

Shrimp:
- 4 tablespoons Spanish extra-virgin olive oil
- 6 cloves garlic, thinly sliced
- 20 large shrimp (about 1 pound)
- 1 dried chile pepper
- 1 teaspoon brandy
- 1 teaspoon chopped parsley
- sea salt

Serves 5–6

To make the gazpacho, chop the tomatoes into quarters roughly and place in a food processor. Peel the cucumber, cut the flesh into chunks. Halve and deseed the pepper, and cut into large pieces. Transfer both to the food processor. Add the garlic and vinegar and blend. Add the oil and season with salt to taste. Pour the gazpacho through a strainer into a pitcher. Place in the refrigerator to cool for at least half an hour. Next, prepare the garnish. Cut the cucumber in half lengthwise and remove the seeds. Sprinkle the flesh with salt and set aside for an hour to allow it to release its water. Rinse the cucumber well and dice into small pieces. Slice the ends off each tomato. Locate the fleshy dividing wall of one segment inside the tomato. Slice into the dividing wall and peel back the skin and flesh to expose the seeds. Remove the seeds taking care to keep the mass of seeds whole. (The point here is to extract the tomato seeds and their surrounding gel intact.) Repeat the process with the remaining tomatoes and set aside. Seed and dice the bell peppers. Dice the shallots. Combine the cucumber, pepper and shallots. Cut the bread into ½-inch cubes and fry in olive oil over medium heat until golden. When the soup is chilled, prepare the shrimp. In a medium sauté pan, heat the olive oil over medium-high heat. Sauté the garlic for 2 minutes, or until browned. Add the shrimp and chile pepper and cook for 2 minutes each side. Pour in the brandy and cook for 1 minute more. Sprinkle in the parsley and season. To serve, remove the gazpacho from the refrigerator. Place 3–4 shrimp and one tomato seed 'filet' in the middle of each bowl. Arrange the cucumber mixture around the edge and sprinkle the chives on top. Place four croûtons in the bowl on top of the cucumber. Drizzle a little extra olive oil over the shrimp and add a few flakes of sea salt. Serve the gazpacho on the side.

Veal cheeks with La Serena mashed potatoes

CARRILLERAS DE TERNERA CON PURE DE PATATAS Y QUESO LA SERENA

- **4 cloves garlic,**
  whole and unpeeled
- **10 veal cheeks (cleaned)**
- **4 cups Spanish red wine,**
  such as a Rioja
- **1 Spanish onion,**
  coarsely chopped
- **1 leek, outer leaves removed,**
  coarsely chopped
- **1 medium carrot,**
  coarsely chopped
- **3 sprig fresh rosemary**
- **4 sprigs fresh thyme**
- **3 teaspoons superfine sugar**
- **3 tablespoons Spanish**
  extra-virgin olive oil
- **all-purpose flour, for dusting**
- **veal stock**
- **1 black truffle**
- **1 tablespoon fresh chervil,**
  chopped
- **1 tablespoon fresh tarragon,**
  chopped
- **sea salt and black pepper**

Potatoes:
- **1 pound potatoes**
  (we recommend Idaho potatoes),
  peeled and cut into chunks
- **½ cup heavy cream**
- **3 ounces La Serena cheese, rind**
  removed, cut into small cubes
- **3 tablespoons Spanish**
  extra-virgin olive oil
- **sea salt**

Serves 5

Split open the garlic cloves by placing them on a chopping board and pressing down on them hard with the flat side of a kitchen knife. In a mixing bowl, combine the veal cheeks with the wine, crushed garlic, onion, leek, carrot, rosemary and thyme. Cover and marinate in the refrigerator overnight. Preheat the oven to 300°F. Remove the meat from the marinade and pat dry. Strain the marinade into another bowl, reserving the vegetables. Combine the sugar and reserved marinade in a small pan over low heat. Cook until the wine reduces by half. Skim off any foam that appears on the surface. Set the pan aside to cool. Drain the vegetables well. Heat 1 tablespoon of the olive oil in a large sauté pan over medium heat. When the oil is hot, add the vegetables and cook until soft and lightly browned. Add 2 tablespoons of olive oil to a pan and heat over medium heat. Season the veal cheeks with salt and pepper and dip both sides in flour, shaking off any excess. Place the meat in the saucepan and cook for 1–2 minutes each side until the meat is brown. Set on kitchen towel to drain and discard the oil from the pan. Place the vegetables in a deep roasting pan. Lay the veal cheeks on top, without overlapping. Pour the reduced wine and sugar mixture over the top and add enough veal stock to cover. Place aluminum foil on top of the pan, and press down until it touches the contents. Transfer to the oven and cook for 2½–3 hours, until the meat is tender. Remove the pan from the oven carefully and, using a slotted spatula, place the veal pieces on a warm serving plate. Strain the remaining sauce through a fine strainer, into a bowl. Discard the vegetables and let the sauce sit for 5 minutes until the fat separates. Remove the fat. Place the veal cheeks and the strained sauce in a clean pan over low heat. Cook until the sauce thickens and add salt to taste. Bring a large pot of water to a boil, add the potatoes and cook for 20 minutes until soft. Drain and mash thoroughly. In a small pan, heat the cream to boiling point. Set aside 1 tablespoon and add the rest to the potatoes. Mix with a wooden spoon until thoroughly combined, then add the cheese mixing vigorously until the cheese is fully incorporated. Gradually add the oil, stirring constantly until thoroughly combined. To serve, place a spoonful of mashed potato in the center of each plate and top with two veal cheeks and a little of the veal-cheek sauce. Shave black truffle sparingly over the top and drizzle with a little truffle oil. Add a few flakes of sea salt, some chervil and tarragon to garnish.

Homestyle flan with crema catalana foam

FLAN CASERO CON ESPUMA DE CREMA CATALANA

- ½ cup half-and-half Jersey milk
- ½ cup heavy cream
- 1 vanilla bean, split
- peel of 1 lemon
- 1 stick cinnamon
- 9 ounces superfine sugar
- 3 large eggs
- 2 large egg yolks
- orange supremes (see Note)
- mint

Caramel:
- ¾ cup superfine sugar

Espuma de crema catalana:
- quart half-and-half Jersey milk
- 1¼ cups heavy cream
- 1 cup sugar
- 12 egg yolks

Serves 4

Preheat the oven to 275°F. To make the caramel, put the sugar in a small pan and cook over low heat. After 5–6 minutes, the sugar will start to turn light brown. Cook for another 7–8 minutes until it becomes dark brown. Be careful to watch the mixture carefully as you don't want it to burn. Remove the pan from the heat and carefully add ½ cup water. The caramel will sputter and release steam as it hardens. Return the pan to the heat and, after about 5 minutes, the caramel will become thick and syrupy. Remove from the heat and let cool a little. Coat the bottom and sides of 4 small ramekins with the caramel, using your fingers or a spatula. Next, make the flan. In a medium pan, combine the Jersey milk and the cream. Add the vanilla bean and seeds, along with the lemon peel, cinnamon, and the sugar. Bring to a boil over medium-high heat, removing the pan from the heat just as the liquid reaches boiling point. In a large bowl, whisk together the eggs and egg yolks. Carefully pour the hot cream mixture into the eggs, whisking vigorously. Strain the mixture into another bowl then fill the ramekins. Set the ramekins in a deep roasting pan. Carefully pour hot water into the pan to come halfway up the sides of the ramekins. Transfer to the oven and bake for 45 minutes. Remove and let the ramekins cool. (The flans can be stored in the refrigerator overnight.) While the flans are cooling, prepare the espuma. Combine the Jersey milk, cream and sugar in a small pan and bring to a boil. Gradually mix the eggs with about half the hot liquid, then add the remaining liquid, return the mixture to the pan and cook over low heat for about 5 minutes, until thick. Remove the pan from the heat and let the mixture cool. Place in an iSi bottle or soda siphon with 2 charges of gas and charge. To serve, place a ramekin in the middle of a serving plate. Garnish with some of the espuma, and the orange supremes and mint leaves.

Note: To make orange supremes, remove the skin, pith, membranes and seeds of the fruit and separate into wedges.

Pepe Balaguer

Restaurant: La Pepica, Valencia

The restaurant La Pepica was a favorite of Ernest Hemingway, and has been popular with Spanish royalty and the food-loving public since it opened in 1898. La Pepica is widely credited with serving the best paella in Valencia.

Lobster paella

PAELLA DE BOGAVANTE

- 1 pound white fish
  (croaker, haddock, grouper
  or any available white fish),
  cut into small chunks
- 1 carrot, finely chopped
- 1 onion, finely chopped
- 1 tomato,
  peeled and coarsely chopped
- 2 cloves garlic
- 2 sprigs fresh flat-leaf parsley,
  finely chopped
- 1 tablespoon olive oil
- 1 large live male lobster
- 1 teaspoon smoked paprika
- 1 tomato, peeled, de-seeded
  and cut into thin julienne strips
- 14 ounces paella or risotto rice
  (such as Calaspara or canaroni)
- a few strands saffron
- salt

Serves 4–6

To prepare the stock:

Heat 5 pints water in a large Dutch oven or stock pot and, when simmering, add the fish, carrot, onion and chopped tomato and cook for 45 minutes. Remove from the heat and pass through a strainer or vegetable mill into a large bowl. Crush 1 of the cloves of garlic with the parsley and olive oil in a mortar, or small bowl and set aside.

To prepare the rice:

Cut the lobster in half. Place a paella pan, measuring 17 inches in diameter, over medium heat and pour in a dash of olive oil. Add the halves of lobster and sauté them with the second, chopped, clove of garlic, the smoked paprika and the julienne strips of tomato. Add the rice and sauté. Next, pour in the stock, using two measures of liquid to one of rice (to a total volume of approximately 1¾ pints). Stir, then add the saffron and salt to taste. Bring to the boil and cook for 10 minutes over high heat, then add a spoonful of the garlic and parsley mixture, reduce the heat to low and continue to boil for 10 minutes more. Remove the paella pan from the heat and let stand for 5 minutes (if you can resist that long!) Serve this special paella straight from the pan.

Sam & Sam Clark

Restaurant: Moro, London

Sam and Sam Clark, business partners and husband and wife, opened the award-winning southern Mediterranean restaurant Moro in 1997, after spending three months traveling through Spain, Morocco and the Sahara. They were inspired by the local ingredients and regional cooking they had experienced and their passion and ideas can be seen in the Moorish cuisine and tapas they serve.

Grilled chicory with sherry vinegar and jamon

ENDIBIAS CON VINAIGRE DE JEREZ Y JAMON

- 2 large white chicory heads
- ½ small bunch flat-leaf parsley, roughly chopped
- 5½ ounces jamon pata negra or Serrano ham, thinly sliced

Dressing:
- 6 tablespoons sherry vinegar
- ½ clove garlic
- ½ teaspoon fresh thyme leaves
- 3 tablespoons extra-virgin olive oil
- salt and black pepper

Serves 4

To make the dressing, put the sherry vinegar into a small pan and place over low heat until reduced to about 2 tablespoons (be careful not to let it cook for too long as it reduces very quickly). Crush the garlic and thyme with a good pinch of salt, preferably in a mortar with a pestle, to a smooth paste. Transfer to a bowl, add the reduced vinegar, some freshly ground black pepper and the olive oil. Set aside. To prepare the chicory, cut off the very end and remove any old, discolored leaves, but keep the head intact. Cut the chicory heads in half lengthwise and cut each length into thirds. Place the chicory on a hot griddle pan, barbecue or broiler over medium heat, and, when one side is slightly charred, carefully turn the chicory and grill the other side (this will not take very long). Add the dressing immediately, along with the parsley. To serve, fan the chicory out on a serving plate, and serve the jamon alongside.

Note: This recipe balances the rich, salty jamon with the nutty sherry vinegar and bitter chicory.

Whole baked sea bass with roast beetroot and almond and sherry-vinegar sauce

LUBINA RELLENA AL HORNO

- 1 large (3¼-pound) sea bass, scaled and gutted
- 1½ teaspoons Maldon sea salt
- ½ teaspoon coarsely ground black pepper
- 4 flat-leaf parsley stems

Preheat the oven to 450°F. Rinse the fish inside and out, pat dry, then season inside and out with the sea salt and pepper. Stuff the cavity with the parsley stems, lemon slices, fennel stalks, fennel seeds and bay leaves. Toss the sliced fennel bulb and red onion with 4 tablespoons of the olive oil, the white wine, and a little salt and pepper. Spread the sliced vegetables in a thin layer to cover the

- 4 thin slices lemon
- 2 medium fennel bulbs,
  stalks removed and reserved,
  bulb sliced into ¼ inch-thick
  wedges
- 1 teaspoon whole fennel seeds
- 2 bay leaves
- 1 red onion, thinly sliced
- 6 tablespoons extra-virgin
  olive oil
- 6 tablespoons white wine
- salt and black pepper

Serves 4

base of a large roasting pan, then place the fish on top. Drizzle the fish with the remaining oil, and transfer to the oven. Bake until just cooked through (this will take about 35–40 minutes). Remove from the oven and set aside to rest for 5 minutes before serving, either in the roasting pan or on a serving dish with the fennel on the side.

Note: A whole baked fish is perfect for a dinner or lunch party, hot or at room temperature. In the summer when fennel is at its peak, it is a great way to use up a glut of this delicious vegetable.

Roast beet:
- 2¼ pounds young beet, washed
  carefully and halved
- 3 sprigs fresh thyme,
  leaves picked
- ½ clove garlic crushed with salt
- 5 tablespoons olive oil
- 1 tablespoon red-wine vinegar
- salt and pepper

Serves 4

Roast beet with thyme

Place the washed beet in a mixing bowl. Sprinkle over the thyme, add the garlic, olive oil, vinegar and a little salt and pepper and toss well. Transfer to a roasting pan and cover tightly with aluminum foil. Place in the preheated oven and cook for 30 minutes (see recipe above), then remove the foil and continue roasting for 20–30 minutes more or until the beet are tender. Serve as a side dish with the Whole baked sea bass and the Almond and sherry-vinegar sauce (see above and below).

**Almond and sherry-vinegar
sauce:**
- 5 ounces whole
  blanched almonds
- 1 ounce stale white bread, crusts
  removed, soaked in water
- 1 clove garlic, crushed with salt
- ½–¾ tablespoon sherry vinegar
- 1½ tablespoons capers, soaked
  in water, squeezed and finely
  chopped (optional)
- sea salt

Serves 4

Almond and sherry-vinegar sauce

In a food processor, grind the almonds to as fine a consistency as possible. Add 3 tablespoons water and process until the almonds form a paste. Squeeze the bread of excess water and add to the almonds along with the garlic. Combine until smooth. Mix together 5 tablespoons water with the sherry, then slowly add the almond mixture, until you end up with a thick cream with a smooth consistency similar to mayonnaise. Transfer to a bowl, add the capers, if using, and season with salt to taste.

Malaga raisin ice cream

HELADO DE PASAS DE MALAGA

- **1 pint heavy cream**
- **½ pint milk**
- **1 small cinnamon stick**
- **1 vanilla pod**
- **7 egg yolks**
- **½ cup superfine sugar**
- **3½ ounces raisins covered with 3½ fl oz Pedro Ximenez sherry or Pedro Ximinez Malaga wine**

Serves 8 (makes just over 1 litre)

Place the cream, milk and cinnamon stick in a large pan. Split the vanilla pod in half lengthwise and scrape the tiny seeds into the pan, discarding the pod. Heat until just below boiling point, then remove the pan from the stove. In a bowl, beat the egg yolks and sugar together for 5–10 minutes until the mixture is pale and thick. Loosen the egg mixture by stirring in a little of the cream and milk mixture, then pour the egg mixture into the saucepan, scraping the bowl out with a spatula. Whisk well to mix everything properly and return to low heat, stirring constantly. Heat gently but be careful not to curdle the mixture. When it thickens and just before it bubbles, remove from the heat, pour into a bowl and place over ice water to cool. Churn in an ice cream machine, in batches if necessary, adding the raisins and sherry towards the end of the churning. (For those without an ice cream machine, you can freeze the ice cream by hand, but remember to stir every half-hour to prevent ice crystals forming. Stirring will also help to distribute the raisins evenly as they tend to sink to the bottom before the ice cream is hard enough to suspend them.) The churning process will take about 2 hours, depending on the temperature of your freezer or the specification of your ice cream maker. Serve the ice cream with a chilled glass of Pedro Ximenez on the side or poured over the top.

Note: Although this is a very simple recipe (using a basic custard for the ice cream) complexity and flavor is provided by the sherry. The raisins are soaked in Pedro Ximenez sherry, a treacly, sweet, raisiny sherry made from Pedro Ximenez grapes, that have been first dried in the sun to concentrate their sugar and taste.

Ramón Freixa

Restaurant: El Raco d'en Freixa, Barcelona

Ramón Freixa's passion for cooking began in his grandparent's bakery. He has worked in some of the best kitchens of Europe and, in 1998, after four years at his father's restaurant, Ramón was given control of the kitchen. From this point, he has continued to create award-winning food at El Racó d'en Freixa – and also finds time to promote Spanish cuisine in newspapers, radio, television and in three cookbooks, making him a worthy winner of many awards.

Minted baby beans with cucumber and algae ice-cream

BOCADILLO DE HABITAS A LA MENTA CON COHOMBROS Y HELADO DE ALGAS

- 18 fl oz liquid cream
- 18 fl oz whole milk
- 14 ounces fresh algae (such as sea lettuce or laver bread)
- ¾ ounce ice cream stabilizer
- 12 egg yolks
- ½ pint of mint water
- ¼ ounce xantana gum
- 1 pound 2 ounces fava beans, cooked
- 1 clove garlic, finely chopped
- 3½ fl oz olive oil
- 1 loaf rustic bread, thinly sliced
- 1 handful ficoide glacial (ice plant)
- 1 handful Ceylon spinach
- 1 handful mitzuna
- 1 handful frisee
- 1 head Belgian endive
- 'Picada Catalana' oil, for drizzling
- 1 tablespoon chervil, chopped
- 14 ounces cucumber
- 1 tablespoon groundnut oil

Serves 8–10

To make the algae ice cream, put the cream, milk, algae, ice cream stabilizer and egg yolks into a blender and pulse until thoroughly combined. Strain the mixture and set aside in the refrigerator for 12 hours. Pour into an ice cream maker and follow the manufacturer's instructions. (If an ice cream maker is unavailable, place the mixture in a deep dish and freeze, stirring every 20 minutes to prevent ice crystals from forming.) To make the mint jelly, bring the mint water to a boil and add the xantana gum. Leave to set in a shallow tray or pan and when solid, cut into cubes. Once the ice cream and the mint jelly have been made, you can start to make the other components of the recipe. Rinse the fava beans, blanch them, then remove their pale skins. Mix the chopped garlic with the olive oil. Preheat the oven to 340°F. Cut the bread into long, thin slices and brush with the garlic-infused oil. Bake the coated bread slices for 10 minutes, then set aside and keep warm until ready to serve. Dress the salad leaves with the Picada Catalana oil, and add a little chopped chervil. Set aside until ready to serve. Peel the cucumber and cut off the ends. Slice lengthwise and scoop out the seeds. Cut the flesh into slices ¼ inch thick. Heat the peanut oil in a skillet and add the cucumber. Cook over medium heat until begining to shine. Remove from the pan and keep warm. To serve, place several slices of warm garlic bread on a plate and top with the beans, then add another slice of bread and the cucumber and salad leaves. Place a spoonful of the chopped mint jelly and a ball of algae ice cream to the side.

Note: To make mint water, twist or bruise 1 handful mint leaves, place in a clean 2½ pint container and fill with still mineral water. Chill in the refrigerator for 24 hours, strain and use. Xantana gum is available from online retailers but, if not available, subtitute gelatin leaves. The 'picada' oil, which is a Catalan specialty is made with olive oil, raisins, pine nuts and hazelnuts and is available from online suppliers. Ice plant, Ceylon spinach, mitzuna, frisee and Belgian endive may be hard to obtain. If so, try substituting a different selection of salad leaves and experiment until you find a combination you like.

Hazelnut cream with pheasant and truffle ravioli
CREMA DE AVELLANAS CON RAVIOLI DE FAISAN I TRUFA

- **7 ounces pumpkin (squash)**
- **2 tablespoons peanut oil**
- **1 shallot, chopped**
- **7 ounces roast pheasant, finely chopped**
- **1 semi-sweet biscuit, crushed**
- **1 black truffle (melanosporum), very finely chopped**
- **12 sheets ravioli pasta**
- **1 egg, lightly beaten**
- **salt and pepper**

Smoked milk foam:
- **4 sheets gelatin**
- **2 teaspoons smoked salt**
- **1¾ pints milk**

Cream of hazelnut :
- **1 pound 2 ounces hazelnuts, toasted in their skins**
- **1¾ pints chicken stock**
- **14 fl oz of liquid cream**

Contrasting Garnishes:
- **alpine or wild strawberries**
- **quince jelly**
- **enoki or other fresh mushrooms, raw or lightly fried**
- **toasted pine nuts**
- **black truffle, thinly sliced**

Serves 6

First, make the filling for the ravioli. Roast the pumpkin in the peanut oil for 30 minutes in a hot oven. Fry the shallot until transluscent and add the roast pumpkin and the pheasant. Mix in the crushed biscuit and the truffle, season to taste with salt and pepper and set aside. Next, assemble the ravioli. Lay out half the pasta sheets and place a generous teaspoon of the pheasant mixture at regularly spaced intervals on the pasta. Add the pasta 'lids', seal with the beaten egg, cut, and set aside. To make the smoked milk foam, first soak the sheets of gelatin in warm water until spongy. Add the smoked salt to the milk and bring to a boil. When the milk is boiling, add the sheets of gelatin and leave the mixture to thicken. Place in a soda siphon with 2 charges of gas and set aside. To make the cream of hazelnut, finely chop the hazelnuts. Pour the chicken stock and cream into a deep pan and heat gently. When the milk and stock mixture is hot, add the hazelnuts and strain. Add salt and pepper to taste and strain again. Place the pan over a bowl of hot water to keep it warm. Bring a large pan of water to a boil and cook the ravioli until al dente. When cooked remove from the pan and transfer to a ridged skillet coated with a little peanut oil to 'mark' them. To serve, arrange a selection of the contrasting garnishes in an irregular pattern on each plate alongside the pheasant and pumpkin ravioli. Top with the smoked milk froth and serve the cream of hazelnut separately in a soup tureen.

Note: To prepare roast pheasant, first ensure it is clean and free from feathers. Preheat the oven to 340°F and truss the bird(s) as you would a chicken. Rub the skin with half a tablespoon goose fat and roast breast-side down in a deep pan for 40 minutes, covered with foil. Then turn the bird over and cook for 20 minutes at 400°F with the breasts covered with bacon if you like. Smoked sea salt is available from specialty retailers.

Chocolate mousse tartlets

TARTALETA DE MOUSSE COCIDA

Pastry:
- 1 pound 7 ounces butter
- 12 ounces superfine sugar
- 14 ounces ground almonds
- 1 pound 14 ounces
  all-purpose flour
- 11 ounces unsweetened cocoa
- ¾ ounce salt
- 1 pound eggs

Filling:
- 9 ounces gianduja chocolate
  (70 % cocoa solids)
- 3½ ounces butter
- 4 ounces egg yolks
- 3 ounces superfine sugar
- 5½ ounces egg whites

Serves 8–10

To make the pastry, cut the butter into cubes, place in a food processor with a mixing blade and add the superfine sugar, ground almonds and 14 ounces of the flour. When the mixture is smooth, sift the remaining flour with the cocoa and salt into a clean bowl and add the eggs, mixing well until fully incorporated. Let the dough rest in a cool place until needed. Preheat the oven to 340°F. To make the mousse filling, melt the gianduja chocolate with the butter in a double-boiler. In a large bowl, whisk the egg yolks with half the sugar until fully incorporated. In another bowl, whisk the egg whites until they form peaks. Pour the melted chocolate into the egg yolks and mix until combined, then carefully fold in the whites. Roll out the pastry and use it to line 2 ¾ inch tartlet tins tartlet tins. Add baking beans or pastry weights and bake 'blind' for 10 minutes. Remove the baking beans or pastry weights and fill the pastry cases with the mousse mixture. Increase the oven temperature to 360°F, return the tartlets to the oven and cook for 8 minutes.

Andy Nusser

Restaurant: Casa Mono, New York

Andy Nusser grew up in Spain in the 1970s, where he began his career in food as a dish washer at Casa Nun restaurant in the village of Cadaques. Andy went on to New York where he cooked with Mario Batali in the tiny kitchen of Po before becoming executive chef of the award-winning Babbo. Nusser and partners opened the popular Casa Mono and Bar Jamon in 2003, which has gone on to be the number one Zagat-rated Spanish restaurant in New York City.

Langoustines with Gazpacho Salad

LANGOSTINOS CON GAZPACHO ENSALADA

- 8 large langoustines or Dublin Bay prawns
- ½ loaf baguette, cut in ½ inch dice
- ⅔ cup olive oil
- 1 red onion, sliced into 6 wedges
- 4 piquillo peppers
- 6 tablespoons red-wine vinegar
- salt and pepper

Spicy Candied Tomatoes:
- 1 pint cherry tomatoes
- 2 cups sugar
- 1 tablespoon kosher salt
- 1 tablespoon crushed red bell pepper
- 1 cinnamon stick

Gazpacho salad:
- ¼ pound sea beans
- 1 cucumber, peeled and cubed
- 8 piquillo peppers, sliced into ½-inch strips
- salt and pepper

Serves 4

Cut the langoustines from head to tail down both sides with kitchen scissors. Peel off their shells and drop them into boiling salted water and cook for two minutes. Plunge the cooked langoustines into a bowl of ice water and then dry on a clean towel. Next make the spicy candied tomatoes. Bring a medium pan of water to a boil and blanch the tomatoes for 15 seconds each before plunging them into a bowl of ice water to cool. In the same saucepan, combine 1 cup water with the sugar, salt, red bell pepper and the cinnamon stick, sim-mering over medium heat until the sugar has dissolved. Drain and peel the tomatoes, then place them in a dry bowl. Strain the sugar syrup over the tomatoes and let stand until cool. To make the croûtons, preheat the oven to 350°F and toss the diced bread on a baking tray with 2 tablespoons of the olive oil. Season to taste and bake for about 10 minutes until golden brown. On another baking tray, toss the onion wedges with 2 tablespoons of the red-wine vinegar and 2 tablespoons of the remaining olive oil. Season with salt and pepper and add to the oven to bake for 20 minutes. After the onions are cooked, cool and separate 4 of the wedges into 'petals'. To make the gazpacho salad, bring a medium pan of water to a boil. Add the sea beans and blanch for 15 seconds. Plunge the beans into ice water to cool and then drain on a clean towel. Add the cucumber and pepper stips. Finally, to prepare the gazpacho vinaigrette, combine the 2 whole wedges of the roasted onion, 4 spicy candied tomatoes and four piquillo peppers with the remaining red-wine vinegar and the remaining olive oil in a blender or food processor and pulse until fully combined. To serve, toss the different elements of the dish in the gazpacho vinaigrette, top with the langoustines and dress with more vinaigrette.

Note: Sea beans are also known in the US as marsh samphire, sali-cornia, sea pickle or glasswort. They are available fresh along the at-lantic and pacific coasts but can also be bought pickled and in jars. In north-western Europe, a very similar plant called samphire is more common, though not commonly available. Both varieties of plant have a salty or even fishy taste and are prized among gourmands.

Sweetbreads with Fennel al Mono
MOLLEJAS CON FENNEL AL MONO

- 2 ¼ pounds sweetbreads
- 12 baby fennel bulbs,
  fronds attached
- 2 cups olive oil
- 1 tablespoon anchovy paste
- ½ cup Anis del Mono
- ¼ cup white-wine vinegar
- 1 cup ground almonds
- 1 cup Wondra flour
  or all-purpose flour
- salt and pepper

Almond vinaigrette:
- 1 cup salted and fried
  marcona almonds
- 1 cup almond oil
- ¼ cup sherry vinegar

Serves 6–8

Rinse the sweetbreads under cold running water and then soak them overnight in 1 ¾ pints of cold water combined with ¼ cup white-wine vinegar. The next day, blanch them in boiling seasoned water for 1–2 minutes before plunging them into ice water and laying them out to drain on a towel-covered tray. Remove the membranes and divide the sweetbreads into portions, each made up of 3 pieces and weighing 5–6 ounces. Trim the baby fennel bulbs, reserving the fennel fronds, then blanch in seasoned boiling water for 5 minutes, before plunging into ice water to stop the cooking process. Dry on clean towels, then cut the bulbs in half lengthwise. Heat ½ cup of the olive oil in a skillet and cook the baby fennel until golden. Add the anchovy paste and the Anis del Mono, stirring until combined. Remove from the heat and set aside to cool. To make the almond vinaigrette, first grind the marcona almonds coarsely in a food processor. Transfer to a clean bowl and fold in the almond oil and sherry vinegar with a spoon. Heat the remaining olive oil in a skillet over medium-high heat. Prepare a dusting mixture by combining the ground almonds and flour in a bowl. Season the sweetbread portions, dust them thoroughly in the almond mixture and pan fry in the olive oil until golden brown and crispy. Remove from the pan and drain on kitchen towels, seasoning again to taste. To serve, place three pieces of fennel al mono on each plate, top them with 3 fried sweetbreads and add the almond vinai-grette. Garnish with the reserved fennel fronds.

Note: Marcona almonds are native only to Spain. They are large and flat in shape and have a more delicate and sweet flavor than other almonds. Wondra flour is a variety of wheat flour to which some malted barley flour has been added; if it is not available, you can substitute Instant Flour or all-purpose flour.

Rhubarb Flan

RUIBARTO FLAN

- 1 quart heavy cream
- 1 cinnamon stick
- 1 vanilla bean
- 3 sheets gelatin, softened
  in warm water until spongy
- 8 egg yolks
- 1 cup superfine sugar

Rhubarb Marmalade:
- ¼ cup grenadine
- 2 tablespoons brown sugar
- 4 stalks rhubarb (including
  whites), cut into small dice
- 2 sheets gelatin, softened
  in water until spongy

Serves 6–8

Preheat the oven to 325°F. Place the cream, cinnamon stick and vanilla bean in a large pan and heat gently. When the cream is almost boiling, add the sheets of the softened gelatin to the cream, one sheet at a time, stirring constantly. Whisk the egg yolks and the sugar in a large bowl until smooth and then whisk in half of the hot cream. Pour back into the large pan and heat, stirring the mixture with a wooden spoon, to a point at which the back of the spoon is coated with the custard when stirring. Ensure the ingredients are incorporated thoroughly but be careful not to overcook the mixture and remove the pan from the heat if necessary. Strain the mixture through a cone shaped strainer, pressing the vanilla pod against it to ensure you extract as much flavor as possible. Pour the mixture into a heatproof jug and then three-quarter fill 6–8 ramekins or individual cocottes. Place these in a roasting pan and add cold water to the pan to come halfway up the sides of the ramekins. Cover the roasting pan with aluminum foil, transfer to the oven and bake for 35 minutes. To make the rhubarb marmalade, bring the grenadine and brown sugar to a boil over medium heat. Add the rhubarb, stirring constantly. Do not look away at this point as the rhubarb cooks in less than 5 minutes. Process the mixture in a blender or food proc-essor. Add the softened gelatin sheets. Top each flan with one tablespoon of the rhubarb mixture. Remove the foil carefully from the roasting pan and check that the custard has set. Place the ramekins in the refrigerator to cool.

José Manuel Pizarro

Restaurant: Tapas Brindisa, London

José Manuel Pizarro spent his early years working in a number of Spain's best restaurants and has been cooking in London since 2002. He is currently the head chef at Tapas Brindisa, the restaurant named after and supplied by the much-loved Brindisa shops owned by Monika Linton, who has been sourcing the best Spanish produce for her shops in Exmouth and Borough markets for years. Her specialist knowledge of local Spanish producers means Tapas Brindisa is able to source ingredients such as cheeses, charcuterie and store-cupboard provisions from local producers all over Spain. José then uses his flair and imagination to turn them into a delicious range of tapas.

Cecina with Pomegranate and Endive Salad

ENSALADA DE CECINA CON GRANADA Y ENDIVIAS

- **7 ounces cecina**
- **3 tablespoons olive oil**
- **1½ tablespoons moscatel vinegar**
- **1½ tablespoons orange blossom honey**
- **seeds of one small pomegranate**
- **1 small endive**
- **1 tablespoon chopped fresh parsley**
- **salt and pepper**

Serves 4

Divide the cecina among 4 plates and season with black pepper to taste. In a bowl, mix the oil, vinegar and honey until well combined and then add the pomegranate seeds. Place the endive and parsley in another bowl, dress with the vinaigrette and season to taste. Arrange the endive on top of the cecina and serve.

Note: Cecina is similar to the Italian cured meat bresaola in texture and appearance. The best-known cecina is Cecina de Leon, which is Spanish air-dried and smoked cured beef made from the hind legs of cattle. Moscatel vinegar is a pale amber vinegar made from moscatel grapes, which is much prized for its bittersweet flavor.

Pan-fried chicken with Romesco sauce

POLLO CON SALSA ROMESCO

- 2 whole baby chickens
  (poussins), deboned
- 2 tablespoons olive oil
- 1 tablespoon chopped
  parsley
- salt and pepper

  Romesco sauce:
- 1 ñora (dried red bell pepper)
- 3 tablespoons olive oil
- 1 clove garlic, chopped
- 1 small slice rustic bread
- 7 ounces roasted tomatoes
- 1 ounce toasted almonds
- 1 teaspoon sherry vinegar
- salt and pepper

  Serves 2

First make the Romesco sauce. Leave the ñora to soak overnight before you begin cooking, then scoop out its center. Heat 2 tablespoons of the olive oil in a skillet and cook the garlic and the slice of bread until golden, then remove and leave to cool. Put the pepper, garlic and bread mixture into a food processor or blender. Add the roasted tomatoes, toasted almonds and vinegar, and mix until smooth. Season with salt and pepper to taste. Heat the olive oil in a skillet. Season the chickens and fry until golden brown all over. To serve, place a tablespoon of Romesco sauce in the centre of two dinner plates and position the baby chickens on top. Sprinkle with a little olive oil and add the chopped parsley before serving.

Note: Instead of the ñora variety, bell peppers of varying sweetness or hotness can be used, depending on taste.

Fillet steak on toast with caramelized onion and torta de barros

FILETES DE SOLOMILLO CON CEBOLLA CARAMELIZADA Y TORTA DE BARROS

- 1 tablespoon olive oil
- 4 fillet steaks
  (approx. 7 ounces each)
- 7 ounces torta de barros cheese,
  cut into 4 pieces
- 4 slices of rustic bread, toasted
- 1 tablespoon fresh oregano,
  chopped
- salt and pepper

  Caramelized onion:
- 6 tablespoons olive oil
- 1 pound 9 ounces onions,
  finely sliced
- 1 teaspoon superfine sugar
- 1 small bay leaf

  Serves 4

To make the caramelized onion, heat the oil in a large pan with a lid and then add the onion, sugar and bay leaf. Cover and cook over low heat, stirring occasionally, until the onion turns a deep brown. This will take approximately 60 minutes. Heat the oil in a skillet, add the steaks and cook to taste. Season and add the cheese to one side of the pan so that it begins to melt. To serve, put a spoonful of caramelized onion on each slice of the toasted bread, add the steaks on top and then sprinkle with the oregano.

Alexandra Raij

Restaurant: Tia Pol, New York

Alexandra Raij is the chef and partner of two Manhattan tapas bars, Tia Pol, and El Quinto Pino. She cooks alongside her Basque husband Eder Montero, who is a native of Bilbao. Together the two have set a new standard for Spanish food and the tapas tradition in New York. Alex's preoccupation with good cooking and eating was cultivated at home where her food-passionate parents exposed her to the pleasures of cooking, eating and gathering around the table. Her parents, originally from Argentina, embraced the diversity of cuisines available in the US. This encouraged her deep interest in new flavors and ways of eating and gave her an enduring love of cookbooks.

Baby romaine hearts with Spanish anchovy vinaigrette

COGOLLITOS CON VINAGRETA DE ANCHOAS

- 12 baby romaine heads or 6 commercially-grown romaine hearts
- 18 Spanish or other mild anchovies, packed in oil
- 1 cup extra-virgin olive oil
- 2 cloves garlic, minced
- ⅓ cup Panko breadcrumbs
- 1½ tablespoons Smoked Pimenton de la Vera
- 2 tablespoons seasoned rice wine vinegar
- ¼ teaspoon salt

Serves 6

Trim the ends of each lettuce without detaching the leaves from the stalk. Cut each lettuce head in half, vertically through the stem end, and submerge in cool water shaking off any dirt or sand (if using commercial romaine hearts cut them in quarters lengthwise). Pat the lettuces dry and set aside, cut side down, on kitchen towels until ready to use (in the refrigerator if cleaning ahead). To make the vinaigrette, heat a small pan over medium heat with 12 of the anchovies (the best anchovies are from Ondaorroa), breaking them up with a spoon as they 'melt'. Add half of the oil, and the garlic and breadcrumbs and stir until both are brown and you have a paste. Remove from the heat and add the paprika. Stir to combine and add the vinegar. Add the salt and 2 tablespoons water to a blender or processor, turn the motor to its lowest setting and slowly add ½ the anchovy paste. Add the remaining oil in a thin stream and follow with the rest of the anchovy paste. Season to taste and adjust the salt or acidity as needed, remembering that vinegars have different acid values and you want the vinaigrette to be slightly acidic. Set aside in the refrigerator if not using immediately. To serve, place 2 baby romaine heads (4 halves), cut side up on each plate. Spoon the thick vinaigrette over the lettuces. Cut the remaining anchovies into long thin slices and drape over the lettuce halves, drizzling with extra olive oil.

Note: The vinaigrette can be made a day ahead of serving. You can substitute the seasoned rice wine vinegar with sherry vinegar with

1 tsp sugar dissolved in it. This recipe is wonderful in the summer when the farmers' markets are full of the small baby lettuce heads that are so prized in Spain. However, if you are not lucky enough to find them, commercially grown romaine hearts can be substituted.

Salt-baked sea bream with green olive and pinenut vinaigrette
DORADA A LA SAL CON SALSA MARIANITO

- **3 sea bream (1½ pounds each), filleted, skin on**
- **2 cups kosher salt**

Vinaigrette:
- **4 tablespoons pinenuts, toasted**
- **4 tablespoons pitted and chopped green manzanilla olives**
- **3 tablespoons minced red onion**
- **3 tablespoons thinly sliced scallion (light green and white parts only)**
- **4 tablespoons Spanish pickled green guindilla pepper**
- **1 teaspoon sugar**
- **1 cup best-quality Spanish extra-virgin olive oil**
- **3 tablespoons rice wine vinegar**
- **1 tablespoon sherry vinegar**
- **salt, to taste**

Serves 6

To make the vinaigrette, mix all the ingredients together in a bowl and reserve until the fish is ready. To prepare the fish, first remove the pin bones and pat dry. Lightly oil a baking sheet with olive oil and place the fillets on it, skin side up. Mix the salt and 1 cup water to make a rough paste and divide among the fillets, making sure the salt mixture stays only on the skin and does not touch the flesh. Place under a pre-heated broiler about 4 inches from the heat for approximately 5–7 minutes. The salt will form a hard crust and promote an even cooking. When the fish is ready, remove the salt crust carefully by lifting it off each fillet with the help of a small spatula. Carefully pull back the skin, which should come off without resistance. Discard the skin, transfer the fillets to individual plates and top with 2–3 teaspoons of the vinaigrette.

Note: If Spanish pickled green guindilla pepper is not available, you can substitute mild pepperoncini. The vinaigrette may be made up to one day ahead, but make sure that you bring it back to room temperature 1 hour before serving.

Orange flan

FLAN DE NARANJA

- **2 cups sugar**
- **1 ¾ cups orange juice**
- **½ cup cold water**
- **2 whole eggs**
- **8 egg yolks**
- **juice of 1 lemon**
- **1 teaspoon cornstarch**

Serves 6

First, place half the sugar in a small pan and add water to cover. Heat the mixture without stirring until the sugar dissolves and turns medium-dark amber in color. When it reaches this stage, quickly pour this mixture into the bottom of 6 (4 ounce) ramekins and set aside to cool completely. Preheat the oven to 300°F. Bring the orange juice and half of the remaining sugar to a boil and then cool slightly by adding ½ cup cold water. In a medium bowl, whisk the eggs, extra yolks, remaining sugar, lemon juice and cornstarch. Slowly add the orange juice mixture to the egg mixture, whisking constantly until combined. Pass the mixture through a fine strainer to remove the fruit pulp and egg membranes. Place the sugared ramekins in a roasting pan and fill them with the custard mixture. Pour hot water into the roasting pan to come three-quarters of the way up the sides of the ramekins and cover the roasting pan with aluminum foil. Pierce the foil many times to allow steam to escape during cooking. Carefully place the pan on the middle shelf of the oven and bake for 20 minutes. Lift the foil to let more steam escape and continue baking until the custard is set, which should be approximately another 10–15 minutes. Allow the custards to cool at room temperature then cover and chill in the refrigerator. To serve, run a warmed knife around the inside edges of the ramekins and tip the custards out onto individual plates.

Note: This is a very fresh and light flan due to the absence of cream.

The Roca Brothers

Restaurant: EL Celler de Can Roca, Gerona

Joan, Joseph and Jordi are the third generation of a family that has been dedicated to the restaurant business since the 1920s. Since 1986, they have run El Celler de Can Roca, in Gerona, near Barcelona, where Joseph is in charge of the dining room and wines, Jordi the baking, and Joan is the chef. The three, who are noted exponents of the art of 'Molecular Gastronomy', have won international recognition and awards for everything from their food to the wine, cigars and, baking of their restaurant.

Asparagus with Viognier

ESPARRAGOS CON VIOGNIER

- 1 pound 2 ounces asparagus
- ¾ cup liquid cream
  at room temperature
- 1½ ounces powdered egg white
- 2 g xantana
- truffle oil
- crystallised lemon peel,
  to garnish
- powdered holm oak, to burn

Metil celulosa:
- ⅔ cup mineral water
- 5 g metil

Viognier:
- ⅔ cup Viognier
- 1 g xantana

Serves 4–6

Cut off and reserve the tips of the asparagus spears. Heat a grill plate or barbecue grill to hot and cook the asparagus. When cool enough to handle, peel the asparagus and mix them in a bowl with the cream. Add the egg white and xantana. Chop and strain. Put into a soda siphon with two charges of gas and keep in a bain marie or double boiler (we use a Roner) at 62°C/143°F. To prepare the metil celulosa, mix the mineral water with the metil and leave to stand at 3°C/37°F for approximately 12 hours. Mix the Viognier and the xantana and leave to stand. Preheat the oven to 300°F. Cut the asparagus tips lengthwise into thin slices and blanch in boiling water. Cut strips of greaseproof paper to line the inside of metal cooking rings of 4 inch diameter. Place the paper flat, putting the asparagus slices, overlapping, along the length of the paper, like a picket fence. Pour the metil through a fine strainer to cover the asparagus. Line each ring with a strip of paper and asparagus and bake for 5 minutes to allow the metil to solidify. Move the rings to individual serving plates and fill the centres with the asparagus froth. Remove the ring and the paper. Finish the dish with the Viognier, crystallised lemon peel and truffle oil. Cover each round with a glass dome, place the powdered holm oak in a specialist culinary pipe, burn it and introduce the smoke into the dome. Take the dome off the dish at the table.

Note: Xantana is used to thicken sauces and soups and is available from online retailers. Metil is a form of gelatin (available as a powder), extracted from the cellulose of vegetables. When used cold it acts as a thickener but jellifies when heat is added. Powdered egg white is available from online retailers.

Oyster in cava

OSTRA AL CAVA

- **4 oysters**
- **1 Royal Gala apple, cored**
- **1g agar agar**
- **1.6g xanatana**
- **1 ⅓ cups Cava, or other sparkling white wine**
- **toasted, sliced almonds**
- **breadcrumbs made with spiced bread**
- **curry powder**
- **crystallised lemon**

Serves 4

Make an apple compote by liquidizing the apple. Cool and decant the liquid, eliminating the pulp and leaving a clear, transparent water. Measure ⅓ cup apple water and add the agar agar. Leave to set, then blend to form a purée. For the Cava soda, mix the xantana and Cava in a blender, then place into a soda siphon with 2 charges of gas.To serve, line the individual dishes with the apple and agar purée. Place an oyster in each dish and surround with the Cava soda. Garnish with the other ingredients and serve.

Note: Agar agar is a form of gelatin derived from sea vegetables. It is also known by its Japanese name, Kanten. See note on opposite page for information regarding xanatana.

White Cromaticism

CROMATISMO BLANCO

Crema de Haba Tonka:
- **2 teaspoons sugar**
- **0.5g salt**
- **1g agar agar**
- **⅓ cup distilled Haba Tonks**

Coffee gelatin:
- **2 teaspoons sugar**
- **0.5g de agar agar**
- **⅓ cup distilled coffee (made from an infusion of 250 ml coffee and 50g coffee beans)**

Iced passion fruit drink:
- **0.5g gelatin**
- **15g dextrose**
- **⅓ cup distilled passion fruit (made from scant 1 cup passion fruit juice)**

Cocoa sorbet:
- **⅓ cup distilled Haba Tonka**
- **25g sprayed glucose**
- **15g dextrose**
- **0.6g stabiliser**

Make the following elements of this dessert separately, then arrange a small amount of each on individual serving plates. To make the crema de Haba Tonka, mix the sugar, salt and agar agar in a small pan and add half the distilled Haba Tonka. Bring to a boil before mixing in the other half of the Haba Tonka. Cool, and then emulsify in a blender. To make the coffee gelatin, mix the sugar and agar agar in a small pan and add half the distilled coffee. Bring to a boil, and then add the other half of the coffee. Leave to set in a medium sized container and once cold, cut into cubes measuring ⅛ x ⅛ inch. To make the iced passion fruit drink, dissolve the dextrose and gelatin with half the distilled passion fruit juice and then mix in the rest. Put into a container and place in the freezer. To make the cocoa sorbet, mix the glucose, dextrose and stabiliser in a small pan with 2 tablespoons water and heat to 185°F. Mix in the distilled Haba Tonka and put into an ice-cream maker (we use a paco jet). Freeze, and just before serving, mix with an electric whisk.

Notes: Only metric measurements have been supplied for the ingredients in this recipe due to the exact quantities required. Distilled Haba Tonka can be made from scant 1 cup water and 1¾ ounces Haba Tonka cocoa beans.

Carme Ruscalleda

Restaurant: Carme ruscalleda—Sant Pau, Sant Pol de Mar

Carme Ruscalleda and her husband Toni Balam grew up in Sant Pol de Mar, near Barcelona, where they now own and run the restaurant Sant Pau. This award-winning restaurant is a favorite amongst media, gastronomic guides and the public. Carme's cooking is inspired by seasonal produce and by the reinterpretation of traditional Catalan cooking. She has received numerous awards and published a number of cookbooks.

Green noodles

FIDEUÁ VERDE

- 2 ounces green garlic
- 9 ounces very fine fresh noodles (n° 0)
- 3 ½ ounces fresh spinach, cut into julienne strips
- 3 ½ ounces zucchini, green part only, cut into julienne strips
- 3 ½ ounces tender green beans, cut into julienne strips
- 2 ounces very tender peas
- 2 ounces baby fava beans
- 2 ounces parmesan cheese, grated
- olive oil, for frying
- salt and white pepper

Vegetable stock:
- 3 ½ pints still mineral water
- 1 onion, finely chopped
- 2 carrots, finely chopped
- 2 leeks, finely chopped
- 2 cloves garlic, chopped
- 1 stalk celery, finely chopped
- ¼ bay leaf

Serves 4

To prepare the stock, heat the mineral water in a large saucepan over medium heat and, when boiling, add the vegetables and bay leaf. Cook for 20 minutes. Add salt and pepper to taste, then strain and set back on the heat to keep warm. Cut the green garlic into julienne strips, then blanch in boiling water with a little salt for just 15 seconds. Drain, rinse and set aside. Preheat the oven to 380°F. Brown the noodles in a little oil in a non-stick paella pan or skillet. When they are golden brown, but before they start to burn, add the zucchini strips and the green beans. As soon as the vegetables begin to fry lightly, add the strips of fresh spinach leaves, the green garlic, and the peas and beans. Season with salt and white pepper. Just cover with the very hot vegetable stock, bring to a boil and leave to cook over high heat for 1 minute. Sprinkle the grated parmesan cheese over the noodles and vegetables and then finish cooking the dish in the hot oven for 5 minutes. Serve immediately.

Note: Green garlic is unripe garlic and has a mild and delicate flavor. It is difficult to obtain commercially but is sometimes available in spring from farmers' markets. Perhaps the best solution, however, is to grow your own supply by planting separated unpeeled cloves of garlic, pointed side up, in a shallow bed or pot. Green garlic is ready to harvest when the stalks are tender and have reached the length of an average scallion.

Quick shrimp soup

SUQUET RÁPIDO DE GAMBAS

- 16 large shrimp, unpeeled
- 3¼ pounds waxy potatoes
  (such as Charlotte or
  BF 15), cut into regular
  sized pieces
- olive oil
- salt and white pepper

  Stock:
- 6 cloves garlic
- 1 small slice fried bread
- 20 fried parsley sprigs
- 2 small dried red bell peppers,
  soaked to rehydrate
- 2 ounces almonds,
  peeled and toasted
- ¼ cup dry sherry
- 3½ pints mineral water
  Serves 4

Peel the shrimp and remove their heads, reserving the peeled tails in a cool place. Sauté the heads in a pan with a little oil until golden brown, then add the stock ingredients except for the mineral water and leave to cook over high heat for 2 minutes. Heat the mineral water in another pan until boiling, then add to the pan with the shrimp heads. Season to taste, and leave to cook for 15 minutes over medium heat. Pass the mixture through a vegetable mill and pour the stock into a large pan. Add the potatoes and cook for 15 minutes over medium heat, until cooked. Add salt to taste and leave to stand, with the heat turned off, for 4 minutes. Dress the shrimp tails with a little oil and salt and fry them lightly in a non-stick skillet. Add them to the pan just before taking the soup to the table to serve.

Apricot sponge

BIZCOCHO DE ALBARICOQUE

- 15 fresh apricots
- 2 tablespoons apricot liqueur
  or Kirsh)
- 4 eggs
- 9 ounces superfine sugar
- 4½ ounces all-purpose flour
- 1 teaspoon baking powder
- ¾ ounce brown sugar
- ¼ ounce sifted chemical yeast
  Makes 1 cake to serve 6–8

Put the apricots into a bowl, cover with the liqueur and leave to mari-nate. Preheat the oven to 380°F. Put the eggs into a large bowl with the sugar and beat the mixture with an electric mixer or a hand whisk until frothy and firm. Sift the flour and baking powder into the mixture a little at a time and stir in carefully. Line a rectangular baking tray (approximately 12 inches x 8 inches) with baking paper suitable for use in the oven. Pour in the mixture and arrange the marinated quarters of apricot over the top. Sprinkle with the brown sugar. Transfer to the oven and cook for 20 minutes. Leave to cool before turning out; the baking paper will make the sponge easy to remove from the tin. Serve freshly baked.

Santi Santamaría

Restaurant: El raco de Can Fabes, Sant Celoni, Barcelona

Santi Santamaría was born in Sant Celoni, where in 1981 he opened El Raco de Can Fabes with his wife Àngels Serra. Countless awards later, El Raco continues to evolve and is one of Spain's favorite restaurants. Santi has published a number of cookbooks, writes for newspapers, and contributes to television, championing the bridge from classical to modern food, and in his own words 'creating a cuisine that weds craft and art.'

Sautéed clams and Swiss chard
SALTEADO DE ALMEJAS Y ACELGAS

- 1 tablespoon olive oil
- 1 clove garlic, chopped
- 1 pound 2 ounces Swiss chard
- 6 slices Serrano ham
- 16 good quality clams from Carril
- 1 small teaspoon chopped
  fresh parsley

Serves 4

Heat the oil in a skillet over medium heat. Add the garlic and cook for 5 minutes until brown. Add the Swiss chard, sauté and add salt and pepper to taste. Set aside a couple of slices of ham, chop the remainder, and add to the Swiss chard. Sauté until brown. Transfer the Swiss chard and ham to a serving plate. Cook the clams in the same skillet until they open. Remove them from their shells and add them to the serving plate, along with the cooking juices from the skillet and the chopped parsley.

Charcoal grilled duck foie gras with endives
FOIE GRAS DE PATO A LA BRASA CON ENDIVIAS

- 16 ounces foie gras,
  cut into four slices
- 2 endives
- 7 ounces Brussels sprouts
- 2 mandarin oranges, segmented
- sugar, to taste
- 3 tablespoons brandy
- juice of one mandarin orange
- ½ tablespoon butter
- grating of mandarin orange peel
- 1 teaspoon grey salt
- pepper

Serves 4

Preheat the oven to 360°F. Season the foie gras to taste, then char quickly over a hot barbeque or charcoal grill before transfering to the oven for 5 minutes. Cut the endives down the middle lengthwise and sauté, along with the sprouts. Saute the mandarin-orange segments in a separate pan, then add to the sprouts with a little sugar. Pour in the brandy, add the extra mandarin-orange juice and leave to reduce until the segments are almost caramelized. Add the butter and continue to cook until the sauce is sticky and glutinous. Arrange the vegetables on a serving plate and very finely grate a little of the mandarin peel over the top. Add freshly ground pepper and grey salt on top of the foie gras.

Note: Grey salt, which is also referred to as sel gris or Celtic sea salt, is a 'moist' and unrefined sea salt usually found on the coastal areas of France. If it is unavailable, you can substitute sea salt.

Angel hair tart with fruit

TARTA DE CABELLO DE ÁNGEL CON FRUTAS

- **8 ounces angel hair or kadaif**
- **3½ ounces butter, plus extra, melted, for brushing**
- **superfine sugar, for sprinkling**
- **4 Calanda peaches**
- **1 vanilla pod**
- **5 fl oz muscatel wine**

Serves 4

Preheat the oven to 360°F. Spread the angel hair on a baking tray, brush with a little melted butter and sprinkle with the sugar. Spread the mixture out to make a circle, creating a hollow in the centre. Transfer to the oven and cook for 7 minutes, until golden brown and crispy. Peel the peaches and cut into wedges. Sauté in the butter in a small pan over medium heat and add the seeds from the vanilla pod. Add the muscatel and reduce until the peach juice thickens. Add the hot fruit to the angel-hair base and serve immediately.

Note: Angel hair is a type of fine vermicelli-like pastry made from Malabar gourd and sugar syrup. If you cannot find it, you may be able to find kadaif, which is similar in appearance to angel hair and is often used in middle-eastern pastry making. If Calanda peaches are not available, you can substitute apples, mangoes, pineapples or pears.

COOKING
INFORMATION

Tips

Aluminum To prevent aluminum pans and pots turning black when something is cooked in them, put half a slice lemon or a piece of lemon rind into the water during cooking.

Baking pans and molds, sticking To prevent pastry dough or cake mixture sticking, never wash baking pans and molds with detergent. Clean them as thoroughly as possible with paper towels or a cloth, then rinse them in clean water, and dry thoroughly.

Baking pans and molds, greasing When greasing pans and molds with butter, put a pat of butter into the pan or mold and stand it somewhere warm, near the stovetop for example. When it has melted, use a brush to spread it all over the base and sides, then let cool. Sweet butter is best for greasing, as it is less likely to burn.

Beet This will retain its color if cooked with its stalk intact.

Burnt stews If a stew burns and sticks to the base of the pan, put the pan into a container with a little vinegar and let stand for a while. Then transfer the stew to a clean pan, without scraping in the burnt part.

Cauliflower To make sure cauliflower stays very white, add a generous dash of milk to the cooking water.

To prevent it from disintegrating, add salt only at the last minute.

See also Odors.

Custard If custard curdles during cooking, pour it into another pan or bowl and beat vigorously with a balloon whisk until cold. The liquid will once again come together and be smooth.

Dishtowel For recipes that use dishtowels to submerge meat, etc., it is important to use a flour-sack-style dishcloth or several layers of cheesecloth as towels made of terry cloth or similar will shed fibers on the food.

Eggs, boiling To prevent eggs from cracking when they are boiled, pierce the shell with a needle or pin at the round end.

Eggs, peeling To make hard-cooked eggs easier to shell, add 1–2 tablespoons of salt to the cooking water.

Eggs, raw These can carry harmful bacteria, such as salmonella and other foodborne illnesses. To avoid food poisoning, it is important to handle, cook and store eggs properly, especially where young children, the elderly or pregnant women are concerned. Always use the freshest eggs available and discard any cracked or broken ones. Many of the recipes in this book use raw egg as an ingredient. If concerned about the health implications of this, please contact your doctor for advice.

Eggs, storing The refrigerator is the best place to store eggs. This guarantees that they will be firm when beaten or whisked.

Eggs, whisking When whisking egg whites, add a pinch of salt or 3 drops of lemon juice before you start. Use a ceramic, glass, or metal bowl (not plastic) and make sure it is completely grease-free.

French fries When making French fries, once the potatoes have been peeled and cut, let them soak in plenty of cold water for 30 minutes so they can release their starch.

Fruit tarts Once the pie dough has been put layed into the pan, use a flat brush to glaze the base with a little lightly beaten egg white, then let dry for 15–20 minutes. When completely dry, fill it with fruit and cook in the usual way.

Garbanzo beans To make sure garbanzo beans turn out tender, put them into warm water to cook. If more water has to be added during cooking, make sure that it is hot.

Garlic To crush garlic more easily in a mortar or small bowl, add a little salt.

Garlic and shallots To prevent indigestion, cut garlic or shallots in half lengthwise and remove the green shoot from the middle before cooking.

Legumes All legumes apart from garbanzo beans should be put into cold water to cook. If water has to be added during cooking, it should

always be cold. When cooking dried beans, stop them from boiling on three separate occasions by adding some cold water, even if extra liquid is not required. This way they will have a softer texture.

Mayonnaise It is important to note mayonnaise is made from raw eggs, which can contain harmful bacteria. If using raw egg, it is best to use the freshest eggs and consume the sauce as soon as possible. If you do not have time to make your own mayonnaise, use good quality bottled.

Mayonnaise, making If mayonnaise curdles while you are making it, that is, if the oil separates from the egg, there are three ways to solve the problem: **1.** Put an egg yolk into a bowl and gradually beat in spoonfuls of the curdled mayonnaise, a little at a time. When this is done, add salt, vinegar, or lemon juice etc. to taste. **2.** Mash a piece of boiled potato about ¾ inch thick, then gradually stir in the curdled mayonnaise, a little at a time. **3.** Put a piece of bread, without crusts and about the size of a walnut, into a bowl, soak it in vinegar or lemon juice, and beat in the mayonnaise.

Meat If it seems that stewed meat is going to be tough, add a large, clean cork (kept solely for this purpose) to the sauce while it is cooking. This helps tenderize it.

Meat, cooking To avoid foodborne illness caused by bacterial contamination, cook meat to the temperature at which the bacteria are destroyed. Use an instant-read thermometer to check the temperature. Ground beef should be cooked to an internal temperature of 155°F. Other cuts of beef can be cooked to 120–145°F for medium-rare, 140–145°F for medium, 155–165°F for medium-well and 170-180°F for well done. Lamb tends to favor slightly lower internal temperatures and can be cooked to 125–130°F for medium-rare, 135-145°F for medium or 165°F for well done. Pork does well at no more than 155°F for boneless loin, 160°F for bone-in loin, and 185°F for the roasted leg and shoulder.

Meat, marinating Prepare the meat for cooking before you marinate; meat should not be trimmed after marinating. Make sure the marinade completely covers the meat and turn every half hour to ensure the flavor is absorbed. Use glass, ceramic or plastic containers for marinating, avoid aluminum or metal containers altogether as this can affect the taste. Always store raw meat in a sealed container away from cooked meat or other food to avoid cross-contamination. Though some marinades and spices keep the levels of bacteria down, it is still advisable to marinate in the refrigerator. Do not re-use marinades that have been used with raw meat, fish or poultry.

Milk To prevent milk from acquiring an unpleasant flavor when it is boiled, rinse out the pan with cold water first.

Odors When cooking brassicas (cabbage, Brussels sprouts, or cauliflower) put a piece of lemon, squeezed gently to remove the juice, into the cooking water. Alternatively, add a piece of day-old bread, soaked in vinegar and wrapped in cheesecloth, to the cooking water.To remove the smell of onion or fish on the hands, dampen them and rub in 2 tablespoons salt. Rinse well.

Oil Which cooking oil to use is often a matter of personal taste, but some are better than others. Sunflower oil is a near flavorless oil made from sunflower seeds. It is a good all-purpose oil, suitable for frying and deep-frying, though care must be taken as it can burn at high temperatures. Vegetable oil is a bend of different refined oils extracted from a number of sources, such as sunflower seeds, rapeseeds, cottonseeds, safflower seeds, corn, soybeans, and peanuts. It is often the cheapest oil, good for frying and deep-frying, but it is not the healthiest. Canola or rapeseed oil is the lowest in saturated fats and is mild in flavor and aroma, also making it a good all-purpose oil. Olive oil is a healthy oil, high in monounsaturated fats and polyphenols, and is good for sautéing and stir-frying. It comes in a variety of different flavors, colors, textures and aromas, from mild to strong. Extra-virgin olive oil comes from the first pressing of the olives and is considered to have a superior flavor to other olive oil, though it's distinctive taste can be strong. It is best for salads, pastas and marinades. Peanut or groundnut oil is made from pressed peanuts to produce a clear, mild oil that does not absorb or transfer flavors. It is good for salads.

Oil, cooking To prevent oil from foaming too much when deep-frying, put a large, brand new iron nail (kept solely for this purpose) into the pan; or add some half egg shells to the pan.

To prevent it from splattering when it is heated, sprinkle in a little salt.

Onions To prevent onions from making your eyes water when you're peeling and chopping them, first put them into the freezer for 10 minutes or into the refrigerator for 1 hour.

Paella Valencia Rice This rice is the ideal choice for this traditional Spanish dish but it can be difficult to find outside Spain. It is a short-to-medium grain rice and Italian risotto rice is not a suitable substitute as paella should not have a creamy texture and is not cooked in the same way. If you can't get Valencia rice, your usual type of long-grain rice is probably the best choice.

Paprika To retain the lovely red color, remove the pan from the heat when adding paprika to a dish.

Pastry for little tarts Add a dash of peanut oil to the dough to make the tarts crustier.

Pressure cookers Cooking times for pressure cookers are about one-third of conventional cooking times. For example, potatoes which take 30 minutes cooked conventionally will be done in about 10 minutes in the pressure cooker once it comes to pressure.

Refrigerator, cleaning Wash the lining well with a damp cloth and a little baking soda, then rinse it with another damp cloth well wrung out in warm water. The refrigerator will then be perfectly clean with no detergent smells to taint the food.

Rice To make sure the grains stay separate during cooking, add 3–4 drops of lemon juice to every 4 cups of cooking water.

Salty stews If you have added too much salt to a stew, add a couple of slices of peeled raw potato, about ¾ inch thick. Leave the stew over low heat for 30 minutes, then remove and discard the potato slices, as they will have absorbed the excess salt.

Another method is to add 1 teaspoon sugar, stirring it into the sauce until dissolved. It will improve the flavor noticeably.

Sponge cake Leave sponge cakes to cool in their pan until just warm or almost cold. Then turn out onto a wire rack to cool completely.

Strawberries If you have to wash strawberries, do it quickly and hull them afterward to prevent water from getting into the fruit and destroying its delicate flavor.

To enhance their flavor, put the strawberries into a glass or china bowl, sprinkle them with a little sugar, and pour in 1 tablespoon balsamic or sherry vinegar for each 2 ¼ pounds strawberries. Chill in the refrigerator, stirring occasionally.

Sautéing vegetables If vegetables (peas, beans, pieces of carrot, etc.) are to be cooked in butter, put them into the skillet first and put the butter on top. If they are to be cooked in oil, put the oil in first, heat it a little, and then add the vegetables.

Sweetening desserts For rice pudding, add sugar to the rice after it has been cooked. For puréed compotes, add sugar to the fruit after has been cooked and passed through a food mill.

Tomatoes To make tomatoes easier to peel, use a very sharp knife to make a cross in the end opposite the stalk, then put them into vigorously boiling water, and leave for 1 minute. Drain and immediately refresh under cold water so the flesh remains firm.

Yeast Three main types of yeast are used as rising agents in baking. To prepare fresh yeast, cream it in a bowl with the lukewarm liquid specified in the recipe, then mash well with a fork to make a paste. Fresh yeast is available from health food stores and bakers' supply stores, but may be difficult to obtain elsewhere. To prepare dried yeast, dissolve a teaspoon of sugar in the amount of lukewarm liquid specified in the recipe in a bowl, then sprinkle the dried yeast on the surface. Let stand for 10–15 minutes, until frothy, then stir well to make a paste. Rapid-rise dried yeast can be added with the flour; there is no need to mix it with liquid first. Dried yeast and rapid-rise dried yeast are both widely available from super-markets. The equivalents are: ½–1 oz fresh yeast = 2 teaspoons dried yeast = 1 envelope rapid-rise dried yeast.

Glossary

Aspic A cold dish of cooked ham, poultry, foie gras, seafood, or vegetables set in flavored gelatin.

Bain marie Also known as a double-boiler, this is a water bath that allows food to be cooked slowly and gently. To use a bain marie in the oven, put the mixture into an ovenproof dish, place the dish in a roasting pan, and pour in boiling water to come about halfway up the sides. Bake for the specified time. A roasting pan, double saucepan, or a heatproof bowl placed over a pan of barely simmering water, may be used on the stovetop. A bain marie is also a convenient way of keeping delicate foods, particularly sauces, warm.

Bake blind This technique of partially cooking prevents a pie shell from becoming soggy when a filling, such as fresh berries or eggs and cream, is added. Once the pie shell has been put into the pan, prick the base all over with a fork to prevent it from rising, then line with waxed paper, foil, or baking parchment and half fill with pie weights. Ceramic and metal pie weights are available from kitchenware stores or you can use uncooked rice or dried beans kept solely for the purpose. Bake the pie shell for the time specified in the recipe, then remove the pie weights and lining. For some recipes the pastry case is then returned to the oven and baked until the base turns golden brown.

Beards The wiry tuft that protrudes from the hinge of mussel shells is known as the beard and should be pulled off before cooking.

Blanch To cook briefly in boiling water to remove salt or bitterness, or to soften or to firm up vegetables. Blanching also means to soak briefly in boiling water to make it easier to peel off skins from ingredients such as tomatoes and nuts.

Bouillon strainer This conical strainer with an ultra-fine mesh is used with a tapered wooden pestle to strain and press down ingredients to make a very smooth purée. It is often used for making sauces.

Bouquet garni An aromatic mixture of fresh herbs tied together and added to stocks, soups and casseroles, to provide added flavor. A classic combination is 3 fresh parsley sprigs, 2 fresh thyme sprigs, and 1 bay leaf tied together with a strip of leek or celery. Envelopes of dried bouquet garni herbs, rather like tea bags, are available. Whether fresh or dried, the bouquet garni should be removed and discarded at the end of cooking and before a mixture is puréed or served.

Braise To cook slowly in a small amount of liquid at a low temperature on the stovetop or in the oven.

Brochettes Long metal or wooden skewers onto which all kinds of ingredients may be threaded.

Brown To let food acquire a pleasing golden color when cooked in oil or melted fat, such as butter. In the oven this is achieved by glazing the top with egg or milk or by sprinkling cheese or bread crumbs over the dish.

Carpaccio An Italian appetizer of meat or fish, originally beef, cut into wafer-thin slices and marinated in lemon juice or vinegar.

Croûtons You can buy these in packages in your local supermarket, but it is better to make them yourself. Cube some day-old French bread and toss the cubes in a generous quantity of olive oil. Then either bake in a preheated oven, turning once, or fry them until they are golden brown and crispy. For additional flavor you can toss the croûtons afterwards in Parmesan and chopped fresh herbs such as oregano or basil, or cook with garlic to make garlic croûtons. You can also add a few drops of chile sauce to the oil to make spicy croûtons.

Dress To season salad greens with a dressing, such as vinaigrette or mayonnaise.

Dutch oven Sometimes called a cocotte, this is a cast-iron pan with straight sides, a heavy base, and a very well fitting lid used for cooking stews.

Fumet A concentrated aromatic stock, usually made from fish but sometimes from poultry, used to flavor other stocks and sauces.

Gelatin This is available in powdered form or as leaves. To use powdered gelatin, pour the liquid into a heatproof bowl and sprinkle the gelatin over the surface. Let sponge, that is, soften, for 5 minutes, then place over a pan of barely simmering water until dissolved. To use leaf gelatin, put the required number of leaves in a bowl of cold water and let soak for 5 minutes. Squeeze out the excess water, place in a bain marie, and heat until the gelatin has dissolved. It is best not to stir gelatin with a spoon, but simply to swirl the bowl a few times, if necessary.

Julienne Very thin strips or sticks of vegetables, most easily cut with a mandoline.

Lard To thread strips of fat through lean meat to keep it moist during cooking.

Macédoine A mixture of diced vegetables or fruits.

Marinate To put raw meat or fish into a mixture of wine, vinegar, citrus juice, or oil, together with vegetables, such as carrots and onions, and aromatics, such as garlic, bay leaves, and spices, so that it absorbs flavors before being cooked. Marinades also often help to tenderize meat.

Meat extract This is a seasoning that can add a meaty, salty flavor to sauces, soups and stews. One popular brand is Bovril. If you can't find it, use Maggi Seasoning or some beef bouillon.

Mixed herbs A collection of commercially available dried herbs.

Papillote To make a package of meat, poultry, or fish with other ingredients in foil, baking parchment, or waxed paper and cook it.

Pinch The quantity of a solid ingredient, such as salt or saffron threads, that can be held between the tips of the thumb and forefinger or on the point of a knife.

Poach To simmer very gently in water without any large bubbles breaking the surface.

Roll out To smooth out pastry dough to an even thickness with a rolling pin. Always roll in one direction, not backward and forward, turning the dough frequently.

Salpicon Very finely diced ingredients bound with a sauce or, in the case of fruit, a syrup. A salpicon is eaten cold.

Sauté To fry lightly in a skillet or sauté pan, sometimes covered, other times not. The process may involve shaking the pan to prevent the food from sticking.

Scald To dip food into boiling water to remove impurities or sharpness.

Set To make a delicately textured mixture or a liquid thicken or solidify.

Singe Briefly to pass poultry, game birds, suckling pigs, kids, or animals' legs through a flame to remove the remains of feathers or hairs that may still be on the meat.

Skim To remove scum or foam that rises to the surface of the liquid when cooking meat or jam. Use a skimmer or a slotted spoon.

Stew To cook slowly in plenty of liquid at a low temperature on the stovetop or in the oven.

Thicken To augment or thicken a liquid by stirring it with a wooden spoon over low heat and/or adding all-purpose flour, cornstarch, potato starch, or egg yolks.

Tomato sauce This is a versatile sauce made with fresh tomatoes that is delicious as a pouring sauce or with pasta and can be used as a base for a number of different recipes. If you do not have time to make your own tomato sauce you can use good quality bottled. Tomato passata is readily available in most supermarkets along with a huge variety of other tomato sauces.

Vegetable mill Sometimes also called a food mill, this consists of a container with a selection of metal straining discs. As you turn the handle, a metal blade forces the food through to produce a coarse, medium, or fine texture purée.

Vinegar There are a number of types of vinegar. Red-wine vinegar has quite a strong taste and is perfect for vegetable salads, marinades for meat or game, or for some strong sauces. Two particularly famous ones are Jerez vinegar, made from the wine of the same name, and balsamic, a concentrated vinegar produced in the region of Modena in Italy. White-wine vinegar is perfect as an accompaniment to fish. Aromatic vinegars are usually wine vinegars to which herbs, spices, fruits or condiments with aromas have been added. Cider vinegar has a milder taste than white-wine vinegar, and can be served to season a fruit compôte or liven up some strawberries, as well as be added to concentrated fish stocks. Vinegar with alcohol is colourless and without aroma, and is mostly used for conserves.

Vinegar, to make To make vinegar with aromatic herbs the herbs should be cleaned well with paper but not washed. Mash them lightly in a mortar or small bowl and put them into a sterilised jar. Fill the jar about ¾ full and then pour previously warmed vinegar (which should not have reached a boil) over the herbs.

Directory

The following sources specialize in high quality Spanish products such as chorizo, Serrano ham, olive oil, cheese and other items used in these recipes and will ship directly to your home. Additionally, most specialty food stores carry or will order the items for you as well.

East Coast

Despana
408 Broome Street @ Lafayette
New York, New York 10013
212-219-5050
www.despananyc.com

South East

A Southern Season
Hwy 15-501 @ Estes Drive
University Mall
Chapel Hill, NC 27514
800-253-3663
www.asouthernseason.com

La Tienda
3601 La Grange Parkway
Toano, VA 23168
1-800-710-4304
www.latienda.com

Midwest

Zingerman's
422 Detroit Street
Ann Arbor, MI 48104
734-663-3354 (DELI)
www.zingermans.com
(for online sales)
www.zingermansdeli.com
(for info, news and events)

West Coast

The Spanish Table (4 locations)
1426 Western Avenue
Seattle, WA 98101
206-682-2827
www.spanishtable.com

1814 San Pablo Avenue
Berkeley, CA 94702
510-548-1383

123 Strawberry Village
Mill Valley, CA 94941
415-388-5043

109 N Guadalupe Street
Santa Fe, NM 87501
505-986-0243

Online Stores

Casa Oliver
1-888-80 Spain
www.casaoliver.com

Igourmet
1-877-igourmet (877-446-8763)
www.igourmet.com

Canada

Pasquale Bros. Downtown Ltd.
16 Goodrich Road
Etobicoke, Ontario
M8Z 4Z8
416-364-7397
www.pasqualebros.com

Pusateri's Fine Foods
1539 Avenue Road
Toronto, Ontario
M5M 3X4
416-785-9100
www.pusateris.com

INDEX

F

Simone Ortega has been writing about food for over fifty years and has become the foremost authority on traditional Spanish cooking. Generations of Spaniards have learned to cook through her books. Her daughter **Inés Ortega** has collaborated with her mother from a young age.

Javier Mariscal is one of the most highly respected illustrators and designers working in Spain today. His work covers a multitude of disciplines, from graphic and industrial design to textiles, furniture, interiors, animation and multi-media projects. In this, his first cookbook, he celebrates the vibrancy of the Mediterranean with an explosion of color and exuberance.

Note

Phaidon Press Limited
180 Varick Street
New York, NY 10014

www.phaidon.com

First published in 2007
© 2007 Phaidon Press Limited

ISBN 978 07148 4836 5
(US edition)

Text first published in Spanish
as *1080 Recetas de Cocina*
by Alianza Editorial, S.A.

All rights reserved. No part of this publication may be reproduced, stored in a retrieval system or transmitted, in any form or by any means, electronic, mechanical, photocopying, recording or otherwise, without the prior written permission of Phaidon Press Limited.

Designed by Estudio Mariscal
Illustrated by Javier Mariscal
Photographs by Jason Lowe
Translated from the Spanish
by Equipo d'Edición
Printed in China

All cup and spoon measurements are level. 1 cup = 8 fluid ounces; 1 teaspoon = 5 ml; 1 tablespoon = 15 ml.

Unless otherwise stated, milk is assumed to be whole.

Unless otherwise stated, eggs are assumed to be large and individual vegetables and fruits, such as onions and apples, are assumed to be medium.

Unless otherwise stated, pepper is freshly ground black pepper.

Cooking times are for guidance only, as individual ovens vary.

If using a fan oven, follow the manufacturer's instructions concerning oven temperatures.

Some recipes include raw or very lightly cooked eggs. These should be avoided particularly by the elderly, infants, pregnant women, convalescents and anyone with an impaired immune system.